America's Humor

After Boasting about Their Bravery, Two Cowardly 17th-Century *Commedia dell' arte* Captains Run Away from One Another. From a series of etchings of *commedia* captains by Jacques Callot. (*The Metropolitan Museum of Art, Bequest of Edwin De T. Bechtel, 1957*)

After Boasting about His Bravery, a 19th-Century Kentucky Ring-Tailed Roarer Decimates a Backwoods Settlement. (*Crockett's Almanack 1841*)

America's Humor

From Poor Richard to Doonesbury

WALTER BLAIR

HAMLIN HILL

OXFORD UNIVERSITY PRESS

Oxford   New York   Toronto   Melbourne

Oxford University Press
Oxford London Glasgow
New York Toronto Melbourne Wellington
Nairobi Dar es Salaam Cape Town
Kuala Lumpur Singapore Jakarta Hong Kong Tokyo
Delhi Bombay Calcutta Madras Karachi

Copyright © 1978 by Oxford University Press, Inc.
First published by Oxford University Press, New York, 1978
First issued as an Oxford University Press paperback, 1980

Library of Congress Cataloging in Publication Data

Blair, Walter, 1900-
America's humor: from Poor Richard to Doonesbury.

Includes bibliographical references and index.
1. American wit and humor—History and criticism.
I. Hill, Hamlin Lewis, 1931- joint author. II. Title.
PS430.B495   817'.009   77-23829   ISBN 0-19-502756-6 pbk

Printed in the United States of America

To our wives,

*Without whose nagging this book
never would have been completed.*

Preface

MOST "AUTHORITIES" AGREE
that laughter is a highly subjective response. So writers who are
foolhardy enough to discuss the humor which does or doesn't
produce it are an endangered species. Usually they are kicked
around for allegedly proving that they themselves have no humor
whatever. It is customary to complain that they are unamusing
nitpickers. Often they are scolded for saying too much about
minor authors—or minor works by major authors—because those
authors or their works tickle the funnybones, not of normal readers, but of the commentators. Again, they are sneered at for leaving out a long treatise on somebody's favorite comic. (Loving
admirers of Will Cuppy are forewarned: This is the only mention
of him in this book.) So, even though we expect to be unjustifi-
ably abused, in order to dodge as much flack as we can, we want
to say at the start what we have tried to do in this study.

Our aim, stated modestly, has been to trace American humor—
high-falutin and low-falutin; rustic, frontier and urban; white,
black, blue and parti-colored—from colonial times to the present.

Although at times our prejudices influenced our samplings and
our evaluations, we have tried throughout to do justice even to
humor that we think unfunny, provided it was influential, typical or widely enjoyed. This is because we believe that for two reasons humor, loved as well as loathed, unfashionable as well as
fashionable, merits detailed consideration:

1) As probably the most popular creative achievement of our
countrymen, our humor reveals a great deal about America's
history.

2) Much of it, whether forgotten or still admired, is fine
enough as literature to justify critical analysis.

So our study has been of comic works as historical documents,
artistic achievements, or both.

Yielding to our interest in the ways historical events shaped
humor in this country, we have written about the comedy that

crossed the Atlantic Ocean and the "localizations" and "Americanizations" of it in its new environments during changing times. We trace the effects of our free—and at times polluted—air on several eternal laugh-provoking types who came here lugging trunkfuls of age-old jokes. We monitor the changing qualities, fortunes, and appeals of funny pedants and ignoramuses, prissy prudes and rascally cheats, braggarts and self-deprecating men and women, as they were pictured by our comic writers. We argue that many mutations were both profound and revealing.

Cultural influences fascinate us, so we describe the almost immediate and often long-lasting reactions in humor to social, political, and intellectual events—the exploration and settlement of the New World, the Revolution and subsequent wars, the westering frontier, widening education, expanding suffrage, the aftermaths of the Civil War, urbanization, scientific developments, the new psychologies, the proliferation of mass media, and the growth of the counter-culture. We also suggest a few interrelationships between these phenomena and their impacts.

Aware that individual humorists, like more reputable writers, are unique, or at any rate have reasons for being impatient with historians who pigeonhole them too neatly, we have done away with some old labels and stressed neglected kinships and individual traits. We have also taken a new look not only at common qualities and skills but also at unusual ones. To make sure that at least some individual works were done justice, we analyze several at length—Benjamin Franklin's war satires, "The Legend of Sleepy Hollow," "Rip Van Winkle," "The Big Bear of Arkansas," "Parson John Bullin's Lizards," "Jim Baker's Blue-Jay Yarn," "The Secret Life of Walter Mitty," *The Great American Novel*, the Doonesbury comic strips, *The Bank Dick*, and Lenny Bruce's standup assaults and batteries. Though we know that these won't get everybody's vote for the funniest or most important comic American writings, we believe that each, as a representative of a time, a place, and an outstanding artist, deserves a close look.

Recognizing how consistently our comics whacked away with twigs, bladders, slapsticks, and bludgeons at pedagogs and pedants, we have tried not to be stuffier than was necessary, and minimized dates and titles. At the risk of catching it for slighting readers' favorites, we have deliberately omitted mentions of some humorists, abbreviated our discussions of others, and at several points chucked lengthy lists of names into footnotes which readers (if they like) can skip. When we treated the post-Civil War "Local Colorists" and "Phunny Phellows," for instance, instead of being exhaustive, we scrutinized only a few representative figures and footnoted many others. Recent books, articles, and even a couple of scholarly journals focus on American humor and broadcast the valuable discoveries and insights of dozens of scholars and critics. We acknowledge our major indebtednesses not in footnotes but in the text and in brief bibliographical notes at the end of the book.

Relevance, we believe, has dictated our choice of illustrations. Some show significant resemblances—e.g., the picture of *Chap-Book's* monacled dandy of the 1890's and *The New Yorker's* monacled Eustace Tilley of the 1920's. Some show incongruities that humorists played with—those, say, between reality and fantasy, between humorists and the eccentrics or clowns that they created, or between an invented character and that character's fantasy-image. Some make it possible to put side by side significantly different versions of the same comic story.

In our eagerness to avoid as many errors as possible, we have tried the patience of friends and colleagues by inflicting parts of the manuscript on them. Richard Amacher, E. W. Baughman, John Bryant, Leon Howard, George Kernodle, and Henry Nash Smith read parts of the book and made invaluable suggestions. James Raimes of Oxford University Press abided our delays and missed deadlines with amazing grace.

Each of us inflicted rough drafts on typists—Shirley Clark and Sue Ann Strickland in Chicago and Gloria Baca in Albuquerque—who struggled, survived, and even made some kind of sense out of them. We thank them.

We have incorporated passages, or versions of passages, from publications by both of us. We thank the initial publishers for letting us draw from the following:

Walter Blair: "Burlesques in Nineteenth-Century American Humor," *American Literature* 2:236-47 (1930); "Popularity of Nineteenth-Century American Humorists," *ibid.*, 3:175-94; "Introduction" to *Native American Humor* (New York, 1937; San Francisco, 1960); *Horse Sense in American Humor* (Chicago,

1942; New York, 1962); "Mike Fink in History, Legend, and Story," in *Half Horse Half Alligator: Growth of the Mike Fink Legend* (Chicago, 1956), pp. 3-40; *Mark Twain and "Huck Finn"* (Berkeley, 1960, 1973); "Introduction" to E. B. White, *One Man's Meat* (New York, 1964); " 'A Man's Voice, Speaking': A Continuum in American Humor," in *Veins of Humor*, ed. Harry Levin (Cambridge, 1972), pp. 185-204; " 'The Big Bear of Arkansas', T. B. Thorpe and His Masterpiece," in *The Frontier Humorists*, ed. M. Thomas Inge (Hamden, 1975), pp. 105-17; "Mark Twain's Other Masterpiece," *Studies in American Humor* 1: 132-47 (1975); and "Charles Mathews and 'A Trip to America,' " *Prospects* 2 (New York, 1976), pp. 1-23; " 'Americanized' Comic Braggarts," *Critical Inquiry* 3:331-49 (1977).

Hamlin Hill: "Modern American Humor: The Janus Laugh," *College English* 25: 170-76 (1963); "Black Humor: Its Cause and Cure," *Colorado Quarterly* 17: 57-64 (1968); "The Durability of Old Southwestern Humor," *Mississippi Quarterly* 29: 119-23 (1975-1976); and "Black Humor and the Mass Audience," in *American Humor, Essays Presented to John C. Gerber*, ed. O M Brack, Jr. (Scottsdale, 1977), pp. 1-11.

We planned the book together, consulted about it frequently, and each submitted all of his copy to his collaborator for corrections and suggestions. So some of our errors were joint achievements. Some, however, we made on our own without anybody's assistance. So that the correct perpetrator of such mistakes may be identified, we list the chapters for which each of us was primarily responsible: Walter Blair—Chapters 1-13, 20, 22-32, 37, 42-44 and "Afterword;" Hamlin Hill—Chapters 14-19, 21, 33-36, 38-41, 45 and 46.

W.B.

H.H.

Contents

Illustrations

Part One

Starters

No
End
of Jokes

They tell sweet lies of Paradise . . .
And lies—and lies—and lies!
—Anita Owen, "Dreamy Eyes," *ca.* 1894.

1.
The Lies
of the Land

EUROPEANS WHO WROTE OR talked about the New World during the sixteenth and seventeenth centuries implied that visitors with a few minutes to spare could easily dig up or liberate from royal treasuries silver, gold, and precious jewels. And they could do this anywhere in the area between the Arctic Ocean and the Caribbean Sea. The returned travelers had good news about other attractions. During endless summers, their story went, wine, plants that cured all ailments, fruit, fish, fowl, and every sort of game were so plentiful that nobody had to stir to get them; stretch out a hand and, like love, they came a-tricklin' down. Indians were noble savages built like Renaissance nudes, easygoing about wealth, and with no sticky notions about personal property. If they were heathens, all the better; this meant they were ripe for conversion into Christians, laborers, mechanics, or perhaps slaves.

Late in the sixteenth century, John Donne showed what he had heard about lands overseas in, of all places, a rhapsody about his mistress preparing for bed:

> O my America! my new-found-land,
> My kingdom, safeliest when with one man manned,
> My mine of precious stones, my empery,
> How blest am I in this discovering thee!

3

Indians were noble savages built like Renaissance nudes. Engravings by Theodore de Bry, based on paintings by Jacques le Moyne de Morgues. From *America* (Frankfurt, 1591). (*Rare Book Division, New York Public Library*)

But settlers soon found that precious stones and metals always were out beyond the edges of their settlements. The living was not quite as easy as promotional tracts advertised. Master George Percy told how it was in Jamestown in 1607:

There were never Englishmen left in a foreign country in such misery. . . . We watched every three nights, lying on the bare cold ground, what weather soever came; [and] warded all the next day: which brought our men to be most feeble wretches. Our food was but a small can of barley sodden in water, to five men a day. Our drink, cold water taken out of the river . . . very salt [or] full of slime and filth; which was the destruction of many . . . three or four in a night; in the morning, their bodies being trailed out of their cabins like dogs, to be buried.

The grim statistics: of one hundred and four men and boys in the colony, within six months fifty-one died of starvation and disease.

The experience was all too typical. A few years later at Plymouth, "in two or three months half their company died," often "two or three a day," victims of the New England winter, malnutrition, and sickness.

Early periods were the worst, but for decades, settling in the New World was riskier than Russian roulette. Understandably, even as things became better, rumors proliferated about natural and supernatural forces hell-bent on crushing newcomers. However bad the weather—fierce winds, tornadoes, waves, currents, hail stones the size of bowling balls, tropical heat, and arctic cold—reports predicted worse. Earthquakes, one of which gulped down a river without a hiccup, were said to be rampant. Lists of fauna included not only fierce beasts that actually were ready to prey but also nonexistent tigers, lions, crocodiles, and sea serpents. After King Philip's War wiped out a tenth of the males in Massachusetts Bay Colony and brought rapes, scalpings, and mutilations, red men were pictured as devils incarnate—torturers, murderers, cannibals. Stories had it that—even worse—hordes of fiends temporarily in human form fanned out over the countryside to horrify and harass. On one occasion, four men—all there were left of a party of six hundred colonists and soldiers—"heard much tumult and great clamor of voices, the sound of timbrels, flutes and tambourines as well as other instruments," and almost at once saw their boat teetering on a tree top—surely the work of sorcerers. A visitor to both Southern and Northern colonies in the seventeenth century wrote that the land was cursed with "witches too many, bottle-bellied witches amongst the Quakers, and others that produce many strange apparitions if you will believe report."

Howard Mumford Jones summarizes scores of travel books and settlers' accounts:

If the modern reader has . . . a feeling of a vague, rich jungle of repellent or terrifying things, animals, plants, and men, it is the impression he would have received, I suggest, had he been a literate European . . . interested in reading about the new-found land. . . . The unpredictable, the abnormal, the inhuman, the cruel, the savage, and the strange in terms of European experience were from the beginning part of the image. . . . The New World was filled with monsters animal and monsters human; it was a region of terrifying natural forces, of gigantic catastrophes . . . where the laws of nature tidily governing Europe were transmogrified into something new and strange.

The gulf between the El Dorado, Cockaigne, Arcadia, and Utopia of promotion tracts and the hell on earth of all-too-palpable fact and all-too-inventive rumor provided ample incongruity for the genesis of rib-tickling comedy.

Of course, for the actual production of comedy, conditions had to be right. Colonists who believed that if only they could get out to it, El Dorado was waiting, could not be funny about their impossible dream. A touch of skepticism was needed. As far back as the twelfth century, an Irish author had shown the way when he became dubious about the glorious Otherworld which reverent old narratives had often celebrated—just such a paradise of milk and honey as credulous writers about the New World had pictured. Full of doubts about a host of religious beliefs, the author of *The Vision of MacConglinne* parodied the lot of them. When MacConglinne rows across milk lakes, through seas of soup, and by islands of cheese, as Vivian Mercier puts it, "most of the Otherworld literature . . . is summed up and annihilated in a single devastating work." The lasting appeal of this satire was shown when it was twice adapted in recent times for public performance—on the stage in 1936 and on radio in 1953.

Colonists who were being buffeted by nature, stalked and pounced on by wild critters, besieged by Indians, and hexed by witches were hardly in the mood—even if they could find the leisure—to turn out much foolery. As well as skepticism, distance in space or time was helpful.

English playwrights George Chapman, John Marston, and Ben Jonson, an ocean away, could be less involved and more frivolous. Mocking promoters and their wild press releases, this trio in *Eastward Ho!*—performed in London in 1604-05 and revived in 1751 and 1775—had a rascally ship's captain, Seagull, ladle out lies to some potential backers. The Indians, said he, so loved the New World offspring of Britons and squaws that "all the treasure they have they lay at their feet":

I tell theè, gold is more plentiful there than copper is with us. . . . Why, man, all their dripping-pans and their chamber-pots are pure gold; . . . and for rubies and diamonds, they go forth on holidays and gather 'hem by the sea-shore, to hang on their children's coats. . . . As [pleasant a country as] ever the sun shined on; temperate and full of all sorts of excellent viands. . . . And then you shall live freely there, without sargeants, or courtiers, or lawyers, or intelligencers. . . . You may be an alderman there, and never be a scavenger: you may be a nobleman, and never be a slave. You may come to preferment enough, and never be a pander; to riches and fortune enough, and have never the more villainy nor the less wit.

Once they had acquired the distancing they needed, Americans too would be able to burlesque wild claims of promoters, realtors, Californians, Texans, Alaskans, Chambers of Commerce, and perveyors of publicity everywhere.

Black humor surfaced briefly when time provided distance, and the Rev. W. Simmonds looked back at the winter of 1609 that he underwent in Jamestown. When the silly colonists sent John Smith home "to answer some misdemeanors," they rid that settlement of the only leader who could run it. Within half a year, of about five hundred "not past sixty men, women and children" survived. These miserable wretches fought starvation by eating "roots, herbs, acorns, walnuts, berries, now and then a little fish . . . even the very skins of our horses." One man murdered his wife, "powdered" [i.e., salted] her and, says Simmonds, "had eaten part of her before it was known; for which he was executed, as he well deserved. Now whether she was better roasted, boiled, or carbonado'd [broiled] I know not; but such a dish as powdered wife I never heard of." Since, as a rule, hardships of one sort or another—or maybe both—were always in good supply here for centuries, wags who were frivolous enough would produce black humor about them or exaggerate them and heap them atop one another until they became laughable.

Writing "from Bristow the 13 of November, 1578," Anthony Parkhurst could set down for Richard Hakluyt "merry tales" about the Newfoundland of some years earlier—the sort, as he said, he told "when I please to be merry with my old companions" or when talking to "those that are desirous of strange news." One was about squid, "which I may sweep with brooms on a heap, and never wet my foot." Another was about "trees that bare oysters." His friends, he says, figure these are "notorious lies, but they laugh . . . when they hear the means how each tale is true." Squid, he explained, are chased by cod into shallows, from which they are washed ashore "by the surge of the sea on the pebbles and sands"; and boughs of trees on the shore "hung in the water, on which both oysters and mussels did stick fast, as their property is, to . . . timber." Since peculiar things were always happening in America and uninformed newcomers always lusted for strange news, over the years merry fellows could unwind incredible yarns about flora, fauna, natives, and geography and then give true or untrue but more or less plausible explanations.

Once they had come to be funny on purpose, the lies that old-timers told to explorers, tourists, immigrants, and tenderfeet who were credulous, or to other old-timers who were in on the joke, might serve several purposes. In practically every instance, the humorous liars—peeved or amused by false claims about the splendors or horrors of the new country—parodied them. Some, disgusted by hardships or frightened by rumored menaces, lied about them to exorcise the damned things. Some trotted out lies to befool and show up strangers, or perhaps to initiate them into a new community. And some, the creative ones, revised or invented and embroidered whoppers for their own pleasure and that of appreciative listeners or readers. "A traveller," said one of the most famous of all liars, Baron Münchausen, "has the right to embellish his adventures. . . , and it is very unpolite to refuse that deference and applause they deserve."

As early as 1521, a native of the Cape Fear region, carried home by a Spanish explorer, astonished his hosts with longbows such as the one about neighbors of his who reared themselves up a gigantic king by softening and stretching his serene majesty's bones when he was an infant. Colonists instructed a Swedish scientist about the way a bear usually killed a cow—"bites a hole in the hide, blows with all his power into it, till the animal swells excessively and dies." Inspired no doubt by their own rainy season, natives of Southern California told a Spanish explorer about a tribe that slept under water. A British scientist of sorts heard from helpful New England hosts about a Cape Cod sea serpent, a Casco Bay merman, and a bird called the pilhannow big enough to prey on fawns and jackals. George Washington, famous for being honest though a public figure, passed on lore to a British traveler that did nothing for his reputation: "He was never so annoyed by mosquitoes as in the Skenesborough, for they used to bite through the thickest boot." Hundreds of other stretchers dot sixteenth-, seventeenth-, and eighteenth-century travel books.

Nineteenth-century Americans, still going strong, often had fun feeding fascinating data to tourists who, they believed, would rush home to deliberately libel them. James Kirke Paulding, a popular New York writer, was not completely candid when he told about the reaction of his countrymen to Captain Basil Hall's *Travels in North America in 1827-28*, published in three volumes after he "went grumbling his way, from one end of Jonathan's farm to another, collecting everything." "Jonathan's tenants, who are in the main a cute set of fellows, often bantered him with all sorts of tough stories, which he would write down in his log-book; but little they thought that he was going to put them out as gospel when he got home." The fact was that Americans did their best to deceive strangers and then eagerly watched for printed repetitions of their windies.

A favorite target was Mrs. Frances Trollope, whose *Domestic Manners of the Americans* (1832) irked them because it held that they had no manners, domestic or of any other sort. Mark Twain cited one story that she picked up aboard a river boat as a good example of "stupid and silly lies" natives told tourists so that they could "laugh at them for believing and printing them." It told in gory detail how a Mississippi River crocodile and her young one morning breakfasted on large helpings of a squatter's wife and five children. The story seemed doubtful, since no crocodiles ever have been found in that river—only alligators, which do not relish human flesh. Mrs. Trollope herself seems to have smoked out another yarn she was told at the same time, for though she included it in her manuscript, she left it out of her book in spite of claims that it was "perfectly true." A bear, she was told, evicted an Indian from his canoe, took his place, emptied an abandoned whiskey flask down its throat, and then sailed into New Orleans. The townspeople, she said, had profound discussions—clearly storytellers' exuberant elaborations:

Some declared it was a savage of a nation hitherto unknown, others that it was an Indian conjuror, in one of their quaint disguises; others again (these were the travelled men) were strongly of opinion that it was an Englishman of fashion, dressed in a driving coat. Some few ventured to differ from the rest, and said they thought it looked very like a bear. A quiet Yankee . . . suggested that, be what it might, they should have a better chance with it on land than on water, and proposed that a hook, attached to a cord of prudent length, should be cast in such a manner as to enable them to draw the canoe to shore. The proposal was acted upon. The prow again touched the land, and the stranger, uttering one loud growl that speedily cleared him a passage, gave another spring that placed him high and dry on land . . . ran through the wondering throng . . . and soon found shelter in the woods.

The Indian, on repossessing his canoe and finding the whiskey gone, philosophized: "Did he too learn to love it? . . . Poor beast! If he tasted it, how could he help it?"

During the 1830's, Mrs. Trollope, renamed Mrs. Wollope, Mrs. Truelip, and the like, as one historian says, "was such a familiar and ridiculous figure to American audiences that comedies seemingly could hardly be without her"; and an obligatory joke was about her credulity. Paulding had at her in a play, a satire on travel books, and a novel. In the next decade, an actor boasted that he had victimized the lady by telling her that Mammoth Cave contained "a natural fountain of pure brandy." Half a century after *Domestic Manners* appeared, Mark Twain—though he liked the book—still got laughs by giving samples of its author's gullibility.

Like other jokes, lies that natives fobbed off on strangers were recycled in different times and places and refurbished to play up local phenomena. In 1714, a stuffy visitor to North Carolina announced that he had "been informed" about a huge tulip tree "wherein a lusty man had got his bed and household furniture, and lived in till his labour got him a more fashionable mansion." In 1837 Westerners substituted a pumpkin for the tree; and in 1951 Vance Randolph included in a book an Arkansas version about a phenomenal potato. He called his book *We Always Lie to Strangers*.

Once America was partially colonized and settled, in addition to reporting on the strange weather, the awful geography, the peculiar flora, and the disquieting fauna, travel writers had much to say about the fascinating men and women. Almost exclusively at first, as superior subjects for humor, they discussed the men.

They tended to play up two flaws—crudity and ferocity. They found the first of these everywhere—in the Northeast, the South, and the West. Visitors reported widespread ignorance, insolence, inquisitiveness, and gaucherie. Just about everybody, they kept saying, was impudent and bad-mannered. Anyone who got half a chance pried into strangers' affairs which were none of his business, asking question after unwelcome question. Everybody spoke the most outlandish patois and assassinated grammar. Every male, seemingly, chawed tobacco. Standard outcries against spitting gave the impression that the settled parts of the continent—and much of the frontier—were shiny, brown, and slippery.

The mayhem, writers believed, was more localized than the disgusting manners—very bad in the South, even worse on the frontier. In both areas, men were hot-tempered, and the heavy drinking of mint juleps, brandy, or kill-devil whiskey fired their ferocity. In no-holds-barred rumpuses, many a poor devil, the books said, had his cheeks clawed, his nose or ear gnawed off, or his eye gouged out. Englishman Isaac Weld in the 1790's put into his book typical if extreme tales about eye-gougings in Maryland and Virginia and "worst of all" a habit fighters had of trying "to tear out each other's testicles." He saw, so he said, "four or five instances . . . of men being confined in their beds from injuries received of this nature in a fight."

Touchy natives and settlers hurried to point out that often reporters of widespread ruffianism on frontiers were not exactly objective. Several foreign writers said frankly in Introductions to books that they hoped their horror stories would keep governments at home from shifting toward radical democratic ways rampant in the New World in general and on its frontiers in particular. Others, less frank, gave away the fact that they were biased by sternly scolding their hosts. Domestic rivalries also brought distortions. Some New England writers, for instance, wrote with the hope that they might slow down their neighbors' stampedes to the West. Only a moron would expect frontiersmen to be pictured as cooing doves in a book titled *Western Migration. Journal of Jeremiah Simpleton's Tour of Ohio Containing an Account of Numerous Difficulties . . . which the Doctor and His Family Experienced . . . in that Highly Extolled Country*. Some adverse reports were oral. A Yankee tin-trader, Paulding wrote, who had been caught cheating and who had been walloped, when he got home "of course told terrible stories of gouging and the like; so that in time [his attackers] came to be thought little better than bullies . . . though people who were best acquainted with them knew better."

Humor made use of such calumnies when frontiersmen or playful writers parodied or exaggerated them. Some pranksters put on shows for travelers; others cooked up elaborate lies. In Louisville a gang of young bucks staged a fake free-for-all with horrendous casualties for a genteel visiting man of letters, then enjoyed reading about the carnage in his book. A frontiersman solemnly told a visitor that the best way to gauge the safety of a tavern was to size up its patrons and count missing ears and eyes. A landlord cheerily listed as a morning's task collecting in a bucket eyes, ears, and noses left lying around the night before.

By 1809 Washington Irving, without leaving his native Manhattan, could put together a playful picture of Marylanders drawn from travel reports, burlesques of them, or both:

a gigantic gunpowder race of men, who lived on hoe-cakes and bacon, drank mint juleps and brandy toddy, and were exceedingly expert at boxing, biting, gouging, tar and feathering, and a variety of other athletic accomplishments, which they had borrowed from their cousins german and prototypes the Virginians, to whom they had ever borne a considerable resemblance. . .

Eastern stay-at-homes were better equipped to picture such hell-raisers than one might guess. For they had read about English roisterers with somewhat similar ways; they personally knew American kindred spirits; and they themselves just might be part-time libertines. For years British authors made fun of country squires who were boors, fanatical huntsmen, and toss-pots. Fielding's Squire Western in *Tom Jones* (1749) was a famous example, and in Goldsmith's *She Stoops To Conquer* (1773), shabby fellows in a country ale house praised the late Squire Lumpkin because "for winding the straight horn, or beating a thicket for a hare, or a wench, he never had his fellow," and because "he kept the best horses, dogs, and girls in the whole country." When his son Tony sang a song damning bookish schoolmasters and Methodist preachers, and glorifying the fun of getting a skinful, the carousers cheered him and let him buy them drinks. British sporting journals and sketch writers pictured and catered to a drinking, hunting, cock-fighting, and wenching set—"Corinthians," "Nonesuches." A very popular fictional pair of the 1820's, Tom and Jerry, had a hot rum concoction named after them which Americans still drink.

Encouraged, perhaps, by this crowd's example, bucks in the Old South or in Eastern American cities carried on in much the same way. In New York, Washington Irving was a member of a jolly group called the Kilkenny Cats. His pal, collaborator, and fellow member, Paulding, must have been aware of a resemblance between his crowd and Southerners when in 1812 he said the latter were men who "amuse themselves pretty considerably with horse-racing, cock-fighting, barbecues and the like . . . wonderful boys for what they call antifogmatics, being certain mint juleps . . . supposed to make a man somewhat belligerent."

The bully-boy title, held for years by "Southerners," galloped westward ahead of the edges of civilization. "Backwoodsmen" and "Kentuckians" took over for a time. In 1830, a New Englander at home after Western wanderings nominated or reported on a new group of title-holders:

. . . the character of the citizens of Kentucky . . . is on the whole estimable. . . . I am well aware that it by no means corresponds with the prejudices of the generality of the citizens of the other states. . . . One circumstance which tends to perpetuate the prejudice is the conduct of the Kentucky boatmen on the Ohio and the Mississippi, some of whom appear to pride themselves on the roughness and rudeness of their manners. . . .

A book published in 1847 by an English explorer who had met or heard about some of the mountain men trapping in the Rockies told the world that this group, "callous to any feeling of danger," was closer "to the primitive savage . . . than perhaps any other class of civilized men"; their good qualities were "those of the animal"; they were "White Indians." In the 1850's Texas newspapers broadcast a poem that celebrated a ferocious rumpus between Texans:

> They fit and fit,
> And gouged and bit,
> And struggled in the mud
> Until the ground
> For miles around
> Was kivered with their blood,
> And a pile of noses, ears, and eyes,
> Large and massive reached the skies.

Nevada, Montana, and Alaska were waiting.

These are only a few ways that our country's history inspired and localized laugh-provoking, imaginative works. The history was unique, but the works contained old materials that had been refurbished. Because this process will be repeated in our history again and again, at this stage an initial look at it is useful.

Portraits of bully boys, some of them comic, that we have traced in their essentials changed very little. But—as other portraits would—they changed. As the frontier moved westward, the men's habitats, habits, talk, manners, and occupations were affected. And historic developments during both the nineteenth and twentieth centuries that we'll notice, some of them traumatic, brought additional changes in lifestyles and comic picturings.

Jokesters, we have seen, played with amusing contrasts between America as a reality, on the one hand, and mythical lands—Arcadia, Utopia, El Dorado, and Cockaigne—on the other hand. Arcadia, dreamed up by the ancient Greeks and Romans, was written about during the Renaissance. Utopia—at least under that name—had been invented in England in 1516, and El Dorado in Spain a few years later. These were visions of satisfied longings—for pastoral innocence, perfect order, and boundless riches. Such wishful fantasies invited mocking parodies. Versions of Cockaigne which appeared long before Columbus sailed the ocean blue provided such take-offs—the Gaelic *Vision of MacConglinne* in the twelfth century; a French fabliau, *Cocagne*, and an English poem, *The Land of Cockagne*, during the thirteenth. These three imaginative burlesques use a similar setting. In a typical version it is a never-never realm soused by wine-filled streams, where roast fowl and suckling pigs with handy knives in their ribs waddle between crepe-roofed cake houses and free delicatessens along pastry-paved streets. Each Cockaigne, though, is pictured in such a way as to enable its creator to satirize his own place and time. The Irishman kids over-pious "visions" of saints, the Frenchman, Avalon—his day's "Island of the Blessed"—the Briton, life in monasteries.

Over the centuries other artists, each in his own way, imagined and portrayed a dream, a nightmare, or a ridiculous world, each using details that hinted at foibles and aberrations of the world in which he himself lived. Aristophanes gave Greek audiences a Cloud-Cuckoo Land inhabited by activist birds; Rabelais and

Pieter Brueghel, "Das Schlaraffenland" (1567) Old World bountiful land—roofs with pies for tiles, trees loaded with food and drink for the taking, fences consisting of fat sausages and roast pigs carrying utensils, and overfed gluttons. Since one sluggard is a Spanish soldier and another an elegantly dressed official, some critics hold that the picture satirizes Spain's exploitation of the Netherlands. (*Ale Pinakothek, Münich*)

Breughel, their own lusty imaginings of Cockaigne and Schlaraffenland; Jonathan Swift, Lilliput, Brobdingnag, Laputa, and Houyhnhomland. Breughel's painting of Schlaraffenland satirizes Spain's exploitation of the Netherlands; Swift's fabulous countries have England's quirks.

In America, William Byrd located his Lubberland on the North Carolina frontier; Washington Irving (helped by Rabelais) had Diedrich Knickerbocker's New Amsterdam and Sleepy Hollow flow with milk and honey; T. B. Thorpe placed his "creation state . . . without a fault" on Shirt-Tail Bend in Arkansas; Mark Twain loosed a wry Connecticut Yankee on a Twainized Camelot; hoboes hymned "The Big Rock Candy Mountain"; Al Capp drew Dogpatch and Slobbovia; Walt Kelly, Okefenokee Swamp; Ken Kesey, the Cuckoo's Nest.

Our aim will be to see, first in a general way, then in particular ways, how jokes got to the Western side of the Atlantic, underwent transformations, and as time went by were renovated again and again for the entertainment of Americans and appreciative foreigners.

. . . jestbooks . . . which derive
mainly from one another, and seldom from coeval folk sources—are
not so much being alimented by folk sources as constituting, them-
selves, a main source of the jokes in oral transmission. As to their copy-
ing from one another, that is only one intermediate step in their migra-
tions: from one mouth to another, one book to another, one land to
another. . . . This answers the question . . . "Who invents jokes?"
Jokes are not invented; they are evolved. And they arrive to us from
other countries and older civilizations, by way of oral and printed in-
filtrations over a period of centuries, and along certain massive and
rather well delimited cultural highways. . . .

—Gershon Legman, 1968.

2.
Evolving Jokes

HANK MORGAN, MARK TWAIN'S
Connecticut Yankee in King Arthur's Court (1889), wrote unhappily about weatherworn, well-traveled jokes that hadn't been
renovated. After being conked with a crowbar in nineteenth-
century Hartford and carried to sixth-century Camelot, he had to
listen to a court jester's after-dinner monologue:

I think I never heard so many old played-out jokes strung together in
my life. . . . It seemed peculiarly sad to sit there, thirteen hundred
years before I was born and listen again to poor, flat, worm-eaten jokes
that had given me the dry gripes when I was a boy thirteen hundred
years afterwards. It about convinced me that there isn't any such thing
as a new joke possible. Everybody laughed at these antiquities—but
then they always do; I noticed that, centuries later.

Anyone who doesn't share Hank's suspicion that new jokes are
impossible to find will probably acquire it after he samples a few
of the countless joke books dating from early Christian times to
the present. He'll find that over the centuries, joke after joke has
been endlessly repeated and that gags hoary with age still are
getting guffaws.

For example, glance at one item in the most famous of thousands of British joke books, *Joe Miller's Jests* (1739). Entirely

17

made up of gems lifted from earlier collections, this compilation
had a prolonged senility—eight editions during its first seven
years, then innumerable printings on into the present century.
(As recently as 1937, a New York publishing house boasted that
its *Joe Miller's Jest Book* repeated all the best of Joe's purported
inventions.)

One oldie in the 1739 edition and several later printings clearly
forecasts the late Jack Benny's most durable gag. Jack, between
his forty-sixth and seventy-ninth birthday—from 1940 to 1974—
time after time wowed theater, radio, and television audiences by
solemnly claiming that he was only thirty-nine years old. The
"original" *Joe Miller's Jests* has:

99. A Lady's Age happening to be questioned, she affirmed, she was
but *Forty*, and called upon a Gentleman that was in Company for his
Opinion; Cousin, says she, do you believe I am in the Right, when I say
I am but *Forty?* I ought not to dispute it, Madam, replied he, for I
heard you say so *these ten Years*.

To this day, an overage joke is called "a Joe Miller," often with
reason. But it still can get laughs.

Painful though slouching through a mess of joke books is, the
ordeal is a regular saturnalia compared with a more scientific
testing of Hank's hunch. This kind of investigation, made possible by the drudgery of several heroic scholars, almost certainly
will end all doubts. The scholars scanned acres of pages in many
languages in kilometers of books, classified types and motifs of
comic narratives that surfaced over the ages throughout the Western world, assigned numbers, and then published their records in
the formidable indexes which we list in a footnote.*

Thanks to these compilers, anyone who has encountered any
joke anywhere probably can track down in these indexes a sum-

---

* Antti Aarne and Stith Thompson, *The Types of the Folk Tale*, 1928; 2d revised
edition (Helsinki, 1961); Stith Thompson, *Motif-Index of Folk Literature*, 1932-1936,
revised edition (Helsinki and Bloomington, Ind., 1955-58), 6 vols.; Ernest W. Baughman, *Type and Motif-Index of the Folktales of England and North America* (The
Hague, 1966); Gershon Legman, *The Rationale of the Dirty Joke* (New York, 1968)
and *No Laughing Matter: Rationale of the Dirty Joke, Second Series* (Wharton, N.J.,
1975); Frank Hoffman, *An Analytical Survey of Traditional Anglo-American Erotica*
(Bowling Green, Ohio, 1973). Useful, though more specialized are D. P. Rotunda,
Motif-Index of Italian Novella in Prose (Bloomington, 1942) and Nikita Elisséeff,
Themes et Motifs des 'Mille et Une Nuits' (Beyrouth, 1949).

mary of that same joke from which practically every smidgeon of humor has disappeared, get a list of versions, and then read every version. The conclusion, based upon excruciating research, will be that essentially the same joke—in fact, every conceivable joke—has been told everywhere again and again.

Most readers probably will be happy to forego this grim experience and settle for a summary of such a check on America's favorite tall tale. A version of this simple-minded little yarn—called by folklorists "The Wonderful Hunt"—was published in *The Farmer's Almanack for 1809*. Thereafter, hundreds of "Wonderful Hunt" stories appeared in other almanacs, newspapers, and books, locating the lie and the liars who told it at points scattered throughout the United States.

The 1809 liar, George Howell, claimed that once when he was hunting along the Hudson River, he shot at a buck. "The very moment" he fired, a sturgeon jumped from the then unpolluted water. The ball passed through and killed the fish, then the deer, then hit a wild bee honeycomb in a hollow tree, whereupon honey gushed out:

"I sprung round to find something to stop the hole with, and caught a white rabbit—It squeaked just like a stuck pig; so I thrash'd it away from me in a passion at the disappointment, and it went with such force that it killed three cock partridges and a wood cock."

The indexes, typically, give a grim summary: "Type 1890 A-F, Motif X 921.1, X 1124.3 and A 20: Humor of Lies and Exaggeration. Münchausen Tales. Accidental discharge of gun kills much game. Gun kills a bird which falls on loose limb of tree, which falls on bear, etc., etc." Citations show that before this kissing cousin of "X 950: Schlaraffenland . . . in which impossible things happen" became an American favorite, it had a long history. It had invaded every corner of Europe and had joined the lies told by Baron Münchausen.

The picture is of jokelore, like a huge amorphous glob in a horror movie, relentlessly oozing from the Old World to the New, swept along by explorers, invaders, curious visitors, travel book writers, settlers, governors, actors, merchants, slaves, and journalists. Like matter, the stuff is indestructible.

But as it rolls along, it usually changes. The Joe Miller-Jack

Benny lie of eternal youth underwent a minor revision: it attached to a well-known personality. The "Wonderful Hunt" underwent a few more: over the years, the hunter, the locale, the slaughtered fauna, and the chain of mischances were somewhat localized. Other jokes changed more, in ways that compilers of indexes, who were most interested in transmissions, usually didn't study. Historians of humor, by contrast, are interested not only in likenesses but also in mutations.

They therefore share and exploit an insight Mark Twain had long before the indexes were made. "Americans are not Englishmen," he wrote, "and American humor is not English humor; but both the American and his humor had their origin in England, and have merely undergone changes brought about by changed conditions and environment." Americans and their humor, to be sure, came from many countries in addition to England; but if Twain's statement is amended to take account of that fact, it is valid.

In order to appeal to changing hearers, watchers, or readers, jokes more often than not evolve. And on migrating to the United States, they were so transformed that some Britons figured they sank in mid-ocean and never got here, while others were convinced that this country had produced comedy that was entirely unique. Mrs. Trollope in the 1830's and Dickens in the 1840's reported—to quote the latter—that Americans "certainly are not a humorous people, and their temperament always impressed me as being of a dull and gloomy character." But during the same decades, London theatergoers were calling American actors' comic stories about New Englanders exotic; and other invaders from overseas were succeeding in equally non-British roles—those of Yankees, blacks, and frontiersmen. British publishers were selling *American Broad Grins* and books such as Davy Crockett's *Sketches and Eccentricities*, and reviewers were calling the importations "national and original" and "unmitigated in their nationality." One generalized: "The humours of our own flesh and blood transported to America, and often located in wildernesses, are like nothing in the family which has remained at home."

After studying the mutations of a couple of ancient European jokes that were fairly complex, Jan Harold Brunvand decided that if preserved by European families, ethnic groups, or folk in isolated regions, they kept best. By contrast:

Whenever such a story *does* pass into the mainstream of Anglo-American narrative folklore it is likely to be adapted to the "joke" form—that is, the characters become popular comic stereotypes, the plot is abbreviated, and the story develops a "punchline" ending. This joke, then, if it survives for very long, will be adapted to the new time and place as well as to narrators' various needs and uses for that particular story.

Brunvand's guess (subject, he says, to further testing) was largely based upon his study of about three hundred tellings (between the Middle Ages and the twentieth century) of the "Taming of the Shrew" story. (Motif T251.2.3. "Wife becomes obedient on seeing husband slay a recalcitrant horse.") National groups "from India to Ireland and to the New World" contributed. Sure enough, after crossing the Atlantic, what had been a long, complicated narrative became a brief anecdote with stereotyped characters and a simplified plot, ending with a snapper. Thereafter, the bit was adapted, to become an episode in a musical comedy, Cole Porter's *Kiss Me Kate* (1948) and a less well-known short story, Warren Kliewer's "The Death of a Patriarch" (1963).

In the interest of equal time, we've surveyed in a rather haphazard way the history of a liberated woman's answer to the shrew-taming story, and found it underwent the kinds of modifications Brunvand describes. Of the many versions, the "Beauty and the Beast" fairytale is the best known. It celebrates a bewitched "Loathly Lady" who regains her well-stacked figure only after she persuades a prince to marry her or (if he's lucky) to give her a "disenchanting kiss." Pundits list variants and analogues in Sanskrit, Turkish, Kaffir, Old Icelandic, German, Old Irish, English, and American.

One early telling, Chaucer's fourteenth-century "Wife of Bath's Tale," is a relatively complex long poem. In it, a hag lets her young bridegroom choose: Which will he have her—ugly, tyrannical, and faithful, or a beautiful, freewheeling swinger? When he chooses unlovely supremacy, she turns into a luscious and faithful young bride.

An American version of this tale wandered around orally during the 1960's and in 1968 appeared in *Still More Playboy's Party*

Jokes: A young executive was in big trouble. His hundred-thousand-dollar embezzlement was about to be uncovered; his wife was set to leave him; he was broke. He was on the verge of drowning himself when an ugly old hag stopped him.

"I'm a witch," says she. "I work magic. I'll conjure away each of your troubles for a night of lovemaking."

They spent three nights in a motel. After each, the crone cackled, "Open Sesame!" "Abracadabra!" "Alakazam!" or some such nonsense, then told her exhausted bedmate that she'd covered his thefts, balanced his books, rewon his wife's love, and slipped three hundred thousand dollars into his bank account.

On the last morning, the hag asked, "How old are you, Buster?"

"Thirty-five. Why?"

"And you swallered all the crud about witchcraft! Boy, no wonder you're in all those messes!"

In the United States of the 1960's, plot twists had been straightened, the length cut, the scene moved to a motel, the prince changed to a crooked boss, and the enchanted beauty into a sex-starved old woman. And whereas tellers of Old World versions took for granted that the hag had supernatural powers, cynical American raconteurs used disbelief to put down an executive and supply a punch line.

Any joke-monger, of course, can get into the act at any stage— shrink a long narrative into a one-liner or swell a one-liner into a short story, a novella, or even a drama or a novel. What we suspect came over here as a brief joke in time became a longish story. William Byrd, Esq., of Westover Plantation, a witty Virginia gentleman, jotted down in his notebook an anecdote he heard in London in the 1720's:

Two gentlemen who pretended a wonderful nicety in distinguishing of wine went to a merchant and, tasting a particular pipe, one of 'em said it tasted of iron and the other of leather. And after it came to be drawn out of the cask, they found at the bottom a small key fastened with a piece of leather, which showed a very distinguished faculty and great success in the sense of tasting.

Byrd's note didn't get into print until the 1950's, but the story (Type F647.1.2. "Marvels, marvelous sensitiveness") was passed along, if not by Byrd by other importers. In 1853 a second Virginian had a judge in Alabama pinpoint the area that produced some hooch by sniffing a cork. Versions surfaced in Arkansas newspapers in 1906, elsewhere in 1916, 1934, 1939 (in *Esquire*), 1942 (*Time*), and in books of 1948, 1949, 1958, 1962, and 1963.

Vance Randolph, a great collector of Ozark oral stories, in 1934 heard a version worth a look because, as folklorist Herbert Halpert says, Randolph's yarns "are so thoroughly localized in place and time, so completely Ozarkian in tone and coloring, that the unsuspecting reader might well accept them as local yarns."

Randolph's Arkansas experts judge not wine but whiskey. One is a doctor, the other a more localized type, an auctioneer who "used to cry sales so everybody calls him Colonel." Reconnoitering a new keg of bourbon, "Doc says it smells like leather, and there must be an old shoe in the barrel." His pal "rubbed a few drops on the back of his hand and smelled it, and then sipped a little," then opined he got "a slight trace of iron" because "maybe somebody has drove a rusty nail into the keg." Drinking into the night, the pair trade witty insults. Doc specifies, "Why, the Colonel couldn't find an anvil in a pile of manure." Both in time get sore, fight, and knock one another off. Paragraphs describe the emptying, then the opening of the fateful keg. A tavern patron spots "a round piece of leather no bigger than a dime with a rusty carpet-tack stuck through the middle." The last paragraph is ironic:

"Gentlemen," says the fellow that run the tavern, "the drinks is on the house." So then everybody went back to the bar, and a pleasant evening was had by all. It's a pity that Doc and the Colonel couldn't be there to enjoy it.

Randolph's version was seven times the length of Byrd's note. In 1962, William Price Fox published "You Don't Smell It: You Drink It" in *Southern Fried*—nine times as long as Randolph's telling. In it, Lamarr Peevy, a Monck's Corner, S.C., bumpkin, spins the yarn. Lamarr, in "the wholesale corn whisky business" (making moonshine), goes to New York to see a customer who griped because Lamarr shipped his schnapps in Coca-Cola barrels. At a saloon in the buyer's chain, Lamarr sips a shot and at once decides that the customer has been cutting his ten-dollar-a-gallon corn in half, canting it into fancy "Lord Calvert's" bottles, and peddling it for $115 a gallon. The moonshiner brags he knows ardent spirits, is challenged to bet, and stakes $4,000 on his ability to "break down the blends, you know," in five un-labeled glasses:

Well sir, I started on the left. It was a simple cheap blend. I called the proof at eighty-six point five and that was right on the head. The blend broke down to sixty per cent rye at three years old, twenty per cent bourbon at four years old. The other twenty per cent was neutral spirits with a real nasty echo taste. . . .

The second glass was a good Tennessee sour mash whisky and the proof was a ninety and every drop was between six and seven years old . . . this whisky was made in Moore County, Tennessee, or pretty close by, 'cause I was familiar with the water there. Then I told them how they drip the whisky over a special hard-maple charcoal, also how their kegs were all center-cut maple.

You know that crowd was real impressed. . . .

Well, the other three whiskys were all simple blends and one straight rye and I went through them pretty fast. I mean there wasn't any question about who won the bet.

Lamarr collects. Then, sensing that his customer is "scared to death I was going to announce that Lord Calvert and all the bar whiskys were corn and not government-bonded and taxed . . . I let him hang there for a while." Lamarr spends several minutes answering patrons' questions before finally joining his customer in a back room, teases him some more, and then lets him be "right obliging" by agreeing to allow Peevy to use any containers he likes and submitting to a fifty per cent price hike.

Fox's long version of the old story features a character Americans always have loved, a rustic who seems naïve but really has know-how. In a clash as old as Western comedy, of which Americans long have been fond—rube versus city slicker—the rube puts down big-town smarties and the boss who tries to bully him. And his leisurely way of telling the story, deadpan, in the American idiom, as well as the highly localized background and characterization, thoroughly change and naturalize a little story that William Byrd heard in London more than two centuries before Fox wrote it.

Historic happenings, social and political changes, and new ways of talking, living, feeling and thinking, had helped bring about such Americanizations. A continuing concern of our study will be such forces and their effects. The next chapter will indicate how three peculiarly American groups—oral storytellers, readers, and writers—were influential in evolving "a folk journalism."

The anecdote was oral. Before he existed as a recognizable person, the American was a story-teller. . . . He told stories endlessly. . . . His story-telling was the foremost art of his civilization and the men who first confided it to type were raconteurs before they were writers. Something of the earlier, more indigenous art exists in the sophisticated development—so that the rhythms of speech, of voices skillfully preparing effects, are widely recognizable on the printed page. . . . But that the humor . . . specifically the anecdote of character, rests on a basis of folklore does not mean that its emergence into print is in any particular unconscious. The newspaper humor that becomes its vehicle is not a symbolism shaped by some mystical pattern in the folk mind, but the conscientious work of writers, frequently intelligent and sometimes very talented, who knew quite well what they were doing. —Bernard DeVoto, 1932.

3.
Folk Journalism

BEFORE LANDING FOR HIS FIRST visit to America in 1638, John Josselyn chatted with colonial sailors encountered offshore. They told him stories on which he, as "a scientist," made notes—"of a general earthquake in New England, of the birth of a monster in Boston, in Massachusetts Bay a mortality." After Josselyn went ashore, neighbors told him about a lion and some dancers who disappeared.

Even that early, as his records show, our ancestors entertained and instructed visitors by spinning yarns. This, as our first chapter indicated, was just one of many instances of such benevolence.

There is abundant evidence that the storytelling habit that flourished here accommodated not only strangers but also settlers, immigrants, and natives. Think of the modern sources of fun which do for us today what this one form did for Americans of the past—the theater (to a large extent), movies, radio, television, and (to some extent) quantities of reading matter—and one reason becomes clear. Also, during much of our history, other conditions were favorable. When families, friends, or neighbors gathered for parties, ceremonies, reunions, corn huskings, quiltings, house raisings, court sessions, picnics, musters, political speeches, and elections, they told and retold stories. When men got together to hunt game or—during wars—to hunt one another, they spent long evenings around campfires trading yarns.

Another thing: Americans, with itching feet and a continent to roam, were habitual movers. Crossing wilds, mountains, and deserts, they would have been fools not to travel together for mutual help and entertainment. Much migration was westward, but our countrymen milled around in every direction to do business or find places to better themselves. Crammed into coaches, steamboats, or railway cars, wanderers enjoyed their portable pastime of storytelling.

"Of all the stories I meet with," wrote a wide-ranging Yankee in 1839, "none are so delightful to me as those I *over*-hear on board a steamboat or a stage-coach . . . *live* stories I call them. . . . Books might be made of the stories you hear in a single evening, and capital books too . . . brimful of energy and vivacity and truth [and] irresistibly impressive."

Books were so made. Scottish Andrew Lang, a pioneer student of folklore and oral diffusion, who knew his field well, in 1889 wrote:

All over the land [American] men are eternally "swopping stories" at bars, and in the long, endless journeys by railway and steamer. How little, comparatively, the English "swop stories"! The Scotch are almost as addicted as Americans to this form of barter, so are the Irish. The Englishman has usually a dignified dread of dropping into his "anecdotage."

During an hour's stroll through a large library, the present authors unshelved books in which writers between 1638 and 1940 described storytelling sessions on stagecoaches in Connecticut, Pennsylvania, and West Virginia; in a Massachusetts hayloft; on Missouri River keelboats; on Mississippi steamboats; in a North Carolina gunsmith's shop; in an Ohio livery stable; by hunters' campfires in five states; alongside a cowboys' chuckwagon in Wyoming; in army tents in Maryland, Georgia, and Montana Territory; and in doggeries, taverns, country stores, and saloons scattered over eleven states. Most of these sessions took place during the nineteenth century and the first two decades of the twentieth.

Some pundits say that storytelling has dwindled in recent years because circumstances have changed and anecdotes are no longer traded as they once were.

No way. Bars and taverns teem with anecdotists, and oral tellers get together in restaurants for coffee breaks, four-martini lunches, and expense-account dinners. In night clubs, amateur raconteurs around tables or under them are entertained by professionals on platforms—Myron Cohen, George Carlin, Joan Rivers, Phyllis Diller, and many others. College and country fair committees pack auditoriums and grandstands by hiring these stars, as well as Bob Hope, his opposite, Dick Gregory, and others. Introduced by hosts who lace monologues with anecdotes, these same entertainers spin yarns for radio listeners and television viewers. Recurrent talk show guests who aren't primarily storytellers "ad lib" humorous anecdotes—Forrest Tucker, David Niven, Joyce Brothers, and novelists, exposé writers and scholars plugging their books.

From the start, American storytelling tended to be democratizing and democratic. Unlike those in Boccaccio's *Decameron*, New World storytelling groups usually were made up of several classes. Travelers marveled at the way guides, innkeepers, and farmers acted, talked, and thought of themselves as being as good as aristocrats, educated men, and the rich. Early in the nineteenth century, a lowly coachman in an astonished Briton's travel book "entertained us with many humorous stories, and always had something smart to say to every waggoner or person who passed us," including "several persons of consequence in the country who . . . took his jokes in good part." Unlike those abroad, American railways and steamboats didn't have second-, third-, or fourth-class passengers; a motley mixture survived long journeys by telling stories.

Today's coffee break, dinnertime, night club, and talk show performers come from backgrounds as diversified as those of earlier anecdotists and gather yarns from as many sorts of places. Radio and television audiences, outnumbering in a few evenings all audiences for all stage productions of Shakespeare's plays, could hardly be more miscellaneous.

"The stories thus collected in America," wrote Andrew Lang, "are the subsoil of American humour, a rich soil in which the

plant . . . grows with vigour and puts forth fruit and flowers."
Lang praised Bret Harte as one of the most popular American
humorists for being de-Anglicized by "the changed atmosphere,
the new conditions." Harte claimed that our humor, "of a quality as distinct and original as the country and civilization," was
"at first noticeable in the anecdote . . . orally transmitted . . .
in the barrooms, the gatherings in the 'country store,' and finally
at public meetings."

Joel Chandler Harris, another native humorist, and, like Lang,
a folklore authority, held that the oral "literature of the common
people," "the pungent and racy anecdote, smelling of the soil,"
embodied "the humor that is characteristic of the American
mind—that seems, indeed, to be its most natural and inevitable
product [one that] can be found in no other nation under the
sun."

True, he exaggerates the uniqueness bit. Nevertheless, plentiful evidence both outside and within printed humorous works
links oral storytelling with their origin and their nature. Biographies and statements such as those by Harte and Harris show
humorists retelling overheard stories. Folklorists hold that re-
usings of the types, motifs, and characters of age-old oral tales
also indicate oral origins.

Three plot patterns that thrive in oral storytelling have been
imported and used often. One meanders scandalously, one details
a conflict in which a weak character licks a strong opponent, and
one soars to a comic climax.

James H. Hackett, an actor who specialized in Yankee roles, in
1827, Mark Twain, in 1895, and Max Eastman and Stephen Leacock, in 1936, described the first pattern—and all called it typical of oral storytelling and characteristically American. Eastman saw this handling as one that makes "slow progress, or no
progress at all, or progress backwards," with humorist and audience playfully enjoying "a mess, the messier it is, within the
limits of patience, the better."

Folklorists Axel Olrik and Max Lüthi cite worldwide uses of
the second structure: a simple conflict ending in "the defeat of
the great by the small, the mighty by the apparently powerless"
(e.g., hunters who conquer mighty beasts; and tricksters, peddlers, slaves and confidence men who triumph).

The third pattern has been described by Norris Yates: "Event is piled on event and detail on detail, each taller than the last, until the apex, the tallest incident of all, is reached." This often is the way of the tall tale which many foreign critics called the *American* prototype.

Oral sources, possibly, and oral influences, certainly, are indicated when "a framework" pictures a storyteller spinning his yarn and an audience listening, while within this framework a narrative is quoted directly. The same shaping forces are indicated, though less clearly, when the author omits the framework but quotes the narrative in the words of a vernacular raconteur. The resulting narrative might be called "a mock oral tale." Both the story enclosed in a frame and the mock oral tale constantly imitate common speech. The prevalence of dialect is often noticed by foreign critics.

During the late eighteenth and the nineteenth century, circumstances in this country encouraged writers—journalists, typically—to use the materials and methods just discussed, and gave them a sizable audience which read and liked their work. Though the circumstances and the productions changed as time passed, some writers have moved in quite similar directions down to the present.

The educational system created an unusual reading public. The colonies, then the states, worked to make literacy (like storytelling) a democratizing force. For a long time, so far as whites were concerned, they made remarkable progress.

In 1642 a Massachusetts Bay Colony law held parents responsible for the elementary education of their children. A bit later, legislators required Massachusetts and Connecticut settlements of fifty families or more to hire schoolmasters to teach "all such children as shall resort to them to write and read." Towns of a hundred or more families had to set up grammar schools that emphasized reading. Ichabod Cranes packed textbooks and hickory sticks and fanned out to teach in Sleepy Hollows all over the country. Impressed tourists wrote that they saw practically no one of school age or above who couldn't read.

So started the brave attempt by our educators—which theoretically continues—to teach everybody who wasn't an idiot (and many who were) to read. As a result, until well into the

nineteenth century, though minority groups were too long neglected, literacy was more widespread here than anywhere else
in the world. Noah Webster boasted that

the American yeomanry . . . are not to be compared to the illiterate
peasantry of England. The yeomanry of this country consist of substantial independent freeholders, masters of their own persons and
lords of their own soil. These . . . not only learn to read, write and
keep accounts; but a vast proportion read the Bible, sermons, treatises
and newspapers every week.

These freeholders read few books and practically no home-
made *belles-lettres*. Printing books was expensive; sales were
puny. As late as 1830, this country imported three-quarters of
its books. Preachers harangued against ungodly plays, actors,
and novels. Even intellectuals thought fiction corrupted. Imports
were better than domestic products and, thanks to stupid copyright laws, were reproduced here without royalty payments.
This made book and magazine publishers prefer them.

Readers weren't sad, however, because they lacked the chance
to read *belles-lettres* by compatriots because *useful* literature was
their choice, and plenty of talented countrymen supplied that to
best-selling media. Farmers and city folk every year bought almanacs, and Bibles were found in every home. Newspapers prospered. By 1785, this country sold 70 percent as many newspapers
as Great Britain, whose population was twice its size. By 1833,
the Atlantic seaboard supported twelve hundred. In new settlements, promoters generously supported weeklies or dailies.
"Sometimes," one editor admitted, "these represented things
that hadn't gone through the formality of taking place." Dickens, touring and griping in 1842, noticed this foible and learned
that "an enormous class . . . must find their reading in a newspaper, or they will not read at all." The novelist was too irked by
America's bad habits (among them, pirating his writings) to
notice any humor worth mentioning in "the herd of journals."

His oversight wasn't too surprising, since for decades comic
interludes nudged into almanacs and newspapers between notices, news, advertisements and other informative matter. Most
were brief, but their number grew when editors found that
longer humorous pieces sold issues. Books which collected them
became best sellers.

The writers gathered material the way travel book writers, joke book compilers, and playwrights who wanted to picture quaint rustics had: They listened to natives and reworked their talk into comic subliterature—almanac and newspaper fillers, joke books, contributions to humorous magazines, and the like. Such "lowbrow printed matter, fertilized by vulgar humor and popular imagination," as Daniel Boorstin has said, "for a turbulent, mobile, self-conscious, sanguine, and literate people . . . took the place of belles-lettres."

A gifted raconteur (such as John Wesley Jarvis, as we shall show) could give humorists galore their best stuff. Most talkers, though, if they got credit at all, had to settle for the vague kind Augustus Baldwin Longstreet gave in the preface to his *Georgia Scenes* (1835) where he mentioned that he had based them upon "the comments of the wits . . . in their own dialect. . . ."

All the same, writers in the East, South, Southwest, and (in time) Midwest and Far West showed indebtedness. Aphorisms, jokes, sketches, monologues, and stories hurried from firesides to print, back to firesides, then back to print again. Finding a comic hit with an unsmirched oral or printed ancestry came to be about as easy as rescuing a virgin out of a seven-woman brothel. Because laws allowed postage-free exchanges of newspapers and magazines, editors everywhere clipped and republished favorite tidbits. A funny poem, a parody of a sermon, or a tall tale could catch on throughout the nation. It was as if word-of-mouth humorists, writers, editors, and readers massed together in a countrywide campfire jamboree.

Origins, types, motifs, borrowings, transfers, and variations of the products resembled those of Old World folklore. But as folklorist Mody Boatright noticed, "in a literate society," despite anguished howls, "verbal folklore" was kidnapped from both the folk and scholars by hacks, journalists, fiction writers and even literati, who tinkered with it to suit themselves, the media, and the audiences. The mingling of folklore and journalism, Franklin Meine suggested, is peculiar enough to deserve a distinctive name—"folk literature." We suggest that although, in many instances, the writings were excellent as literature, a more distinctive name would be more accurate—"folk journalism."

It is essential to notice that both talkers *and* writers collaborated to create this hybrid. "The origin and perpetuity of many of our queer and out-of-the-way phrasings," a humorist wrote in 1853, might be traced to court house, store, and groggery gatherings, where "every new expression and queer tale is treasured up, and new ones manufactured. . . ." Philologists have been delighted by the New World's prodigal enrichment of the language. As an old man, Walt Whitman compared colloquial speech to a jester who cavorted into "the majestic audience-hall" of feudal society's King Language and bludgeoned stuffy expressions to smithereens. "The attempt of common humanity to escape from bald literalism, and express itself illimitably," Walt believed, had breathed new life into the nation's "fancy, imagination and humor." Ignorance or defiance of rules spawned assaults on grammar; geography, flora, fauna, and history stimulated the use of words in new ways and the invention of original tropes. These helped commoners spin amusing yarns and voice shrewd insights. Storytellers, as we have mentioned, used characters and plots that hadn't been fashionable recently in bookish circles.

American authors differed from the overseas breed. As Jefferson bragged, "We have no distinct class of literati in our country." Writers on farms and plantations and in cities were close to the rank and file who read their words. They felt no constraints against reworking oral materials into funny written pieces.

But although they were hampered by no constraints, they did have problems. As they soon learned, it wasn't enough to put down the exact words of informants. In 1834, after a successful dramatist published anecdotes he'd found sidesplitting when a master storyteller recited them, he apologized because he knew he'd failed dismally to create in print "the hilarity that greets [a story] when it is heard." He headed a long parade of writers who bemoaned the impossibility of making the transfer. "It's the despair of the writing man who has known the best storytellers," J. Frank Dobie summarized in 1961, "that he cannot translate the oral savor into print."

Have a look at articles and books in which folklorists have accurately transcribed tape recordings of oral storytellings or speeches. Except to scholars whose overriding interest is accuracy, these are worse than painstaking: they are pains giving. Or look at books in which three of today's popular anecdotists—Joey Adams, Harry Hershfield, and Myron Cohen—tried to get sure-fire routines into writing. Hardly an item is in the same ball park as their word-of-mouth renditions.

Three other recent collections generally are much better. H. Allen Smith's *Buskin'* (1968) and *Rude Jokes* (1970), and Leo Rosten's *The Joys of Yiddish* (1968) consistently make printed anecdotes almost as toothsome as the oral versions. We suggest that they succeed because the authors were skilled writers who found ways to compensate for the play-acting ploys that enhance vocal tellings but are incommunicable, such as gestures, intonations, and facial expressions. (That meticulous recorder of folktales, Vance Randolph, has confessed that even he maneuvers his texts to make up for a disastrous loss of what Mark Twain called "an exceedingly important feature" of the humorous story told "by word of mouth, not print"—the pause.)

Creative journalists, less concerned about accurate recording than about effects, modify and invent in whatever manners meet their needs. Let us count the ways:

1) Some simply out-imagine monologists on their own grounds. Says Ben C. Clough:

The fireside, the cracker-barrel, and the tent are the backgrounds against which our robust imagination likes to spread its wings inordinately, but it is the gentlemen of the press who go furthest when they indulge in a vacation from fact. . . . The folklorist properly seeks out the hunter, the trapper, the lumberman, the railroader, and the oldest villager, but he sometimes makes a fetish of oral transmission. Let him step into a country newspaper office, let him talk with the leg-men of a metropolitan daily, let him find one of the underpaid lucky fellows who are allowed some freedom in "special stories"—and he will learn something to his advantage.

Again, H. L. Mencken, a passionate lover of colorful vernacular phrasings, says of the money writers: "These wags really made 'tall talk' the fearful and wonderful thing that it became during the two pre-[Civil] war decades, though no doubt its elements were derived from authentic folk speech." We later cite evidence that many humorous writers, because they gave the illusion that they were literally transcribing speech, deserved the credit that these experts gave them.

While pop writers were often belligerently slangy and unliterary, they were alert enough to what respectable authors were doing to filch from them everything that they could use.

2) Colonists, and for several decades citizens of the new nation, copied eighteenth-century overseas writings. Benjamin Franklin, a journalist, learned from these models how to impersonate homespun philosophers as well as genial and malignant chumps. From them, too, he learned how to write primordial tall tales. The procedures were useful to writers who followed him and Americanized the telling.

Two trends in later British writing affected both this country's reputable writers and many lowbrow humorists during the nineteenth century:

3) A trend that Stuart Tave describes in *The Amiable Humorist* (1960) was a shift from the belief "that the function of comedy is to copy the foolish and knavish originals of the age and to expose, ridicule, satirize them." The newer notion was "that the best comic works present amiable originals, often models of good nature, whose little peculiarities are not satirically instructive, but objects of delight and love." Like crowd-pleasing English writers (Dickens, for instance), our humorists often, we shall show, genially pictured rascals, subversives, or trash, and made readers at least half-like them. (This didn't keep some of the same humorists, in some moods, from engaging in skepticism, deflation, and vituperation.)

4) Another helpful tendency was initiated when Walter Scott, Maria Edgeworth, and others forsook generic characterizations and settings and wrote about men and women who followed rules, nursed prejudices, and spoke lingos of groups of certain kinds in specific areas. Soon after this movement started, an American critic noticed that "the old school . . . underwent a complete French Revolution in England, and, by a natural consequence, in this country."

Differences between American and English humor, Constance Rourke believed, came about in part because of the use of localized *settings:*

Nowhere is this plainer than in relation to the physical scene. . . . Our comic similes, our humor, have abounded in scenes. The wild scene with its white oaks, raccoons, possums, bears, sprawling rivers, and lush growth made a subject of which our early humorists never

seemed to tire. Comically, poetically, yet exactly, they drew these subjects again and again, and this turn of absorption makes one of the
fresh imaginative contours which our humor has followed.

The *people* pictured against this background were also localized.
Before long, Longstreet was making a claim that other humorists
in this country soon duplicated—that his sketches gave "the
manners, customs, amusements, wit, dialect, as they appear in
all grades of society."

Stereotypes, it is true, never vanished. But as a result of the
revolution, many comic writers took more care to give dialogues
or monologues a lifelike sound and to create more complex characters, even enriching some portrayals with pathos. Some peopled pages with enough family members, friends, and neighbors
to evoke a community. Seba Smith, in a sketch of the 1830's, has
Uncle Joshua tell how his son left for the wars with Downingville's militia:

I told Joel it was time to be off; so he took his gun, and his knapsack,
which was pretty well stuffed, for each of the children had put in a
doughnut or an apple, or a piece of cake, after their mother had
crammed in as much as she thought he could carry, and then he
marched away like a soldier up to the tavern . . . they had to come
down by our house and go up over a rise of land t'other way about half
a mile, before they got out of sight. So we all stood out in a row by the
side of the road. . . . Father got out as fur as the doorstep and stood
leaning on his staff, and mother stood behind him with her specs on
. . . and the rest of us, with the children, and cousin Debby, and all,
went clear out to the side of the road. Pretty soon they come along by,
my son at the head, . . . and my wife called out to him, "Now do
pray be careful, Joel, and not get shot." . . . And the children called
out all together, "good-by, Joel, good-by, Joel." . . . Joel looked around
and nodded once, when his mother called out to him, but the rest of the
time he held his head up straight and marched like a soldier. We stood
and watched 'em till they got clear to the top of the hill . . . and in a
minute more they were out of sight.

This passage, though less amusing than others, shows what
often happened. Its style is shaped to sound colloquial, and its
simplicity and restraint are remarkable. It thus illustrates the
effects of imports on some writers, and the ways subliterature in
the 1830's and 1840's prepared the ground for more subdued and
compassionate postbellum local-color writing and even late-
nineteenth-century realism.

5) When nonliterary writers represented common speech, they did more than prove that they had listened to talk. Especially when they set down the circumstances of the storytelling, showed who the storyteller was, and described listeners' reactions, they took steps to reincarnate in writing a physical and mental experience. Of course, the gambit wasn't new: Raspe and his imitators had used it in Münchausen books, and Scott had used it. So, it was probably another technique for which we must give writers more credit than speakers.

One way a skillful writer could use the boxed story structure had been illustrated superbly by Chaucer's "Wife of Bath's Tale." To be more precise, two of Chaucer's prologues—one to *The Canterbury Tales* as a whole and one to the good woman's story, plus the story itself—bring Wife Alice vibrantly to life. Chaucer calls this storyteller "a good fellow," and with justification. Physically, she is as vivid as a figure in Breughel's festive paintings—blowsy, steatopygous, a huge hat on her head, scarlet stockings crisscrossed on her plump legs, her soft shoes spurred to prod her horse. Jolly, hearty, fast-talking, worldly wise, this five-time widow on the hunt for her next spouse knows how to win every trick in the love game. She proves this by giving a treatise on men and marriage in a story frame that takes twice as many lines as her enclosed tale does. And the lively interplay between Alice and her listeners adds to the reader's pleasure.

As has been mentioned, a number of our humorists—journalists and writers of popular fiction—have used structures exactly like the one Chaucer used here. As we'll demonstrate, they collected large dividends. (We analyze three masterpieces in later chapters.) Additional humorists—Mark Twain, Saul Bellow, and Philip Roth, for example—got analogous results in mock oral tales. Both kinds of authors created vivid narrators or speakers who, in their own right, became focuses of the readers' interest. Readers are led to watch for hints about the intelligence and the intention of each monologist: Has he been deceived because he was credulous? Is he, like natives who lie to travelers or like Western humorists, deliberately trying to fool us? Perhaps he is playing a game: "Now you know and I know that I'm kidding, but let's pretend that I'm not. Let's enjoy together the way I make a case for impossible happenings." These are only three of a huge range of possible procedures.

In any case, though oral storytelling or social conversations inspired or even initiated the work, the journalist-writer's skill has been responsible for important accomplishments.

The fact that our comic writers used techniques similar to those of Chaucer, Raspe, Scott, and others doesn't mean that their accomplishments were the same. For one thing, what Huck Finn said about an inventor applied to some British writers: "He hadn't no harm in him, and was just a genius . . . which wasn't his fault." Despite all its boasted wealth, our country produced few geniuses. But more than differences in skill was involved. The American folk journalists, the vernacular storytellers to whom they were indebted, their media, their audiences—and consequently their merits—were all peculiar to the country. Therefore, they could re-create unique local and national experiences with vividness that no import could achieve.

*A portion of American literature
has become national and original . . . that which in all countries is
always most national and original—because more than any other by
the collective mind of the nation—the humourous . . . impregnated
with the convictions, customs, of a nation. . . . The Americans are a
democratic people; a people without poor; without rich; with a "far
west" . . . with no endowments for the support of a learned class . . .
Englishmen who never had feudalism on their soil. . . .
National American humour must be all this transformed into shapes
which produce laughter . . . institutions, laws, customs, manners,
habits, characters, convictions—their scenery whether of the sea, the
city or the hills,—expressed in the language of the ludicrous, uttering
themselves in the tones of genuine and heartfelt mirth.
—H. W., Westminster Review (1838).*

4.
Favorite
Incongruities

TRAVELERS WHO STUDIED THEIR
predecessors' books, conned newspapers, visited part of the country, questioned natives, and then published their impressions decided that Americans had two irritating habits:

1) They bragged too much.
2) They distrusted everybody.

Simultaneously and more or less independently, foreign and
domestic literary critics read American humorous writings and
generalized about them.

Put the travelers' findings alongside the critics' insights, and
you'll notice interesting correlations.

Friendly and hostile visitors alike tore into Americans for
boasting. Here, written in 1818, is a typical complaint:

The *national vanity* of the United States surpasses that of any other
country, not even excepting France. It blazes out everywhere and on
all occasions,—in their conversation, newspapers, pamphlets, speeches
and books. They assume it as a self-evident fact, that Americans sur-
pass all other nations in virtue, wisdom, valour, liberty, government
and every other excellence.

Commentators could back claims like this with direct quotations from the media mentioned. They held that flush time speculators and developers of new territories talked too much like the rhapsodists that we quoted in our opening chapter. Also, the visitors repeatedly said, all too often Americans enlarged just as imaginatively on their own capabilities.

The charge that Americans were suspicious skeptics was elaborated by Charles Dickens in the "Concluding Remarks" to his *American Notes*, where he wrote at length about "one great blemish in the popular mind . . . strongly presented at every turn, full in the stranger's view"—"Universal Distrust":

The American citizen plumes himself upon this spirit . . . and will often adduce it . . . as an instance of the great sagacity and acuteness of the people, and their superior shrewdness and independence.

"You carry," says the stranger, "this jealousy and distrust into every transaction of public life. . . . Any man who attains a high place among you, from the President downwards, may date his downfall from that moment; for any printed lie that any notorious villain pens, . . . appeals at once to your distrust, and is believed. You will strain at a gnat in the way of trustfulness and confidence, however fairly won and well deserved; but you will swallow a whole caravan of camels, if they be laden with unworthy doubts and mean suspicions. . . ."

The answer is invariably the same: "There's freedom of opinion here, you know. Every man thinks for himself, and we are not to be easily overreached. That's how our people come to be suspicious."

Using different terms to attack the same traits or very similar ones, other commentators took cracks at the citizen's cold practicality, cautiousness, hard-boiled cynicism, shrewdness, or sharpness.

When literary critics decided that our writers were creating distinctive humor and tried to define its nature, they spotted an outstanding element that was closely related to boasting: *exaggeration*. Clarence Gohdes, burrowing through piles of British magazines, found a repeated refrain: "By the middle of the [nineteenth] century the critical conclusion was pretty generally fixed that the essence of American humor was exaggeration." Over the years, this sweeping generalization was constantly repeated. "It is customary," Max Eastman wrote in 1936, "to say that American humor is distinguished from British by exaggeration. . . ."

One batch of statistics neatly backs this belief. Ernest Baughman, compiling his type and motif index for English and North American folktales, found that besides outjoking Britons by a ratio of five to one, American writers outdid them even more teetotaciously with extravagant anecdotes: "The tall tale . . . is an overwhelming American form (3,710 American variants, 29 English variants)"—nearly a hundred and twenty-eight to one. Many of the tall tales, of course, were comic exaggerations of the boasts of promoters and bully boys or of the feats (including "Wonderful Hunts") of the latter.

A more inclusive name that critics most often gave the humorous quality that corresponded to Dickens's "universal distrust" was "irreverence." Disrespectful funmaking debunked not only men but also traditional faiths of many sorts. A British theorist who in 1852 confidently defined "the spirit of similarity that pervades all American humour" remarked, after noting its exaggeration, that it is "at times sly and sarcastic . . . as fond of exposing a presumed simplicity of ignorance, as it is of dressing up an act of cleverness utterly regardless of principle; [and it is] almost always rude." Nearly four decades later, Andrew Lang compared our comic writers with Aristophanes, who habitually kidded Greek gods, and with medieval playwrights, who "habitually buffooned . . . saints and more sacred persons." "There is nothing of the social flunkeyism," he said, "which so often marks our own satirists. The most peculiarly American fun has . . . lacked reverence . . . has always dared to speak out."

On this side of the Atlantic, over the years several of those who knew our humor well agreed. Josh Billings claimed in 1868: "Americans love caustick things . . . prefer turpentine tew colone-water, . . . must have [humor] on the half-shell with cayenne." Jesse Bier, in *The Rise and Fall of American Humor* exactly a century later, commented: "American comedy is voracious, deflationary, skeptical, cynical, pessimistic, blasphemous, and black, not by turns or accident but in an inevitable sliding scale of function. . . ." Also writing at the end of the 1960's, Richard Boyd Hauck agreed that many of our best humorists, to paraphrase the song, accentuated the negative and all but eliminated the positive when they wrote what he called "absurd humor." And in 1973, Louis D. Rubin decided that the "Great

American joke" came into being when skeptics of a particular kind constantly based their humor on the disparity between the American dream and the reality—"between what men would be and must be."

Some critics have noticed that our dexterous humorists have often managed to juggle the equivalents of "exaggeration" and "skepticism." Constance Rourke contrasted a British expression of 1670 and 1785 with an 1835 American adaptation which made fun of boasting. The former went: "as lazy as Ludlam's dog, that leaned his head against the wall to bark." The latter was part of a Yankee peddler's badmouthing of a section—so poor, said he, that "tears came into the kildears' eyes when they flew over old fields" and "lean, lank labbersided pups . . . had to prop up against a post-and-rail fence, 'fore they could raise a bark at my tin-cart." Short though it is, Rourke claimed, the American passage contains "that combination of highly concrete description with magnified overflow which has been characteristic of our humor." Here the identification of the earthy speaker, and the substantiality and localization of the scene, both contrast with and contribute to "magnified overflow" or "inflated fancy."

Again, Rourke held that "a peculiar American bent" intertwined "mythologies," or "fantasies," and "disbelief" to produce a long line of popular funny characters:

Many mythologies have been created in which men believed; the inflated fancy belongs to all myth. But where, except on our frontiers, have been invented mythologies which men disbelieved in and still riotously enjoyed, heaping invention upon invention? And this special form of mythology has sprung up not once or transiently among us but many times and in many places, having to do with Mike Fink, Crockett, Paul Bunyan, John Henry, and a host of minor figures.

Though, as we shall notice, comic demigods were not as uniquely American as Rourke and quite a few other critics believed, they were long-time favorites of our folk, our writers, and our readers. And when folk journalists kidded their bully boys and agrophiles, they simultaneously mocked critical travelers, burlesquing both the native bravado and the native skepticism the travelers had criticized.

What Rourke called "magnified overflow" or "inflated fancy"

and foreigners called "exaggeration" also joggled with "skepticism" or "irreverence" in comic social and political commentaries. Naturally, men who wanted their fellows to believe that they were heroic statesmen or full-time Christians—or even better, both—were targets. Lincoln's enemies had him look at heaps of corpses on a battlefield and say, "That reminds me of a little joke." "Piety is a good kind of disease for a man to have," Josh Billings wrote, "but when he has so much of it that he has to go behind the door on Sunday to drink his whiskey it will do to watch him the rest of the week." "Trust everyone," said Mr. Dooley, "but cut the cards."

When Jimmy Carter, in the 1976 presidential campaign, presented himself as both a statesman and a religious man, Mark Russell, night club monologist, told about the candidate's trip to Philadelphia for the Bicentennial: "Jimmy laid his hand on the Liberty Bell and the crack was healed! Hallelujah!"

Characters portrayed by the humorists embodied the high talk and low motives. A procession of comic men and women whose life work combined imaginative lying with cynical cheating has been one of the most persistent groups that our humor has portrayed. Its members, like America's ring-tailed roarers, changed locales and labels over the years; but the jokes about them all dealt with an unchanging theme: the disparity between fantastic promises and dirty tricks.

Ned Ward, an English satirist and tavern-keeper, without even bothering to sail to America, by 1699 had heard enough about New Englanders to bawl them out for having traits which helped them lie and cheat: "Though they wear in their Faces the Innocence of Doves, you will find their Dealings as Subtile as Serpents. . . . The Gravity and Piety of their Looks . . . make Strangers that come amongst them give Credit to their words. . . . They are Traders without Honesty. . . ."

Probably because many Yankees became wandering peddlers, this representation for a long time was commonplace. "To yankee" someone came to mean to cheat him; "a yankee trick" was a one-sided bargain. Mrs. Rip Van Winkle left this world after she "broke a blood-vessel in a fit of passion at a New-England peddler" who'd outclevered her.

In the 1840's, a *London Magazine* contributor was puzzled

about a strange attitude of Americans toward peddlers: Our
countrymen had a low opinion of the rascals because many had
been caught perpetrating "ingenious frauds and deceptions."
However—

when a peddler is detected in having sold you, from the store of his
spice box, wooden nutmegs instead of the true and genuine East Indian
article, instead of any particular odium attaching to him for having
cheated you, you get heartily laughed at for having suffered yourself
to be imposed upon, while he escapes with the fruits of imposition and
the general remark, "I guess it was only a regular Yankee trick."

A recurrent fable shows that, true enough, Americans found
such shenanigans amusing. Time without end our countrymen
recited and laughed at its elements—the innocent and stupid
look of the swindler, a silver-tongued sales pitch cataloguing the
incongruous offerings, cunning tricks to bilk the victim, the
buyer's cockiness before and during the deal, his dismay when
he at last sees how he has been taken, and the diddler's clever
exit with a whole undamaged skin.

By 1821 the formula had so thoroughly jelled that Alphonso
Wetmore, a young army paymaster in St. Louis, could in forty-
eight hours knock together a play, *The Pedlar*, that dramatized
it. The cliché-crammed pasticcio, based on Wetmore's own experience (he was a transplanted Yankee), oral lore, and his
reading in newspapers and almanacs, was performed by ama-
teurs "with great applause" in 1821, 1825, and 1835.

Peddler Nutmeg, the title character, modestly admits that
he's "the greatest genius in the universe, ready to cheat [a cus-
tomer] out of what he is worth." This New Haven "traveling
merchant" sells cockle for onion seeds and stone coal for indigo.
Soon he peddles a lantern to every member of a large household
in need of one lantern and diddles Harry Emigrant in a horse
swap. And though he's caught finagling and his goods are auc-
tioned off, thanks to his cleverness he's in fine shape when the
play ends. The listing of his miscellaneous items as usual gets
laughs, partly because it's so varied and partly because it included so much boob bait:

One case of family medicines, consisting of doctor Rodger's vegetable
pulmoniac detirgent concoction, Lee's Scotch Ointment, Relf's cough
drops, Lee's patent Windham bilious pills . . . Redheiffer's patent

cathartic perpetual motion, . . . gingerbread, John Bunyan's Pilgrim's Progress—One odd volume of select Tricks upon Travellers—three boot Jacks, and a small keg of pickled herring—one gallon bottle of Cider Brandy—three pounds and a half of dried peaches—one Merino sheep skin—four tin pans—three hundred and twenty rifle-flints—one package of artificial nutmeg . . . several newly invented patent bee-hives, and thirty three unfinished powder-horns.

With this inventory in mind, it is worthwhile to look next at part of another list of items in a peddler's pack: "inkles, cadisses, cambric, lawns . . . as white as driven snow; . . . gloves as sweet as damask roses; . . . golden quoifs and stomachers, for my lads to give their dears; pins and poking-sticks of steel; [and a ballad] to a very doleful tune, how a usurer's wife was brought to bed of twenty money-bags at a burden; and how she longed to eat adders' heads and toads. . . ." The ancient language at once shows that this collection was hawked during an age and in a country other than Nutmeg's. But here is another smooth-talking salesman: "You would think a smock were a she angel he so chants," says a customer. Since this fellow too cozens hayseeds into buying his junk (including "counterfeit stones") they don't need, his story and its comic appeal are identical.

But this peddler, Autolycus in Shakespeare's *A Winter's Tale*, plying his trade three centuries before Nutmeg, lists stuff that for the life of us we can't identify without a historical dictionary. Many of its items were obsolete when Nutmeg packed his cart with items we still can recognize. Humble though it is, there-fore, Nutmeg's inventory signals historic changes. Tristram Pot-ter Coffin correctly says that the Yankee is a "world type" nat-uralized by our folk journalists in part because they moved him "to the western and southwestern frontiers where he matched wits with roarers and braggarts developed there." Autolycus's as-sociates were Mopsa, Dorcas, Florizel, Camillo and Perdita; Nut-meg's included Oppossum, Old Prairie, Old Continental, Harry Emigrant, and Mike Fink. The very names tell a great deal about the different settings and the contrasting comedy.

Autolycus engages in some deviltries that are rather more for-midable than Nutmeg's—cutting purses, burglary, impersona-tions, and blackmail. The line is a hard one to draw, but he would seem to belong to a group that Americans, beginning in

Old World Tricksters *vs.*
New World Tricksters
Scapin in Moliére's *Les
Fourberies de Scapin*
(1671). Engraving by
Pierre Brissart.

the 1840's, would call "confidence men" and would often use in
comic writings from that day to this. Mitford Mathews' *Dictionary of Americanisms* cites earliest appearance of the term in a
New Orleans newspaper story of 1849 that was widely repeated.
(The story, incidentally, contained several references to Autolycus.) The elements of the confidence game obviously correspond
to those of a Yankee trick—an innocent-looking operator who
takes advantage of the victim's confidence in him, swindles the
easy mark, and then escapes.

Again we have an age-old figure. Shakespeare had surely seen
confidence operators at a Bartholomew Fair in Smithfield and in
Stratford on Mop Day; and he couldn't have missed reading
about prototypes in cheap booklets by his contemporaries. Before and after Elizabethan times, motif indexes note, hundreds
of items appeared about clever fellows, mischief makers, cheats,

Confidence man Simon Suggs of Alabama outmaneuvering Colonel Bryan, confidence man. Engraving by O. C. Darley in Johnson J. Hooper's *Adventures of Simon Suggs* (1845). (*Library of Congress*)

and tricksters who befool, bedazzle, and cozen unwary—or even wary—victims; and anyone who has prowled around in literature a little can quickly think of many Old World comic uses of the type. (We list a few in a footnote.) *

* The earliest bedevilers were gods, such as the Greek Hermes and the Norse Loki. In Roman comedies, tricky slaves choused their betters. Storytellers in the Middle Ages celebrated vice figures—Tyll Eulenspiegel of Germany and his British avatar Owl Glass and Reynard the Fox of Flanders, France, Germany and England. Rabelais cre-

Sixteenth-century peddler.
Woodcut by J. Amman

Life in the New World and our countrymen's ingenious know-how brought into being spanking new trickeries. John Robert Nash crowded nearly four hundred pages of his bestselling *Hustlers and Con Men* (1976) with biographies, innovative exploits,

ated Panurge, a master of skulduggery who throws loaded dice, cuts purses, and sets off stink bombs under theologians' benches. Mid-sixteenth-century comedy in England offered a small group of playgoers Mathew Merygreek in *Ralph Roister Doister*—a cunning parasite who wheedles and abuses Ralph to get his way. Ben Jonson in 1614 wrote *Bartholomew Fair*, in which Edgeworth picks pockets and his accomplice Nightingale lulls victims by singing while he robs them. In seventeenth-century France, Moliere wrote a slapstick masterpiece, *Les Fourberies de Scapin*, in which the glib protagonist hornswoggles a number of dupes. (In the 1970's, a British revival delighted audiences in both England and the United States.) In eighteenth-century France, Alaine-René Lesage, improving on some Spanish models, wrote a classic picaresque novel, *Gil Blas*, which showed a wily young man learning a different kind of deviltry from each of his successive masters. Pierre Augustin Caron de Beaumarchais, himself a clever social climber and part-time secret agent, created a finagler who to this day amuses opera-goers—Figaro. Meanwhile in Great Britain, many writers imitated Moliere's Scapin. Tobias Smollett translated *Gil Blas* and made use of its example when he became a leading writer of novels about rogues and connivers with many followers.

Swindling Yankee (1839)

a long chronology, and a glossary of technical terms to detail the proud record. Some milestones: first mail order con game, 1800; rigged insurance claim, 1811; big-time riverboat sharping, 1830. As new frontiers opened, imaginative inventors took advantage of new conditions. They speculated in land grants, carried medicine shows to the suffering, salted mines, and so on *ad infinitum*. Daniel Drew started his climb to great wealth when he fed cattle salt, besogged the thirsty critters full of water, then quickly sold them as literally "watered stock." Going on to more remunerative skin games, such as manipulating politicians and stocks, he made them pay so well that in time he could found a great theological seminary dedicated to preaching the word of God.

Newspapers and magazines constantly printed stories about the flim-flams of smart con men—and a large share, instead of being objective or admonitory, were playful and comic. Humorists portrayed new trickeries set against changing backgrounds. A few scattered samples: The anonymous *Col. Crockett's Exploits and Adventures in Texas* (1836) and Herman Melville's *The Confidence Man* (1857) had characters engage in sundry artful dodges aboard Mississippi steamboats; in 1845 Johnson J. Hooper's Simon Suggs cheated at cards, worked camp meetings, gypped speculators, and impersonated a rich relative on the Alabama frontier; in 1873 Mark Twain gave readers United States Senator Dilworthy, oily political crook; in 1908 O. Henry's "Gentle Grafter" took in many victims; in 1927 Sinclair Lewis's evangelical scalawag piously and profitably undid the Lord's work; also in the 1920's and the 1930's, Chico Marx and his brother Groucho, as well as W. C. Fields, engineered rambunctious cheats in movies that are still popular; in the 1940's *How to Succeed in Business Without Really Trying* had a crafty young man bluff his way to the top of a corporation in a popular book, musical, and movie; a bit later con man Harold Hill in *The Music Man* gypped the folk of River City; and during the last decade *Addie Pray* and *The Sting* sold well as books and then succeeded as award-winning motion pictures.

The most fascinating real-life confidence man our fecund nation ever fathered was the showman Phineas T. Barnum (1810-1891). Presidents and ex-Presidents hailed him as "the most famous American in the world, eclipsing even generals, statesmen and inventors." His autobiography was a bestseller for forty years. His name is still attached to a circus which modestly, and perhaps defensibly, calls itself "The Greatest Show on Earth." Melville acknowledged his supremacy in *The Confidence-Man*. Two years after the first printing of Barnum's autobiography, one of our most successful humorists, Charles Farrar Browne, made his debut in the role of a patent imitation—Artemus Ward, "genial showman." Mark Twain, the only contemporary American whose renown rivaled the impresario's, often wrote admiringly about him.

A great deal of Barnum's success came about because he blatantly admitted—in fact, he boasted about—his sharp tricks. He planted newspaper stories about triumphant fakeries; his autobiography recalled them at length. In his *Humbugs of the World*, he set himself up as not only a great practitioner but as *the* authority on humbuggery throughout the ages. Born in Connecticut, trained to cheat—he proudly said—by experts there, he exploited human foibles and frailties throughout his long life.

"Real merit," he wrote, "does not always succeed as well as humbug." The generalization clashed head on with a pious hope fostered by American religionists: "Good guys prosper," or—in the words of Miguel de Cervantes and Benjamin Franklin—"Honesty is the best policy." Honesty pays! Americans at least half believed in each aphorism. Such an ambivalent attitude is not only the source of fascination, it also is the stuff of comedy.

Barnum and what he represented had other aspects that appealed to the folk journalists. Neil Harris defined these when in his 1973 study, *Humbug*, subtitled "The Art of P. T. Barnum," he raised these questions: Why did Americans flock to the rascal's American Museum and other displays when they had healthy hunches—in fact, when they were sure—that the people and objects on display were out-and-out fakes? And why, even after the shows had been proved to be phony, did they keep on going?

Harris decided that, instead of acting as a brake, "the universal distrust" that Dickens wrote about was a cause for the infatuation with trickery. Widespread education, self-reliance, and contempt for abstract learning caused Americans to enjoy deciding for themselves what to believe and disbelieve. Though Harris doesn't mention this, there was at the same time an uneasy respect for expertise, a nagging worry that, as will be seen, helped some of our most durable and popular jokes exploit incongruities between book learning and true wisdom.

The defiance of erudition, and the joy that thinking for themselves gave them, led Americans, Harris believes, to love hoaxes and kindred deceptions. An obituary that applauded Barnum for creating "the comedy of the harmless deceiver and the willingly deceived" stated the formula and indicated the attitude. Barnum ingratiated himself, it is likely, because he talked frankly about his trickery and thus shared the joke.

Harris lists numerous hoaxes in addition to Barnum's that were admired, and he might easily have listed many more. Beginning in colonial times, as we've seen, countless natives enlightened visitors with spoofs. Nineteenth-century magazines thrived on them. Examples: *The Massachusetts Ploughman* in 1845 solemnly discussed arctic seabirds that fed on electric fish, defecated once a year, and as a result produced the most fertile manure ever known. Unhappily, though, the precious stuff wasn't usable since its effluvia was "fatal to the olfactory nerve of man." Just as deadpan, *The American Railroad Journal* detailed complicated plans that had been perfected to construct "a railroad from *Bellecentre*, Ohio, to the *North Pole*." And Pacific Coast wits at about the same time came up with some ingenious specimens that became internationally famous.

Or were they tall tales? As Norris W. Yates has said, "The humorous newspaper hoax is a form of both the practical joke and the written tall tale." The popularity of all three must have had identical causes. So too must the popularity of comic stories about smooth-talking peddlers, about medicine show vendors with "scientific" proof that their potions could cure anything from constipation to leprosy, and about confidence men with plausible schemes to make quick fortunes. The characters these stories celebrated—along with frontier roarers who claimed they were mightier than they really were, professors and scientists who flaunted more learning than they actually had, and meek men who dreamed they were tigers—were favorite comic types we'll encounter again and again. They were all imposters.

A tall tale—that art form so beloved by Americans—might be seen as an imposter in the guise of a narrative: a story that, for laughs or satire, pretends to be more veracious than it is. A hoax makes the same sort of a pretense but (at least for a while) tries to get away with its confidence game. As we look, next, at some of the writings of Benjamin Franklin, we'll see that this writer for newspapers, in the days before folk journalists, made early contributions to the art of the tall tale and the hoax.

First, though, we'll watch Franklin—again quite early—take advantage of another strong, long-lasting affection of his countrymen: for the comic figure who is the opposite of the imposter—the unpretentious man, the self-deprecating, common-sense philosopher. We'll see how, even in Franklin's day, conditions on this side of the Atlantic made Poor Richard and his ilk appealing, and how Franklin discovered and made use of their attractiveness.

"A Harmonious
Human
Multitude"

*Pieces of Pleasancy and Mirth have
a secret charm in them to allay the heats and humors of our spirits.*
—Franklin

5.
Franklin:
Muddied Giant

DURING HIS EIGHTY-FOUR YEARS
(1706-1790), Benjamin Franklin, to put it mildly, did many
things. Anne Robert Jacques Turgot, a French contemporary,
spoke for the Old World in a tribute to a giant: "He snatched the
lightning from the skies and the sceptre from the tyrants." A
scholarly twentieth-century biographer, Carl Van Doren, was a
bit more restrained, but still hardly temperate, calling him "a
harmonious human multitude." His deeds in just one of half a
dozen areas could make men living normally frenetic lives feel
like lallygagging sluggards. Unschooled, he learned to stumble
around in five languages, and mastered three sciences—natural,
political, and social—diplomacy, and economics. Starting poor,
he prospered so well as a printer, shopkeeper, publisher, and
businessman that he was able to "retire" at age forty-two and
devote himself to scientific study, philosophy, and public service. He begat a university and the American Philosophical Society, practically invented the Philadelphia municipal government, and as a diplomat, legislator, and architect of the United
States government did the work not of one founding father but
of a dynasty.

Part of his activity was as a writer, and a fraction of his writings were humorous. John Adams, who often worked with him, who was usually upstaged by him, and who was suspicious of his motives and jealous of his fame, was warm in his praise of this fraction:

He had wit at will. He had humor that, when he pleased, was delicate and delightful. He had satire that was good-natured or caustic, Horace, Swift or Rabelais, at his pleasure. He had talents for irony, allegory, and fable, that he could adapt with great skill to the promotion of moral and political truth. He was a master of that infantine simplicity which the French call naiveté, which never fails to charm, in Phaedrus and La Fontaine, from the cradle to the grave.

Whether his comic writings deserve such lavish compliments or not, they demand attention in a history of American humor, partly because of their great variety and partly because they made important contributions to the development of that humor. For Franklin was an early discoverer of the most enduring American comic type—the homespun, unlettered, but shrewd man of common sense—and our longest-lasting joke about that type. He was also, in ways that heretofore have not been recognized, a pioneer in developing a form of humor that worked particularly well here—the tall tale. Some details concerning his reputation and his career will suggest why and how he did this pioneering.

It might seem that a public benefactor and amusing writer such as Franklin could not be, as the popular phrase puts it, "all bad." But judgments of him through two centuries imply he came close. The same John Adams who praised his humor called him an idler, a diplomatic ignoramus, a hypocrite, a wheeler-dealer, a publicity hound, a lecher, a sybarite, and an embezzler. This would appear to cover the ground pretty well, but journalist William Cobbett, another contemporary, added a few epithets—deist, quack, fornicator, and infidel. Adams passed along texts and the tone to subsequent Adamses, a durable family of prolific writers; and both he and Cobbett furnished caricatures useful to diehard Federalists and other politicos.

Friends came to Franklin's rescue—textbook tycoons and writers for the young—who, it turned out, were as rough as his enemies on his reputation. The McGuffeys, whose *Readers* uplifted generations of moppets; Parson Weems, who gave Washington his little hatchet; edifying Noah Webster, and others wrote preachy biographies. These gave the world a cheerful charmer, an efficiency expert who used "frugality, industry, system, method in all his business" and became the first and best-known American rags-to-riches success.*

When Herman Melville put Franklin into an 1855 novel, he mixed details from both hostile and preachy portrayals. His Franklin is "a lady's man . . . the caressed favorite of the highest born beauties of the Court," a sly conniver who affects rusticity—"a practical magian in linsey woolsey." He preaches with "condescending affability": in a few pages, in "most graciously bland flowing tones," he calls a young visitor "my good friend" three times, "my friend" six, and "my honest friend" sixteen. His pitches are "thrifty, domestic, dietarian, and, it may be, didactically waggish."

Two decades later, Mark Twain left out Franklin's amorousness but jabbed at him as a foxy purveyor of puritanical platitudes—a "vicious" conniver who "early prostituted his talents"—the sort who will "work all day, and then sit up nights, and let on to study algebra by the light of a smouldering fire, so that all other boys might have to do that also, or else have Benjamin Franklin thrown up at them [, and who] had a fashion of living wholly on bread and water. . . ."

Attacks ran on into the twentieth century, still sniping at precisely the virtues that antebellum biographers praised—perhaps the fiercest penned by D. H. Lawrence in 1923:

Most moral Benjamin. Sound, satisfied Ben! . . . setting up this unlovely, snuff-coloured little ideal of a pattern American . . . this dry, moral, utilitarian little democrat, has done more to ruin the old Europe than any Russian nihilist. . . . And now . . . clever America lies in her muck heaps of gold, strangled in her own barbed wire of shalt-not ideals and shalt-not moralisms, while she goes to work like millions of squirrels in millions of cages. . . . Let Hell loose, and get your own back, Europe!

"Early to rise and early to bed," chanted James T. Thurber in 1956, "makes a male healthy and wealthy and dead." As re-

* The quoted phrase is "Peter Parley's" [Samuel Goodrich's] in *The Lives of Washington and Franklin*. Ralph D. Miles cites it in a study we are largely summarizing, "The American Image of Benjamin Franklin," *American Quarterly*, IX (Summer, 1957), 117-143.

cently as 1968, an author of a scholarly book jeered at Franklin for being a secretive, hypocritical spouter of sanctimonious saws.

But scholars studying chargers and charges cast doubt on both. Some, though not all, of John Adams's remarks about flaws have to be discounted because Adams was strait-laced, irked, and prejudiced. His claims that Franklin was lazy and ignorant about diplomacy are piffle. Research during more than a century has found no support for his talk about malfeasance. Cobbett, whose apt pen name was "Peter Porcupine," was a professional pamphleteering backbiter.

Is there more of a basis for the charge that Franklin was a smug, self-appointed paragon? The most casual delver into easily available writings by him can learn that although he did not come within leagues of Rousseau, Franklin frankly admitted many failings. For all his praise of frugality, he admitted, it was "a virtue I never could acquire myself." "In truth," he said, "I found myself incorrigible with respect to *order*." He decided that honesty was the best policy only after trying the opposite. Extant beer and wine bills show that he was quite a bibber. His "Dialogue between Franklin and the Gout" and several attacks of gout and the "miseries" show that he both ate and drank more than was healthy. He admitted to carnal excesses and acknowledged a common-law marriage and an illegitimate son. And an array of writings suggest a variant on one of Poor Richard's sayings, "An old young man will be a young old man:" "A dirty young man will be a dirty old man." Albert H. Smyth, editor of what was long the best edition of Franklin's works (published 1905-1907), explained why he omitted or bowdlerized some: "His humor is coarse and his mood of mind Rabelaisian. His 'salty imagination' delights in greasy jests and tales of bawdry. . . . he remained to the end of his life the proletarian, taking an unclean pleasure in rude speech and coarse innuendo." Smyth of course used a Victorian yardstick, but he was an admirer who painstakingly edited ten volumes of Franklin's writings.

All the same, textbook and Sunday school moralizers, and cynics who believed them and sniped at Franklin, were not the sole begetters of the image of a money-grubbing striver who went around wearing a home-made halo. Paradoxically, some of

Franklin's own writings—his most famous ones at that, *Poor Richard's Almanack*, *The Way to Wealth*, and the *Autobiography*—helped greatly.

The first of these, published annually between 1732 and 1758, contained the standard mélange of facts and predictions. More memorable were autobiographical bits and wise saws credited to the fictitious compiler, Richard Saunders. Bit by bit, these tidbits introduced a man, hard working and hard pressed, an almanac maker with a sound—though not brilliant—mind who lives out in the country with his good and "careful" but sometimes spunky wife Bridget. The aphorisms—"instructive hints in matters of morality and religion," their author called them—gave practical advice in homely language.

Educated British gentlemen in the eighteenth century belittled proverbs and their coiners. So Poor Richard's spawning of "moral sentences, prudent maxims, and wise sayings, many . . . containing much good sense in very few words," showed them he lacked couth. Unnoticed because no one at the time bothered to track down sources was the fact that most of the aphorisms were repeated or reworded. Modern delvers have found earlier versions in Montaigne, (1603), Bacon (1625), Herbert (1640), Quarles (1641), Howell (1659), Virgil (translation, 1697), Gay (1727), three books by Fuller (1727, 1731, 1732), and many additional writers.

One folklorist snipes at Franklin for implying that Richard recited popular adages when his "usual contribution [consisted] of making a literary aphorism appear like a folk product." A more thoughtful way to put it would be that Franklin skillfully revised literary maxims into sayings such as an uneducated but acute man might think up because his experience had taught him lessons. A few comparisons illustrate this. Halifax's wording was: "As soon as men have understanding enough to find a fault, they have enough to see the danger of mending it." Franklin cuts wordage, alliterates "m's," and replaces abstractions with a metaphor: "Men take more pains to mask than mend." Howell wrote: "Nor wife, nor wine, nor horse ought to be praised." Even this Franklin simplifies, reorders climactically, and makes more homely: "Never praise your cider, horse, or bedfellow." Fuller has: "He had a mouth for every matter."

Franklin's Richard rhymes his version by inserting a character with an appropriate name: "Henry Smatter has a mouth for every matter." Handy proof that Franklin gave Richard's saws the sound of folk talk is the way many actually became part of common speech.

Some sayings may well surprise readers who remember only those they met in school. They are in character because, like the conventional preachments, they are based upon sound thinking about experience. However, though they will not seem to modern readers to justify Smyth's term "coarse," they are salty enough to show that Richard was not schoolmarmish:

> There's more old drunkards than old doctors.
> Keep your eyes wide open before marriage, half shut afterwards.
> Neither a fortress nor a maidenhead will hold out long after they begin to parley.
> Let thy maid-servant be faithful, strong, and homely.
> After three days men grow weary of a wench, a guest, and rainy weather.
> He who marries for love without money has sorry days and happy nights.

Until recent scholars resurrected these lines, Americans somehow managed to forget them. Instead, they endlessly recalled the moss-covered maxims that urged early rising, pennies saved, diligence, and the like. And they tended to identify the creator of Poor Richard with the preachy fellow who uttered them.

Why? The reason, some say, is that the copybook pieties preached America's go-ahead gospel so effectively. There was another reason. Though the *Almanacks* sold ten thousand copies a year and were read and reread by purchasers, a packaging of the more stuffy aphorisms was the most widely read piece that Franklin ever wrote—a piece whose popularity left that of all his other works far behind. This was *The Way to Wealth*, a preface to the 1758 edition of the *Almanack*, and later a pamphlet. As a separate item, it had appeared in "nearly 500 editions" when somebody made a count about a decade ago. It was translated into more languages than any other American work except, perhaps, that other blockbuster, *Uncle Tom's Cabin*. And it drew together from previous *Almanacks* a hundred or so precepts urging hard work, prudence, and frugality. Introducing it, Poor

NOTICE! GENTLEMEN MUST TAKE OFF THEIR HATS AND KNEEL, WHEN ADDRESSING HIS MAJESTY.

A humorist's caricature of Franklin. "It looked odd to the English to see him come into the royal presence, and, leaning his wet umbrella up against the throne, ask the king, 'how's trade?' " Illustration by F. Opper in Bill Nye, *History of the United States* (1894)

Richard tells what he heard one Father Abraham, "a plain clean old man, with white locks," say in a speech to a crowd at an auction. Richard confessed that he was gratified to listen to this digest of "all I had dropt on those topicks during the course of five-and-twenty years." One paragraph illustrates:

Methinks I hear some of you say, *Must a man afford himself no leisure?*—I will tell thee, my friend, what Poor Richard says, *Employ thy time well if thou meanest to gain leisure;* and *since thou art not sure of a minute, throw not away an hour.* Leisure is time for doing something useful; this leisure the diligent man will obtain, but the lazy man never; so that, as *Poor Richard* says, *a life of leisure and a life of laziness are two things.* Do you imagine that sloth will afford you more comfort than labour? No, for as *Poor Richard* says, *Trouble springs from idleness, and grievous toil from needless ease. Many without labour, would live by their WITS only, but they break for want of stock.* Whereas industry gives comfort, and plenty, and respect: *Fly pleasures, and they'll follow you. The diligent spinner has a large shift;* and *now I have a sheep and a cow, every body bids me good morrow;* all which is well said by Poor Richard.

Other paragraphs parade the bromides most often ascribed to Franklin by prissy friends and skeptical foes, here credited to Poor Richard. Richard's final paragraph shows an undercutting but amusing response to the old man's harangue: "The people heard it, and approved the doctrine and immediately practised the contrary, just as if it had been a common sermon. . . ."

The *Autobiography*, written in four installments between 1771 and 1790 and published in part in a French translation in 1791, was not issued complete until 1868. Clinton Rossiter finds it has been "translated and retranslated into a dozen languages, printed and reprinted in hundreds of editions, read and reread by millions of people, especially by young and impressionable Americans." "The influence of these few hundred pages," he adds less demonstrably, "has been matched by that of no other book." Partly this was because the McGuffeys, Weemses, Peter Parleys, and their ilk drew upon the *Autobiography* almost exclusively for excerpts or life stories.

For three reasons, this account plays up its author's rise from rags to riches and gives detractors evidence that Franklin was smug. 1) The memoirs are incomplete, breaking off when the author had just started to perform his finest public services; so far, his climb had been his chief achievement. 2) Franklin wrote the first part to instruct his son and "posterity," the other installments for a wider immediate public with the hope that his story would benefit readers. 3) He wrote the installments at ages sixty-five, seventy-eight, eighty-two, and eighty-four—when he was what tactful insurance companies call "overage." Gaffers tend to gloss over their failures, enlarge their better deeds (if any), and make even their unlovely deeds look as good as possible. For these reasons, Franklin does a bit more preening (especially in the passages written during his seventies and eighties) than modest folk may approve.

Despite these rather pathetic fallacies, few readers find the book as annoying as Franklin's detractors do. Self-deprecatory and playful rather than vainglorious and somber, most of it is charming. The relative objectivity, the dry wit, or the wary skepticism with which the author unfolds what is actually quite a success story gives it the look of relative modesty. Anecdotes play up an amusing disparity between glistening aims and dingy

shortcomings. During an ocean voyage, the author's boat is be-
calmed and the crew hauls aboard a catch of codfish:

Hitherto I had stuck to my resolution of not eating animal food; and
. . . I considered . . . the taking of every fish as a kind of unpro-
voked murder, since none of them had or ever could do us any injury
that might justify the slaughter. All this seemed very reasonable. But
I had formerly been a great lover of fish, and when this came hot out
of the frying pan, it smelt admirably well. I balanced some time between principle and inclination: till I recollected, that when the fish
were opened, I saw smaller fish taken out of their stomachs: Then
thought I, if you eat one another, I don't see why I mayn't eat you. So
I dined upon cod very heartily and continued to eat with other people,
returning only now and then . . . to a vegetable diet. So convenient
a thing it is to be a *reasonable creature* since it enables one to find or
make a reason for every thing one has a mind to do.

Telling a simple story at some length, with a lack of regret or
justification and a grave recital of what, after all, is a pretty obvious moral, are typical of Franklin. So is the style. Compared
with carefully built, convoluted sentences admired at the time—
those, say, by Edward Gibbon and Samuel Johnson—Franklin's
are childlike. Most of the words are commonplace, or short, or
both. Critics have aptly called the writing sensible, unpretentious, relaxed, plain, colloquial, and homespun.

Another thing: compared with the Franklin of reality, Daddy
Ben of the memoirs is an unlearned man. Many authors he mentions or quotes were those being read by anybody and everybody—Defoe, Addison, Steele, Richardson, and the like. Less
than half land among the seventy-six that Frank Luther Mott
and Chester E. Jorgenson list merely to "suggest only the most
prominent writers" the real Franklin knew well. There is not a
word, for instance, about Plato, Pliny, Herodotus, Epictetus,
Tacitus, Seneca, Sallust, Tully, Bacon, Fénelon, Temple, Swift,
Voltaire, Boyle, Burke, [Erasmus] Darwin, [Adam] Smith,
Hume, Turgot, Priestley, and Condorcet—all shapers of Franklin's thought and style.

Beyond question, differences between the real-life Franklin
and the fictional "I's" of the three works just discussed are huge.
The actual Franklin was a city dweller most of his days; Richard and Abraham were rustics, and Daddy Benjamin's "homespun" style made him sound like one. The actual man was a

complex person—a shrewd politician, a sophisticated diplomat, and an elusive genius whose true nature is still debated. He was a keen and original thinker, an inventor, a scientist, and a well-read, learned man. The characters we meet in the *Almanack*, *The Way to Wealth*, and the *Autobiography* are simple, straightforward, easily plumbed, down-to-earth, and far less bookish. The confusion about Franklin's character has been fed not only by others' writings about him but also by his own best-known works.

In America there is little to be observed except natural curiosities. The new world must have many vegetables and animals with which philosophers are but little acquainted. I hope you will furnish yourself with some books of natural history, and some glasses and other instruments. . . . Trust as little as you can to report; examine all you can by your own senses. I do not doubt but you will be able to add much to knowledge. . . .

—Samuel Johnson to Dr. Staunton, 1791.

6.
Teachers

How did Franklin come to write as he did in the *Almanack*, "The Way to Wealth," and his *Autobiography?* J. F. Ross, in 1940 studying Franklin's first published writings and some influences that shaped them, came up with useful clues. Sixteen-year-old Ben, an apprentice to his brother James, helped him put out his newspaper, the *New England Courant*; he set type, ran the press, and peddled papers. Reading the *Courant*, he found that contributors often signed humble names to their writings—Betty Frugal, Timothy Turnstone, Homespun Jack, and Ichabod Henroost, for instance. They wrote pretty much the way folk with such names might talk—in a style closer to the speech of bumpkins and laborers than to that of learned men and women. They wrote, as one of them put it, "in a very easy and familiar manner, so that the meanest ploughman, the very meanest of God's people can understand." Another member of the group justified the practice: "Say not who hath written, but consider what is written. . . . Say not that he is a mechanic, and an illiterate man; for there is good metal sometimes under mean soil." "He is no clown that drives the plow," Poor Richard would write, "but he that does clownish things."

When young Franklin submitted his own early efforts, the contributors liked them and backed their acceptance. This was understandable, for Ben wrote much as they did. His fictitious author was Silence Dogood, a countrywoman, poor, frugal, hard-

working, friendly with farm folk and leather-apron men, fond
of "useful and desirable knowledge," but contemptuous of flossy
writing "in the learned languages." She expressed herself in a
fashion that, for the time, was colloquial, slangy, even at times
earthy. Now and then because she was unsophisticated, she was
unwittingly satirical, as when she trustfully wrote a recipe for
concocting a fashionable funeral elegy that was sure to be trite
and bathetic. At other times, because she had good sense and
had benefited from experience, she thought up homely aphorisms or attacked frauds, such as Harvard men who slipped
through examinations with the help of tutors, graduated "as
great blockheads as ever, only more proud and self-conceited,"
and then accumulated bags of money. Clearly she was a blood
relation of the *Courant's* fictitious commentators and also of Poor
Richard, Father Abraham, and the Daddy Benjamin of the *Autobiography*.

Franklin, interestingly, says nothing about learning to create
a character of this sort from his brother's "writing friends"—
merely that their praise pleased him and that they "perhaps
were not really so very good [judges] as I then esteem'd them."
A likelihood is that another influence was more important—one
he speaks of in four different passages in his *Autobiography*. It
merits more notice than it has received because in addition to
being acknowledged by him, it gives Franklin's most popular
characterizations a long and honorable line of ancestors. Also,
defining this source will help trace the ancestry—and the mutations—of what even today is probably America's most beloved
joke.

In the first passage of the *Autobiography*, Franklin recalls
that in his sixteenth year (when he created Widow Dogood),
"intent on improving my language," he learned from books he
studied about "dispute in the Socratic method." He was "charm'd
with it, adopted it," and long used it successfully. In the second
passage, he tells how, arguing religion in his twenties, he
constantly "trepanned" a fanatical friend "with my Socratic
method." In the third passage, he says that, having blandly decided "to live without committing any fault at any time," he
listed thirteen virtues and rules for acquiring each; for "Humility," he said, "Imitate Jesus and Socrates." In the fourth pas-

II Mon. **April hath xxx days.**

Kind Katharine to her husband kiſs'd theſe words,
' Mine own ſweet *Will*, how dearly I love thee!
If true (quoth Will) the World no ſuch affords.
And that its true I durſt his warrant be;
For ne'er heard I of Woman good or ill,
But always loved beſt, her own ſweet Will.

1	G	All Fools.	1	29	5	32	7	*Great Talkers,*
2	2	*Wet weather, or*	2	♈	5	31	7	*little Doers.*
3	3	7 * ſet 9 0	2h	29	5	30	7	New ☽ 3 day,
4	4		3	♉	5	29	7	at 4 morn.
5	5	*Cloudy and likely*	4	29	5	27	7	☽ ſets 9 29 aft.
6	6	*for rain.*	5	♊	5	26	7	*A rich rogue, is*
7	7		6	18	5	24	7	*like a fat hog, who*
8	G	2 Sund. p. Eaſter	6h	♋	5	23	7	*never does good til*
9	2	☉ enters ♉	7	26	5	22	7	*as dead as a log.*
10	3	7 * ſet 8 50	8	♌	5	21	7	Firſt Quarter.
11	4	Days 13 h. 20 m.	9	22	5	20	7	☽ ſets 1 46 mo.
12	5	*Wind or Thunder,*	10	♍	5	19	7	*Relation without*
13	6	☍ ☉ ♃	10	16	5	18	7	*friendſhip, friend-*
14	7	☌ ♄ ♀	11	28	5	17	7	*ſhip without pow-*
15	G	3 Sund. p. Eaſter	12	♎	5	16	7	*er, power without*
16	2	7 * ſet 8 21	1	22	5	15	7	☽ ſets 4 7 mor.
17	3	*and rain.*	2	♏	5	14	7	Full ● at 10 at
18	4	*Beware of meat*	2h	16	5	13	7	night.
19	5	*twice boil'd, & an*	3	28	5	12	7	*will, will witho.*
20	6	*old foe reconcil'd.*	4	♐	5	11	7	*effect, effect with*
21	7	Days inc. 4 h. 26	5	22	5	10	7	☽ riſ. 11 aftern.
22	G	4 Sund. p. Eaſter	6	♑	5	8	7	*out profit, & pro-*
23	2	S George ☍ ♃ ♀	6h	16	5	7	7	*fit without ver-*
24	3	Troy burnt	7	29	5	6	7	*tue, are not*
25	4	St. Mark, Evang.	8	♒	5	5	7	Laſt Quarter.
26	5	*Cloudy with high*	9	24	5	4	7	*worth a farto.*
27	6	*winds, and perhaps*	10	♓	5	3	7	☽ riſ. 1 31 mor.
28	7	7 * ſet 7 47	11	22	5	2	7	
29	G	Rogation Sunday	12	♈	5	0	7	Days 14 hours
30	2	☌ ☉ ♀ *rain.*	12	22	5	59	S	7 * ſet 7 54

Page from *Poor Richard's Almanack* (1733-58) displaying a punning poem and several italicized aphorisms.

sage, he tells how, at age twenty-nine, he wrote "a Socratic dialogue" to read to his literary club and to publish in the *Pennsylvania Gazette*.

Socrates (470?-399 B.C.), like Widow Dogood and young Franklin, was hard up. His appearance was that of modern Street People—a year-round coat, no shoes, no shirt, a beard. A teacher before the publish-or-perish rule, he published nothing and his fame would have perished if secondary sources had not immortalized him. The Delphic Oracle called him the wisest of men, but he posed as a simpleton. Because, he plaintively explained, he knew nothing and his respondents knew much, he just had to ask questions. Franklin describes the steps he took when he became a teen-age follower:

I . . . dropt my abrupt contradiction, and positive argumentation, and put on [the character of] the humble inquirer and doubter. . . . I found this method safest for myself and very embarrassing to those against whom I used it, therefore I practis'd it continually and grew very artful and expert in drawing people even of superior knowledge into concessions the consequence of which they did not foresee, entangling them in difficulties out of which they could not extricate themselves, and so obtaining victories that neither my self nor my cause always deserved.

In time, Franklin says, he "left" this way of arguing. But, realizing that some Socratic tools were useful, he kept them—"retaining only the habit of expressing my self in terms of modest diffidence, never using . . . the words, *certainly*, *undoubtedly* or any that gave the air of positiveness," and saying, instead, "I conceive . . . or it is so if I am not mistaken." He follows with a discussion of a favorite theme, the virtue of modesty, obviously proud of his own superb stock of it.

What he clung to, in other words, was the habit of playing a self-deprecatory role. The Greeks had a word for a person with such a habit—*eiron* (the root of our word *irony*). And when Franklin's critics identified the actual man with his most famous fictional creations, they unwittingly repeated the attacks of the Athenians against Socrates. Since varied enactments of parts like those of Poor Richard and his kind recur again and again in our humor, and there isn't a satisfactory English equivalent, we'll have to use the word *eiron* often and so must define it with some care. A brief history of the word will be useful, partly to show kinships and partly to uncover modifications in meaning hastened by life in the New World.

Aristotle defined *eiron* in his *Ethics* as "the mock-modest man" who is "apt to disclaim what he has or to belittle it." F. M. Cornford, a scholar of Attic comedy, calls this type the "ironical man"—one who "is given to making himself out worse than he is." A Greek dictionary calls him "one who says less than he thinks."

We can perhaps sense the original meaning best if we think of an artist making himself out much worse than he is. Think of the ventriloquist Edgar Bergen, smooth, sophisticated, debonair, dangling on his knee his dummy, Mortimer Snerd—goggle-eyed, buck-toothed, weak-chinned, wearing a vapid grin, an out-moded suit, a red tie, and a brown derby. Snerd is funny because every stupid thing that his creator makes him say in "his" ade-noidal dumb fashion proclaims him a moron. Bergen, enacting with his voice the characterization that the dummy makes visi-ble, is being—in the original meaning of the word—an *eiron*. Red Skelton puts on the rumpled overalls and battered hat of farmer Clem Kadiddlehopper, crosses his eyes, loosens his lower jaw, and muffles his voice as Klem says idiotic things; Skelton too is impersonating someone far below him in intelligence. In *The Canterbury Tales* Geoffrey Chaucer, who actually was a shrewd, learned, and articulate poet, portrays himself as slow on the uptake and inarticulate. Arthur Heiserman describes the role that John Skelton, a poet, scholar, teacher, and rector, took in the fifteenth century: he wrote as "a plain, honest, uncompli-cated, vulgar, . . . simple, unlettered . . . plowman," Colin Clout.

Sixteenth-century jesters took advantage of their role to voice truths that others didn't dare to express. Thomas Fuller praised one: "Jesters often heal what flatterers hurt, so that princes by them arrive at the notice of their errors, seeing jesters carry about with them an act of indemnity for whatever they do. . . . Our Tarlton was master of his faculty. When Queen Elizabeth was *serious* (I dare not say *sullen*) . . . he could *undumpish* her at his pleasure." Pretending innocence but speaking with forked tongues, Shakespeare's fools and others, like Tarlton (pos-sibly the prototype of Yorick), undumpished and at the same time chided royalty, thus indicating the satirical values of the pose. Characters in plays and novels, humble and unlearned speakers "by chance" of truths, were pages such as Jack Wilton in Nash's *Unfortunate Traveller* (1594), squires such as Don Quixote's Sancho Panza (1605, 1615), servants such as the za-nies of the sixteenth- and seventeenth-century *commedia dell' arte*, and valets such as Bertie Wooster's Jeeves in the twentieth century.

In America, characters of this sort were destined to have status

miles higher than that of a court jester, page, squire or valet.
Thanks to a new status, they would be laugh-provoking oracles—
quoted, admired, and even depended upon for insights. A complete listing would include at least thirty masculine and feminine commentators on American life during two centuries.
Some, as will be indicated, were famous enough to have their
words—or their characters' words—quoted with relish and respect long after they were in their graves. As late as the 1970's,
the self-deprecatory "folk humor" of the late Harry S. Truman
and Senator Sam Ervin not only amused millions of Americans
but also won their hearty praise.

Why? The reason is that developments in the New World
helped Franklin and a long procession that followed him become
more than mere comic figures—respected utterers of important
truths. Thanks to some European help and to the American environment, by the eighteenth century a mutation of the Old
World distrust for pedantry had occurred. In some segments of
our population, overt hostility had developed. Many now might
say that when an educated man pretended to be illiterate, perhaps he wasn't "making himself out worse than he was." Possibly
he was assuming a virtue when he had it not, and thus *improving* his image. Contrary convictions in some Establishment
groups, and vestigial remnants of respect—or actual ambivalence—in the general populace were what continued to make
the unlearned pose derogatory.

It is possible to see stages in the development of this changed
attitude that helped Americanize humor and satire. A writer for
the *Courant*, it will be remembered, said that "sometimes" an
illiterate person might be wise. Two years before Franklin was
born, Sarah Kemble Knight, a Boston gentlewoman, after watching "Bumpkin Simpers" and "Joan Tawdry" behave in a way
that exposed their countrified upbringing, moralized: "We may
observe here the great necessity and benefit both of education
and conversation; for these people have as large a portion of
mother wit, and *sometimes a larger* [italics ours] than those who
have been brought up in cities; but for want of improvements,
render themselves almost ridiculous." Madam Knight was a
schoolteacher (Franklin's for a time, perhaps) and therefore possibly oversold education; but her belief that country folk might
be wiser than urbanites marked a stage in an interesting trend.

By the time Franklin matured, four groups—religious reformers, Deists, "natural historians" and anti-intellectuals—had advanced the even more radical belief that prospered prodigiously in this country—that a lack of education actually *helped* an experienced person with a good mind acquire wisdom. And Franklin had ties with every single one of these groups.

The religious reformers—early Puritans in England—favored an educated ministry. From 1640 on, though, when the faith spread to lower-class "Diggers" and "Levelers," such "dirty people of no name" badmouthed education. A cobbler who served as a lay preacher subtitled his popular book *A Treatise to Prove Humane-Learning to be no Help to the Spiritual understanding of the Word of God*. A pastor who "would rather hear a plain country man speak in church, that came from the plough, than the best orthodox minister" welcomed to his pulpit the unschooled tinker John Bunyan. When Puritans and other anti-Establishment groups crossed the Atlantic, they cultivated similar attitudes. Samuel Gorton, jailed in Boston for blasphemy and persuaded to move to Rhode Island, gloated in 1646, "I was not bred up in the schools of human learning; and I bless God that I never was, lest I had been drowned in pride and ignorance . . . as millions are and have been." Quakers compared learned ministers to shopkeepers who clanged churchbells to lure customers, and then conned them into buying worthless goods. During "the Great Awakening" which swept the colonies between 1734 and 1750, a Boston minister noticed that "many [revivalists] speak slightly of our schools and colleges" and wish they could "rase them to their foundations." A typical Methodist circuit rider sniffed at the "sapient, downy D.D." whose "paper words" put one in mind of "a gosling that had got the straddles by wading in the dew." Franklin, reared in Puritan Boston by a pious father, played with Puritan children, heard the great preachers and read their books. He imitated Bunyan's mixture of narration and dialogue. His Widow Dogood got her last name from a famous Puritan book which Franklin praised, *Essays to Do Good*. He lived for years in Quaker Philadelphia. Admiring the sermons of George Whitefield, a founder of Methodism and an instigator of the Great Awakening, he became his friend and financial backer.

Many seventeenth- and eighteenth-century non-sectarians

called Deists also discredited formal learning. "My own mind," wrote Deist Tom Paine, "is my own church"; his best-selling pamphlet was *Common Sense*. "State a moral case to a ploughman and a professor," wrote another Deist, Thomas Jefferson. "The former will decide it as well, and often better than the latter, because he has not been led astray by artificial rules." Much study of moral philosophy, he held, wasted time. From his early years until his death, Franklin read Deists' books and often expressed Deist beliefs. Collaborating with Jefferson on the Declaration of Independence, he proposed the very important words, "We hold these truths to be self-evident," which derive from the Deist belief that some laws—the most important ones, in fact—can be understood and followed by the humblest man if he has not had the bad luck to be born an idiot.

Another New World group—explorers, settlers, surveyors—who learned important truths quite incidentally became important "natural historians." In the seventeenth century, a soldier of fortune like John Smith, a curious (and often credulous) inquirer like John Josselyn, a theocrat like William Bradford; in the eighteenth century, an unschooled collector of plants like John Bartram and surveyors like Charles Mason and Jeremiah Dixon; in the early nineteenth century, soldiers Meriwether Lewis and William Clark all made and recorded invaluable observations about a previously unknown country, its flora, and its fauna. Typically, William Byrd of Virginia, who in 1728 surveyed the Virginia–North Carolina border, as a matter of course set down valuable facts about Indian mores, rattlesnake root, hickory nuts, wild grapes, cane brakes, opossum, polecats, buffalo, bears, and wild turkey, though he had no scientific training whatever. Also as a matter of course, he was a member and an informative correspondent of the Royal Society of Great Britain. As Daniel J. Boorstin says, "In Europe, discovering something new in the natural world required the concentration of a philosopher, the researches of a scholar, or the industry of an encyclopedist. In America it took effort to avoid novelty."

Completely self-trained though he was, Franklin made worldshaking contributions to scientific knowledge in the field of electricity. In addition, he studied the movement of cyclonic storms, the Gulf Stream, the effects of oil on troubled waters, the cure for the common cold, and other problems which today would be tackled only by specially trained scientists. Like Byrd, he was elected to the exclusive Royal Society for what, though important, were basically "amateur" studies.

If George Perkins Marsh of Vermont is to be believed, even Franklin's broad interests and activities were typical of Eastern colonists: "Every man," he said approvingly, "is a dabbler, if not a master, in every knowledge . . . a divine, a statesman, a physician, and a lawyer to himself, as well as a counsellor to his neighbors, on all the interests, involved in the sciences appropriately belonging to those professions."

Finally, anti-intellectualism was gaining strength in America. Two years after Franklin's death, Hugh Henry Brackenridge ironically prescribed a lack of learning as a prerequisite for success in several fields:

I feel myself disposed to agree with those who reject human learning in religious matters altogether. More especially as science is really not the fashion at the present time [and] even in the very province of science it is dispensed with; that of natural philosophy, for instance. In state affairs, ignorance does very well. . . . I am for having all things of a piece; ignorant statesmen, ignorant philosophers, and ignorant ecclesiastics.

In time, the irony faded. As Richard Hofstadter says in his fine history, *Anti-Intellectualism in American Life* (1964), "At an early date . . . it seemed to be the good of the common man in America to build a society that would show how much could be done without literature and learning—or rather, a society whose literature and learning would be largely limited to such elementary things as the common man could grasp and use."

Whatever he himself believed, Franklin could not have failed to see that the intellectual climate in America had readied audiences for characters such as Silence Dogood, Poor Richard, Father Abraham, and old Daddy Ben. As will be seen, historical developments after Franklin's death continued to make these characters and others of their kind some of the best-loved figures in our humor.

They would all perpetuate what is surely the most dependable American joke—the one based upon the way educated people

miss the truth by using book learning while humble, unlearned
people find truth by using their horse sense. Again and again,
Americans would find hilarious the fact that a man's education
is likely to make him think and act like a damned fool. "The
learned fool," says Poor Richard, "writes his nonsense in better
language than the unlearned; but still 'tis nonsense." Again:
"Tim was so learned, that he could name a horse in nine languages. So ignorant, that he bought a cow to ride on."

In "On the Price of Corn, and Management of the Poor," a
letter to a newspaper in 1766, Franklin followed the formula to
perfection. The writer states in the first paragraph, "I am one
of that class of people, that feeds you all . . . a *farmer*." The
signature, "Arator," shows that the purported writer, like the
medieval Colin Clout, "the meanest of God's people," for whom
the *Courant* crowd wrote and Jefferson said can often decide a
moral problem "better than a professor," is a plowman. A bit
later, to prove that he knows what he is talking about, Arator
says, not that he has read books (though he quotes "the good
Book" twice), not that he is educated, but "In my youth, I travelled much, and observed in different countries." Using his experience, his good eyes, and his head, he has learned truths
which he states with a sharpness and economy not unlike Poor
Richard's, e.g., "When you are sure that you have a good principle, go through with it." (Davy Crockett's most famous maxim
would be, "Be sure you're right, then go ahead.") In the plain
but forceful words of a farmer, he could tear into the claim that
a ban on exporting certain farm products would cut prices on
manufactured goods:

I have heard my grandfather say, that the farmers submitted to the
prohibition on the exportation of wool, being made to expect and believe, that, when the manufacturer bought his wool cheaper, they
should also have their cloth cheaper. But the deuce a bit. It has been
growing dearer and dearer from that day to this. How so? Why, truly,
the cloth is exported; and that keeps up the price.

Now, if it be a good principle, that the exportation of a commodity is
to be restrained, that so our people at home may have it the cheaper,
stick to that principle, and go through-stitch with it. Prohibit the exportation of your cloth, your leather, and shoes . . . to make them
cheaper at home. And cheap enough they will be, I will warrant you;
till people leave off making them.

To polish off his opponents ("some folks," he calls them), the farmer shrinks their stand to an absurdity by saying that they "seem to think they ought never to be easy" until their country "becomes another Lubberland" where "streets are paved with penny-rolls, the houses tiled with pan-cakes and chickens, ready roasted, cry, 'Come eat me.' "

About this time [aged sixteen] I met with an odd volume of the Spectator. *It was the third. I had never before seen any of them. I bought it, read it over and over, and was much delighted with it. I thought the writing excellent, and wished, if possible, to imitate it. With that view I took some of the papers, and, making short hints of the sentiment in each sentence, laid them by a few days, and then, without looking at the book, tried to complete the papers again by expressing each sentiment at length, and as fully as it had been expressed before, in any suitable words that should come to hand. Then I compared my* Spectator *with the original, discovered some of my faults, and corrected them.*

—Benjamin Franklin, *The Autobiography* (1771).

7.
Varied Masks

DISSENTING CHURCHMEN HAD decided that a "popular style" that would "strike home to the capacity and humour of the multitude" was best. "Words easy to understand," Bunyan said, "do often hit the mark, when high and learned ones do only pierce the air." A co-signer of the Declaration of Independence with Franklin bawled out politicians for debauching good usage—evidence that even then, "public persons," as he called them, mangled grammar because they had learned that doing so brought votes. "If the author does not intend his piece for general reading," wrote Franklin, "he must exactly suit his style and manner to the particular taste of those he proposes for his readers." His own "style and manner" in piece after piece are tailored to a character that he is impersonating— one skillfully created to carry the message. As Larzer Ziff points out:

Each [piece] reflects a sharp recognition of the audience . . . in the point of view from which it is presented. Is it the object to ridicule the mores which condemn the fallen woman while overlooking the man? Then the speaker is the amiable, good-hearted, yet guilty Polly Baker. Is the object to drive home a collection of proverbs on economy? Then the speaker is Father Abraham, a trim and successful old man who has benefitted from the best of such sayings. . . .

Franklin's brilliant creation of the appropriate *persona* for the literary task at hand is a feature of almost every piece. . . .

The number of characters, masks, or *personae* is huge— roughly a hundred, in pieces that have been with some certainty ascribed to Franklin. The variety is so abundant that it led one modern critic to guess that if he had tried, the author might have done well as a novelist. The creatures range from "veracious" and logical spokesmen with whom the writer is sympathetic and with whom readers are expected to be sympathetic to disgusting monsters. There are blood brothers of Poor Richard, such as "an old tradesman, homespun and chearful." Politically, the figures align variously. There are colonists—a New England man, a tradesman of Philadelphia, and a Virginian. There are residents of Great Britain who take a variety of positions—colonists' advocate, a London manufacturer, a friend to military government.

Some, though flawed, are not vicious. Anthony Afterwit is an honest tradesman who doesn't know how to cope with an extravagant spouse. A traveler credulously swallows impossible stories about America's fauna. Alice Addertongue, " a young girl of about thirty-five," is overfond of gossip. A roguish scientist playfully and punningly enters a Royal Academy contest by suggesting experiments to learn ways of making stomach gas less offensive. Another prankish fellow, this time a man of the world, advises a young man to marry, but if this is impractical, to get himself an older rather than a younger woman for a mistress. He gives many reasons:

Because . . . their minds are better stored with Observations, their Conversation is more improving and more lastingly agreeable . . . there is no Hazard of Children, which irregularly produced may be attended with much Inconvenience. . . . Because the sin is less. The Debauching of a Virgin may be her Ruin, and make her Life unhappy. . . . Because the Compunction is less. The having made a young girl miserable may give you frequent bitter Reflections; none of which can attend making an old Woman happy . . . and lastly, They are so grateful!

The monsters are monstrous in sundry ways. They are foolish, arrogant, violent, inhuman, hypocritical, or several of these

combined. Since their origins, their uses, and their literary prog-
eny differ greatly from those of the more sympathetic *personae*,
they will be discussed separately in the next chapter.

Readers of leading eighteenth-century British essayists will notice some likenesses between Franklin's non-monsters and "the
feigned persons of the authors" in the essays. The resemblances
are not entirely incidental. After all, throughout his life, except
for the few last years, Franklin was a British subject. After his
eighteenth birthday, he spent a good third of his life abroad,
much of it in England. Until the eve of the American Revolution, he was not at all sure that he favored a break. And, as the
saying goes, all his days some of his best friends were English.

"Extremely ambitious," as he put it, "to be a tolerable *English*
writer," he made no bones about imitating contemporary authors. Scholars have traced their influence through a large share
of Franklin's pages. One who particularly shaped his humor and
satire was Joseph Addison (1672-1719).

Home from London after serving his apprenticeship there,
Franklin's older brother James spread the fame of the *Spectator*
and its fashionable and popular creators, Addison and Richard
Steele. He and his contributors emulated them. So did young
Ben. The *Autobiography* tells how he thought up and worked
at time-consuming, tricky exercises which he hoped would teach
him to write like these models. His good opinion of them lasted
throughout his life. In 1749 he named Addison among authors
the youth of Philadelphia should study to perfect their grammar
and master clear, concise styles. Two years later, outlining a cur-
riculum for the Philadelphia Academy, he had second-class (i.e.,
year) students learn grammatical rules, the writer's intention,
the scope, "the meaning of every sentence, and every uncommon
word" by studying carefully "easier" *Spectator* essays. In the
sixth and final class, the students would read and explain "the
best English authors," among them Addison and "the higher
papers in the *Spectator* and *Guardian*." In his old age, Franklin
still praised these works.

His first published *Dogood Papers*, and a bit later the *Busy-
Body Papers*, clearly show the influence in his formative years.
The first *Spectator* gives the "feigned person's" account of him-
self:

I have observed, that a reader seldom peruses a book with pleasure till he knows whether the writer of it be a black or a fair man, of a mild or choleric disposition, married or a bachelor, with other particulars of the like nature, that conduce very much to the right understanding of an author. To gratify this curiosity, which is so natural to a reader, I design this paper, and next, as prefatory discourses. . . .

The first *Dogood Paper:*

And since it is observed that the generality of people, now a days, are unwilling either to commend or dispraise what they read, until they are in some measure informed who or what the author of it is, whether he be poor or rich, old or young, a scholar or a leather-apron man, and give their opinion of the performance . . . it may not be amiss to begin with a short account of my past life and present condition. . . .

Addison's "Spectator" plays up the fact that he was a grave child and a sullen youth, and that in the university "I distinguished myself by a most profound silence . . . indeed I do not remember that I ever spoke three sentences together in my whole life. . . ." He says that he writes his papers because friends think it a pity that "so many useful discoveries . . . should be in the possession of a silent man." Franklin's widow's first name is "Silence." She is a "spectator" who, like her British counterpart, watches from the sidelines, comments on foibles and fashions (topics often discussed by her predecessor), and relays the views of friends. About half of one of her pieces quotes *Spectator 185;* another obviously imitates the allegorical vision of *Spectator 3.* Of course, there are great differences. The British series was for upper-class English readers; Franklin consciously addressed lower-class American colonists. The chief likeness, in fact, is in manner rather than matter—a pervasive tone of geniality and good will appropriate for the fictional author. When Addison in *Spectator 35* implied that his objective was to write "true humour," the descendant of "truth, good sense, wit and mirth," he also defined his admirer's objective in his essays or skits which he hoped would amuse and cajole his readers.

By contrast, a number of interesting and influential pieces written by Franklin in some ways resemble what Addison called "false humour." These seem to originate in what the *Spectator* calls "an imagination that teems with monsters, a head that is filled with extravagant conceptions."

Although, as has been shown, the American tendency to admire ignorance somewhat rusted the irony of Franklin's satires
in the "Poor Richard" mode, the irony of the "monster" pieces
was unharmed. Feelings about the hideous faults of the repulsive
creatures didn't change in the colonies—still haven't, for that
matter. Therefore, when Franklin created "monster" roles, no
one could doubt that he made himself out worse than he was.

Franklin learned to create such *personae* from teachers other
than those discussed above. Their preachments are beamed to
different audiences than those reached by his more genial speakers, and the aims of the pieces in which they appear are different. The pieces initiate other trends—quite important ones—in
American humor, some of them continuing to the present. Rep-
resentatives of this group of writings, masterpieces of their kind,
will receive detailed treatment in the next chapter.

KO-KO. *Well, a nice mess you've got us into, with your nodding head and the deference due to a man of pedigree!*

POOH-BAH. *Merely corroborative detail, intended to give artistic verisimilitude to an otherwise bald and unconvincing narrative.*

PITTI-SING. *Corroborative detail indeed! Corroborative fiddlestick!*

—W. S. Gilbert, *The Mikado, or the Town of Titipu* (1885).

8.
Franklin's Monsters— and Some Offspring

ON APRIL 15, 1774, A PSEUDON-ymous letter in the London *Public Advertiser* offered a plan to "quiet the disturbances in America, . . . make our royalty master a king *de facto* [and] procure a round sum towards discharging the National debt." Let "a few regiments of bold Britons, appearing with ensigns displayed, and in all the pomp of war," half led by General Gage, half by one of the great orators in Parliament, "accompanied with a detachment from the artillery," march through North America. The colonists, "a dastardly set of poltroons, . . . will fly like sheep pursued by a wolf." Next, enroll all colonists in the militia, where they will be subject to martial law, appoint officers "from among the conquered people," try any rambunctious colonist by court martial, and have him lashed, "according to the nature of his offenses," one hundred to one thousand times. Set up a military dictatorship, collect taxes until the colonists are bankrupt, and sell them and their land to either France or Spain. Two million pounds collected in this way, the writer estimates, will enable Lord North to reduce the national debt and win "the blessing of the poor . . . by taking off the halfpenny duty on porter."

A second letter in the same newspaper on May 21, 1774, suggested even more drastic measures to humble "our rebellious vassals." Let General Gage lead five battalions through several towns, accompanied by a hundred sow-gelders. In every town or village, assemble the males and have them all castrated. The pseudonymous writer demolished objections and predicted tremendous gains: (1) "In the course of fifty years it is probable we shall not have one rebellious subject in North America." (2) Instead of importing castrati from Italy at great cost, managers of opera can use our own more cheaply and keep the money at home. (3) As a service to the Levant trade, we can furnish seraglios and harems with eunuchs and "with handsome women, for which America is as famous as Circassia." (4) Emigration from England, far too popular, will halt.

Absolute proof is lacking, but authorities on Franklin are virtually certain that he wrote both of these letters—about as black in their humor as any modern bitter satire.

What was a nice American colonist doing in wolf's clothing like this? He'd learned from teachers quite different from easygoing Socrates and Addison how to put on masks different in important ways from those he wore in his most famous works.

James Franklin had brought home from London the writings of a pair which were stirring British readers—Daniel Defoe (1660–1731) and Jonathan Swift (1667–1745). Brother Ben liked both and learned from them. They perhaps helped him learn to impersonate sympathetic monologists, for both had done this. More important, though, they—or close imitators—taught him to be an *eiron* in what was more obviously the original way —to be possessed by the personalities of monsters. A look at the satirical masterpiece of each and at some of Franklin's most effective ironical writings will show this indebtedness.

In *The Shortest-Way with the Dissenters* (1702), Defoe immersed himself in the role of a speaker who wasn't inferior to his creator in relatively blameless ways (e.g., lacking money or education) but who was far below him morally—in tolerance, humanity, and self-control. Readers today can hardly imagine the ferocity with which Church of England fanatics in the early eighteenth century hated dissenters. A typical hater called them "a breed of vipers . . . treasonable . . . clamourous, insatiable, church-devouring malignants," and said they should be "treated like growing mischiefs, or infectious plagues." Defoe played the role of just such a livid churchman. To deal with them, said the fanatic he impersonated:

If one severe law were made, and punctually executed, that who ever was found at a [Protestant] Conventicle should be banished . . . and the preacher be hanged, we should soon see an end. . . . *Alas the Church of England!* What with Popery on one hand, and Schismatics on the other; how has she been crucified between the thieves.

Now, let us crucify the thieves . . . let the obstinate be ruled with the *rod of iron . . . that the posterity of the sons of error may be rooted out from the face of this land for ever.*

The fanatical author parades arguments for sending Protestant preachers to the gallows and their congregations to the galleys.

Defoe said that his aim in this "irony" was "to speak in the first person of the party" that he opposes and to say *"the very thing they drive at"* in "plain English [so that] the whole nation will start at the notion, and condemn the author to be hanged for his impudence"—to exaggerate to the highest absurdity High Church fanaticism but not to give away the fact. He succeeded. Some opponents, caught off guard, wildly cheered his harsh attack, only to learn that they'd been bamboozled.

What *The Shortest-Way* was for Defoe, *A Modest Proposal,* twenty-seven years later, was for Swift—a masterpiece among his shorter works. It uses quite similar tactics but differs in one significant way. Swift impersonates an Irishman harrowed by the suffering of Irish men and women who are forced to beg food for their helpless children and then watch them grow up, become thieves, join foreign armies, or "sell themselves to the Barbadoes." The writer presents "a fair, cheap and easy method of making these children sound and useful members of the commonwealth":

I do therefore humbly offer it to public consideration, that of the hundred and twenty thousand children, . . . twenty thousand be reserved for breed [and] that the remaining hundred thousand, may, at a year old, be offered in sale to the persons of quality and fortune, through the kingdom; always advising the mother to let them suck plentifully in the last month, so as to render them plump, and fat for a good table. A child will make two dishes at an entertainment for friends; and when the family dines alone, the fore or hind quarter will make a reasonable dish; and seasoned with a little pepper and salt, will be very good boiled on the fourth day, especially in winter.

The piece is like *The Shortest-Way* in justifying a horrible course of action with what the writer offers as overwhelming arguments (e.g., it will decrease the number of Catholics, add to the country's income, and lift the standard of living).

But as the writer outlines the problem, he is factual rather than intemperate, compassionate rather than cruel. The sight of begging mothers and children everywhere *is* what he says it is, "a melancholy object." Voluntary abortions and the murdering of infants, as he says, *do* move to pity "the most savage and inhuman." As the reader peruses such paragraphs about Ireland's problems, therefore, he agrees and is sympathetic. When the reader moves to the paragraphs proposing a remedy, though, he comes upon startling signs that the voice is that of a fiend who blandly recommends cannibalism and offers what he thinks are rational arguments for it. There is a contrast between the humane passages and unfeeling calculations or mad gloatings, such as, "a young healthy child, well nursed, is at a year old, a most delicious, nourishing, and wholesome food, whether stewed, roasted, baked, or broiled . . . in a fricasee, or ragout," and "I rather recommend buying the children alive, and dressing them hot from the knife, as we do roasting pigs." The contrast proclaims and underlines the irony.

Toward the close of the essay, the mask is briefly lowered and, as Wayne Booth says: "For a moment all comic disparities are dropped; Swift, his speaker, and we readers are all united in a despairing vision of just how bad conditions are—since they have been made to seem morally worse than the modest proposal." The final paragraph returns to the mode of irony as the speaker piously boasts that he makes his suggestion without the least personal interest, his only wish being to promote "the public good of my country"; "I have no children, by which I can propose to get a single penny; the youngest being nine years old, and my wife past child-bearing."

Likenesses between *The Shortest-Way* and *A Modest Proposal* are clear. In each, the fictitious author urges an action so repulsive that the reader recoils in disgust. In a sense, there is guilt by association. Church of England clergymen and oppressors of Ireland are defiled because their champions propose such wretched solutions. Their stand is exaggerated and, paradoxically, reduced to absurdity. But there is an important difference. Though each puts on a Halloween mask, Defoe keeps his on from start to finish, whereas Swift at intervals drops his to show the world a face more like his own. Unless the reader of Defoe's piece decides for himself that the author is playing a role, he may be the victim of a hoax. Swift, by contrast, provides anti-hoax insurance.

The two pieces in the *Public Advertiser* of 1774 are in the mode of *The Shortest-Way*. In each, an unmitigated rapscallion says "the very thing" the opponents "drive at" in English so plain that readers may well "start at the notion." Intemperate writers to newspapers actually had come very close to saying the same things shortly before these caricatures of their remarks were published. And in neither of Franklin's pieces is the mask lowered.

Defoe's method was also the one Franklin used in what several admirers consider his satirical masterpiece, "The Sale of the Hessians." As a climactic paragraph in the Declaration of Independence shows, the colonists hotly resented England's sending of "large armies of foreign mercenaries to complete the works of death, desolation and tyranny, already begun."

The monster that Franklin impersonated in "The Sale of the Hessians" was one Count de Schaumberg of Hesse, who is joyously raking in payments for attritions to an army he'd sent across the seas and using the blood money to live lavishly. This heartless hypocrite has sent this letter, purportedly, to Baron Hohendorf, "commanding Hessian troops in America." The count has heard with delight about the carnage wreaked upon his men in the Battle of Trenton. He's ecstatic because so many were killed—at so much a killing—and because so few escaped. He even hints that it will be a dandy thing if a number of those wounded pass away. In accordance with instructions given—

. . . you will not have tried by human succor to recall the life of the unfortunates whose days could not be lengthened but by the loss of a leg or an arm. That would make them a pernicious present, and I am sure they would rather die than live in a condition no longer fit for my service. I do not mean by this that you should assassinate them; we should be humane, my dear Baron, but you may insinuate to the surgeons with entire propriety that a crippled man is a reproach to their profession, and there is no wiser course than to let every one of them die when he ceases to be fit to fight.

The count will soon send new recruits, and he urges the baron not to "economize" them: "Remember glory before all things" —before money, say, since love of it "degrades" soldiers.

Schaumberg lovingly remembers the three hundred Lacedae-monians who all died defending Thermopylae: "How happy should I be could I say the same of my brave Hessians!"

The baron hurries to tell why he himself doesn't need to join his men and gloriously perish, as Leonidas did: "things have changed, and it is no longer the custom for princes to go and fight in America for a cause with which they have no concern." He adds arguments: 1) Someone has to be in Europe to collect the pay for each man killed. 2) He must stay abroad to replace troops lost—a harder and harder thing to do, since men are be-coming scarce and must be supplanted by boys. He ends by out-lining ways casualties (and therefore, of course, glory) may be increased and the war prolonged. This is very desirable, since "I have made arrangements for a grand Italian opera, and I do not wish to be obliged to give it up." He ends with a pious greeting: "Meantime I pray God, my dear Baron de Hohendorf, to have you in his holy and gracious keeping."

The technique is that of Defoe's masterpiece—the exaggera-tion of actual attitudes in the monologue of an unmitigated scoundrel to whom bloody deaths in battle or even wantonly contrived by doctors bring "unspeakable pleasure." And the mingling of hypocritical maunderings about bravery, glory, and God with the disgusting instructions makes them all the more repulsive. Moses Coit Tyler says in his *Literary History of the American Revolution:*

In some respects, this is the most powerful of all the satirical writings of Franklin. More, perhaps, than is the case with any other work of his, it displays, with marvelous subtlety and wit, that sort of genius which can reproduce with minute and perfect verisimilitude the psychological processes of some monstrous crime against human nature,—a crime which it thus portrays both to the horror and the derision of mankind.

A letter that Franklin wrote his son from London gave details showing that another much admired piece of his was more in the manner of Swift than Count Schaumberg's dramatic mono-logue—"An Edict by the King of Prussia." By good luck, the American was breakfasting with some British gentlemen when a Mr. Whitehead "came running in to us, with the paper in his hand."

Here! says he, here's news for ye! *Here's the King of Prussia, claiming a right to this kingdom!* All stared, and I as much as anybody; and he went on to read it. When he had read two or three paragraphs, a gentleman present said, *Damn his impudence, I dare say, we shall hear by next post that he is upon his march with one hundred thousand men to back this.* Whitehead, who is very shrewd, soon after began to smoke it, and looking in my face said, *I'll be hanged if this is not some of your American jokes upon us.* The reading went on, and ended with abundance of laughing, and a general verdict that it was a fair hit. . . .

As Whitehead indicated, in his purported "edict," King Frederick claims that, since Germany is England's "mother country," it has a right to do what Great Britain is doing—command obedience and levy taxes on "colonies." England therefore is ordered to let Prussia regulate its commerce and manufactures under threat of trial and punishment for treason.

Anyone looking at the piece as it first appeared is bound to suspect that Mr. Whitehead wasn't very bright. An introduction said that the "editor" had separated the edict from "the usual articles of *foreign news*" because of its "extraordinary" nature, and he wondered whether it was "serious" or "merely one of the king's *Jeux d'Esprit*." In other words, Franklin (who wrote this), like Swift, predicted the irony by using a contrasting voice. Anyone who missed this early sign, as well as clear indications in the work itself, got a final chance when the "editor" put at the end a far-too-innocent criticism:

All here think the assertion [the edict] concludes with, "that these regulations are copied from acts of the English parliament respecting their colonies," a very injurious one; it being impossible to believe, that a people distinguished for their love of liberty, a nation so wise, so liberal in its sentiments, so just and equitable towards its neighbors, should from mean and injudicious views of petty immediate profit, treat its own children in a manner so arbitrary and tyrannical!

This fuses irony forged from innocence with irony forged from corruption, and the "editor" joins the "king" to create satire.

A less famous skit in the manner of Swift is still more ingenious and, we think, one of Franklin's sharpest hatchet jobs. Setting this up must have been time-consuming and hard. On his own press in far-off Passy, France, in 1782, the ex-printer painstakingly reproduced the make-up—headlines, type design—the works—of a newspaper published across the ocean, then printed a *Supplement to the Boston Independent Chronicle* and had copies distributed in England. All this paraphernalia might seem to suggest a hoax. So might the elaborate use of three different writers. But the sheer complexity, plus the lavishly invented, preposterous, and grisly details, in the end give the bloodcurdling show away.

The target is a ploy that enraged the colonists even more than the homeland's importing of mercenaries—the use of Indians and payment of bounties for scalps. The satire, Franklin said, "places in a striking light, the English barbarities . . . particularly those committed by the savages at their instigation. The *form* may perhaps not be genuine, but the substance is truth."

After giving a dateline, "an editor" supplies a heading: "Extract of a letter from Captain Gerrish, of the New England Militia, dated Albany, March 7." Gerrish's report, then quoted, says that he and his men captured booty during a recent expedition and "were struck with horror to find among the packages 8 large ones, containing SCALPS" of "our unhappy country-folks" taken during three years by Senecan Indians and sent by them, with James Crauford's covering letter, to the governor of Canada for transmission to England.

Crauford's letter, which comes next, introduces a blood relation of Swift's Irish advocate of baby-munching. (We suspect, though, that he couldn't have been created if Franklin hadn't read not only rhetoric but also fiction by Defoe and Swift in which they showed uncanny ability to climb into characters' hides and speak with their voices in first-person log books crammed with concrete experiences, precise facts and vivid sensory impressions.) Completely without signs of emotion, Crauford sets down a businesslike invoice, numbering, counting, and classifying eight packs of scalps, one thousand sixty-two in all, "cured, dried, hooped, and painted with all the Indian triumphal marks." The hieroglyphs—Franklin's most ingenious inventions —help him with his icy-blooded descriptions:

No. 2. Containing 98 [scalps] of farmers killed in their houses; hoops red; figure of a hoe, to mark their profession; great white circle and sun, to show they were surprised in the day-time; a little red foot, to show they stood upon their defence, and died fighting for their lives and families.

No. 7. 211 girls' scalps, big and little; small yellow hoops; white ground, tears; hatchet, club, scalping-knife, &c.

No. 8. This package is a mixture of all the varieties above mentioned; to the number of 122; with a box of birch bark, containing 29 little infants scalps of various sizes; small white hoops; white ground; no tears; and only a little black knife in the middle, to shew they were ript out of their mothers' bellies.

(The "little black knife"—more precisely, its translation—probably is the sort of invention Defoe had in mind when he spoke of "miraculous fancy.") Crauford then quotes an oily speech made by Seneca Chief Conejogatchie, addressed to "Father," piously protesting friendship, whining about poverty and hardships, and urging better payment for scalps. Crauford's concluding paragraph blandly recommends "further encouragement to these honest people," and promises to pass out "presents . . . sent for them . . . with prudence and fidelity." His unemotional catalogue and his tacit approval vivify him and disgust the reader.

Now comes Captain Gerrish's final paragraph, reporting plans to use the grisly trophies to further the colonists' efforts. They will be carried to England and hung "some dark night on the trees in St. James Park, where they could be seen from the King and Queen's Palaces," with the hope that they will stir "compunction of conscience." En route, they will probably reach Boston a few days after the letter.

The story ends with the "editor's" announcement that the scalps have got to Boston. There, thousands of townspeople are "flocking to see them . . . and all mouths are full of execrations." The story takes a final turn with the news that the plan to tack the scalps on trees had been junked and another has replaced it:

It is now proposed to make them up in decent little packets, seal and direct them; one to the King, containing a sample of every sort for his museum; one to the Queen, with some of the women and little children; the rest to be distributed among both houses of parliament; a double quantity to bishops.

The superbly marshaled, concrete details, the antiphony of voices, and the striking personalities all work together to give this bizarre and imaginative document great power.

Lewis Leary, in discussing Franklin's writings in 1973, claimed that he "exhibits almost all the tendencies and attitudes discoverable in succeeding American authors of his kind." Leary goes on to note that "under Franklin's aegis, the ventriloquist writer invaded the new world," with his humor serving as "a hedge from behind which many who followed him would exploit the comic view." He points to the two-hundred-year-old heritage of sympathetic, horse-sensible American monologists who, though untutored, rough-cut diamonds, could wittily back sound attitudes and policies: such men as Hosea Biglow, Abe Lincoln, Josh Billings, Mr. Dooley, Will Rogers, and Harry Truman.

This pioneering alone justifies our treating Franklin at length in a history of American humor. But this book-nurtured journalist was a leader or foreshadower in other important ways as well. In addition to these kinsmen of Poor Richard, there would be many heirs of such unlovable speakers as heartless James Crauford, vicious Count de Schaumberg, and the swaggering, pietistic, and unfeeling King of Prussia. Later American *eiron*-humorists would don the disguises and speak with the voices of fools, rascals, and fiends to urge views and actions at odds with those of their creators. At intervals, men such as Abraham Lincoln and Mark Twain would play the role of numskull or heel. For longer stretches, humorists would have ventriloqual spokesmen back attitudes and actions that they themselves opposed. James Russell Lowell, a hater of the Mexican War, would have silly Birdofredum Sawin, fired with enthusiasm, enlist, serve ingloriously, and—brutalized by war—turn into a cynical conniver. Two popular comic creations of the Civil War period would be a boozelogged, grafting Copperhead limned by a Northerner, and as his opposite, a traitorous truckler to the North, created by a pro-Confederate Georgian. Ring Lardner would have his storytellers unconsciously expose their warped natures by reciting or writing first-person narratives. William Faulkner would have Jason Compson expose his dishonesty and meanness, and those of Southerners like him, by narrating a section of the novel *The Sound and the Fury*. And in *Our Gang*, Philip Roth would let the speeches of politician Trick E. Dixon show him up as a villain unworthy of public trust.

Students of Franklin have also learned that on at least one

occasion, he was an early purveyor of tall tales much like those which would burgeon later. In 1765, satirizing credulous British journalists who wrote about America, he sent to the *London Advertiser* a letter signed "A Traveller" and boasting that he was a "coffee-house student of history and politics." One sentence ran: "The very tails of the American sheep are so laden with wool, that each has a car or waggon on four little wheels to support and keep it from trailing on the ground." Another sentence backed the claim that codfish and whales, though salt water denizens, were found in the Great Lakes: "Cod, like other fish, when attacked by their enemies, fly into any waters where they think they can be safest; . . . whales, when they have a mind to eat cod, pursue them wherever they fly; and . . . the grand leap of the whale in that chase up the fall of Niagara is esteemed by all who have seen it, as one of the finest spectacles in nature!"

We find a still more striking kinship which, we believe, hasn't up to now been remarked—between American windies and Franklin's versions of *The Shortest-Way* and *A Modest Proposal*.

Norris W. Yates, a leading authority on the tall tale, defines it as "a fantastic yarn rendered temporarily plausible by the supporting use of realistic detail." With no emendations whatever, this definition perfectly describes *Supplement to the Boston Independent Chronicle* and the convincing "realistic details" about those grisly bundles of scalps. If we make the phrase "realistic *and logical detail*"—a defensible modification—resemblances between the tall tale and other writings discussed in this chapter are clear. In each, starting with a fantastic—a grotesque, extravagant, capricious, or ridiculous—happening or proposal for an action, the writer follows up with justifications, developments, and consequences which are in a sense realistic and logical.

As Franklin did in "The Sale of the Hessians," some future spinners of outrageous yarns would wear a deadpan mask from start to finish. As Franklin did in "An Edict by the King of Prussia," some future unfolders of such tales would alternately don and doff solemnity. The reactions of listeners or readers would show resemblances: They might be hoaxed throughout the telling; they might catch on part way through; or they might from the start know that the narrator was playfully or satirically

building a pyramid of impossibilities on a preposterous foundation. Carl Sandburg represents this reaction in *The People, Yes:*

> "Do tell!"
> "I want to know!"
> "You don't say so!"
>
> "Tell me some more.
> I don't believe a word you say
> but I love to listen. . . ."

As we shall indicate later, no single formula or source for so
complicated a thing as the American tall tale will serve. Authors
as varied as Herodotus, Tenaud, Rabelais, and Goldsmith have
been nominated as sources for the sheep-with-trailers satire, and
what motive-indices call the "humor of lies and exaggeration" is
worldwide. But surely, likenesses between the genre and the
monster fabrications of Franklin deserve a place among contrib-
utory sources. As early as December 31, 1777, a writer for *The
New Jersey Gazette* obviously had learned from Franklin how to
embroider in the manner of future humorists when he announced that the great man would soon

produce an electrical machine of such wonderful force that, instead of
giving a slight stroke to the elbows of fifty or a hundred thousand men
who are joined hand in hand, . . . will give a violent shock even to
nature herself, so as to disunite kingdoms, join islands to continents and
render men of the same nation strangers and enemies to each other;
and . . . by a certain chemical preparation from oil, he will be able
to smooth the waves of the sea in one part of the globe, and raise tem-
pests and whirlwinds in another, so as to be universally acknowledged
for the greatest physician, politician, mathematician, and philosopher,
this day living.

Finally, it is not hard to believe that when Franklin treated
broadly, comically, and with great frankness such matters as
false piety, deceit, bodily functions, prostitution, illicit sex, violence, mutilation, and massacres, he mined a vein that a great
deal later would be mined by today's writers of black humor.

These were remarkable foreshadowings. But it is necessary,
now, to apply the brakes, and to notice that after all, his achievements were primordial. Franklin was of a time and place quite
different from the United States of a later day. He came close to
living—and what is more, dying—an Englishman. His birth

date of 1706 indicates that if he had gone to his reward at the end of the Biblical three score and ten years, it would have been only months after he threw in with the colonies against the motherland, and during the year the Declaration of Independence was written. He spent a third of his maturity abroad and was in this country during no more than an eighth of the Revolution. He learned most of his comic writing skills from foreigners—naturally, since these were by far the best writers. Further, as Lewis Leary shrewdly observes, "too great a departure from saying things as they had always been said" would make him "seem eccentric or isolated" and play hob with the persuasive powers of an author who made no bones about writing largely to teach and to persuade.

As he showed clearly in a piece (much of it swiped from Rabelais) of 1738, he knew enough about dialects to chide a Pennsylvanian for calling a panther "a painter," a New Yorker for saying "dis" instead of "this," and a Yankee for calling a cow a "keow." But compared with his successors, he used vernacular quite sparingly. Home after nine years in France, he was irked to find the country crawling with Americanisms, and asked Noah Webster to help him stamp out the worst of them. He did not waver in his hope that his countrymen would make the best English of Great Britain "our standard."

Later Americans—those folk journalists we talked about—learned to their surprise, and eventually to their delight, that they had not only a fine language of their own but also their own traits and foibles. Authors in England and America with new ideas about what was funny and what was the best way to write about it would help humorists find ways to use them. Another force—one that was not very important to Franklin—would join, and sometimes all but supplant, printed works as sources: the talk of men and women in daily exchanges and in storytelling sessions.

We look next at a superlative raconteur whose influence during the first third of the nineteenth century on journalists, actors, and playwrights was truly remarkable—John Wesley Jarvis. In helping others to discover the values of storytelling in dialect, which looms so large in America, he performed an invaluable service in the development of American humor.

Cast
Typing

> *[John Wesley Jarvis's]* stories, *particularly those connected with his southern tours, abounded in motley scenes and ludicrous occurrences. . . . His humour won the admiration of every hearer, and he was recognized as the master of anecdotes.* —John W. Francis, New York physician and antiquarian.

> *The* Yankees *are* Enterprising *and* hardy—cunning *in* bargains . . . *very fond of telling* long *stories without any* point. . . .
> —James H. Hackett, actor, private note, 1827.

> *I say . . . there's no mistake in me; . . . I can jump higher—squat lower—dive deeper—stay under and come out dryer! There's no back out in my breed—I go the whole hog. I've got the prettiest sister, fastest horse, and ugliest dog in the deestrict—in short. . . . I'm a horse!*
> —Nimrod Wildfire, in James K. Paulding, *The Lion of the West* (1830).

9.
John Wesley Jarvis, Storyteller

BENJAMIN FRANKLIN LEARNED how to create lovable homespun philosophers and repulsive monsters largely by studying literary models; and from his day on, American comic writers borrowed skills and materials from his published writings. The next chapters will show how some humorists were also helped mightily by oral stories and their printed retellings.

One of the strongest oral influences is provided by John Wesley Jarvis (1780–1840). This amateur humorist told stories that one professional after another put to his own literary uses during the second quarter of the nineteenth century and well beyond.

His anecdotes provided—at the very least—ingredients for stage performances by three popular monologists, a burlesque travel book, some sketches, and at least six plays. A good case can be made for the claim that the Jarvis stories set off a chain reaction that exploded American dialect comedy.

Jarvis, though born in England, was carried to America at the age of five, so long before he grew up he was thoroughly Americanized. And he got around. A portrait painter ingratiating enough and good enough to get many commissions, he lived for weeks, months, often years in his home base, New York, and in Boston, Philadelphia, Baltimore, Charleston, Richmond, Savannah, New Orleans, Nashville, and many points in between. Because he was a striking figure, a jolly good fellow and an incurable wit, he made friends and picked up stories wherever he worked and played.

John James Audubon, who met Jarvis in New Orleans in 1820, described him in painterly detail—short, barrel-chested, with an over-size head; hat, boutonniere, frilled shirt, all white; coat green; waistcoat pink; trousers yellow; a baby alligator peeking from a pocket and furnishing a touch of brown. On a visit to the studio, Audubon nervously watched his host prove he could hit the mark by pinking targets set up on the spot.

Others who knew the painter wrote about his free and easy ways of loving and living. Early biographers delicately wrote about his "mysterious marriages"—made extralegally (and no doubt economically) with concupiscent models—and his habit of getting drunk at every stop with cronies—artists, actors, writers, ne'er-do-wells, politicians, and the like. Everywhere, his witticisms, word play, practical jokes, and anecdotes tickled his companions.

He did popular one-liners, like the one about a portrait of Andrew Jackson on a Cincinnati tavern sign: "I'll rub a dog's tail on a pallet and he'll *wag* a better likeness." A few witticisms were racy, like his comment on someone's guess that if successive generations of dogs had their tails chopped off, tailless species might evolve: "That's capital logic—I wonder that Jews now have any tails!" At least one practical joke was grisly. After watching a dissection while studying anatomy, Jarvis entertained a sensitive guest at dinner. At the table, he snatched away a cloth and "the gentleman saw before him a human head on a charger—boiled."

Storytellers scattered through the North, South, and Southwest helped build a huge store of anecdotes, character sketches, outrageous puns, and tall tales. In New York, Jarvis was active in two literary clubs famous for good talk. (One had the same name as his favorite joke, "The Kilkenny Cats.") He spent many festive nights at New York's first art center trading jibes and jests with fellow painters who "would have made good actors." In Charleston, he won a liars' contest by playing an ancient trick—solemnly saying that he knew the leading liar's every word was true as gospel.

John Neal raved about his skill in print four times—twice in 1824, again in 1835, and finally in 1868. Some tellers of tales, Neal said, messed up everything and bored listeners to death. But give a true artist a go at "one of the oldest and commonest Joe Millers" that ever flooded newspapers, and he so transformed it that it became uniquely his. Take Jarvis:

Did you ever hear his Kilkenny Cats? . . . Jarvis would tell you that story, old as it is and foolish as it is, so that you wouldn't forget it to your dying day. I have known him to repeat it to the very same persons, in the very same way, year after year; and yet every man of them would go fifty miles to hear it again. I heard it once after having seen two or three celebrated imitations, fully determined not to make a fool of myself—and why should I—what was there to laugh at, in such a story? —And I did not get over it for a month.

When Neal was an old man of seventy-five and Jarvis was mouldering in his grave, Neal still fondled the memory of the way "the best storyteller that ever lived" had told that chestnut half a century before to a Baltimore club, with a "running accompaniment of growling and sputtering and flashing" that threw the glummest listener into convulsions and decimated even those who had heard it before. "Some of the club actually shouted until they lost their breath and tears stood in their eyes."

William Cullen Bryant, not an easy man to amuse (his most famous poem was about the pleasure of being dead), called Jarvis's drollery "irresistible," and others who went for his jokes in a big way made up that era's Knickerbocker writers *Who's Who* —Paulding, Drake, Halleck, Samuel F. B. Morse, Gulian Verplanck, Irving, and Cooper. (He painted portraits of the last three.) T. B. Thorpe, whose "The Big Bear of Arkansas" would become a landmark in Southwestern humor, fell under Jarvis's spell when a teen-age art student, and forty-five years later fondly remembered Jarvis's "fluency in speech" and his "happy manner of description and story-telling."

William Dunlap, a fellow member of the Bread and Cheese Club in New York, writing about the portrait painter in his history of American art, used ten long and quite irrelevant pages to retell some of Jarvis's anecdotes and praise his wizardry as a raconteur. At the end he figured that he had failed completely, partly because "the aid of a bottle" as a rule made Jarvis's listeners more receptive than most readers of a two-volume history were likely to be but chiefly because print never could catch the painter's most important skills—dialect, regional phrasings, intonations, expressions, mannerisms, and gestures.

Dunlap spoke with authority because (among other things) he was a successful playwright and producer. As such he belonged to one crowd that Jarvis had as lifelong friends. His first portrait was of a comedian; Jarvis decorated an oyster bar wall with a painting of a famous stage character; and for a time he was the New Orleans roommate of a comedian whose performances he went to regularly anyhow. Several actors heard his anecdotes and adapted them to their uses.

To writers and actors, stories that Jarvis told about three groups—French immigrants, Yankees, and frontiersmen—were often useful.

Three stories in which Jarvis skillfully used French dialect were successful on the stage—one very successful.

The actor who first adapted them was a remarkable British comedian, Charles Mathews (1776-1835). Although—or possibly because—he was painfully skinny, crooked-jawed, somewhat crippled, paranoid, manic-depressive, an insomniac, and a hypochondriac, Mathews became one of England's most admired comedians. A score of England's and America's top authors praised him to the skies—Dickens, for instance, who applauded him "whenever he played," and Macaulay, who called him "certainly the greatest actor I ever saw."

Mathews had to be good to be tremendously popular in sketchily scripted annual one-man performances—*At Homes* or *Trips to* this or that country—a twenty-seven-year-long series. (In the 1970's, Jonathan Winters and Lily Tomlin put on somewhat similar shows.) Typically, Mathews offered a loose narrative about encounters with a number of varied characters. Helped by grimaces, pantomime, ventriloquism, dances, patter songs, monologues, and lightning costume changes, he impersonated contrasting men and women. Each gallery portrayed characters representing a wide range of locations, nationalities, types, professions, ranks in society, educations, and economic positions. During a tour of the Eastern United States in 1822–23, Mathews picked up material for his next marathon show. *A Trip to America*, given in England in 1824–26 and in America in 1834, was a hit. This was true largely because, by a great stroke of luck, the British actor became acquainted with John Wesley Jarvis. The artist's stories were by far the best source of usable sketches.

An old hand at using French dialect himself to win laughs, Mathews glaumed onto three anecdotes in Jarvis's repertoire featuring Gallic immigrants. Two were impressive only because the painter and the actor performed them with great skill. In one, a sprightly Frenchman deflated a self-important general who threw his weight around in an inn by doubling every one of the officer's arrogant orders: "Give me a candle, sir!" says the general. "Bring me, sair, *two* candaile!" shouts the Frenchman. "Quick, sir, show me to a bed." "Quick, sair, . . . show me to *two* beds." Jarvis evidently told this both well and often, for in addition to Mathews, two others who heard him made use of it— Paulding in a burlesque travel book, *John Bull in America*, and Dunlap in a play, *A Trip to Niagara*.

More impressive was Mathews's dramatization of a Jarvis yarn about a French admirer of Andrew Jackson. The sketch and the song, which can now be appreciated only in their historical context, contained sharp satire which Jarvis must have added to prick pretensions very topical and quite typical in the young nation—instances of the bragging that infuriated legions of travelers. An extreme example was the overweening pride manifested in a song about the Battle of New Orleans.

The War of 1812, as futile a military conflict as any ever fought, brought disaster after disaster to America and ended

MR. MATHEWS'S

Lecture on Peculiarities, Characters and Manners, founded on Observations and Adventures during his late

TRIP TO AMERICA.

PART I.— Exordium — Tourists — Embarkation on board the *William Thompson*—Speaking Trumpet—Whimsical coincidence of names—Yellow fever—In sight of New York—New Brunswick—English Importations—Jack Topham and his Cousin Bray—Waterloo Hotel, Liverpool, contrasted with Jack Rivers's Hotel at Elizabeth Town—American phrases expounded—Cool Landlord—Hot wine—Arrival at Bristol (in America)—First appearance at Baltimore—Philadelphia—Steam Boat and Stage Coach Characters—Arrival at New York.

Song—"Mrs. BRADISH's BOARDING-HOUSE."

More characters—American fun—Mr. Raventop, the American jester—Major Grimstone; *"very well!"*—Mr. Pennington—American strictures on English tourists—Jack Topham's fancies—Native Indians—Black Tragedian: *"to be or not to be!"*

Song—" OPOSSUM UP A GUM TREE."

(REAL NEGRO MELODY.)

American Army—Irregular Regulars—Muskets and Umbrellas—Swords and fishing rods—

Song—" MILITIA MUSTER FOLK."

PART II.—Hiring a *help*, (*Anglice*, a servant)—War—Public Dinner —General Jackson—French Poet Laureat——

Song—"ODE TO GENERAL JACKSON."

Definition of the word *Yankee*—Jack Topham on the natives—Arrival at Boston —Bunker's Hill—Monumental Inscriptions—A REAL YANKEE, Jonathan W. Doubikin, and his Uncle Ben—Winter sets in—Natives rising and Snow falling—Sleighs, (*Anglice*, sledges)—John and Jonathan, or *"I guess,"* and *"you know."* —Mons. Mallet—Election—

Song—" BOSTON POST OFFICE."

Providence—Enticements for Mr. Mathews to perform—Charter a Coach—Fiddling Negro—Worcester—Another particularly cool Landlord—Court of Justice—Charge to the Jury—Emigration discouraged by a British Farmer—Disabled goods and chattels—

Song—" ILLINOIS INVENTORY."

Maximilian the Nigger (*Anglice*, Negro) and the snuff-box—Preparations to depart—

" THE AMERICAN JESTER'S SONG."

AND

" FAREWELL FINALE."

PART III.—A MONOPOLOGUE, called

All Well at Natchitoches.

COLONEL HIRAM PEGLAR....A Kentucky Shoe-maker.
AGAMEMNON ....A Poor run-away Negro.
JONATHAN W. DOUBIKIN ....A real Yankee, (his Master.)
MONSIEUR CAPOT..........A French Emigrant Tailor.
MISS MANGEL WURZEL......A Dutch Heiress.
Mr. O'SULLIVAN ....An Irish improver of his Fortune.

Program summary for Mathews's "Trip to America," for which storyteller Jarvis furnished comic portrayals of French immigrants, Yankees, and a Kentucky colonel.

with a treaty which did not even mention what the President had called its chief causes. But after the instrument was signed and before news about it had crossed the Atlantic, old Injun fighter Andrew Jackson led a frontier army that licked a strong British force in the Battle of New Orleans. Somehow this victory gave many patriots the happy illusion that the United States had won the war. Inevitably Jackson became a hot prospect for the presidency, nominated in 1822 by the Tennessee legislature and elected—to the Senate—in 1823. Beginning in 1821, he had been celebrated in a smarmy and strangely rhymed song that was astonishingly popular—Samuel Woodworth's "The Hunters of Kentucky." This chauvinistic piece was made famous the length of the Mississippi in the 1820's by a buckskin-clad actor, the flamboyant Noah Ludlow. In a showy production, Ludlow time after time drove audiences wild with the climactic stanza:

> But JACKSON, he was wide awake,
> And wasn't scared of trifles;
> For well he knew what aim we take,
> With our Kentucky rifles;
> So he led us down to Cypress swamp,
> The ground was low and mucky;
> There stood John Bull in martial pomp,
> AND HERE WAS OLD KENTUCKY.

Here the actor flipped off his coonskin cap, brought up his rifle, and took aim at imaginary redcoats, while audiences cheered wildly and nearly drowned out his refrain:

> Oh! Kentucky, the hunters of Kentucky,
> THE HUNTERS OF KENTUCKY.

During Mathews's visit the piece, originally published in New York, was popular not only along the river but throughout the country.

"The general," says Matthews's scenario for *A Trip to America*, "accepts an invitation to a banquet commemorating the War of 1812 on condition that he pass unnoticed, and that no speech shall be made, or desired from him." Everything goes well until

. . . a little grinning Frenchman rises, and pays the General a most ridiculous compliment, by comparing him to Alexander the Great, and assuring him, he is able to shoot all the English that ever was, and everybody else that will be; and kill them all to death with his own grand sword. He then informs the General and the company, that he was intended to be von poet laureat, having such great talent . . . preparatory to delivering an ode of thirty verses, in praise of the General, which he has written, and begs leave to sing.

The "Ode to General Jackson" which is then performed—thirty awful verses of it and, to judge from sample lines sung by Mathews, laced with fulsome compliments—boasts about American prowess and uses rhymes as comic as those in Woodworth's doggerel:

> Then vive brave General Jackson,
> Who led de grand attacks on,
> And beat de British Saxon,
> Huzza! huzza! huzza!

The little Frenchman's *gasconnade*, besides giving Mathews a chance to get laughs with his Gallic dialect, neatly pinked the boastfulness that was widely thought to be an outstanding American flaw.

The third French émigré anecdote that Jarvis presented to Mathews, when dramatized, brought the British actor his greatest triumph. It grew from a sketch to a play, and served a second actor—an American—very well. This one depended for its point upon an American's ignorance about a French pronunciation and for its humor upon the Frenchman's un-American (and therefore funny) way of talking.

The story is this. Day after day, Monsieur Mallet goes to the Boston post office and anxiously asks: "Pray, Sare, I beg your pardonne. Avez vous von lettre pour Monsieur Mallet (pronouncing his name Mallay)?" As he explains, he is eager to hear from his only daughter, who lives in Bordeaux. Week after week, he gets the same answer: "Mallay, no, no letter of that name." Mallet's despair grows until, one day, he happens to learn that a letter has been waiting for him but that the postman has not recognized the French pronunciation. "Why don't you learn to pronounce your name properly?" asks the clerk:

"Vot you mean by dat?" (seizing the letter, which he rapturously kisses, and affectionately presses to his bosom, . . . then returning to his former indignation) "Vot you mean by dat, I say? to keep my lettre all dis time, ven I come so oft, and tell you it was from my dear daughter. . . . You are very neglect, insolente, ignorant man. I shall complain of you to Congress. If I had learn vot de Aungliesh call de box, I would blow your nose for you." The postman retorting in turn, his apathy and conduct so provoke the poor Frenchman, that in his rage he tears up the letter he has sought so long; and is only aroused to a sense of what he has done by the laughter of the republican. . . .

A synopsis of the sketch ends: "His despair at the circumstance, and the manner in which he departs, are, as Mr. Mathews delineates them, beyond description, and must be seen to be appreciated." Contemporary comments prove this bit was a high spot in the *Trip*. ("We never beheld anything more complete, masterly, and affecting," one reviewer said.) What is more, the story was enlarged into a full-length play, *Monsieur Mallet; or, My Daughter's Letter*, by W. T. Moncrieff. With Mathews in the title role, the play opened in London in January, 1829. It had a long run there and in the provinces. "I have gained more real reputation by [this performance]," Mathews wrote a friend, "than by all I ever did in the legitimate wildernesses. Mallet, almost serious, perfectly tragic in some scenes, is the finest part I ever had."

Those words—"almost serious" and "perfectly tragic"—probably define a quality which did much to make the sketch and the play so popular. In addition to the outlandish gallicisms, volatility, and hot temper which Jarvis's other Frenchmen shared with Mallet, the episode had a touch of pathos. This mingling of pathos with comedy, as Stuart Tave has shown in *The Genial Humorist*, was increasingly fashionable in this period—an important aspect of sympathetic humor.

Of course, Mathews cherished his French émigrés partly because they were like his earlier un-American characterizations; they were only marginally American. But soon after it was introduced, the Mallet anecdote would acquire an American connection.

This was due to James H. Hackett (1800–1871), a brash young American actor with little experience and great admiration for Mathews. In 1827 Hackett went to London and put on in Covent Garden an old play in which Mathews had starred, tinkered to give him a chance to do a one-man show blatantly modeled after a Mathews *Trip*. This fledgling, in other words, had the chutzpa to invade Mathews's home grounds and do the same things the beloved comedian did—tell stories (several used earlier by his idol), shuffle costumes and roles, mimic dialects, and give "impressions" of Mathews. One of the stories, his notes show, was "Mons. Mallet & the Letter."

The show bombed, and critics pulverized Hackett for his inferior aping of Mathews. But Hackett sailed home, advertised that he was fresh from a London triumph, frequently performed

Six of Mathews's twenty-odd impersonations of American characters in 1824. Left to right: Miss Mangel Wurzle, a Dutch heiress; Colonel Hiram Pegler, a bibulous Kentuckian; Mr. O'Sullivan, an unhappy Irish immigrant; Mr. Raventop, a funereal American jokester; M. Capot, a French immigrant tailor; and Agamemnon, a runaway black fiddler. Pegler, Raventop, and Capot were based upon Jarvis's anecdotes.

the Mallet sketch, and in time made the play *Monsieur Mallet* a feature of his repertoire.

After his less than glorious launching, Hackett was to go on to higher things. In time, he would better Mathews in his handling of Jarvis's stories about Yankees, and with Jarvis's help,

he would do much to make famous a comic American type that
Mathews had missed in his *Trip to America*—the frontiersman.

Localizing touches did little to make Mathews's émigrés great
novelties. By contrast, a pair of Yankees introduced by Mathews,
Jonathan Doubikin and his Uncle Ben—also courtesy of Jarvis—
struck London playgoers as brand new. They also had a great
impact in America. There, beginning in 1787, a few New England characters had strutted their brief hour upon the stage and
had even spun yarns in dialect. But in America as in England,
no actor good enough to get much attention had played such a
role. Mathews changed this.

"A story that Jarvis happened to hear once, and which he happened to repeat in the presence of Mathews" inspired the British
actor's greatly admired Yankee impersonation. Mathews
"whipped it over" and then, mimicking Jarvis's facial expressions, bits of business, vocabulary, pronunciations, and intonations, retold it on London's Adelphi stage "night after night,
and month after month." Later he carried it, as part of his *Trip*,
to the provinces and, years later, to the United States.

To introduce his dramatization of the yarn, reminiscing about
his visit to Boston (to quote the synopsis), "Mr. Mathews becomes acquainted with a real *Yankee*, one Jonathan W. Doubikin, one of the happiest, most original, and most characteristic of
all Mr. Mathews's personations in the present entertainment"—
brought about when Jonathan unfolds a "particularly amusing
and well told" story about his Uncle Ben's hunt. A squirrel that
Ben shoots does not fall from the tree, and Uncle Ben promises
Jonathan a shilling if he'll climb up and bring it down. Jonathan
gets the squirrel but, though he tries and tries, fails to collect
"that ere little trifle" he was promised. Time after time, whenever Jonathan circles back to his demand, Uncle Ben comes up
with excuses not to pay. Reviews show that the sheer repetition
of the running gag—Jonathan's requests for that ere trifle and
of Uncle Ben's refusals—convulsed English theatergoers. "To do
him justice," one reviewer wrote, "Doubikin certainly does make
a great deal out of nothing."

Once more, a sketch was such a hit that Mathews found it paid
to expand it to a play. The actor and a collaborator huddled to-

gether and wrote *Jonathan Doubikins* (the final "s" was added), or *Jonathan in England*, with the running gag about that ere trifle moving through a maze of plots. It allowed the actor, as Jonathan, to spout Yankeeisms lifted from a glossary and to ape Jarvis. It was a great success.

Two American actors who specialized in Yankee roles followed Mathews in retelling Jonathan's yarn about Uncle Ben. They also appeared in the play about him, somewhat revised. John Neal in 1835 calculated that British playgoers had paid half a million dollars to hear this story, Americans as much more, and said that Mathews and the American actors were still peddling it to full houses, even though many in their audiences had heard it half a dozen times.

The first of the two Americans was Hackett, with indebtedness apparently a two-way street. A remark of Mathews and a private note written by Hackett both seem to show that though Jarvis told Mathews Jonathan's yarn about that ere trifle, so did the young actor. Just the same, as Francis Hodge says, Hackett "was undoubtedly encouraged" to use it "by Mathews' big success with it in London."

This note of Hackett's and another in the same batch are interesting because they record his belief about Yankee storytellers' ways and give a full text of Jonathan's story "as near as I can commit [it] to paper to what I give [it] on the stage." The passages have merit partly because Hackett (unlike Mathews) knew Yankees rather well. Some years before he turned actor, as a clerk for a wholesale grocer trading out of Utica, New York, Hackett talked and bargained daily with western New England customers in the area. So, though he himself was not a Yankee, when he imitated the species, he could draw upon a good fund of personal observation.

New England countrymen, Hackett had decided, were "very fond of telling long stories without any point." The minute the yarns "appeared to approach" a payoff, they were "diverted to some new digression," so it was hard to tell when they ended. Hackett's, then, is an early description of what Mark Twain seven decades later called *the* American humorous story—"spun out," Twain said, "to great length, and arriv[ing] nowhere in particular"—and Max Eastman more than a century later called

distinctively American: "loose, rambling, fantastically inconse-
quential monologues" whose chief charm is "a total want of
structure"—"a mess, the messier it is, within the limits of patience, the better."*

Hackett's script for Jonathan's story follows this formula, de-
ploying twelve hundred words to tell an anecdote that could
have been told in a hundred. The author lavishly characterizes
Uncle Ben's wife, though she has nothing to do with the plot
("genteel," "shocking clever," "ugly," "misable fat," "makes
good pumpkin pies"). He gives these completely irrelevant facts
about Uncle Ben: he disliked cussing and loved powerful preaching, dumplings and molasses; he was buried in "churchyard at
New Haven, fourth turn from the entrance on the right hand
side as you go in, *marvel* tombstun." When Jonathan finally gets
to the hunt, he quotes a long conversation, enumerates all the
problems Ben faces and solves before he shoots, repeats a long
discussion ending with Ben's promise to pay his nephew nine-
pence for dislodging the squirrel, describes the way he chucks it
down, and then traces the endless postponements of "that trifle."
The conclusion, even with some deletions, shows how the story
meanders:

I never *seed* him from that day. . . . I hope he's gone to the *Devil* for
lying—and I don't believe his *grace* ever went higher than the wall,
and though he never got *drunk* on *parade* day . . . he used to get *blue*
as a *rason* every *Saturday* night,—whenever he could get brandy for
nothing—he'd fill a tumbler, and just *chip* her up and *swigg* her down
. . . saying if his mammy had gin him sich milk, he never would have
left off sucking under heaven, howsom-never, the Deacon lectured him
every week, when he promised he never would do so agin—one day
the Deacon cotch'd him drunk, two days running—so says the Deacon—"Well now Uncle Ben, this is *too* bad—how can you do so—I'm

* Americans have been very fond of the form from Hackett's day to the present.
Examples include Frances M. Whitcher, "Hezekiah Bedott" (1855); Mark Twain,
"Jim Blaine and His Grandfather's Old Ram," *Roughing It* (1872); Ed Wynn's
monologues on the stage, radio, and television in the 1920's, 1930's, 1940's and 1950's;
and *Willie Remembers* (1973). Of course, the belief that the form is *uniquely*
American is unjustified. As G. Legman points out in *Rationale of the Dirty Joke*
(New York, 1968) I, 9: "The rambling story or pointless anecdote, nowadays known
as the 'talking horse' or 'shaggy dog' story" is "mistakenly believed to be a new
genre, though it is a special art in, for example, *Joe Miller's Jests* (1739) No. 79—
modeled on Apuleius' *Golden Ass*, and Balaam's ass centuries earlier [as well as]
Laurence Sterne's *Tristram Shandy* (1767). . . ." (Scholars have found scores of
"sources" for Sterne's novel.)

sorry really" so says Uncle Ben to him—"are you so sorry Deacon?" says he "I am, really sorry"—well then" says Uncle Ben, "if you *are really sorry* Deacon—I forgive you."

When Hackett first tried to wind his leisurely way through this convoluted yarn and others in London, the audience shouted him off the stage, and reviewers called his stories "tedious" and "far too long." Since Mathews had got hearty laughs with the same sort of storytelling, the reason must have been that Hackett had not mastered the artistry such comedy demanded. Later, in his homeland, after he had acquired experience and skill, he pleased many audiences by telling the stories in the play *Jonathan Doubikins* (which did better in America than it had with Mathews in England). And in several other "Yankee plays," Hackett told long-winded dialect stories that were warmly appreciated.

In his definitive history of Yankees on the stage, Francis Hodge sums up Hackett's contribution and points to a further development. Granted, Hodge says,

he took his incentive, direction, and something of his style from Charles Mathews . . . he moved quickly in original directions. . . . The over-all result . . . was the establishment of a line of comedy which could be acted by only native actors. He clearly pointed the way [and] so successfully popularized the Yankee on the stage that he directly encouraged other young American actors to take up his line and compete with him. One of these was George Handel Hill.

Hill (1809–1849), Boston born, was the first native New Englander to star in Yankee roles and was probably their most authentic performer. As a teen-ager, Hill imitated on home-made stages actors he had seen and Massachusetts bumpkins he knew personally, and throughout his life, though he wandered widely, he often got back home to pick up fresh impressions.

Hill, therefore, copied nature, but he also learned his art from non-New Englanders, especially Mathews and Jarvis. When he was fourteen, he may have seen Mathews in a Boston theater. Regardless, over the years, he read about him and profited from his example. He came to know Mathews's teacher, Jarvis, still better. Hill played in New York, Jarvis's home base, as early as 1826, and then or a bit later, the two became close friends. In

1835, when Hill was performing in New Orleans, Jarvis roomed
with him and slogged to the playhouse "through the mud"
nightly, he said, to watch and coach the actor.

Hill, a star at twenty-three, acted in some forty Yankee plays
in his remaining seventeen years to win the nickname "Yankee"
Hill. Inevitably, among the popular dramas, one was *Jonathan
Doubikins*. Like Mathews and Hackett, Hill larded this and
other dramas with anecdotes in dialect, many of them Jarvis's
standbys. And he gave evening-long solo performances during
which he mimed, sang songs, and told jokes—including, of
course, Jonathan's story about Uncle Ben and that ere trifle.
Newspapers and periodicals printed "Yankee Hill's Latest," and
a publishing house that specialized in bestselling humorous
books issued *Hill's Yankee Stories and Reciter's Own Book of Popular Recitations*.

When Hill acted in London, reviewers compared him with
Mathews and often found him better—at least in his favorite
role. They particularly praised his subtlety, his deadpan style,
and his rapport with audiences. "The audience," wrote one, "relished the sly humor with which he told . . . barefaced lies . . .
and the solemn mockery of seriousness with which he confirmed
them; and he seemed established in favour with them before he
had been ten minutes on the stage." Another reviewer said:

The true merit of his acting is, that he gives a perfect picture of a very
odd character, hitherto very slightly known on our stage, and proves
that in that power of humour which is somewhat rare, and which is
always highly attractive, he can fairly take his stand among the best
low comedy actors we possess. He was received with great applause, his
jokes produced abundant laughter.

In Hill's homeland, too, critics rated him above his predecessors.
So did audiences, often Yankees, who obviously were judges of
authenticity.

When the young actor's skill and popularity in Yankee roles
grew, Hackett tapered off New England rustic roles that he
himself played until, at last, he practically yielded his rival the
field. Yankee Hill, it appears, was enough of an artist to learn
from nature and a study of the performances of older actors, and
improve upon both. So he climaxed a development which had

begun when John Wesley Jarvis told a British visitor a story about Jonathan, his Uncle Ben, and that ere trifle.†

We shelve chronology briefly in order to polish off the history of Jarvis's Yankee story by tracing its final transmogrification, which carried it to the frontier. Augustus Baldwin Longstreet (1790–1870), Georgia lawyer, pamphleteer, and humorous writer, in 1835 published *Georgia Scenes*, a famous and influential early collection of frontier sketches. He furnishes a terminus to the Uncle Ben odyssey. In 1838 he wrote a sketch for an Augusta magazine, *The Mirror*, reprinted in the *Southern Literary Messenger* and, as late as 1858, in *The Georgia University Magazine*.

This sketch begins with a stuffy introduction that brings in phrenology and Horace to sidle up to the claim that a garrulous man can torment a listener. For proof, Longstreet tells the story of an illiterate Georgia farmer whose monologues were unusually horrible for two reasons: (1) He "never quit a subject until he carried it through the most minute, circumstantial, dry, tantalizing details that ever afflicted a patient ear." (2) Because he was buck-toothed, he "never used his upper lip in talking [but] transferred its office to his upper teeth," so that what in normal speech were "b" sounds he replaced with "v" sounds and "p" sounds with "fs."

The treatise on talkativeness raises a suspicion. This grows when Longstreet says that his torturer, Benjamin Grinnolds, "was usually called Little Ben, to distinguish him from an uncle of the same name," and the suspicion is confirmed when at long last little Ben tells his story and we wade through ambushes of misplaced v's, f's, and irrelevant details to learn that Uncle Ben once shot a squirrel and promised Little Ben "a trifle" if he brought it down from its tree. The story ends:

I flung down the squir'l and s'ys I to uncle Ven, where's that trifle you were going to gi' me? . . . Oh s'ys he I do 'n know, I'll give it to you some o' these days. So I waited two weeks, and I meets uncle Ven at the muster, and s'ys I uncle Ven, where's that trifle you were going to gi' me, old feller? Oh s'ys he I do 'n know Ven, I'll give it to you some o'

† Josh Silsbee (1813-1855), an inferior but quite successful Yankee actor, provided an anticlimax by appearing in *Jonathan in England*. This was one of a dozen plays that he purloined from earlier actors. His death, says Hodge, "brought to a close the era of Yankee theatre."

these days. So I waits about three weeks, and I meets uncle Ven at the
Court House, and s'ys I to him uncle Ven where's that trifle you were
going to gi' me old feller? Oh s'ys he I don' know I'll give it to you
some o' these days, and ding the trifle have I seen to this day—vut I
never see uncle Ven that I don't run him about that trifle, and I reckon
he hates it the worst o' any thing you ever seed.

This, as a friend of Longstreet said, "loses almost all its interest
on paper." But the friend claimed that when Longstreet rendered
it orally "in its proper cadence, tone, emphasis and pronunciation," it was side-splitting. The comment reminds us of those
Dunlap made about Jarvis's stories. Longstreet indicated that he
had heard the story. Was it told by Jarvis, one wonders, during
one of the artist's forays into Georgia? Or had the humorist heard
it told by Mathews, Hackett, Hill, or some other echoer of Jarvis?
    Whatever the source, Longstreet's retelling not only equipped
its yarn spinner with protruding teeth, it moved him, his Uncle
Ben, and the squirrel out of New England to the frontier of that
day, the Old Southwest, and turned him into a red-necked Georgia farmer.
    Jarvis himself, of course, had visited the area, and one New
York friend of his believed he picked up his best stories there.
(Jarvis had, one remembers, given Mathews the only example
in his *Trip* of the tall talk which, jokelore had it, was the frontier's chief export—the little Frenchman's song about Jackson.)
The portrait painter's acquaintance with Southwestern humor
and his use of it in social gatherings probably led to his playing
a role in making it famous.
    James K. Paulding (1778–1860), a prolific Knickerbocker au-
thor, as has been said, tucked Jarvis's anecdote about the sassy
Frenchman and the stuffy general into his burlesque travel book.
He and Jarvis were fellow members of that leading New York
literary and carousing group, the Kilkenny Cats. In and out of
meetings, the two were friends and fellow bibbers even after
Jarvis illustrated one of Paulding's books and painted his portrait.

    In 1830, Hackett, now a producer as well as an actor, offered
what in those uninflated days was a fabulous prize—three hundred dollars—for the best "original comedy" adaptable to Hack-

ett's "powers and style of acting . . . whereof an American
should be the leading character." Soon after, repaying a visit of
Jarvis, Paulding stopped by the studio and left a reminder of a
promise:

My good friend,
  I called to return your visit . . . and want to impress upon you the
obligation You will confer upon me by furnishing me with, a few
sketches, short stories and incidents, of Kentucky or Tennessee manners, and especially of their peculiar phrases and comparisons. If you
can add, or *invent* a few ludicrous Scenes of Col. Crockett at Washington, You will be sure of my everlasting gratitude. "D—n You," as the
Kentucks say.

Yours very truly

Studying this note, Joseph J. Arpad recently made a plausible
guess—that it disclosed "the source material for Paulding's characterization of Colonel Nimrod Wildfire, the 'half horse-half
alligator' backwoods Congressman from Kentucky, who appeared in Paulding's . . . play *The Lion of the West, or, A Trip
to Washington*." This play, winner of the prize, opened in New
York in 1830, with Hackett as Wildfire. Twice revised by playwrights other than Paulding, and eventually titled *The Kentuckian, or A Trip to New York*, the drama gave Hackett his best
role. It went as well in England as in America, and Hackett appeared in it for more than twenty years.

The revisions make it impossible to be sure what Jarvis contributed to the final (and only surviving) version. Reviews containing quoted dialogue suggest that the adapters modified the
cast, plot, and setting but changed Nimrod Wildfire's traits and
comic speeches hardly at all. Such revisions could be minimal,
since Wildfire, like comic Yankees of the day, stays out of the
plot until the last minute, and then ambles in and unmasks the
villain. Again like the stage Yankees, the Kentuckian is there
largely to make laughable mistakes and to use queer expressions
and tell yarns such as those Paulding asked Jarvis to furnish.

Wildfire's most peculiar phrases had brief histories or no histories at all before 1830, the year of the play. The authoritative
Dictionary of Americanisms (Chicago, 1951), edited by Mitford
M. Mathews, discovers the first use of "lion of the west" ("a
frontier ruffian or bully") in an 1828 song. The dictionary places

other words used by the Kentuckian later—"te-to-taciously" and "exfluncated" in 1831; "catawampus" in 1839; and "catfish" meaning "lawyers," in 1857. ("I call catfish lawyers," says Nimrod, " 'case you see they're all head, and their head's all mouth.")

In addition to furnishing words such as these, Jarvis could well have come up with Wildfire's one-liners—"whimsical extravagance of speech" which, another character explains, "results from mere exuberance of spirits and . . . total ignorance of conventional restraint." "Wildfire boasts about his high spirits: "I'm ready for anything from a barbecue to a war dance— heigh! . . . I want something strong—some music of about 300 horse power." He praises Kentucky soil: "The ground's so rich that if you but plant a crowbar over night *perhaps* it will sprout ten penny nails afore mornin'." He tells about past fights: "He'll come off as badly as a feller I once hit a sledge hammer lick over the head . . . he disappeared altogether; all they could find of him was a little grease. . . ." He brags about what he will do in a duel: "You have called me out, and if you think to get rid of me without exchanging a shot, you might as well try to scull a potash kettle up the falls of Niagara with a crowbar for an oar." Again—"I'll plug you like a watermelon." Wildfire's repeated shout, "Wake, snakes, June-bugs are coming," seems to have made its debut in the play; the first example in the *Dictionary of Americanisms* came in 1835. Reprintings of these bon mots and others in the drama from 1833 on show that they were widely appreciated.

Jarvis may have suggested that Wildfire should bellow, as he did every now and then, a variant of his boast: "I'm half horse, half alligator, a touch of the airthquake, with a sprinkling of the steam-boat." If Jarvis made the suggestion, he certainly did so with full knowledge that such talk was hoary with age. As later chapters will show, it had the most venerable ancestors. And even in America since 1809, it had been repeated in print scores of times. By 1830, a writer could launch it, then cut it off and be confident that readers would end it, e.g., "Boatmen appeared to pride themselves on the roughness and rudeness of their manners—'half horse, half alligator, &c.' "

Two boasts like this one, often extended, were standard parts of a pattern endlessly repeated in the United States, frequently in a simple little yarn spun by a vulgar Westerner. Two roughs meet; each shouts his brag; they fight; one wins. Paulding had included a version of this narrative in *Letters from the South* in 1817; Nimrod Wildfire tells the story in the play. A contrast between the travel book account and the one in *The Lion of the West*, as Arpad says, gives us clues about Jarvis's contribution:

> In the revised text, there is an attempt to capture the back-woods vernacular, to replace descriptive statements with segments of dialogue, and to impose the spontaneity of the spoken word into the rhythm of the narration . . . in revising the anecdote . . . Paulding did not attempt to dramatize it . . . to make the fight an integral part of the plot. Instead, he merely changed the written narration to oral narration [which] reveals that Wildfire was presented to his audience in the role of an oral humorist and story-teller. . . . Not only did [Jarvis] provide Paulding with information on western character, humor, and vernacular, but he also provided a model for oral traditions in story-telling. . . .

Newspapers, almanacs, and books reproduced the story as it was told in the drama time after time, often attributing it to Davy Crockett.

Crockett was identified with Wildfire, not without reason, from the start. And the play encouraged the tendency by making Nimrod a candidate for reelection to Congress. Jarvis quite possibly helped Paulding write a speech for him, combining his boast with political satire—one in which he proposes to settle the whole tariff question:

> The moment the Tariff Bill comes upon the floor I'll jump upon the table and I shall say to the speaker, Look here, Mr. Cheerman, just stop your steam! Now about these Tariff duties—warn't my father the first man that ever lopp'd a tree in old Kaintuck? warn't he the first to float down Kentucky river with a hogshead of tobacco, when the Ingens stood so thick upon the banks you couldn't see the trees for um? I say, Mr. Cheerman, about this here Tariff—there's no mistake in me; of all the fellers on this side the Alleghany mountains, I can jump higher—squat lower—dive deeper—stay under longer and come out drier! There's no back out in my breed—I go the whole hog. I've got the prettiest sister, fastest horse, and ugliest dog in the deestrict—in short, to sum up all in one word on these here Tariff duties, Mr. Cheerman— I'm a horse!

Like Wildfire's fight story, this political speech was reprinted many times, once in a *Crockett Almanack*. Obviously contemporaries appreciated the overwhelming logic.

The most interesting of Jarvis's probable donations was a yarn that would resurface again and again—in Thoreau's *Walden* (1854), for instance, and as late as 1951 in a collection of Ozark windies. Wildfire's version:

Look you here now, tother day, I was a horseback paddling away pretty comfortably through Nobottom swamp, when suddenly—I wish I may be currycomb'd to death by 50,000 tom cats, if I didn't see a white hat getting along in mighty considerable style all alone by itself on the top of the mud—so up I rid, and being a bit jubus, I lifted it with the butt end of my whip when a feller sung out from under it, Hallo, stranger, who told you to knock my hat off? Why, says I, what sort of a sample of a white man are you? What's come of the rest of you? Oh, says he, I'm not far off—only in the next county. I'm doing beautifully—got one of the best horses under me that ever burrowed—claws like a mole—no stop in him—but here's a waggon and horses right under me in a mighty bad fix, I reckon, for I heard the driver say a spell ago one of the team was a getting a leetel tired. . . . So, says I, you must be a pretty considerable feller on your own, but you had better keep your mouth shut or you'll get your teeth sunburnt.

In several ways, this is typical of America's favorite tall tales. The phrasing is talk-like, the details are homely, and the depth of the Kentucky mud is developed climactically. And the heaped "facts" are delivered in a deadpan style. (They cause a credulous English visitor who hears the yarns to call it "the first well authenticated anecdote" that she has picked up for the travel book she is going to write.)

John Wesley Jarvis, then, deserves to be a star witness for historians who claim that an oral storyteller could be highly influential on American humor. The contributions this one superb raconteur made to the development of French, Yankee, and frontier dialect humor were prodigious.

Other oral storytellers joined published writers in creating the tales about American geography, wild creatures, men, women, and comic demigods to which we next turn.

You've all on you, heered of Mike Fink, the celebrated, an self-created, an never to be mated, Mississippi roarer, snag-lifter, an flatboat skuller. Well, I knowed the critter all round, an upside down; he war pretty fair among squaws, catfish, an big niggers. . . . —Crockett's Almanac, 1851.

10.
Mike Fink

BEGINNING IN THE 1820's, oral storytellers and folk journalists transformed Mike Fink (1770?–1823), a bully boy on three frontiers, into a distinctively American comic demigod. And though both raconteurs and journalists helped assemble lore about the legendary Mike, it was the writers, evidently, who gave the generally unlovable creation his longest-lasting appeals.

During a good part of his lifetime, Mike was a leading roughneck on a series of frontiers, each in turn notorious for its violence. Born in Fort Pitt, he became a meat hunter and Indian scout in the surrounding area before he was fully grown and for several years carried out dangerous missions. After the treaty of Greenville brought a degree of peace to the Pennsylvania frontier and he could no longer earn a living with his rifle there, Mike became a keelboatman on the Ohio and Mississippi Rivers. For years he helped wrestle vessels up and down those treacherous waterways in his working hours, and for recreation, whomped all challengers of his right to wear in his hatband the red feather of the champion of all the boatmen. When steamboats nudged many keelboats off the rivers, he joined a trapping expedition that fought its way up the Missouri River and on to the Rockies. He was murdered in a frontier fort near the mouth of the Yellowstone River.

"Whilst still a stripling," said a journalist who grew up in Pittsburgh during Mike's ranger days, "Mike acquired a reputation for boldness and cunning far beyond his companions. A thousand legends illustrated the fearlessness of his character."

The total may be too big. Nevertheless, until quite recently, stories about Mike, his scouting, and his marksmanship circulated in the Pennsylvania of his youth.

Two years before Fink died, Alphonso Wetmore's play, *The Pedlar*, dramatized oral lore about the boatman. Thereafter for years, much evidence shows, oral stories about him in his longest-lasting role, that of a boatman, flourished all along the river route between Pittsburgh and New Orleans. Young Abe Lincoln probably heard some of them in 1825, when he lived near the mouth of Anderson Creek and helped operate an Ohio River ferryboat, or in 1828 and 1831, when he made flatboat trips to New Orleans. A decade or so later, the boy Sam Clemens almost certainly heard some in riverside Hannibal, Missouri. In 1847 a widely traveled actor-turned-newspaperman swore he had picked up "anecdotes and stories" about Mike in Cincinnati, Louisville, New Orleans, Natchez, and St. Louis. Folklorists have cornered old-timers and picked up venerable yarns about the boatman in several river towns well into the present century.

In the mid-1840's an army lieutenant on an expedition into New Mexico, camping near Valverde and warmed by "fine claret and good old brandy," heard tales of Mike's doings in the Rocky Mountain region. And toward the end of the decade, an explorer was told that a grave alongside the Yellowstone River was that of "the *celebrated* Mike Finch [sic.]"

Hosts of writers with varied backgrounds, aims, and talents helped cluster stories about the westering ranger-boatman-trapper. The list of the media for which they wrote is as varied as it can be—a couple of plays, a ladies' gift book, a pamphlet on navigating the Ohio and Mississippi Rivers, government reports, local histories, humorous books, books of sketches, travel books, anthologies, several almanacs, many magazines, and innumerable newspapers. Every part of the country that had a print-shop swelled the total.

The tales about Mike, like most American legendry, intermarried folklore with journalism and fiction. Because printed narratives hungrily devoured oral narratives, and vice versa, to separate one from the other is impossible.

Today it often is almost impossible for us to tell apart the episodes that were meant to be taken seriously and those that were intended to get laughs. And staring bemused at most of the stories at which nineteenth-century readers seem to have laughed, we are likely to find ourselves, like Queen Victoria, saying sourly, "We are not amused." Our attitudes are remarkably different from nineteenth-century attitudes; this must be the reason. It is not enough for us to understand that readers in those distant days must have regarded Western barbarians and their archetype, Mike Fink, much as Swift's eighteenth-century readers did Yahoos and Al Capp's present-day fans do degraded Dogpatchers such as Moonbeam McSwine and Earthquake Magoon—as sub-humans. Still more difficult, if we're to laugh at the stories, we also have to be as amused as our forebears evidently were by drunkenness, recklessness, racism, male chauvinism, violence, and sheer cruelty.

In Wetmore's *The Pedlar*, Mike marches onto the stage "with red shirt and tow trowsers on—a little drunk, singing soundings" such as, "Quarter less twain!" Soon he fights a frontiersman after agreeing that there will be no gouging or ear-biting, and out of sheer habit his rival does a little gouging anyhow. Mike roars that he wants a swig of Monongahela whiskey because "for a *picayon* I can get happy as a lord; and for a *bit*, dead drunk."

Two years before Mike's death, therefore, legends were put into writing which made him a guzzler and a brute. Later stories, both oral and in print, enlarged on his drinking with a statistic: he could gulp a gallon of liquor in twenty-four hours and neither stagger nor slur a syllable. His craving was so great that if a shipper entrusted an alcoholic cargo to his care, he siphoned out pitchersful, downed them, and replaced them with water.

Just as "sidesplitting" was the way the Mike of the stories treated women. He took loose women on cruises and slept with floozies during overnight stops. His method of attacking an old problem was illustrated by his handling of "his wife" when his boat docked one day. He made a bonfire and forced Peg to lie down in it and stay there by swearing he would shoot her if she moved:

Peg, through fear of Mike, stood it as long as she could; but it soon became too hot, and she made a run for the river, her hair and clothing all on fire. In a few seconds she reached the water, and plunged it. . . .

"There," said Mike, "that'll lern you to be winkin at them fellers on the other boat."

He sometimes had one of his women help him show what a fine shot he was:

He would compel her to hold on the top of her head a tin cup filled with whiskey, when he would put a bullet through it. Another of his feats was to make her hold it between her knees, as in a vice, and then shoot.

Most sensational of all, in a day when females did their best to hide their legs (at the time called limbs), he had his love hoist her skirts to the Lord knows where and hold the cup between her thighs until he pinked it with a rifle ball.

Other times, to show off his shooting skill, Mike used the help of unwilling animals. He massacred game in profusion and let it rot. As his keelboat bobbed on the river, he shot off a cat's ears or the curly tails of a litter of piglets. Not only to parade his power with a shooting iron but also to get free meat and drink, he victimized a sheep-owning settler. Spying a fine flock of sheep, he went ashore and rubbed snuff on the faces of half a dozen. They leaped around, rubbed their noses in the turf, and sneezed. Calling the settler, he explained that the frantic animals were victims of a current plague of the black murrain. To keep the rest of the flock from catching it, he would shoot into the mass, pick off only those that were afflicted, and toss them into the river. The owner agreed, paid Mike with two gallons of old French brandy, and watched with relief as the boatman dumped the carcasses into the water. After dark, the crew "hauled the sheep aboard, and by daylight had them neatly packed away and were gliding merrily down the stream."

Some of Mike's pranks as popular lore pictured them were most amusing to people with strong racial prejudices. Because the shape of a riverside Negro's heel "offended Mike's eye" when the boatman noticed it from the deck of his keelboat, he shot it off, and later told a judge who tried him: "I've jest altered his breed, and arter this his posterity kin warr the neatest kind of a boot!" An 1852 almanac published in New York, Boston, and Baltimore told about a trick he played on some redmen:

The celebrated Mike Fink once observed some Indians stealing into a widow's milk-cave, from which they had frequently stolen quantities of cream, meat, cheese, etc. He watched them until they got in, fastened the door outside, and then bored holes through the bank above. He and his son then commenced pouring hot water down on them, until they yelled, kicked, and fainted, telling their people that the milk-cave rained hot water.

Another time, just for the hell of it, he shot the scalp-lock off of an unoffending Indian. Later, when the victim hunted him down, Mike put bullets through his head and the heads of his tribesmen.

He was not exactly kind to white men, either. As his boat moved along the rivers, he and his crew howled insults at shore people and other boatmen, and if they failed to find the badinage amusing, he beat them up. The lucky man who was a close friend had a rare treat in store. When the pair of them had tied one on, Mike would let him prove his loyalty by standing sixty, seventy, or eighty yards away with a whiskey cup atop his head and letting Mike shoot it off.

"The boatmen," wrote Bernard DeVoto, "were the sublimate of frontier hardness. And America, incurably artistic, demanded a culture hero. Mike Fink . . . became the symbol . . . the boatman apotheosized. He was the marksman who could not miss, the bully-boy who could not be felled, unmatchable in drink, invincible to wenches . . . immortally violent. . . ."

In time, anecdotes wedded Mike and a fitting mate. This dame chased a Snake Indian who had swiped a venison ham, wounded him, "came up to him, secured the ham, tied the villain's hands together, dragged him back to the cabin, and kept him prisoner until her husband returned" from a hunt. Mrs. Fink learned to stand "as still as a scarecrow in a cornfield" while her spouse entertained a guest by shooting off half her comb.

Sal Fink was a worthy—and more amusing—offspring. Attacked by a bear and its cubs, she kicked the cubs into submission, then "with her naked fists, (for she scorned the use of her side arms on the occasion)" knocked the mother bear down, grabbed a boulder, killed Mrs. Bruin with a single blow, and dragged the beast home. Sal's greatest feat:

One day when she war out in the forest, making a collection o' wild cat skins for her family's winter beddin, she war captured in the most all-sneaken manner by about fifty Injuns, an' carried by 'em to Roast flesh Hollow, whar the blood drinkin wild varmits determined to skin her alive, sprinkle a leetle salt over her, an' devour her before her own eyes; so they took an' tied her to a tree, to keep till mornin'. . . . Arter that, they lit a large fire in the Holler, turned the bottom o' thar feet towards the blaze, Injun fashion, and went to sleep to dream o' thar mornin's feast; well, after the critturs got into a somniferous snore, Sal got into an all-lightnin' of a temper, and burst the ropes about her like an apron-string! She then found a pile o' ropes, too, and tied all the Injun's heels together all round the fire,—then fixin a cord to the shins of every two couple, she, with a suddenachous jerk, that made the intire woods tremble, pulled the intire lot o' sleepin' red-skins into that ar great fire, fast together, and then sloped like a panther out of her pen, in the midst o' the tallest yellin, howlin, scramblin and singin'. . . .

Unlike Fink, whose spoor occur in quite a few historical records, neither his spouse nor his daughter left traces in documents that have been found. Writers for almanacs and newspapers simply appear to have decided to give him a worthy helpmeet and a doughty daughter. Legendry and anecdotage work that way, inventing appropriate mates and pals.

By analogy, the folklore-and-journalistic Mike attracted a cluster of tales that had been told about others but that also fit him. The historian who recorded Mike's sheep-and-snuff trick spotted an earlier version about a James River bargeman. Still earlier British bargemen on the Thames in the days of Charles II, like Fink, were famed for "river talk"—insults bandied with one another and shore people, and leading to fisticuffs. An anecdote about Mike's ride, buck naked, aboard a bull, on three occasions had been told about completely different men.

The most interesting forerunners are those of stories which seem to be the most localized, individualized, and authentic— tales about Mike's skill with a rifle which enabled him to shoot off half of his wife's comb, and to pink whiskey cups clenched between women's legs or perched on pals' heads, without injuring women or pals. The report of Fink's death in the *Missouri Republican* on July 16, 1823, says that just before he was murdered he "was engaged in his favorite amusement of shooting a tin cup from the head of another man"; and contemporaries who had known the man often mention this peculiar pastime, so apt for a reckless frontiersman. But striking parallels in earlier lore cast doubts on the reliability of these reports. In Greek myth, for instance, Hercules's companion, Alcon, saved a son when a serpent coiled around him by shooting a fatal arrow into the

Colonel Crockett, beat at a shooting match with Mike Fink. *The Crockett Almanack*, 1840

reptile without harming the boy. About 1200, Saxo Grammaticus told about a similar performance by the Dane Toki. In the fifteen-century *Malleus Maleficarum*, a candidate for initiation had to shoot an apple or a silver penny from his son's cap. And, of course, the reference to the apple reminds one, as it did several writers about Mike Fink, of fourteenth-century William Tell's famous bow-and-arrow shot—enacted in plays by Lemierre (1766) and Schiller (1804) and celebrated in Rossini's opera in 1829. Folklore, cooperating with print—as was its habit in this literate country—attached variants of the old narratives to a New World comic demigod.

Whatever their ancestry, stories about Mike were obsessed with his violence, his boorishness, and his contempt for law to such an extent that they fail to turn on most modern readers. Searching through the Fink literature for something that can still amuse, two keen-eyed critics at last hit on the same element. Constance Rourke, though she was puzzled by the fact that while tales of this lawless brawler "exhibited the broad, blind cruelties of the backwoods, . . . many of them insisted that Fink was good," found him outstanding in one way: "His language was one of his glories, matching his power to push a pole." Mark Van Doren agreed, saying, "As a talker, he is sublime."

Definitive proof is impossible, but we believe that what the two admired—what Miss Rourke called Mike's "loosely strung poetry"—was put into his mouth by writers. A four-verse ballad and a fragment of another that Mike actually composed and that a fellow mountain man carefully recorded have no sparkle whatever. The earliest samples of his utterances are just as undistinguished. Only after journalists and fiction writers, years after his death, have begun to "quote" Mike at length does he do himself proud as a talker, let alone a poet. And it is probably worth noticing that the writers came along after critics and pioneering authors had recognized the value of vulgar speech as a means of portraying low characters.

Not until 1839 does a writer tell us, in an almanac, that after Mike announced that he is tough, he shouted, "and if any man dare doubt it, I'll be in his hair quicker than hell could scorch a feather." In 1842, Mike was made to lament the dullness of a peaceful period: "If the Choctaws or Cherokee or the Massassip don't give us a brush as we pass along, I shall grow as poor as a strawed wolf in a pitfall." In 1847, he told of a "cussed old cow" that "had the orfullest holler hind its shoulders you ever did see, and the old folks being petiklar careful about the crittur, they jest insisted that I should foller it around in wet weather and *bail its back* out." And in 1848, in the midst of a novel crawling with melodrama, Mike's oration to his keelboat crew during a storm is quoted:

"Boys, this here's a night—well it is . . . and ef I war poetically made, I'd describe it to you in a way to make your har stand' like the tail o' a full blown peacock. How the wind rolls and tumbles about like a dying craw-fish, and sprinkles the water in your faces, my hearties; and all fur your good, too, if you warn't so thunderation blind you couldn't see it, and the night warn't so dark. Why, ef it warn't for sech times like this, what in natur would become on ye, my angels?—fur ye never git water nearer to ye nor the river, and you're afearder o' that nor a dog that's got the hydrobothoby, or sum sech curious jaw-breaking name. . . . ."

In the poetic rhapsodies that writers claimed Mike intoned most often, the frontiersman, like Walt Whitman, celebrated himself and sang himself. The earliest of these boasts were poor things, e.g., in 1829: "Mike made proclamation—'I'm a salt river roarer; and I love the wimming, and how I'm chockfull of fight,' &c." However, over the years one writer after another used his imagination to make his hero's vaunting soar. An outstanding invention was the one by T. B. Thorpe, whose masterpiece, "The Big Bear of Arkansas," will be discussed at length in a later chapter. Thorpe's "The Disgraced Scalp-Lock" (1842), to be sure, prettifies the roughneck hero by endowing him with a romantic love of nature and a nostalgia as incongruous as a frock coat would be.* But the tale uniquely quotes some of Fink's profanity and has him say to his crew as his keelboat nears Natchez:

"Well, I walk tall into varmint and Indian, it's a way I've got, and it comes as natural as grinning to a hyena. I'm a regular tornado, tough as a hickory withe, long winded as a nor'-wester. I can strike a blow like a falling tree, and every lick makes a gap in the crowd that lets in an acre of sunshine. . . . Whew, boys! if the Choctaw devils in them ar woods thar, would give us a brush, just as I feel now, I'd call them gentlemen. I must fight something, or I'll catch the dry rot—burnt brandy won't save me."

Such talk may not convulse modern readers, but more because of its style than anything else, it probably will come closer to doing so than the records of Mike's rough pranks do. It will also relate Mike as he is pictured in popular stories to another comic demigod who, became famous a bit later than Mike and whose renown lasted much longer—the legendary Davy Crockett.

---

* Kenneth S. Lynn holds that the nostalgia reflects Thorpe's longing for the vanished days when his Whig party was in its prime—a clairvoyant feat since during the year the story appeared Whig politics and Thorpe as a Whig politician were still flourishing.

*. . . as early as the same can be
completed, I shall put to press a Narrative of my life; in which I . . .
shall strive to represent myself as I really am,* a plain, blunt Western
man, *relying on honesty and the woods, and not on learning and the
law, for my living.* —Letter to the Public, Washington City, December
30, 1833, signed "The public's most obedient servant, David Crockett."

11.
David versus Davy

"I HAVE MET WITH HUNDREDS,
if not with thousands of people," wrote Congressman David
Crockett of the Twelfth District, Tennessee, "who have formed
their opinions of my appearance, habits, language, and every
thing else. . . . They have almost in every instance expressed
the most profound astonishment at finding me in human shape,
and with the *countenance*, *appearance*, and *common feelings* of
a human being."

There was rather more truth to this claim than there is to some
that politicians make. Witness the item in a Pennsylvania newspaper about a stop the congressman made in little Columbia in
1834, the year he wrote the complaint: "Col. David Crockett
. . . went 'ahead' after a delay of fifteen minutes, and leaving
persons who expected to see a wild man of the woods, clothed in
a hunting shirt and covered with hair, a good deal surprised at
viewing a respectable looking personage, dressed decently and
wearing his locks much after the fashion of our plain German
farmers."

Crockett was peeved about the way a book had misrepresented
him; but the book's anonymous author had drawn upon oral
storytellers (including the congressman himself) and on journalists for his matter and manner. During the next two decades
and far beyond, books, magazines, newspapers, and a run of almanacs would add and repeat anecdotes about the man, and
most would be untrue. The trouble was that the storytellers,
none of them under oath, gussied up or even invented these

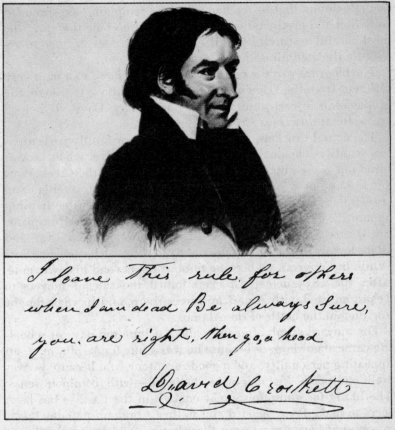

*I leave This rule. for others
when I am dead Be always Sure,
you. are right, then go, a head*

David Crockett

David Crockett. Watercolor portrait by Anthony Lewis DeRose. *The New-York Historical Society*

stories to suit their purposes. Because Crockett was in politics, his backers and coat-tail riders pictured him favorably and his haters unfavorably. When he switched parties, everybody sashayed to the other side. Well, not everybody: some storytellers, uninterested in propaganda but eager to be amusing, shaped their accounts accordingly. And since all these caricatures were being circulated widely at the same time, it is not hard to see why contemporaries were confused. When James Atkins Shackford wrote a scholarly biography that appeared as recently as

1956, he found that he too had reason to complain: "So shrouded in fiction and myth and error has Crockett become that only the most careful research into all available sources can hope to recapture the man himself."

The biography of the real David Crockett shows us a man very different from the Davy of popular lore. But the actual man, the propagandistic caricature, and the legendary Davy all helped create the funny Davy Crockett.

The actual Crockett, born in 1786 to a poor family in Tennessee, scantily schooled, started work at age twelve, when he was hired out to neighboring farmers. He served in the Creek War, got a name as a hunter, militia officer, genial storyteller, and crowd-pleasing campaigner in the hustings, and after holding appointive offices was elected to the state legislature. He ran for the United States Congress in 1825 and lost, won in 1827 and 1829, lost in 1831, won again in 1833, and was beaten in 1835. While in Congress, he became famous far beyond his own state. After the 1835 defeat, Crockett joined the tide of movers to Texas, enlisted with American forces there, and in 1836 fought and died in the battle of the Alamo.

His upward climb after only about a hundred days of schooling came about largely because he was a fine figure of a man, an appealing personality, and a good raconteur, and because he was well equipped—his neighbors believed—with common sense. The liking for gumption, great enough in the East, as has been seen, to make Poor Richard and Father Abraham popular there, was perhaps even greater on the frontier. A historian points out a reason. Life out West (the Southwest of that day) was a superb leveler: "Common hardships, common poverty, common ignorance, and the utter inability to get more out of life than coarse food, coarse clothes, and a rude shelter, reduced all to a level of absolute equality which existed nowhere else."

Frontiersmen were likely to distrust anyone who had to learn how to think or what to do by reading books instead of by depending upon his hard head and the lessons that experience had taught him. A Texas judge told off lawyers for lugging a stack of books into his courtroom: "Once and for all, I am appointed, not to judge the nice points of law, but to give my decisions according to the simple dictates of justice and common sense." Crockett, when he was a Tennessee squire, worked the same way and thought he got good results:

My judgements were never appealed from, and if they had been they would have stuck like wax, as I gave my decisions on the principles of common justice and honesty between man and man, and relied on natural born sense, and not on law and learning to guide me; for I had never read a page in a law book in all my life.

Aboard a Mississippi steamboat in 1829, Count Alexis de Tocqueville learned from Tennesseans that a distrust of books and reliance on horse sense had helped elect Crockett to Congress. The people of his district, the Frenchman was told, voted in this clod "who has no education, can read with difficulty, has no property, . . . dwelling continuously in the woods," because—"Full of pride and ignorance, the electors want to be represented by people of their own kind." Crockett's defeated rival was an educated man "of wealth and talent." Later, in his fine book, *De la Démocratie en Amérique*, the brilliant French commentator held that the strange belief of Davy's constituents was that of most of his countrymen—that "almost all the inhabitants of the United States conduct their understanding in the same manner, and govern it by the same rules:"

To evade the bondage of system and habit, of family maxims, class-opinions, and, in some degree, of national prejudices; to accept tradition only as a means of information, and existing facts only as a lesson used in doing otherwise and doing better; to seek the reason of things for oneself alone; to tend to results without being bound to means, and to aim at the substance through the form; such are the characteristics of what I shall call the philosophic method of America . . . in most of the operations of the mind, each American appeals to the individual exercise of his own understanding alone.

Congressman Crockett showed that he went for this attitude in a speech that he made in Boston, as he reported it in his *Tour to the North and Down East*:

I ain't used to oily words; I am used to speak what I think, of men, and to men. . . . I have made my way to the place I now fill, without wealth, and against education; I was raised from obscurity, and placed in the high councils of the nation, by the kindness and liberality of the good people of my district . . . and according as God has given me judgment, I'll use it for them, come of me what may.

The stand Crockett took appealed to the men of Tennessee who elected him and to the New Englanders who heard this speech.

In the election that shocked De Tocqueville, Crockett ran and won as a pro-Jackson Democrat. By the time, some years later, that he spoke in Boston, he had turned against Jackson and had become an ardent Whig. Whatever his party tie-up, this professional frontiersman could count on supporters who believed that when it came to making decisions, horse sense was a better guide than book learning. First Democratic publications and later Whig publications congratulated their readers on having the frontiersman's homespun wisdom on their side.

Then as now, though, Americans were of two minds about the value of rusticity, rough manners, and scanty book learning. In some moods and situations, they thought these were God's marks on wise leaders; in others, they thought they were blemishes. In 1820 in *Letters on the Eastern States*, William Tudor showed he believed that the rural upbringing of Connecticut writers boggled them when they tried to produce "satire and sportive wit" *because* they had "imbibed rusticity:" "The consequence has been that even genuine wit was degraded by its association, till it became mawkish to correct taste." Nevertheless, within a few years, comic writers would be amusing large audiences *because* they had "imbibed rusticity."

We shouldn't find it hard to sympathize with such ambivalence. Practical Americans who in the 1930's and 1940's scoffed at Franklin D. Roosevelt's brain trusts, who in the 1950's jeered at Adlai Stevenson and his "egghead" followers, and who in every decade downgraded academics knocked themselves out to put their offspring through college and bragged when their young were given high grades and Phi Beta keys by "those professors." And Americans kidded rigid rules for social behavior at the same time they made etiquette guides whopping bestsellers.

Out of such inconsistencies come satire and comedy, and a journalist could amuse readers by picturing Davy as either one of Nature's Noblemen or a Stupid Lout, whichever suited his purpose. As Shackford put it:

. . . while Crockett was a Jacksonian, the Democratic press polished him up with little reference to the true man, and the Whig papers, with just as little regard for fact, tried to laugh him out of Congress as a blundering bull in the sanctified halls of gentlemen. When David changed his alliances, the Democratic papers were prone to take up the old line initiated by the Whigs and enlarge upon that, while the Whigs refined upon the earlier tradition which the Democrats had so carefully built up.

One account of Davy's behavior at a particular White House dinner showed him acting quite properly and "wittily routing President Adams's son when that young man attempted to ridicule him." Another report of the same affair had him greedily grab a huge helping of goose, rudely bawl out a waiter for swiping his plate, slurp water from his finger bowl, and collect six cups of sherbet. The Congressman (or his press agent and ghost) called the process followed in the latter account libelous, "magnifying the plain rusticity of my manners into unparalleled grossness and indelicacy."

Political pamphleteers were not the only ones who got laughs with jokes about the canebrake politician. Storytellers and journalists, usually without ulterior motives, told yarns about this "original" whose habit of talking tall about his surroundings and speaking humorously about himself made him a natural.

The stories did not have to have roots in reality and often were not new. The real Crockett was well-built, handsome, and ruddy-cheeked. But for centuries, traditional jokes had made ugliness a funny quality. Falstaff claimed Bardolph's crimson proboscis glowed with a flame that made torches inoperative. *The Spectator* in 1711 told about "Spectator's" election to England's Ugly Club. Seventy years later Charleston, S.C., had a branch.

Joke 177 in *Joe Miller's Jests* (1739) was about the British kingdom's champion ugly man. When Gus Longstreet entered law school in Litchfield, Connecticut, in 1813, a student welcomed him: "Here, sir, is a knife always given to the ugliest student. . . . Until now it has been mine, but beyond doubt, sir, since you are here, I have now no right to it any longer." Andy Jackson, "Old Hickory," won a like award. (So, in time, would Lincoln.) In Mike Fink's ballad about Neal Hornbeck—

> He were crook'd back'd, hump'd shoulder-ed
>   And with thick lips is blessed,
> And for to make him ug-i-ly,
>   The Lord has done his best.

Lore had it that Davy was so repulsive-looking that if he just grinned at a raccoon, it tumbled from its tree. Once, worried because he grinned and grinned without bringing down his victim, he was relieved when a close look showed he had mistaken a knot for a beast. All the same, he had grinned all the bark off the branch.

Stories about other men gravitated to the more famous Davy. Out in Fort Smith, Arkansas, in 1818, another raccoon learned that the dog which had treed it belonged to the famous sharp-shooter Martin Scott, and Scott was at hand. "The coon cried in anguish and despair, that he was a *gone coon;* rolled up the white of his eyes, folded his paws on his breast, and tumbled out of the tree. . . ." Davy displaced Scott in some versions of this anecdote. In one, looking down at the hunter, the raccoon hoisted his paw like a schoolboy and asked, "Is your name Crockett?" Told it was, says Davy—

"Then," said he, "you needn't take no further trouble, for I may as well come down without another word." And the cretur walked rite down from the tree, for he considered himself shot.

I stoops down and pats him on the head, and sez I, "I hope I may be shot myself before I hurt a hair of your head, for I never had sich a compliment in my life."

"Seeing as how you say that," sez he, "I'll jist walk off for the present, not doubting your word a bit, d'ye see, but lest you should kinder happen to change your mind."

This story and others, ostensibly told by Crockett, though he had no part in their telling, were ground out by almanac writers, hack biographers, and other folk journalists. Like Mike Fink anecdotes, these often personalized old tales about the ferocious American Westerner but had much older ancestors—ancestors dating back to the ancient Greeks. Just as the Greeks had a name for the type Franklin represented, the *eiron*, they had one for the type Davy Crockett represented, the *alazon*.

Since we'll meet many incarnations of this type, a great American favorite, we now must define it and look at some of its Old World ancestors preparatory to contrasting them with New World mutants.

For the Greeks, the *alazon* was the opposite—often the foil—of the *eiron*, who, it will be remembered, made himself out worse

"And the cretur walked rite down from the tree, for he considered himself shot." *Davy Crockett's Almanack, 1841*

than he was. The *alazon*, in Aristotle's words, was "apt to claim the things that bring glory when he hadn't them, or to claim more than he had." Max Eastman was the first critic, we think, to label the Poor Richard purveyor of "dry humor" an imported *eiron* and the personification of American boasting an imported *alazon*. Eastman called the former "the soft-spoken, poker-faced boy, canny and restrained, who always has something more in mind than he is telling you." He said that the *alazon* was a "blustering, swanking, cock-and-bull-story-telling lad like Davy Crockett or his biographers . . . the loudmouthed backwoodsman, 'gamecock of the wilderness' with his tall tales and preposterous asseverations of prowess."

Like other translations, though those by Eastman have merit, they aren't quite inclusive enough to meet our needs. While the *eiron*, true enough, can be a modest, kindly commentator, he can also be a Uriah Heep, a ferocious satirist, a wily politician, or a humorist playing a role. An *alazon*, true enough, can be a bully-boy braggart; but he also can be a professorial pedant, a show-off physician or scientist, or even (we're afraid) a historian of humor. He has been known to materialize as a politician who really knows fewer answers than he claims he knows in campaign speeches. And at times he has been a humorist pretending to be one of these many types.

For these reasons, though we'd love to scrap two somewhat intimidating Greek terms, we're going to continue to talk about *eirons* and *alazons*.

The long history of the *alazon* goes back to Aristophanes' *The Frogs* (405 B.C.), in which Dionysius merrily wagged his vaunting tongue. In his *Nichomachean Ethics*, Aristotle defined the character as "he who claims more than he has" and contrasted him with "the mock-modest man." Plautus (c. 254-184 B.C.), who used the *alazon* in seven comedies, gave one of the plays the title that critics often use when discussing such a figure—*Miles Gloriosus*—braggart warrior, and gave the hero a name that mocks his vainglory: Pyrgopolinices—Tower-Town-Taker. During the Renaissance and on down to the present century, writers of many sorts in many countries created their versions, a few instances of which are cited below.*

Some of these characters were very popular. The type loomed large in dramatic performances throughout Europe and in England from about 1550 to about 1750. Jonson's Bobadill in *Every Man in His Humor* won laughs in 1598 and in many revivals thereafter; in the Victorian period, the part was Charles Dickens's

* Sir Dinadin and Sir Kaye in Thomas Malory's *Morte D'Arthur* (1485); Martano, Ludovici's *Orlando Furioso* (1515, 1533); Tinca, Pietro Aretino's *Talanta* (1542); Ralph, Nicholas Udall's *Ralph Roister Doister* (c. 1553); Braggadocio, Edmund Spenser's *Faerie Queene* (1590-1611); Parolles, Shakespeare's *All's Well That Ends Well* (c. 1596); Falstaff, Shakespeare's *1 Henry IV* (c. 1579); Falstaff and Pistol, *2 Henry IV* (c. 1598) and *The Merry Wives of Windsor* (1599); Bobadill, Ben Jonson's *Every Man in His Humour* (1598); Capitanos Metamoros, Spavento, Cocodrillo, Rodomonte, Rinoceronti, Spezzafero, Fricasso, and Scaramucia *in commedia dell' arte*, sixteenth, seventeenth, and eighteenth centuries; Captain Face, David Barry's *Ram Alley* (c. 1608); Besus, Beaumont and Fletcher's *A King and No King* (1611); Matamora, Pierre Corneille's *L'Illusion Comique* (1635); Jodelet, Paul Scarron's *Jodelet* (1645); Drawcansir, George Villiers and Others', *The Rehearsal* (1671); Bluff, William Congreve's *The Old Bachelor* (1693); Brazen, George Farquhar's *The Recruiting Officer* (1706); Bob Acres, Richard Brinsley Sheridan's *The Rivals* (1775); Münchausen, Rudolph Erich Raspe's *Baron Münchausen's Narrative of His Marvelous Travels and Campaigns* (1786). More recent examples: Sergius, George Bernard Shaw's *Arms and the Man* (1894); Cyrano, Rostand's *Cyrano de Bergerac* (1897), performed as a special on television, 1975; Eiluf, Brecht's *Mother Courage* (1941), revived on Broadway, 1975. Also in T. H. White's adaptation of *Morte D'Arthur*—a quartet of novels collected as *The Once and Future King* (1939-1958) and in *Camelot* (1960), the musical based upon it, the boastful knights were recycled.

favorite role. (Bobadill claimed he gave London's masters of defense public lessons: "They have assaulted me some three, four, five, six of them together. . . . I have driven them afore me the whole length of the street. . . . By myself, I could have slain them all.") The Duke of Buckingham and others in *The Rehearsal* (1663, 1671) lampooned Dryden's bombastic heroes by creating Drawcansir, a braggart who spoke in couplets. ("I, the blood of thousands daily spill/ . . . If they had wings, and to the gods would flie, / I would pursue and beat 'em through the skie.") During London theatrical seasons for a century and a half, the name Drawcansir became in England a widely used synonym for braggart. Münchausen's vainglorious tales, written by Raspe (1786), went through edition after edition, and as early as 1800 had been translated into five languages. References by the score to "American Münchausens" and innumerable retellings of the baron's stretchers—several by Davy's ghost writers—prove that he was famous and influential in the United States.

In their vauntings, these swaggerers did more than promise to do great things in the future. A few years ago, John Wardroper, an unabashed lover and collector of ancient jokes and their reincarnations, showed what often happened when he included two versions of the same anecdote in an anthology, *Jest upon Jest*. In 1595, a joke book had: "A gallant threatened one, saying, 'If thou offend me, I'll throw thee so high into the element that rather mayst thou fear famishing than falling.'" In 1639, another collection had:

A terrible braggart boasted how it was his chance to meet with two of his arch-enemies at once. "The one," saith he, "I tossed so high in the air, that he had at his back a baker's basket full of bread, though he had eaten all the way, he would have been starved in the fall ere he would have reached the ground." And the other he struck so deep into the earth that he left him no more to be seen above ground but his head and one of his arms—and these to no other end than to put off his hat to him as he had occasion to pass that way.

By shifting from the future to the past tense, a braggart turns a boast into a *fait accompli*—an episode in his autobiography. He adds some vivid details and ties to it a related jest.

Not surprisingly, as Richard M. Dorson has noticed, when the

feats of Crockett celebrated by almanacs, newspapers, and
pseudo-autobiographies are ordered chronologically, they unfold a life story that comically echoes romances, epics, and sagas
in which heroes at their very best are celebrated in earnest. The
Crockett legends "possess the leading motives and conform to
the growth structure of all Old World heroic story." Dorson cites
likenesses between Davy's fabulous biography and those of
Prince Marko, Cu Chulainn, Hector, Siegfried, Beowulf, Roland,
Antar, and others. Just barely tied to the subject's actual life, the
mythical story, Dorson finds, gives him a strange birth and precocious strength, quotes his awesome boasts about his muscles,
weapons, animals, and women, and tells about his "fierce hand-
to-hand encounters and conquests, ardent wooings, travels in far
lands, and superhuman exploits." C. Grant Loomis, in a similar
study, found parallels between Celtic saints' legends—of all
things—and stories about the fabled Davy.

Captain. *Naturalists say that by
nature the lion roars, the snake hisses, the bear growls; by nature the
bull bellows, the horse neighs, the wolf howls, the dog barks, and that
by nature Captain Fear always threatens and always menaces . . .
since I am by nature threatener, slasher, slayer and killer, I have to
slash, slay, quarter and cut to pieces some human creature every day.*
—*The Boasts of Captain Fear of Hell Gulch* (1607).

*I'm a leetle the savagest crittur you ever did see. . . . I can outlook
a panther and outstare a flash of lightning: tote a steamboat on my
back and play at rough and tumble with a lion, and an occasional kick
from a Zebra. Goliath was a pretty hard colt but I could choke him.
. . . I can walk like an ox; run like a fox, swim like an eel, yell like
an Indian, fight like a devil, and spout like an earthquake, make love
like a mad bull, and swallow a nigger whole without choking if you
butter his head and pin his ears back.*
—"Speech of Colonel Crockett in Congress,"
Davy Crockett's Almanack of Wild Sports in the West, 1837

12.
Davy versus Captain Fear
of Hell Gulch

A CONTRAST BETWEEN THE LEG-
endary Davy and another famous braggart may be at least as
useful as Dorson's comparisons. The other fabulous *alazon* was
quite as popular as Davy; his fame, in fact, spread to more countries. His name suggests kinship—Captain Fear of Hell Gulch.
In the printed lore about the pair, both killed herds of animals
and used up or annihilated dozens of single opponents and a few
armies. Both traveled all over the world and through a good part
of the sky. But since Captain Fear belonged to a time and a place
two centuries and thousands of miles from the Tennessee canebrakes, a contrast throws light on the way a stock character was
naturalized and made amusing to nineteenth-century Americans.

The version of the hero's name given above is a free translation from the Italian—Capitano Spavento della Valle Inferna.
This was the most popular and widely copied braggart soldier

among a score in *commedia dell'arte*—"the comedy of professional players,"* theatrical pop art (as contrasted with learned)
from the middle of the sixteenth century to the middle of the
eighteenth, not only in Italy but also, to a surprising extent, in
much of the rest of Europe and in England. This theater appealed to aristocrats as well as peasants and influenced such famous dramatists as Jonson, Shakespeare, Moliere, and Goldoni,
as well as others less famous.

A chief reason for the success of Italian repertory companies
at home and in England, France, Spain, Germany, Austria,
Poland, and Russia was the skillful way performers improvised
monologues, dialogues, mime, music, dance, and even acrobatics
to flesh out characterizations and plots barely sketched in the
brief scenarios which were their only guides. Each company had
specialists, often for their lifetimes, in stock roles: doddering old
gaffer, pedantic doctor, clever valet, stupid lackey and others.
(One sign of the long life of the tradition: the *commedia* name
for comic servants, *zannis*, persists as a word we still use with a
related meaning, "zany.")

The braggart soldier was one of the most durable and best-
liked among these stereotypes; and a great actor in the role was
Francesco Andreini (1548?-1624), so thoroughly identified with
performances as Capitano Spavento that he was often spoken of
by his stage name. Andreini starred in the early and durable
Gelosi Company, which appeared with great success in Italy,
Austria, and France. More is known about him than about any
other *capitano* because of the company's fame, the publication
in 1611 of fifty scenarios used by the group, and the preservation
in print of Andreini's *The Boasts of Captain Fear of Hell Gulch*,
the most complete set of such brags that survives.

The ways Davy and Spavento talked about their ancestry contrast sharply. The Old World captain claimed that his forebears
were of noble blood and had bequeathed him matchless digni-
ties. Democratic Davy traced his untitled family no further back
than his grandparents, and he spoke about nothing but its lon-
gevity and its prowess. At the age of one hundred and twenty,
his grandmother coughed on an attacking Indian until he not

* Other captains included Mountain-Splitter, Moor-Killer, Crocodile, Rhinocerous,
Iron-Buster, Black-Ass, Lion-Tamer, and Earthquake.

Il Capitano (1668).

only surrendered but also "died of the full-gallop consumption."
At one hundred and forty-eight, Davy's mother "could jump a
seven rail fence backward, . . . spin more wool than any of
your steam mills [and] cut down a gum tree ten feet around."
His father, at one hundred and forty-nine, was "a venerable
sample of white oak" with a trunk "so all flinty hard that you
could strike fire from it with a sledge hammer."

Spavento played up his warlike qualities and achievements.
"Since by nature," he remarked, "I'm menacer, slasher, slayer
and killer, I have to slash, slay and quarter some human creature every day." His birth and childhood forecast a great army
career, and his training furthered it. He was born "clad in
breastplate and coat of mail . . . washed in melted lead,
swathed in red-hot steel bands, and fed on hemlock and gunpowder. . . . While still a boy, I learned from a murderer how
to wound, kill and chop people to tiny pieces." His sword, en-
graved "For the Champion Hired Killer," knocked off soldiers
without mutilating their bodies, sharpened itself by butchering
officers, and brightened when he dipped it into the blood of
colonels. He fought in all the great sieges and battles, leveled
many cities, and made whole continents pay tribute to his glory.
When America refused, he kicked it out of the world, readmit-
ting it only after forty Indian ambassadors (dressed in parrot
feathers, yet) brought gifts of amber, musk, and precious stones.

Davy's babyhood and training readied him for hunting rather
than for warfare. There was nothing bellicose about his swath-
ing—a simple blanket made of rattlesnake skins. True, he was
washed with bear's gall, but only because his aunt had heard
that it "brought forward the intellectures." He was watered on
buffalo milk, weaned on whiskey and raw rattlesnake eggs, and
then fed—not gunpowder—but roast ducks, bear meat, and venison hams. He used his favorite weapons—fists, thumbnails, rifles,
and "the longest knife in all Kentuck"—to demolish gigantic
wild beasts and men one at a time. His favorite pets were not
battle steeds but hunting dogs and domesticated forest animals,
which helped his wife keep house and carried him from place to
place. He got into battles and wars only incidentally, and though
he did well when he took on armies of Sandwich Island cannibals, Haitians, and Mexicans (made their heads fly like "horse

chestnuts in a hurrycane"), his battlefield performances were puny compared with Spavento's.

To reward Spavento for a favor, Venus gave him amatory powers that made Italy's leading courtesans long to have him as a lover. The noblest cavaliers with unwed daughters made his life a hell by begging him to take their darlings to the altar. Just to end all the tiresome bickering, he considered taking a wife, though he was sure that no mate could be "a consort" simply because "no woman could match my quality and partake of my dignity and honors." This probably was a lucky break, since any spouse of the captain certainly would have worn herself out bearing the prolific fellow's children. When another champion challenged him to a fertility contest, "In a single night Hercules got fifty damsels with child, and in half a night I got two hundred." This was only the start; in time, Spavento announced: "If all of my bastards had to be housed in a foundling hospital, the whole world would be too small."

Despite the fact that when—as he delicately put it—Davy "went a-galling," he "had a right smart chance of sweethearts," he was not in the captain's league. The women he went for, every time, were not in the captain's league either. Each was a giantess and an Amazon comparable with Mike Fink's daughter. Sal Fungus, one of Davy's typical girlfriends, met up with a huge Indian in the forest one morning: "Sal kicked his fundaments, and he slapt her face; then she wrung his nose till the blood spurted and that war what made him so mad." That too war what fired Davy's passion, for soon "we courted, hunted and walked together night and day." Her charms:

She could scalp an Injun, skin a bear, grin down hickory nuts, laugh the bark off a pine tree, swim stark up a cataract, gouge out alligators' eyes, dance a rock to pieces, sink a steamboat, blow out the moonlight, tar and feather a Puke [a Missourian], ride a painter bare-back, sing a wolf to sleep and scratch his hide off.

In a passage that burlesques sentimental excesses, Davy tells how Sal reacted when he left for the wars: "She died with a bursted heart—it war too big with love for me, and its case war not big enough to hold it."

The maiden that Davy wed, Sally Ann Whirlwind Crockett,

was another hellion. She beat Mike Fink, no less, until "he swore he had been chawed up and swallered by an alligator." The pair produced three daughters, "the tallest and fattest, and sassyest gals in America," and among the strongest and toughest.

Quite a few almanac stories show that Davy was not completely faithful; he tells about carrying on with several "doxies." He mentions no illegitimate offspring, though, and since he says nothing about having remarkable reproductive prowess, we must assume that he did not.

Spavento's speeches, like those of other *commedia dell'arte* characters, were spattered with dialect. In his case, it was a Spaniard's mispronunciations of Italian words, since, as his uniform indicated, he was a caricature of the arrogant Spanish military men who dominated the Italian peninsula in Andreini's day. Nevertheless, he paraded learning in every scientific field— geography, physics, chemistry, astronomy; in politics and world affairs; and in the humanities—classic mythology, poetry, music, rhetoric, the dance, and philosophy. He dropped cloudbursts of names. Jove was a pal who did him favors. His sword was forged by Vulcan and owned, before he got it, by Xerxes, Cyrus, Darius, Alexander, Romulus, Tarquin, and Caesar. With it he killed Hercules, Apollo, and Cupid. When he licked the Amazons, Homer, Virgil, Ovid, Dante, and half a dozen other great poets celebrated the victory. His style was a pretentious parade of highfalutin figures of speech and Ciceronian cadences.

The Davy of the legend was like the true-life Crockett in having little use for learning. The only time he tried "a larned courting"—to win bluestocking Kitty Cookins—he found that he could not "keep up his end of the log," and he had no regrets:

She axed me if I war fond of reading, and I telled her that I had read the catekise when I war a child, and thort it only fit for children, but that I could draw a bead on a squirrel at three hundred paces. . . . She lookt down and begun to trot her little foot, and said thar war no defined people in the clearing, and how she inferred litter-a-toor and novelties, and loved to look at the moon, and the clouds, and how she liked . . . Sally Tude and vartue, and war going to cultivate bottiny and larn the use of yarbs. And then she read a little out of her book, and axed me if I war fond of poetness and duplicity. I telled her I didn't know about them kinds of varmints; but I liked a bear-steak, or a horn of mountain dew, and had drunk two sich fellers like her sweetheart under in one evening.

Here Davy's ignorance caused him to macerate grammar, spell atrociously, and substitute words he knew for unfamiliar ones— "defined" for "refined" and "infer" for "prefer": frontier malapropisms—without giving a damn.

However, in tales about Davy, an anomaly often occurs. Because it is related to the American ambivalence noticed a few pages back, the deviation is important enough to deserve a close look. And some facts about a time-worn Old World joke help with the scrutiny.

In Europe for centuries, a comic butt, as we've mentioned, was the imposter who pretended that he had more knowledge than he actually had. In *commedia dell 'arte* a recurrent type was the pedant—usually a windy old doctor (in numerous Gelosi scenarios, Doctor Gratiano). One earmark of a pretender to learning was a habit of peppering his talk with Latin phrases or latinate words. Rabelais, for instance, wrote a chaper, "How Pantagruel Met with a Limosin who Affected to Speak in Learned Phrases." In it "a handsome spruce young scholar" bewilders Pantagruel with sentences full of sixteenth-century double talk, e.g., "We transfretate the sequam at the dilucal and crepuscul; we deambulate by the compites and quadrives of the urb. . . ." Pantagruel says, "he doth only flay the Latin," and Rabelais draws a moral: "that it becomes us to speak according to the common language, and shun all strange words." In *Tom Jones*, Fielding has an eighteenth-century counterpart, a surgeon, pay two calls on his hero and each time completely confuse his listeners with what the author ironically calls his "great learning."

"Of wounds, indeed [says he], it is rightly and truly said, *Nemo repente fuit turpissimus*. I was once, I remember, called to a patient who had received a violent contusion in his tibia, by which the exterior cutis was lacerated, so that there was a profuse sanguinary discharge; and the interior membranes were so divellicated that the os, or bone, very plainly appeared through the aperture of the vulnus. . . ."

In the *Crockett Almanack* published in 1835, Davy, supposedly delighted because he has not been smirched by an education, uses these sentences:

My throat and jaws were so *exfluctoficated* with the influenza that I even snored hoarse.
[Wildcats] scratched her backsides so *tarnaciously* they've never itched since.

A *monstratious* great he-alligator . . . came on a ranting gallop out of the water.

Latinate coinages such as these, if we credit popular anecdotes (and we are mad fools if we do), were commonplace not only in Davy's talk but in frontier talk in general in the days of Andy Jackson. (A few others: "to absquatulate" [sneak away]; "to obflisticate" [obliterate]; and a word still in use, "rambunctious.") Davy's—and fictional frontiersmen's—concoctions are in the same class as terms used for centuries by folk who, like Davy, lack learning. But they have been used before by men eager to do something quite out of character for the Tennessean—to convince hearers that they are erudite. Instead of being contemptuous of book larning, in other words, those who used them were overeager to make others think they had it. The hacks who made the almanacs were out for laughs—and with luck, felicitous phrases—even if they had to be inconsistent in picturing Davy.

Just the same, when the legendary Davy and other funny story Westerners flung around words so out of keeping with a contempt for books, they showed a kinship with Captain Spavento. There was a tremendous difference, though, between Davy and other Southwesterners, on the one hand, and Spavento, on the other hand. And the difference was closely allied with other highly significant contrasts between the Italian and American creations. Spavento consistently pretended he was learned and at the same time exposed his misinformation. As Daniel C. Boughner says:

While posing as a traveler, Spavento actually betrays his ignorance of foreign countries. . . . He ornaments his statements with Dantesque epithets—though true to his type he sometimes bungles these. . . . The fun of his role requires that he utter howlers with an air of solemn assurance, and he casually commits egregious blunders. [Defying chronology] he mixes up his own exploits with ancient myths and treats classical lore with . . . airy contempt for accuracy. . . .

And learning was not the only virtue Spavento assumed when he had it not; in every respect, he was a fake.

A bit of the scenario for one of the plays in the Gelosi repertoire shows Captain Fear's real nature: "Flavio enters, attacks the Captain, . . . knocks the Captain down. When the Captain begs for his life, Flavio lets him go." The big joke about this braggart was that all his boasts were buncombe; he was not learned, a noble, a triumphant lover, a worldwide traveler, a great warrior, or a brave man. Though he claimed to be all these in spades, as Marvin T. Herrick says, "Actually he was a poverty-stricken nobody, a coward, an ignoramus, the laughing stock of women. His one genuine accomplishment is a flow of language usually devoted to colossal lies."

The incongruity was as venerable as the type. From Aristophanes on, the glaring contrast in the Old World was between the gaudy claims of the *alazon* and the actuality. Usually the boaster's appearance gave him away: huge-bellied or spindly-legged—perhaps both—he looked like neither a paladin nor a lothario. When he fought, he made sure it was with a woman, a sissy, a eunuch or (in one instance), a butterfly. Challenged by a formidable opponent or even by a coward who outbragged him, the *miles gloriosus* quibbled. ("The captain replies that he never fights unless he has the permission of Mars and the town gallants looking on, and goes off.") When two braggarts who were equally fearful collided, each ran away from the other. When a boaster was forced to fight, he was quickly beaten and humiliated. In the field of love, the boaster was always on the sidelines, glued to the bench. As Shakespeare's Parolles says in *All's Well that Ends Well* (IV, iii, 374-376):

> Who knows himself a braggart
> Let him fear this; for it will come to pass
> That every braggart shall be found an ass.

Frontier ways of living may have had something to do with it. So might two traditions which, as has been shown, were strong in the New World—the plausible tall tale and Western ferocity. Whatever the reason, when the *miles gloriosus* crossed the Atlantic, trudged on to the frontier, and became an American ring-tailed roarer, he underwent a change. Here he was not a poltroon or a sissy. He was a mighty athlete; he was spoiling for a fight; he was tough. He did not run away but fought no-holds-barred and well. His opponent was another superbly conditioned tall talker who was brave, strong, and hard to beat. They fought fiercely; both were battered; and the battle did not end until one of the men was licked. This was the pattern for story after story about Davy Crockett and other frontiersmen.†

† Since there are no new jokes, we oversimplify when we speak of Old World and New World formulas. There were exceptions:

Professor George Kernodle has reminded us of the long-lived British mummers play. It may well have taken form in the time of the Crusades, and it was given frequently well into the present century. Its chief event is a combat. Each of two rivals—St. George of England, St. Denis of France, Bold Slasher, Cromwell, George IV, Napoleon or some other—shouts a boast about his great deeds in war and love and threatens to lop off his rival's buttons and cut him into mince pies. They then fight. One is killed but is resurrected. The resurrection is brought about by a third *alazon*, a doctor who, like a *commedia doctora* or a frontier medicine show spieler, claims he can cure anything—"the itch, the stitch, the palsy and the gout/ Pains within and pains without." A bumpkin helps collect money from the audience:

> In come I, as ain't been yet,
> With my big head and little wit,
> My head so big, my wit so small,
> I will dance a jig to please you all.

The temptation is to call *him* an *eiron*, but we have resisted it.

In the United States in *Davy Crockett's Almanack 1837*, "a corncracker," i.e., a Kentuckian, tells about a run-in he had with a Yankee peddler. Peddlers, he says, "Although the greatest chaps in creation for brag and sarce, . . . always play possum when there is danger; and skulk out the back door over the fence in no time." The Kentuckian found one of the rascals romancing his doxy; the Yankee talked tall but quickly ran away when the Kentuckian threatened him.

"A good inch from the [squirrel's] eye—and after all my teaching too!". . . . *"I never drew a knife across the throat of one of 'em [hostile Indians] without a shudder."* . . . *"I ain't fit to breathe the same air as you. What am I? Nothing but an ignorant backwoodsman!"*—Davy Crockett, in Frank Murdock and Frank Mayo, *Davy Crockett: Or, Be Sure You're Right, Then Go Ahead (1872-1896).*

13.
Davy II, Davy III, and Mose

TWO REINCARNATIONS OF THE legendary Davy, the first in a play which was on the boards between 1872 and 1896 and the second in a television series, a motion picture, a comic strip, and a number of books between 1955 and 1957, show that picturings of a demigod may change tremendously with the passage of time. The successive portrayals show our hero becoming less funny (intentionally, at any rate), more noble, and, for adults, less appealing.

Richard M. Dorson correctly says of the first legendary Davy, who was popular between 1830 and 1856:

Davy represents frontier crudity, violence, anti-intellectualism, chauvinism, and racism. He butchers the varmints of the forest, sneers at book learning and educated Easterners, despises niggers, Injuns, and Mexicans, and arrogantly trumpets the supremacy of Uncle Sam . . . Crockett is self-reliant and individualistic, scornful of cultural institutions, intensely confident and braggart, and a thorough nationalist.

The second coming of Davy was the work of actor-playwright Frank Murdoch and character actor Frank Mayo—the play, *Davy Crockett; Or, Be Sure You're Right, Then Go Ahead*, a blockbuster. Starting in 1872 at the age of thirty-three, Mayo impersonated twenty-five-year-old Davy throughout the United States and in England continuously until two days before his death, aged fifty-seven, in 1896. Mayo counted two thousand

143

stagings, got tired, and stopped far short of the total for what was
the most successful drama in its category during its era.

This vastly popular melodrama contains only vestigial reminiscences of the crude, bellicose, horse-sensible, tall-talking
Davy—even of the comic Davy. This Crockett is brave, gentle,
chivalrous, eloquent and sensitive. (After he slew forty-two Indians, he considerately remarked, "I never drew my knife across
the throat of one of 'em without a shudder.") An ideal hero for
an 1870's melodrama, this paragon today can get only unintentional laughs. For instance:

On a dark and stormy night, Davy has welcomed the half-
frozen heroine (properly chaperoned, of course) to his woodland
hut. To thaw out the sixteen-year-old maiden, the frontiersman
has burned the bar to the door. At this inconvenient moment, a
pack of ravenous wolves arrive, hell-bent on eating the hut's suc-
culent occupants. They plan, naturally, to come through the un-
barred door. "Nothing," deduces Eleanor, "can save us!" Davy
disagrees:

DAVY. Yes, it can!
ELEANOR. What?
DAVY. The strong arm of a backwoodsman. [Davy bars door with his
    arm. The wolves attack the house. Heads seen opening in the hut
    and under the door]
                              TABLEAU
                              CURTAIN

When the curtain rises on the next act (TIME: SEVERAL HOURS
LATER), our hero still is using his arm to bar the door. The
wolves still are howling and gnawing at the cabin "with such incredible ease," recalls a playgoer, "that I wondered what kind of
logs had been used." Davy now gets off his best line, truly a
thing of beauty:

"THIS IS GETTING KIND OF MONOTONOUS, THIS BUSINESS IS."

The arm holds out until a rescue party arrives, and Davy can
rest it until he needs it to perform its next good deed. On this
one, Sir Walter Scott collaborates. The frontiersman has been
moved by Eleanor's reading of "Lochinvar" to him. ("Well,
there's something in this rough breast of mine that leaps at the

The heroic David Crockett, pictured on the cover of *Davy Crockett's Almanack, 1837*

telling of a yarn like that.") He realizes he "ain't fit to breathe the same air as you." But on her wedding day, he borrows a stallion, rescues her from an unloved groom, and carries her away, hollering: " 'Whoop,' says the knight, 'I'm Lochinvar. Who dares to follow?' "

Davy III, thanks to the miracle of television, collected more fans than either earlier Davy, lasted a shorter time (1955-1956), and was less amusing—even unintentionally. A nationally televised work of art produced by Walt Disney, it consisted of a series of weekly episodes which unfolded a fictional biography that was supposedly authentic. Preceding each segment, Davy I was briefly celebrated in a lively, tuneful ballad hailing "Davy, Davy, Davy Crockett, king of the wild frontier" and the tall tales about him. The ballad for months made the hit parade, was blatted from juke boxes everywhere, and sold millions of copies. But the old-fashioned tall-tale characterization had only the vaguest possible connection with the dramatic one.

The series starred a beautiful leading man—tall, handsome, muscular, immobile of face but frenetically active, who performed a great many heroic deeds. He solemnly spoke a humorless dialect, so even his talk was unamusing. Bereft of comic touches though the Mayo-Murdoch Davy was, he was a laugh riot compared with this demigod as Fess Parker played him. Davy III was everything that Davy II was—gentle, chivalrous, sensitive, eloquent, and brave. In addition, he was noble to the point of being downright stuffy. The series had some broadly comic touches. But they were supplied, not by the gallant hero, but by a sidekick—a Sancho Panza to an unamusing Don Quixote. The partner was played by Buddy Ebsen, a character actor who went on from the series to star as a hillbilly clown in a long-enduring slapstick television series, "The Beverly Hillbillies."

The Davy Crockett series of the mid-fifties captivated millions of adults and still more millions of children who sat entranced before television sets on Crockett nights. Right away, all the kids had to have rifles and fringed jackets, or at least coonskin caps like their idol's. In a few months, the cost of raccoon tails shot up 1900 percent. In some stores, a tenth of the juvenile-wear sales were of Crockett-linked items. A score of books, some old, some new, were rushed off the presses and snapped up at bookstores. One had an advance sale of a million copies. A daily Crockett comic strip was syndicated to more than two hundred newspapers.

One hundred and nineteen years after the real Crockett died, in other words, a mythic picture of him could dehumorize him into a man too good for this naughty world. It seems likely that the times had something to do with such a stuffy character's stupendous success. Stuffy or not, he was heroic, and we needed a hero. Two months before the Crockett series started, the television exposure of Joseph McCarthy had brought about his censuring by the Senate. Eisenhower had been elected President on a peace-and-tranquility ticket. America, at least juvenile America, found that an all-out hero who was unfunny (but who had a funny pal) was appealing.

The fad died almost as quickly as it had begun. A movie condensation of the series had only moderate success. Crockett books were remaindered; rifles, coonskin caps, and fringed shirts stuffed garbage cans from sea to shining sea.

From 1848 to the mid-1850's—between the appearance of Davy I and the advent of Davy II—New York City provided the nation with an urban ring-tailed roarer, Mose the fireman. Though British fiction and drama about London's Tom and Jerry inspired his creators, Mose was as legitimate a son of New York City as the legendary Davys were of the frontier. He was a Bowery "b'hoy," the city's most colorful and most amusing tough about town. Since his neighbors recognized him as not only typical but also funny, we can glimpse reasons why so many media—plays (twenty or more), novels, newspapers, humorous periodicals, lithographs, circuses, and (of all things) ballets which starred him—did well in New York. "Glimpse" is not too weak a word, for even more than Davy's, his peculiar charm seems to have weathered. And why he should tickle, as he did, the folk of two dozen cities other than New York, where plays about him prospered—from Montreal to Charleston, from Chicago to New Orleans, and from Louisville to San Francisco—is something of a problem. Probably, like the Western swaggerers whose popularity overlapped his, Mose appealed because the nation at that time went for tall talkers, because he blatantly—even defiantly—shared widespread gaucheries, and because in an era when sections were different from—and curious about—one another, he was so localized a figure.

Like keelboatmen and frontiersmen, or in fact like toughs of any place and period, Mose wore a costume and a hairdo that made him stand out like a bandaged thumb: shiny plug hat worn slantwise over a close-shaven phiz (since the period thought beards effeminate) and hair—short in back and long in front—glistening with bear grease, fancy vest cut low to display fancy shirt and suspenders, long black frock coat, pants tight from buttocks to knee, then bell bottom or rolled below.

Like other heroes in our country's obstreperous youth, Mose loved to fight and kept telling the world: "I'm bilein' over for a rousin' good fight wit' some one some where. . . . I ha'n't had no muss, 'cept a little blow out last night, for a'most a whole week. If I don't have a muss soon, I'll spile! . . . How I could lam him or any other *he* tonight! . . . Bring on a cord or two! We can lick de crowd! We're all loaded an' primed. . . . I'll give him thunder over de coconut." In plays, stories and pam-

**Handbill advertising a
Mose play.**

phlets, Mose, in the elegant words of the New York *Herald*, was
"the hero of a hundred musses." In New York, Mose fought
members of gangs such as the Plug Uglies, men of rival fire
companies, or complete strangers who irritated him in brothels
or other social gathering places. He could crush bones with a
heavy slingshot, but usually he picked up weapons from streets—
paving stones, staves, and brickbats. A great traveler, like Davy
(to England, France, Araby, China), he found chances for musses
outside of New York. In California, for instance, he fought a

bear, Indians, and Forty-niners. Except in rare instances, the pattern of his musses was that of other antebellum free-for-alls. Fierce and fearless rivals sounded off, then battled until one of them was whomped.

Like barbaric Westerners, this urban hero was both loved and laughed at because he lacked learning and social grace. He had a way of flicking cigar ashes and spitting on fine rugs. At a banquet speaker's table, he whacked the table top for order and yelled, "Are you all on hand at the station? Then start her lively!" When he wanted his girl friend Lizey to sing, he told her, "Blow your horn!" and when she finished, he said, "I'm be blowed if it ain't slap up. You can sing a few!" In London, though he found the mummies in the British Museum interesting, he scoffed at them because "they ain't no good to nothin'." Presented at court, he voiced a hope that the royal children were "pretty, bright and sassy." At the fashionable Vauxhall Gardens, he showed he was with it by telling the waiter, "Bring us a plate o' pork an' beans. Say, a big piece o' pork. An' don't stop to count de beans!" Though he preferred oysters with catsup to corned beef and cabbage, his savoir faire and culture were those of an early Jiggs or Moon Mullins.

His talk signaled his crudity. He used "d's" for "th's"; his grammar was horrible; he spouted slang phrases: "He's one o' de b'hoys! . . . We ain't—I won't do—I don't mean—nothin' else! . . . Gass! He's a stuffin you! . . . Look here hoss-fly!"

Mose's part-time job—or hobby—as a volunteer fire-fighter (Company 40, de Marta Washington) was as heady, as skilled, and as proletarian an activity as Mike Fink's Indian scouting, keelboating, and trapping; and much of his talk showed he went for it to de hub: "I love dat ingine better dan my dinner. Last time she was at de corporation-yard, we plated de brakes, an' put in new condensil pipes; and de way she works is about right, I tell you. She trows a three-inch stream de prettiest in town." Phrases he made famous came from fire-fighting: "Sykesy, take de butt! . . . Get off dem hose or I'll hit yer wid a spanner! . . . We're goin' in—we be." Climactic scenes showed him performing heroic rescues.

For all his crudities, Mose had a heart, to coin a phrase, of gold. As a playbill boasted, he was "always found defending right against wrong; protecting the weak against the assaults of the strong." He saved greenhorns from con men, senior citizens from muggers, the poor from the greedy rich. And whenever a dastardly villain abducted a pure maiden and made ready to accomplish his foul purpose, Mose dashed up and rescued the helpless virgin. If he was praised, he turned modest and said simply, "Ain't I doin' my duty?" When it came to righting wrongs, Mose was as infallible as Superman.

Audiences that saluted Mose with cheers as an old friend when he swaggered onto the stage contained a bigger share of "b'hoys" than earlier audiences had. "The boxes," said a soured contemporary Manhattan critic, "no longer shown [sic] with the elite . . . the character of the audiences was entirely changed, and Mose . . . was in the pit, the boxes, the gallery." He must have exaggerated. The fireman's pals alone never could have filled two theaters in New York City and one in Newark night after night to see three plays about Mose that were being performed simultaneously. Playgoers from other groups in New York and in other cities must have enjoyed vicarious visits, along with the comic fireman, to places of many sorts—ballrooms, a woman's gymnasium, a bowling parlor, saloons, gambling hells, waterfront dives, fish markets, the Tombs, the Astor House, the Soup House, and the Battery.

Actor Francis S. Chanfrau (1824-1884), who originally played Mose, who made the part famous, and who outlasted half a dozen others cast as Mose, explained why even the most successful dramatization featuring the fireman lost its pull early in the 1870's:

It is a conglomeration of scenes—a piecemeal affair altogether—and the local hits and slang phrases, while they were understood by everybody when the play was new, are utterly incomprehensible to the present run of play-goers. When *Mose* was born, he was simply a representative of a well-known class in New York. The era of the steam fire-engines changed all that, and Mose no longer exists.

If Herbert Asbury is to be believed, a few vestiges lingered on and were still around after he got to New York in 1915. Old-timers in flophouses and bars with whom he talked (after he stood them drinks, we suspect) told him, sure, they had heard of Mose the fireboy. What they claimed they had heard were not snatches of antebellum stories but stuff about a giant. Their Mose was twelve feet tall, as strong as ten men, had feet as big as East River barges, and wore a beaver hat two feet tall or—on duty—a helmet the size of a pup tent. He carried a horse-car in one hand, mowed down gangs with uprooted lamp-posts, blew ships along the East River by puffing cigar smoke into their sails, and swam the Hudson with two strokes. These representations are so much like those about Paul Bunyan which were current when Asbury published them in *The Gangs of New York* (1928) and *Ye Olde Fire Laddies* (1930) that one suspects that either the old-timers or Asbury imbibed printed rather than oral inspirations.

Part Two

The Golden
Age of
American
Humor

A National Phenomenon

If the time ever should arrive that we shall possess a domestic theatre, with authors and actors who have been accustomed, from infancy, to observe and feel the nice shades of local peculiarities, the comic muse will have some worthy offerings for this section of the country. The class of clowns in European comedies, have here their counterparts, but greatly varied by the institutions under which they live. An equal degree of awkwardness, rendered more ludicrous, by a greater degree of education; a good deal of native shrewdness, with a large portion of social simpleness, will give rise to many scenes of comedy. Go a step or two higher, and take individuals of both sexes, who have lived in seclusion, with some natural tendency to eccentricity, and have got all their ideas of society, from books, and of dress, from their own fancy; and watch them when they make an incursion into the world, and the comedian will find them replete with excellent matter.

—William Tudor, *Letters on the Eastern States* (1821).

14.
Oppositions

EVEN THOUGH MANY RAW MA-
terials and methods of American humor were universal, by the
1830's it had been decisively molded by the national character.
The exaggeration, the anti-intellectual bias, and the interest in
native characters and their modulations of the spoken language
came together during the antebellum years in ways that would
characterize much of our humor for a century.

Beginning in the late 1820's and early 1830's, comic characters poured from literary pens, and Americans were made acquainted with such folks as Mike Fink (in 1821), Davy Crockett
and his prototype Nimrod Wildfire (in 1830), Jack Downing
and his family (in the same year), and Hosea Biglow, Birdofredum Sawin, Major Joseph Jones, Mrs. Partington, Widow Bedott,

and Sut Lovingood in the 1840's. Leading authors who produced humor frequently and consistently during these years included Augustus Baldwin Longstreet, Johnson J. Hooper, Sol Smith, Thomas Bangs Thorpe, William Tappan Thompson, George Washington Harris, and John S. Robb, among those usually called the humorists of the Old Southwest; and Seba Smith, James Russell Lowell, Charles A. Davis, Thomas Chandler Haliburton, and Benjamin Shillaber, among humorists of Down East. These, and others, flooded newspapers and periodicals with their humor and collected it in books that often went into reprintings. Comic periodicals—most of them short lived—sprang up, and at least one publisher—Dick & Fitzgerald—exploited the field of humor almost exclusively. In short, the impulse to write humor coalesced into something close to a national phenomenon.

Contradictions, and consequently incongruities, were rampant in the reasons for this coalescence. The happy illusion that they had won the War of 1812 helped make Americans truculent, cocky, and boastful; and the superciliousness of travel-book critics of American inferiority and newness made them more so. In a nation still proud of all men's equality, both Whigs and Democrats voted for slavery. Both parties therefore backed Southern planters and New England factory owners, but both parties wooed the votes of poor and middle-class whites. College-bred New England men of family and Southwesterners who were educated and well-to-do found some disreputable fellows companionable and amusing, though they defined them differently. Principles of justice and fair play often seemed to be discarded as reputable men admired and laughed at horse-traders, sharpers, peddlers, and confidence men who went for W. C. Fields's motto, "Never give a sucker an even break."

However many paradoxes underlay the antebellum humor, there were some assumptions—largely unformulated—on which much of it was based. A tension existed between the intellectual and the ignoramus. Though naturally each favored members of his own group, each could find the collisions laughable.

One possibility for comic collision (the least significant one) lay in political allegiances. Vastly oversimplified, Whig ideals and those of the Jacksonian Democrats were antithetical. The black and white picture showed Whigs favoring a limited elec-

torate of enlightened and propertied voters; the Democrats
wanted universal male suffrage, opening the polls to penniless
semi-literates. That overgeneralization could produce humor
which satirized politicians of either party or ridiculed the specific political issues of the day (as with Jackson's banking policy
or Polk's involvement with the Mexican War). Theoretically, at
least, Whig humorists might be expected to depict common men
as repulsively stupid, vicious, and amoral; and Democrat humorists might be expected to represent Whigs as erudite eggheads,
fastidious, stuffy, and so overly intellectual that they would have
trouble tying their own shoes.

But, of course, politics is never that simple. Both David Crockett and Abraham Lincoln were elected to office as Whigs; and
Emerson voiced at least a tentative endorsement of the Democrats. James Russell Lowell, rather than a staunch conservative,
was whatever seemed right at the moment—Whig, Democrat,
Republican. His typical attitude: On election day of 1850 he
wrote, "I shall vote the Union ticket (half Free Soil, half Democratic), not from any love of the Democrats, but because I believe it to be the best calculated to achieve some practical result."
In his poem "A Fable for Critics," Lowell even made fun of his
own penchant for "isms":

> There is Lowell, who's striving Parnassus to climb
> With a whole bale of *isms* tied together with rhyme. . . .
> The top of the hill we will ne'er come nigh reaching
> Till he learns the distinction 'twixt singing and preaching.

Joseph Glover Baldwin (one of the most genteel humorists of the
1850's) praised Jackson's "fairy work, in converting the bank
bill back again into rags and oak-leaves." Augustus Baldwin
Longstreet was a John C. Calhoun Whig, while Johnson J. Hooper
and William Tappan Thompson were Henry Clay Whigs.* And
neither party was the exclusive domain of the stereotype eggheads and anthropoids. Alexander Saxton has recently pointed
out that in Jackson's Democratic Party, "the new urban working
class played a significant but not dominant role." Old Hickory
himself delighted in the semi-Whiggish humor of Seba Smith's

* The philosophies and platforms of these groups are less important here than
that a vast spectrum of beliefs existed, making a Whig-Democrat dichotomy an oversimplification.

Jack Downing, commenting, "Depend on it, Jack Downing is only Van Buren in masquerade."

Only at the extreme of caricature, then, does the black-and-white opposition of Whig pedant and Jacksonian bumpkin seem historically valid. And in fact, two recent scholars, Norris Yates and Richard Boyd Hauck, have argued convincingly that two of the leading antebellum comic periodicals, William T. Porter's *Spirit of the Times* and George W. Kendall's New Orleans *Picayune*, shared a major editorial policy: they avoided political issues as a basic ingredient of the humor they printed.

A more important collision for humorous exploitation was the geographical one. Throughout most of the nineteenth century, regional peculiarities (always sure-fire sources of humor) attracted the attention of Americans, as they did that of English travelers. Despite subtle gradations, the Yankee, the backwoodsman, the New England bluestocking, the New York Dutchman, and the Southern aristocrat were all distinguishable from one another, and one fairly persistent contrast good for laughs pitted the Eastern seaboard against the back settlements. James K. Paulding noticed that "between the tenants of Down East and those of the Southlands there did exist a deal of ill will . . . partly owing . . . to differences of manners and customs, for the former abhorred horse-races, cock-fights, and mint-slings, preferring thereto apple-brandy, tea, cucumbers, pumpkin-pies, thanksgivings, general trainings, and other harmless luxuries."

Together with regional peculiarities went defensive and offensive regional pride. Like modern Texans, humorous characters of every section gloated about the virtues of their towns, counties, and states. It was the custom, it would seem, to exaggerate the beauty, the fertility, the affluence, or the other superlative qualities of a region until claims soared into tall tales. The Yankee, traditionally portrayed as self-effacing and laconic, could boast about himself and his section as rapturously as the ring-tailed roarer.

More important, writers noticed that both serious and comic tensions could be exploited by moving a character from one region to another. Cooper's Harvey Birch in *The Spy*, Dr. Obed Bat in his *The Prairie*, and Melville's cast of characters in *The Confidence-Man* represent relatively serious applications of the

The comic Davy finds a Yankee peddler with his gal friend. *Crockett's Almanack, 1837*

formula; but comic migrations seemed felicitous years before those books appeared. Rural Yankees—Joe Strickland, Enoch Timbertoes, Jack Downing, and Sam Slick—wandered into towns and cities, gawking and mystified, then reported back to the home folks the wondrous and peculiar ways of city residents. Crude outsiders from the mountains, sticks, or canebrakes appeared in more civilized settlements, too—Sut Lovingood, Davy Crockett, Major Joseph Jones, and Simon Suggs, for instance— looking with suspicion at the new territory. Crockett's speech in Boston (recorded in *An Account of Colonel Crockett's Tour to the North and Down East* in 1835) made fun of his preconceptions of New England:

We have been taught to look upon the people of New England as a selfish, cunning set of fellows, that was fed on fox ears and thistle tops; that cut their wisdom-teeth as soon as they were born; that made money by their wits, and held onto it by nature; that called cheatery mother-wit.

Similar incongruities could occur when the Yankee wandered beyond the boundaries of his own region. As complex a character as American humor has invented, the Yankee could be shrewd and cunning—"a wily, cozening trickster, poised under a mask of ingenuousness and seeming good will," as Richard Dorson has called him. When he wandered into the backwoods, with his pack of notions to peddle, he was, if Sut Lovingood of the Tennessee Knobs is to be believed, the man who invented "new fangled doctrines fur the aid of the devil. In fact [New England] am his garden, whar he can grow what won't sprout any whar else." But when he went into town, as Dorson also notes, comic picturings showed him to be "a fool, an ignorant countryman, baffled by urban ways, befuddled by modern machinery, legitimate game for dupes and hoaxes. . . . Inevitably the bewildered rustic found himself cozened by city sharpers."

Throughout the country, in short, comic collisions might follow the placing of an "alien" regional type in a culture foreign to him. Understandably, the way the type was represented depended in large part on the geographical loyalties of the humorous writers. Yankees were sympathetic yokels when limned by many New Englanders, villains when described by a humorist on the frontier. Backwoodsmen were hardy, pragmatic heroes in the Old Southwest, but often became monsters when a writer on the Eastern seaboard depicted them.

Whatever the political or regional affinities of a writer, another possibility for comic collision lay in contrasting social levels. Most humorous authors who flowered in the antebellum decades were educated. Many were professional men—lawyers, judges, doctors, or journalists who were patrician in their lifestyles and world views. Practically any of them—Davy Crockett and George Washington Harris are the most notable exceptions— might be expected to champion erudition, dignity, and decorum rather than common sense, rowdiness, and rascality. In fact, though, both in the East and on the frontier, loyalties were strangely divided.

Some Eastern humorists best remembered for staid and genteel humor lived lives not above reproach. Washington Irving, for instance, in his youth belonged to the club, the Kilkenny Kats, whose membership was notorious for raising cain and getting pie-eyed. He scandalized respectable New Yorkers with the broad humor in his *Knickerbocker's History*, and all his days he was an outrageous flirt. Oliver Wendell Holmes was noted for his bawdy and off-color lectures to medical school students. He began his lecture on female genitalia by observing, "My subject this afternoon is one with which I trust you young gentlemen are not familiar," and he compared the birth canal with an express company, "Because they both *contract* to make/ *Delivery of freight*." And he made raucous fun of religious fanatics, like "The Moral Bully":

> The Moral Bully, though he never swears,
> Nor kicks intruders down his entry stairs,
> Though meekness plants his backward-sloping hat,
> And non-resistance ties his white cravat. . . .
> Hears the same hell-hounds yelling in his rear,
> That chase from port the maddened buccaneer,
> Feels the same comfort while his acrid words
> Turn the sweet milk of kindness into curds,
> Or with grim logic prove, beyond debate,
> That all we love is worthiest of our hate.

He ridiculed prissy female education and Brahmin inbreeding which had produced a "compromised and lowered vitality" among that caste—in which Holmes was himself a charter member. And James Russell Lowell, later professor of modern language at Harvard, as a youth was an anti-establishment political radical of dimensions rivaling the inhabitants of Haight-Ashbury in the late 1960's, getting rusticated out of Harvard for drinking and cavorting indecorously in chapel. A Southwestern humorist like Augustus Longstreet could be equally ambivalent about his society—Georgia gentry—and uncouth commoners. In fact, humorists could find snobs and stuffed shirts everywhere in the United States, and egalitarians hypnotized by the emerging horse-sensible American. It's even more true, probably, that the so-called opposition between stuffed shirts and egalitarians is an oversimplification. Most humorists, whatever their political, geographical, and cultural allegiances, saw the ludicrous possibilities of, say, having an ignorant Yankee of the servant class invade an upper-crust drawing-room, of having a simpleminded hunter from Tennessee swig water from his finger-bowl at an elegant dinner under the delusion it was soup, or of having a prissy stranger try to maintain his dignity while undressing before the members of a rural family whose single bedroom he has been forced to use for the night.

Clearly the wealth of incongruities created an embarrassment of comic riches. It also created confusion. As a result of their attempts to find order in the chaos, commentators have chosen to oversimplify the forces at work in antebellum humor. Some of the generalizations which will not survive close scrutiny: (1) that Yankee humor did not exploit gross exaggeration, tall tales, and boasts, which are still often said to be the exclusive ingredients of frontier humor; (2) that William T. Porter's *Spirit of the Times* was a "house organ" for Southwestern humor, when in fact it included humor from all parts of the country; (3) that the terse mother-wit aphorism was the sole property of the New England almanacs, when in fact Crockett's almanacs included, in addition to the tall tales which are better known, the same kind of filler; and (4) that the "frame story," with a dignified narrator controlling the description of a backwoodsman, was the form most often used for telling a Southwestern story, when in fact it was less frequent than other forms.

The confusion is compounded by the struggles of various writers to accommodate, through a series of literary strategies, their personal sympathies and distastes. It is essential to ask (and often difficult to decide) how close the writer of humor came to holding the views which the narrator expressed. Simply because a genteel narrator framed a story, we can't assume that the writer shared the narrator's position. Distance and detachment, ironic poses, and varying degrees of aloofness from and identification with vernacular characters produced a complex art. One man's wisdom was another man's arrogance, just as one man's innocence was another man's ignorance. When there was no framework—in a mock oral narrative by an illiterate, or an ungrammatical letter composed by a yokel—a deviation from a norm provided comedy. A silent but ever-present contrast was provided by the literate and elegant prose upon which the public was fed during most of the nineteenth century.

It could be argued that each writer, whatever his "school," whatever his regional affiliations or political registration, however high- or low-browed he might himself be, responded to the oppositions just discussed in a unique way. To complicate matters even more, he responded—depending on his mood, to the temper of the times, and the evolving possibilities for creating humor—in different ways on different occasions.

Still, a useful way to categorize this humor is to examine its comic effect. Some humor, whoever wrote it, tended to exalt tra-

ditional values. It upheld order over disorder, decorum over unbridled license, and a rigid social hierarchy over the fluid egali-
tarianism of the frontier. Whether written by an author on the
Atlantic Coast, in New England or the tidewater South, or a
"Southwesterner," its biases were essentially conservative and
restrained. It might use a vernacular character either as a sorry
example of lawlessness or as a mother-lode of common sense. It
might make tolerant fun of the self-importance and erudition of
its pedants. But, in spite of almost limitless modulations, it essentially championed a moral and predictable universe. It was
reputable.

Humor of the opposite sort—humor which was anti-Establishment—was also written by authors of both the East and the
West. Some of the time, at least, it was the work of a terrified
prude who recorded his shock and indignation at the wild and
raucous characters he described. This *subversive* humor portrayed indelibly drawn characters whose code of behavior affirmed disorder, violence, and amorality. Its author (as distinguished from its narrator) was fascinated and charmed by the
moral chaos its main characters embodied and the dangerous
logic with which they supported it. Vernacular characters found
metaphors for an inscrutable and unpredictable universe in a
"creation bar," devised similes and analogies that animalized or
mechanized human beings, and created such codas as "It is good
to be shifty in a new country." Few writings seem to urge the
ultimate anarchy that such a position implied; but over and
over, with an enormous range of modulations, this humor describes characters in a hostile universe, dependent on their physical prowess, their cunning, or their common sense to survive. In
their society, stratified caste systems, "civilized" laws, and book
learning simply did not seem to work. Though they were icono-
clasts, lawbreakers, or even sadists, they were also vivid and
funny. Genteel readers might be terrified by them, but their creators found them irresistible. Quite possibly, some of the authors
might complain, with Prufrock, that this was not quite what
they meant. Nevertheless, they allow a dynamic rascal to flaunt
the law, decency, modesty, and abstract notions of right and
wrong, and elevate him to a high point in American humorous art.

The next seven chapters will sketch the outlines of reputable and subversive humor. This dichotomy is perhaps as fragile as other ones, but it has the advantage of divorcing the humor from narrow political limits and of refusing to cram it into biographical and geographical pigeonholes. First, however, it will be useful to look at a writer who glimpsed the comic possibilities of both the reputable and the subversive humorists in 1819.

*He [Ichabod Crane] was, in fact,
an odd mixture of small shrewdness and simple credulity. His appetite
for the marvellous, and his powers of digesting it, were equally extraordinary; and both had been increased by his residence in this spellbound
region. No tale was too gross or monstrous for his capacious swallow.*
—Washington Irving, *Legend of Sleepy Hollow.*

15.
Ichabod and Rip

WASHINGTON IRVING, WHO HAD
a good eye for stereotypes, in his *History of New York* (1809)
sketched several who would be developed more fully later—the
maundering pedant (Diedrich Knickerbocker), the Dutchman,
the Yankee, the settler, the ring-tailed roarer, and the backwoods
squatter. When he pictured Ichabod Crane in "The Legend of
Sleepy Hollow," using the voice of old Knickerbocker, he looked
forward to the parading of "reputables" in the Golden Age. And,
again with the help of his narrator, in representing Rip Van
Winkle, he anticipated picturings of "subversives." As set-pieces,
the two stories clarify those two terms, "reputable" and "subversive." But they also suggest the complexity of a writer's attitude,
since they embody apparently contradictory responses on Irving's part; and it is important to underscore the variety of humorous responses a single writer might crystallize.

The main outlines of "Sleepy Hollow"—the wooing of Katrina
Van Tassel by greedy and gluttonous Ichabod Crane, and his disappearance when a headless horseman (his rival, Brom Bones)
scares him out of the community—are familiar. But in a complex way, there are touches in Irving's tale of thwarted love that
make it an early high point in reputable humor. Tarry Town
and Sleepy Hollow, as the narrator makes explicit, unlike the
constantly shifting frontier, are settled, entrenched communities
where

population, manners, and customs remain fixed; while the great torrent of migration and improvement, which is making such incessant

changes in other parts of this restless country, sweeps by them unobserved.

This static society produces order, affluence, and (highly important to Irving's story) a hoary tradition of folklore:

Local tales and superstitions thrive best in these sheltered long-settled retreats; but are trampled underfoot by the shifting throng that forms the population of most of our country places. Besides, there is no encouragement for ghosts in most of our villages, for they have scarcely had time to finish their first nap, and turn themselves in their graves, before their surviving friends have travelled away from the neighborhood.

Into this closed, comfortable, lush community comes a Yankee, a Connecticut school teacher whose frame and features are a caricature of Brother Jonathan:

He was tall, but exceedingly lank, with narrow shoulders, long arms and legs, hands that dangled a mile out of his sleeves, feet that might have served for shovels, and his whole frame most loosely hung together. His head was small, and flat at top, with huge ears, large green glassy eyes, and a long snipe nose, so that it looked like a weathercock perched upon his spindle neck, to tell which way the wind blew.

Ichabod Crane, "an odd mixture of small shrewdness and simple credulity," had an insatiable appetite. As soon as he catalogued the thriving Van Tassel family wealth, Crane decided to woo the daughter. He imagined himself the master of the Van Tassel estate, with "the blooming Katrina, with a whole family of children, mounted on the top of a wagon loaded with trumpery, with pots and kettles dangling beneath." Ichabod's plot, in other words, is to sell off the Van Tassel farm and invest the money "in immense tracts of wild land, and shingle palaces in the wilderness." It is he, then, with his schemes for enterprising speculation, who endangers the harmony and order of the New York Dutch community.

If Ichabod, "setting out for Kentucky, Tennessee, or the Lord knows where," has some qualities of the restless backwoodsman, his nemesis in the story is a backwoodsman who proposes to preserve the status quo by vanquishing the Yankee interloper and himself marrying Katrina. Brom Bones has all the marks of a frontier ring-tailed roarer. He wears "a fur cap, surmounted with a flaunting fox's tail"; he fights, frolics, races, fights cocks, plays practical jokes, and "would be heard dashing along past the farm-houses at midnight, with whoop and halloo, like a troop of Don Cossacks." There is something strangely un-Southwestern, though, about Brom: "The neighbors looked upon him with a mixture of awe, admiration, and good-will; and when any madcap prank, or rustic brawl, occurred in the vicinity, always shook their heads, and warranted Brom Bones was at the bottom of it." This indulgence—"admiration and good-will"— was never destined to be the lot of Sut or Simon Suggs on the frontier; and the truth is that, no matter how much Brom appears in frontier garb or seems to be a backwoodsman, he in fact is the native who banishes Ichabod from the community and allows it to return to its sleepy, entranced condition. So Brom, a mock-disreputable, saves Katrina (for himself), restores order and evicts Ichabod, and frustrates his attempt to subvert order.

"The Legend of Sleepy Hollow" fits the pattern of reputable humor in other ways. Ichabod, a son of Puritan New England, believes in a supernatural world that is decidedly theological. The Tarry Towners enjoy their legends of ghosts, wizards, and apparitions:

They are given to all kinds of marvellous beliefs; are subject to trances and visions; and frequently see strange sights, and hear music and voices in the air. The whole neighborhood abounds with local tales, haunted spots, and twilight superstitions. . . .

Ichabod, by contrast, has a sterner, Calvinist explanation of such goings-on. Steeped in his Cotton Mather's "direful tales," Ichabod sees such spooky events as the "devil and all his works," and has himself "been more than once beset by Satan in divers shapes." He really believes in and fears the things that go bump in the night, while the community he invades treats them with the same good-natured indulgence that it bestows on Brom Bones. Because he is not an "insider," poor Ichabod is especially vulnerable to the specter that Brom creates to terrify him out of the community.

Another significant character in "Sleepy Hollow" is its narrator, old Diedrich Knickerbocker, who adds a postscript to the story which sounds like a burlesque of both a *Farmer's Almanack* anecdote and a frontier tall tale. Insisting that he is recording the story precisely as he heard it, Diedrich explains that it was told at a corporation meeting by a "sadly humorous" man who was confronted as soon as he finished by "one of your wary men, who never laugh, but upon good grounds—when they have reason and the law on their side." The listener, in what would be a proper New England or respectable fashion, demands to know "what was the moral of the story, and what it went to prove." The storyteller pauses, then offers a majestically insane syllogism:

"That there is no situation in life but has its advantages and pleasures—provided we will but take a joke as we find it;

"That, there, he that runs races with goblin troopers is likely to have a rough riding of it.

"Ergo, for a country schoolmaster to be refused the hand of a Dutch heiress, is a certain step to high preferment in the state."

The sober gentleman, "sorely puzzled by the ratiocination of the syllogism," then announces that he doubts whether the story is entirely truthful. " 'Faith, sir,' replied the story-teller, 'as to that matter, I don't believe one half of it myself.' "

The tale appears to have some qualities of subversive humor— in its caricature of Ichabod the Yankee, its description of Brom as a frontiersman, and its mockery of the demand for some moral significance by a humorless listener. But that listener has, in fact, been gulled by the storyteller. "The Legend of Sleepy Hollow" deftly controls those impulses that might lead to raucous or lawless comedy. Irving's—or Knickerbocker's—prose is elegant, genteel, and erudite (the narrator quotes or alludes to James Thompson, Milton, and Shakespeare); and in the entire story the rural characters are not allowed more than a half-dozen lines of dialogue. A closed society with a rigid caste system rejects the threat to its own security; and affluence, material prosperity, and elegant living are described and relished in ways that mark the narrator, in spite of his gentle satire, as a member of the conservative and patrician reputables.

Rip Van Winkle, by contrast, is a prototype of the frontiersman whose picture would be elaborated in the subversive humor of the Golden Age. Rip is a ne'er-do-well whose greatest talents lie in avoiding work, raising hell, and completely relaxed hunting:

He would sit on a wet rock, with a rod as long as a Tartar's lance, and fish all day without a murmur, even though he should not be encouraged by a single nibble. He would carry a fowling-piece on his shoulder for hours together, trudging through woods and swamps, and up hill and down dale, to shoot a few squirrels or wild pigeons. He would never refuse to assist a neighbor even in the roughest toil, and was a foremost man at all country frolics for husking Indian corn, or building stone fences. . . . In a word, Rip was ready to attend anybody's business but his own; but as to doing family duty, and keeping his farm in order, he found it impossible.

In addition, Rip possesses one of the greatest attractions of the lazy rascal type: he is a master storyteller. To the children, "he told . . . long stories of ghosts, witches, and Indians." And with his group of guzzlers at the tavern, Rip "used to sit in the shade through a long, lazy summer's day, talking listlessly over village gossip, or telling endless sleepy stories about nothing."

Predictably, in a New York Dutch community much like Tarry Town, Rip's behavior violated the principles of thrift, prosperity, and material comfort. "One of those happy mortals, of foolish, well-oiled dispositions, who take the world easy, eat white bread or brown, whichever can be got with least thought or trouble, and would rather starve on a penny than work for a pound" has to have a nemesis. Rip does, in the person of his wife, Dame Van Winkle. Chasing after her husband and his dog "Wolf," she (as Huck Finn was later to complain of another apostle of civilization) combs him all to thunder. Rip has a refuge, though—the wilderness. There, he can escape responsibility, work, and his wife. Literally, he can be a small boy running away from home when he walks in the hills and woods of the Catskills; and on his fateful day, he can make an escape that will last twenty years. The ghosts of Henry Hudson's crew are perhaps not quite the same supernatural beings as Jim Doggett's creation bear (in "The Big Bear of Arkansas," to be discussed in Chapter 20), but Rip—according to his chronicler—regards them in somewhat the same way: "there was something strange and incomprehensible about the unknown, that inspired awe."

The contrast is a bewitchingly prophetic one, too: a forest that represents a safety valve and an escape from restraint and conformity; the pleasures of lager and nine-pins, in a world without nagging wives—a world that is, in fact, starkly silent, in con-

Rip Van Winkle and His Scolding Wife. Engraving by F. O. C. Darley. "If left to himself [Rip] would have whistled life away in perfect contentment; but his wife kept continually dinning in his ears about his idleness, his carelessness, and the ruin he would bring on his family."

trast with the nagging Dame Van Winkle—and, finally, a twenty-year sleep that relieves Rip of wife, property, and even a pang of remorse: "He had got his neck out of the yoke of matrimony, and could go in and out whenever he pleased." And what Rip pleased to do was to tell his story "to every stranger that arrived at Mr. Doolittle's hotel . . . and not a man, woman, or child in the neighborhood but knew it by heart."

The contrast with "The Legend of Sleepy Hollow" is impressive: Rip tries to escape the bonds of his society—estate (however dwindled it was under his mismanagement), matrimony, and labor—and he succeeds! Like a Lord of Misrule, Rip is the master of revels in his community; and not only does he successfully violate all the canons of his society, he even passes on his legacy to a son who "evinced an hereditary disposition to attend to anything else but his business." Rip Junior, it might be argued, was the first inheritor of a tradition that thumbed its nose at "decency," dignity, and propriety and headed out for the territory when the forces of decorum began to overburden him with their rules and regulations.

A further element in "Rip Van Winkle" uses a narrative technique often employed by later frontier humorists. The story is encased within a preface, a note, and a postscript that introduce two narrative voices into the tale. One of these is the voice of old Diedrich Knickerbocker, who does something that any artist telling a whopper is likely to do: he insists on the absolute truth and accuracy of the story. The old man even claims that he got his yarn from Rip himself:

I have even talked with Rip Van Winkle myself, who, when last I saw him, was a very venerable old man, and so perfectly rational and consistent on every other point that I think no conscientious person could refuse to take this into the bargain. . . . The story, therefore, is beyond the possibility of doubt.

And some of Knickerbocker's notes add an air of authenticity and folklorish accuracy, too.

But as if Diedrich's testimony isn't enough, another narrator begins the story with a testimony for Knickerbocker. The old man's *History*, he says, had as its "chief merit" "its scrupulous accuracy" and "unquestionable authority." And even the epigraph which begins the story announces that "Truth is a thing that ever I will keep."

The formula is a perfect one: an outrageous tall tale moves from the cold fact of the preface further and further into the wildest improbabilities as it enters into the deepest part of the forest, and then, as it returns again to the village, edges back to cold, authentic fact. Over and over in later humor, the value of multiple narrators and the tall-tale formula would serve to establish the contrasts between regions, philosophies, and even cultures.

In a sense, Irving saw the possibilities and the potential for the wide range that local color, the common man, and the conflict between eggheads and rustics could contribute to humor. And his two masterpieces charted the territory that was to be so abundantly explored a few years later.

The
Reputables

No rude shows of a theatrical kind;
no minstrel with his harp and legendary ballad, nor gleeman, with an
ape dancing to his music; no juggler, with his tricks of mimic witchcraft; no Merry Andrew, to stir up the multitude with jests, perhaps
hundreds of years old, but still effective, by their appeals to the very
broadest sources of mirthful sympathy. . . .

. . . Their immediate posterity, the generation next to the early
emigrants, wore the blackest shade of Puritanism, and so darkened the
national visage with it, that all the subsequent years have not sufficed
to clear it up. We have yet to learn again the forgotten art of gayety.

—Hawthorne, *The Scarlet Letter*, Chap. 21.

Shrill, querulous women, sour and sullen men,
Untidy, loveless, old before their time,
With scarce a human interest save their own
Monotonous round of small economies,
Or the poor scandal of the neighborhood;

*   *   *   *   *

Church-goers, fearful of the unseen Powers,
But grumbling over pulpit-tax and pew-rent,
Saving, as shrewd economists, their souls
And winter pork with the least possible outlay
of salt and sanctity. . . .

—John Greenleaf Whittier, Prelude to
"Among the Hills."

16.
"To Laugh
Newenglandly"

HAWTHORNE AND WHITTIER,
some might claim, exaggerated the glum look of New Englanders; others might say that they knew what they were talking about. Whether its creators were sourpuss Puritans or not,

several New England humorists supported conventional notions about propriety, decorum, restraint, and morality. Their comedy therefore was strikingly different from that to be discussed in the following chapter. Reputable humor of the sort they produced was not confined to the country east of the Hudson River. But there were striking relationships between some qualities of the New England mind and more decorous humor.

Seventeenth-century Puritans *did* laugh, of course—not often enough, perhaps, and perhaps at jokes within rather narrow limits. Like fellow Britons across the Atlantic, American settlers found puns, acronyms, anagrams, paradoxes, and similar brain-teasers to their liking. They reveled in comic elegies, finding complicated word plays in the name of the deceased (as in John Fiske's "Upon the decease of Mris Anne Griffin"), and concocting extended comic metaphors that strained the limits of ingenuity (as in Nicholas Noyes's "To My Worthy Friend, Mr. James Bayley, Living [If Living] In Roxbury"). When they engaged in this somewhat ascetic frivolity, the Puritans followed two rules that would shape reputable humor long after the Puritan theocracy was overthrown and secularized.

First, the colonists insisted that humor must be moral. Levity, used sparingly, might help educate and preserve dignity and decorum. No comic debauches, orgies, or fights would have been proper to Puritan humor, unless they served to show the evils of such behavior. Except in promotional tracts extolling the virtues of New England life or chiding the wicked, no wanton excesses of hyperbole, which might seem like untruths, would be very appropriate. No mockery of parsons, pedants, or officers of the law (temporal or theological) would have been tolerated, since it would pose a threat to the stability of society and to its authority. Instead, moral precepts—saws like those of Nathanael Ward, whose writing in the guise of a simple cobbler foreshadowed Franklin's homespun wisdom—were the proper stuff for humor. As a result, much of the humor was oppressively didactic, and the rest, unoppressively didactic. It championed virtue, frugality, the status quo, and the social hierarchy. If it satirized "evil living," it did so to show that deflections from grace inevitably brought damnation.

Second, with few exceptions—such as Ward's "Simple Cobbler of Aggawam"—colonial humor was the property of a dignified, literate, intellectually superior writer. More often than not, he was a minister; invariably he was a wit. He paraded his ingenuity, his mental agility, and his complex logic in ways that were distinctly self-conscious. Like his Old World counterparts, he called attention to himself, in short, with pedantry and self-satisfaction. While we don't profess to know what Edward Taylor was thinking when he wrote his poem "The Preface," we are willing to believe that he must have felt especially smug when he penned his famous metaphor for God's creation of the earth and sun:

> Who in this Bowling Alley bowld the Sun?
> Who made it always when it rises set:
> To go at once both down, and up to get?

The image is so unexpected, so startlingly clever (God with three fingers stuck in the sun while—to the modern mind, at least—clad in a silk bowling shirt), that when the paradox of the rising-setting, down-up conceit is added, the lines call attention not only to their agility but also to the mind that composed them.

As a result of the speaker's self-consciousness, several things happen. Since the dignified author retains complete control, the frame technique is rarely used; wit or intellectualized verbal humor is the rule rather than raucous comedy of action or vernacular idioms. And more often, sophisticated forms (the short essay, the letter, or the poem) rather than the anecdote or tall tale are the modes cultivated.

Even in the late eighteenth and early nineteenth centuries, when New England was no longer a Puritan stronghold, respectable colonial humor exerted influence. The Revolutionary War triggered political satire—to redress wrongdoing of a social rather than a religious nature. A school of humorists who worked under the loose label "The Hartford Wits" (John Trumbull, Joel Barlow, Timothy Dwight, and a few others) wrote tediously long epic poems and satire "directed," as Lewis Leary has said, "against the absurdity of anyone disagreeing with solid, New England views." And the flood of New England almanacs (of which Robert B. Thomas's *Old Farmer's Almanac* was the most durable) used comic material as filler for columns on planting, harvesting, and cooking.

Especially in the almanacs, one can see the heritage of the Puritans or the moralizing Hartford Wits. A famous story in a New England almanac was a character sketch of "Neighbor Freeport," in 1813. A literate narrator describes the decline and fall of Freeport, who spent too much time drinking, telling jokes, and enjoying "a crowd of jovial fellows." Freeport's farm is sold for taxes, his wife returns to her father, and his children get shipped to an orphanage. Freeport himself "became an outcast, a vagabond, and died drunk in the highway!" As an exemplum against the dangers of pleasure (the oversimplifying H. L. Mencken defined a Puritan as a person who was terrified that someone, somewhere, was having fun), there is little humor in Freeport's demise. But in the midst of his sermon, the narrator works in some complicated humorous imagery. A lengthy musical analogy describes the situation at Freeport's house: "While Freeport was so musical at the tavern his affairs got out of tune at home. His wife took a high pitch, and often gave him an unwelcome solo." After summarizing Mrs. Freeport's complaints, the author solemnly meanders through a sentence that takes a sly dig before it concludes with a homely simile:

"To hear all this and ten times more was not very welcome to the ears of Freeport, whose heart was naturally tender and humane, so to get rid of it, he used to return to the tavern like a sow to her wallowing."

A play on words tells of a worsening condition: "His shop bills run up fast, while his character was running down." The narrator commits a not-too-subtle pun when he explains that a creditor, "Plunkett, the cobbler, . . . had lent him nine pence several times and now had cobbled it up to a court demand." Other creditors are given names like those in Restoration comedies: Scrapewell, Screwpenny, and Stephen Staball, the butcher. All this produces comedy reminiscent of the colonial humorist: Using mildly comic devices to flavor his sermon, a witty narrator takes swipes at deviations from propriety.

Far along into the nineteenth century, Ralph Waldo Emerson wrote an essay, "The Comic," which exemplified Yankee biases. "The perpetual game of humor is to look with considerate good-nature at every object in existence, *aloof*, as a man might look at a mouse, comparing it with the external Whole." *Aloof*, though ambiguous, probably means that the humorist looks at an object alone, estranged from nature. It might imply superiority—even superciliousness—of a humorist-onlooker; certainly it implies the high moral insight of the humorist. Further along, Emerson states anew an old belief—that the function of humor is to reveal (and presumably to remedy) defects in men and society: "The presence of the ideal of right and of truth in all action makes the yawning delinquencies of practice remorseful to the conscience, tragic to the interest, but droll to the intellect."

A term borrowed from the Hindus to identify the intellectual, dignified New England man of letters in the nineteenth century was *Brahmin*. It was a compliment, not a slur; and it was perfectly acceptable for a Brahmin to indulge in comic writing, as long as he did not lose his dignity in the process, did not champion rowdiness or impropriety, and found the key for "Sutthin' combinin' morril truth with phrases sech ez strikes," as Birdofredum Sawin put it when talking about a vernacular rhetorician named Enoch Timbertoes.

At the same time that Brahmin humorists like Oliver Wendell Holmes and James Russell Lowell were writing (part of the time) patrician humor for a highbrowed New England audience, Lowell (in the "Biglow Papers") and another group of writers were exploiting what might be called the popular-culture branch of reputable humor, a group known as the Down East humorists and their counterparts in other areas of the country. Predominantly newspaper or periodical humorists rather than writers of books, this school (including George W. Arnold of New York, Asa Greene and Seba Smith of New England, and Charles Augustus Davis of New York) followed many of the precepts of Brahmin comic theory. But perhaps because they were writing for a popular audience, they chose not to claim some of their Puritan inheritance. For instance, they experimented with less embarrassment with slang and ungrammatical vernacular language. Though they still used established literary forms such as epistles, poems, and essays, instead of retaining a learned speaker they let homespun characters talk for them. Finally, they managed through a series of comic characters, Joe Strick-

land, Timbertoes, Jack (or J.) Downing, and Sam Slick, for instance, to define for literary purposes the reputable vernacular
character in American humor, one who has persisted down to
the present in Pa Kettle, the "Bert and I" long-playing record,
and even in contemporary television advertising for the baked
products of Pepperidge Farm.

James Russell Lowell's phrase, "the tongue of the people in the
mouth of the scholar," aptly lists the two ingredients of pro-
Establishment humor: native qualities, especially colloquial
speech, filtered through and restrained by the well-mannered
and conventional narrator. Fairly early in the nineteenth century, the school that followed such a creed found a magazine to
serve as its house organ. Lewis Gaylord Clark's *Knickerbocker*
provided an outlet and even the name for one group of genteel
authors (several of them emigrant New Englanders) who struggled with the paradoxes of their Whig politics and their literary
nationalism.

The pages of the *Knickerbocker*—billed as an "Original American Magazine"—bristled with witty pieces by Oliver Wendell
Holmes of Boston, Washington Irving of Sunnyside, and Charles
Frederick Briggs of New York—plus more somber works by
Hawthorne, Longfellow, and Whittier of Massachusetts. A typical contributor was likely to be a patrician, a son of an impressive
family, and if not Harvard educated at least a believer in a natural aristocracy of the intellect. He viewed both Jacksonian
Democrats and his Transcendental half-brothers with more than
slight suspicion, and kept a close eye on British models of good
writing (Swift, Scott, Bulwer, and most of all, Charles Lamb) so
that he could imitate them. But he kept saying that American
literature needed to assert its independence and make use of its
own resources. He loved wit, good food, wine, leisure, and the
quality of "fastidiousness." And he believed that literature was
the by-product of his affluent lifestyle—the mark of a cultivated
man that he could make pay only if he was lucky. Now and then
he might in fact become a scholar—as Lowell did when he became a professor at Harvard or Henry Cary of Pennsylvania did
when he was made the president of Columbia College in 1849—
but more often he had to be satisfied to be a professional dilet-
tante. (One of the few comic representations of the type—at a

later period—is Bromfield Cory in W. D. Howells's *The Rise of Silas Lapham*.)

Whether the reputables were Boston bluebloods, New Yorkers, or residents of other areas in the East, their main impulse was to write literature, not humor. Paradoxically, it is a curious truth that though Holmes, to pick a representative, wrote thousands of pages of histories, biographies, essays, and fictional works, he is remembered today by most Americans for a slim and generally atypical selection of comic materials. "The Deacon's Masterpiece" and "The Ballad of the Oysterman" are perhaps the only writings from his pen familiar at the present time. Beyond modern imagining is the embarrassment of these dignified gentlemen at the bizarre thought that they might be remembered chiefly because they were on occasion thought to be funny. Holmes wrote a facetious poem called "The Height of the Ridiculous," which told how he composed some verses, so comic that the first man who read them dissolved into such hysterical laughter that "since, I never dared to write / As funny as I can." Joke though it was, that punch line probably reflected a suspicion of too much levity for its own sake. On another occasion, in a letter to Lowell, Holmes described humorous verse:

I hold it to be a gift of a certain value to give that slight passing spasm of pleasure which a few ringing couplets often cause, read at the right moment. Though they are for the most part to poetry as the beating of a drum or the tinkling of a triangle is to the harmony of a band, yet it is not everybody who can get their limited significance out of these humble instruments.

The admiration is at best mitigated by Holmes's notions about the triviality of comic poetry.

But Holmes, the roly-poly little occasional poet, physician, and author of what he called "psychological" novels, produced a verse at the drop of a hat, a college class reunion, the birthday of a friend, or for practically any other occasion. His most famous poem, "The Deacon's Masterpiece or, The Wonderful 'One-Hoss Shay,' " combined (in 1858) those elements we have been discussing in an ideal mixture. To begin with, there is a rustic and colloquial Deacon, who speaks in tangy New England dialect when he decides

He would build one shay to beat the taown
'n' the keounty 'n' all the kentry aroun';
It should be so built that it couldn't break daown:
"Fur," said the Deacon, " 't's mighty plain
Thut the weakes' place mus' stan' the strain;
'n' the way t' fix it, uz I maintain,
                    Is only jest
T' make that place uz strong uz the rest."

The Deacon's simple, twangy speech reflects his simple logic in constructing a shay in which every single piece will be equally indestructible. The shay lasts exactly a century, but then it collapses

                    in a heap or mound,
As if it had been to the mill and ground!
You see, of course, if you're not a dunce,
How it went to pieces all at once,—
All at once, and nothing first,—
Just as bubbles do when they burst.

Even if that were all there were to Holmes's poem, it would be a fascinating bit of nonsense, flavored by the Deacon's speech and his engineering "masterpiece."

But Holmes had more in mind than a splash of local color. Like any good moralist, he wanted to embody a useful truth in his humor. Allusions to the Lisbon earthquake of 1755 and to the Deacon's logic about no single part wearing out first have persuaded erudite readers that Holmes was writing a comic exemplum, ridiculing the airtight logic that Jonathan Edwards worked out in his essay *On the Freedom of the Will* (the effects of which Mark Twain once compared favorably with a three-day drunk). Just as the Deacon did not take into account the possibility of all the parts wearing out at the same instant, so Edwards's apparently unassailable theology wore out from the mere passage of time. Thus Holmes added a camouflaged didacticism, which might even be universalized into a message about rigid schemes and closed minds. New England would have found that a laudable mixture of levity and high purpose.

O Molly, what shall I say of London? All the towns that ever I beheld in my born-days are no more than Welsh barrows and crumlecks to this wonderful sitty! . . . One would think there's no end of the streets, but the land's end. Then there's such a power of people, going hurry skurry! Such a racket of coxes! Such a noise, and hulliballoo! So many strange sites to be seen! O gracious! my poor Welsh brain has been spinning like a top ever since I came hither!—Win Jenkins, in Tobias Smollett, *The Expedition of Humphrey Clinker* (1771).

17.
The Yankee
and the Major

ALTHOUGH THE ACADEMIC group of reputable humorists dabbled occasionally with the homespun, cracker-barrel New England type, it took popular humorists to refine the stereotype of the Yankee from its broadest outlines into a full-color comic portrait. Building upon the endemic appeal of the Yankee in anecdotes, plays, and sketches, discussed above, canny authors and journalists appropriated him for literary use.

In 1825, George W. Arnold created Joe Strickland and used him for comic purposes in a series of letters which appeared in the New York *National Advocate* and *Enquirer* (though they were supposedly written by a Vermonter) sporadically throughout the rest of that decade. As Allen Walker Read has shown, although the letters were begun as a gimmick for advertising Arnold's lottery parlor, several unpredictable things happened. Joe's letters became popular in a flash, and the sincerest form of flattery overtook them. Rivals got into other newspapers to plug other lottery parlors. Arnold added to the appeal of his own pieces by having Joe talk about current happenings and popular topics. Joe's letters, as a comic device that did not require an uppity narrator, managed to hang on in their unwavering illiteracy for five years. And the formula of Joe's writing about the strange doings in the big city to a fictional clan "back home" in Vermont allowed for time-tested humor of the country mouse–city mouse variety.

Joe views the marvels of New York as many visitors since him have—with awe. "Such a place as this is you never see," he told his Uncle Ben; "the housen are all jamed in so tite to one another that you cant git your finger in between um, and the fokes are as thick as todes arter a rain." A perpetual motion machine, the drama, a mechanical chessplayer, and a boat that was allowed to drift over Niagara Falls all pass in review in Joe's commentary.

More important, Joe discovers early that his own native shrewdness beats book learning: "A man put in the papers here that he koud larn enny boddy ritin & rithmytik, in foretean lessons, so I went, and I hadnt bin butt fore times, befour I koud spel ass wel ass he, and koud tel that thre tymes leven was atyfore." Invited to a club for "fokes here in yawk that kawl themselves Good Sosiety . . . tha are awl darn big buggs, arn putty much awl hum-buggs," Joe discovers that he can beat the members at cards and taunts their highfalutin ways.

After Joe Strickland, the deluge. His letters managed, no doubt because of their homespun dialect, their championing of mother wit over book learning, and the hint of satire they contained, to create an immediate flood. Humorous periodicals sprang up with *Yankee* in their titles: *Yankee Miscellany* in Boston, *Yankee Blade* in Portland, and *Yankee Notions* and *Yankee Doodle* in New York, for instance.* By 1843, a reviewer in the *Knickerbocker* would complain about "all the 'down-east' letters which have been inflicted on the public *ad nauseam*." Among the cast of Yankees responsible for the nausea were Seba Smith's ubiquitous Major Jack Downing, whose entire family took to composing semi-literate humorous letters, first to Smith's Portland *Courier* and later to other papers; Davy Crockett in some of his guises (i.e., the "David Crockett" of chapter 11); Sam Slick, Thomas Chandler Haliburton's Nova Scotia peddler, who sold clocks of dubious value but gave away pawky insights into human nature through almost a dozen books that went into countless editions in the 1830's, 1840's, and 1850's; Hosea Biglow,

---

* Fillers at the bottom of almanac columns, "letters" on editorial pages, and even front-page "reports" recounted the doings of Yankee clodhoppers.

Lowell's firebrand Yankee abolitionist; and, with that exceptional quality that proves the rule, John Winslow's Billy Warrick and Mrs. Bass of the Pine Woods; C. F. M. Noland's Pete Whetstone of North Carolina; John S. Robb's Sugar of Missouri; and—most notably—William Tappan Thompson's humorous character, Major Joseph Jones (usually bunched in with the humorists of the Old Southwest). Literally hundreds of other "Yankee types" cropped up fitfully in almanacs, jest books, and burlesque writings.

Seba Smith began the comic letters of Major Downing, which over the years were collected in several volumes, reprinted in dozens of editions, and imitated by Charles Augustus Davis's very popular *Letters of J. Downing, Major . . .* , which had appeared in another dozen editions by 1836. Smith used a formula much like the one that Arnold began. On January 18, 1830, Jack, a rustic yokel from Downingville, wrote a letter back home describing his first trip to Portland. Smith, as he said later, hit upon "the plan to bring a green, unsophisticated lad from the country into town with a load of axe-handles, hoop poles, and other notions, for sale, and while waiting the movements of a dull market, let him blunder into the halls of the legislature, and after witnessing for some days their strange doings, sit down and write an account of them to his friends at home in his own plain language." Like Joe Strickland, Jack is overwhelmed by the big city: "If I could tell ye one half I've seen, I guess you'd stare worse than if you'd seen a catamount." After Jack exhausted the possibilities for Maine politics and Portland's newfangledness in twenty-eight letters, in April, 1831, he traveled to Washington to help Andy Jackson run the national government. As a fictional member of Andy's Kitchen Cabinet, Downing sent back to the eager folks in Downingville (and to the growing audience for his letters) letters that made fun of the political scene, burlesqued the antics of identifiable politicians, and used practical mother wit to solve most of the problems of the President. Although Daniel Boorstein has acutely called Jack "omni-partisan," some of his political positions seemed so effectively pro-Jackson that Davis used his *J.* Downing as an anti-Jackson propaganda weapon.

Smith continued to use Jack as a satiric blunderbuss to pepper nullification, manifest destiny, and the administration of James K. Polk. He added pictures of backgrounds and characterizations by having Downingvillers like Cousin Nabby and Uncle Joshua alternating with Jack to pen screeds about the events at home. Such descriptions would be called "local color" after the Civil War. For the present, though, they allowed for folksy depictions of the oddities of rural life and championed the domesticity, the patriotism, and the moral standards of the Downingvillers. Those standards, by the way, might be slippery and open to criticism—as when Jack and his Uncle Joshua boast of outfoxing someone else; but all the same, they were time-tested and almost ritualistic ones.

When he moved out of New England, though, the Yankee became a terror. Constance Rourke begins her book *American Humor* with a description of a Yankee peddler entering a backwoods settlement:

Doors banged and windows were shut. The peddler moved relentlessly nearer, reached a doorway, and laid his pack on the half hatch. The inhabitants had barred their doors and double-locked their money-tills in vain. With scarcely a halt the peddler made his way into their houses, and silver leapt into his pockets. When his pack was unrolled, calicoes, glittering knives, razors, scissors, clocks, cotton caps, shoes, and notions made a holiday at a fair. . . . In the end he invaded every house. Every one bought. The Negroes came up from their cabins to watch his driving pantomime and hear his slow, high talk. Staying the night at a tavern, he traded the landlord out of bed and breakfast and left with most of the money in the settlement.

Under the circumstances, it is little wonder that Sut Lovingood considered Yankees children of the devil. He once defined New England as "the frosty rocks, where nutmaigs am made outn maple, an' whar wimmen paints clock-faces an' pints shoe'paigs, an' the men invents rat-traps, mantraps, an' new fangled doctrins fur the aid ove the devil."

Richard Dorson has limited the outlines of this side of the Yankee character: "the Yankee appeared as a scheming knave and fertile prankster who matched his wits against a suspicious world, both for business and pleasure. Ingrained in the Yankee fable lay the conception of a wily, cozening trickster, poised under a mask of ingenuousness and seeming good will for a shrewd

deal or an act of mischief." What is fascinating about this facet
of the Yankee, though, is that the character, both in fable and in
the person of Sam Slick, does not become a criminal. His abilities
at bargaining merely dramatize the fact that he is thrifty, frugal, and laconic. He constantly forgets, for example, to mention
that the horse he has just traded is blind. If he is never totally
honest about his "swaps," he is not often overtly dishonest,
either. He enters his bargains preceded by a reputation that
spells out "Let the buyer beware" as plainly as if it were tattooed
on his forehead, so that there is an almost ritualistic challenge
to get the better of the other bargainer—without malice and
without the injustice and amorality that so often accompany the
true con man.

The final figure we will look at in our gallery of reputable
comic characters is not a Yankee at all. Major Joseph Jones of
Pineville, Georgia, created by William Tappan Thompson in
the early 1840's, was as prolific a letter writer as the two Major
Downings Jack and J. The fact that he was a Georgian, finan-
cially well off, and a slaveholder, made it almost predictable
that the Major would be a reputable comic character. Just as
some sections of New England had been wild enough in colonial
times to find subversive humor congenial, so Pineville was settled and respectable enough in the 1840's to delight in that
brand of humor which reaffirmed the social code. Moderate affluence and enough education to sprinkle his letters with quotations from classics and with foreign phrases influenced the re-
spectability of the Major's opinions. So did a heritage that was
Yankee-like: in 1897, Professor W. P. Trent called the Georgian
"the Southern Yankee [who] has much of the native shrewdness
and push that mark the genuine Down-Easter, and he has a considerable share of that worthy's moral earnestness." *Major
Jones's Courtship*, as the title suggests, made lighthearted fun of
the highly civilized rituals of flirting, proposing, and marrying.
And, dramatically unlike the frontier, at least as funmakers
showed it, Pineville is a world where nice young ladies blush
at the word "stocking." There are practical jokes and good-
natured high-jinks in the major's Pineville—but not an eye-
gouging in his county.

That domestic flavor of Pineville disappeared from Thomp-

Jack Downing. This picture by A. Hoppin from *My Thirty Years Out of the Senate* (1859) shows the first great comic Yankee at the beginning of his career. It also shows the character who for many years represented the United States in cartoons. Uncle Sam's costume derives from Jack's.

Major Joseph Jones, as pictured in 1847 by F. O. C. Darley. This reputable man's costume looks like the one worn by the reputable Jack Downing.

son's later collection, *Major Jones's Sketches of Travel* (1847). Perceiving, as Arnold and Smith had done before him, the value of taking an insular character on travels during which he would tell about his comic responses to new sights and metropolitan scenes, Thompson sent the Major up North to Philadelphia, Washington, D.C., and New York. From there, Jones imitated the traditional model by making an ass of himself on occasion but more often by seeing through the shams and frauds of the big city. His transfer to a Northern scene also allowed the Major to comment satirically on national politics—whacking at abolitionists and free blacks, and cheering the virtues of the slavocracy back home.

But if the Major did not share the political attitudes of his Yankee brethren, his creator nevertheless had him create humor in similar ways. Like them, the Georgian believed in the underlying morality of the universe that his letters reflected; like them, he mixed the quaintness of regional peculiarities with attempts at reform; and like them, he showed contradictory traits when he mixed illiterate spelling with the erudite quotations which sprinkled his letters.

It is a long jump from Edward Taylor and other colonial humorists to these semi-literate Yankees. Morality had become secularized, virtue more fluid, pedantry more thoroughly mixed with rustic language. But at least in broad outlines, the affinities were there. Humor still preached much of the time, and when it did not, it pictured a stable, domestic tranquility (as in B. P. Shillaber's Mrs. Partington or Frances M. Whitcher's Widow Bedott) in which tradition, decorum, justice, and sanity played significant parts. It was especially felicitous, then, that the illustration of Jack Downing became (in spite of his Yankee tricks and political audacity) the model for "Uncle Sam."

Subversives

> *Some men are liars from interest*
> *. . . some are liars from vanity . . . some are liars from a sort of*
> *necessity . . . some are enticed away by the beguilements of pleasure,*
> *or seduced by evil example and education. Bolus was none of these; he*
> *belonged to a higher department of the fine arts, and to a higher class*
> *of professors of this sort of Belles-Lettres. Bolus was a natural liar, just*
> *as some horses are natural pacers, and some dogs natural setters. . . .*
> *He lied with relish: he lied with a coming appetite, . . . he lied from*
> *the delight of invention and the charm of fictitious narrative.*
>
> —Joseph G. Baldwin, "Ovid Bolus, Esquire" (1853).

18.
The Profile
of a Prude

A YOUNG MAN WHO CONFESSED
himself a "nat'ral born durn'd fool" is weaving a yarn to a group
assembled around a campfire—among them, an encyclopedia
salesman. When the narrator mentions the wedding of the characters in the story, the pedantic salesman intrudes into the narrative:

"Allow me to interrupt you," said our guest; "you do not quote the
marriage ceremony correctly."
"Yu go to *hell,* mistofer; you bothers me."

And thus Sut Lovingood pronounces the essential and eternal
verdict of every self-reliant hell-raiser on the stuffed shirts who
pester him. Lawyers, judges, preachers, Yankees, schoolteachers,
and anyone whose function is to restrict unbridled zest for life
are included in the indictment Sut delivers. And the punishment
inflicted on these apostles of the status quo ranges from minor
social embarrassment to something approaching a mini-apoc-
alypse.
The authors of subversive humor allowed the rascal to carry on
his unseemly and asocial behavior in a wide range of settings—

187

both in the city and the backwoods; and they sometimes recounted his carrying on through the voice of a dignified narrator who disapproved of the events he related. The paradox—one that has bothered Americans for many years—was that the character with frontier attributes of self-reliance, disrespect for authority, and gumption might in fact be an outstanding all-American. On the other hand, he might be the lawless radical who acknowledges no authority but strength and cunning. (A version of each of these possibilities, Jim Doggett in "The Big Bear of Arkansas" and Sut Lovingood, is discussed in Chapters 20 and 21.)

Whichever alternative was represented, there was an amazingly consistent exploitation of the confrontation between a settled culture and an unsettled one. Much of the time, caste and social levels were distilled into the personalities of a pedantic narrator and an ignorant central character. The contrasts between their language, their social graces, their notions of propriety, and their legal attitudes could all make for comic incongruities.

Usually when a hell-raiser appeared in literary humor, there was an almost predictable snob lurking somewhere to describe him. And many times the cultivated antagonist was also the narrator of the humor—correcting or apologizing for "bad" language, interpreting uncouth behavior, revising "whoppers" until they came more in line with hard fact, and even denying that a rascal's antics were socially acceptable on the frontier. Sometimes the joke itself was so embedded in character description, pedantic asides, and similar artsy-craftsy irrelevances that it could be lost on all but the most persistent reader.

But the device of including a stuffed shirt in subversive humor could serve another function. By ridiculing pompous, fastidious, or pedantic characters, an author (as opposed to a narrator) could make fun of the status quo. From a vast array of possible examples, here are four which suggest the variety of ways in which acceptable behavior could be undermined through the presentation of a model who becomes a laughingstock: two straight men from Longstreet's *Georgia Scenes*; a myopic narrator who attempts to convert the schemes of a con man named Simon Suggs into a heroic epic; and an effete New England egghead, the Rev. Homer Wilbur, who is unknowingly absurd.

Two sanctimonious halves of a single personality, named Hall and Baldwin, narrate the stories in *Georgia Scenes*. Hall's duty is to relate stories about men, while Baldwin's stories are about women. Hall gets the choicer tales to tell, but his own attitude toward the gander pullings, horse swaps, and miscellaneous fights he catalogues is one of fastidious disdain. In "The Gander Pulling," for instance, he has to describe that traditional event on the frontier when a gander, heavily greased from breast to neck, is hung from a pole while a group of riders attempts to pull his head off for a purse of quarters. Hall, superior and supercilious to the last, provides readers with a history of Augusta, Georgia—down to the last metes and bounds of the older villages on the site—and as he watches the gander being greased, descends into a meditation of Wordsworthian dimensions:

For myself, when I saw Ned dip his hands into the grease, and commence stroking down the feathers from breast to head, my thoughts took a melancholy turn. They dwelt in sadness upon the many conjugal felicities which had probably been shared between the *greasess* and the *greasee*. I could see him as he stood by her side, through many a chilly day and cheerless night, when she was warming into life the offspring of their mutual loves, and repelled, with chivalrous spirit every invasion of the consecrated spot which she had selected for her incubation. . . . And now, alas! an extract from the smoking sacrifice of his bosom friend was desecrated to the unholy purpose of making his neck "a fit object" for Cruelty to reach "her quick, unerring fingers at."

There is more of this vein of exalted recollection, but the point is that Hall's distance from the characters, events, and settings he describes can be measured only in light-years.

After describing "The Fight" in one of the more famous stories in *Georgia Scenes*, Hall moralizes that "Thanks to the Christian religion, to schools, colleges, and benevolent associations, such scenes of barbarism and cruelty as that which I have been just describing are now of rare occurrence. . . . Whenever they prevail, they are a disgrace to that community. The peace-officers who countenance them deserve a place in the Penitentiary." Such a high moral tone contrasts impressively with the slaughter and mayhem that in fact occur in the story.

Baldwin is, if anything, even more moralistic as he relates the stories of masculine disenchantment with feminine behavior. A story about "The 'Charming Creature' as a Wife"—counting up the domestic sillinesses of a bride who turns her husband to drink and death because of her lack of huswifery—concludes with the admonition that the tale should "be a warning to mothers against bringing up their daughters to be 'Charming Creatures.' "

Hall and Baldwin are both addicted to more than didacticism and bombast, however. Both have an unwholesome fondness for quoting from poetry, for placing robust and colloquial language in italics or quotation marks, and (worst of all) for pedantic footnotes that sprinkle their own erudition along the bottom of their pages. Each feels a strong urge to authenticate stories with specific dates and exact locations:

If my memory fail me not, the 10th of June, 1809 found me, at about 11 o'clock in the forenoon, ascending a long and gentle slope in what was called "The Dark Corner of Lincoln."

In the year 1807 I resided in the city of Augusta and, upon visiting the market-house one morning . . .

Shooting-matches are probably nearly coeval with the colonization of Georgia. They are still common throughout the Southern States, though they are not as common as they were twenty-five or thirty years ago. Chance led me to one about a year ago. I was travelling in one of the northeastern counties, when . . .

Such comments suggest that in many of these stories the narrator wants to confirm the historical accuracy of the tales. And the Preface to *Georgia Scenes* makes clear the motivation behind this desire. It says that such horrible shenanigans were true and representative of the community only "at an earlier time," implying that moral order was now the rule. The Preface insists that the stories, which the narrator never intended to print except for the clamor of his friends to have them available, "consist of nothing more than fanciful *combinations* of *real* incidents and characters"; but even that was not a satisfactory apology. The "authors" were embarrassed at the "introduction of some things into them which would have been excluded were they merely the creations of fancy," and felt it necessary to offer excuses for "the coarse, inelegant, and sometimes ungrammatical language" in them.

But their impulse for a moral in their stories seems dramatically different from that of the reputable humorists. Hall and Baldwin were both prigs whose language, attitudes, education, and refinement isolated them from the actions they described. Louis J. Budd has pointed out that Longstreet "satirized the elite" and enjoyed the "sandpapering of overpolished spots in upperclass Augusta," in addition to feeling contemptuous of "whites who fell short of gentility."

If Longstreet was equivocal about his gentry, making them sometimes ridiculous with their inflated language and highfalutin airs, Johnson J. Hooper created an anonymous narrator for *Simon Suggs's Adventures* whose rhetoric was as purple as Hall's and Baldwin's and whose ridiculousness was even more dramatic. Hooper intended to burlesque campaign biographies, so he chose for his subject a rascal (one whose likeness to Old Hickory was unmistakable) and for his narrator a man who could work up to fever pitch over that rascal's skulduggery. "Would that thy pen, O! Kendall, were ours!" "Had not Romulus his Rome? Did not the pugnacious son of Philip call his Egyptian military settlement Alexandria? . . . Who then shall carp, when we say that Captain Simon Suggs bestowed *his* name upon the spot strengthened by his wisdom, and protected by his valour!"

Such rhapsodic carrying on inflates Simon's activities to heroic and monumental proportions; as it turns out, Simon is running only for sheriff of Tallapoosa County, Alabama. The narrator is able to ignore Simon's illegal and immoral intentions and to convert Simon's schemes and plots into valorous engagements. In short, although Hooper may have intended to ridicule Jackson, he also makes fun of the mock-heroic response to Simon that the narrator expresses. Blind to the true con-man attributes of Simon's biography, bombastic in his elegant praise, and ridiculous in his admiration of Suggs, the narrator is himself a fool— the character in the book whom Simon cons most successfully of all.

Fourth in the parade of educated idiots is one who cannot possibly be taken seriously, though he is dull enough to inflict trances on many readers. When James Russell Lowell revised his *Biglow Papers* for book publication, he expanded the character of a narrator, the Rev. Homer Wilbur, a pure pedant who maunders at such tedious length that only the intrusions of Hosea Biglow and Birdofredum Sawin—illiterate, rural New Englanders—relieve what could easily be the fatal effect of Wilbur's comic erudition. Quoter of Latin and Greek, apologist for the slangy exuberance of Hosea and Birdofredum, long-winded egomaniac, Homer Wilbur is without doubt the most foolish wise man in all American literature. And, although he is responsible for forwarding the poetry of Hosea and Birdofredum to the newspapers and approves of some of their political and social ideas, the Reverend is too much an apostle of sweetness and light to accept all of the ideas which Lowell couched in their rural verse. Wilbur reports that Hosea "is also (*horresco referens*) infected in no small measure with the peculiar notions of a print called the Liberator, whose heresies I take every proper opportunity of combating, and of which, I thank God, I have never read a single line." Wilbur feels compelled to apologize for the dialect of the poems and barely manages to restrain his own impulse to write a "brief dissertation touching the manner and kind of my young friend's poetry."

It seems likely to us that Lowell built up Wilbur in the book version of the *Biglow Papers* to elevate its tone. He confessed that he was bothered about "the risk of seeming to vulgarize a deep and sacred conviction" by expressing it solely through the mouth of Hosea. And Wilbur's pedantry, bookwormery, and classicism are faults that afflicted Lowell himself. Still, Wilbur is a clown, so if he is a disguised version of the author himself, he is very much like the self-portrait Lowell included in *A Fable for Critics:* inept, confused, and comically indecisive.

The range, then, that a humorist could exploit with an educated character was vast. Like Hall and Baldwin, he can disparage the rogues he describes and yearn for an orderly and balanced universe that doesn't exist; like the narrator of *Simon Suggs's Adventures*, he can confuse the antics of a rascal for noble and heroic feats; or like Homer Wilbur, he can be so obtuse that he becomes a contrasting comic figure in his own right. But whatever the technical functions he serves, he is always the apostle of decorum, of logic, of self-control; and he is always beset by an environment, by actions, and by a cast of subversive characters that disrupt and defeat him.

> *Men were made a-purpos jis' to
> eat, drink, an' fur stayin awake in the early part of the nites: an'
> women were made to cook the vittles, mix the spirits, an' help the men
> do the stayin awake. That's all, an' nothin more. . . .*
> —*Sut Lovingood's Yarns* (1867).

19.
A Gallery
of Rogues

POKING SLY FUN AT THE GEN-
try, and calling into doubt the principles of virtue, integrity, and
morality that they championed, is a pretty sly way, though, to
spread subversion. And this mode of humor fronted the issue directly with a set of characters who ranged from unprepossessing
to almost mythic in stature, but who were united in their suspicion of authority, gentility, and book learning.

Ransy Sniffle, in Longstreet's "The Fight," was

a sprout of Richmond, who, in his earlier days, had fed copiously upon
red clay and blackberries. This diet had given to Ransy a complexion
that a corpse would have disdained to own, and an abdominal rotundity
that was quite unprepossessing. Long spells of the fever and ague, too,
in Ransy's youth, had conspired with clay and blackberries to throw
him quite out of the order of nature. His shoulders were fleshless and
elevated; his head large and flat; his neck slim and translucent; and
his arms, hands, fingers, and feet were lengthened out of all proportion
to the rest of his frame. His joints were large and his limbs small; and
as for flesh, he could not, with propriety, be said to have any. Those
parts which nature usually supplies with the most of this article—the
calves of the legs, for example—presented in him the appearance of so
many well-drawn blisters. His height was just five feet nothing; and
his average weight in blackberry season, ninety-five.

Sut Lovingood, too, presented an appearance that not even a
mother could approve. He was

a queer looking, long legged, short bodied, small headed, white haired,
hog eyed, funny sort of a genius, fresh from some bench-legged Jew's
clothing store.

A portrait of Simon Suggs by F. O. C. Darley.

Simon Suggs was perhaps the most repulsive of all the cast of rogues:

His head is somewhat large, and thinly covered with coarse, silver-white hair, a single lock of which lies close and smooth down the middle of a forehead which is thus divided into a couple of very acute triangles, the base of each of which is an eye-brow, lightly defined, and seeming to owe its scantiness to the depilatory assistance of a pair of tweezers. Beneath these almost shrubless cliffs, a pair of eyes with light-grey pupils and variegated whites, dance and twinkle in an aqueous humor which is constantly distilling from the corners. Lids without lashes complete the optical apparatus of Captain Suggs; and the edges of these, always of a sanguineous hue, glow with a reduplicated brilliancy whenever the Captain has remained a week or so in town, or elsewhere in the immediate vicinity of those citizens whom the county court has vested with the important privilege of vending "spirituous liquors in less quantities than one quart." The nose we find in the neighborhood of these eyes, is long and low, with an extremity of singular acuteness, overhanging the subjacent mouth. Across the middle, which is slightly raised, the skin is drawn with exceeding tightness, as if to contrast with the loose and wrinkled abundance supplied to the throat and chin. But the mouth of Captain Suggs is his great feature, and measures about four inches horizontally. An ever-present sneer— not all malice, however—draws down the corners, from which radiate many small wrinkles that always testify to the Captain's love of the "filthy weed." A sharp chin monopolizes our friend's bristly, iron-gray beard. All these facial beauties are supported by a long and skinny, but muscular neck, which is inserted after the ordinary fashion in the upper part of a frame, lithe, long, and sinewy, and clad in Kentucky jeans, a trifle worn.

And Birdofredum, preparing to return from the Mexican War, inventories the loss of a leg, an eye, his left arm and all the fingers on his right hand, a comprehensive mutilation that he is sure will suit him perfectly as a politician.

Others among the subversives—like Bob Durham and Bill Stallings in "The Fight" or Jim Doggett in "The Big Bear of Arkansas"—are large, strapping variations of the Kentuckian, the keelboatman or the mountain man, and rounders whose gusto and verve somehow require a frame larger than usual to contain them. Like the tall tales they enjoyed spinning, they almost burst the limits of physical probability.

Whatever their physical aspects, the subversive characters have one trait in common: their distrust of and disregard for the rules. At the least dangerous level, such indifference becomes clear in their defiance of the laws of truthfulness and honesty. A tall-tale teller is, by definition, a raconteur who trifles with veracity, who dupes or pretends to dupe his listener with a whopper deliberately soaring beyond the mundane and believable levels. Joseph Glover Baldwin, whose "Ovid Bolus, Esquire" (in his *Flush Times in Alabama and Mississippi*) is a model for the inventive liar, analyzes the credible foundation to Ovid's yarns: "The truth was too small for him. Fact was too dry and commonplace for the fervor of his genius. . . . He adopted a fact occasionally to start with, but . . . he had long torn down the partition wall between his imagination and his memory. He had long ceased to distinguish between the impressions made upon his mind by what came *from* it, and what came *to* it: all ideas were facts to him." Except to give his outrageous lies credibility, no tall-tale teller would have had Hall's and Baldwin's penchant for the historical placing and dating that we noted in *Georgia Scenes;* and Sut's admonition to "go to hell, mistofer" would be exactly the proper one to the literal-minded and unimaginative auditor who brought up inconvenient facts.

There are almost as many variations on the tall tale as there are examples of the form, and we analyze in the next chapter the one we consider the perfect version, "The Big Bear of Arkansas." But there has to be a listener or listeners to the stretcher. Sometimes, as in Mark Twain's "Bemis and the Bull" story from *Roughing It* or the Charles William Allbright tall tale in *Life on the Mississippi*, the listeners refuse to be "sold" and taunt the yarn-spinner; sometimes the teller himself is bewitched by the tale (as in "The Big Bear"); and sometimes the deception is ritualized, when a group around a campfire retells stories, attempting to top one another's flights of imagination.

Often, though, a character begins a narration punctuated by ungrammatical phrasing, slangy diction, and homespun metaphors and similes, building up a bizarre and improbable story so skillfully that the listener has not noticed that a realistic form of telling has been invaded by fantastic content. And finally the listener (often a gullible stranger, unused to having the truth wrenched beyond the breaking point) discovers that he and his naïveté are the actual butts of the joke—that he has become the rhetorical equivalent of that perennial cartoon character who steps off a cliff and keeps going for a dozen paces before realizing he is walking on air.

When the deliberately deceitful tall tale is converted into action, it becomes a hoax. The subversives were addicted to such practical jokes, frequently for the sheer joy of duping and outfoxing someone else. Like young Crockett, they could resell the same

skin at the trading post over and over, or like young Mark Twain
return an unripe but stolen watermelon to the farmer and get a
satisfactory one. They were con men who tricked unwary purchasers, selling them blind horses, magically therapeutic elixirs,
and tickets to theatrical performances like the showing of the
terrible guyascutus or the Burning Shame in *Huckleberry Finn*.
Simon Suggs could captivate a camp meeting with his bogus
conversion and depart with the collection. And Simon's motto,
"It is good to be shifty in a new country," pinpoints the credo
of the con man as hoaxer. But the antics of the subversive move
on occasion beyond the harmlessness of an improbable story told
to an ingenuous listener and beyond the hoax played on a gullible and avaricious foil into a world where pain and anguish and
moral anarchy are the human condition.

Of course, pain and anguish have always been a dependable
source of laughter, from the time of air-filled bladders and slapstick to that of the custard pie. And when rogues themselves suffer some kind of comic punishment, readers sense a comfortable
justice in the world. Birdofredum's mutilation in the Mexican
War and the catalog of bugs, vermin, and nuisances he suffers
in Mexico ("I felt a thing go thru my leg,—'t wuz nothin' more
'n a skeeter!") are the result of his own gullibility in volunteer-
ing for the war. And, of course, Birdofredum manages to convert
his various tribulations to his own advantage when he decides
that what is left of him will be fine for political appeal and voter
sympathy:

> Ef, wile you 're 'lectioneerin' round, some curus chaps
>   should beg
> To know my view o' state affairs, jest answer WOODEN
>   LEG!
> Ef they aint settisfied with thet, an' kin' o' pry an'
>   doubt
> An' ax fer sutthin' deffynit, jest say ONE EYE PUT OUT!
> Thet kin' o' talk I guess you 'll find 'll answer to a
>   charm,
> An wen you 're druv tu nigh the wall, hol' up my
>   missin' arm.

When Birdofredum tries to capture a free black family and sell
it into slavery but is himself caught by the blacks, who "kep' me

One of Justin Howard's illustrations for *Sut Lovingood's Yarns* (1867) shows Sut watching his buck-naked daddy on the run. It was unusual at the time to picture characters so informally unattired. It wasn't unusual for a character in one of Sut's yarns to be chased by angry hornets.

pris'ner 'bout six months, an' worked me, tu, like sin," we sense perfectly proper comic retribution.

The same sense of justice operates when Sut, himself a lethal practical joker, is blown up with soda or skinned by an over-starched shirt.

Frequently, though, the rascal in subversive humor manages to injure, quite deliberately, various innocent bystanders, little old ladies, sheriffs, men of the cloth, and his own parents. When Simon Suggs decides to leave home, he cheats his father at a game of cards to win a horse, broods on "the doting love of his mother," and then tiptoes "into his mother's room, and nicely load[s] the old lady's pipe with a thimble full of gunpowder." Thomas Bangs Thorpe's recounting of the pranks of Mike Fink included incidents both sadistic and homicidal. When Pete Whetstone has Dan Looney tell about a big fight in Illinois, he has Looney confess that he kept on gouging his opponent's eyes after the man had surrendered: "I played my thumbs into his eyes, and he sung out; but before they got me off, I reckon my right thumb got mighty near to the fust jint." Henry Clay Lewis, who wrote about his medical practice in Louisiana under the name of Madison Tensas, catalogues malpractices, desecrations of cadavers, and the inflicting of greater pain than the ones his patients had called him in to cure. And Sut, that unique mixture of fool and fool-killer, strews death and desolation through Tennessee like the grim reaper on an International harvester and with the impartiality of "crabs" in a fraternity house.

Most of the time, this physical anguish—or even mayhem—is told about so comically and is fitted so artistically into the panorama of frontier life that readers laugh. But occasionally, at least, the conviction is unshakable that there is more than just a note of desperation to the values lying beneath subversive humor: might does indeed make right, it is vital to be shifty in *any* country, and the best defense is to be as offensive as possible. Survival itself depends on brutality and victimization. Logical and moral precepts just do not work in a world where the good are punished and the hell-raisers go scot free. If this hypothesis is correct, then some subversive humor has a significantly modern flavor. Some of it aims, in one of its channels, directly toward contemporary black humor and comic savagery.

We now propose to look closely at two samples of subversive humor which suggest the limits within which the formula operated. One story, "The Big Bear of Arkansas," is optimistic about a backwoodsman who lives beyond civilization and by his own rules; the other, *Sut Lovingood's Yarns*, carries rebellion against law and order to the point of anarchy.

Two Masterpieces

Heracles visited Mount Tretus, and presently descried the lion coming back to its lair, bespattered with blood from the day's slaughter. He shot a flight of arrows at it, but they rebounded harmlessly from the thick pelt, and the lion licked its chops, yawning. Next, he used his sword, which bent as though made of lead; finally, he heaved up and dealt the lion such a blow on the muzzle that it entered its double-mouthed cave, shaking its head—not for pain, however, but because of the singing in its ears.

—Robert Graves, 1958.

20.
"The Big Bear of Arkansas"

FRED SHAW, LATE PROFESSOR OF English in the University of Miami, in mid-summer 1954 got word that he was to show William Faulkner around Miami during a stopover between planes. Shaw and a graduate student met America's greatest living novelist and at once escorted him to the nearest air-conditioned bar. The student mentioned that he was writing a dissertation about a relationship not yet much explored—between Faulkner and antebellum Southwestern humor. Faulkner spoke of his great admiration for such humor and in particular

paid a fine compliment to Thomas Bangs Thorpe's "The Big Bear of Arkansas." The student said he thought he could detect similarities between that story and Faulkner's "The Bear." Faulkner looked surprised. Then: "That's a fine story. A writer is afraid of a story like that. He's afraid he'll try to rewrite it. A writer has to learn when to run from a story."

Faulkner's reaction to talk about resemblances was a typical writer's response, and no doubt he was unconscious of any. Just the same, the likenesses between his short story and Thorpe's are impressive.

Important as an influence, "The Big Bear" also merits praise as a classic. On its first appearance in 1841, William T. Porter, knowledgeable editor of one of the leading outlets for such a story, warned readers "on no account" to miss "the best sketch of backwoods life, that we have seen in a long while." Porter printed the story in both *The Spirit of the Times* and a second periodical he edited, and in 1845 featured it in a collection of his favorites—*The Big Bear of Arkansas and Other Sketches*. Meanwhile, the piece had been reprinted in sporting magazines and newspapers throughout the United States and Europe. And thereafter, down to the present, it would be published and called a masterpiece again and again.

The subtitle of Porter's anthology, itself a landmark in American humor, suggested an important appeal of Thorpe's story and others like it: "Illustrative of Characters and Incidents in the South and the Southwest." Porter's introduction praised "a new order of literary talent" for blazing "novel and original" trails by writing "in a masterly style . . . valuable and interesting reminiscences of the pioneers." The new breed, Porter said, were men "who live at home at ease" in the midst of the life which they portray. Porter borrowed his epigraph from Dogberry: "This is your charge; you shall comprehend all vagrom men." Like the vagrom men about whom they wrote authentically, Porter said, his writers had "exteriors 'like the rugged Russian bear,' " were "gifted with . . . good sense and knowledge of the world," "fond of whiskey," and loved telling stories.

To the rough exterior, the description fit Thorpe: "a poor little fellow with an awful face," a friend called him, looking "like an embodiment, in semi-human form, of a thick fog on the Mississippi, at half past three in the morning to a man who has just lost his last dollar at poker." The friend perhaps exaggerated, but even portraits—usually flattering—show that Thorpe was short and pudgy, with a big flat nose, auburn hair, and a sour phiz; he resembled a pug dog with russet sideburns.

But his attractive personality helped him comprehend vagrom men, as did his knowledge of the world. The friend went on to say that Thorpe's "grave and saturnine countenance quite belies a kind and playful spirit that seems to live in light and loveliness beneath the madness and gloom of his character." And at twenty-five, when he wrote his masterpiece, Thorpe had had varied experiences. Though born a Yankee, he had lived during most of his childhood and youth in Albany and New York City. In Manhattan he studied painting under a pupil of John Wesley Jarvis, John Quidor; and starting in his teens, Thorpe exhibited —and even sold—paintings. More important for his writing, from the time he was an adolescent, he sat in on story-telling sessions of artistic Bohemians—Gilbert Stuart, Henry Inman, the ubiquitous Jarvis, and others. During more than fifty years, every now and then he praised in print this group, particularly the three men mentioned—their mimicry, their "fluency in speech, their happy manner of description and story-telling." As late as 1872 he recalled the feat of one artist: "Ingham was only remarkable for telling one story, and that one only at the regular meetings of the National Academy. And this story, for a long period of time, was absolutely told every twelve months with mathematical precision as to circumstance, manner, and words."

For a couple of years (1834-1836), Thorpe went to Wesleyan University in Connecticut. Then bad health, invitations by fellow students from the South who liked him, and chances for portrait commissions led him to move to Louisiana. By 1841, he had married, settled down in Feliciana Parish on the Mississippi River, and launched a career as both painter and writer.

In addition to the oral stories of Jarvis and his pals, he knew Irving's writings "by heart." (Like his teacher, Quidor, he had painted illustrations for Irving's comic narratives.) He had read sketches and books by and about Davy Crockett, sermons by critics urging his countrymen to create a national literature, and guesses that the frontier might produce The American Character. He had seen at first hand life in New Orleans, aboard riverboats, and on riverside farms and plantations. Thanks to the hospitality and breezy ways of his neighbors, he was hunting, getting sozzled, and swapping stories with Feliciana planters, and between jollifications, painting portraits of his friends, their wives, and their daughters. On a recent visit to New York, he had called on a couple of editors, sold one a painting, and got orders from both for magazine pieces. He had placed writings with *Knickerbocker Magazine* and *Spirit of the Times*. "The Big Bear of Arkansas" first appeared in the March 27, 1841 issue of the *Spirit*.

In this piece, the high point of a long and prolific career, young Thorpe discovered new possibilities for a vernacular style, comic characterization, and imaginative invention. A look at it may suggest why, for all its brevity and its look of artlessness, it caused scholars to dub a whole group of great humorists "The Big Bear School."

Like units in Boccaccio's *Decameron* and Chaucer's *Canterbury Tales*, "The Big Bear of Arkansas" is a story within a story. It has two narrators, a writer who tells about the gathering of an audience aboard a riverboat, and an oral narrator who unfolds an enclosed tale about a bear hunt.

The first sentence is: "A steamboat on the Mississippi frequently, in making her regular trips, carries between places varying from one to two thousand miles apart; and as these boats advertise to land passengers and freight at 'all intermediate landings,' the heterogeneous character of the passengers on one of these up-country boats can scarcely be imagined by one who has never seen it with his own eyes." The language—even for a day when most writings were quite formal—is stilted and unimaginative: its lightest touch is a drab quotation from an advertisement. The ponderous tone, the big words, and the sentence construction show up the first narrator as a bit stuffy. So does his next sentence, also highfalutin, its sole figure of speech (here italicized) smelling of the lamp: "Starting from New Orleans in one of these boats, you will find yourself associated with men from every state in the Union, and every portion of the globe; and a man of observation need not lack for amusement or instruction in such a crowd, if he will take the trouble to read *the great book of character so favourably opened before him*." As he continues, this narrator proves to be the sort that marks off phrases barely edging towards slang—e.g., "latest paper" and "social hall"—in apologetic quotation marks.

Nevertheless, he soon shows he relishes the motley steamboat crowd and popular nicknames: "Here may be seen jostling together the wealthy Southern planter, the pedlar of tin-ware from New England—. . . a venerable bishop and a desperate gambler—. . . Wolverines, Suckers, Hoosiers, Buckeyes, and Corn-crackers, besides a 'plentiful sprinkling' of the half-horse and half-alligator species of men, who are peculiar to the 'old Missis-sippi'. . . ." And when he boards the *Invincible* for a brief trip from New Orleans, he at once notices that the crowd is as miscellaneous as usual and decides that, because of special circumstances, he will not, on this trip anyhow, peruse "the great book of character" they open.

When the second narrator, Jim Doggett, arrives, the writer tells of his offstage shouts, describes and quotes him at length, remarks his pleasant effect on the crowd, and—because he will only see "so singular a personage" briefly—persuades him to tell a long story. Jim's yarnspinning skill delights him:

His manner was so singular, that half of his story consisted in his excellent way of telling it, the great peculiarity of which was the happy manner he had of emphasizing the prominent parts of his conversation. As near as I can recollect, I have italicized them, and given the story in his own words.

Once Jim gets going, the writer quotes him without interrupting. When Jim ends, the educated narrator describes an aftermath that fascinates him. Stuffy though his language makes him appear, then, this narrator, no aloof and prissy Whig aristocrat, has a lively interest in his fellow passengers and an even livelier one in Jim.

Jim first lifts his voice at the bar, shouting stock frontier boasts. "Hurra for the Big Bar of Arkansaw! [I'm a] horse! [I'm a] screamer! [Alongside me] lightening is slow!" Having noisily identified himself, the Big Bear strolls into the cabin, sits, hoists feet onto the stove, greets the crowd, says he feels at home, and soon charms his motley audience:

Some of the company at this familiarity looked a little angry, and some astonished; but in a moment every face was wreathed in a smile. There was something about the intruder that won the heart on sight. He appeared to be a man enjoying perfect health and contentment: his eyes were as sparkling as diamonds, and good-natured to simplicity. Then his perfect confidence in himself was irresistibly droll.

Clearly no clownish caricature, this is an interesting personality attractive to men of all "creeds and characters," of all classes and parts of the country.

So close to the stodgy utterances of the writer, Jim's quoted words, phrasings and rhythms are by contrast informal, idiosyncratic, and imaginative. His homage to his dog Bowie-knife is typical:

. . . whew! why the fellow thinks the world is full of bar, he finds them so easy. It's lucky he don't talk as well as think; for with his natural modesty, if he should suddenly learn how much he is acknowledged to be ahead of all other dogs in the universe, he would be astonished to death in two minutes. Strangers, the dog knows a bar's way as well as a horse-jockey knows a woman's; he always barks at the right time, bites at the exact place, and whips without getting a scratch. I never could tell whether he was made expressly to hunt bar, or whether bar was made expressly for him to hunt; any way, I believe they were ordained to go together as naturally as Squire Jones says a man and woman is, when he moralizes in marrying a couple.

Jim's zest creates hyperbole and the flood of details that support wild claims. Affection helps Jim read Bowie-knife's mind and endow the beast with human virtues—intelligence and modesty. One of the unhackneyed similes, the trope which cites the well-informed horse-jockey, signals his worldly wisdom. His praise of the timing of Bowie-knife's bark and bite, and his use of "whips" show his precise knowledge of a great hunting dog's tactics. His philosophical discourse about the predestination of either the hunter or the hunted is distinctive. So is a respect for what is "natural" which comes out two other times as he tells his story.

In addition to being exuberant, an acute observer, and a do-it-yourself philosopher, Jim is a superb yarnspinner. He orders expository details and events in a masterful fashion and marshals hosts of particulars and witty comments on them. Although his story (in large part because of its salty style) seems artless, it makes comical use of two anticlimaxes, mounts to its climax, and then ends.

The introduction of the two narrators, of Jim's audience, and the detailing of Jim's talk with the crowd occupy more than half of Thorpe's pages before the Big Bear begins his account of his greatest hunt. These preliminaries initiate a pattern which Doggett's yarn develops and completes—essentially one of contrasts and expansion.

After saying that he feels entirely at home among the cosmopolitan steamboat crowd, Jim launches talk about a contrast that is analogous to that between his vernacular style and the formal style of the writer:

"Perhaps," said he, "gentlemen, . . . you have been to New Orleans often; I never made *the first visit before,* and I don't intend to make another in a crow's life. I am thrown away in that ar place, and useless. . . . Some of the gentlemen thar call me *green*—well, perhaps I am, said I, *but I arn't so at home;* and if I ain't off my trail much, the heads of them perlite chaps themselves wern't much the hardest; for according to my notion, they were the real *know-nothings,* green as a pumpkin vine—couldn't, in farming, I'll bet, raise a crop of turnips; and as for shooting, they'd miss a barn if the door was swinging. . . ."

Jim has had trouble talking with these dandies. If they speak of "game," they mean not "Arkansaw poker and high-low jack" but fowl and wild animals, which Jim calls "meat." Moreover, New Orleans game is tiny stuff, "chippenbirds and shite-pokes"— "trash" that Arkansans think beneath contempt. Jim says that at home he will not shoot a bird weighing less than forty pounds.

Arkansas is "the creation state, the finishing-up country. . . . Then its airs—just breathe them, and they will make you snort like a horse." Even when Jim admits that mosquitoes there are enormous, he defends them in a way underlining the contrast between Arkansas and the rest of the world. Natives or settlers are impervious to them, and the one injury they caused was to a Yankee—"a foreigner" who "swelled up and busted, . . . super-ated . . . took the ager . . . and finally took a steamboat and left the country."

To end his argument, Jim lists his state's features in the order of their size: mosquitoes, and then—"her varmints are large, her trees are large, her rivers are large." Next—as if climactically—he comes to the bears. They differ not only from bears anywhere else but of any other time: "I read in history that varmints have their fat season and their lean season. That is not the case in Arkansaw, feeding as they do upon the *spontenacious* productions of the sile, they have one continued fat season the year round" and running one "sort of mixes the ile up with the meat," and if you shoot one, "steam comes out of the bullet hole ten feet in a straight line." When a "foreigner" asks, "Whereabouts are these bears so abundant?" Doggett introduces the greatest district in this marvelous Cockayne, Schlaraffenland, Lubberland, Arkansas—"Shirt-tail Bend" on the Forks of Cypress—Jim's own clearing.

Shirt-tail Bend is called "one of the prettiest places on the old Mississippi," but soon this mild claim gives way to claims that "the government ain't got another such place to dispose of" and that three months after planting beets are mistaken for cedar stumps, potato hills for Indian mounds. *"Planting in Arkansaw is dangerous,"* Jim warns. Dangerous for bears are Doggett, "the best bar hunter in the district"; his gun, *"a perfect epidemic among bar;* if not watched closely, it will go off as quick on a warm scent as my dog Bowie-knife will," and the aforesaid super-dog.

Soon after Jim has jocosely praised his settlement, two paragraphs in the highfalutin style of the writer return to the contrasting steamboat cabin. There skeptics briefly dispute with him, but the first narrator asks for "a description of some particular bear hunt," describes the Big Bear's singular manner, then without interrupting, lets him give his account in his own salty words.

Repeating the pattern of contrast and enlargement, Jim mentions two ordinary hunts—ordinary, that is, for the Forks of Cypress—then promises to give "an idea of a hunt, in which the greatest bar was killed that ever lived, *none excepted.*"

A customary hunt for Jim is "about as much the same to me as drinking." "It is told," he says, "in two sentences—a bar is started, and he is killed." This hunt, by contrast, requires many sentences, since the varmint was the giant beast which eluded Jim, his epidemic gun, and the incomparable Bowie-knife two or three long years.

Jim first learns about this critter by measuring the height of bite marks made on sassafras trees—marks which, experience proves, show "the length of the bar to an inch." These are "about eight inches above any in the forest that I knew of. Says I, 'them marks is a hoax, or it indicates the d-----t bar that was ever grown.' In fact, . . . I couldn't believe it was real, and I went on. Again I saw the same marks, . . . and *I knew the thing lived*. That conviction came home to my soul like an earthquake."

Jim tells about hunting the bear and wasting away in flesh

because of his frustration over many months before he again happens to mention the critter's size. This time the beast is "a little larger than a horse." Still later, when Jim gets a final shot at him, the bear "loomed up like a *black mist*, he seemed so large." After Jim's shot, "the varmint wheeled, gave a yell, and *walked through the fence* like a falling tree would through a cobweb." Thus, like Cypress Forks beets and potatoes, the bear of bears grows at an astonishing rate.

Though this account has traced the bear's growth by degrees in Jim's narrative to his greatest size, it has not noticed a second climactic development that is not made explicit until the very end.

Soon after that earthquake conviction has proved to Jim that the giant animal lives, he has a startling thought: "Says I, 'here is something a-purpose for me: that bar is mine, or I give up the hunting business.' " The way everything goes wrong during the first pursuit of the bear is disquieting because it is "past my understanding." Other happenings prove to be just as inexplicable. Jim's flesh begins to waste away "faster than the ager." He becomes obsessed—sees the bear in everything he does. But when at last he gets close enough to see the beast plainly, he reacts strangely, exclaiming, "But wasn't he a beauty, though? I loved him like a brother."

A companion's shot strikes the animal's forehead: "The bar shook his head, . . . and then walked down from that tree as gently as a lady would from a carriage. 'Twas a beautiful sight. . . ." Now Jim takes careful aim "at his side just back of his foreleg" and pulls the trigger; his gun snaps. The bear leaps into a lake, has a fight in the water with the dog, sinks, and stays submerged. Jim dives, brings up the carcass, and thinks all is over. But—

"Stranger, may I be chawed to death by young alligators, if the thing I looked at warn't a she bar, and not the old critter after all. The way matters got mixed . . . was onaccountably curious, and thinking of it made me more than ever convinced that I was hunting the devil himself. I went home that night and took to my bed—the thing was killing me. . . . I grew as cross as a bar with two cubs and a sore tail."

Kidded by his neighbors, Jim decides "to catch that bar, go to Texas, or die," and he makes preparations for a final hunt. But the day before that hunt is planned, at a most inopportune moment the bear comes along. Jim manages to fire a shot. The beast wheels, walks away, and Jim hears him "groaning in a thicket nearby, like a thousand sinners." When Jim reaches him, he is dead.

At this point, ending his story, Jim states a deduction for which his yarning has prepared:

". . . strangers, I never liked the way I hunted and *missed him*. There is something curious about it, I never could understand,—and I never was satisfied at his giving in so easy at last. Perhaps, he had heard of my preparations to hunt him next day, so he just come in, like Capt. Scott's coon, to save his wind to grunt with in dying; but that ain't likely. My private opinion is, that that bar was an *unhuntable bar*, *and died when his time come.*"

So the biggest bear in Shirt-tail Bend, domicile of the biggest bears in Arkansas, a state which itself is greater than any other country—such a bear in the end is slain not by bullets but by the inscrutable fate which has brought him and the Big Bear of Arkansas together. And from the first sentence to this point a parade of details prepare for this climax.

This climax has some relevance to remarks that Faulkner made during his talk with Professor Shaw and the student about bear stories. Shaw had suggested that the bear in bear stories was "the big test—the medieval dragon." Faulkner agreed: "Yes, the bear was a symbol; he was the wilderness. On the frontier . . . things could be pretty hard. Here was a farmer trying to beat back the woods, trying to make a crop, and not having a very easy time of it; and here was the bear. If he could kill him, he had licked the wilderness."

The comment provides a useful gloss on the work about which Faulkner was talking, his own "The Bear." But since that superb story is a serious one which uses symbols to convey its profound significations, the remarks have relevance to Thorpe's story only as much as a solemn treatise on Mississippi farming would have to Faulkner's hilarious "Spotted Horses." For however noteworthy are the realism and the characterization of "The Big Bear of Arkansas," in essence it is a comic story. Its different narrators and styles, its incongruities and expansions, its fantastic imaginings as well as its initial reception and subsequent history make this clear to all readers except a few thesis-ridden scholars.

Important aids to the humorous effect are the changes in Jim's attitude and that of his listeners while he tells his tall tales, and two strategically placed anticlimaxes.

En route to the cabin, Jim pauses at the bar. Soon he is shouting a cheer for himself, boasting that he is a horse and a screamer, and alleging that compared with him lightning is slow. After he joins fellow passengers, they are at first startled or irritated. But soon "something about the intruder"—his *joie de vivre*, his *Gemütlichkeit* and his "irresistibly droll" self-assurance—win every heart and cause everyone to smile. As he joyously pours out one whopper after another, the listeners' reactions show that they know very well that he is putting them on. When he talks about shooting only forty-pound turkeys, "twenty voices in the cabin at once" proclaim disbelief. When he piles on details about the fatness of one of these birds, "a cynical-looking Hoosier" asks "Where did all that happen?" and a bit later he interrupts Jim's claim that Arkansaw is without a fault by saying, "Excepting mosquitoes." Undeterred, Jim makes even more outrageous claims, whereupon a gentlemanly Englishman, "foreigner" though he is, laughs and voices disbelief, and "a 'live sucker' from Illinois . . . has the daring to say that our Arkansaw friend's stories 'smell rather tall.' "

Jim argues with this skeptic surely in a playful spirit with no hope that he will close yawning credibility gaps. And though the listeners do not interrupt Jim's yarn about his biggest hunt, as he launches it they cannot be unaware of Jim's exaggerations or unappreciative of his witty way of phrasing them.

But as the story moves along, Jim's attitude and that of his listeners change. At the start, fresh from the bar, Jim is high spirited, jocose, humorous. His eyes sparkle as he invents and exaggerates wildly improbable details. But signs that he and his listeners are amused decrease. When he finishes, both he and his audience are solemn:

When his story was ended, our hero sat some minutes with his auditors in a grave silence; I saw there was a mystery to him connected with the bear whose death he had just related, that had evidently made a strong impression on his mind. It was also evident that there was some superstitious awe connected with the affair,—a feeling common with all "children of the wood," when they meet with any thing out of their everyday experience.

The picture is of a man who tells a beautiful lie—such a superbly imagined and performed work of art that he convinces not only his audience but also himself. Fantastic Cypress Forks, which Jim has created out of thin air (and a fact or two) becomes a reality for him. The bear, which he has imaginatively enlarged beyond all reason and even gifted with supernatural powers, has overawed Jim's auditors and—still more impressive —Jim himself. Thanks to his own soaring eloquence, paradoxically, Jim has confused the real and the imagined.

Overwhelmed though he is, Jim manages to recover before his silenced listeners: "He was the first one, however, to break the silence, and jumping up, he asked all present to 'liquor' before going to bed,—a thing which he did, with a number of companions, evidently to his heart's content."

As the style indicates, after Jim ends his story, his salty language gives way to the stuffy style of the first narrator—latinate words, apologetic quotes, long sentences. Simultaneously, Jim and his audience are plopped down again in the mundane cabin. The final sentence of "The Big Bear of Arkansas" rounds out the contrast between Jim's clearing and the world of the writer: "Long before day, I was put ashore at my place of destination, and I can only follow with the reader, in imagination, our Arkansas friend, in his adventures at the 'Forks of Cypress' on the Mississippi."

The shift in style marks an anticlimax. Another anticlimax which occurs earlier was probably even more impressive in 1841.

The period, recall, was by modern standards an incredibly prissy one when the slightest hint of blasphemy or obscenity shocked Americans beyond belief. An instance: Jim, in a passage quoted a few paragraphs back, said that his gigantic bear groaned "like a thousand sinners." Because the simile somehow sounded irreligious, the words were cut out of a number of early reprintings. Whole books have been written about taboos in force against references to sex. Following the publication of Herman Melville's *Typee*—five years after Thorpe's "Big Bear"—so many wails would be raised about its frankness that numerous passages would be excised from subsequent editions—passages which readers today often study with complete bewilderment, unable to imagine what the readers of those quaint times found suggestive in them. Even rarer than references—including vague ones—to sex were scatological passages. Melville, in the final chapter of *The Confidence–Man* (1857) would write about what a character called "a life preserver"—described as "a brown stool with curved tin compartment underneath" which smells bad—and alert readers somehow managed to discover that the passage refers to a toilet seat. In our own dear enlightened era when folk are daily uplifted by televised Curses on Constipation and Paeans to Regularity or by bits about bodily functions in respected books, plays, and movies, we need a translation for a passage that in 1841 was unique—part of Jim's story:

". . . I went into the woods near my house, taking my gun and Bowie-knife along, *just from habit*, and there sitting down also from habit, what should I see, getting over my fence, but *the bar!* Yes, the old varmint was within a hundred yards of me, and . . . he walked . . . towards me. I raised myself, took deliberate aim, and fired. Instantly the varmint wheeled . . . I started after, but was tripped up by my inexpressibles, which either from habit, or the excitement of the moment, were about my heels. . . ."

This translates: Accompanied by his dog and carrying his gun, as usual, Jim entered the woods to take his daily crap. Squatting there, he looked up, saw the bear approaching, and fired at him. The bear turned. Jim started after him, but his pants ("inexpressibles" in 1841!) fell about his heels and tripped him. Combined with this account, shockingly frank for 1841, were phrases that are indicated above by dots: "the way he walked *over that fence* —stranger, he loomed up like a *black mist*, he seemed so large," and "he *walked through the fence* like a falling tree would through a cobweb." In other words, at the very moment when Jim's imagining carries the picture of the bear to a climax of physical grandeur, he also tells about having a bowel movement, letting his pants fall, and being tripped up by them. And the clauses following the quoted passage are those which tell about the bear's groaning and his mysterious death.

This combination of the earthy with the fantastic makes for a superb anticlimax—an incongruous coalescence that is not only typical of American humor and the tall tale but also one of their superb achievements.

> *My pint am in taking aboard big*
> *scares, an' then beatin enybody's hoss, ur scared dog, a-runnin from*
> *under em agin. I used to think my pint an' dad's were jis' the same,*
> *sulky, unmixed king durned fool; . . . when I gits his 'sperience, I*
> *may be king fool.*
>
> —George W. Harris, *Sut Lovingood's Yarns* (1867).

21.
Sut Lovingood and
the End of the World

JIM DOGGETT WAS A MAN WHO, in addition to having superb storytelling qualities, lived in a world that refused to play according to the rules. Remember, Jim discovered that he was "useless" in New Orleans; his proficiency at farming and shooting was of no value there. And, more important, the course of his comic story charts, as we pointed out in the last chapter, that his prowess didn't really conquer an inscrutable wilderness and a bear that wouldn't play by the rules, either. Fascinatingly, William Faulkner was equally impressed with another ripstaver in a ruleless world, Sut Lovingood. Faulkner said of Sut,

I like Sut Lovingood from a book written by George Harris about 1840 or '50 in the Tennessee mountains. He had no illusions about himself, did the best he could; at certain times he was a coward and knew it and wasn't ashamed; he never blamed his misfortunes on anyone and never cursed God for them.

But although Edmund Wilson admired the imaginative language and the power of George Washington Harris's *Sut Lovingood's Yarns*, he had a less charitable opinion of the young man in its title: "Sut Lovingood is something special. He is not a pioneer contending against the wilderness; he is a peasant squatting in his own filth."

It is possible that what Wilson deplored and Faulkner (and a small but growing band of scholars) admired was the identical earthy celebration of an amoral universe and the reprehensible carrying on of Sut. For that matter, the essential difference between Faulkner's and Wilson's responses was prophesied back in 1867, when the *Yarns* first appeared in book form and a young journalist writing under the name of Mark Twain predicted that "it will sell well in the West, but the Eastern people will call it coarse and possibly taboo it."

In fact, what George Harris managed to infuse into some of the most riotous comic happenings in American humor was a philosophy that an attentive reader could well find coarse, and even fatalistic and anarchical. Sut announces, as the first of his five cardinal points of his credo, "Firstly, that I haint got nara a soul, nothin but a whiskey proof gizzard" (which might explain why Sut doesn't bother to curse God, by the way). He proposes that "Men were made a-purpos jis' to eat, drink, an' fur staying awake in the early part ove the nites: an' wimmen were made to cook the vittles, mix the spirits, an' help the men do the staying awake. That's all, an' nothin more. . . ." Such hedonism would be bad enough to an Easterner, probably, but Sut elaborates even further in a later story:

Jus' so the earth over: bishops eats elders, elders eats common people; they eats such cattle as me, I eats possums, possums eats chickens, chickens swallers worms, and worms am content to eat dust, an' the dust am the end of it all.

In such a world, it is not especially surprising that Sut twice even contemplates suicide. At the end of one of his stories, he suggests to "George," his educated auditor, that "I orter bust my head open aginst a bluff of rocks, an' jis' would do it, ef I wasnt a cussed coward." At the conclusion of another yarn, he speculates,

I feel like I'd be glad to be dead, only I'se feared of the dyin. I don't care fur hereafter, for its impossible fur me to have ara soul. Who ever seed a soul in jis' such a rack heap of bones an' rags as this? I's nothin but some new-fangeled sort of beast, a sort of cross between a crazy ole monkey an' a durned wore-out hominy-mill.

Fortunately for us—and unfortunately for the Tennessee Smokies in which he lives, though—Sut does manage to resist the temptation to bust his head open.

Instead, he puts into operation another aspect of his philosophy: he takes sadistic revenge on a world in which he ranks be-

tween the common people and the possums. He makes this part
of his philosophy explicit, then tries to define

universal unregenerate human nature: if ever you does anything to
enybody without cause, you hates em always afterwards, an' sorter
wants to hurt em agin. An' here's another human nature: if anything
happens sum feller, I don't care if he's your bes' frien, an' I don't care
how sorry you is for him, there's a streak of satisfacktion 'bout like a
sewin thread a-runnin all thru your sorrow. You may be shamed of
it, but durn me if it ain't there. . . . An' here's a little more; no odds
how good you is to young things, or how kind you is in treatin them,
when you sees a little long legged lamb a-shakin its tail, an' a-dancin
staggerinly under its mam a-huntin for the tit on its knees, yer fingers
will itch to seize that tail, an' fling the little anxious son of a mutton
over the fence among the blackberry briars, not to hurt it, but jis' to
disappint it. Or say, a little calf, a-buttin fast under the cow's fore-legs,
an' then the hind, with the point of its tongue stuck out, makin sucking
motions, not yet old enough to know the bag end of its mam from the
hookin' end, don't you want to kick it on the snout, hard enough to
send it backwards, say fifteen feet, jis' to show it that butting won't always fetch milk? Or a baby even, rubbin' its heels past each other,
a-rootin an a-snifflin after the breast, and the mam doing her best to
git it out, over the hem of her clothes, don't you feel hungry to give it
jis' one percussion cap slap, right onto the place what some day'll fit a
saddle, or a sewin' chair, to show it what's atwixt it and the grave; that
it stands a powerful chance not to be fed everytime it's hungry, or in
a hurry?

And a catalogue of Sut's deviltries suggests that he puts his
theory into admirable practice (though, alas, not with any nursing babies).

Sut's chief targets are the symbols of authority that constantly
torment him: Sheriff Dolton, Parson Bullin, lawyer Stillyards,
and Clapshaw the circuit-riding preacher. In one story, "Frustrating a Funeral," he so terrifies the entire community by dese-
crating a slave's corpse that at the end, Sut can count "Hunicutt
gone, Seize's corpse lost, *doctor* gone, *parson* gone, *sheriff* gone,
and to cap the stack of vexatious things the *doggery keeper* gone.
Why, the county's ruinated."

If Sut's victims were *only* the doctors, sheriffs, parsons, and
lawyers, his apologists would have an easier time justifying his
behavior. He would be just another fool-killer. But Sut's dubious
interest in raising hell extends to Mrs. Yardley, who dies after

Sut looses a horse at her quilting, and to old man Burns, who "went plumb crazy—crazy as a bed-bug in July" after a bull-ride rigged by Sut. Sut sets fire to a tin-ware peddler with two pounds of gunpowder in his hip pocket, and after the explosion "the sittin part of him was blowed to kingdom come, and so were everything else belongin to that region." When Hen Bailey swallows a live lizard, Sut's compassionate solution to Hen's dilemma is to send a live mole up the other end of his digestive tract. And a little later, "here come the lizard tearin out his mouth, the worst skeer'd varmint I ever seed in all my borned days. His eyes were as big as fox grapes, an' most all of them outside of his head, an' dam if he didn't have enough to skeer a lion, for the mole had him fast by the tail, an' were mindin his holt, an' that there interprisin littil earth-borer hadn't a durn'd morsel of fur left onto his hide; it were all *limed* off; he looked right down slick an' funny, with a lizard a-haulin him through the sand." And Sut's own dad is his most persistent target.

Several things save Sut's yarns from being a casebook in abnormal psychology. For one, there are one or two occasions when the jokes are turned on Sut himself—as when Sicily Burns doses him with soda, promising him that he's drinking an aphrodisiac. (Even George, the amused and usually immune auditor of Sut's stories, falls into a full and open outhouse hole in one story.) More important, Harris had, as perhaps the quotations above suggest, an amazingly acute ear for vivid comic metaphor, for astonishingly apt imagery, cadence, and dialect, and a sense of timing that challenges Rube Goldberg. Somehow, as one reads a few of the stories of Sut and his antagonists, these amazing humorous qualities camouflage the underlying anarchy. The "coarse" or amoral, even nihilistic, frame of reference is washed away by a comic genius that dazzles most readers.

Harris's literate narrator, George, served as the recorder of Sut's stories, but without nearly the comic contrast that marks "The Big Bear of Arkansas." Usually Sut and George have stopped by the side of the road to guzzle whiskey or camp in the woods overnight, when—with the slightest of prompting—Sut launches into his story. Once, in fact, George attempts to narrate a tale of his own; and, after his long, nostalgic, tearful scene-opener (in "Eaves-dropping a Lodge of Free-Masons"), reminiscent of Longstreet, Sut interrupts George: "Oh, complicated durnashun! that ain't it," the backwoods critic reacts. "You're drunk, or you're shamed to tell it, an' so you tries to put us all asleep with a mess of durn'd nonsense, about echoes, an' grapes, an' walnut trees; oh, you be durned! Boys, just give me a holt of that there willow basket, with a cob in its mouth, an' that there tin cup, an' after I've sponged my throat, I'll talk it all off in English."

In "Parson John Bullin's Lizards," a reward-notice offering eight dollars in produce for Sut allows for some background information to filter to the crowd scattered around Capehart's Doggery. George questions Sut; and he and we learn that Bullin has caught Sut and a girl frisking horizontally in a huckleberry bush, demanded that Sut appear at the next campmeeting in Rattlesnake Springs, and that as a result of Sut's behavior there, "Ole Barbelly Bullin, as they calls him now," has posted his offer of a reward. George asks Sut questions, acts as a straight man, and retains a modest control over the narrative even if his language and his attitude do not provide comic contrast to those of the central story.

And in a sense, Sut's energy, his violence, and his unleashed imagination when the yarn-spinning fit is on him, are well served by an agent like George, who is appreciative enough to stay out of Sut's way. Also, those critics who suggest that Harris intends us to find Sut completely reprehensible should notice, we believe, that Harris never has George step in to condemn Sut's morals or to offer alternatives to Sut's acts and attitudes. George's function is truncated to omit disclaimers—no alibis, no dignified rejections. George refuses to be shocked, to condemn, or to help readers discover an alternative to Sut's evaluations of human behavior and method for coping with the world—so persistently, in fact, that it must have been Harris's conscious intention.

Neither, for that matter, does Parson Bullin provide readers with an "acceptable" alternative to Sut. Bullin is an "infernal, hypercritical, pot-bellied, scaley-hided, whisky-wastin', stinkin old ground-hog," not only according to Sut's appraisal but also to what we learn of him from events of the story. He sells cheap whiskey, which he colors with slime from a mud puddle; after promising not to snitch, he tells the girl's mother about catching her with Sut. And he is so physically repulsive that it is impossible to see him (or practically anyone at all, for that matter, in all Sut's stories) as providing some significant contrast, comic or ethical, to Sut's own world view.

By the time that the frame to "Parson John Bullin's Lizards" has ended and Sut launches into his version of the fun at Rattlesnake Springs, we have been prepared to anticipate and to relish the possibility that Sut has successfully dished out retribution to the parson. The reader has subtly been made an ally to a character who is outlawed, who ridicules a parson, and who has apparently demolished religion for miles around.

As he tells the story, Sut enters the camp meeting and sits on the mourner's bench just in front of the pulpit, "as solemn as a old hat cover on collection day." And Parson Bullin begins a sermon "powerfully mixed with brimstone, an' trimmed with blue flames." Sut has brought along a bag filled with seven or eight lizards, though; and just when Bullin reaches the fever-pitch of his sermon on hell's serpents—telling the women of the congregation "how they'd coil into their bosoms an' how they *would* crawl down under their frock-strings, no odds how tight they tied them, an' how some of the oldest an' worst ones would crawl up their legs, an' travel *under* their garters, no odds how tight they tied *them*"—Sut sees his chance, unties his bag, and lets his lizards scoot up the preacher's pants leg. "Quick as gunpowder they all took up his bare leg, makin a noise like squirrels a-climbin a shell-bark hickory. He stopped preachin' right in the middle of the word 'damnation,' and looked for a moment like he were a listenin for somethin—sort of like a ole sow does, when she hears you a-whistlin for the dogs."

Bullin's theology then takes a decidedly enthusiastic turn. The lizards come out of his shirt collar, sport themselves in his pants, and torment him "about the place where you cut the best steak outen a beef." After a brief burst of humility—"Pray for me brethren an' sistern, for I is a rastlin with the great enemy right now!"—Bullin begins to strip. First his clawhammer coat, then his shirt, and finally his pants bang against the pulpit; and "nigh onto fifteen shortened biscuits, a boiled chicken with its legs crossed, a big double-bladed knife, a hunk of tobacco, a cob-pipe, some copper ore, lots of broken glass, a cork, a sprinkle of whisky,

a squirt, an' three lizards flew permiscuously all over that meetin-
ground." At this point, Bullin, with "nothin left onto him but a
pair of heavy, low-quartered shoes, short woolen socks, an' eel-
skin garters to keep off the cramp," leaps over the pulpit "among
the most pious part of the congregation" and makes a mad nude
dash for the woods. "He weighed nigh onto three hundred, had
a black stripe down his back, like onto a ole bridle rein, an' his
belly were about the size, an' color of a beef paunch, an' it
a'swingin out from side to side; he leaned back from it, like a
little feller a-totin a big drum, at a muster. . . . There were
cramp-knots on his legs as big as walnuts, an' mottled splotches
on his shins; an' takin him all over, he minded of a durnd crazy
old elephant, possessed of the devil."

When, after a week, Bullin attempts to preach again, there
isn't a woman in the congregation, according to Sut: "Parsons
generally have a pow'ful strong holt on women," Sut explains,
"but, hoss, I tell you there ain't many of em kin run stark nakid
over an' thru a crowd of three hundred women an' not injure
their characters *some*."

Now, there's some obvious poetic justice about Sut's revenge.
A sanctimonious, hypocritical preacher stripped and exposed
to his fundamental nature seems like an appropriate metaphor
for the unmasking of pretentiousness. And if only John Bullin
suffered from the lizards and the exposure, there would be no
dilemma.

But Sut's pranks manage to uncover universal perversity or to
afflict the innocent as promiscuously as the guilty. One of the lizards Bullin lets fly into the congregation "lit head-first into the
bosom of a fat woman, as big as a skin'd hoss, an' nigh onto as
ugly, who sot thirty yards off, a fannin herself with a turkey-
tail":

Smart to the last, by golly, he immediately commenced runnin down
the center of her breast-bone, an' kept on, I spect. She were jis' bound
to faint an' she did it first rate—flung the turkey-tail up in the air,
grabbed the lap of her gown, gin it a big histin an' fallin shake, rolled
down the hill, tangled her legs an' garters in the top of a huckleberry
bush, with her head in the branch an' jus' lay still.

And when he leaps the pulpit, he manages to land right on top
of old Miss Chaneyberry: "He lit a-straddle of her long neck,

a-shuttin her up with a snap, her head atwixt her knees, like
shuttin up a jack-knife." As Bullin lopes for the woods, the
women "jerked most of the children with em, an' the rest he
scrunched." But no one, except the lady in huckleberry bush and
old Miss Chaneyberry, can resist watching his progress:

Some women screamin—they were the skeery ones; some laughin—
they were the wicked ones; some cryin—they were the fool ones,
(sorter my stripe you know;) some tryin to git away with thar faces
red—they were the modest ones; some looking after old Bullin—they
were the curious ones; some hangin close to their sweethearts—they
were the sweet ones; some on their knees wif their eyes shut, but facin
the way the ole mud turtle were a-runnin—they were the deceitful
ones; some doin nothin—they were the waitin ones; an' the most dangerous of em by a durnd long sight.

Notice that Sut's inventory of responses—scary, wicked, foolish,
modest, curious, sweet, deceitful, waiting, and dangerous—
doesn't include a single *sympathetic*, *compassionate*, or *outraged*
member of the congregation.

In effect, what Sut (or, Sut insists, not him but a bag of lizards) disrobes is a microcosm of humanity with practically no
redeeming qualities. We do not weep for John Bullin; but we do
not weep for old Miss Chaneyberry, either, shut up like a jack-
knife and missing all the fun. In Sut's world, as in Melville's in
The Confidence-Man, there are only the gullible and the disreputable, a Conradian "choice of nightmares" saved only by its
raucous hilarity. In his first sermon after the events at Rattlesnake Springs, Bullin mentions Sut as "livin proof of the hell-
desarvin nature of man"; but in the midst of our laughter, it is
fair to ask who in the story is *not* living proof?

Perceptive readers may have noticed that, in addition to the
comic action in "Parson John Bullin's Lizards," there is a fantastically imaginative, humorous language in the quotations
which adds another level to the artistry of these stories. Sut always manages to find not only fanciful but almost eloquent references to compare the physiologies and actions of his enemies to
the natural world. (And, it is true, incidentally, that George is
literal-minded and totally lacking in this poetic image-making
quality.) Sut thinks and talks almost as if he'd read Ralph Waldo
Emerson's theorizings on the use of nature for language.

Such fanciful analogies and similes—Miss Chaneyberry shut up like a jack-knife, Bullin leaning back from his paunch like a little man carrying a big drum or sort of listening like an old sow does when you whistle for the dogs—are inventive genius. Their aptness and vividness combine with their unexpectedness to produce comic incongruity of a high order.

In addition, as Milton Rickels has noted, Sut's imagery consistently finds analogies for human beings in animals, insects, and other forms of "lower" life. Though comic, it reduces Sut's antagonists to a bestial level. John Bullin, for instance, is not only the ground-hog, the mud-turtle, and the crazy old elephant in the passages we have already quoted. He acts like an animal in addition to looking like one. He rubs himself "where a hosses tail sprouts." He squirms under the lizards' torment "as ef he'd slept in a dog bed." He runs "like a ole fat waggon hoss, skared at a locomotive." And he is so terrified of the lizards that his "eyes were a-stickin out like onto two buckeyes flung agin a mud wall, an' he wer a-cuttin up more shines nor a cockroach in a hot skillet."

Sut's dehumanizing tendency in his vivid language (machines like hominy-mills, threshing machines, hay balers, and locomotives are also part of his consistent imagery) extends to himself, to do him total justice, and even in less odious ways to people he likes. And such catholic animalizing assists importantly in allowing us to relish the pandemonium and desolation at Rattlesnake Springs. Only if we accept both Sut's philosophy and the implications of his dehumanizing language is it possible to appreciate the havoc of Bullin stripped, Miss Chaneyberry bent double, and that part of the congregation not scrunched by Bullin's exit reduced to panic.

Finally, if Sut is a more reprehensible rascal than Jim Doggett, they share significant qualities. Both are illiterate "children of nature," dubious of the virtues of civilization. Both rely on innate and instinctive common sense; and both of them manage to capture, in language which raises homely colloquialisms to high art, the qualities that have enthroned the disreputable character as one of the royal figures of American humor.

Tall
Tales
Go West

. . . steel pens, if put into the ground over night, are found to be gold ones in the morning.
—Yankee Blade, 1848.

22.
The Last Frontier

As one wave after another of explorers, then hunters, then settlers rolled from the Eastern seaboard to the Pacific Coast and backwashed into mountain mining towns, many fictional motifs and patterns were repeated. Reports about the first American frontier, it will be remembered, played up fabulous rewards and fiendish hardships. So did mid-nineteenth-century rumors about the Far West.

There was unanimous agreement that just getting out to the Far Western country overland was hell on wheels. Travel at twelve miles per day, as Kevin Starr says, was a nightmare—

a weary succession of prairies, deserts, mountains, painfully measured out in the plod of hooves and the creak of wheels. One could die in a variety of ways: from fever, poisoning, the accidental discharge of guns, gangrene. A wagon could roll backward down a mountain grade and crush those behind it. . . . Men, even good men, under stress, might resort to gun and bowie knife—and be shot or skewered by someone more adept. If one were dying, and things were bad for the others, he could be left on the trailside to die alone. Children lost both parents. Women sat sobbing on the side of the trail as men trekked off to reach water or tried to repair an axle before the main caravan got too far ahead. Gravesites lined the overland trail ("may he rest peaceable in this savage unknown country"). . . .

Going by boat was as bad, whether the Eastern traveler crossed at Panama (a sixty-day journey) or went around the Horn (four to six months, depending on the ship)—rotten meat, stinking water, wormy sea-biscuits, seasickness, scurvy, dysentery, claustrophobia, mounting tensions, at worst insanity, suicide, and even murder.

Once in the West, the traveler found he was in either "the garden of the world or the most desolate place of Creation," depending upon the area visited, the season, and the reporter's prejudices or purposes. The weather might be wonderful, hills green, gardens and orchards burgeoning; dry, hot summers might seem endless, rains torrential, snows deep, deserts and mountains impossible.

Even before Sutter's partner discovered gold, promotional tracts—as always, in a new country—were fulsome. In the 1845 *Emigrants' Guide to Oregon and California*, an inspired writer had a vision:

Soon, when those wild forests, trackless plains, untrodden valleys, and the unbounded ocean, will present one grand scene of continuous improvements, universal enterprise, and unparalleled commerce; when those vast forests shall have disappeared before the hardy pioneer; those extensive plains shall abound with innumerable herds of domestic animals; those fertile valleys shall groan under the immense weight of their abundant products; those numerous rivers shall teem with countless steam-boats, steam-ships, barques and brigs; when the entire country will be everywhere intersected with turnpike roads, rail-roads, and canals; and when all the vastly numerous and rich resources of that now almost unknown region will be fully and advantageously developed.

Once an emigrant had been lured into the Western country by poetic promises like this one, the contrast was gigantic. A visitor summarizes his impression of Washoe, as Nevada was then called, in 1860:

The deep pits on the hill-sides; the blasted and barren appearance of the whole country; the unsightly hodge-podge of a town; the horrible confusion of tongues; the roaring, raving drunkards at the bar-rooms, swilling fiery liquids from morning till night; the flaring and flaunting gambling-saloons, filled with desperadoes of the vilest sort; the ceaseless torrent of imprecations that shocked the ear on every side; the mad speculations and feverish thirst for gain—all combined to give me a forcible impression of the unhallowed character of the place. . . . What had I done to bring me to this? In vain I entered into a retrospection of the various iniquities of my life; but I could hit upon nothing that seemed bad enough to warrant such a fate.

By now, japes about such incongruous picturings were routine. They popped up for the most part in the East, but they also proliferated on the new frontier. As always, the trick was to exaggerate outrageously either bad aspects or good ones. And internal evidence offered no clues to the place of origin.

Is the desert country barren? "Well, the birds that fly over it have to carry their own ration." Is the Sacramento River low in the dry season? "You'd say so if you'd seen what I saw yesterday. I saw a couple of suckers lightening a salmon over the bar." "In Oregon, lately, hailstones fell as large as watermelons. The snowflakes are so big, the ladies put handles onto 'em and use 'em for parasols." A Californian writes that he is so hard run for victuals and other edibles that nothing but a miracle or highway robbery can save him from starvation. For two weeks, he says, he "lived on a piece of oil-cloth boiled with an old boot to give it a meaty flavor." (Cf. Charlie Chaplin's boot dinner in *The Gold Rush*.)

On the other hand: "Strawberries grow in California as big as punkins. To learn if they're ripe, you plug 'em the way Yankees do watermelons. You serve 'em cut into slices, like pineapples. Great country, that Californy." "A California paper says a hunter killed nine thousand snipes with four shots. The air was full of falling birds for several days, not to speak of a great number of cripples hobbling about the ground." "You mean to tell me, boy, that you've got two more California turkeys as large as this?" "Dunno about their being California turkeys, but I know they came over on the same ship as this one, and before they died they were called ostriches." "The climate out here is so healthy, we had to shoot a man before we could start our burying ground."

Are the people pretty tough, then? "Fellow in San Francisco is so strong he can lift himself three feet off the ground by his own coat collar." "An editor out West has to have his boots tapped weekly—wears 'em out kicking loafers out of his office." "Man out West is so dirty, the assessors put him down as real estate." "There is an old maid out West, 'tis said, so tough and rough that they use her forehead for a nutmeg grater." "They shoot folks here somewhat, and the law is rather partial than otherwise to first-class murderers." "Oh it's a lively place, you bet! . . . reely hexcitin'. I look out of the winder every mornin' jist to see how many dead men are layin' around. I declare to gracious the bullets flies around here sometimes like hailstones!" Finally: "A beautifully and ably conducted free fight came off in C street yesterday afternoon, but as nobody was killed or mortally wounded in a manner sufficiently fatal to cause death, no particular interest attaches to the matter, and we shall not publish the details."

Freaks of nature among the volcanic plateaus, painted deserts, and forests of the West, and newly found ore deposits that brought booms and rushes, inspired jokesters to update or concoct lore like that which the earliest Old World visitors had strewn on pages of travel books. When someone out there came upon a silicified tree stump, a contributor to *Knickerbocker Magazine* in 1850 produced an account of a story-telling session in Independence, Missouri, during which a Connecticut spinster asked Harris, a mountain man, about petrifactions he'd seen:

. . . "Oh, yes, ma'am," said he. "About them things I can tell you something interesting, and so strange, that if I had not seen it I should be tempted to doubt the truth myself. As my companions and myself were traveling near the Yellowstone Forks, one afternoon last winter, where the snow was very deep, we suddenly came upon a spot on the side of a mountain, where everything looked fresh and green; the trees were covered with foliage, the birds were singing merrily in the branches, the grass was waving in the breeze, and, in short, ma'am, it looked like a spot of summer dropped into the middle of winter. The sight was so strange, that we concluded to camp. . . . So, unpacking my mule, I took a hatchet and went to a log, thinking to hew us some kindling wood. I struck, and the hatchet glanced. I looked at the edge; it was turned! That log, ma'am, was petrified! I then went to a tree that looked green, with birds singing on its branches. That too, ma'am, was petrified; and, ma'am, the very leaves and grass were petrified; and stranger still, ma'am, the birds themselves were petrifactions." "Ah, yes!" said the lady, smiling exultingly, as though she had now caught him. "But you said the birds were singing!" Harris was perplexed. He had gone too far, but resolving not to back out, he exclaimed, "Yes, ma'am, by Jesus, they were! The very notes in their throats were petrified."

In January 1849, the *Yankee Blade* quoted advice by a man who had returned from California when he was asked what was the most important item for a gold seeker to take to the diggings: "Green spectacles, by all means, for they are needed to protect

the eyes of the gold diggers from the brilliancy of the metal."
The Boston *Herald* was soon reporting that settlers in Shasta,
California, had hit upon a new way to get rich: "The gold grows
to the roots of the grass. The grass is pulled up and the gold
shaken off, as gardeners pull up the vines to shake off young potatoes." *Yankee Notions* had this: "It is stated that in a certain
locality in California the quartz is so rich that a pound and a
half of gold is extracted from every pound of rock."

Soon after the discovery of the rich Comstock lode in Virginia
City, a visitor to San Francisco found that gold was nowhere,
nearby Washoe had become "a second California," and a silver
mania had taken over:

Speculation peered into the silvery heavens in search of new lodes; nay,
the genius of enterprise pointed toward the regions of everlasting woe
as an appropriate sphere for the smelting interests. Tons of ore were
piled in heaps along the curb-stones in the streets; every office was an
emporium for the purchase and sale of feet; every desk in every store
was a stall at which millionaires browsed upon paper; every window
glared and dazzled the sight with gorgeous engravings of stocks; every
man of the hundreds and tens of thousands that stood at every corner,
and in every saloon, and before every bar, carried feet in his pockets
and dividends in his eyes; and every walking thing, save horses and
dogs and rats and mice, talked stocks and feet from morning till night,
and dreamed dividends from night till morning. Young ladies would
hear of no propositions from any gentleman with less than a thousand
feet; no gentleman, however ardent, would compromise himself without asking, "Is she on the Wild-Cat or Legitimate? How many pay feet
does she offer? and what assessments are due her?"

Mark Twain would mine a great many feet of the same vein
as late as 1872 in *Roughing It*.

Far Western comic writers turned out pieces which, though
related to older American humorous works, often bore imprints
of their own birthplace and time. In at least one important way,
this last frontier differed from earlier ones: the mapping of its
features, the discovery of its rich deposits, and their mining on
a huge scale all demanded scientific knowledge and know-how.
Thanks to the best of luck, science was ready to do what was
needed.

The first half of the nineteenth century had been a great period for scientific advances. Many had been in one field—geol-

ogy. Amazing progress had transformed this study from speculation to a science based upon solid facts. In the nick of time,
geological time charts had been perfected, rocks classified, surveys made, and findings published. Further, several great scholars had made giant leaps for mankind in geological study, and
two of the best had helped interest Americans in it.

Charles Lyell of England in the 1830's published two brilliant
and popular works which informed thousands of readers about
the principles and elements of geology. In 1841 and 1845, Lyell
came here and told Americans interesting facts about three matters of local concern—the speed at which Niagara Falls was re-
ceding, the amount of mud heaped up each year in the Mississippi Delta, and what was going to happen in a few centuries to
the vegetable matter in Virginia's Great Dismal Swamp. Also,
like several other British visitors, he wrote a couple of travel
books which were widely read in America.

Louis Agassiz, a Swiss naturalist and geologist trained in three
of Europe's most prestigious universities, in 1846 came to Boston
to deliver lectures and was hastily seated on a professorial chair
in Harvard's brand new Lawrence Scientific School. He was the
sort of appointee that university presidents pray for—usually in
vain: an imaginative investigator, a prolific writer, a superb
teacher, a great administrator, a popularizer the general public
quickly came to adore, and a fund raiser par excellence. He
promptly proceeded to publicize new findings and to revolu-
tionize the teaching and study of zoology and geology.

These scientists, of course, were both involved in the great
dispute about evolution. Charles Darwin, formulator of the evolutionary hypothesis, constantly used Lyell's data. "The second
volume of Lyell's Principles," William Irvine says in *Apes, Angels & Victorians* (1955), "was really *The Origin of Species*
without Darwinism, or at least explicit Darwinism. In almost the
same sequence, Lyell took up the problems of the *Origin* . . .
and did everything but solve them." As a leading disbeliever in
evolution who happened to be well informed, Agassiz gave the
theory and the facts upon which it was based (his facts as well
as Darwin's) wide circulation.

Thanks to such advances and such interest, geological explora-
tions, surveys, maps, and reports came to be the rage. Especially

when covered by colorful and articulate reporters, a wide public actually read about them. An outstanding instance occurred in the early 1840's, when a flamboyant young lieutenant, John Charles Frémont, guided by the picturesque Kit Carson, led expeditions into the Far West and—with the help of a wife who had a flair for writing—recorded them. Thousands of copies of *Report of the Exploring Expedition to the Rocky Mountains, 1842, and to Oregon and North California, 1843–44* were read by prospective and actual movers westward. After 1845, Americans debated fiercely about the best route for a continental railway. (Frémont, guided this time by Old Bill Williams, led one expedition surveying possible passes.) As George R. Stewart says:

the bootblack or the cabdriver could argue the advantage of central, southern, or northern routes; any number of elaborately organized expeditions were being sent out by Congress and were reporting back voluminously upon the topography, geology, meteorology, zoology, botany, and ethnology of the country adjacent to the particular parallel of latitude which they had been instructed to explore . . . the final thirteen tomes of railroad expeditions now form a real monument in the history of exploration. . . .

Three men who were as different from one another in backgrounds and careers as a trio could be were alike in one thing: they scored successes by producing humor that took advantage of this widespread interest in science, scientific inventions, and geological surveys. The three were an army engineer, George Horatio Derby; a mountain man and wide-ranging guide, Jim Bridger; and a reporter for a Nevada mining town newspaper, William Wright.

*To a man of a mathematical turn
of mind—to a student and lover of the exact sciences these inaccuracies
of expression—this inability to understand* exactly *how things are
must be a constant source of annoyance; and to one who, like myself,
unites this turn of mind to an ardent love of truth, for its own sake—
the reflection that the English language does not enable us to speak the
truth with exactness, is peculiarly painful.*

—John Phoenix [George Horatio Derby],
"A New System of English Grammar" (1854).

23.
Derby, Alter Egos:
Phoenix and Squibob

GEORGE HORATIO DERBY (1823-
1861), born and raised in Massachusetts, trained at West Point,
and wounded after brief action in Mexico, prepared for his most
important military work by serving in the Washington, D.C.,
Topographical Bureau and on the upper Mississippi. In 1849 he
went to the Pacific Coast on an exploratory and mapping assignment. During the next seven years, tours of reconnaissance,
mapping, and engineering chores took him to the lower Colorado River, to Oregon, northern Washington, and many parts of
California.

During his years in California, this lively young army officer
won a name throughout the state for his ingenious practical
jokes. At a Sonoma party, for instance, he sneaked into the room
where the babies had been stashed, swapped their blankets, and
let parents discover his deviltry only after long buggy-rides
home. (Owen Wister had his hero play the same prank half a
century later in his best-selling novel, *The Virginian*.) Derby
introduced his bride and his mother after telling each that the
other was very deaf, and then listened to their shouting for ten
minutes before confessing that he had lied. (An antebellum
sketch, "The Coquettes," had used the same trick earlier; so had
Brusquet, court fool of Francis I of France, in the sixteenth cen-

tury.) Again, sitting in for a time for the editor of the San Diego *Herald*, Derby completely reversed the newspaper's politics, ferociously attacked the candidate whom the editor had backed and praised to the sky the man he had been opposing. These were only three of many boisterous dirty tricks.

On leaves in San Francisco, Derby was a welcome member of an informal crowd of army officers, journalists, editors, artists, actors, politicos, and other jolly good fellows who regularly congregated for rough male fun in a famous saloon on Montgomery Street. Literary men in this free-and-easy group encouraged Derby to write for newspapers and magazines and eventually gathered his pieces in two popular books, *Phoenixiana; or, Sketches and Burlesques by John Phoenix* (1855) and the posthumous *Squibob Papers by John Phoenix* [Capt. Geo. H. Derby] (1865).

In 1915, when many in the American professorial Establishment still sniffed at even the classic writers of our country, an innovative scholar, Fred Lewis Pattee of Pennsylvania State College, had the gall to read, discuss, and praise (with reservations) "the new humor of the West." He believed Abe Lincoln first made this comedy famous since he himself a "man of the West . . . stood in the limelight of the Presidency, transacting the nation's business with anecdotes from the frontier circuits, meeting hostile critics with shrewd border philosophy, and reading aloud with unction" his favorite low-brow humorists. Among these, Pattee had a favorite:

The greatest of them all, the real father of the new school of humorists, the man who gave the East the first glimpse of the California humor, was George Horatio Derby. . . . He had little time for books, and his writings . . . were the result wholly of his own observations upon the picturesque life that he found about him in the West. In his Phoenixiana . . . we find nearly all the elements . . . the solemn protestation of truthfulness followed by the story that on the face of it is impossible . . . grotesque exaggerations [used] deliberately and freely as provocative of laughter . . . irreverence . . . euphuistic statements . . . Yankee aphorisms . . . unexpected comparisons and whimsical *non sequiturs*. . . . Not much was added to Western humor after Derby [whose] art [he] learned . . . from contact with the new West . . . the humor of the gathering of men under primitive conditions . . . often crude and coarse . . . elemental.

Pattee paid the price an innovator must: he made errors which later scholars were happy to correct—in his geography (which joined in unholy matrimony the Old Southwest, the Midwest, and the Far West and called the amalgam "the West"); in his chronology; and in his assignment to "new" humorists comic techniques which were by no means peculiar to them.

His worst guess—probably made because Derby was a rough-living engineer, rowdy practical joker and two-fisted drinker—was that the humorist surely could not have learned a smidgeon of his art from books, but must have acquired it solely from "contact with the new West." Like a majority of the "Westerners" of gold-and-silver-rush days, Derby had been reared in the East. He was educated in a Boston school, the Andover Teachers' Seminary, Northfield Academy, and West Point (where he was seventh in his class). He lived in the Transcendental Concord of Emerson and Thoreau and the eloquent Washington D.C., of Webster, Clay, and Calhoun; he taught school for a year; and he read widely. As George R. Stewart says:

> He was . . . a well-educated gentleman [with] fair training in French, at least some smattering of Latin [and] frontier Spanish. . . . He was also well read [in] the Bible . . . could amaze friends by reciting whole chapters. He is almost as much at home with classical mythology. In addition one can note in his far from voluminous works easy allusions to and quotations from Virgil, Horace, Shakespeare, Ben Jonson, Cervantes, Milton, Sterne, Boswell, Henry Carey, Scott, Byron, Longfellow, Poe, Irving, Charles Lever, G. P. R. James, Thackeray, Macaulay, and (most of all) Dickens.

This impressive list can be enlarged with these additions: Sappho, Cicero, Chaucer, Spenser, Pope, Swift, Goldsmith, Samuel Johnson, Newton, Hugh Blair, William Herschel, Thomas Hood, John Stuart Mill, Emerson, Agassiz, Richard Henry Dana, and Harriet Beecher Stowe.

William Dean Howells, who riled many less prissy critics by being too refined, actually faulted Derby for being too bookish for his own good—so "weighed upon by literary tradition" that "he was 'academic' at times." An example of "Phoenix's" bookishness is the description of the editor's return to his San Diego office after his playful standby had made a shambles of the *Herald's* political campaign. Words lifted from Holy Writ say that the editor "cometh, and 'his driving is like that of Jehu the son of Nimshi for he driveth furiously.' " Another quotation tells how he looks: "In shape and gesture proudly eminent, stood like a tower: . . . but his face deep scars of thunder had entrenched, and care sat on his faded cheek; but under brows of dauntless courage and considerable pride, waiting revenge." The source, almost certainly quoted—accurately—from memory, is Milton's description of the deposed Satan in *Paradise Lost*. The editor's defiant shout takes the form of a heroic couplet. Next, Phoenix borrows legal terminology to report that the dispute has been settled "without prejudice to the honor of either party." The finale is a description of Phoenix's battered self, which the reader will find comic only by conjuring up a memory of sixteenth-century portraits: "We write this while sitting without any clothing, except our left stocking, and the rim of our hat encircling our neck like the 'ruff' of the Elizabethan era. . . ."

Ancestors of the Phoenix, the Squibob, and the other creations of Derby who made fools of themselves in numerous sketches have been noticed in previous chapters: they were the *alazon*–pedants who over the centuries tried to impress others with learning that they didn't have. Using burlesqued bluffers such as these was Derby's favorite hold.

In "A New System of English," Phoenix with typical modesty calls himself "a student and lover of the exact sciences . . . thoroughly acquainted with every ancient and modern language." In a San Francisco *Herald* sketch Derby published in 1855, one "Amos Butterfield," a dealer in flour and pork, expertly describes ladies' costumes:

She wore a white crape illusion with eighteen flounces, over a profusely embroidered tulle skirt, looped up on the side with a bouquet of Swiss meringues. Her boddice was of seagreen tabbinet, with an elegant pincushion of orange-colored *moire antique* over the bertha. Her headdress was composed of cut velvet cabbage leaves, with turnip *au naturel*, and a small boned turkey secured by a golden wire, *"a la maitre d'hotel*," crowned the structure.*

* Compare Mark Twain's suggestions about reforming the German language in *A Tramp Abroad* and his reports by a society reviewer in 1863, 1865, and 1866. Example: "Mrs. F. F. L. wore a superb *toilette habillee* of Chambry gauze; over this a charming Figaro jacket, made of mohair, or horse-hair, or something of that kind; over this again, a Raphael blouse of *cheveux de la reine*, trimmed round the bottom with lozenges formed of insertions, and around the top with bronchial troches. . . ."—"The Lick House Ball," *Golden Era*, September 27, 1863.

In another piece he posed as an informed music critic evaluating "The Plains. Ode Symphonie par Jabez Tarbox"; in still another, as a learned astronomer eager to "disseminate the information he has acquired among those who, less fortunate, are yet willing to receive instruction," and so on.

As Derby pointed out during a serious moment, "the discharge of his duties" as a member of the Corps of Topographical Engineers "required the utmost familiarity with the higher and more abstruse branches of science." No doubt both his familiarity and his addictive playfulness led him to kid scientific learning as often as he kidded other kinds—or even more often. It is also likely that his wide reading acquainted him with earlier burlesques and satires directed at scientists and inventors.

Ben Jonson, for instance, some of whose work he knew, in a 1625 comedy had played with fanciful fabrications about the invention of a submarine; Galileo's burning glass, which might be used to set fire to fleets; and a new sauce that would cause American cannibals to "forbear the mutual eating of one another"—all described with such an air of reality that Jonson thought it wise to add a note to say he was joking.

Eighteenth-century writers, a group Derby favored, living (as he did) in an age when science prospered, had fantasized about flying machines, some of which went to the moon.† They had also told scientific tall tales about the discovery of "the cause of the law of gravity," the extraction of sunshine from cucumbers, and the enumeration of London's population by the study of its excrement.

In the New World, from the very start of immigration, science fiction, whether accidentally or intentionally funny, had flourished. A sixteenth-century Spanish physician learned that American sassafras cured liver trouble, kidney stones, gout and syphilis, and a seventeenth-century scientist was assured that grated

† Cyrano de Bergerac's *Comical History*, translated into English in 1687, described a visit to the moon. So did David Russen's *Iter Lunare* (1703) and Daniel Defoe's *A Journey to the World in the Moon* (1705). Thomas Shadwell had Gimcrack in *The Virtuoso* (1676) say: "I am so much advanc'd in the Art of Flying, that I can already out-fly that pond'rous Animal call'd a *Bustard*. . . . Nay, I doubt not, but in a little time to improve that art so far, 'twill be as common to buy a pair of Wings to fly to the World ir the Moon, as to buy a pair of Wax Boots to ride into *Sussex* with." Eleven years later, Mrs. Aphra Behn had a moon-struck character "discourse as gravely of the [Moon] People, their Government, Institutions, Laws, Manners, Religion, and Constitution, as if he had been bred a *Machiavel* there."

beaver testicles, swallowed with wine, ended flatulence. Franklin wrote a mock *Letter to the Royal Academy* in which he set forth with great gravity a plan "to discover some Drug wholesome & not disagreeable, to be mix'd with our common Food, or Sauces, that shall render the Natural Discharges, or Wind from our Bodies, not only inoffensive, but agreeable as Perfumes." In the nineteenth century, Poe had perpetrated famous scientific hoaxes; humorous magazines had satirized scientists; and even rustic comedians had solemnly delivered "scientific lectures."

Derby's most successful jokes evidently were about science. Apocryphal stories about him played up such japes—had him court-martialed for announcing to superior officers who did not share his love for frivolity impossible but somewhat plausible "scientific improvements in the important branches of the military art." These included a newly invented cannon that shot around a corner and whacked the gunner in his *os coccyges*, or a stinky gas to distress and disperse the enemy. It was said that he was punished when he prepared "an illustrated report upon the coyote [that] offered views of the animal from front, side, and rear elevations, and engaged in all its habits and functions."

The friend who edited *Phoenixiana* began it with a take-off on government surveys of possible continental railway routes, "Official Report of PROFESSOR JOHN PHOENIX, A.M., Of a Military Survey and Reconnaissance of the route from San Francisco to the Mission of Dolores, made with a view to ascertaining the practicability of connecting these points by a Railroad." The joke was that this pretentious document covered a route only two miles long through the heart of the city and out to a suburb. At a cost of forty thousand dollars, the professor has led seventeen experts (seven of them his brothers and cousins) and a hundred and eighty-four workmen on this hazardous expedition, with the city's finest groggeries providing the chief hazard. The report, illustrated with a worthless map, gives invaluable facts about the terrain, the climate, and the inhabitants. And throughout, the language, whether it is that of Dr. Fogy L. Bigguns, Ethnologist, that of Dr. Abraham Dunshunner, LL.D., Geologist, or that of Professor Phoenix, Principal Engineer and Chief Astronomer, is highfalutin and somber.

"REMARKABLE DISCOVERIES IN OREGON AND WASHINGTON TER-
RITORIES," an 1855 article by Derby, gave the world the words of
one Dr. Herman Ellenbogen, M.D., about some of "the most interesting" findings in the field of natural history made by an
"Expedition organized by the Government for the survey of the
Railroad route to the Pacific coast." Specimens of "birds, reptiles
and mammals, hitherto rare or entirely unknown," have been
sent to the Smithsonian Institution, says the doctor. He tells at
length what was learned about two animals, the gyascutus
(*Gyascutus Washingtoniensis*) and the prock (*Perockius Ore-
goniensis*). Both had been celebrated mythical animals in the
comic bestiary created by oral storytellers and journalists over
the years. (Mark Twain in *Huckleberry Finn* would retell a yarn
about the former which he had heard in a California mining
camp.)

Ellenbogen provides a pseudo-learned etymology of the gyascutus's name (fifth book of the *Aeneid*) and then patiently
proves, by describing skeletal remains, that popular lore about it
is libelous. The prock had been vulgarly called a "side-hill
winder" because legends had held that it could perambulate nowhere but on hills, and only in one direction. The reason? One
pair of the creature's legs was shorter than the other. Hunters
therefore had no trouble capturing or killing procks galore.
Procks that escaped and got to the top of a mountain were unable
to descend, and either froze to death or starved. Utter nonsense,
said Ellenbogen: skeletons show that the beast's legs were all of
the same length, but were so articulated at the hip and shoulder
that the beast could easily adjust them and go either uphill or
downhill. "I need scarcely say that the traditions of [the prock's]
being unable to turn, and the consequent method of capture, are
mere inventions."

Derby's alter egos spread news about many sciences and scientific inventions. They gave the world two jocose lectures on astronomy and a doubletalk lecture on biology, pontificated about
the causes of Oregon's rains, prescribed an antidote for California's fleas, reviewed an erudite tome on gyroscopes, and
poured out news about a Massachusetts Dental Association meeting. "Phoenix's" interest in dentistry led him to interrupt a

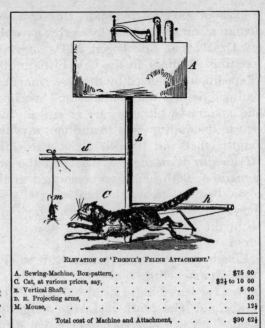

ELEVATION OF 'PHŒNIX'S FELINE ATTACHMENT.'

A. Sewing-Machine, Box-pattern, ...	.	$75 00
C. Cat, at various prices, say, ...	$2¼ to	10 00
B. Vertical Shaft, ...	.	5 00
D. H. Projecting arms, ...	.	50
M. Mouse, ...	.	12¼
Total cost of Machine and Attachment, . . .	.	$90 62¼

One of Phœnix's brilliant inventions. *Knickerbocker Magazine, July 1857*

travel letter to recount feats of a tooth-pulling machine invented by a dentist with "a strong mechanical genius." The machine combined "the lever, pulley, wheel and axle, inclined plane, wedge, and screw." Particularly remarkable was the way it somewhat damaged a little old lady who needed to have a tooth pulled:

at the first turn [it] drew the old lady's skeleton completely and entirely from her body, leaving her a mass of quivering jelly in her chair! Tushmaker took her home in a pillow-case. She lived seven years after that, and they called her the "India-Rubber Woman." She had suffered terribly with the rheumatism, but after this occurrence never had a pain in her bones. The dentist kept them in a glass case. After this, the machine was sold to a contractor . . . , and it was found that a child of three years of age could by a single turn of the screw, raise a stone weighing twenty-three tons. Smaller ones were made . . . and . . . used for boning turkeys. There is no moral to this story whatever, and it is possible that the circumstances may have become slightly exaggerated. Of course, there can be no doubt of the truth of the main incidents.

"Phoenix" himself, by his account, was a great inventor, especially of devices and machines which were forerunners of the complicated inventions of Rube Goldberg in the twentieth century. "J. Poole's Patent Snipe Jagger," advertised in a circular, was an elaborate contraption meant to do away with snipe hunts such as greenhorns conducted.

In the course of [Jim Bridger's] checkered life he saw marvels enough to have formed a stock in trade of a regiment of fair-weather travelers, and of novelists. . . . But the actual marvels of which he had seen so many never satisfied Jim Bridger; he delighted in tough yarns. . . . [He was] the greatest liar on the American continent.—E. A. Curley, Special Correspondent of The London Field, *writing from Wyoming, 1873.*

> *Here lies the famous Dan De Quille,*
> *He lied on earth; he now lies still.*
> *His F-lying soul somewhere did soar,*
> *There to lie forevermore.*
> *—Virginia City* Daily Union, *December 2, 1864.*

24.
Jim Bridger and William Wright

Born in Virginia, Jim Bridger (1804–1881) started his westering at age eight, when his family moved to frontier Missouri. A few years later, he was on his own. He farmed, ran a ferryboat, worked as a roustabout for riverboatmen, and spent five years in a smithy before going out to the Rockies with the Ashley-Henry trapping expedition in 1822. He was still in his teens. Mike Fink, one of that party, was murdered that winter; but Jim lived the hard life of a trapper, Indian fighter, and guide until just before his death at age seventy-seven.

Toward the end, he was commonly called by a nickname as pat as any thought up by a fiction writer, for a man of his sort—Old Gabe. Bernard DeVoto, a leading historian of mountain men, called him "the great" and worshipped him. As Desdemona loved Othello, the writer venerated Old Gabe for the dangers he had passed. He also admired Jim because he was omniscient about the whole Far West—its geography, trails, climate, and topography, and its animal and human inhabitants. Further, he had great skill and fame as a storyteller.

Thanks to chroniclers of the life of the West, Bridger's exploits and personality were discussed in print for many years. There is agreement about his physical makeup—an eagle eye, about six feet tall, well-built, "straight as an arrow," on the slender side, "quick in movement, but not nervous or excitable." Either because he became less assertive or—more probably—because the fashion in heroes changed, as years passed, more and more often writers about him mentioned that he was plain, unassuming, and quiet.

Too often, however, Jim was far from quiet. This was the claim of an army captain whose party Old Gabe led on one expedition. When the group wintered at Fort Laramie, the captain was quartered with him. You get the impression that Jim, though he was often called "polite," left something to be desired as a room-mate. Four times he talked about murdering the captain and was not joking. He had more lice than any one man needed and shared his wealth. And he supported the claims of some historians that frontiersmen adopted animal and Indian ways by ignoring clocks and eating or sleeping whenever he felt like it. Any time sleepiness came—as a rule, early in the afternoon—Jim went to bed. After four, five, or six hours, he got up, built a fire, roasted meat (just about his only food), and devoured it. He was likely to spend the rest of the night beating on a tin pan tom-tom fashion and tunelessly chanting Indian songs.

The captain, finding these habits rather disruptive, did his best to keep his companion awake until at least nine at night by reading to him. He first chose Longfellow's *Hiawatha*, a poem in unrhymed trochaic tetrameter which its author believed was about a race of men which Gabe thought he knew pretty well. The guide hunched down with his gaunt arms wrapped around his knees and listened until some bit that seemed incorrect distressed him, then jumped to his feet, paced, swore at length, with eloquence and feeling, and ended his critique: "It's an infernal lie! No such God-damned Injuns ever lived!"

Fireside readings from Shakespeare fascinated Old Gabe a good many more hours, but in the end got almost as bad an assessment. Enraged by Richard III's faulty morals, Gabe hollered that the Bard of Avon "must have been as devilish mean as a Sioux to write such scoundrelism," and plopped the bard's collected plays into the flames. Some culture rubbed off, though, and the mountain man often uplifted groups by quoting long passages from the plays—accurately, too, except for frequent cusswords with which he embroidered the lines.

Interesting and innovative though these dramatic recitations were, they did not bring Bridger his greatest fame as a campfire performer. His oral storytelling was what won him his chief notoriety throughout the country. His stories took a while to get into print. Major General Grenville Dodge, in his authoritative biographical sketch of 1905, claimed that the "Jim Bridger stories" that survived were not produced until 1860 or even later and were as much the creation of others as of Old Gabe. In particular he blamed E. Z. C. Judson (pen name of Ned Buntline), who had a fantastically varied life (midshipman, soldier, scout, trapper, Indian fighter, temperance lecturer, and journalist) and almost as remarkable a flair for building the fame of various American heroes. In the late 1840's, he initiated the buildup for Mose the Fire b'hoy; later he helped make famous Jim Bridger, Big Foot Wallace, Texas Jack, and Buffalo Bill. He was not as a rule intentionally funny:

In 1860, Buntline

[hunted] up Bridger at his home . . . and Bridger gave him enough adventures to keep him writing the balance of his life. Bridger took a liking to Buntline, and took him across the plains with him on a trip. After a while, Buntline returned to the East, and not long afterwards the Jim Bridger stories commenced to be published. One of these was published every week, and Bridger's companions used to save them up and read them to him. Buntline made Bridger famous.

J. Cecil Alter, the mountain man's most informative biographer, agrees that it was Buntline who transformed the yarns "into chunks of pure gold" so that their teller soon became less known as a frontiersman than as a purveyor of whopping lies. He claims that storytellers all over the place "greedily seized upon" the stories, subjected them to "countless metamorphoses," and blamed them on Bridger. "He happened to encounter the right journalists," says DeVoto, "and his name got attached to the folklore of winter nights that were the profession's rather than his."

Alter was sure that many of the tales assigned to Old Gabe "were hoary with senility when Bridger was born," and that many, in a time-hallowed fashion, had been scrounged from other men and attached to the newer celebrity. Some yarns about extremes of climate in the Far West had a lineage running back to the days of the earliest explorers. A story about Jim's fight with a bear was purloined from Captain R. B. Marcy. The unhappy man whose winter quarters the guide had shared "gives a short version of a popular and widely circulated tale of personal adventure": Six Indians chased Jim to the rim of the Grand Canyon. He killed five, but the sixth—"tallest I ever see"—fought him hand-to-hand with butcher-knives:

> "We wus nearin' the edge of a deep and wide gorge . . . an' a fall to the bottom meant sartin death. . . . It wus a long and fierce struggle. One moment I hed the best of it, an' the next the odds wus agin me. Finally—"
> Here Bridger paused as if to get breath.
> "How did it end?" at length asked one of his breathless listeners anxiously.
> *"The Injun killed me."*

The windy about the petrified forest that *Knickerbocker Magazine* in 1850 had Harris, the profane mountain man, tell the scandalized old maid became Bridger's invention in a dozen variations. In several, Jim showed his illiteracy by mispronouncing "petrified"; the fact adds humor and interest to a variant that tacked on an inspired climax. Jim looked around, the story went, and saw with astonishment that everything—sagebrush, trees, foliage, fruit—was p*ee*trified. He sauntered around, pulled emeralds, rubies, and sapphires as big as black walnuts off branches, and stuffed them into his pockets. Stone rabbits, sagehens, and other critters all stood motionless under p*ee*trified trees, and the air was sweet with p*ee*trified perfumes and the p*ee*trified music of p*ee*trified birds. Riding his horse, Jim suddenly noticed that the animal had stepped off a cliff. He expected to fall to his death on the rocks far below, but the horse trotted across the gulch. Why? "That's just the main wonder of it—the *laws of gravitation* was p*ee*trified!" (This version of the punch line was written by Mark Twain in his notebook for 1889. Unfortunately he wrote no more of the story.)

The historian who cited several variants of this anecdote in his book about Yellowstone Park believes, with Alter, that at least the bit about the law of gravitation "is clearly the work of some later interpolator." A striking thing about "Jim Bridger's lies" was that, when they got into print after 1860, many of them showed more knowledge than a trapper and guide who could neither read nor write was likely to acquire. Popular scientific lore had become mingled with the mountain man's folklore.

The "decidedly scientific nature" of another story attributed to Jim caused another writer to include it in his account of the exploration of the Yellowstone River. Old Gabe, it went, told about a remarkable experience that he had when fishing in the headwaters of the Columbia River high in the mountains. The mountain trout he pulled out were cold as ice. But he found that just by lowering them, still on your hook, to the bottom, you could cook your catch. You see, down there the water runs over the rocks so far and so fast that sheer friction brings it to a boil.

Jim remembered the Winter of the Big Snow in the Great Salt Lake valley. Seventy days the stuff fell without stopping, averaging a foot a day, until the whole country was piled high with seventy feet of snow. All the buffalo herds in the valley were caught in the storm and froze to death. Their carcasses were perfectly preserved, though, and "when spring came, all I had to do was tumble 'em into Salt Lake an' I had pickled buffalo enough for myself and the whole Ute nation for years."

Salt water figured in another "Bridger Lie"—the one about Old Gabe's sure way to learn the altitude of any place: "Just bore down until you strike salt water, then measure the depth."

"You been here long?" a tenderfoot asked Bridger. "Well, you see Scott's Bluffs over there? About four hundred feet high. When I first came here, there warn't no bluffs there—only a deep gulch."

The knowledge of geology which made it possible for the journalists' Jim to make this calculation also enabled him to make a joke about gauging the passage of time in a fertile area: he noticed that a stone which he had tossed across the Sweetwater grew up and became Independence Rock.

Finally, there was the time Jim—so he said—sighted a huge elk, took aim, and fired. The elk paid no heed whatever, just stood there chewing his cud. Jim fired three more carefully aimed shots, and the elk still ignored him. Steaming with anger,

Jim decided to club the ornery critter to death, grabbed his rifle by the barrel, and rushed toward him. Next thing Jim knew, he had smashed against something that was hard, immovable, and invisible; it sent him sprawling. What he had hit was a crystal rock mountain, so flawless that it worked like a telescopic lens and made an animal twenty-five miles away appear to be within easy shooting distance. Talking with other old-timers, Bridger found that by good luck, they had learned about the thing less painfully:

You see, a lot of bones and carcasses of animals an' birds wus found scattered all around the base. You see they ran or flew against this invisible rock and jest killed themselves dead. You kin feel the rock an' that's all. . . . It's a good many miles high, for everlastin' quantities of bird's bones are jest piled up all around the base of it.

Derby emigrated from New England, Bridger from Virginia and later Missouri, and William Wright (1829–1898) from the Midwest. Wright's birthplace was Ohio; Iowa was his home when, still in his teens, he started as a reporter. In 1857, at age twenty-eight, he moved to the Far West. He mined in California and Washoe before getting a job in 1862 reporting for the Virginia City *Territorial Enterprise*. This newspaper, having been in business two years, was the area's oldest. Put out by a rip-roaring gang of editors, writers, and printers, it was also the liveliest, and most popular in the Nevada Territory and beyond. For a while, it had a larger circulation in San Francisco than did any local paper, and some of its pieces traveled as far as the Eastern seaboard and even crossed the Atlantic.

Wright was a top *Enterprise* reporter and editor until it suspended publication in 1893. He contributed acres of items signed "Dan De Quille" not only to it but also to other newspapers and magazines, Western, Midwestern, and Eastern. After Virginia City had nearly died, had been revivified by new finds and had been clouted by a disastrous fire, he put together the best history of the Comstock Lode, *The Big Bonanza* (1876). Mark Twain, who had been a co-reporter, room-mate and hellraiser with him in the 1860's, invited him to travel to Hartford and be his guest so that he could give him a hand in writing. Twain then peddled the history to his own publisher with an introduction signed "Mark Twain."

During his thirty-one-year stint on the *Enterprise*, Dan ground out copy of every sort, ranging from deadly serious to playful and from low-grade to superior. The quality and nature of the humor also varied a great deal. Often Dan reused the oldest jokes, perhaps routinely, perhaps with original touches. Twice in just thirteen pages of *The Big Bonanza*, he told the fashionable postwar anecdote about the braggart who feared to fight and ran away. The first account—about the Wild Boar of Tehama and the little miner who scares him into jumping head-first out of a saloon window—is undistinguished. The second and longer version, featuring "the Taranterler of Calaveras, a war horse from the hills and the fighter from hell," has some good moments when the cowardly braggart thinks up excuses for not fighting— a feature of European tales which Americans tend to neglect: "Mr. Jones, this man is a friend of yours. I can't fight any friend of yours. . . . Now, your friend is of the right stripe; I like his looks. Thar's no use of two good men a-fightin' for nothin'. . . . I can't fight in a room . . . never had a fight in a room. I don't like it." The list of illnesses and cures that De Quille works into his explanation of the duties of a Nevada state mineralogist has ancestors that date back to the Middle Ages and include American medicine show spielers; but it has a few new twists:

He is to discover earthquakes and provide suitable means for the extermination of the same; also, for book-agents, erysipelas, corn doctors, cerebrospinal meningitis and the Grecian bend . . . splice out short rainbows, cure warts free of charge, and furnish antidotes for harelip, nightmares, corners in stocks [and] twins. . . . Should he at any time discover in any part of the State indications of milk sickness, female suffrage, poison-oak or choke-damp, he will forthwith proceed to make an assay of the same, and, having extracted the cube root, will deposit it among the Pacific Coast Pioneers; with a recommendation to the mercy of the Court.

This pretty well covers the essential thing: it shuffles together highly incongruous items. And the modernization of the Super Ugly Man joke—about Mark Twain's looks after a boxing instructor "busted Mr. Twain on the snoot"—is fairly amusing:

His nose is swollen to such an extent that to fall on his breast would be an utter impossibility. . . . After dark, he ventured forth with his nose swollen to the size of several junk bottles—a vast, inflamed and pulpy old snoot—to get advice about having it amputated. None of his friends recognize him now, and he spends his time in solitude, contemplating his ponderous vermillion smeller in a two-bit mirror. . . . we know his nose will never be a nose again. It always was somewhat lopsided; now it is a perfect lump of blubber. Since the above was in type, the doctors have decided to amputate poor Mark Twain's smeller. A new one will be made for him of a quarter of veal.

(This was written more than three decades before Rostand penned *Cyrano de Bergerac*.)

De Quille shows he knows about at least one forerunner of his when he writes that "Judge Grand," seven of whose yarns he retells, "most assuredly deserved the title of 'Münchausen the Second,' which was sometimes applied to him." Grand, he says, known to hundreds of Westerners under another name, "always [lied] about his own wonderful exploits, and [told] such outrageously whopping whoppers" that no ten-year-old child could swallow them. "He would relate his stories with such wonderful gravity that I believe he had become firmly convinced that every word he uttered was true as gospel."

By contrast, Dan De Quille's lies, though grave, were deliberate concoctions carefully adorned with "scientific" plausibility. C. Grant Loomis, who explored vast stretches of De Quille's writings, picked a bouquet of his tall tales, analyzed them, and decided what this humorist's sole "departure from the usual tradition of lying" was: "The most successful and certainly the most widely publicized and generally remembered . . . fabrications are those which depend upon a belief in the miracles of the scientific age, whether it be on the side of natural lore or in the vastly expanding field of amazing inventions." Loomis thought this belief flourished when Dan's scientifantasies appeared because discoveries and inventions publicized daily had led readers to be "immediately open to any suggestion of new wonders, provided the matter was put forth in an authoritative and documented presentation." De Quille took full advantage of this ready-made credulity.

Dan's Nevada was as full of stupefactions as the New World had been for Elizabethans. He told about world-shaking discoveries such as that of "a hot spring of considerable size, the water of which, when properly seasoned . . . cannot be distinguished from the best chicken soup"—the source of a cheap supply for eateries and a boon for "invalids with weak stomachs." Another find was a pile of stones that constantly emitted "a peculiar, low musical tinkling sound . . . coming and going like the notes of an aeolian harp." Other stones, scattered on a level surface, mysteriously "began traveling toward a common center, and then huddled up in a bunch." Dan gave news of inventors who made seventeenth-century sorcerers and ingenious nineteenth-century Yankee inventors look like pikers. One used a pump encased in an air-tight cylinder to extract an *Enterprise* editor's rheumatism from his leg and stretched him until he became a giant "thirteen feet six inches in length." One attached a plunger-pump column to a bell-shaped muzzle and used the contraption to suck schools of fish out of Lake Tahoe. Other inventions were a crematorium which reduced any cadaver to ashes for six bits; a "Tabaksine" that stored tobacco smoke and ended the need to carry tobacco and cut down risks of fires; and a windmill rigged "to hoist loose sand during hours when the wind blew, in addition to the usual load of water, and to arrange for having this sand operate turbine wheels and thus keep on pumping after the wind had died"— perpetual motion.

De Quille salted his "quaints," as he called articles about these and other phenomena, with learning picked up in mines and behind his mining-town newspaper desk—statistics, explanations, dates, "natural" laws, Latin terms, and the names of places, discoverers, inventors, testers, witnesses, and authorities. The aim was to "prove" his stories true— to bring about a willing suspension of disbelief permanently, or at least for a long, long time. Dan, in other words, wrote in the tradition—discussed in the chapter on Franklin's monsters—of *The Shortest-Way* and "The Sale of the Hessians" rather than that of *A Modest Proposal* and "Rules by Which a Great Empire May Be Reduced to a Small One." Typically, he tried to fool his readers, and he was tickled pink when he succeeded.

So he gloated when a Boston engineer wrote an article in a professional journal okaying Dan's perpetual-motion machine and calculating the exact horsepower it could produce. He was pleased when P. T. Barnum offered him "ten grand" to stage performances of the traveling stones in his circus and when a

German society studying electromagnetic currents had its secretary ask "Herrn Doktor Dan De Quille, Physiker von Virginiastadt" for more particulars about the stones. He was disappointed when his longest, most detailed and documented quaint—the one about "a 'Silver Man' found in a mine between Esmeralda and Owen's River"—failed to take in anybody.

Dan's most famous scientific tall tale, "Sad Fate of an Inventor," told the story of how "Mr. Jonathan Newhouse, a man of considerable inventive genius," tested his suit of solar armor, an elaborate apparatus which the writer described in detail. The thing was "intended to protect the owner from the fierce heat of the sun in crossing deserts and burning alkaline plains" by keeping its wearer refrigerated:

Mr. Newhouse went down to Death Valley, determined to try the experiment of crossing that horrible place in his armor. He started out into the valley one morning from the camp nearest its borders, telling the men at the camp, as he laced his armor on his back, that he would return in two days. The next day an Indian who could speak but a few words of English came to the camp in a great state of excitement. He made the men understand that he wanted them to follow him. At the distance of about twenty miles out into the desert the Indian pointed to a human figure seated against a rock. Approaching, they found Newhouse still in his armor. He was dead and frozen stiff. His beard was covered with frost and—though the noonday sun poured down its fiercest rays—an icicle over a foot in length hung from his nose. There he perished miserably, because his armor had worked too well, and because it was laced behind where he could not reach the fastener.

Reprinted in newspapers in America and overseas, this bagged a great many victims. A friend sent De Quille a marked copy of the London *Times*, to which an officer had written a letter urging that British soldiers in India be supplied with the armor. The London *Daily Telegraph* asked for "some additional confirmation before we unhesitatingly accept [the tale]." De Quille welcomed the chance to supply proofs and to scuttle some silly rumors that had been published about the device. "A Mystery Explained," a much longer piece than the original one, added facts galore that had been "made available" since the first report appeared. These had been supplied by "one David Baxter, who states that he is Justice of Peace and ex officio Coroner of Salt Wells, a station in Inyo County, California, situated at the head of the sink of Amargosa River, at the north end of Death Valley." Having held an inquest, Baxter was able to correct inadvertent errors in the first piece. For instance, he could now say that the content of the India rubber sack used to soak the armor was not simply water but a mixture of seven chemicals with water. This was a typical elaboration.

Ironically, Wright's playful label for his pseudo-scientific pieces now seems more apt than he could possibly have guessed. Today's readers cannot help but feel that, sure enough, his ingenious fabrications are "quaint." Inventors and men of science who succeeded in outmoding so many ancient values have played hob with old-time Far Western humor. Yesterday's wildest imaginings have become today's probabilities. For instance, we, with freezers and air-conditioners, who have watched astronauts in lunar armor lope around on the moon, cannot find improbable the idea of a fool inventor in solar armor freezing to death out on a California desert. And when the fantasy behind the scientific tall tales of Derby, Bridger and Wright eroded, their jests lost much of their comic impact.

Other times, other fantasies. Even nightmares have to be modernized now and then before we can laugh at them or melt them into science fiction.

Part Three

"And the War Came"

Changes in Jokelore

> Both of [the bragging raftsmen]
> was edging away in different directions, growling and shaking their
> heads and going on about what they were going to do; but a little
> black-whiskered chap skipped up and says:—
> "Come back here, you couple of chicken-livered cowards, and I'll
> thrash the two of ye!"
> And he done it, too. He snatched them, he jerked them this way and
> that, he booted them around, he knocked them sprawling faster than
> they could get up. Why, it war n't two minutes till they begged like
> dogs. . . . Little Davy made them own up that they was sneaks and
> cowards. . . .—Huckleberry Finn on his visit to the raft in Mark
> Twain, *Life on the Mississippi (1883).*

25.
Twilight of the Comic Demigods

IN 1852 AN OBSCURE PLAY-
wright, George L. Aiken, dramatized that year's best-seller, Harriet Beecher Stowe's *Uncle Tom's Cabin*. After making a stir as
a serial, this sensational crusading work in book form sold
305,000 copies in twelve months: a per capita sale today would
be 2,750,000. Aiken played up and enlarged theatrical elements
in the story and threw in crowd-pleasers of his own, and the play
had long runs in Northern cities.

That was just the start. Sales of the book dwindled and at last
ended. But in provincial theaters from the Atlantic to the Pacific,
in showboats on the waterways and wide-ranging tent shows, the
play was a box-office bonanza for more than a century. God-
fearing men and women who stayed away from other plays
went, whenever they had a chance, to *Uncle Tom's Cabin*. The
characters and scenes that the public came to know weren't, as

a rule, those of the book but those in the six-act drama. Though surprises were no longer possible, viewers still loved the exciting parts. They also doted on two kinds of scenes that Aiken alternated in almost equal doses with thrilling segments. One kind brought tender tears, the other belly laughs. Since many audiences like to died laughing at them, these fantastically popular scenes show what consistently tickled hordes of Americans between the 1850's and the 1950's.

The nearest thing to a folk play that this country has produced got guffaws by having an array of comic stereotypes do their traditional stuff.

Topsy, a favorite clown, had a first entrance line that placed her: "I 'spects I's de wickedest critter in de world." She would repeat the catch phrase each time she came onstage. So she was a mischievous kid who played pranks on nervous oldsters. Soon a stage direction further type-cast her: "Song and dance introduced." It, too, would be repeated. Here and elsewhere, blacked-up Topsy, dressed in bright tatters and spouting dialect, sang, joked, and "jumped Jim Crow"—a minstrel show darky chucked into a drama.

She was by no means the only such character. Records show, surprisingly, that in many performances, saintly Uncle Tom, taking off his halo, did *entr' acte* minstrel-show hoedowns, songs, and Brother Bones monologues. As if this wasn't enough, two other men in blackface, Sambo and Quimbo, played ethnic tricks on white villains.

White characters are just as easy to spot as holdovers. Phineas, a low-comedy Kentucky roarer, talked the old lingo: "Chaw me up into tobaccy ends! . . . Bring us a jug of whisky instantaneously, or expect to be teetotally chawed up! . . . That river looks like a permiscuous ice-cream shop come to an awful state of friz." For an added incongruity, when this fire-breather was made to fall in love with "the teetotalist pretty girl" along the Mississippi, she converted him to her Quaker faith and he mixed "verilys," "thees," "thous" and pleas for peace with his "chaw me's" and "vamooses."

Gumption Cute, a Yankee gyp artist, did everything that brought a dishonest dime—spirit rapping, displaying sideshow freaks (like his acknowledged model, Barnum), "speculating" (like Simon Suggs), playing on sympathies for war veterans (like Timbertoes and Sawin), and doing a spot of blackmailing. His talk recalled that of Wetmore's auctioneer and foreshadowed that of W. C. Fields when he called Topsy "Charcoal," "Stove Polish" and "My Ebony Angel." At least once he was treated to a ride out of town on a rail. (This hilarious punishment dated back in our humor to 1782.)

Ophelia was a pious and prissy Vermont spinster who vainly tried to bring Yankee organization to the chaotic St. Clair household—a natural victim of Topsy's rambunctious ripoffs. And during a series of farcical misunderstandings, she was wooed and won by another type of character, a successor to Parson Wilbur— the sanctimonious and pedantic Deacon Perry.

So the play gathered a bouquet of antebellum posies, and thanks in large part to these, long after slavery was outlawed, the comic-sentimental melodrama was one of the most popular of all American plays. The comedy actually was broadened over the years until *two* Topsies and *two* minstrel-show Uncle Toms doubled the fun. And for decades after the Civil War ended, as has been indicated, other plays with big helpings of prewar humor—about Yankees, Davy Crockett, and Mose the Fire b'hoy— kept delighting audiences.

Books helped the plays reincarnate humor. Whenever it is possible to count editions, enumerations show that popular writings from the golden age of comedy long endured. Between 1852 and 1880, at least a hundred and thirty editions of books by ten leading Eastern and Southwestern humorists were issued. During the same period, nineteen anthologies helped circulate such writings. *Sut Lovingood's Yarns*—the greatest humorous book of the antebellum decades—wasn't compiled by its author until 1867; thereafter, for at least seven decades, the book was never out of print. Reminiscent Southerners say that many men in their section kept *Sut* hidden behind respectable volumes on the backs of library bookshelves.

This, of course, doesn't mean that the Civil War and the revolution which it speeded and confirmed did not shape so vital an expression as our humor. The irresistible drive toward the conflict, the awful war, and the disturbing aftermath shaped every type of expression, no matter how high or low.

Today, perhaps better than at any other time, Americans should be able to understand and sympathize with the psychic reactions to the traumas of the second half of the nineteenth century. These included shifts in power, disorderly demonstrations, raids, riots, executions, burnings, the bloodiest war in history up to that time, a nation torn in two, lynchings, feuds, the discovery of corruption in high places, the assassination of one President and the impeachment of another, and a revolution in the ways of living.

Tomes have been written about the tremendous changes that the Civil War dramatized and quickened. Political dominance, the studies notice, moved from states and sections to the country's capital. A rising industrial North and an agricultural Midwest bullied a South that was hard hit by economic problems, then defeat in war, and then by what ironically was called "the Reconstruction period." The Great West, soon made accessible by railways, became increasingly important. The railways, steel mills, factories, banking houses, stock markets, and the tycoons that they enriched, all flourished prodigiously.

Leading authors show that the changes brought great uneasiness and even distress. Walt Whitman's faith in the antebellum years had led him to say in his Preface to the 1855 edition of *Leaves of Grass:*

The United States themselves are essentially the greatest poem. In the history of the earth hitherto the largest and most stirring [nations] appear tame and orderly to their ample largeness and stir. Here at last is something in the doings of man that corresponds with the broadcast doings of the day and night.

The contrast of his later attitude, as he stated it in *Democratic Vistas* in 1871, is striking:

The depravity of the business classes of our country is not less than has been supposed, but infinitely greater. The official services of America, national, state, and municipal, in all their branches and departments, except the judiciary, are saturated in corruption, bribery, falsehood, mal-administration; and the judiciary is tainted. The great cities reek with respectable as much as non-respectable robbery and scoundrelism. . . . I say that our New World democracy . . . is, so far, an almost complete failure. . . .

When Henry Adams came back to America after spending the Civil War years in London, this scion of an old family found his homeland so changed that—so he said—he hardly recognized it. In his novel *Democracy* (1880), he had a cynical ambassador summarize his own personal disillusionment:

I have lived seventy-five years, and all that time in the midst of corruption. . . . Rome, Paris, Vienna, Petersburg, London, all are corrupt. . . . Well I declare to you that in all my experience I have found no society which has had elements of corruption like the United States. The children in the streets are corrupt. . . . Everywhere men betray trusts both public and private, steal money, run away with public funds. . . . you gentlemen in the Senate very well declare that your great United States . . . can never learn anything from the example of corrupt Europe. You are right—quite right! The great United States needs not an example.

A couple of authors of a satirical novel of 1873 paused a minute to make a serious forecast:

The eight years in America from 1860 to 1868 uprooted institutions that were centuries old, changed the politics of a people, transformed the social life of half the country, and wrought so profoundly upon the entire national character that the influence cannot be measured short of two or three generations.

The prediction, in *The Gilded Age*, by Charles Dudley Warner and Mark Twain, was sound except in two particulars. The change started rather earlier than 1860—about 1854 or 1855. And the guess about how long the upheaval would affect American life was too conservative. More than a hundred years later, it still shaped aspects of our life, our thinking, and our literature.

Since many forces are usually at work, it is easy to oversimplify causes for changes in even an uncomplicated area—such as most believe humor is. But it seems safe to say that the war and the transformations accompanying it were largely responsible for changes in (1) the ancient American pattern of jokes about fighting braggarts, including our comic demigods, (2) the comedy in regional fiction, and (3) popular newspaper and lecture-hall humor.

Look first at what happened to the swaggerers who had fought so fiercely with one another during prewar days: *Götterdämmerung*.

Two swaggering bully boys—Americanized *alazons*—ring-tailed roarers—bandy boasts, have a fierce fight in which both powerful fighters get battered; the better man is the winner. This was the older three-part story told about frontiersmen and the legendary Mike Fink. Davy Crockett, in sanctified reincarnations courtesy of melodramatists and Walt Disney, became a little less boastful but carried on in much the same way. Of course, the pattern was not discarded; it has not disappeared to this day.

But during the new era, a different pattern which has some very good points turned up more and more often. In it, the man who claims to be more than he is meets a man who's self-deprecating—an *eiron*. Max Eastman's description of the joke in the form that tickled the ancient Greeks and others in the Old World will help define the increasingly popular design:

It is characteristic of the Greek view of life that the triumph of the *eiron* over the *alazon* became almost a settled convention of their comic theater. . . . Comedy, you might say, was born into the world as a playing off of the one against the other. And the word *irony* arose out of this crude clash. It described the "taking down" of the big talker [the *alazon*] by the man who says less than he means [the *eiron*]. . . . Unfortunately our national comedy, which ought to have brought into conflict these two characters, never got written. Here as elsewhere American literature is unachieved.

"Never" is too strong a word. The soft-spoken character actually took the braggart down in "A Row at 'Natchy Under the Hill,' " *Davy Crockett's Almanack 1838*, a story that Davy tells about a clash he saw in one of the gathering and fighting places for Mississippi boatmen:

Close to the wharf, upon the deck of a broadhorn, stood a fellow of powerful muscular appearance, and every now and then he would swing around his arms and throw out a challenge to any one *"who dared come and take the rust off of him,"* styling himself a *"roarer,"* and declaring that he hadn't had a fight in a month, and was getting lazy. . . .

Presently a little stubbed fellow came along, . . . stepped up, and in a dry kind of style looked up in his face and inquired, "Who might ye be, my big chicken, eh?"

"I'm a high pressure steamer," roared the big bully.

"And I'm a snag," replied the little one, as he pitched into him, and before he had time to reflect, he was sprawling upon the deck. A general shout of applause burst from the spectators, and many now, who before had stood aloof from the braggadocia, jumped on board the boat and enjoyed the manner in which the little fellow pummeled him.

In 1852, a sketch called "The Dandy Frightening the Squatter" appeared in an Eastern humor magazine, *The Carpet-Bag*. The setting was a woodyard on the Mississippi at which a steamboat was docked. "A spruce young dandy, with a killing moustache, &c. who seemed bent on making an impression," sighted a woodsman quietly leaning against a tree. The dandy boasted that he would scare the fellow, stuck a bowie knife into his belt, took a horse pistol in each hand, swaggered ashore, and told the loafer: "Say your prayers! . . . you'll make a capital barn door, and I shall drill the key-hole myself!" "The squatter calmly surveyed him a moment, and then, drawing back a step, he planted his huge fist directly between the eyes of his astonished antagonist, who, in a moment, was floundering in the muddy water of the Mississippi." As the boat's passengers shouted approval, the "crest-fallen hero" sneaked back to the boat, and his conqueror spoke for the first time: "I say, yeou, nest time yeou come around drillin' key-holes, don't forget yer old acquaintances!" The sketch, crude though it is, has been studied endlessly because scholars have decided that, coming as it did from Hannibal, Missouri, and signed "S.L.C.," it was the first published piece by one Samuel L. Clemens who, a bit more than a decade later, would become the famous Mark Twain.

The Crockett sketch and "The Dandy Frightening the Squatter," among others, show that the old plot and the payoff—even in the former, Spenser's "Braggadocio" misspelled—weren't unknown in the New World. Nevertheless, Eastman's claim about the conflict between the blow-hard and the ironic man is correct if it is slightly amended: the confrontation of the pair, and the triumph of the latter over the former, was relatively infrequent up to a point. In defining that point, one can't be precise, since what Eastman calls "the man who says less than he means" defies definition. But a portent can be noticed, then a definite change.

Beginning about 1850, in newly surfacing stories, Mike Fink was unable to lick anybody. (In "Deacon Smith's Bull, or Mike Fink in a Tight Place," which appeared in the Milton, Pa., *Miltonian*, *The Spirit of the Times* [New York] and the Hannibal, Mo., *Courier* in 1851, the author, Scroggins, has Mike tell the story of his encounter with a bull which bested him. He quotes one of the onlookers: "Mike Fink has got the *wust of the scrim-*

mage once in his life!") And his opponents had some resemblances to traditional *eirons*. The victor who in an 1850 story "battered poor Fink so that he fainted away" was a female; the man who gave Mike his lumps and made him pray, in a story published five times between 1850 and 1860, was a preacher; and the fellow who in an 1874 anecdote knocked him cold was a Sunday school type who had promised his mommy not to fight. But since the female was the helliferous Mrs. Crockett, the preacher had "a herculanean fist" and made threats, and the mother-loving youth had a pate hard enough to bang Mike's head into insensibility, they were all a bit too tough to qualify.

The story about Mike printed in 1883, though, conformed quite well to the Old World pattern. Mike, whom it called "an extravagant boaster" and a "regular 'Salt River Roarer,' " ashore at Westport, told jokes and made it perfectly clear that listeners had damn well better laugh heartily at them. "In a corner sat a small, quiet-looking man, evidently much abstracted, and deeply bent on attending to his own business." When he failed to laugh at several jokes, Mike went over to him, touched him, and told him:

it would pay him to heed the first-class jokes . . . , for if he didn't, somebody would get hurt. "Ah," said the quiet man, "is that so," and he immediately lapsed into his reverie.

The next joke was told and duly enjoyed, but no laugh came from the corner of the quiet man, and Mike . . . went over to him, and told him he intended to whip him. "Ah, indeed," said the man, "is that so?" and hardly were the words out of his mouth, than with a tremendous blow under the ear he struck the giant, felling him. . . . Fink made for the stranger, who slipped down upon his back and began that fight with the feet for which so many of the borderers were noted, and in a few minutes a worse whipped man than the jolly flatboatman was never seen.

When Fink called for quarter, or, as he expressed it, "hollered calf rope," the quiet man said to him: "I am Ned Taylor, sheriff of this county; if you don't board your boat and push off in five minutes, I'll arrest you and your crew." To this Fink did not demur, and was soon floating down the Ohio.

The same year this account of the sheriff's triumph appeared, "by way of illustrating keelboat talk and manners," Mark Twain published in *Life on the Mississippi* the finest American version of the old, old story, written in 1876 for *Huckleberry Finn* but not included in that book. It was part of Huck's report of what he heard and saw one night when he swam out to a raft, hid among some bundles of shingles, and eavesdropped on a crew of spifflicated raftsmen. Corpse-Maker, the biggest of the lot, and the Child of Calamity each in turn told how ferocious he was. Their boasts were inventions that even we, the authors, enjoyed reading—even after a wide-ranging search which ended with our getting a little fed up with comic boasts.

Corpse-Maker leaped three times and cracked his heels together with each jump, then hollered statistics about his family, his appetite, and other matters. Sample: "Sired by a hurricane, dam'd by an earthquake, half-brother to the cholera, nearly related to the small-pox on my mother's side! . . . I take nineteen alligators and a bar'l of whiskey for breakfast when I'm in robust health, and a bushel of rattlesnakes and a dead body when I'm ailing! . . . Blood's my natural drink, and the wails of the dying is music to my ear!"

The Child of Calamity outdid him. During acrobatic gyrations (standard ornaments of brags), he twice got cheers by performing what must have been an *entrechat-six* ("jumped and cracked his heels together three times before he lit"). And he told about mishandlings of cosmography that rival similar feats in Rabelais and Davy Crockett's *Almanack* story about loosening the earth's axis:

"When I'm playful I use the meridians of longitude and parallels of latitude for a seine, and drag the Atlantic Ocean for whales! I scratch my head with the lightning and purr myself to sleep with the thunder! When I'm cold, I bile the Gulf of Mexico and bathe in it; when I'm hot I fan myself with an equinoctial storm; when I'm thirsty I reach up and suck a cloud dry like a sponge; when I range the earth hungry, famine follows in my tracks! Whoo-oop! Bow your neck and spread! I put my hand on the sun's face and make it night in the earth; I bite a piece out of the moon and hurry the seasons; I shake myself and crumple the mountains! . . . The massacre of isolated communities is the pastime of my idle moments, the destruction of nationalities the serious business of my life!"

After shouting these fine words, the two raftsmen, Huck says, made even more dire threats, but in time it was evident that neither was going to strike a blow, and eventually, they started

Little Davy knocked Corpse-Maker and the Child of Calamity sprawling, from *Life on the Mississippi* (1883).

to edge away from one another. Then came the passage which appears as an epigraph to this chapter (p. 251), wherein the little black-whiskered Davy steps up and wallops the both of them.

About the time this was published, so Mody Boatright says, a story was current on the frontier which by now had replaced Kentucky, the Mississippi River, and the Rockies as the land of the toughest—cowboy country.

An Easterner came into a cow town, galloped up and down the street howling and firing his six-shooter, and marched into a saloon "chanting a boast he had recently heard":

> Just then the marshal, who had been sitting quietly at a table, arose and addressed him.
> "So you are a wolf, are you?"
> "Yes, I'm a wolf."
> "Well, what kind of a wolf are you?"
> "Oh, me? I'm just a little old coyote."

And in 1884, A. J. Sowell, in *Rangers and Pioneers in Texas*, claimed that the standard procedure was for the braggart to be put down by a quiet friend:

> Occasionally in some Western village, you will hear a voice ring out in the night air in words something like these: "Wild and wooly," "Hard to curry," "Raised a pet but gone wild," . . . "Hide out, little

ones," and then you may expect a few shots from a revolver. It is a cowboy out on a little spree, but likely he will not hurt anyone, as some friend who is sober generally comes to him, relieves him of his pistol, and all is soon quiet again.

George Hendricks's wide reading about Wild West ruckuses, summarized in *The Bad Men of the West* (1941), led him to decide that "the swaggering, blustering, or bragging kind" of a tough guy was not the typical bad man; the real article "was usually quiet, soft-spoken, mild-mannered."

H. L. Davis in his 1952 *Winds of the Morning*, enlivened a paragraph by briefly referring to the postwar version:

. . . a little sandy-mustached man with glasses who had been telling around that he was from a country where people used rusty barbed-wire for toilet paper and the canary birds sang bass, and that he had been run out of it for being too tough . . . stretched out on the [jail] floor limp and subdued, sleeping it off as meek as a moon flower in a meadow.

Skip to the present decade. When young Richard Pryor, one of the most successful American comedians, performed in 1975, his audiences shouted requests that he act out one of his most popular characterizations: "Do Oilwell! Do Oilwell!" In the sketch, a belligerent black street-corner tough swaggers and yells his answer to policemen who tell him to move along. "I'm Oilwell, six-foot-five, two hundred and twenty-two pounds of *Mannn!* I ain't goin' no *Where!* He go'n to *Mooove* me!" Thereupon Oilwell is thoroughly beaten up by the men in uniform, and the audience—largely black—howls with laughter. "It does not matter," writes James McPherson, "that Oilwell is beaten. . . . What matters is that Pryor's audiences can laugh at Oilwell's pretensions."

The comic strip "Rick O'Shay" for January 25, 1976, had a braggart cowboy tell another cowboy, Hipshot, the hero of the cartoon, that he is calling him out. "All right, kid," says Hipshot. "But first, what sort of *funeral* arrangements would you like?" In a series of panels, he reads from the local undertaker's brochure descriptions of various options. The challenger shows growing distress, and in the last panel stumbles away, saying, "I . . . I've got a feelin' that even if I *beat* him, I'd lose."

A few months later, in a news story, Charles Mohr reported

Jimmy Carter's use of "a rare joke" during his campaign for the Democratic presidential nomination. It was "about a mild young man who settles a barroom dispute with a bully by using a tire tool." Mohr added: "The joke is almost a trademarked part of Gov. George C. Wallace's repertoire."

As conscientious historians, we of course wonder about the reasons for changes which so often occur in the plot of the boast-and-battle story. We think of five that don't have to be mutually exclusive.

As Boatright, Sowell, and Hendricks imply, the later version perhaps became popular simply because it was truer to life. Another possibility: it became widespread because it was funnier. Still another possibility: after a time, becoming tired of the older formula, authors were attracted by a different one. And since the Old World plot had been kicking around for centuries, and since even hack writers probably read books and saw plays, literary influences may have got in some licks as well. Probably the cataclysmic Civil War and its aftermath also helped bring about this change.

*His first wife, a delicate, pretty
little woman, had suffered keenly and secretly from the jealous suspicions of her husband, until one day he invited the whole Bar to his
house to expose her infidelity. On arriving, the party found the shy,
petite creature quietly engaged in her household duties, and retired
abashed and discomfited. But the sensitive woman did not easily recover from the shock of this extraordinary outrage. It was with difficulty she regained her equanimity sufficiently to release her lover
from the closet in which he was concealed, and escape with him. She
left a boy of three years to comfort her bereaved husband.*

—Bret Harte, 1872.

26.
The Local
Colorists

WHILE BITTER PEACETIME DE-
bates, a devastating war, and a contentious Reconstruction period tore the nation apart, a paradoxical change took place in regional fiction. A large group of its authors drifted or marched
into ways of writing that—it was believed—fostered national
unity. The group, which reigned well beyond the end of the century, were the local colorists.

Looking back, we see signs of the drift which at the time were
not much noticed. There is, for instance, the remark of a critic in
1853: "Local reality is a point of the utmost importance." Between 1850 and 1860, a dozen novels or collections of stories
backed his claim by portraying in detail the folk and the life of
New York City, rural New England, Southern plantations, and
frontier Ohio, Michigan, Alabama, and Mississippi.

Through the 1870's and beyond, growing numbers of regional
stories appeared. Newly founded periodicals, much more high-
toned than the newspapers and specialized magazines that had
printed antebellum regional humor, were increasingly hospitable: *Harper's Monthly* (1850-   ), *Putnam's Monthly* (1853-
1910), *Harper's Weekly* (1857-1916), *The Atlantic Monthly*
(1858-   ), *Appleton's Journal* (1869-1881), and *Scribner's*

Monthly (1870-1881, renamed *The Century* and published under that name, 1881-1930). Most stories featured in these magazines came out in book form. The books were issued by houses which were, for the most part, far more respectable than the sleazy publishers of prewar humorous books. Local colorists were encouraged by payments not only in cash but also in prestige.

Two writers who had become famous in the prewar period for crusading antislavery writings became important local colorists. Both had written about New England life and characters earlier without anything like the success that they now achieved with regional writings. In 1866, John Greenleaf Whittier published *Snow-Bound: A Winter Idyl*, which he called "a picture of an old-fashioned farmer's fireside"—a loving evocation of boyhood remembrances. His first royalty check signaled a cordial response that would last for years; it was for ten thousand dollars. Harriet Beecher Stowe in 1859, 1862, and 1869 published three highly praised and successful books re-creating life in Massachusetts and Connecticut as she and her husband had known it in childhood. The last had a representative title, *Oldtown Folks*.

In 1870 young Bret Harte made such a stir with regional pieces that some contemporaries credited him with launching, single-handed, the local color movement. *The Luck of Roaring Camp, and Other Stories* assembled narratives recently published in *Overland Monthly* and reprinted throughout the country. That same year Harte's humorous poem, "Plain Language from Truthful James," attracted even wider attention. In 1871, with a fat contract from the *Atlantic* for twelve months' exclusive output, Harte left California for the East, never to return. For the rest of his life, he would work (and eventually exhaust) the rich Gold Rush vein.

Harte's sensational success speeded the movement. Along with the *Atlantic*, other prestigious magazines pleaded for manuscripts of the fashionable sort. Some actually sent out scouts to hunt down and sign up new regional fictionists. Local colorists got into the act everywhere. A footnote which lists more than fifty of the most prominent ones, along with the territory of each, gives an idea of the thorough way they covered the nation.*

---

* James Lane Allen (Ky.), Gertrude Atherton (Ca.), Sherwood Bonner (Ms., La., Tn.), Virginia Frazer Boyle (Tn.), Alice Brown (N.H.), George W. Cable (La.),

A passage in Alfred Henry Lewis's "The Man from Red Dog" (1897), a yarn spun by the Old Cattleman about Arizona, has a familiar ring:

"All promenade to the bar," yells the Red Dog man. . . . "I'm a wolf, an' it's my night to howl. . . . I hears sech complaints constant of this yere camp of Wolfville, I takes my first idle day to ride over an' line things up. . . . I finds you-all is a lawless, onregenerate set. . . . By next drink time I climbs into the saddle, throws my rope 'round this den of sin, an' removes it from the map."

"Nacherally," says Enright, some sarcastic, "in makin' them schemes you ain't lookin' for no trouble whatever with a band of tarrapins like us."

"None whatever," says the Red Dog man, mighty confident.

The rest of the story is cut to the fashionable pattern: the braggart interloper is eliminated by a less talkative cowhand.

Here and elsewhere, kinship between older humor and local color is clear. When, in the new period, a pair of old-time humorists just kept on writing the way they always had, nobody worried about their being anachronistic. Bret Harte's belief was that his short stories and those by his fellows had as ancestors prewar humorous tales. As ancestor-hunters often do, Harte oversimplified; many additional writings were influential. But as critics had noticed even before Harte spoke up, family resemblances justified their calling him a typical American humorist. Some postwar writers admitted indebtedness. Mary N. Murfree, who wrote under a masculine pseudonym, manfully confessed

---

Esther B. Carpenter (R.I.), Alice Cary (Oh.), Mary Hartwell Catherwood (Oh., In., Il., Mn.), Charles W. Chesnutt (N.C.), Kate Chopin (La.), S. L. Clemens (Mo.), Rose Terry Cooke (Ct.), Rebecca Harding Davis (Pa.), Margaret Deland (Pa.), Philander Deming (N.Y.), Harry Stillwell Edwards (Ga.), Edward Eggleston (In.), Chester B. Fernald (Ca.), Mary Hallock Foote (Ca., Id.), John Fox, Jr. (Ky.), Mary Wilkins Freeman (Ma.), Alice French (Octave Thanet, Ark., Ia.), Zona Gale (Wi.), Hamlin Garland (Ia., Wi.), William N. Harben (Ga.), Joel Chandler Harris (Ga.), Bret Harte (Ca.), Ella Higginson (Wa.), Thomas Allibone Janvier (N.M.), Sarah Orne Jewett (Me., N.H.), Richard Malcolm Johnston (Ga.), Grace King (La.), Caroline Matilda Kirkland (Mi.), Alfred Henry Lewis (Az.), Charles F. Lummis (N.M.), Helen R. Martin (Pa.), Philip Verrill Mighels (Nv.), Mary N. Murfree (Charles Egbert Craddock, Tn.), Frank Norris (Ca.), Thomas Nelson Page (Va.), Sidney Porter (O. Henry, N.Y.), Harriet Elizabeth Prescott (Ma.), James Whitcomb Riley (In.), Rowland E. Robinson (Vt.), F. Hopkinson Smith (Va.), Harriet Beecher Stowe (Ma.), Ruth McEnery Stuart (La., Ar.), Bayard Taylor (N.Y., Pa.), Maurice Thompson (In.), William Allen White (Ka.), John Greenleaf Whittier (Ma.), Owen Wister (Wy.), Constance Fennimore Woolson (Mi., S.C., Fl.), Lillie B. Wyman (Ct.).

that she had been enlightened by George Washington Harris and his friend Sut Lovingood. Some were less frank. Edward Eggleston, a Hoosier novelist, said that a Frenchman's book on Flemish art had primed him, but he incidentally mentioned Down East and "coarse, boisterous, rollicking" Southwestern writers; and scenes and characters in his books knock out any doubts about their influence.

Just the same, as we have said, the later group generally had qualities that set them apart from the earlier crowd.

When they wrote for magazines that had as subscribers more cultivated readers than prewar humorists usually had, the newer fictionists tried to be more refined. In consequence, much of the gusto, the look of spontaneity, the downright earthiness, got lost. As Harte did in the passage quoted at the start of this section and as Lewis did a few paragraphs back, the new school often deployed a style that Claude Simpson rightly called "a synthetic compound of formality and slang held together with expertly fractured grammar." Listen to O. Henry's con-man narrator in "The Ransom of Red Chief" early in the present century:

There was a town down there [in Alabama], as flat as a flannel-cake, and called Summit, of course. It contained inhabitants of as un-deleterious and self-satisfied a class of peasantry as ever clustered around a Maypole.

Bill and me . . . needed just two thousand dollars more to pull off a fraudulent land scheme. . . . Philoprogenitiveness, says we, is strong in semirural communities; therefore, and for other reasons, a kidnapping project ought to do better there than in a radius of newspapers that send reporters out in plain clothes to stir up talk about such things. We knew that Summit couldn't get after us with anything stronger than constables and, maybe, some lackadaisical bloodhounds and a diatribe or two in the *Weekly Farmers' Budget*. So, it looked good.

At another extreme, until well into the 1880's, some members of the newer group of fiction writers had a growing tendency to go all out to record dialects. Henry James, over in England, talked about this:

Nothing is more striking than the invasive part played by the element of dialect in the subject-matter of the American fictions of the day. Nothing like it, probably—nothing like any such predominance—exists in English, in French, in German work of the same order.

Quite a few authors so thoroughly reproduced vernacular speech that reading them is boggling. Murfree, for instance, quotes a Tennessee mountaineer: "Eph, he owed me a haffen day's work; I holped him ter plow las' month, an' so he kem ter-day an' hoed along cornsider'ble ter pay fur it." A Louisiana Creole in a story by George W. Cable says, "You can strike me dead if thad baril sugah din fedge the more high cost than any other in the city." And here, Thomas Nelson Page quotes a Virginia ex-slave:

"Ole marster (we didn call 'im *ole* marster tell arfter Marse Chan wuz born—befo' dat he wuz jes' de marster, so)—well, ole marster, his face fyar shine wid pleasure, an' all de folks wuz mighty glad, too, 'cause dey all loved ole marster, and aldo' dey did step aroun' right peart when ole marster was lookin' at 'em, dyar warn' nyar han' on de place but what, ef he wanted anythin', would walk up to de back poach, an' say he warn' to se de marster."

Given a choice, many readers today would rather plough an acre of concrete than read a whole story as obsessed with lingo as Page's all-too-representative "Marse Chan" was.

Why did these writers and others in their school try so hard to give thorough phonetic transcripts? An overweening aim, they insisted, was to make everything they wrote just as accurate as they could. This included the dialogue, since a general idea was that nothing was more redolent of a region. A good local-color story, Harte said firmly, had to treat American life "with no fastidious ignoring of its actual expression, or the inchoate poetry that may be found in its slang." Even when, like Alfred Henry Lewis, local colorists somewhat sullied the pure and poetic vernacular to get laughs, they were as ostentatious as the rest in parading local habits, occupations, and backgrounds. From the start, the group did well by settings. "In doing this work," wrote Stowe, "I have tried to make my mind as still and passive as a mountain lake, and then to give you merely the images reflected there." Several authors wrote scenic descriptions nearly half as wordy as Cooper had written and treatises on interior furnishings that predicted Sinclair Lewis's exhaustive catalogues.

Were these fictions, then, realistic? Well, yes, within limitations fathered by the *Zeitgeist*. Today's readers will be struck by the fact that instead of writing about contemporary scenes, local colorists wrote about them as they supposedly had been a few decades back. Stowe's New England was the one of her childhood or earlier, and she was born in 1811; Harte looked back to the California of the forty-niners; the huge group of Southern local colorists specialized in the period "befo' the waw." And realism was softened by nostalgia.

Harte gave stay-at-homes a California peopled entirely with fascinating men and women who made Establishment people (Eastern as well as Western) look pretty drab: whores, gamblers, stagecoach drivers, Virginia colonels, highwaymen, pocket miners, lonely, lovely and innocent ladies, raffish doctors—a picturesque crowd. His appealing—and for the time, devilishly daring—habit was to specify that some of the least reputable and toughest of these had hearts of gold. These characters did noble deeds and committed heroic sacrifices that made possible a good cry.

Writers about New England let their characters prove that laconic, cantankerous, and dour though they had seemed, Yankee men and women had been mighty appealing. Hear a local colorist tell about a family reunion in Maine: "Each heart is warm and every face shines with the ancient light. Such a day as this . . . easily makes friends of those who have been cold-hearted, and gives to those who are dumb their chance to speak, and lends beauty to the plainest face." Now hear one of Stowe's characters tell the world what a wonderful place old New England was—

a simple, pastoral, germ-state of society . . . forever gone. Never again shall we see that union of perfect repose in regard to outward surroundings and outward life with that intense activity of the inward and intellectual world, that made New England . . . the vigorous, germinating seed-bed for all that has since been developed of politics, laws, letters, and theology, through New England to America, and through America to the world.

Dozens of stories and novels made the prewar South the most idyllic place in dear, prewar America. Harte had Colonel Culpepper Starbottle carry out to the Pacific Coast the chivalry, eloquence, bravery, and honor of the area, but native storytellers made clear that the exportation brought no shortage. Many obviously agreed with Thomas Nelson Page when he said that with all its faults, "the social life of the Old South" was "the purest, sweetest life ever lived." They implied that life on the planta-

The idyllic South fondly remembered in 1873. Wood engraving by R. N. Brooke. From *Harper's Weekly*, XVII, June 28, 1873. (*Library of Congress*)

tion, which nobody had doubted was dandy for Massa, Mistus, and the beautiful children, more surprisingly was a great treat for "childlike" and "faithful" slaves, too. Antebellum white trash and mountaineers, seen through the pink glasses of memory, looked just as happy.

Nostalgia wasn't new, even in America. As early as 1817, William Wirt pictured old-time plantation life as idyllic. That same year, James K. Paulding, as he traveled in the South, heard about days of glory that had ended. A year later, Paulding's fellow New Yorker, Samuel Woodworth, remembered how dear to his heart were the days of his childhood when fond recollections presented them to view and wrote "The Old Oaken Bucket," an instant hit. In 1823, wandering 'mid the pleasures and palaces of Europe, John Howard Payne longed for home, home, sweet,

sweet home, and wrote another deathless classic. Stephen Foster's songs did something he told his lady she shouldn't do—wept about the departure of a period when the sun shone bright, before hard times come a-knocking at the door.

What was new about the postwar period was the way a huge body of leading fiction writers positively wallowed in nostalgia. There were several historical causes for their obsession. In 1844, Ralph Waldo Emerson, noticing the way locomotives and steamboats were annihilating distance, binding the whole continent together and bringing "hourly assimilation," guessed that "local peculiarities" couldn't possibly survive. The trend, of course, speeded up after the war, and others in addition to Emerson who were fond of parochial quirks worried about their disappearance. One aim of the local colorists, in those rapidly changing times, was to preserve some of these memories.

A dividend, it was hoped, might be the broadening of sympathy between diverse sections. As Claude M. Simpson has said:

The concept of the Union had been established. . . . But the difference between legal unity and cultural diversity was as great as ever, and many persons seem to have felt a pressing need for a depth of understanding that slogans and propaganda had made impossible during the era of conflict. . . . Jealousy of the East . . . was increasingly evident as voices from the rest of the country insisted on their capability and dignity, and clamored to be recognized. . . . Thus the psychological need to interpret local character, local geography, local fauna and flora, local idiom and folkways seem to underlie the impulse that kept a generation of essayists and storytellers busy. Their method was to excite by emphasizing the exotic and the picturesque, or to idealize by glorifying a noble past, or to seek sympathy and understanding by showing "things as they are."

Edmund Wilson thought he knew why Northern magazines and their readers were eager to come upon stories, in particular, about the halcyon days of the old South that were gone with the wind:

Having devastated the feudal South, the Northerners wanted to be told of its glamor, its old-time courtesy and grace. . . . A rush of industrial development had come at the end of the war, and the cities of the North and the West, now the scene of so much energetic enterprise which rendered them uglier and harsher, were losing their old amenities; and the Northerners wanted, besides, a little to make it up

Joel Chandler Harris's
faithful Uncle Remus.
Drawing by E. W. Kem-
ble (1888).

to the South for their wartime vituperation. They took over the Southern myth and themselves began to revel in it. . . . The Northerners,
after shedding so much blood, illogically found it soothing to be told
that slavery had not been so bad, that the Negroes were a lovable but
simple race, whose business was to work for the whites.

Quite a few Southern writers were avid to make their sympathetic picturings help foster reconciliation. Harris had Uncle
Remus, an antebellum plantation slave, remain loyal to his
marster throughout the war and on into the harried postwar period because he was fond of him. Harris had the old man tell his
folktales to a little white boy whom he loved and who loved
him—symbols, it was implied, of the warm affection between
races in the Old South. Though the fact is probably no longer remembered by anybody but scholars, Harris also wrote at length
about whites who didn't live on plantations, and again he tried
hard to make his stories healing agents. President Theodore Roo-

sevelt, in a speech that the bashful Harris heard in 1905, said that though Georgia had done much for the Union,

she has never done more than when she gave Joel Chandler Harris to American literature. . . . one of his greatest services is that he has written what exalts the South in the mind of every man who reads it, and yet has not a flavor of bitterness toward any other part of the Union. There is not another American anywhere who can read Mr. Harris's stories—I am not speaking at the moment of his wonderful folklore tales, but of his stories—who does not rise up with a more earnest desire to do his part in solving America's problems aright.

Later, Roosevelt said, "I regard Harris as the greatest educator in the South along the lines he has written of."

These were the origins, the methods, and the services of the local colorists. What about the achievements of these part-time humorists in the field of American humor?

Anyone reading them today may find now and then sentences, paragraphs, chapters, or even a few whole stories amusing. These still come across pretty well: Harte's witty commentaries on California types, many of whom became standard figures in Westerns; Stowe's recitations of yarns told by a talkative Yankee loafer, Sam Lawson, and her comic clashes between dogmas or between principles and deeds; Eggleston on some Hoosier crudities and quirks; Harris's renditions of Negro fables with their sly satire concerning blacks and even more mischievous digs at whites; O. Henry's tales about the Gentle Grafter and about poor or middle-class dwellers in New York City.

But we believe that few general searchers for amusement will read many local colorists or many stories by any one of them. They will find more restraint and refinement, less zest, and fewer laughs than they like. Granted, the school's use of pathos (a skill learned largely from Dickens) helped soothe wartime wounds. It enriched humorous characterizations (e.g., those of Huck and Jim). It moved fiction toward realism. But most readers today will find the writing sentimental in ways that we now sniff at. (We haughtily refuse to be touched by any sentimentality that isn't fashionable). The dialect will be too hard to read. The preachment will be too obvious.

Because the writings that contain it do so many things that we find unappealing, practically all of the humor in the vast body of local-color fiction has lost its savor for modern readers.

Edmund Clarence Stedman, a successsful Wall Street broker and anthologist who wrote poetry like that of Tennyson and also published genteel criticism, in 1873 keened about the "wretched, immediate [literary] *fashion* of this demoralized American period." Two writing groups, he had decided, were "almost equally responsible . . . for the *horrible* degeneracy of the public taste." One was the local colorists; he mentioned Harte as an example. The second group was made up of humorists; he specifically mentioned Josh Billings. The full-time comic writers, like the local colorists, became top dogs after the war. Stedman accused them of helping the regional fiction writers gain applause for "slang and nonsense spiced with smut and profanity."

The next chapters will show that the humorists who irked this critic did join the lovers of dialect and peculiar local phrases in making language perform acrobatics. Since for a period they were overfond of cacography, and since their contemporaries thought them amusing, they came to be called "Phunny Phellows."

Phunny
Phellows

> Let [the humorists] seek to em-
> body the wit and humor of all parts of the country. . . . Let them
> form a nucleus which will draw to itself all the waggery and wit of
> America.   —North American Review, *1866*.

> In the course of extensive travels through the United States in *1861 I*
> had often met with the name of "Artemus Ward" attached to articles
> of a peculiarly quaint and comic character, copied and recopied in the
> newspapers of the North and South. . . . The originality of the style
> and the eccentric spelling caused me to wish for information relative
> to the author. . . . Among the humorists who rose to eminence dur-
> ing the American War, Artemus Ward was the raciest . . . and most
> genial.   —Edward P. Hingston,1870.

> "People laugh at me more because of my eccentric sentences than on
> account of the subject matter. . . . There is no wit in the form of a
> well-rounded sentence." —Artemus Ward, as quoted in Melville
> Landon, "Traveling with Artemus Ward," 1871.

27.
Charles Farrar
Browne/Artemus Ward

AT THE RIPE AGE OF THIRTY,
Lewis Mumford had learned enough about American literature
to explain in *The Golden Day* (1926), to his satisfaction, why it
went to the dogs after the Civil War. Following the villainous
conflict which "cut a white gash across the history of the country" and "dramatized in a stroke the changes that had begun to
take place during the preceding . . . years"—

"the promise of regionalism" was exterminated for fully two generations. Local life declined. . . . On one side [of the gash] lay the
Golden Day, the period of . . . a well-balanced adjustment of farm

and factory in the East, of a thriving regional culture, . . . an age in which the American mind had flourished and had begun to find itself. When the curtain rose on the post-bellum scene, this old America was for all practical purposes demolished. . . .

Mumford held that it was the loss of regional ways of living that afflicted the nation with the writings discussed in the last chapter: "Presently the novel of 'local color' appeared—proof enough that the color had washed out."

Oversimplifying no more than the young Mumford did, we suggest that while the local colorists looked wistfully and genially back at the past, the less refined and more popular Phunny Phellows joked for a nation that was limping toward unity. In their writings, comedy of locale—a standby of popular antebellum humorists—shrank or tended to disappear, and a kind of comedy unanchored in any region took charge.

A look at what happened to two magazines in 1861 signals important changes in popular humor. After a life of thirty years, *The Spirit of the Times*, in which "The Big Bear of Arkansas" and many other fine regional sketches appeared, suspended publication. The nine-year-old *Yankee Notions*, in an issue that came out during the month the War Between the States began, showed adaptability to changing tastes that would enable it to live on until, in 1872, it reached an antiquity remarkable for a humorous magazine in the era.*

The April, 1861, issue of *Yankee Notions* was updated in several ways. Nine cartoons, one on the cover, and a plentiful sprinkling of wisecracks and jokes commented on controversies of the day. More important, interrupted by a limited number of never-absent moss-covered jokes, there was a long parade of items of a

---

* Though numerous, comic magazines had rough going in nineteenth-century America. An early example, *Salmagundi*, issued by Washington Irving, his brother William, and James K. Paulding, lasted about two years—1807-1808—as did a second *Salmagundi*, issued by Paulding in 1819 and 1820. The short runs were typical. Midway through the century, *The Carpet-Bag* and *The Lantern* had equally brief lives. Newspapers and magazines that were famous for humorous matter did better if they covered additional ground. For example, *The Spirit of the Times* (1831-1861) did well to advertise that it was a "Chronicle of the Turf, Agriculture, Field Sports, Literature and the Stage." Beginning in the middle of the century, some magazines devoted to humor did better—*Yankee Blade* (1845-1890), *Yankee Notions* (1852-1872), and *Comic Monthly* (1859-1876.) By comparison, though, three comic periodicals born late in the century were remarkably long-lived—*Puck* (1877-1918), *Judge* (1881-1939), and *Life* (before its reincarnation as a pictorial, 1883-1936).

new-fangled sort. As if on cue to summarize the newer pattern for a fight story, for instance, "The Case-Hardened One" told a story about Bill Rigden. "Blowing considerable," Bill trotted out antique ring-tailed roarer boasts—"run faster, jump higher, dive deeper, come out dryer . . . than any man in the crowd." A skin-and-bones, fever-wracked squatter accepted the challenge, whomped Bill in wrestling matches, jumps, card games and drinking bouts, then played a trick that made Bill admit: "I give up. I'm beat." Thereupon: "Amid the roars of the crowd, the pale gent mounted his pony and cantered away."

Anyone paging through the issue will be struck by the predominance of bad spelling as a device. Typical sentences: "Not one living thing is thear to Be seen were I sit except a large Sea Gull wich with its wild and Pearcing Cry made me lift my eyes and Paws. . . . my fren said that the old kardinils always wore petticotes to show that they were as holy as old mades, and I allowed my respeck for the seks to quiet my internal kriticism." Now, cacography no doubt had been imported from England, where *Spectator Papers* essayists used it and Smollett had fun with it in *Humphrey Clinker*. Here writers in almanacs, joke books, and newspapers had been using it for years. As Allen Walker Read suggests, a native institution doubtless helped make it fashionable (and for a time it was very fashionable):

> The common schools had as one of their principal aims the teaching of traditional spelling, and good spelling was a symbol of cultural achievement. The astronomical sale of Noah Webster's "blue-backed" spelling book was further bolstered by the institution of the spelling bee. The strong pressure towards uniformitarian spelling was bound to produce some kind of rebellion, and the humor of intentional misspelling was the result.

True; but misspelling was only one of many kinds of funmaking in the April, 1861, *Yankee Notions* that on page after page got laughs by playing with words—puns, malapropisms, assaults on grammar, weirdly shaped sentences, dialect distortions, parodies and burlesques of dramas and fictional works. Like discombobulated spellings, none of these tricks with words was new. Aristophanes, Plautus, Rabelais, Shakespeare, Swift, Addison, Franklin, and Edward Lear had peppered writings with playful homonyms. What was novel in this cheap American comic magazine was a positive inundation of pranks with diction which all but drowned the popular humor of localized characters that had flourished during the golden age of American humor.

The author of the longest piece in the April issue, Mortimer N. Thomson, in a preface to his *Doesticks What He Says*, as far back as 1855 had described both the sketches in his book and the stuff in *Yankee Notions:* "Many of the thoughts are not novel in themselves, but are merely whimsically put, and not a few of the whims are borrowed. . . . They are dressed up in a lingual garb so quaint, eccentric, fantastic, or extravagant, that each lender will be sadly puzzled to recognize his own. It is undoubtedly this trick of phrase, this affectation of a new-found style, which has caused their widespread notoriety."

The humorist who more than Thomson, more in fact than any other American, made the "new-found style" popular, by April, 1861, had his career well under way. He was in New York, working for a comic magazine, *Vanity Fair*. Soon he would become its editor, publish his first book, carry the latest sort of comedy across the nation and then across the ocean, and collect many followers. This was Charles Farrar Browne, better known under his pen-name, Artemus Ward.

Charles Farrar Browne was born in 1834 in a respectable Maine town to God-fearing parents. Nevertheless, after slightly more schooling than Crockett had and a short apprenticeship, Browne became a tramp printer. The craft had a bad name. A man who started his own career in this role but who later became respectable sketched the breed: "his wallet stuffed with one shirt and a hatfull of handbills, for if he couldn't get any type to set he could do a lecture. . . . all he wanted was a plate and bed and money enough to get drunk on."

Before he was eighteen, Browne quit or got fired from jobs on five New England newspapers. In 1851, he hit Boston, got hired by a humorous magazine, *The Carpet-Bag* (1851-1853), worked for it for two years, and had his first pieces published in it. Then he drifted in a westerly direction as far as Ohio. There he set type for six scattered newspapers before winding up on the Cleveland *Plain Dealer* at the generous salary of forty dollars a month.

Along the way, he proved his versatility by teaching school in

Kentucky (though only for a week) and writing news items and fillers. Somehow he managed to persuade the *Plain Dealer* editor that he could cover markets, arriving travelers, courts, meetings, fires, thefts, murders, swindles, and racetracks. If news about them was scarce, he could promptly grind out enough brief items, quaint thoughts, and jocosities to fill a column that he was to provide.

Some months short of his twenty-fourth birthday, Browne wrote and published a filler:

Pitsburg, Jan. 27, 18&58

The Plane Deeler:
Sir:
i write to no how about the show bisnes in Cleeveland i have a show consisting in part of a Calforny Bare two snakes tame foxies &c also wax works my wax works is hard to beat, all say they is life and nateral curiosities among my wax works is Our Saveyer Gen taylor and Docktor Webster in the ackt of killing Parkman. now mr. Editor scratch off few lines and tel me how is the show bisnes in your good city i shal have hanbils printed at your offis you scratch my back i will scratch your back, also git up a grate blow in the paper about my show don't forgit the wax works.

yours truly,
ARTEMUS WARD
Pitsburg Penny

P S pitsburg is a 1 horse town.   A. W.

After working their painful way through the capricious capitalization, the ailing grammar, and the misspelling, readers today might well predict that a feeble little item so hard to decipher couldn't possibly have caused a stir. Wrong. For whatever reasons, America was ready to welcome the "genial showman," Artemus Ward, his finagling, and his freakish style.

It did so, in spades. There was much talk about this piece. Letters to the paper praised it; it was picked up by many exchanges. During the next few weeks, Browne followed it with several more screeds from the illiterate imposter he had created—reports of the ramshackle show's progress from town to town in Ohio, proudly adding plugs for the mangy menagerie and "wax statoots of celebrated piruts and murderers, etc., ekalled by few, and exceld by none." Ward kept trying to inveigle the Plane Deeler editor into "gitting up a tremendus excitement in yr Pa-

Charles Farrar Browne, comic lecturer, pictured in *Vanity Fair*.

per." And the escalating fame of the letters launched Browne—or Artemus Ward, as he was soon to be called—on a most successful career.

Plain Dealer sales leaped to a new high. The publisher of a top New York comic monthly, *Vanity Fair*, bought simultaneous rights to the Ward letters and then lured Browne away to join the staff and, a bit later, to become the magazine's managing editor. Meanwhile, Browne had figured out a new way to cash in on his popularity and build it. He became a humorous lecturer throughout the Midwest, the East, the South, and the Far West. In 1862, his first book had a tremendous sale for that time—40,000 copies. (Comparable sales today per capita would be about 265,000 copies.) In 1864, preceded by his fame, he sailed to England, was immediately signed as a regular contributor to the leading comic magazine, *Punch*, drew big royalties on his second book, and during a seven-week run in London lectured in Egyptian Hall, Piccadilly, to full houses. Prestigious newspapers printed laudatory reviews. Within eight years, 250,000 copies of his first book had been sold in the United States and England.

Browne was sickly from his youth, and his enjoyment of the printers' favorite pastime didn't improve his health. A biographer finds that when he lived in Cleveland, if not before, he "established bacchanalian habits." A San Francisco lecture manager telegraphed a question: "What will you take for forty nights in California?" Browne's answer, "Brandy and water," evidently was accurate except for its failure to mention that he also would take supplements of champagne, whiskey, and other stimulants. When he found how hospitable the Virginia City newspaper crowd was, the lecturer stretched a stay from two to ten nights and tied one on every night. He wrote to one of his hosts, Sam Clemens, from Austin, Texas:

Why did you not go with me and save me that night—I mean the night I left you drunk at that dinner party. I went and got drunker, beating, I may say, Alexander the Great in his most drinkinist days, and I blackened my face at the Melodeon and made a gibbering idiotic speech. God-damit! . . . Some of the finest intellects in the world have been blunted by liquor.

After Browne's triumphant invasion of England, British conviviality (courtesy of the Savage Club, the Garrick Club, and private benefactors), exhaustion, and worsening illness were followed by his death a few weeks before his thirty-third birthday.

As the "18&58" letter signed "Artemus Ward" shows, Browne made use of the tricks that *Yankee Notions*, no doubt encouraged by his success, would use in 1861. Ward couldn't spell, and as consequence he stumbled (unwittingly, of course) into puns and malapropisms.

He could have come upon such comedy in a dozen places. In *The Carpet-Bag*, for which he set type, John Greenleaf Whittier's brother Matthew had his character, Ethan Spike, make comic mistakes because he knew no better, e.g., "It will make your hairs stand on eend like quills on the frightened konkerbine." Ruth Partington, created by the editor of the magazine and constantly featured in its pages, was the most popular user of malapropisms in antebellum America.

Ward's use of word play would continue. He wrote about "the moral bares," "the soshul bored," "highly manured" prose and "women's rites." He told why he swapped daguerreotypes with President Lincoln: "so we can gaze upon each others' liniments." He made lavish use of malignant grammar.

This showman's creator made famous one favorite device and gave an example of it: "People laugh . . . more because of my

eccentric sentences than on account of the subject-matter. . . .
There is no wit in the *form* of a well-rounded sentence. If I say
Alexander the Great conquered the world and then sighed because *he could not do it some more*, there is a funny mixture."
He is illustrating *anticlimax*, a favorite misstep, as in Artemus's
touching story of his leaving his dear old father and his boyhood
home: "I thought I saw tears tricklin' down his venerable chin,
but it might have been tobacco juice. He chawed." Other kinds
of "eccentric sentences," conceits, overstatements, understate-
ments, twisted clichés, and euphuisms were all meat for Browne.
In his romps with words, he was wonderfully versatile.

"I wait," he explained, "until some fancy strikes me, which
by and by is followed by another. When there are a half-dozen
or so I put them on paper." The "fancies" must usually have
been aberrant phrasings, for those—rather than character portrayals or skilled narrations—were his specialty. Alert readers
noticed a disappearing act like that of Lewis Carroll's Cheshire
cat: The shady con man and his tacky show dropped out of the
writings, and misspellings became less frequent and vanished
from some of them. The illustrations looked less like the plump,
baldheaded showman and more like lank, curly-headed, mus-
tached Charles Farrar Browne.

Some reasons: A reviewer slapped at bad spelling as a shopworn trick in 1863; others downgraded it; humorists used it less
and less. As Browne traveled the lecture circuit, reporters wrote
about contrasts between "Artemus Ward, Showman," and his
creator, and audiences and illustrators came to associate his real-
life physical presence with his humor. Browne/Ward gradually
shucked off rascality and blatant illiteracy.

This didn't mean that he assumed a role that was completely
new. Before he became a popular lecturer, he wrote a piece about
the type. "Humbugs," he called such performers, who "cram
themselves with high sounding phrases. . . . ain't overstocked
with brains, but they have brass. . . ." He posed as such a fake,
spouting purple prose before descending to anticlimaxes, misquoting Shakespeare and other authors, and pouring out misinformation—all with ponderous solemnity. Anticipating later humorists, he exposed a mind that was confused and that erratically
sashayed among irrelevancies. *The London Spectator* was fascinated by his vagaries:

Artemus Ward and Mrs. Ward in the Showman's Museum. Charles Farrar Browne peers at them through the doorway.

The character he likes best to fill is that of a sort of intellectual Hans—the world simpleton of the German stories—in the act of confiding himself to the public. In the German stories Hans only makes a practical fool of himself in all sorts of impossible ways. But Artemus Ward intellectualizes him, shows the inner absurdity of his thoughts with pathetic earnestness. . . . He yields a literal obedience to every absurd suggestion of thought and language, just as Hans does to the verbal directions of his wife and mother, and gets into intellectual absurdity just as Hans gets into practical absurdity. This with the melancholy earnest manner of a man completely unconscious that there is anything grotesque in what he says, conveys an effect of inimitable humour.

Hearing himself happen to say, "Why is this thus?" and worried about such like-sounding words nudging one another, his lecturer tries to make quick repairs but continues to be victimized. "Why is this thusly?" he asks, then still dissatisfied, he really balls everything up with: "Why thus this thusness?"

Said the delighted *Spectator* critic, "He cannot evidently help developing at length the subtle suggestions of verbal confusion that strike everybody's ear with an idiotic jingle of fascination." (In Woody Allen's 1971 film *Bananas*, Fielding Mellish's girlfriend had somewhat similar trouble. "Full of pith," says Fielding. "Lithen," she says.) Again, a rhythm catches him and won't let him go. Some women tell him: " 'Base man, leave us, oh, leave us!'—and I left them, oh, I left them." During an illustrated lecture, he points to a picture of a lion and says: "Yonder lion, you will observe, has a tail. It will be continued *for a few evenings longer.*"

Far Western funmakers in the sixties, it will be remembered, were burlesquing topographical surveys and learned scientific treatises. During the same decade, Browne, as Brom Weber says, "burlesqued the lecturers—philosophers, politicians, ministers, travelers, generals, professors—who for years zealously traveled about the country, and with serious mien, dispensed wisdom, edification, and inspiration." He became, for purposes of comedy, a dry-as-dust bluffing authority—an *alazon* of the pedant class. John Bright, a dedicated reformer who'd been born into a frivolous world without any sense of humor, criticized the lecture on Mormons in terms that must have delighted Ward: "Its information was meager and presented in a desultory, disconnected manner."

As a writer, too, Browne went in for parodies. He had met the genre when he worked for *The Carpet-Bag*; he had gone to New York when playhouses minted money by presenting one after another. He wrote at least twelve literary burlesques, and as James C. Austin says, they ridiculed practically all the kinds of popular romances—"the French romance, the romance of adventure on the high seas, the romance of the noble red man, the romance of the American countryside after the style of Washington Irving, and a few more." Representative titles included "The Fair Inez: Or the Lone Lady of the Crimson Bluffs. A Tale of the Sea," "Roberto the Rover," and "Woshy-Boshy, or the Prestidigitating Squaw of the Snakeheads." His song titles, like his lectures, used verbal plays: "Dear Mother, I've Come Home to Die by Request" and "Dearest, Whenest Thou Slumberest, Dostest Thou Dreamest of Me?"

Three very successful humorists found Browne's ways of writing, his lecturing, and his prosperity attractive. Starting unknown, each imitated him and won remarkable success—Henry Wheeler Shaw, David Ross Locke, and Charles Henry Smith, creators, respectively, of Josh Billings, Petroleum Vesuvius Nasby, and Bill Arp.

> *"How 'bout my Cabinit, Mister Ward?" sed Abe.*
>
> *"Fill it up with Showmen sir! Showmen is devoid of politics. They hain't got any principles! They know how to cater for the public. They know what the public wants . . . A. Linkin, adoo!"*
>
> —Artemus Ward, 1861.

> *Mr. Linkhorn, sur, privately speakin', I'm afeard I'll get into a tite place here among these bloods and have to slope out of it, and I would like your Skotch cap and cloak that you travelled in to Washington.*
>
> —Bill Arp, 1862.

> *"Linkin," sez I, "ez a Dimekrat, a free-born Dimekrat, . . . knowin also that you er a goriller, a feendish ape, a thirster after blud, I speek."*
>
> —Petroleum Vesuvius Nasby, 1863.

28.
Shaw, Locke, and Smith

HENRY WHEELER SHAW, LIKE Browne a native Yankee, was kicked out of college early in his sophomore year. He shuttled from job to job in the Midwest, then backtracked. He was a struggling real estate agent and auctioneer in Poughkeepsie, New York, when the first Ward letters came out. Shaw read one and remembered a piece he had published in a local paper with no response—"Essay on the Mule." He disinterred this and rewrote it in the Ward manner as "Essa on the Muel." ("The muel iz half hoss and haf Jackass, and then kums to a full stop, nature diskovering her mistake. . . .") Shaw mailed his essa, signed "Josh Billings," to a New York newspaper, collected payment (a dollar and a half), and soon saw reprints in three comic magazines.

"I think," he said, "I've struck oil." He sold other Ward-like pieces and saw them picked up by exchanges. With his carpet-bag stuffed full of clippings, he visited Browne in New York, swigged a liquid lunch with him, and then, as Browne read his drolleries aloud, joined his host in gusty guffaws. The next day Browne talked his own publisher into issuing *Josh Billings, His Sayings*.

This was the first of ten successful books bearing Josh's name. Shaw heard how profitable his host's platform appearances were and went to a lecture. He himself began to give comic lectures; they ran twenty seasons and carried him all over the country and into Canada. Takings from these, newspapers, and books were augmented and at times topped by those from *Josh Billings' Farmer's Allminax*. Illiterate comic aphorisms in it led to sales during one decade of more than a million copies.

A second Phunny Phellow who followed the trail that Browne had blazed was David Ross Locke. He, like Browne, started in his native East (New York) as a printer's devil, meandered out to Ohio as a tramp typographer, and during the 1850's and 1860's set type for several newspapers in that state. He met Browne there. In 1862, assuming the guise of a Ward-like uneducated but cunning heel, he began to write a series for the Findlay *Hancock Jeffersonian*; they were continued later in the *Toledo Blade*. They were in the comic illiterate style that Browne and Shaw had helped make fashionable, and tradition has it that Browne helped him find a name for his rapscallion—Petroleum Vesuvius Nasby. Here is a sample, with most of the verbal perversities quietly repaired (as they will be in quotations that follow) for readability:

TO THE DEMOCRACY OF THE COUNTRY:
   I announce myself as a candidate for ary one of the offices to be filled this autumn . . . , the reasons for taking this step . . . run as follows:
1st. I want a office.
2d. I need a office.
3d. A office would suit me; therefore,
4th. I should like to have a office. . . .
I have done the party some service. . . . I have fought and bled for the cause, have voted as often as three times at one election, and have worn mourning around my eyes for three weeks after each campaign. . . . No man has drunk more whiskey than I have for the party—none has done it more willingly.

The newspaper contributions, several books, a long-running dramatization, and lectures made his a rags-to-riches story.

Petroleum Vesuvius Nasby. Thomas Nast drew the frontispiece for *Swingin Round the Cirkle* (1867).

Nasby's writings and others by Locke used devices and materials Browne favored. Horrible spelling and delinquent grammar have been mentioned. As Browne/Ward's writings in time became less illiterate, so did Locke/Nasby's. Both early and late, his letters performed Ward-like verbal acrobatics. For the best of reasons, most of Locke's writings other than the Nasby letters had less impact and have been forgotten: his teacher's came earlier and were funnier. All the same, several burlesques closely resemble Browne's. They kid travel books, Oriental vaporings such as Thomas Moore's *Lalla Rookh*, and gothic or sentimental romances. A brief sample:

There came hissing through his teeth the deadly words:
  "R-r-reven-ja—ha! ha! ha!". . .
  "I have yet time!" he shrieked. . . . "I can save her—and marry her."
  Away he sped. The gazelle never sped faster. As speeder he did well. . . . The house was in sight. One convulsive bound and he was in front of it—another, and he had burst open the door. . . .
  "Bridget!" he shrieked.
  There was no answer. In the center of the room lay a smouldering mass of kitchen girl and clothes. . . .

"Too late—too late!" he moaned. . . . "Speak to me, Bridget," he moaned, rocking over the charred mass.

But she did not speak to him. Charred masses never do, and it was really absurd of him to ask it.

If anyone were given this excerpt and a typical bit of a burlesque by Browne, with no names attached, he would be able to ascribe them correctly only by a lucky accident.

A third wartime and postbellum humorist who found Browne's formula profitable, though sired by a Yankee, was a Georgian by birth and lifelong residence and a Southerner in sympathies. Charles Henry Smith, unusually well-schooled for a humorist of that period, graduated from Franklin College, learned enough law to get admitted to the bar, and was a Confederate officer when, at age thirty-five, he turned part-time author.

He had read letters signed Artemus Ward and books by Benjamin Franklin. When he first wrote newspaper pieces, he was clearly influenced by the former; eventually, he became more like Poor Richard and Josh Billings. His initial writings, letters signed "Bill Arp," and addressed to President Abraham Lincoln, were reminiscent of Ward's interviews with Lincoln and Jefferson Davis. (They were also reminiscent of accounts which Sut Lovingood wrote in 1861 telling how Sut—so he claimed— helped a quaking Abe Lincoln travel in disguise to Washington. Possibly Smith, in turn, provided hints to Locke, who, like Harris and Smith, had his character collaborate with the enemy.) The first letter was a friendly note from "a good Union man and law-abiding citizen," answering Lincoln's demand in April 1861 that the Southern armies disperse:

Mr. Lincoln—Sir: These are to inform you that we are all well, and hope these lines may find you in status quo. We received your proclamation, and as you have put us on very short notice, a few of us boys have concluded to write you, and ask for a little more time. The fact is, we are most obliged to have a few more days, for the way things are happening, it is utterly impossible for us to disperse in twenty days. Old Virginia, and Tennessee, and North Carolina, are continually aggravating us into tumults and carousements, and a body can't disperse until you put a stop to such unruly conduct. . . .

Equally cooperative letters which followed, ostensibly with the best intentions, kept digging at Lincoln and the Northern armies. After Lincoln's assassination, Bill Arp wrote a letter in the

Artemus Ward gives President Lincoln helpful advice. From *Vanity Fair*, Dec. 9, 1860

same sympathetic spirit to "Mr. Artemus Ward, Showman," styling himself "truly your friend," and gently telling him what a tough time "we Rebs, *so called*," had when they tried to "harmonize" with their conquerors.

Obviously Smith borrowed from Browne. Both, at the start of their writing careers, spelled horribly and pulverized grammar, but in time both became more literate. Before and after reforming, neither somehow could avoid puns. (Arp called refugee days "the times that tried men's soles" and said that as a Southerner eager for peace, he was "all for hominy.") Arp joined Ward in misquoting classical authors: "As General Byron said at the Battle of Waterloo, I ain't what I used to was, and my spirits are fluttering, faint and low." Edmund Burke launched Bill toward an anticlimax: "But fare thee well, my friend, and before you cross another Rubicon, I advise you, 'Consider, old cow, consider.'" Annie May Christie, who cites these gaffes and others, notices that, like Browne, Smith frequently ridicules not only *belles-letters* but also oratory that takes rhetorical flights. He does this by using anticlimax—a very helpful device in burlesque: "He soars high in recollected phrases, but falls suddenly to his character's homely level."

After the war, Smith found it impossible to support a growing family (final count, thirteen children) just by practicing law, storekeeping, politicking, and farming. Sporadically at first, in time regularly for a salary, he capitalized on the huge stir his wartime pieces had made by turning out Bill Arp letters for newspapers and magazines. He collected these in five books, and beginning in 1878 he delivered several hundred lectures, most of them humorous, that carried him into thirteen states.

In this period, realizing (as he said) that the earlier Arpian satire had succeeded because "it was pertinent to the occasion and impertinent" to its victims—and that conditions had changed—Smith revised his style. His mode was now that of a humorist he praised for being "Aesop and Ben Franklin condensed and abridged"—Henry Wheeler Shaw/Josh Billings. He complimented Josh for doing several things that he himself did. Josh, for example, used "metaphors and striking comparisons" from "nature and everyday life." Smith thought "the masses" admire these because they make use of "the contrast between [an uneducated speaker's] mind and his culture." When "an old thought that has been dressed up for centuries . . . suddenly [appears] in everyday clothes," he believed, it gets to American readers for a familiar reason: "It is curious how we are attracted by the wise, pithy sayings of an unlettered man." Examples of Smith/Arp's aphorisms: "There are some men who, if they owned the whole world, would want a tater patch outside. . . ." "Government officials always have friends."

Browne, Shaw, Locke, and Smith were only a few of the Phunny Phellows who rose and prospered between 1855 and 1895. A complete list would be a long one, for this was a period when such writers proliferated. But because they don't do at all well when read in quantity, we shall dump a mere forty names of their most prominent fellows into the long footnote below*

---

* Joseph C. Aby (Hoffenstein), William Livingston Alden (The Times Man), George W. Bagby (Mozis Addums), James M. Bailey (Danbury News Man), William P. Brannen (Vandyke Brown), Robert J. Burdette (The Hawkeye Man), Charles C. Clark (Max Adeler), W. W. Clark (Gilhooley), Roger F. Coffin, Edward E. Edwards, George B. Goodwin (Dennis Muldoon), J. C. Goldsmith (The P.I. Man), A. Miner Griswold (Fat Contributor), Charles G. Halpine (Miles O' Reilley), Charles H. Harris (Carl Pretzel), Charles Hoyt, Stanley Huntley (Spoopendyke), W. J. Lampton (Topnoody and Waxem), Melville D. Landon (Eli Perkins), George T. Lanigan, W. H. Levinson (Julius Caesar Hannibal), C. B. Lewis (M. Quad), Henry Clay Lukens (Erratic Enrique), J. W. Morris (K. N. Pepper), Idora Plowman

and let the quartet typify the breed. While all these writers differed somewhat from one another, our extensive samplings, we believe, justified this handling. If you read many, you remember the remark that the bungling politician made about slums: "When you've seen one you've seen them all." The remark, crass and inexcusable when made about ghettoes, applies all too well to these humorists. And the four we have introduced, since they are representative, will enable us to generalize about the lot.

Like our four, most were both popular and prosperous. Newspapers gave such humorists unprecedented exposure, thanks to the exchange system early in the post-war period and to syndication at the end. The writers' wide-ranging lecture tours did for them something vaguely comparable to what television talk shows do for authors today. Subscription books and paperbacks had large sales.

During the angry years before and during the war, several of them helped readers blow off steam by producing pretty ferocious stuff. Writing against abolitionists, secessionists, and then draft dodgers and battlefield bunglers, Ward hit hard at groups unpopular in the North. Bill Arp and Petroleum Nasby managed to be even fiercer by working in the tradition of Franklin's monsters and Lowell's Birdofredum Sawin. Arp wanted to collaborate with the enemy; Nasby did collaborate.

A fellow drinker asked Locke, "Just what kind of a man is Nasby, really, as you write about him?" "Why," Locke said, "he's something like you—a sort of a nickle-plated son of a bitch." Exactly. He was a fool, loafer, drunkard, coward, braggart, bigot, hypocrite, bigamist, thief and—for purposes of political satire—a corrupt politician and traitor.

One example of his viciousness will prove that his creator was right—a nauseating bit about the burning of a Negro schoolhouse: "The cry of the nigger children which couldn't escape,

---

Moore (Betsy Hamilton), Robert Henry Newell (Orpheus C. Kerr), Edgar Wilson Nye (Bill Nye), George W. Peck, Marcus M. Pomeroy (Brick Pomeroy), Samuel W. Small (Old Si), Alexander Edwin Sweet, Mortimer M. Thomson (Doesticks), G. A. Townsend (Gath), Thomas Small Weaver (Job Shuttle), Charles H. Webb (John Paul), A. M. Weir (Sarge Plunkett), P. H. Welch, Henry Ten Eyck White (The Tribune Man), William Albert Wilkins (Hiram Green), John H. Williams (B. Dadd).

symbolized their deserted condition, and the smell of 'em, as they roasted, was like unto incense, grateful to our nostrils." Locke was right when he said that this version of Defoe's Shortest-Way advocate "represented a sort of madness." A hundred years before Archie Bunker, Locke satirized bigotry and reaction in much the way creators of Archie would. Compliments paid him by relatively temperate men show that even they found him attractive. "I should be willing to resign the Presidency," said Lincoln, "if I could write such letters." Grant offered Locke an ambassadorship as a tribute.

Though, in his lectures, he alternately spoke as Nasby and as Locke, thus at times dropping his mask, he resembled other literary comedians. Long after the war, he continued to inject venom into controversial issues. In this, he differed from most other literary comedians. Nearly all of the others withheld from the characters that they assumed hot prejudices and eccentric quirks such as would have individualized them. The characters' spelling, their syntax—even more important, their touches of dialect—became less idiosyncratic. Their backgrounds were shrouded in mist. With few exceptions, the professional comic writers handed over to local colorists a privilege their predecessors had particularly treasured—the fun of evoking provincial ways of feeling, living, and talking. Like that conniving Yankee showman turned Hoosier, Artemus Ward I, and that overly obliging Georgia redneck, Bill Arp I, firmly rooted and palpable men and women absquatulated from their pages.

What most Phunny Phellows shared was a way of dressing the pieces that they wrote in what one critic has called a "quaint, eccentric, fantastic, or extravagant . . . lingual garb." In piece after piece, they got their laughs by performing feats with word play of the sort we have seen our four men performing.

To find a school of American writers as fond of philological contortions, we have to peer back to early Puritan days. Seventeenth-century colonial savants, it will be recalled, also doted on games with words—in that era puns, conceits, anagrams, palindromes, and "inkhorn coinages." But the likeness comes about for fairly clear reasons. The seventeenth-century word jugglers put on their act to flaunt their own learning; nineteenth-century comic writers parodied their performance—staged *their* act to flog displays in their period of pedantry and literary affectations. Posing as showoffs, they intermingled weird wordings, eccentric sentences, and misquotations with learned jargon, purple prose, oratorical flights, and tender tears. The result was hundreds of burlesques and parodies of lectures, orations, plays, poems, and fictional works that readers and their parents had only recently found impressive and touching.

During Browne's editorship of *Vanity Fair*, an editorial which he perhaps wrote boasted, "We are engaged in a noble work. We are doing for literature what actors are doing for the stage—we are simplifying matters—stripping them of their excrescences, and proving that anything is susceptible of being burlesqued."

On occasion, Browne recited bathetic poetry, it appears, with warm appreciation. At a libatious banquet in Virginia City hosted by the *Territorial Enterprise* crowd, he recited a lachrymose poem about little Baby Bell to wild applause but not a standing ovation. At the poem's end, he asked that "every man 'at loves his fellow man and 'preciates a poet 'at loves *his* fellow man, stan' up" and drink a toast to the poet. After everyone in the entranced audience made "fervent, enthusiastic, and sincerely honest attempts to comply"—and failed—Browne amended his proposal: "Well—*consider* it stanning and drink it jush as you are." But habitually in his humor he took off on sentimentality in broad burlesques.

As *Yankee Notions* burlesques—and those by all four of our Phunny Phellows—indicate, the most generalized sort of character can be the author of such takeoffs. It was enough for him to be a pretentious imposter—one who lets on to have excruciatingly tender feelings and fancy literary skills which he lacks. When he played this role, he clearly belonged to the long line of intellectual *alazons* we have been tracing.

To provide the laugh a line which readers of the period evidently enjoyed, the Phunny Phellow didn't hesitate to play a completely opposite role, that of an uneducated bumpkin who has lots of gumption and therefore can say wise things about human quirks and the life of his day. "With me," Henry Wheeler Shaw said, "everything must be put in two or three lines." "Everything" was a mother-wit aphorism that he had sweated over for several hours "to get just right"—a combination

31 Days. DECEMBER. 1872.

Q.—How did robins git their name?

A.—By robin cherry-trees.

The farmer leads an eazy life,
12 hours a day ends hiz labors;
Evenings pares apples for cider sass,
Or hauls over the coals hiz nabors.

Days		Kalkulashuns.	GIN AND MILK.
1	G	☉ △ *Kold and*	How fast will the "*comeing man*" probably travel? I kant tell to a dot; but if he kant beat 2.25, he better stay whare he iz.
2	M	*snowsome* ♃	
3	T	≌ Yankee doodle	
4	W	born 1659 ●	
5	T	● *mutch kold* ♈	
6	F	✳ Yankee doodle	
7	S	still livs ♓	
8	G	*snow 60 foot deep*	A man with a phew branes iz like a dog with one flea on him—dredful oneazy.
9	M	♀ Yankee doodle	
10	T	iz	
11	W	a lively cuss ♏	
12	T	☍ *grate kold* □	
13	F	♅ now hammer	
14	S	out oats ☉	
15	G	(☽) *kolder* [☐]	Be humble, and yu are sure tew be thankful; be thankful, and yu are sure tew be happy.
16	M	expekt sla rides ♀	
17	T	♈ *sharp, but kold*	
18	W	⊕ thou shalt	
19	T	not	
20	F	covet thi nabor's	
21	S	jackass ♂	The more yung ones in a family, the eazier they are tew raize. One chicken alwus makes more klucking for a hen than a dozen duz.
22	M	♏ *snow inkreases*	
23	T	⊕ now murder	
24	W	hogs ♋	
25	T	⚌ *wind shifty*	
26	T	♈ now tear up	
27	F	wood ♃	
28	S	< *big kold* >	Blessed iz he who kan pocket abuse, and feel that it iz no disgrace tew be bit bi a dog.
29	G	⚏ the grass hopper	
30	M	haz fled ☍ ♃ ♀	
31	T		

Calendar page, *Josh Billings' Farmer's Allminax, 1872.*

of Josh Billings's rusticity and wit. "Next to William Shakespeare," Lincoln said, "Josh Billings is the greatest judge of human nature the world has ever seen."

Shaw was unusual in sticking to this single role throughout his career. Others switched from one impersonation to the other or alternated as *alazon* and *eiron*. Locke's character, Nasby, consistently pretended to be more than he was, but when Locke lectured, he would be Nasby for several paragraphs and then a commonsensible commentator for several. Smith, after starting in one role, dropped it and took on its opposite—the one that he praised Shaw for playing well. Though Smith knew the Bible

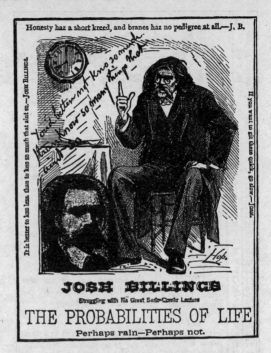

Flyer advertising a lecture
by Josh Billings, which
contrasts the character
with his creator.

and the writings of Josephus, Horace, Shakespeare, Pope, Johnson, Burke, Goldsmith, Scott, Coleridge, Byron, and others, Bill
Arp II spoke in the words of a hayseed about the things he had
learned by observation and hard work. Charles Farrar Browne
in his writings had Artemus, his creation, shuttle back and forth
between pretentious ignorance and ineptitude, on the one hand,
and unread wisdom and insight, on the other. But when he lectured, he consistently took the part of a humbug who was doing
his damnedest to pass himself off as a learned teacher but who
was debunked by his uninformed and chaotic mind.

Dressed in their brilliant bumpkin overalls, comic writers
spoke up in aphorisms for old American beliefs.

"Common sense," said Josh Billings, "is the vernacular of
truth. . . . I have learned more from common people than I
have from the uncommon ones. . . . Life consists not in holding
good cards but in playing those you do hold well. . . . The devil
enters the idle man's house without knocking." Shades of Poor
Richard!

Bill Arp II as a rule was even more orthodox than his idol. He was the contented farmer, the happily married man, and the lover of his family, the community, the country (as opposed to the city), and mankind. A typical passage:

I . . . look over my farm and see the wheat and the oats . . . waving so beautiful in the breeze and I feel proud and serene for I sowed that wheat myself and helped to prepare the land, and it is my wheat and my oats and come honestly and wasn't made out of somebody else. . . . It beats money made by luck all to pieces.

But this is only half of the story. The postwar period was one of great disillusionment. Business tycoons profited in spectacular ways and thumbed their noses at the public. American inventiveness and know-how found new ways to make governmental corruption highly profitable, and when non-participants had this growing industry brought to their notice, they took a dim view of it. Even that champion antebellum optimist, Walt Whitman, in 1871 was calling the national scene "appalling" and finding "hypocrisy throughout." "The depravity of the business classes of our country," he claimed, "is not less than has been supposed, but even greater [and in politics] corruption, bribery, falsehood, mal-administration." Novelists joined poets in proclaiming that the country was depraved. Edward Bellamy, in his best-selling novel, *Looking Backward*, spoke of the hopelessness of "the best of men" who saw no chance to reform "the crying abuses of the existing social arrangement." He related the widespread despair to the period's comic writings: "Just here you will find the explanation of the profound pessimism of the literature [between 1863 and 1888], the note of melancholy in the poetry, and the cynicism of its humor."

Bellamy could easily have quoted scores of sourpuss fulminations by the most popular humorists to prove that in fact they were a bunch of sneering skeptics:

Artemus Ward: "Had I been liberally educated I could, with my brilliant native talents, have been a great thief—I believe they call 'em defaulters. . . . I venture to say that if you search the earth all over with a ten-horse power microscope, you won't be able to find such another pack of poppycock gabblers as the present Congress. . . ."

Petroleum V. Nasby: "A lie, well started, vigorously stuck to, and energetically pushed, answers just as well as the truth, and will live a long time. . . . I don't put these thoughts of mine upon paper for amusement. There hain't been anything amusing in Democracy for the past five years. . . . Seven-tenths of mankind is bad in a greater or less degree; . . . the devil has a warranty deed on four-tenths, a quit-claim on two-tenths, and a mortgage on another tenth. Them in which he has a present or prospective interest are very largely in the majority."

Disillusionment was only to be expected, of course, of a confidence man like Artemus Ward I, that sodden S.O.B. and crook, Petroleum V. Nasby, and that collaborator with the enemy, Bill Arp I. But good old Josh Billings, Bill Arp II, and dozens of other Phunny Phellows used their aphoristic skill to make mean remarks about a great many old beliefs:

Josh Billings: "Progress seems to be the ideal of creation, but all progress seems to end in destruction rather than perfection. . . . Politics is the apology of plunder. . . . Every man has a weak side, and some have two or three. . . . 'The law of nations'; iron clad gun boats. . . . My opinion of mankind as a brilliant success needs a good deal of nursing. . . . I don't think the world has any civilization to spare, but I think she has more than she can manage well."

Bill Arp: "Looks like there is always something preying on something, nothing is safe in this sublunary world. . . . Didn't our four fathers fight, bleed, and die about a little tax on tea, when not one in a thousand drunk it? Because they succeeded, wasn't it glory? But if they hadn't, I suppose it would have been treason. . . ." (The second of these bits is close enough to a crack by Artemus Ward to make almost certain that it is an echo.)

Artemus Ward said of himself and other genial showmen: "They hain't got any principles! They know how to cater to the public." The remark possibly applied equally well to Phunny Phellows who gave those that liked them homely old sentiments and those that didn't, cynical aphorisms. A possibility is that in those changing times, the masses were ambivalent and didn't worry about any inconsistencies.

Not only did the literary comedians assail orthodox sentiments in their letters, essays, and epigrams; they also tilted at them—

and at pious sentimentality—in their burlesques. See how Browne mocked accepted moralists as he concluded "The Fair Inez" with some completely irrelevant clichés:

> Gentle reader, has not my story a moral? Do you not see that honesty is the best policy, and that procrastination is the thief of time? Is not virtue its own reward, and should we despise a man who wears a ragged coat? Dress does not make the man, and try to lay up something for a rainy day. Live within your means! Pay your debts, and remember that the race is not to the swift. If you would thrive rise at five. Subscribe for your county paper!
>
> Gentle reader, my story is done. It is hard to part, but try and bear up under it. Farewell, farewell!

The night before he finished his nine-volume history of early America in 1890, pessimistic Henry Adams summarized its bleak outcome: "All my wicked villains will be rewarded with Presidencies and the plunder of the innocent; and my models of usefulness and intelligence will be fitly punished and deprived of office and honors." Innumerable Phunny Phellows reduced their disbelief in the old notion of poetic justice to comic proportions by burlesquing Sunday school stories. In "Affairs round the Village Green," Browne told how a brilliant youth became a fishmonger, a lunkhead became a great lawyer, and two Good Little Boys became, respectively, a "failing merchant" and a convict.

An attitude that modern readers comprehend only with great effort was an attack on emotional writings just as subversive as the one on preachy romances. A quaint old belief was that only the most admirable people were easily and deeply touched—a heritage of a period when a man or woman "of feeling" was a model.

In 1843, Thomas Dunne English wrote a poem, "Ben Bolt," about a girl everybody in a country parish called "sweet Alice." She *was* accomplished: "she wept with delight when you gave her a smile, and trembled with fear at a frown." These remarkable responses were mentioned not to bring sniggers but to prompt cheers. She got them. The poem was endlessly reprinted and was set to music twenty-six different times. The awed respect for Alice's overreactions was like that which caused a high faintality rate, innumerable blushes, and quarts of tears among

THE INDIAN GIRL OF STORY.   THE INDIAN GIRL OF FACT.

Indian maiden of romance vs. Indian maiden of humor. F. Opper illustrated
a contrast drawn by Phunny Phellow Bill Nye in his *History of the United
States* (1894): "They were shown . . . as graceful and beautiful in figure;
but in those days when the Pocahontas girls went barefooted till the age of
eighty-nine years, chewed tobacco, kept Lent all winter and then ate a brace
of middle-aged men for Easter, the figure must have been affected by the
irregularity of meals."

heroines in nineteenth-century novels. The taste for sloshing
around in emotion nurtured bathetic obituary poems. It helped
maudlin preachers and orators fetch the huzzas of listeners.

   Therefore, when irreverent Phunny Phellows wrote burlesque
romances in which heroines—and even heroes—went on regular
emotional benders, and when they wrote or spouted historical
anecdotes, sermons, and orations that soared to emotional eloquence and then bellyflopped to bathetic depths, the humorists
added to their assaults on accepted moral precepts another attack on hallowed convictions.

Charles Dudley Warner in *Washington Irving* (1881) held that "in this seething time," when "the lighter literature took a sentimental tone, and either spread itself in manufactured fine writing, or relapsed into a reminiscent and melting mood . . . suddenly and completely this affectation was laughed out of sight by . . . the 'humorous' writer, whose existence is justified by the excellent service performed in clearing the tearful atmosphere." He was, of course, over-sanguine. In the 1890's, George Du Maurier's astonishingly popular heroine, Trilby, sang a version of "Ben Bolt" and revived its remarkable popularity, and writers continued to turn out mawkish fiction throughout the rest of the century. Just the same, one of the good deeds performed by the Phunny Phellows was an assault on moralizing and sentimental debaucheries.

This motley crowd was historically (if not artistically) important in other ways. Thanks to the level of their funmaking and the many outlets they found, they brought laughter to a far larger audience than their predecessors had. It was a less localized audience than a national one. Thanks to the delight they brought and to their fame and prosperity, as authors they won more respect from the man in the street than earlier American writers, serious or humorous, had. And by coining cynical aphorisms and whacking away bravely at sentimentality and pretentiousness, they helped express and popularize new attitudes and disbeliefs in the postwar years.

Part Four

Mark Twain

Mark Twain's Chestnuts

> *Thanne telle I hem ensamples many oon*
> *Of olde stories longe tyme agoon,*
> *For lewed peple loven tales olde;*
> *Swiche thynges kan they wel reporte and holde.*
> —The Pardoner in Chaucer's *Canterbury Tales.*

29.
"The Jokes
That Never Die"

IN A LETTER OF 1890, MARK Twain held that "the most valuable capital, or culture, or education usable in the building of novels is personal experience." He figured that therefore he was well equipped, and to prove it, he ticked off the many kinds of life with which he was familiar— "boy-life out on the Mississippi," which had "a particular charm" for him, work as a traveling printer in several cities, Mississippi River steamboat pilot, Western miner and prospector, newspaper reporter for years, lecturer, entrepreneur, and publisher: "And I have been an author for 20 years and an ass for 55." He downgraded literary influences, boasting that his "wide culture" was "all of it real, none of it artificial, for I don't know anything about books."

The weight of the evidence suggests that he was putting on the sort of act Ben Franklin had put on in colonial days. Or perhaps he was forgetful. Take the matter of jokes.

Hank Morgan, Twain's visitor to medieval England, we noted in an early chapter, gloomily listened to a court jester's monologue, cussed out "poor, flat, wormeaten jokes" that the silly Fool told, and was "almost convinced . . . that there isn't any such thing as a new joke possible." Not long before he published this fictitious gripe, the humorist had cussed overage jokes in his private notebook: "God damn the *old* jokes, the jokes that never die —that tortured Cain and brought murder into the world—&c. The mother in law—big footed girls—he lit the fire with petroleum, funeral at 3."

He was a dandy one to talk.

Twain put a variant of an ancient flatulence story (1607) into his *Dated 1601 Conversation as It was by the Fireside in the Court of Queen Elizabeth*. Did he believe it was new? Impossible. He confessed that he wrote *1601* after reading Old English books: "In one of these I came across a brief conversation which powerfully impressed me . . . with the frank indelicacies of speech permissible among ladies and gentlemen in that ancient time. I was immediately full of a desire to . . . contrive one of those stirring conversations out of my own head." He could have found exactly such talk in many dusty tomes. After canvassing jest books published between 1483 and 1751, John Wardroper reported that "many stories about farts in mixed company could be given"; the one closest to Twain's variant, we think, was in Thomas D'Urfey's early-eighteenth-century collection of songs. But even if he had not found a dialogue about uncontrolled gas in some ancient anthology, since the story was orally circulated down to the very present, he could have learned about such chats from one of many storytellers who entertained him over the years.

Other fireside exchanges echo a favorite eighteenth-century diarist he identified in the foreword: "The following is supposed to be an extract from the diary of the Pepys of that day." One conversationalist claims that he got a story from Boccaccio's *Decameron*. This is incorrect, but the mistake is an understandable one since the prototype of the tale is in a book imitating the *Decameron* which Clemens had recently bought and read—the *Heptameron*, by Margaret of Angoulême, queen of Navarre.

It was acute, of course, of Twain to insert ancient jokes in what was intended to be a bantering exchange that would "out-Rabelais Rabelais." No such justification—if one is needed—can be offered for his use of a medieval gambit in a skit that he wrote out in Nevada soon after he got his first newspaper job there in 1862.

The chief joke in "The Petrified Man"[*]—one that the humorist himself admitted missed fire—was pretty clearly lifted from Chapter XIX of *The Second Book of Rabelais, Treating the Heroic Deeds and Sayings of the Good Pantagruel*.

The piece was in another old tradition—that of Swift's "Modest Proposal" and the satires by Franklin, notably "Rules by which a Great Empire May be Reduced to a Small One." For both Swift and Franklin did what Twain specifically said he did —presented a discourse "with an unfair pretense of truth" but included self-destructing details. (Twain pretty clearly derived from Franklin's *Autobiography* the idea for an amusing passage in "The Facts Concerning the Recent Carnival of Crime in Connecticut," wherein, like Franklin, Twain's narrator listens to a long sermon and, as it progresses, revises again and again the amount that he plans to drop into the collection plate.)

Twain's griper about old jokes called some "worm-eaten." If ever a jest was honeycombed with worm-holes, it was one of which John Wardroper, that great student of "journeyings of jests across frontiers and across countries," said: "A Greek joke that is found among the Arabs (and, in turn, throughout Europe) is of a man who hears that one of a pair of twin brothers has died. When he meets the other twin, he asks, 'Was it you who died, or your brother?' "

This jape turned up during the fifteenth century in a Greek jestbook, in 1630 in a British jokebook, in 1864 in *Shakespeare Jest Books*, in the 1880 *Modern Joe Miller*, the 1883 *Wit and Humor of the Age*, the 1888 *Book of Noodles*, the 1902 *Masterpieces of Wit and Humor*, and the 1965 collection of Ozark jokes called *Hot Springs and Hell*. There, editor Vance Randolph gives much of this long history but concludes, "I am sure that I read this in one of Mark Twain's books years ago, but am unable to locate it now."

He should have looked at an anthology, *Lotus Leaves* (1875), where W. F. Gill printed the sketch by Twain that used the jape. (Gill did so without paying, thus infuriating the humorist, who was a money writer.) Or he should have looked at Twain's *The Stolen White Elephant Etc.* (1882), a book on which Clemens collected royalties. In "An Encounter with an Interviewer," Twain told about his exchange with a "nervous, dapper, 'peart' young man" from the *Daily Thunderstorm* who questioned him on a morning when "I was not feeling bright":

Q. . . . Who is this a picture of on the wall? Isn't that a brother of yours?

A. Oh! yes, yes, yes! Now you remind me of it; that *was* a brother of mine. That's William,—*Bill* we called him. Poor old Bill!

Q. Why? Is he dead, then?

A. Ah, well, I suppose so. We never could tell. There was a great mystery about it.

Q. That is sad, very sad. He disappeared, then?

A. Well, yes, in a sort of general way. We buried him.

Q. *Buried* him! *Buried* him without knowing whether he was dead or not?

A. O, no! Not that. He was dead enough.

Q. Well I confess that I can't understand this. If you buried him and you knew he was dead—

A. No! no! We only thought he was.

Q. O, I see. He came to life again?

A. I bet he didn't.

Q. Well, I never heard anything like this. *Somebody* was dead. *Somebody* was buried. Now, where was the mystery?

A. Ah, that's just it! That's it exactly. You see, we were twins—defunct and I,—and we got mixed up in the bath-tub when we were only two weeks old, and one of us was drowned. But we didn't know which. Some think it was Bill. Some think it was me.

Q. Well, that *is* remarkable. What do *you* think?

A. Goodness knows! I would give the whole world to know. This solemn, this awful mystery has cast a gloom over my whole life. But I will tell you a secret now, which I never have revealed to any creature before. One of us had a peculiar mark—, a large mole on the back of his left hand,—that was *me. That child was the one that was drowned!*

People who speak of milking a joke will have to agree that Twain here churned one into butterfat. (The authors stole the butterfat bit from Bob Hope.)

Twain resuscitated the doddering jokes so far mentioned during the first fifteen years of his career as a professional writer. It may be that at first he did not notice what was going on. Beginning in the 1870's, however, he saw and said that any author, himself included, inevitably reworked not only used jokes but aged materials of all sorts.

A speech, notes in book margins, and letters show this. He seconded Alexandre Dumas's claim that a man of genius did not steal from other writers but conquered and annexed territory to an empire that he peopled and ruled. Twain cited an example: "Shakespeare took other people's quartz and extracted gold from it—it was a nearly valueless commodity before." He endorsed a "truth" stated by Oliver Wendell Holmes: that "we all unconsciously work over ideas gathered in reading and hearing, imagining they were original." Going further, he told a friend that he himself sometimes knowingly transplanted the ideas of other storytellers into his own narratives.

There is a good chance that he noticed this dependence during these years. Again and again, he directly quoted other authors at length and adapted to his own needs narratives that he had read and heard told. He dumped into factual works pages of quoted matter. One scholar found that even without counting the long, second-hand passages that made up the appendices, *Roughing It*, for instance, has nearly eleven thousand borrowed words. Since *The Prince and the Pauper* was a historical novel, he was driven to notice that from start to finish it is built of twice-told tales. Other borrowings, though less patent, were quite as useful.

Also, because *Roughing It* recounts Mark Twain's Western experiences, he perhaps became aware as he wrote it of the tremendous value to him of stove-side gatherings during a visit to Angels Camp in the winter of 1864–65—a visit which, we argue later, was a turning point in his writing career. There he heard a story which, when he retold it, won him his first national—indeed, international—fame, plus others that he would retell for several decades. And though the Angels Camp harvest was unusually rich, oral stories that he heard elsewhere constantly served him well.

His reading, wider ranging from the 1870's on, also provided much matter that he conquered and annexed to his territory. Because *Huckleberry Finn*, started during this decade, was his masterpiece, its possible sources have been hunted down with great zeal. And scholars have learned that they were remarkably numerous and varied.

Not surprisingly, as they have shown, this professional humorist trotted along in the tracks of funny American writers; he echoed more than a baker's dozen of them in this book alone. The oldest, Augustus Baldwin Longstreet, had published his pioneering book, *Georgia Scenes*, the year Clemens was born. The youngest, Joel Chandler Harris, thirteen years Clemens's junior, was just beginning his career.

More surprisingly, foreign authors scattered over centuries were sources of passages in a book supposedly by an uneducated country kid. These included Old Testament authors, Cellini, Cervantes, Shakespeare, Bunyan, Pepys, Defoe, LeSage, Saint-Simon, Casanova, Goldsmith, Scott, Moore, Trollope, Carlyle, Dumas, Dickens, Reade, Taine, and W. E. H. Lecky. Others probably were influential; we list only those about whom there can be little or no argument. And though some passages by these writers which Twain transmuted were not humorous in either earlier forms or in the novel, most were originally humorous or were transformed into humor by Twain.

> *Troop after troop of citizens came to serenade Wilson, and . . . shout themselves hoarse over every sentence that fell from his lips—for all his sentences were golden, now. . . .*
>
> *And as each of these roaring gangs of enthusiasts marched away, some remorseful member of it was quite sure to raise his voice and say—*
>
> *"And this is the man the likes of us have called a pudd'nhead for more than twenty years. He has resigned from that position, friends."*
>
> *"Yes, but it isn't vacant—we're elected."* —Mark Twain, *The Tragedy of Pudd'n head Wilson* (1894).

> *The little pretending to be the big . . . it's like a cat letting on to be a cataract.* —Mark Twain, *Notebook* #23, Spring, 1889.

30.
Eiron *and* Alazon

EARLY IN HIS CAREER, MARK Twain made an important discovery—that the two ancient comic types called (by the Greeks, but not by him) the *eiron* and the *alazon* could be used again and again in many ways for purposes of comedy. He used them often as characters in third-person narratives. With greater effectiveness in "autobiographical" and fictional works, he used them as first-person narrators.

Represented by a third-person narrator, both of them appeared in an amateurish anecdote, "The Dandy Frightening the Squatter," in 1852, which scholars are persuaded that Sam Clemens wrote when he was a sixteen-year-old printer's apprentice. Though characters are sketchy stereotypes, descriptions and happenings ineptly handled, and the style blah, it has been studied with care because it shows what he was up to at the start of his career.

The story begins with the docking of a Mississippi steamboat at Hannibal. "A spruce young dandy, with a killing moustache, &c., . . . bent on making an impression on the hearts of the young ladies on board," "a formidable-looking bowie-knife" in

his belt and "a large horse-pistol in each hand," marches ashore.
Facing "a tall, brawny woodsman" silently leaning against a
tree, he yells:

"Found you at last, have I? You are the very man I've been looking
for these three weeks! Say your prayers! . . . you'll make a capital
barn door, and I shall drive the key-hole myself!"

The squatter calmly surveyed him a moment, and then, drawing
back a step, he planted a huge fist directly between the eyes of his
astonished antagonist, who, in a moment, was floundering in the turbid
waters of the Mississippi.

The watching passengers shout, the squatter makes a single laconic comment, and the ladies vote "the knife and pistols to the
victor."

Shortly before this was printed, both its plot and many of its
details had surfaced in periodicals; Sam may have put one version into type. But it seems to us that crude though it is, the story
has some ancient ancestors. For here is a boaster, one who claims
to be more than he is. He tries to bluff a quiet man who has the
look of being less than he is. In other words, this is a teen-ager's
version of a confrontation at a Missouri town's woodyard between an *alazon* and an *eiron*.

"The Dandy" moldered in an obscure humorous magazine until antiquarians did some body-snatching. By contrast, Twain's
story of 1865, "The Celebrated Jumping Frog of Calaveras
County," though published obscurely, hopped into newspapers
all over the country, crossed the ocean and—thanks to Twain's
seven remunerative resurrections of it in books and magazines
between 1865 and 1897—enjoyed a long life.

Artful telling, of course, also helped. The anecdote, as scholars
learned after some more exhumations, had been going the rounds
for years without making any stir whatever. Journalists and the
sober-sided mining camp yarn spinner Clemens heard tell it did
little more than summarize the plot, much as Clemens did when
soon after hearing it he wrote:

Coleman with his jumping frog—bet a stranger $50.—Stranger had
no frog and C. got him one:—In the meantime stranger filled C's frog
full of shot and he couldn't jump. The stranger's frog won.

Twain expanded this curt and meager summary into a complex
and comic narrative twenty-nine hundred words long. Refashion-

ing his Angel's Camp experience to make it amusing, he pictured himself as a humorless auditor who listened with angry boredom to the telling of a very funny story by a maundering narrator just as completely without a sense of humor. In addition to his leisurely storyteller and impatient listener, he brought to life Jim Smiley (né Coleman), a fantastically compulsive gambler, the stranger who took him and his money, an ingratiating frog, and a couple of talented animal shills.

The stranger in Twain's version lets Smiley deduce that he is stupid when he looks at the trained frog, Dan'l Webster, and says, "I don't see no p'ints about that frog that's any better'n any other frog." Then when Smiley offers to bet, the stranger touches up the sketch of himself as a plaintive wayfarer ripe for plucking. Finally, while the overeager Smiley rushes out to the swamp, slops around, catches a frog, and brings it back, his visitor pensively stuffs Smiley's Dan'l Webster with quail shot. His nondescript leaper wins the bet, and after collecting, the stranger exits with a gesture and a remark that show he is smarter than he appears to be. We suggest that he is a Calaveras County *eiron*, and —assuming that his sneer at Dan'l Webster's appearance was justified—Dan'l is an amphibian *eiron*.

Wager winners that Smiley collects do not appear to have p'ints about them better'n those of competing pets. But after Smiley has trained them, they no longer look bad after the bets are down. His dog, Andrew Jackson, for example says the story: ". . . to look at him you'd think he warn't worth a cent but to set around and look ornery. . . . But as soon as the money was up on him he was a different dog. . . ." Then there's Smiley's mare, a worthy descendant of equine *eirons* that had been used to diddle Americans in comic racing stories at least since 1792.

By 1833, the horse has acquired a name—Sleepy David—and the look of a natural-born loser: as "lean, slab-sided, crooked-legged, rough-haired, milk-and-molasses-colored a son of a gun as ever went on four legs" and "stood at all times as if he was asleep." The 1854 specimen, Sleepy Davy, not only looks vulnerable but is ridden by a drunk:

"You never saw so bad a looking creeter. . . . He hitched along behind his drunken owner, with his nose down between his knees, his tongue lolling half out of his thin jaws, his eyes nearly closed, and his tail clinging close to his body, while the boys' were in high glee at the prospect of the approaching fun. The bets were all closed . . . the instant the bugle sounded . . . the drunken man vaulted into the saddle, and ten men couldn't have held his horse . . . he had it all his own way. . . ."

Mark Twain shows what a genius can do with similar material:

"Thish-yer Smiley had a mare . . . and he always used to win money on that horse, for all she was so slow and always had the asthma, or the distemper, or the consumption, or something of that kind. They used to give her two or three hundred yards' start, and then pass her under way; but always at the fag end of the race she'd get excited and desperate like, and come cavorting and straddling up, and scattering her legs around limber, sometimes in the air, and sometimes out to one side among the fences, and kicking up m-o-r-e dust and raising m-o-r-e racket with her coughing and sneezing and blowing her nose—and *always* fetch up at the stand just about a neck ahead, as near as you could cipher it down."

In *The Innocents Abroad*, a tourist who pretends to be an utter fool charms his companions by putting patronizing guides in their place: "The doctor asks the questions, generally, because he can keep his countenance, and look more like an inspired idiot, and throw more imbecility into the tone of his voice than any man that lives. It comes natural to him." His finest hour comes when he questions an Italian guide about a mummy: "Is, ah—is he dead?"

A key passage in *Roughing It* introduces a famous animalized *eiron*, the coyote—"a long, slim, sick and sorry-looking skeleton, with a . . . tolerably bushy tail that forever sags down with a despairing expression of foresakenness and misery, . . . always poor, out of luck and friendless . . . so scrawny, and ribby, and coarse-haired, and pitiful." But sick a swift dog on him, especially one that believes he runs fast:

The cayote will go swinging gently off on that deceitful trot of his, and every little while he will smile a fraudful smile over his shoulder that will fill that dog entirely full of encouragement and worldly ambition, and make him lay his head still lower on the ground, and stretch his neck, . . . and move his furious legs with a yet wilder frenzy. . . . And all this time the dog is only a short twenty feet behind the cayote, and to save the soul of him he cannot understand why it is that he cannot get perceptibly closer; and he begins to get aggravated, . . . and next he notices that he is getting fagged, and that the cayote actually has to slacken speed a little to keep from running away from him—and *then* that town dog is mad in earnest, and he begins to strain and weep and swear, and paw the sand higher than ever, and reach for the cayote with concentrated and desperate energy. This "spurt" finds him six feet behind the gliding enemy. . . . then, in the instant that a wild hope is lighting up his face, the cayote turns and smiles blandly upon him once more . . . and forthwith there is a rushing sound, and the sudden splitting of a long crack through the atmosphere, and behold that dog is solitary and alone in the midst of a vast solitude!

Henry Nash Smith notices that this passage is a miniature of the basic situation of *Roughing It*—"a tenderfoot (. . . a representative of the dominant culture) with a higher opinion of himself than he can make good in the Far Western environment; a veteran who looks disreputable . . . but is nevertheless in serene command of the situation; and the process by which the tenderfoot gains . . . quite fresh and new knowledge, at the cost of humiliation." So the whole book, it would seem, can be summarized in terms that also fit the age-old comic conflict.

In *Pudd'nhead Wilson*, Twain developed the conflict as one of several interlaced book-length plots. Young lawyer David Wilson, not much to look at—"homely, freckled, sandy-haired"— makes an ironic remark soon after settling in a stodgy little Southern town, Dawson's Landing, that leads the townspeople to dub him pudd'nhead. But he has a great deal of horse sense, as is proved by his coining of earthy aphorisms which he scribbles on his calendar. ("Nothing so needs reforming as other people's habits"; "It is difference of opinion that makes horse-races.") His canny experiments lead to his discovery, long before Alphonse Bertillon was born, of identification by fingerprints. As a result, he stages a courtroom performance that rivals those of Perry Mason and thereby shows the citizenry that they, not he, have been lummoxes.

Although Twain's greatest ironic characters, as will be shown, were first-person narrators, he wrote about his most appealing boasters in the third person. Quite early, young Sam Clemens met "the little pretending to be the big," as he called them, in literature and in life. As a boy, he got the impression that the whole United States was crawling with chauvinists and big talkers:

everybody bragged, everybody blustered. . . . ours was the only free country the sun had ever looked upon; ours was the highest of all civilizations; . . . and on top of all this, it was our daily custom to strut, and swell, and swagger around, hands under coat-tails, hat tilted over left eye, spoiling for a fight—numerical strength of the enemy, matter of no consequence. Popular song of the time:

> "Englishman he beat
>   Two French or Portugee;
> Yankee-doodle come down,
>   Whip them all three."

In *The Hannibal Journal* of the time, a young man who had been jilted made ring-tailed roaring threats in a poem:

> I'll flog the *Young Earthquake*,
>   The earth I will physic;
> Volcanoes I'll strangle,
>   Or choke with the phthisic.

In Hannibal's streets, the boy heard the disreputable town drunkard, old General Gaines, shout typical keelboatmen boasts, including the words, "Whoops! Bow your neck and spread!"

It is hard not to suspect that Clemens saw one of the plays we discussed in Chapter 13—those starring Mose the fireman—which were shown widely during the 1850's, just when Clemens was wandering. In *Roughing It*, he dresses his Virginia City "stalwart rough," Scotty Briggs, in "fire helmet, flaming red flannel shirt, patent-leather belt . . . , coat hung over arm, and pants stuffed into boot tops." Every detail accurately describes Mose's outfit. And Scotty's comments on his pal, Buck Fanshaw, echo scores of antebellum boasts, including those of New York's fireb'hoys: "He could lam any galoot of his inches in America. . . . He was the bulliest man in the mountains, pard! He could run faster, jump higher, hit harder, and hold more tanglefoot whisky without spilling it than any man in seventeen counties."

Twain was sure that his first superb book-length characterization, Colonel Sellers in *The Gilded Age*, fictionally portrayed a cousin of his. But he must have taken hints—and particulars—from other relatives and from sundry writers. Like Meercraft, the "projector" in Ben Jonson's *The Devil is an Ass* (1616), Sellers thought up myriad wild schemes and inventions that would bring him "millions." The "recovery of drown'd land," curing leather from dogs' skins, "bottle-ale," imported forks, wine made from raisins and blackberries, raising wool on eggshells and grass from marrow bones, cornering toothpicks: these were some schemes he talked about. His "millions" were pounds. Sellers's plans to corner the corn crop and the hog crop, buy up all the wildcat banks in five states (profit: fifty million dollars), build a railroad, and sell his Infallible Imperial Oriental Optic Liniment and Salvation for Sore Eyes all over the world for "God only knows how many millions and millions."

Sellers's less remote ancestors were Goldsmith's Beau Tibbs and Dickens's Micawber. Micawber cheerfully, though without great conviction, keeps predicting that "something will turn up" to mend his tottering fortunes. Sellers has unwavering faith that passeth understanding in his wild schemes, and has an untethered imagination that leaves Micawber's far behind. But the two have likenessses that contemporary reviewers and recent scholars have noticed: both have wild plans, live on hope, and rhapsodize about the future.

A second comic character that Twain portrayed in *The Gilded Age*, Senator Dilworthy, had a real-life prototype, but as Edward Wagenknecht has noticed, a speech he makes sounds very much like one that the Reverend Chadband makes in Dickens's *Bleak House*. Speaking at the Cattleville Sunday school, the politician unctuously nominates himself as a model for his audience by telling his life story—poor boyhood, love for teachers, piety, Sunday school, spurning of temptations "to drink wine, to dance, to go to the theatres," pure mind, hard work, honesty, election to the governorship and then to the Senate, saintly self-sacrifice, and dedicated public service. Actually he is a liar, a payer of bribes, and a receiver of graft—a pious fraud.

The colonel and the senator differ in that the former believes in his illusions and the latter is a hypocritical cynic. But the pair are alike in claiming to be better than they are, and in each case the incongruity is the source of fun.

Colonel Sellers was too useful a fellow to be confined within a single work. Impersonated by an outstanding comic actor in a freewheeling dramatization of *The Gilded Age*, he was for years one of the most popular figures in the American theater.

Sellers was briefly at his fantastic best, though, in Twain's generally inferior *The American Claimant*. This ends with a letter the colonel writes a friend shortly before the friend sets out for England. The inventive Sellers has perfected a sublime scheme "based upon hard, practical scientific laws"—nothing less than the control of sunspots to reorganize "the climates of the earth according to the desire of the populations interested." His charges for weather shifts, though reasonable, will bring him billions. Sellers has an assignment for his friend:

> I would like you to provide a proper outfit and start north as soon as I telegraph you, be it night or day. I wish you to take up all the country stretching away from the north pole on all sides for many degrees south, and buy Greenland and Iceland at the best figure you can get now while they are cheap. It is my intention to move one of the tropics up there and transfer the frigid zone to the equator. I will have the entire Arctic Circle in the market as a summer resort next year, and will use the surplusage of the old climate . . . to reduce the temperature of opposition resorts. . . .
>
> Meanwhile, watch for a sign from me. Eight days from now we shall be wide asunder; for I shall be on the border of the Pacific, and you out on the Atlantic, approaching England. That day, if I am alive and my sublime discovery is proved and established, I will send you greeting, and my message shall deliver it where you are, in the solitude of the sea; for I will waft a vast sun-spot across the disk like drifting smoke, and you know it as my love-sign, and will say, "Mulberry Sellers throws us a kiss across the universe."

The bragging match between the Corpse-Maker and the Child of Calamity, discussed elsewhere, though written for *Huckleberry Finn*, was shifted to *Life on the Mississippi* and left out of the novel. This meant that the pair of comic *alazons* who did their scheming in Huck's story as it was published were the King and the Duke. These two, copied, like others of their sort Twain pictured, from men in life and in books, show kinship with ancient boasters the minute they tell one another how they operate. "What's your line—mainly?" the older man asks:

> "Jour printer, by trade; do a little in patent medicines; theatre-actor —tragedy, you know; take a turn at mesmerism and phrenology when there's a chance; teach singing-geography school for a change; sling a lecture, sometimes—oh, I do lots of things—most anything that comes handy, so it ain't work. What's your lay?"
>
> "I've done considerable in the doctoring way in my time. Layin' on

o' hands is my best holt—for cancer, and paralysis, and sich things; and I k'n tell fortune pretty good, when I've got somebody along to find out the facts for me. Preachin's my line, too; and workin' camp-meetin's; and missionaryin around."

They join Old World fakes in claiming that they have noble blood. On one occasion the King, like pedants and doctors traced back to antiquity (e.g., Plautus's Lidus), concocts pedantic word derivations—in his case to explain why he calls funeral obsequies "orgies." When the pair tread the boards, they advertise them-selves as David Garrick the Younger of Drury Lane Theatre, London, and Edmund Kean the Elder of the Royal Haymarket Theatre, and murder Shakespeare's lines.

In *Personal Recollections of Joan of Arc*, a novel generally—with reason—scorned and spat upon by critics, Twain created a likable and amusing braggart who unfortunately was buried in that historical (and sometimes hysterical) novel. "Edmond Au-brey, called the Paladin, because of the armies he was always going to eat up some day," is a fifteenth-century half horse-half alligator. He is equipped with the over-fancy Spanish costume, the ponderous belly, and the cowardice that are trappings of many Old World boasters. Aubrey is always what Jim Doggett is at the finish of his tall tale—a believer in his creation. He does not lie consciously but has faith in the complete truthfulness of his ever-swelling self-glorifications. When he tells his initial yarn about Joan's first royal audience, he is sad because he was absent. "Next, his talk was full of what he would have done if he had been there; and within two days he was telling what he *did* do when he *was* there." During successive tellings, he ele-vates his imaginary noble ancestry and plays an increasingly im-portant part. In the last version, he has Joan give him a vital task, telling him: "Pluck me this false knave from the throne!" He dangles a little man who is a member of his audience by the scruff of his neck to show how he obeyed her. To provide a cli-max, he has the King send Joan away so that he may star in a scene all his own:

"Then the King dismissed the Maid most graciously—as indeed was her desert—and, turning to me, said, 'Take this signet-ring, son of the Paladins, and command me with it in your day of need; and look you,' said he, touching my temple, 'preserve this brain, France has use for it; and look well to its casket also, for I foresee that it will be hooped with a ducal cornet one day.' I took the ring, and knelt and kissed his hand, saying, 'Sire, where glory calls, there will I be found; where danger and death are thickest, that is my native air. . . .' "

Critics have said that the Paladin's tall talk exports to fifteenth-century France the yarn spinning of the humorist's frontier, and it certainly echoes Western vauntings that Sam Clemens read and heard when he was young. But he had read about or had seen on the stage some British literary characters very like Aubrey who were almost Aubrey's contemporaries. Rather surprisingly, he knew, for instance, Bessus, a swaggering coward created by Beaumont and Fletcher. He knew over a longer time, and more intimately, Shakespeare's Sir John Falstaff. As Howard Baetzhold has proved, a dozen parallels (including several in the passage just cited) establish plump Jack Falstaff as the fat Paladin's ancestor. (An important mutation: Twain, to make the point that Joan was a miraculous leader, has Aubrey, under her powerful influence, overcome his cowardice and fight to the death at her side.) Both are *alazons* who tell imaginative whoppers about their great deeds in desperate fights.

> . . . *there is no merit in ninety-nine stories out of a hundred except the merit put into them by the teller's art; as a rule, nothing about a story is "original," and entitled to be regarded as private property and valuable, except the art which the teller puts into the telling of it.* —Samuel L. Clemens, letter to Alexandra Gripenberg, December 27, 1888.

> *And then the crowd would burst out in a laugh again, and yell at him, and ask him what was his name before he was married, and what . . . was his sister's cat's grandmother's name, and all the things that a crowd says when they've got hold of a feller that they see they can plague. Well, some things they said was funny,—yes, and mighty witty too, I ain't denying that,—but all the same it warn't fair nor brave, all them people pitching on one, and they so glib and sharp, and him without any gift of talk to answer back. . . . They had him, you know. . . . He was a good-enough sort of cretur, and hadn't no harm in him, and was just a genius, as the papers said, which wasn't his fault. We can't all be sound: we've got to be the way we're made. As near as I can make out, geniuses think they know it all, and so they don't take people's advice, but always go their own way, which makes everybody forsake them and despise them, and that is perfectly natural. If they was humbler and listened and tried to learn, it would be better for them.* —Huck Finn commenting on a fool professor who, about 1846, invented an atomic-powered balloon. *Tom Sawyer Abroad.*

31.
"The Art Which the Teller Puts into the Telling"

LIKE SELLERS, HUCK'S CON MEN and the Paladin, boastful pretenders—and ironic pretenders to faults they don't have, too—in anecdotes, poems, plays, and fictional works for centuries gave away their foibles and any virtues they had by what they said. When authors used such characters as narrators, the *alazons* and *eirons* got a chance to show off quirks at length in the first person.

On two occasions, Mark Twain implied or claimed that this way of telling stories—even ancient ones—gave them one of their chief charms. Soon after a journalist published a story that she heard Clemens tell, a reader accused the humorist of swiping it from Boccaccio's *Decameron*. Nonsense, he said: he heard it from his friend F. Hopkinson Smith; Smith had heard it in Virginia, told it often, and eventually published a version in a magazine. Twain thought the *Decameron* version unfunny and without anything worth stealing. "Smith," wrote Twain, "will transmute that dross into his golden words, and by the art of delivery will make you shout." His "way of telling" the story gives it "the only 'originality' that has any value"—and for him, the best way was that of a first-person narrator.

A comparison between Smith's "Ginger and the Goose" and Boccaccio's version shows why Twain felt that his friend "made a good and tellable thing" out of a "curt and meager" anecdote. Aarne and Thompson, in *The Types of the Folktale*, list versions not only in Italian but also in Lithuanian, Flemish, German, Hungarian, Czech, Indian, West Indian, and English. A British version of 1693, 1883, and 1968 features a crane. Then with their customary avoidance of humor, they classify the plot, number it, and summarize it:

785A. *The Goose with One Leg.* Accused of eating the goose's leg, the thief maintains that it had only one leg, and cleverly enforces his point by showing geese standing on one leg. (Usually the master confounds the rascal by frightening the geese so that they use both legs.)

Ginger, who tells the American version, is a young black servant of an old Virginia family who comes through as much more of a personality and a far better raconteur than Boccaccio's Neifile. Ginger evokes a way of living and shows an understanding of personalities and human relationships that have no counterparts in Neifile's brisk recital. He sketches a household and individualizes its members in ways that show why and how they tick—stiff-backed old gentleman ("wen he mek up his min' to do a ting, why, you could hab bet at onst dat it war done"); young Marse Ned; Ned's bride, Miss Carrie, "sot in her ways," feuding with her mother-in-law; the matriarch ("ole Miss kind o' drew in, an' de young people didn't hab de nicest sort ob a time"); the grumbling cook, who refuses to cook the goose because she sides with the old lady; Ginger, who agrees to cook the fowl because he sympathizes with the young couple; his girl friend Dolly, who "kep' on a-triflin' " until she cajoled him into giving her the leg. His carefully recorded dialect and the payoff which characterize him are illustrated by the concluding paragraphs of Smith's story. After dinner, Marse Ned has joined Ginger in the barnyard:

"I like to know," he say, "whar dat oder leg ob de goose hab gone," an' he look me straight in my face.

Now it war jist de time dat our gooses war a-restin', an' I look roun' an' see dem all a stan'in' on deir one leg, an' so I tek Marse Ned by de arm an' I pint to dem all. "What's you a-meanin', Marse Ned?" I say. "Does you see any ob dem gooses wid more'n one leg, dat you 'cuse me ob sich a ting?" An' Marse Ned he jist raise up he han', an' he holler "Shoo! shoo!" an' den in coorse de gooses put down der oder leg, an' dey all run.

An' den I tu'n right roun' at Marse Ned, an' I say, solemn like, an' I say him loud, an' I say him strong, an' I look him straight in de whites ob his eyes—I say, "Marse Ned, when you see dat goose on de table in front ob you, did you 'member to say 'shoo' to dat goose? I jist arsk you dat!" And Marse Ned neber had one word to say.

In "How to Tell a Story," Twain praised recent retellings of another chestnut that, he said correctly, "had been popular all over the world for twelve or fifteen years." This is No. 1225 in the Aarne-Thompson *Types:* "A man's head snatched off by accident and his companions do not see what has happened. Debate: did he ever have a head?" Wardroper reprints the following version in *The Complete London Jester* (1765):

A LYING DOG

In the heat of an engagement a sailor took his wounded comrade on his shoulders—and [as he was] carrying him down to the surgeon, the fellow in his way lost his head. "Why," says the surgeon, "do you bring me a man without a head?"

"Odso!" says the sailor, "he told me he had lost his leg, but he was always a lying dog."

By the time Clemens heard this, a soldier displaced the sailor, the scene shifted to a battlefield, a cannon ball beheaded the wounded man, an officer questioned the numbskull, and the pay-off line was italicized, capitalized, punctuated, and repeated: "It is true, sir, just as you have said. . . . *But he* TOLD *me* IT WAS HIS LEG!!!!! Haw-haw-haw! HE TOLD ME—HO-HO-HO!—IT WAS HIS LEG!!!!! HAW-HAW-HAW!!!!! HE TOLD ME IT WAS HIS LEG!!!!! The changes, so far as Twain was concerned, were made in vain:

"isn't worth the telling . . . no art . . . anybody can do it
. . . very depressing . . . makes one want to renounce joking
and lead a better life . . . a machine could tell it."

James Whitcomb Riley, Twain held, took this contemptible
and pathetic minute-and-a-half *comic* story and glorified it into
a ten-minute *humorous* story that was "about the funniest thing
I have ever listened to." The explanation: Riley expertly played
the role of a perfect narrator for comic effect—"a dull-witted old
farmer who had just heard [the story] . . . , thinks it unspeak-
ably funny, and is trying to repeat it." The gaffer does everything wrong—minces chronology, heaps up irrelevancies, tries
in vain (but at great length) to recall other nonessentials, makes
unimportant mistakes, then painstakingly corrects them, explains why he made them, leaves out important matters, then
goes back and awkwardly inserts them, and so on *ad infinitum*.
The end is a masterly portrait:

> The teller is innocent and happy and pleased with himself, and has
> to stop every little while to hold himself and keep from laughing out-
> right; and does hold in, but his body quakes in a jelly-like way with
> interior chuckles; and at the end of the ten minutes the audience have
> laughed until they are exhausted, and the tears are running down
> their faces.
> The simplicity and innocence and unconsciousness of the old farmer
> are perfectly simulated, and the result is a performance which is thor-
> oughly charming and delicious. This is art—and fine and beauti-
> ful. . . .

In each retelling of a superannuated story, therefore, the teller,
Mark Twain believes, is a chief source of amusement. Not the
plot, not the payoff snapper, but the characterization of the narrator is the cream of the jest. It seems worthwhile to compare the
two fictitious storytellers he praises and to see if they have anything in common.

The best thing in Smith's narrative is Ginger, a clever servant
who, to the delight of young Marse Ned and the reader, blandly
and blatantly pretends to be less than he is—an *eiron*.

And what tickles Twain in Riley's performance is his impersonation of a farmer who believes that he tells a story well when
he tells it very badly. Like, say, a deluded Don Quixote or hundreds of the don's descendants, he is firmly convinced that he is

better than he is. The gap between what he attempts and the minute accomplishment makes him an *alazon*.

Twain had no truck, of course, with fancy Greek labels. All the same, time after time he used a first-person narrator that fits one of them perfectly. This was true whether the first-person narrator was the semi-fictional "Mark Twain" or a fictional Huck Finn, say, or Henry Morgan.

As unaddicted to the use of ancient terms as the humorist, John C. Gerber recently classified the poses the humorist took—the points of view "other than his own" that he used—sometimes in short passages, sometimes in long ones, to get laughs:

Fundamentally, there are two ways to confront life falsely. Either one can pretend that life is more agreeable to the spirit and more amenable to the will than it really is, or one can pretend that it is less so. One can exaggerate his superiority to human affairs or his inferiority to them. As the narrator "Mark Twain," Twain did both. He pretended undue superiority, for example, in posing as the Gentleman, the Sentimentalist, the Instructor, and the Moralist; he assumed undue inferiority in posing as the sufferer, the Simpleton, and the Tenderfoot.

The terms "undue superiority" and "undue inferiority" are good ones for the comic posturings, respectively, of the boaster and the humble man.

Autobiographical and travel books teem with examples of each pose. In *The Innocents Abroad*, the Sentimentalist, for instance, on viewing the alleged Tomb of Adam, proudly drenches it with tears:

The fountain of my filial affection was stirred to its profoundest depths, and I gave way to tumultuous emotion. I leaned upon a pillar and burst into tears. I deem it no shame to have wept over the grave of my poor dead relative. . . . he did not live to see his child. And I—I alas, did not live to see *him*. Weighted down by sorrow and disappointment, he died before I was born—six thousand brief summers before I was born.

The unctuous moralist, after seeing the can-can danced in a Parisian suburb, gives a long, complete description of the spectacle. "I," he says haughtily, "placed my hands before my face for very shame." Then he adds, "But I looked through my fin-

Mark Twain portrays
himself as a skilled artist.

gers." As in the "Petrified Man" sketch, the position of the fingers is the payoff.

When writing *A Tramp Abroad*, Twain told a friend that his
overall plan was to pose as an instructor in three fields and at the
same time to give away the fact that he was an ignoramus in
each:

I allow it to appear . . . that I am over here to make the tour of
Europe *on foot*. I am in pedestrian costume, as a general thing, & *start*
on pedestrian tours, but mount the first conveyance that offers, . . .
endeavoring to seem unconscious that this is not legitimate pedestrian-
izing. My second object here is to become a German scholar; my third,
to study Art and learn to paint. I have a notion to put a few hideous
pen and ink sketches . . . in my book, & explain their merits & defects
in the technical language of art.

Instructor Twain tells Germans how he would reform their ineffi-
cient language:

I would leave out the Dative Case. It confuses the plurals; and, besides,
nobody ever knows when he is in the Dative case, except he discovers

One of his masterly drawings. Illustrations for *A Tramp Abroad* (1880).

it by accident . . . move the verb further up to the front . . . do away with those great long compounded words; or require the speaker to deliver them in sections, with intermissions for refreshments . . . retain *Zug* and *Schlag*, with their pendants, and discard the rest of the vocabulary. This would simplify the language.

Art student Twain smugly shows off his elevated taste in painting:

What a red rag is to a bull, Turner's "Slave Ship" was to me, before I studied Art. Mr. Ruskin is educated in art up to a point where that picture throws him into as mad an ecstacy of pleasure as it used to throw me into one of rage, last year, when I was ignorant. His cultivation enables him,—and me, now, —to see water in that glaring yellow mud and natural effects in those lurid explosions of mixed smoke and flame, and crimson sunset glories; it reconciles him,—and me, now,— to the floating of iron cable-chains and other unfloatable things. . . . A Boston newspaper reporter went and took a look at the Slave Ship floundering about in that fierce conflagration of reds and yellows, and said it reminded him of a tortoise-shell cat having a fit in a platter of tomatoes. In my then uneducated state, that went home to my non-cultivation, and I thought here is a man with an unobserved eye. Mr. Ruskin would have said: This person is an ass. That is what I would say, now.

Elsewhere in the same book, the author—who switches comic masks whenever he feels like it—"assumes undue inferiority" and poses as a simpleton. With a party, "Mark Twain" is climbing a mountain. "Scientific reading" has taught him that "either thermometers or barometers ought to be boiled to be accurate; I did not know which it was, so I boiled both." When he gets no result, he inspects the instruments and finds flaws: "the ball of the thermometer was stuffed with tin-foil." Undaunted, he carries on his "scientific work" and boils something at each stop. At one point, he boils a camera: "a failure . . . I could not see that the lenses were any better." One experiment leads him to adopt a hypothesis which he tests by climbing to the mountain's summit:

I boiled my thermometer, and sure enough, this spot, which purported to be 2,000 feet higher than the locality of the hotel, turned out to be 9,000 feet *lower*. Thus the fact was clearly demonstrated, that, *above a certain point, the higher a point seems to be, the lower it actually is*. Our ascent itself was a great achievement, but this contribution to science was an inconceivably greater matter.

Cavilers object that water boils at a lower and lower temperature the higher and higher you go, and hence the apparent anomaly. I answer that I do not base my theory upon what the boiling water does, but upon what a boiled thermometer says. You can't go behind the thermometer.

In "Old Times on the Mississippi," telling about his apprenticeship as a pilot, the author assumes the tenderfoot role. One who puts biographical facts alongside literary picturings will find that he tinkers with history to suit his purpose. He was in his twenties when he learned the river from pilot Horace Bixby, but he represents himself as a callow teen-ager. He had a river-town boy's thorough familiarity with steamboats and their ways; in "Old Times" he is a complete ignoramus. The first night out, for instance, he is wakened at midnight by the watchman and told to turn out:

And then he left. I could not understand this extraordinary procedure; so I presently gave up trying to, and dozed off to sleep. Pretty soon the watchman was back again, and this time he was gruff. I was annoyed. I said:—

"What do you want to come bothering around here in the middle of the night for? Now, as like as not, I'll not get to sleep again to-night."

The watchman said:—

"Well, if this an't good, I'm blest. . . ."

About this time Mr. Bixby appeared on the scene. Something like a minute later I was climbing the pilot-house steps with some of my clothes on and the rest in my arms. Mr. Bixby was close behind, commenting. Here was something fresh—this thing of getting up in the middle of the night to go to work. It was a detail that had never occurred to me at all. . . . I began to fear that piloting was not quite so romantic as I had imagined it was. . . .

To say that the author, here and in *Roughing It*, poses as a tyro oversimplifies a bit. To be precise, it is a time-battered oldster vaguely resembling Samuel L. Clemens, who does the posing. He tells, with the distancing and amused tolerance that time has brought, about an earlier self who was an inexperienced greenhorn. Such a processing of reality, of course, edges away from "factual" writing and comes close to first person *fiction* in which a created character pictures himself as being more or less than he is.

Mark Twain once said that he was at his best as a fiction writer when he used a first-person narrator: "Experience has taught me long ago that if ever *I* tell a boy's story . . . it is never worth printing. . . . To be successful and worth printing, the imagined boy would have to tell the story *himself* and let me act merely as his amanuensis." His first-person storyteller that critics constantly praise is, of course, Huck Finn.

The very first time Twain spoke of writing Huck's *Adventures*, all he said about characterization and plot was that he planned to "take a boy of twelve and run him through life," and the boy would not be Tom Sawyer because "he would not be a good character for it." But he was firm about the fictional point of view: it would be that of the boy because "I believe it would be fatal to do it in any shape but autobiographically—like Gil Blas."

His comparison shows a kinship. Like Lesage's *Story of Gil Blas of Santillane* (1715, 1724, 1735), Huck's autobiography appears in a parade of works stretching back at least to Juvenal (c. 60–140 A.D.) and including picaresque novels turned out during three centuries. Protagonists and the ground they explore vary. Juvenal's poverty-stricken nobleman, for instance, has a vinegary look at sin-riddled society in ancient Rome. Gil Blas, lower-middle-class, educated, joins up with thieves, servants, actors, doctors, courtiers, and other unsavory folk in much of eighteenth-century Spain. Huck, an ignorant, poor-white pariah, mingles with blacks, trash, quality, and those in between in nineteenth-century towns, farmhouses, and plantations along eleven hundred miles of the Mississippi. Wherever they go, these protagonists (and scores like them) encounter enough people to learn that men, as Twain put it, are "creatures to be ashamed of in pretty much all their aspects."

Such an acrid view may not seem to provide the best stuff for
comedy. But *Huckleberry Finn* is (among many things) one of
America's funniest books. For this, its first-person narrator deserves much of the credit.

"Like Gil Blas," Twain said. Some resemblances: Huck, like
Gil, is on the run; he assumes various disguises and plays several
roles; he lies and steals. But Twain's model posed problems. Tobias Smollett listed one of these when, in *Roderick Random*
(1748), *he* imitated Lesage's novel. Gil, he said, is too frivolous.
He laughs at his disgraces—thinks sin is funny: "This conduct
prevents that generous indignation which ought to animate the
reader against the sordid and vicious disposition of the world."
Smollett reached around and patted himself on the back for managing better: "I have attempted to represent modest merit struggling with every difficulty to which a friendless orphan is exposed, from his own want of experience, as well as from the
selfishness, envy, malice, and base indifference of mankind."

Twain (although he was critical of Smollett) moved away
from his model in a similar direction. He made sure that Huck
would not laugh at his disgraces or at sin by doing two things:
(1) He equipped him with an ulcerated conscience that at times
made life a hell for him. (2) He created a character who in fact
would laugh at practically nothing, since he was as devoid of
humor as an aged country ham. Just naturally as somber all the
time as his creator was when on the lecture platform, Huck concocted melancholy lies about horrendous disasters; and he broke
down and laughed only once throughout scores of hilarious experiences—and then at a joke that really was not there. As added
insurance against his being tolerant of wickedness, Twain justified Huck's fibs and petty larcenies as a vulnerable orphan's
only defenses against a hostile world. And he created a hero with
something finer than "*modest* merit." In fact, he made it clear
that the boy was essentially innocent and sound of heart, nearer
to sainthood than to rascality. Smollett's "generous indignation"
on a large scale was out, though; Twain was sure that it was
death and disaster to his kind of amusing satire. So he let Huck
speak directly about his repulsion only four times—a total of
twenty-five laconic words (four used twice) in a long novel.

Age-old stereotypes of poor whites helped to make Huck believable to American readers. Jokelore had long portrayed South-

western trash as dumbbells with neither humor nor moral standards. And Huck himself was a victim. Loaded with mother wit, he was dead sure that he was stupid. Virtuous, he was convinced that he was hopelessly wicked. In the scene that for years has got the critics' highest praise, the boy makes his finest decision—to help slave Jim escape bondage—and tells himself that he is a wicked fool:

The more I studied . . . the more my conscience went to grinding me, and the more wicked and low-down and ornery I got to feeling. And at last, when it hit me all of a sudden that here was the plain hand of Providence slapping me in the face and letting me know my wickedness was being watched all the time from up there in heaven, whilst I was stealing a poor old woman's nigger that hadn't ever done me no harm, and now was showing me there's One that's always on the lookout, and ain't agoing to allow no such miserable doings to go only just so fur and no further, and I most dropped in my tracks I was so scared. Well, I tried the best I could to kinder soften it up somehow for myself, by saying I was brung up wicked, and so warn't so much to blame; but something inside of me kept saying, "There was the Sunday school, you could a gone to it; and if you'd a done it they'd a learnt you, there, that people that acts as I'd been acting . . . goes to everlasting fire."

It is a neat, ironic touch to have the boy, instead of *pretending* that he is worse than he is, as other *eirons* do, actually *believing* that he is a hopeless sinner.

Like his creator, Huck at times switches roles. Twain wrote his masterpiece when Cervantes's masterpiece, *Don Quixote*, was influencing much of his work. The playing off of an *alazon*, the don, against an *eiron*, his servant, in the Spanish novel had been admired and imitated for centuries. In early chapters of *Huckleberry Finn*, Tom Sawyer is a Quixote to Huck's Sancho Panza, with Tom talking up romantic flimflam and Huck bluntly saying that the stuff "has all the marks of a Sunday school." When Tom has been left in St. Petersburg, though, and Huck and Jim are drifting on their raft, Huck is the pseudo-expert and Jim an earthy commentator who is sometimes a victim of his ignorance and sometimes a voicer of wise insights.

For instance, after Huck, the Biblical scholar, instructs Jim about King Solomon's huge harem, the black man uses his native wit to comment:

"A harem's a bo'd'n-house, I reck'n. Mos' likely dey has rackety times in de nussery. En I reck'n de wives quarrels considable; en dat 'crease de racket. Yet dey say Sollermun de wises' man dat ever live'. I doan take no stock in dat. Bekase why: would a wise man want to live in de mids' er sich a blimblammin' all de time? No—'deed he wouldn't. A wise man 'ud take en buil' a biler-factry; en den he could shet *down* de biler-factory when he want to res'.''

Huck, the self-appointed historian, tells Jim about Henry VIII's villainy during a war that took place more than two centuries after Henry's death:

"Well, Henry he takes a notion he wants to get up some trouble with this country. How does he go at it—give notice?—give the country a show? No. All of a sudden he heaves all the tea in Boston Harbor overboard, and whacks out a declaration of independence, and dares them to come on. That was *his* style—he never give anybody a chance. He had suspicions of his father, the Duke of Wellington. Well, what did he do?—ask him to show up? No—drownded him in a butt of mamsey, like a cat. Spose people left money laying around where he was— what did he do? He collared it. Spose he contracted to do a thing; and you paid him, and didn't set down there and see that he done it—what did he do? He always done the other thing. Spose he opened his mouth —what then? If he didn't shut it up powerful quick, he'd loose a lie, every time. That's the kind of a bug Henry was.''

Although Huck's speech shows him up as an overconfident pretender to learning, he moves along to a conclusion that makes sound horse-sense: "All I say is, kings is kings, and you got to make allowances. Take them all around, they're a mighty ornery lot." In other words, right after he concocts his historical mishmash, this linsey-woolsey thinker reaches a shrewd judgment.

Hank Morgan says something similar: "Dear, dear, . . . there is nothing diviner about a king than there is about a tramp . . . just a cheap and hollow artificiality. . . ." Morgan, hero and narrator of Twain's tall tale, *A Connecticut Yankee in King Arthur's Court*, wafted from nineteenth-century Hartford to sixth-century Camelot, has learned this truth on a journey with the king. When Arthur, traveling incognito, is picked up and sold as a seven-dollar slave, no one notices his sacred majesty. Hank is, in Twain's words, "an ignoramus"—rough-hewn, socially crude, and uneducated. But his perception, his countryman would claim, is of a sort that his superior background and training make inevitable. This blacksmith's son has had rich experiences as a blacksmith, veterinarian, factory worker, and superintendent.

He is, as he boasts, "a Yankee of the Yankees—and practical"—
mechanically ept, inventive, well-stocked with gumption. Clearly
he is in the line of Americanized *eirons*.

In a scene that is the spitting image of one in *Don Quixote*,
Hank and his girl Sandy go on a mission to rescue forty ladies
from an ogre. Coming to a pigsty, Sandy blames some wicked en-
chantment for making her escort think that a castle is a sty and
imprisoned ladies are sows. Humoring her, Hank pays the swine-
herd, drives the animals home, and puts them up overnight:

> We had to drive those hogs home—ten miles; and no ladies were
> ever more fickle-minded or contrary. They would stay in no road . . .
> broke out through the brush on all sides. . . . And they must not be
> struck, or roughly accosted; Sandy could not bear to see them treated
> in ways unbecoming their rank. The troublesomest old sow of the lot
> had to be called my Lady, and your Highness, like the rest. . . .
> There was one small countess, with an iron ring in her snout and
> hardly any hair on her back, that was the devil for perversity. She
> gave me a race of an hour, over all sorts of country. . . . I seized her
> at last by the tail, and brought her along, squealing. . . . We got the
> hogs home just at dark—most of them. The princess Nerovens de
> Morganore was missing, and two of her ladies in waiting. . . . Of
> course the whole drove was housed in the house. . . . Never heard
> anything like it. And never smelt anything like it. It was like an in-
> surrection in a gasometer.

Wild fantasies such as Sandy's are a dime a dozen in Camelot—a world teeming with liars—"a childlike and innocent lot:
telling lies of the stateliest pattern . . . and ready and willing
to listen to anybody else's lie, and believe it, too," dealers in
"tales of blood and suffering" told with "a guileless relish." The
chief rival of the Yankee in a struggle for power is old Merlin,
"the mighty liar and magician," eternally rapping about his
great feats, and never able to carry out his boasts. Hank does
some lying, too. "I am a magician myself," he announces, "and
the Supreme Grand High-yu-Mucka-muck and head of the
tribe, at that."

Blustering, then failing, Merlin follows the Old World pattern. Hank, with know-how, impudence, and a smattering of scientific knowledge, is able to follow the antebellum New World
formula of Mose and Davy Crockett, not only to brag but to live
up to his vauntings. And whenever this plebeian among aristocrats carries out a boast, he puts on a show and gloats.

Typical triumph: A fountain has failed. Merlin, "burning smoke-powders, and pawing the air, and muttering gibberish," tries to reactivate it. No soap. At night, unobserved, Hank and experts he has trained mend the leak but postpone the flow of water and stash away some fireworks until they can collect a crowd and stage a spectacle. While the multitude watches, the Yankee does hokuspokuses, shouts "magic" words, sets off electrical charges, and starts the pumps:

. . . a vast fountain of dazzling lances of fire vomited itself toward the zenith with a hissing rush, and burst in mid-sky. . . . One mighty groan of terror started up from the massed people—then suddenly broke into a hosannah of joy—for there, fair and plain in the uncanny glare, they saw the freed water leaping forth! . . . You should have seen those acres of people throw themselves down in that water and kiss it; kiss it, and pet it, and fondle it. . . . I sent Merlin home on a shutter. He had caved in and gone down like a landslide. . . .

It was a great night, an immense night. There was a reputation in it. I could hardly get to sleep for glorying over it.

Mark Twain must have felt pretty elated too. For he had cooked up a situation and a set of incidents hospitable to a character who was simultaneously an ironic man and a screamer.

This discussion of Mark Twain's use of moss-grown waggeries, though it touches on ways he transformed them, leaves out comments on important aspects of his writings. In "Jim Baker's Blue-Jay Yarn," a segment of *A Tramp Abroad*, Baker's aberration is one that can be traced back to Mopsus, in Greek mythology. The "Mark Twain" who introduces the story parades his whimsy, his sensibility, his imaginativeness, and his knowledge of Teutonic folklore, and then is exposed, jeered at, and humiliated. So, roughly speaking, he can be classified as an *alazon*. The old pocket miner whose yarn he repeats is a homespun philosopher and, again roughly speaking, can qualify as an *eiron*. But each is a great deal more than a comic stock character. Further, the framework and the anecdote it encloses are interrelated in a unique and outstanding work of art. Some of this narrative's qualities, in addition to its lineage, will be discussed in the next chapter. Two final chapters about Mark Twain will deal with new and forward-looking aspects of the humorist's work.

32.
Mark Twain's
Other Masterpiece

GRIZZLED JIM BAKER, THE LONE
dweller in a deserted California mining camp, begins a story
about favorite woodland neighbors by summing up his scientific
findings during seven years:

"There's more *to* a blue-jay than any other creature. He has got
more moods, and more different kinds of feelings than other creatures;
and mind you, whatever a blue-jay feels, he can put into language.
And no mere commonplace language, either, but rattling, out-and-out
book-talk—and bristling with metaphor, too—just bristling! And as for
command of language—why, *you* never see a blue-jay stuck for a word.
No man ever did. They just boil out of him! And another thing: I've
noticed a good deal, and there's no bird, or cow, or anything that uses
as good grammar as a blue-jay. You may say a cat uses good grammar.
Well, a cat does—but you let a cat get excited, once; you let a cat get
to pulling fur with another cat on a shed, nights, and you'll hear grammar that will give you the lockjaw. Ignorant people think it's the *noise*
which fighting cats made that is so aggravating, but it ain't so; it's the
sickening grammar they use. Now I've never heard a jay use bad
grammar but very seldom; and when they do, they are as ashamed as
a human; they shut right down and leave."

Bernard DeVoto thought "Jim Baker's Blue-Jay Yarn," an in-
terlude in *A Tramp Abroad* (1880), typified Mark Twain's humor in part because of the way it combined fantasy and reality.
Baker's furred and feathered friends not only talk but achieve
high levels of diction, metaphors, and even grammar. But Baker,
"a creation from the world of reality," DeVoto says, is born not
of fantasy but of "the sharp perception of an individual." "Fantasy," he concludes, "is thus an instrument of realism and the

humor of Mark Twain merges into the fiction that is his highest reach."

Critics of several persuasions saw Baker's yarn as being what W. E. Henley called it in an early review of *A Tramp Abroad*, Twain "at his best and brightest, . . . delightful as mere reading [and] of a high degree of merit as literature." DeLancey Ferguson, for example, thought it stood out in a book which "contained phrases and passages that were Mark Twain at his best," and added, "were one asked to choose from all Mark Twain's works the most perfect example of the genuine Western tall tale, patiently and skillfully built up . . . , the choice would come down at last" to this story.

A case can be made for the claim that, just as *Huckleberry Finn* is the greatest of Twain's longer comic works, the "Blue-Jay Yarn" is the greatest of the shorter ones. Although it does not have the depth, the scope, or the variety of the novel, it is equally characteristic, and judged on its own terms, in some ways it is superior; it has fewer flaws and greater unity. Besides, it is delightfully funny. So it is worth a close look.

The story's background partly accounts for its pre-eminence and helps one define its genre. Storytelling sessions with some masters of the art in the winter of 1864–1865 helped the humorist not only discover the substance of the yarn but rediscover the form that was appropriate for it. Later practice and analysis helped him give the written narrative qualities that—quite rightly—he prized. And literary traditions and models also contributed in important ways to its excellence.

During the years before he went West in 1861, Sam Clemens constantly heard stories told well. His mother, an "obscure little woman" with an "enchanted tongue," he called "the most eloquent person" he ever met. Ned, his father's slave, told "The Golden Arm" story which Twain retold year after year to lecture audiences. On the Missouri farm where he spent boyhood summers, he enjoyed his uncle's storytelling; at night in the Quarters, he heard Uncle Dan'l "telling the immortal tales which Uncle Remus Harris was to . . . charm the world with, by and by." (Dan'l effectively prepared childish listeners for jimdandy nightmares by unloosing a bloodcurdling ghost story just before he sent them to bed.) During Sam's *Wanderjahren*, fellow jour printers and steamboatmen were memorable yarnspinners.

He grew up when American humorists were trying to catch in print the substance and the manner of oral yarns. At his printer's case in Hannibal and elsewhere, he set up their writings; in his leisure hours, he read them. At the time he went West, however, the Phunny Phellows' new styles were fashionable word-play, topsy-turvy sentences, parodies, and burlesques. Writing for the Virginia City *Territorial Enterprise* and for San Francisco newspapers, Twain ground out comedy of the sort currently popular. Throughout the rest of his life, he would often—too often—write Phunny Phellow humor. But a visit to the California mining country reacquainted him with the stuff and the style of fireside storytelling that shaped many of his best writings.

Clemens, a twenty-nine-year-old San Francisco journalist, peeved officials by publishing feisty exposés. When he found it expedient to absent himself a while, Jim Gillis, pocket miner out in the area where Baker lived, asked him to be a guest. Between December 4, 1864, and February 25, 1865, the budding author stayed with Gillis and his partner, Jim Stoker, in a Jackass Hill cabin or bunked in a nearby Angel's Camp hotel.

The region had once swarmed with gold seekers, but the rich diggings had played out, and now only a few desultory pocket miners dotted fields, hills, and forests. Clemens did a little pocket mining without luck and was kept from doing more by a rainy season which—even for a state where what natives call "unusual weather" flushes houses down hills—was worse than usual. He, his hosts, and soggy neighbors huddled for hours around the cabin fireplace or the hotel bar-room stove. His notebook jottings gripe about endless deluges and the "beans and dishwater" monotonously served by the hotel's French restaurateur. He complains that "4 kinds of soup which he furnishes to customers only on great occasions . . . are popularly known among the Boarders as Hellfire, General Debility, Insanity and Sudden Death." The booze must have been just as corrosive. In a plaint that has the poignancy of a personal reminiscence, Clemens holds that a shot of the tavern's straight whiskey "will throw a man a double somerset and limber him up like boiled macaroni before he can set his glass down."

All the same, looking back, he would call this area a "serene and reposeful and dreamy and delicious sylvan paradise" where he had "a fascinating and delightful time." He fondly remembered dates with the Eves of this Eden, a miner's pneumatic daughters whom he called "the Chapparal Quails." More important, every few years during more than four decades, he praised the purveyors of the chief entertainment aside from drinking— the mining camp yarn spinners. He analyzed their artistry, and at the top of his form imitated them and retold their stories.

There is support for the guess several scholars have made that the mining country visit, because of the impact of those story-telling orgies in Jim Gillis's Jackass Hill cabin and the Angel's Camp caravanserie, brought a turning point in the author's career. The very first sketch he published after he got back to San Francisco had as its best and chief ingredient a vernacular mono-logue by one of the Angel's Camp crowd. One evening he told anecdotes to a group of fellow reporters so well that they lost all track of time. Within months, he decided that he had a "call" to "drop all trifling . . . & strive for a fame" by cultivating his "talent for humorous writing." Soon after this discovery of his vocation, he published one of the tales that he had heard "around the tavern stove"—"the germ," as he put it, "of my coming good fortune," a piece of writing that "became widely known in America, India, China, England—and the reputation it made for me . . . paid me thousands and thousands of dollars. . . ." The story furnished the chief part of the title of Twain's first book, and though he infrequently revised any piece once it had been printed, he carefully—and substantially—revised this one three times. Other retellings of California mining camp yarns came out in 1865, 1867, 1871, 1880, 1884, 1893, and 1907.

The cream of what turned out to be a bumper crop was the "Blue-jay Yarn," covering eleven pages of *A Tramp Abroad*, published in 1880, when the author paused part way through the writing of *Adventures of Huckleberry Finn*.

The "lovable" personality and the skill of the original teller of this story in the mother lode country doubtless helped Twain see its merit. This was Jim Gillis, "gray as a rat, earnest, thoughtful, slenderly educated, slouchily dressed and clay-soiled," but "a gallant creature" whose "style and bearing could make any costume regal . . . a man, and a whole man." "A much more remarkable person than his family and his intimates ever suspected," Jim in the humorist's opinion was a genius—"a born humorist, and a very competent one" who "would have been a star performer if he had been discovered, and had been subjected to a few years training with a pen." Twain identified Jim, who he thought was the best raconteur in the diggings, as the originator of three of his mining-camp tales, though one of them almost certainly was told by Jim's partner. The writer's notebook jottings, his characterizations of the tellers, and his vivid picturings in memoirs and in the stories themselves justify the other attributions.

When inspired, Jim stood with his back to the fire, unleashed his imagination, and spun yarns. Each was a gaudy lie created as he went along but soberly told as "history undefiled." Usually he made his "pard" Stoker the incongruous hero, and Stoker sat smoking, listening solemnly but amiably to his "monstrous fabrications." One of the stories that Twain retold celebrated Stoker's prodigious cat, Tom Quartz, a beast that "had never existed," Twain said, "outside of Jim Gillis's imagination." Another was "Jim Gillis's yarn about the blue jays"—"a charming story, a delightful story, and full of happy fancies." When he theorized about oral storytelling and a writer's adaptation of its ways, he found Jim Gillis a useful teacher.

Twain would call the oral story as Gillis told it "high and delicate art," and would find "no merit in ninety-nine out of a hundred [stories] except the merit put into them by the teller's art." He deliberately tried to use that art in his books. But he repeatedly said that written art had to modify the ways of oral storytelling. If an author merely set down the golden words of a fine storyteller, a funny thing happened on the way to the printer: they turned to dross. Twain prohibited publication of an interview he gave because quoting talk in print is "an attempt to use a boat on land or a wagon on water."

He decided that careful artistry alone could give printed words the sound of free-and-easy speech: "I amend dialect stuff by talking and talking and *talking* it till it sounds right." Measures like those he took to give painstakingly memorized platform monologues the qualities of off-the-cuff utterances helped him write colloquial passages—"a touch of indifferent grammar flung in here and there, apparently at random" but in fact shrewdly deployed; "heaving in . . . a wise tautology"; "sprinkl[ing] in one of those happy turns on something that has previously been said." The chief incongruity in the two-hundred-word opening paragraph of Baker's story—between fulsome praise of book talk and grammar and abysmal ignorance about both—is made apparent by only four assorted, and strategically placed, grammatical mishaps. And the paragraph illustrates "wise tautology" by reiterating half a dozen times the belief that a jay can express whatever it feels.

Twain lauded Gillis for "build[ing] a story as it goes along, careless of whither it is proceeding, enjoying each fresh fancy as it flashes from the brain." In "How to Tell a Story," he held that the very basis of the American art was "to string incongruities and absurdities together in a wandering and purposeless way." He downgraded jokes with payoff lines and praised stories with "pervasive" humor which, like that of William Dean Howells, "flows softly all around about and over." So his aim was to ape in print the leisurely imagining and inundating humor of Gillis and other experts.

Twain makes the "Blue-Jay Yarn" seem to meander, for one thing, by prefacing it with an apparent unhurried digression of his own, and then by having Baker sidle into his monologue at his leisure. The humorist, a continent and an ocean away from the mother lode country, strolls into the woods above the Neckar. Soon, remembering German legends about the area that he has been reading, he falls "into a train of dreamy thought about animals which talk, and kobolds, and enchanted folk." Later, lost and alone in the dense, silent woods, he fancies that he glimpses some of these creatures in the shadows under the trees.

Suddenly, the quiet is shattered by the croak of a raven staring down from a branch at the intruder. A second bird comes along:

The two sat side by side on the limb and discussed me as freely and offensively as two great naturalists might discuss a new kind of bug. . . . They called in another friend. This was too much. I saw that they had the advantage of me, and so I concluded to get out. . . . They enjoyed my defeat as much as any low white people could have done. They craned their necks and laughed at me, (for a raven *can* laugh, just like a man,) they squalled insulting remarks after me as long as they could see me. . . . when even a raven shouts after you, "What a hat!" "O, pull down your vest!" and that sort of thing, it hurts you and humiliates you, and there is no getting around it with fine reasoning and pretty arguments.

The confrontation leads Twain to recall the man who could understand birds and animals—Jim Baker. Baker's background and some of his opinions are detailed. Only after this preamble—one that at first glance appears to be very loosely related—does Baker's monologue start with the remarks about the great skill with which jays communicate. In a passage a bit longer than the first, and therefore an apparent over-elaboration, Jim next argues that "a jay is just as much a human as you be" by mentioning sundry human traits and ("wisely tautological") repeating the claim several times:

> "You may call a jay a bird. Well, so he is, in a measure—because he's got feathers on him, and don't belong to no church, perhaps; but otherwise he is just as human as you be. And I'll tell you for why. A jay's gifts, and instincts, and feelings, and interests, cover the whole ground. A jay hasn't got any more principle than a Congressman. A jay will betray; and four times out of five, a jay will go back on his solemnest promise. The sacredness of an obligation is a thing which you can't cram into no blue-jay's head. Now on top of all this, there's another thing: a jay can out-swear any gentleman in the mines. You think a cat can swear. Well, a cat can; but you give a blue-jay a subject that calls for his reserve-powers, and where is your cat? . . . Yes, sir, a jay is everything that a man is. A jay can cry, a jay can laugh, a jay can feel shame, a jay can reason and plan and discuss, a jay likes gossip and scandal, a jay has got a sense of humor, a jay knows when he is an ass just as well as you do—maybe better. If a jay ain't human, he better take in his sign, that's all."

The impression that Baker is loquacious is heightened by the introduction here of a different type of comedy. These remarks, proving as they do that his birds are human chiefly by arguing that they are depraved in as many ways as human beings are, have the bite of satire. Twain would have said that Jim's equating of humanity with total depravity, in addition to "wandering in an apparently purposeless way," introduces an important component—a philosophical concept about the nature of mankind. "It takes a heap of sense to write good nonsense," he told himself in a note shortly before he wrote the blue-jay yarn. As an oldster, he would marvel at the way his humor outlasted that of more than eighty popular contemporary humorists, thus living "forever." ("By forever," he explained, "I mean thirty years.") His explanation: "I have always preached." The humorist was repeating a judgment of his best friend, Howells, who said that "what finally appeals to you in Mark Twain . . . is his common sense."

The way the tale that follows is unfolded reinforces the impression that it wanders, since—simple though it is—it (in Twain's phrase) seemingly "fools along and enjoys elaboration" for almost thirteen hundred words. It does not, in fact, detour; each of two parts illustrates a claim Baker makes as he starts his monologue:

Part one: Baker describes the comic doings of some jays around a deserted log house near his cabin. One finds a knot-hole in the roof and decides to fill it with acorns. Though he dumps in huge numbers, since the house is "just one big room," he fails. The bird becomes increasingly frantic, frustrated, outraged; and his more and more eloquent orations prove that "whatever a blue-jay feels, he can put into language."

Part two: Attracted by his commentaries, first one, then more jays gather and discuss the phenomenon. Finally one learns what the trouble is and announces his discovery. Thereupon, greater and greater numbers of birds fly in, study the scene, and jeer about the frustrated jay's mistake. The reactions prove that jays are "just as human as you be." When he makes this uncomplicated fable laughable, Twain proves that the effect of a humorous story depends less upon matter than on manner, in a printed story as well as an oral one, if the author of the printed version adapts oral procedures.

Writings as well as oral storytellers, of course, shaped the blue-jay yarn. A beast fable, this narrative is part of a genre that amused audiences, literally, for ages. Even before Aesop, its beginnings, like Aesop himself, are hidden in the mists of antiquity, and from those beginnings to the present, the form has flourished. A few outstanding practitioners were Hesiod, Aristophanes, and Socrates in the ancient world; Chaucer and myriad anonymous celebrators of Reynard the Fox in the Middle Ages; Robert Henryson and William Caxton in the fifteenth century; Francois Rabelais in the sixteenth; Jean de la Fontaine (twelve books; "I use Animals to teach Mankind") and Sir Roger L'Estrange in the seventeenth; Jonathan Swift, John Gay, Gotthold Ephriam Lessing, Bernard Mandeville, Matthew Prior, William Cowper, Johann Wolfgang Goethe, and Benjamin Franklin in

the eighteenth; Leo Tolstoi, Ivan Krylov, Rudyard Kipling, Tri-
lussa (C. A. Salustra), Guy Wetmore Carryl, and others in the
nineteenth.

Since (as scholars have proved) Twain read widely, he knew
several of his remote predecessors in the anthropomorphic field.
About the time he wrote Baker's yarn, his reading had helped
him remember or discover three Americans working in the genre
in the 1880s. As co-editor of a forthcoming anthology, *Mark
Twain's Library of Humor* (1888), he was jotting down in Notebooks 15 and 16 lists of possible inclusions. Four times he mentioned George T. Lanigan (1846–1886) or his *World's Fables*,
and the anthology would include seven of Lanigan's pieces.
Twice he named Ambrose Bierce; one entry recalled fables published in a newspaper as much as thirteen years earlier; and the
anthology had seven of Bierce's fables, at the time still uncol-
lected. In Bierce's "The Robin and the Woodpecker," the latter
bird admits that he does not know why he pecks holes in a dead
tree: "Some naturalists affirm that I hide acorns in these pits;
others maintain that I get worms out of them." Alert source-
hunters will notice the bird's theoretical kinship with Baker's
blue-jay, which dumped acorns into his knot-hole for reasons
that were never clarified. They may also be interested in the fact
that once, when he talked about his story long after he wrote it,
Twain called it "a tale of how the poor and innocent *woodpeck-
ers* tried to fill up a house with acorns."

"Uncle Remus (?) writer of colored yarns," another notebook
entry, Twain made before the yarns had appeared between hard
covers and, evidently before he had learned that the creator's
name was Joel Chandler Harris. Clemens and his co-editors included two of Harris's narratives in their anthology. He read
Harris's tales to audiences, corresponded with him, swapped stories, arranged meetings, called him "a fine genius," and even
tried to get the shy little man to share lecture platforms. It seems
possible that partly because he so admired Harris and, like him,
as a boy had heard black storytellers tell animal legends, he did
well when he exploited what Harris called "that incongruity of
animal expression that is just human enough to be humorous" in
the "Blue-Jay Yarn."

Several passages in Jim Baker's story are enriched by comic

linkings between bird and animal—for instance, the jay's discovery of the hole: "He cocked his head to one side, shut one eye and put the other one to the hole, like a possum looking down a jug"; or the dog-like gesture showing the jay's puzzlement: "he took a thinking attitude . . . and scratched the back of his head with his right foot." (A kinship—perhaps something more—is indicated when one compares a passage in "Uncle Remus Initiates the Little Boy," the first Uncle Remus story and one included in Twain's anthology: "Den Brer Rabbit scratch on one year wid his off hine-foot sorter jub'usly. . . .") More incongruities are of the sort Harris mentioned—between bird and humans. After he drops the first acorn into the hole, the jay

"was just tilting his head back with the heavenliest smile on his face, when all of a sudden he was paralyzed into a listening attitude and that smile faded gradually out of his countenance like breath off'n a razor, and the queerest look of surprise took its place. . . . He cocked his eye at the hole again, and look a long look; raised up and shook his head; stepped around to the other side of the hole, and took another look from that side; shook his head again."

His puzzlement grows; so does his anger:

"He fetched another acorn, and done his level best to see what become if it, but he couldn't. . . . Then he begun to get mad. He held in for a spell, walking up and down the comb of the roof and shaking his head and muttering to himself; but his feelings got the upper hand of him, presently, and he broke loose and cussed himself black in the face. I never seen a bird take on so about a little thing."

Now he decides that he'll be damned if he doesn't fill that hole if it takes a hundred years, and for two and a half hours, he heaves in acorns without stopping:

"Well at last he could hardly flop his wings, he was so tuckered out. He comes a-drooping down, once more, sweating like an ice-pitcher, drops his acorn in and says, 'Now I guess I've got the bulge on you by this time!' So he bent down for a look. If you'll believe me, when his head come up again he was just pale with rage. He says, 'I've shoveled acorns enough in there to keep the family thirty years, and if I can see a sign of one of 'em, I wish I may land in a museum with a belly full of sawdust in two minutes!' "

The culmination of his frantic efforts and his frustration is accompanied by his greatest flight of eloquence:

"He just had strength enough to crawl up on to the comb and lean his back agin the chimbly, and then he collected his impressions and begun to free his mind. I see in a second that what I had mistook for profanity in the mines was only just the rudiments, as you may say."

In addition to the animalization or the humanization of birds, the story as Baker tells it amuses because of its comic picturings. Incongruities, as Max Eastman has noticed, are stressed when they are made highly concrete. Twain creates pictures because, as Howells says, "he is the impassioned lover, the helpless slave of the concrete": the jay peering into the knot-hole, shaking his head, cussing himself black in the face, turning pale with rage, taking a thinking attitude and leaning his back agin the chimbly attest to this slavery.

There are more humanizations and bodyings forth in the second movement of the story. A jay passing by hears the baffled bird "doing his devotions," stops, learns the reason, and calls in other jays:

"They called in more jays; then more and more, till pretty soon the whole region 'peared to have a blue flush about it. There must have been five thousand of them; and such another jawing and disputing and ripping and cussing, you never heard. Every jay in the whole lot put his eye to the hole and delivered a more chuckle-headed opinion about the mystery than the jay that went there before him. They examined the house all over, too."

The figurative comparison to "a blue flush" helps make this vivid, joining earlier figures to give substance and a comic quality to the proceedings and to justify Baker's apercu that a jay's language, sharing a conspicuous merit with written as well as oral American humor, just bristles with figures of speech. In the final paragraphs, after the old jay solves the mystery and announces his findings, his fellow jays become "a blue cloud," manifest vividly additional human traits, and prove their sense of humor is superior to an owl's:

"They all came a-swooping down like a blue cloud, and as each fellow lit on the door and took a glance, the whole absurdity of the contract that the first jay had tackled hit him home and he fell over backwards suffocating with laughter, and the next jay took his place and done the same.

"Well, sir, they roosted around here on the house-top and the trees for an hour, and guffawed over that thing like human beings. It ain't

no use to tell me a blue-jay hasn't got a sense of humor, because I
know better. And memory too. They brought jays here from all over
the United States to look down that hole, every summer for three years.
Other birds too. And they could all see the point, except an owl that
come from Nova Scotia to visit the Yo Semite, and he took this thing in
on his way back. He said he couldn't see anything funny in it. But
then, he was a good deal disappointed about Yo Semite, too."

DeVoto felt that the last sentences "mar the effect of a passage in
pure humor" because "they strain toward a joke, escaping from
the clear medium of the tale itself into burlesque." Those who
have heard an audience respond to the recitation of the sentences
by a master—Hal Holbrook, say—may disagree. Blemish or not,
the sentences (as DeVoto adds) are typical of Mark Twain. And
their mingling of horseplay with delicate fancifulness is typical
of both printed and oral American tall tale humor.

 An exchange between Twain and Joel Chandler Harris indicates that the humorist might well claim that this discussion so
far has failed to deal with the chief charm of this story. Twain
had complimented Harris on his picturing of Uncle Remus as he
told Negro folktales to a boy on an antebellum Georgia plantation. Harris, as modest as he was shy, protested that the folktales
were far more important than characterization: "my relations
toward Uncle Remus are similar to those that exist between an
almanac maker and a calender." Nonsense, Twain answered,
"the principal of life" was in the frameworks. The enclosed tales
were

only alligator pears—one merely eats them for the sake of the salad
dressing. Uncle Remus is most deftly drawn, and is a lovable and delightful creation; he, and the little boy, and their relations with each
other, are high and fine literature, and worthy to live for their own
sakes; and certainly the stories are not to be credited with *them*.

Granted, Clemens overstated, he was sincere in praising an
achievement that he admired and tried to duplicate: the use of
a framework to make up for attritions—over and above those previously discussed—that an oral story suffers when it is reduced
to print.

 When Clemens refused to let that interviewer publish an accurate transcript of an interview he had granted, he explained
that he did so because

an immense something has disappeared from it. That is its soul . . . everything that gave that body warmth, grace, friendliness and charm and commended it to your affections—or, at least, to your tolerance—is gone and nothing is left but a pallid, stiff and repulsive cadaver.

Such is "talk" almost invariably, as you see it lying in state in an "interview." The interviewer seldom tried to tell one *how* a thing was said; he merely puts in the naked remark and stops there. When one writes for print his methods are very different . . . he loads, and often overloads, almost every utterance of his characters with explanations and interpretations. . . . Now, in your interview, . . . you have not a word of explanation; what my manner was at several points is not indicated. Therefore, no reader can possibly know where I was in earnest and when I was joking; or whether I was joking altogether or in earnest altogether. Such a report of a conversation has no value.

A fiction writer, this implies, has a duty to so represent his listener and his storyteller as to relate them to the story. Somehow, by showing the pair in action and reaction, an artist must clarify such matters as why the one listens to a long-winded monologue and why the other gives it the substance and form he does. Somehow, too, the writer must simulate what Twain called "the spontaneity of a personal relation, which contains the very essence of interest."

The "Mark Twain" who listens to the jay story, and enjoys it and repeats it in toto is characterized by the long first-person account of his ramblings in the Black Forest and his recollection of a far away friend.

This "Mark Twain," is a relatively complex and ingratiating person, a fact that is made clear when one compares him with the "Mark Twains" who were auditors for a couple of other mining-camp tales. One of these "Mark Twains," gifted with as little humor, say, as a Canadian owl, is steered by a practical joker into the clutches of a monologist who mercilessly corners him and bores him to death with what he feels are irrelevant maunderings, but which are actually hilarious, before he gratefully escapes. He gives his account because he is outraged. The other "Mark Twain" has his curiosity raised to fever heat by jocose miners. He therefore listens eagerly to a long-winded chatterbox who barely mentions his subject but spins out (very funny) irrelevancies until whiskey overcomes him, he falls asleep, and his listener at long last learns that he has been hoaxed.

By contrast, the Black Forest "Mark Twain" has humor and understanding. He relishes the "deep and mellow twilight" and the silence of the pine wood; he has enjoyed the German *Märchen;* he imagines that he glimpses "small flitting shapes here and there down the columned aisles of the forest." When the ravens jaw at him, he can relish their insults and joke about the way "the thing became more and more embarrassing." His amused and amusing account of his adventures has shown why he can hear Jim Baker's monologue with delight, remember it, and at a much later date lovingly repeat it verbatim. He has prepared the reader for his mock-solemn claims that animals talk to each other, that Jim is the one man he has known who can understand them, and whimsical proof: "I knew he could . . . because he told me so himself."

Jim, like his auditor, benefits when compared with his counterparts in the two Mother Lode stories mentioned above. Both of the other storytellers are non-stop babblers simply because they are cursed with total recall and are allergic to relevance. Besides, one of them is "tranquilly, serenely, symmetrically drunk—not a hiccup to mar his voice, not a cloud upon his brain thick enough to obscure his memory." By contrast, Jim is loquacious because he has an appreciative audience; he has endless leisure; and his way of living has given him his awe-struck reverence for birds which most normal people find completely unlovable.

The biography of this "middle-aged, simple-hearted miner" shows how he discovered that jays can talk and he can understand them. He has been pushed by solitude into a strange companionship that he fondly recalls and celebrates at length. He "had lived in a lonely corner of California, among the woods and mountains, a good many years, and has studied the ways of his only neighbors, the beasts and the birds." Finally—to put it more bluntly than his compassionate portrayer does—this hermit has become a mite touched in the head. Seemingly random sentences give pertinent evidence: "Seven years ago, the last man in the region but me moved away. There stands his house—been empty ever since. . . ." A bit later: "Well one Sunday morning I was sitting out here in front of my cabin with my cat, taking the sun, and looking at the blue hills, and listening to

Jim Baker. Drawing by
E. W. Kemble (1888).

the leaves rustling so lonely in the trees. . . ." The statistics, and
the pathetic fallacy of "lonely" leaves, are doubly poignant because they are unobtrusive. Equally unstressed is the causal relationship between the recluse's history and (1) a misanthropy
that equates the birds' prodigious orneriness with human-ness,
and (2) admiration for creatures that eloquently curse a thwart-
ing world and that band together to jeer damn foolishness. Not
surprisingly, Jim fantasizes about these kin-birds, and as DeVoto
says, "His patient, explanatory mind actually works before our
eyes and no one can doubt him."

Awareness of one of Twain's favorite devices may help the
reader to notice a final touch in his portrayal of Baker. For years,
Twain had been making use of counterpoint—repetitions with
meaningful modulations. While writing *A Tramp Abroad*, he
cited one use of the device and its effect. He would, he said, place
cheek-by-jowl "a perfectly serious description of 5 very bloody
student duels which I witnessed in Heidelberg" and a broadly
burlesqued account of a pretentious but completely harmless
French duel. "The contrast," he predicted, "will be silent but

eloquent comment." Echoing with variations appears in "Blue-Jay Yarn" when the jeering at "Mark Twain" by raucous ravens is followed by the jeering at the befooled blue-jay by other jays. But note the contrast. Whereas the victim richly elaborates on "Twain's" droll humiliation and abject retreat, Baker says not a word about the mental state, the retorts, or the behavior of his embarrassed protagonist. This chief character, in fact, at this point vanishes from the story. The "silent but eloquent comment" that this contrast suggests is: So completely has Jim Baker identified with a woodland neighbor who, like him, has been defeated and, unlike him, has beautifully and directly voiced his feelings that he skips any report on the jay's humiliation.

A way of talking, telling a story, thinking and fantasizing that is delightful and funny is thus made probable by a characterization of Jim Baker which is complex enough to encompass a heart-warming touch of pathos.

Mark
Twain
Pioneers

You have a bastard perception of humor, nothing more; a multitude of you possess that. This multitude see the comic side of a thousand low-grade and trivial things—broad incongruities, mainly; grotesqueries, absurdities, evokers of the horse-laugh. The ten thousand high-grade comicalities which exist in the world are sealed from their dull vision, they are unconscious of their presence. The ten thousand are hid from the entire race.
—Mark Twain, *The Mysterious Stranger* (1916).

33.
Eirons *in the Fire*

EVEN IF HE REALIZED THAT THE old jokes were the most common ones, and borrowed time-tested formulas for making his audiences laugh, in the later years of his career Mark Twain also experimented with plenty of comic techniques that were new. For example, several recent critics have discussed him as a "fabulator"—a foreshadower of existentialism or black humor. While there was nothing completely novel about these parts of Mark Twain's later humor, it prophesied many of the preoccupations of modern humorists. We propose in this chapter and the next to examine some devices that both contribute to Mark Twain's continuing and increasing popularity and anticipate modern humorous writings.

Among the foibles of Jim Baker which we have celebrated, it is important to notice that, though like Jim in *Huckleberry Finn*, "harmless when not out of his head," the miner is as crazy as a woodtick. Unbalanced by years of solitary confinement, he is saved from being a clinical case history illustrating the effects of isolation only by the comic garrulousness of his condition. Alone with the animals for seven years, Jim has personified them, developed empathy with them, and watched them act like (or imagined they acted like) the humans whose company he was denied.

But, harmless as Jim Baker is, he contains the potential for a character who is so out of joint with the world around him that he is a serious threat to it. There are glimpses of such a character as early as Colonel Sellers in *The Gilded Age* and some stronger evidence in Pap Finn's paranoid speech about the gov'ment in *Huckleberry Finn*. By 1883, in a new play about Sellers, the humorist includes scenes "not wholly warranted," as a biographer says, "by the previous character of Sellers, unless, indeed, he has gone stark mad." But not until Hank Morgan in *A Connecticut Yankee in King Arthur's Court* (1889) does a menacing common man become dominant and pervasive. Perhaps because of Mark Twain's own increasing pessimism, the outlines of a "new" character began to clarify themselves: a common man, homespun, democratic, and colloquial, who was less an *eiron* than a crackpot. Such a character's homely wisdom disguised violence, conceit, and instability. Like Hank, he might literally blow up his world; or like Roxy in *Pudd'nhead Wilson*, he might symbolically destroy it by upsetting the entrenched system through the exchanging of a pair of babies. Like the Richardses in "The Man That Corrupted Hadleyburg," "good" characters could destroy themselves through their fear of social disapproval, or, as in *The $30,000 Bequest*, through their vanity and greed. Whatever the brand of destruction he wreaks, this character is a Fool who is also a fool.

Mark Twain's faith in the slangy American *eiron* had eroded slowly. He himself often had proudly posed as one in his early writing. He had seen frontier lawlessness and brutality, but described it in *Roughing It* with, at most, muted condemnation. But his faith in democracy had waned, and with it his belief that common men could consistently embody wisdom and virtue. In the 1870's, he had kidded universal suffrage and the jury system; he had advocated the granting of more votes to educated men than to "ignorant and non-taxpaying classes." In a comic letter, he predicted—and at least half approved—the coming of monarchy to the United States. By 1902, in "Does the Race of

Man Love a Lord?" he was affirming that democracy was doomed by man's essential need for a caste system in his government. Even more broadly, he began in the mid-1880's to congeal his opinions about "the damned human race" and to see man as feckless, self-motivated, and incapable of performing a generous and noble act unless it suited his temperament and training (his heredity and his environment, we would now say). Controlled, machine-like, by the "law of his make," man was by definition incapable of virtue and clear thinking.

Hank, in the opening pages of *A Connecticut Yankee*, displays all the qualities we would expect from Jack Downing or Hosea Biglow. A shrewd Yankee, a self-professed "ignoramus" proud of his lack of formal education, Hank shares with his antecedents a "native" talent and mechanical inventiveness, a colloquial and idiomatic prose style, and a horse-sensible way of thinking. But when Hank gains power and establishes a solid base for putting his homely values into actual practice, something notably unexpected happens. While we as readers await the millennium, we witness instead an apocalpyse—twenty-five thousand knights of the Round Table slaughtered, Gatling guns, electrified barbed wire, torpedo bombs, and the deliberate destruction of an entire civilization. By the end of the novel, Hank has become a homicidal tyrant whose earlier noble sentiments ring false. David Wilson, too, whose caustic aphorisms frequently echo the clear vision and common sense of the *eiron*, produces the ultimate tragedy in *Pudd'nhead Wilson* by restoring the caste system to Dawson's Landing and by wallowing in the adulation of the very society we might have expected him to indict.

Of course, rogues, anti-heroes, and schlemiels have been comic staples in humorous writings forever, but usually as minor or unsympathetic characters. And they are usually contrasted with other types who provide the moral norms for an audience, or they are "defeated" because of their deviations from propriety. Like some of *Sut Lovingood's Yarns*, though, Mark Twain's later writings sometimes focus on characters whose world is amoral and purposeless. A race of damned fools, universally lacking in wisdom of the homespun (or any other) variety, produces a moral chaos. This is decidedly "modern." A catalogue of recent novels based on this identical premise would run for pages and

"After the Explosion," Dan Beard's illustration for *A Connecticut Yankee in King Arthur's Court* (1889): "The deliberate destruction of an entire civilization."

pages: characters who seem to be simple *eirons* turn out to be only simpleminded; homespun precepts to live by turn out to be lethal or uncommunicable; and virtuous actions are less likely to produce beneficent results than immoral ones. Yossarian in *Catch-22*, Nathanael West's Balso Snell and Lemuel Pitkin, and the various fictional characters of Kurt Vonnegut are only the most obvious inheritors of the legacy of the doomed central character in a universe that lies in wait to bash him with a lethal custard pie.

In a short but trenchant attack on unthinking patriotism called

"The War Prayer" (1905, but not published until 1923), Mark Twain tells of an elderly and angelic visitor to a church service who points out to the congregation the illogic of their prayers for a great military victory. Beneath the plea for victory is the unspoken prayer,

O Lord, our God, help us to tear their soldiers to bloody shreds with our shells; help us to cover their smiling fields with the pale forms of their patriot dead; help us to drown the thunder of the guns with the shrieks of their wounded, writhing in pain. . . . Blast their hopes, blight their lives, protract their bitter pilgrimage, make heavy their steps, water their way with their tears, stain the white snow with the blood of their wounded feet!

The implications of their prayer affect the congregation but do not bring repentance, humility, or enlightenment. As Mark Twain puts it, "it was believed afterwards, that the man was a lunatic, because there was no sense in what he said."

Again, in a short dialogue, "The Dervish and the Offensive Stranger," the stranger argues successfully that there is no such thing as a good or evil deed, but good or evil intentions only. "The results" of intentions, the stranger insists, "are not foreseeable. They are of both kinds, in all cases. It is the law."

This raises another problem. If all men are fools, trapped by their heredity and environment beyond all hope of change, and if no virtuous acts can be guaranteed to produce desirable results, then how can humor, satire, parody, or any of the other comic forms that Mark Twain had habitually used to ridicule injustice bring about improvements in human affairs? His answer, in a number of his later "satiric" writings, is unclear, for his impulse to write satire is constantly blocked by the hopelessness of effecting change. The world-view is very close to the one Twain indicated he had when he wrote W. D. Howells concerning Edgar Allan Poe: "You grant that God and circumstances sinned against Poe, but you also grant that he sinned against himself—a thing which he couldn't do and didn't do." Translated to a social or political level, such sentiment removes blame (or censure) and virtue (or praise) from the realm of literature. And as a result, this author who had written scathing attacks on governmental corruption, bureaucratic boondoggling, and social injustice now produced another curiously modern form of writing—"satire" of a nihilistic cast, in which reform is neither suggested nor, for that matter, even possible.

A look at an example or two of this curiously frustrating mode of writing will suggest how Mark Twain's morality came into head-on collision with his philosophy. Stirred up by King Leopold's exploitation of blacks in the Belgian Congo, Twain wrote a long attack, *King Leopold's Soliloquy* (1905), against the monarch and his imperialism. By unfolding the entire narrative in Leopold's own voice, Twain had the option (like Franklin's King of Prussia, Birdofredum Sawin, or Petroleum Nasby in earlier American humor) of having the monarch damn himself by expressing opinions which were the opposite of the actual author's. That seems to have been what Twain intended. Leopold begins his soliloquy with bursts of profanity alternating with the sanctimonious hypocrisy of kissing a crucifix. As he reads over the reports exposing his villainy, he admits the truth of all the charges—murders, mutilations, castrations. But he acknowledges a universal human trait: human beings will cringe at the photographs, turn away from the repulsive facts, and ignore the truth. "Why, certainly," he muses, "*that* is my protection. . . . I know the human race." The "sap-headed and soft-hearted" reformers, as Leopold labels them, will have no success; books can be suppressed, newspapers bribed. And the mass of men—the "average all 'round," as Colonel Sherburn had called them in *Huckleberry Finn*—will be too cowardly or too stupid to recognize the truth. As Leopold puts it,

If men were really *men*, how could a Czar be possible? and how could I be possible? But we *are* possible; we are quite safe; and with God's help we shall continue that business at the old stand. It will be found that the race will put up with us, in its docile immemorial way. It may pull a wry face now and then, and make large talk, but it will stay on its knees all the same.

Such comments, however much Twain believed they were ironic, reflect so much of his own later philosophy that they undercut his hopes for the possibility of reform.

Similar peculiar undercuttings occur in a number of other later works. In "The Czar's Soliloquy" (1905), a later assault on the Russian monarchy, Twain vitiates the satire by allowing Nicholas II some keen insights into human behavior and personality. Standing naked before a mirror, Nicholas sees himself all too clearly: "wax-work head—the face with the expression of a melon—the projecting ears—the knotted elbows," in total, a human "carrot." But he realizes, as Hank Morgan had in *A Connecticut Yankee* twenty years earlier, that clothing makes the Czar. "Clothes," Nicholas soliloquizes, "and title are the most potent thing, the most formidable influence, in the earth. They move the human race to willing and spontaneous respect for the judge, the general, the admiral, the bishop, the ambassador, the frivolous earl, the idiot duke, the sultan, the king, the emperor." And, like Leopold, Nicholas is able to calculate and soothe the mass of men:

A curious invention, an unaccountable invention—the human race! . . . These people are horses—just that—horses with clothes and a religion. A horse with the strength of a hundred men will let one man beat him, starve him, drive him; the Russian millions allow a mere handful of soldiers to hold them in slavery.

In conclusion, the Czar wisely takes the step needed to conceal his bizarre appearance: "There is but one restorative—*Clothes!* I will put them on." Thus, in spite of his confession, Nicholas had enough insight into human nature to make his treachery and duplicity succeed.

Likewise, the essay "In Defense of General Funston" turns on itself to prevent redress of the infamies that an American officer committed in the name of patriotism, while in fact suppressing an independence uprising in the United States' new colony, the Philippine Islands, won from Spain in the Spanish-American War. After a scathing attack on Funston's conduct in the Philippines—conduct that included treachery and torture in order to capture the insurgent leader, Aguinaldo—Twain admits, "Funston is not to blame for his fearful deed." Instead, his "It," as Twain calls it, is responsible:

He did not make his own disposition, It was born with him. It chose his ideals for him, he did not choose them. It chose the kind of society It liked, the kind of comrades It preferred. . . . It had a native predilection for unsavory conduct, but it would be in the last degree unfair to hold Funston to blame for the outcome of his infirmity.

Since, at least in these later polemical writings, Mark Twain's world is made up of the same mixture of fools and knaves which Melville revealed in *The Confidence-Man*, any hope of improving them was foolish. That Twain tried, in a number of other later writings, to preach to his audience for its own good shows the internal conflict he felt, but it does not alter his opinion that "the lowest animal," as he called the human race, was without hope.

Since Mark Twain's death in 1910, this facet of his philosophy has seemed to a lot of writers an accurate diagnosis of the human condition. World wars, technological developments, increasing nuclear weaponry, uncontrolled increases in population, and several thousand other factors have suggested the probability that rugged individualism, intelligent dialogue, and movement toward the millennium might not be quite as certain as they seemed in the nineteenth century. Bitter novelists and bitter humorists have raged against the "system," and against specific abuses within the system. But, like Mark Twain, these writers have suffered from the same inability to offer changes to correct a situation—to write satire with reform as its intent. The laughter is helpless laughter and the prediction is for apocalypse instead of the millennium.

> *"It is true, that which I have revealed to you: there is no God, no universe, no human race, no earthly life, no heaven, no hell. It is all a Dream, a grotesque and foolish dream. Nothing exists but You. And You are but a* Thought—*a vagrant Thought, a useless Thought, a homeless Thought, wandering forlorn among the empty eternities!"*
>
> *He vanished, and left me appalled; for I knew, and realized, that all he had said was true.*
>
> —Mark Twain, *The Mysterious Stranger* (1916).

34.
Nightmares and Silences

LATE IN HIS LIFE, HENRY JAMES was supposedly told that real people did not act like the characters in his novels (a perfectly true observation). James is said to have replied that if real people did not act like that, they certainly ought to. The assumption seems to have been that James's fiction was not intended to be an accurate duplication of real life. Instead, it was a world populated by the imagination of the author, perhaps with characters whom he preferred to those in the outside world.

There is nothing new to the idea that literature creates ideal worlds and peoples them with characters who do not resemble real people. Indeed, H. L. Mencken observed once that "alone among the animals, [man] is dowered with the capacity to invent imaginary worlds, and he is always making himself unhappy by trying to move into them." Unlike Henry James or H. L. Mencken's "man," Mark Twain did not create idealized dream worlds. Instead, in his later writings he became obsessed with delusions, creating a world peopled by split personalities and confusions between dreams or nightmares and reality. Neither alternative made possible an "escape" into tranquility and order.

Earlier in his career, in the 1870's, 1880's, and 1890's, Twain had developed dream-world and split-personality motifs in "The Recent Carnival of Crime in Connecticut," *A Connecticut Yankee*, and *Pudd'nhead Wilson*. In the last fifteen years of his life, though, these themes and patterns became almost compulsive. The facts of his own life—his bankruptcy in 1894, his oldest daughter's death in 1896, his wife's death after a lingering illness in 1904—pushed him toward this kind of writing, one decidedly modern in its surreal atmosphere and psychological implications.

In a letter in 1893, he implied that his entire life had been a dream: "I dreamed I was born and grew up and was a pilot on the Mississippi and a miner and a journalist in Nevada and a pilgrim in the *Quaker City*, and had a wife and children and went to live in a villa at Florence—and this dream goes on and on and sometimes seems so real that I almost believe it is real." In 1897, he decided that his waking self and his dream self, whom he named Watson, were actually dual occupants of a single body, even though the co-tenants, like Cox and Box, never intruded upon one another. And he began working on a series of fragments now known as *The Mysterious Stranger Manuscripts*, a never-finished collection of plots using angelic (or satanic) strangers, dream worlds, and surrogates for characters, and diatribes against human nature, the moral sense, and the indifference of God to man's condition.

In a series of manuscripts which he tried to finish between 1895 and 1910, he returned again and again to elements of what we would now call abnormal psychology: the interior worlds within the minds of characters on the brink of derangement. And perhaps it is some indication of his own identification with this fiction that most of the characters bear striking biographical resemblances to Twain himself, and that he was unable to complete the manuscripts that exploit these themes. Indeed, it is only because of the research of John S. Tuckey and William M. Gibson that they have recently become available to general readers.

A persistent motif in these surreal writings, as John Tuckey summarizes it, is "that of a man who has been long favored by luck while pursuing a dream of success that has seemed about to turn into reality. Sudden reverses occur and he experiences a nightmarish time of failure. He clutches at what may be a saving thought: perhaps he is indeed living in a nightmare from which he will awaken to his former felicity. But there is also the possibility that what seems a dream of disaster may be the actuality of his life." The hook in Mark Twain's fantasy worlds was that they were more dangerous and bizarre than the "real" worlds of his characters. Monsters devoured families, delusions led to insanity, and the desire for a stable and predictable universe—even in a dream—became only a frustrated hope. Though it is unlikely that Twain had any such astute perception in mind, these dream fragments of his later years seem to suggest that he believed the human subconsciousness inhabited a world at least as irrational, meaningless, and distorted as the one that his conscious observation could perceive.

Few literary works, even the most recent fabulations of Barthelme, Kosinski, or Hawkes, chart as inexorably doomed a daydream as Mark Twain's scheme for "The Great Dark." In that twenty-thousand-word fragment, before dinner but after experimenting with a microscope he had bought for his daughter's birthday, Mr. Edwards falls asleep. He dreams that his family is aboard a ship floating on the drop of water that they had viewed under the lens of the microscope. The one-celled animals are now gigantic sea-monsters who prey on passengers and crew; and it is impossible to steer toward safety, because under a microscope there are no stars to guide by. Though Mr. Edwards's forty winks take only a few moments, his dream-time drags on endlessly. It is punctuated—in both the portions Mark Twain finished writing and in the notes that project continuations— with deaths, attempted mutinies, and soul-wrenching agonies. The irony of confusing his dream world and the real world produces an insane brand of humor—that of unrelieved frustration and a satanic undercutting of the central character's wishes and expectations.

In the midst of this novel that he could not finish, Mark Twain included another, lighter brand of humor that echoed some of the irrational quality of the serious parts. From the early days of his apprenticeship, Twain had exploited (as had other Phunny Phellows) the misuse of in-group language for comic purposes. In *Roughing It*, when Scotty Briggs tries to ask a minister to serve at Buck Fanshawe's funeral, the two cannot communicate because Scotty talks in gambler's lingo and the minister speaks in ceremoniously theological language:

". . . You see, one of the boys has gone up the flume—"
"Gone where?"
"Up the flume—throwed up the sponge, you understand."
"Thrown up the sponge?"
"Yes—kicked the bucket—"
"Ah—has departed to that mysterious country from whose bourne no traveler returns."
"Return! I reckon not. Why, pard, he's *dead!*"

The dialogue continues for several pages before the two characters comprehend one another. Other examples abound, from the Oracle in *The Innocents Abroad* to the King or Jim in *Huck Finn*, as staples of verbal humor—malapropisms, euphemisms, misquotations, and misunderstood argot.

These modes of humor are traditionally funny because they are incongruous in a world that is sane. Readers know what words such characters were trying to hit when they missed, what note they were aiming at when they flatted out. That is a different concept from a world where *all* logic is disordered and communication itself is impossible. And in much modern humorous writing, the simple technique of verbal wordplay becomes private language, insanity, or linguistic exhaustion.

It would be wrong to try to make Twain the father of modernist attitudes about language. But it is true, nevertheless, that some of the linguistic humor in later works like "The Great Dark"—because it occurs in a fictional world bereft of rational and objective precepts to gauge the absurdity by—stands somewhere between the verbal gymnastics of the literary comedians and the verbal nihilism of contemporary absurdist humor. In "The Great Dark" Twain exploited the comic potential of misused nautical language, when a mate punctuates his conversations with commands like, "Missen foretop halyards there—all clue-garnets heave and away—now, then, with a will—sheet home!" But no one notices or corrects this meaningless argot; no one imposes sane logic from the "real" world on this linguistic nonsense, as Alice tries to do in Wonderland. And the nonsense turns ominous when Mr. Edwards discovers that there is no other world than the illogical and meaningless one that the language affirms. He tells the "Superintendent of Dreams" (who has plotted the trip under the microscope for him), "You can end the dream as soon as you please—right now, if you like."

He looked me steadily in the eye for a moment, then said, with deliberation—
"The dream? *Are you quite sure it is a dream?*"
It took my breath away.
"What do you mean? *Isn't* it a dream?"
He looked at me in that same way again; and it made my blood chilly, this time. Then he said—
"You have spent your whole life in this ship. And this is *real* life. Your other life was the dream!"

Other stories and fragments—"Which Was It?," "Which Was the Dream?," and a host of working notes and notebook entries—explore obsessively the nightmare world, a hideous and interminable dream which the dreamer can neither halt nor control.

If Mark Twain substantially foreshadowed some of the central elements of contemporary fantastic and black humor—in his universal condemnation of mankind; his conversion of satire to diatribe; his exploitation of schizophrenia and dream worlds; and his movement toward absurdist uses of language—in the final years of his life he also suggested a significantly modern definition of the author-audience relationship.

More than most writers, the popular humorist is a slave to his audience; he measures his success (and his profit) by the yardstick of its laughter. He must gauge his humor by its tastes and whims, adapt to its changing moods, and cater to its prejudices and convictions, or destroy an intimate and fragile relationship. For most of his career, Twain was as sensitively attuned to his readers' expectations as any humorist ever was. He knew that his "wretched and slangy" Western humor could not be served up to an Eastern or national audience in *The Innocents Abroad*, that he circulated among a "submerged clientele" he labeled the "Belly and Members" level of society rather than among a high-browed readership. He planned to publish *The Prince and the Pauper* and actually did publish *Personal Recollections of Joan of Arc* without his name on the title page in order to have them taken seriously. And he exploited topical material, alternated humor with serious passages, and tapped the subscription method of publication in order to reach and appeal to a large audience.

But Twain announced—as it turned out, somewhat prematurely—that *A Connecticut Yankee in King Arthur's Court* was the last book he would write for publication. Even though he published many volumes after that one, there is a sense in which his announcement was accurate. In the last decade or so of his life, he wrote more and more for personal amusement, often set publication dates for his material which would prevent its being issued for decades or even centuries, and piled up that impressive body of unfinished manuscripts which were the legacy of his old age. It is true that he was wealthy enough not to need prodigious royalty checks; it was also true that his aging contributed to his enervation. And it is probable that he thought his readership was unprepared for "shocking" truths which he believed his later literature contained.

Perhaps it is not unfair to see, at least in part, something further of the modernist position in Mark Twain's alienation and estrangement from his audience. Contempt for that damned human race which included his audience, a glimmering of the failure of language to inspire reform or even to communicate, and the ultimately pessimistic laughter of futility and despair may not have been major elements in Twain's symbolic silence; but they hover as potential and partial explanations that have much in common with modern comic authors.

But Twain's self-imposed silence was rather noisy. He delighted in being the most conspicuous person on the planet, absolutely wallowed in adulation and notoriety, continued to give frequent interviews and public speeches, and published many articles and books.

For him, writing was a profession which, even in his final years, he worked at compulsively. But he did decline to complete or to publish much of the writing of this period. His Autobiographical Dictations suggest a wide range of contradiction in his attitude. They were written, supposedly, so honestly that only future generations would be able to tolerate some of their painful insights. Twain changed the rules, however, and printed parts of them in the *North American Review* during his lifetime. In order that he might be completely honest about himself and his thought processes, he dictated sections to a stenographer because he believed it was an ideal method for transcribing autobiography; but toward the end of the manuscript—because he found he could not be honest enough before an audience—he abandoned that procedure. Focusing solely upon himself, writing or not as the mood struck him, interrupting himself to pursue distractions and never regaining the original line of thought, Twain was as indifferent to an audience as he had been sensitive to one for the preceding four decades. He might well have agreed with the faddist manifesto of the 1920's that "the author expresses, he does not communicate."

Dadaist, existentialist, guru, Mark Twain most decidedly was not. But, along with Henry Adams, he was one of the first nineteenth-century Americans to feel and reflect in his last writings that sense of hopelessness, impotence, and rage which has been dubbed the "modern malaise." And in proportions that were unusual for his times, he experimented with some comic (and some not so comic) devices for expressing his sense of helplessness—devices which have become the staples of contemporary humor.

Part Five

Into The Twentieth Century

The Turn
of the
Century,
1895–1905

*Once there was an undersized
Town that had the Corn Fields sneaking up on all sides of it, trying
to break over the Corporation Line. People approaching the Town
from the North could not see it, because there was a row of Willow-
Trees in the Way.*

*Here in this comatose Settlement lived a Family named Pilkins. The
Pilkins were all the Eggs in Smartweed. They owned a big General
Store catty-cornered from the Court-House. It was well known that
they sent to Chicago for their Clothes and ate Ice-Cream in the Winter-
Time. The Pilkins Girls had been away to a Convent to have their
Voices sandpapered and fitted to a Piano and they came back with the
first Gibson Shirt-Waists seen in those Parts. Most of the Girls south
of the Tracks were just getting wise to the Russian Blouse.*

—George Ade, 1900.

35.
Another Transitional
Period

THE DECADE BETWEEN 1895
and 1905 was one of rising discontent and social upheaval in
America. The panic of 1893 was a bad one, with an impact that
lasted for years. The year 1894 brought a march of the unemployed upon Washington, the Pullman strike with army inter-
vention, and a worsening of horrendous conditions on many
farms. The disruptions brought a political realignment of a major sort.

Unhappy Southern and Western Democrats rallied against
what they believed was keeping the people down—the gold

standard. Gold, they claimed, was the money of Wall Street, the rich—the cities. Silver, for them, was the money of the Southern farms, the Western wheatlands, the Far West, and the small towns—the country. So, they figured, if free coinage of silver was instituted, the downtrodden older America would regain the place it deserved.

The Democrats found themselves a champion during the sweltering 1896 convention in Chicago when William Jennings Bryan of Nebraska made a speech that the delegates interrupted again and again with whoops of approval. The peroration:

If they dare to come out in the open field and defend the gold standard as a good thing, we will fight them to the uttermost. Having behind us the producing masses of the nation and the world, supported by the commercial interests, the laboring interests, and the toilers everywhere, we will answer their demand for a gold standard by saying to them: You shall not press down upon the brow of labor this crown of thorns, you shall not crucify mankind upon a cross of gold.

Declared the party's presidential candidate, Bryan, the "Boy Orator of the Platte" traveled thirteen thousand miles preaching his gospel to frenzied audiences.

Mark Hanna, whose man William McKinley had been nominated by the Republicans, gathered huge contributions from city banks, insurance firms, and railroad corporations. New Yorkers talked about seceding if the Nebraskan won. The press was pro-Republican.

Bryan carried the South and the Far West. It wasn't enough. The East and the Middle West swept McKinley into office. The campaign had brought into open opposition the ancient agrarian order against the newer urban and industrial order, and the latter had won.

In no other kind of contemporary writing are these antagonisms in American society in 1895-1905 reflected more clearly than in our humor. Our chief humorists long had been rustic or western. Many of them during the years 1895 to 1915 were country-born but became city dwellers. Beginning about 1915, our most famous humorous writers were to be urban by birth and preference. Such generalizations are riddled with exceptions, of course; but the shift from predominantly "rustic" to predominantly "urbane" humor was a gradual development rather than an overnight one. During the turn-of-the-century period, there was what academics like to label "a transition."

An ambivalence then, as always, created incongruities. Prominent humorists, while they pined at times for the commonsensible "good old days," became more witty and bookread, or at least *tried to become* more witty and bookread, and believed that they succeeded. They made fun on occasion of the crossroads philosophy, but at other times they championed it. They felt the pull of down-to-earth realism, but in their comic writings they explored fantasies, the bizarre, and even pre-Freudian neuroses. Like humorists to come, they basked in the belief that their eggheadery was superior. But, unlike the later *New Yorker* crowd, they were smugly sure that they were on top of a world that they understood.

In a sense, therefore, they weren't all that different from the reputables and the local colorists of earlier American humor, for whom gentility was a prerequisite; and some developments in the final years of the nineteenth century tended to feed their beliefs about their own brand of comicality. When our society became urbanized and cultural centers were formed, bookstores to a large extent could replace the newspaper, the popular subscription book hawked by agents, and the lecture platform. The impulse toward a national norm prompted literateurs to argue about the Great American Novel and to ask themselves earnestly whether *Leaves of Grass* really was poetry. They eroded more of the delight in regional distinctions and peculiarities; and the "mass" media—the phonograph, fledgling radio, and cinema—diverted much popular humor from the printed page to these art forms that were heard and seen. And that streak of inferiority that had deliberately called hyperbolic attention to itself in earlier humor tended, at the turn of the century, to become an embarrassment.

The monthly magazine became, much more than it had been before, the "proper" outlet for genteel humor. Editors such as Charles Dudley Warner, Thomas Bailey Aldrich, and Richard Watson Gilder (to name only three) opened the pages of *Harper's Monthly*, the *Atlantic Monthly*, and the *Century* to humor of a conservative, if not pallid, complexion. (Gilder felt he had to deodorize chapters of *Huckleberry Finn* before they could be serialized in his journal; Mary Mapes Dodge tinkered with *Tom Sawyer Abroad* for young readers of *St. Nicholas*.) Magazine editors and their contributors were nervous about the importance of literature at which people laughed. "As soon as the humorist strains to meet the clamorous demand of a rapacious public," Burges Johnson said, "so soon does he drop from the heights of real literature to the lowest depths of space writing." Clearly, the belief was that a humorist writing monthly instead of daily was likely to have a cultivated instead of a popular audience. Even when he did this, though, he left himself open to some criticism of his high-brow attitude. Early in the century, Charles Johnston was complaining about "that wit which is marred by egotism and vanity, which springs from the desire to shine, to show off, to prove one's self smarter than one's fellows, to air the superior qualities of one's mind." There is something more fascinating about the neat polarities of Johnson's and Johnston's ideas, however. Even if the genteel humorist would never demean himself by getting embroiled in an eye-gouging contest, by the end of the nineteenth century he was willing to debate publicly about the values he felt should supplant "space writing" humor.

When the beginning of the twentieth century understandably led writers and critics to assess and sum up accomplishments in practically all segments of American life, humor was no exception. In 1901, two leading American magazines ran lengthy assessments of the preceding century's humorous triumphs, with James L. Ford in "A Century of American Humor" and W. P. Trent in "A Retrospect of American Humor" providing overviews. While both give thumbnail biographies of the top figures, Trent was acute enough to distinguish between professional humorists and writers—Irving, Holmes, Warner—who were "primarily citizens of the world of letters." And though each critic provided a different list of humorists, both tended to emphasize the Down East humorists and the literary comedians. So there were some value judgments in these two otherwise objective postmortems.

A few years earlier, an even stronger value judgment had contributed to the debate. In 1895, European-born H. H. Boyesen, a Columbia professor, wrote about "The Plague of Jocularity" which he held was infecting Americans. Boyesen admired a few humorists, especially Mark Twain, but deplored "a reckless determination to be funny, in connection with a total want of reverence," which he thought was running wild all over the United States. Such relentless joking was not cultivated, not intellectual, not—worst of all—European! "Instead of that interchange of thought, which with other civilized nations is held to be one of the highest of social pleasures," Boyesen lamented, "we exchange jokes." Similar snobbery marked the call for "The Need of a New Joke" in an anonymous paragraph in the prestigious *Atlantic:* "Our famous American Humor," the writer suggested, was worn out because of "the sin of not showing profound insight."

Defenders of popular humor answered some of these challenges. The same James L. Ford who had composed one of the obituaries came out in violent opposition to "the kindly, genial humor which never hurts any one's feelings"; and the same Charles Johnston who was quoted above lambasted the genteel wit that produced "a certain tickling of the sensations, it is true, but, with it, dissatisfaction, unrest, a sense of vanity, with final bankruptcy staring us in the face."

But the defenders of gentility, as editors of literary journals and contributors to them, stood on a platform that gave them an advantage. In April and June 1902, Burges Johnson opined in *The Critic* that "the rise of a certain group of writers whose oversupply of the joy of life bubbles forth occasionally into streams of nonsense" was something new in American humor. In *The Independent* that same year, W. D. Nesbit (who was himself funny under the pseudonym "Josh Wink" for the Baltimore *American*) praised those humorists who "are doing much to elevate the profession of light and airy writing," and cheered because "slang, vulgarity and profanity have run their course in printed humor." "They have no place, and find none," he revealed, "in the really good work of this day." H. W. Boynton praised Oliver Wendell Holmes as "our greatest legitimate humorist" and relegated other nineteenth-century comic writers to the role of mere "jesters." Finally, Ella MacMahon, in "Is Humor Declining?," announced that she was delighted because at long last, humor of dialect, of pain and deformity, and satire of religion were "looked upon as being in the worst possible taste as well as being on the lowest level of humorous invention."

Among the practitioners of the "new" humor (which, to be sure, had antecedents as far back as colonial times), John Kendrick Bangs was as representative as any. Editor of *Harper's Weekly*, on one occasion an unsuccessful candidate for mayor of Yonkers (who could fashion his defeat into a humorous book, *Ten Weeks in Politics*), Bangs was a man who embraced the most conservative tenets of genteel humor. Indeed, Boynton labeled him "a clever sophomore, with a thumbing acquaintance with the Classical Dictionary," and one of his admirers, John Corbin, characterized him as "dignified and scholarly without foregoing the lightness of touch, the play of humor and satire that is one of the unfailing signs of intellectual strength." Bangs made clear where he stood in the Great American Humor Debate in the *Book Buyer* for April 1900, when he praised those "whose humor has been of the purest, sweetest, rarest sort" that "yielded to the refining processes." "It is not necessary nowadays," Bangs said haughtily, "to be vulgar to be amusing."

The fact was that throughout the 1890's, Bangs had been the leader in the "new" school. His position helped; he was the conductor for most of the decade of "The Editor's Drawer," a prestigious feature of *Harper's Magazine*. (His predecessors had been Lewis Gaylord Clark and Charles Dudley Warner.) An inveterate clubman, he was constantly called upon at the Aldine, the Players, and the Authors clubs for witty after-dinner speeches. And a surprising number of his books, now completely forgotten, made the best-seller lists of the decade: *Coffee and Repartee* (1893), which was compared with *The Autocrat of the Breakfast Table; The Idiot* and *Mr. Bonaparte of Corsica* (both in 1894); and *The House-Boat on the Styx* (1896). Bangs's son touches on the qualities of these literary productions which he, and no doubt readers of the time, believed were admirable (incidentally, revealing a sublime ignorance of his father's predecessors):

There was in most of his books a literary element which marked them as more closely approximating the belletrism of a Christopher Morley than the wise-cracking of a Will Rogers. Sinclair Lewis thinks that Bangs was one of the first popular American humorists to flatter a wide reading public by taking for granted that it could understand and appreciate classical, literary, and historical allusions without the aid of explanatory context.

The claim dramatizes the reliance on book learning and pedantry that a "wide reading public" would accept rather than suspect.

At least as important as Bangs's cosmopolitan attitude and his intellectual background were some of the forms that he used in his humorous writing. *The House-Boat on the Styx* is a fantasy in which Diogenes, Shakespeare, Napoleon, Tennyson, Artemus Ward, Samuel Johnson, and dozens of other famous dead engage in conversations. And *The Idiot*, though to some extent it employs the title character as a traditional American *eiron*, has him make comments as irrational and illogical as any in *Mad Magazine:* One of his reasons for preferring life on a canal-boat to that in a house is "that more people die in houses than on canal-boats." He proposes a hotel with movable rooms, "constructed like an elevator," so that "if you were sleeping in a room next door to another in which there was a crying baby, you could pull the rope and go up two or three flights until you were free from the noise." And he proposes to found a newspaper "that will devote its space to telling what hasn't happened":

Put on your front page, for instance, an item like this: "George Bronson, colored, aged twenty-nine, a resident of Thompson Street, was caught cheating at poker last night. He was not murdered." There you tell what has not happened. It has the charm of the unexpected. Then you might say: "Curious incident on Wall Street yesterday. So-and-so, who was caught on the bear side of the market with 10,000 shares of J. B. & S. K. W., paid off all his obligations in full, and retired from business with $1,000,000 clear." Or we might say, "Superintendent Smithers, of the St. Goliath's Sunday-school, who is also cashier in the Forty-Eighth National Bank, has not absconded with $4,000,000."

Several of Bangs's short stories explore derangement and hallucination, and *Ghosts I Have Known* and *The Water Ghost and Others* convert the supernatural to zany comedy. "The Water Ghost of Harrowby Hall," for instance, is a beautiful but a rather too aqueous young woman who haunts a room every Christmas Eve. One occupant "became like one insane" as she dripped water all over him, "and was found unconscious in his bed the next morning by his host, simply saturated with sea-water and fright, from the combined effects of which he never recovered, dying four years later of pneumonia and nervous prostration at the age of seventy-eight." The young owner of Harrowby Hall tries to steam the ghost into oblivion, and when that fails, one Christmas Eve he freezes her and keeps her permanently in a cold-storage locker.

Bangs was a particularly apt choice to write an introduction to a 1903 edition of Derby's *Phoenixiana*, for there were significant parallels in the two men's humor. Bangs's comments on Phoenix approved "good, wholesome, honest fun" that had "none of the taint of ill-nature." In addition, Bangs must have approved of Derby's zaniness, his erudition, and his bizarre, associational leaps in thought, for they were much like the Idiot's own ways of thinking which dazzle Mr. Pedagog into remarking:

I believe there is no subject in the world which you cannot connect in some way or another with every other subject in the world. A discussion of the merits of Shakespeare's sonnets could be turned by your dextrous tongue in five minutes into a quarrel over the comparative merits of cider and cod-liver oil as beverages, with you, the chances are, the advocate of cod-liver oil as a steady drink.

The suggestion is that, to the extent that Bangs is representative of genteel humor of the 1890's, the exploration of subjective or "abnormal" states of consciousness, the use of modes of fantasy not grounded solidly in reality, and the use of an intellectual and educated protagonist were receiving noteworthy and extended treatment. Bangs did not invent the Perfect Neurotic, but he established a background and an environment that would be associated with that character later on.

> Ah, yes! I wrote "The Purple Cow"—
> I'm Sorry, now, I Wrote it!
> But I can Tell you, Anyhow,
> I'll Kill you if you Quote it!
> —Gelett Burgess, 1896.

> REPROBATION, *n.* In theology, the
> state of a luckless mortal prenatally damned. The doctrine of reproba-
> tion was taught by Calvin, whose joy in it was somewhat marred by
> his conviction that although some are foredoomed to perdition, others
> are predetermined to salvation.   —Ambrose Bierce, 1906.

> He said he preferred Vogner any day in the Week on account of the
> distinct Appeal to the Intellectual Side and the Atmosphere of Mysti-
> cism, whatever that was.   —George Ade, 1899.

36.
Some Urban
Humorists

IN 1929, CLAUDE BRAGDON
commented in retrospect on what he called the "Purple Cow Period" of American periodical literature. He remembered that
during the 1890's in the United States, a group of what he called
"dinky magazines" sprang up. Here, *The Chap-Book*, *The Philis-
tine*, and especially *The Lark* were " 'young,' devouringly ego-
centric and self-assertive."

The Lark was the precursor of both the arty little magazine of
the 1920's and the lunatic-tinged periodicals of the present like
Mad and the *National Lampoon*. Founded by Gelett Burgess,
Ernest Peixotto, and Bruce Porter in San Francisco in 1895, it
lasted for only twenty-four monthly issues—followed by a one-
issue *Epilark* that signaled its demise. Between its covers was an
abundance of heady prose and ornate poetry. Its pages, frequently expensive Chinese bamboo, always unpaginated and un-
cut, were adorned with elaborate illustrations and poster art. In
the midst of such a pretentious art-for-art's-sake decor, there was
an occasional burst of whimsical and far-fetched humor. In the
first issue, Burgess printed his famous "The Purple Cow":

Original printing of "The Purple Cow."

I never Saw a Purple Cow;
I never Hope to See One;
But I can Tell you, Anyhow,
I'd rather See than Be One.

And every subsequent issue contained a short nonsense verse
with an illustration of one of Burgess's "Goops" (boneless, hair-
less creatures who had the look of something like the Pillsbury
flour advertisement man rolled out of dough). Occasionally a
longer poem like Burgess's "The Peculiar History of the Chew-
ing-Gum Man" would appear. And the magazine toyed with
mirror-image illustrations and crude woodcuts labeled with the
titles of famous pictures, and presented a palmist's chart using
the sole of a foot rather than the palm of a hand. The "irresponsible nonsense" extended even to the advertising pages, where,
in several issues, the editors announced the publication of the
Petit Journal des Refusées. This was to be a magazine printed
on black paper with yellow ink that would refuse no manuscript
accompanied by a rejection slip from a leading periodical. The
advertisement for the *Petit Journal* ("More artistic than a Bicycle Catalogue. . . . Weird as a Hasheesh Dream") was followed by an even more outrageous announcement: the impend-
ing publication of a magnificent volume called *L'Arkitecture*

Moderne (one illustration was to be of L'Ark de Triomphe) in an edition of three copies—bound, respectively, in half-chicken, crushed mouse-skin, and Irish bull.

Even more impressive than the pure zaniness of this humor was the reaction of the press throughout the country to it. By the end of its first year, *The Lark* could (and did) quote notices from nearly three dozen newspapers and periodicals in which the words most often used to describe the magazine were *flippant*, *unconventional*, *curious*, *quaint*, and *preposterous*. The New York *Critic* noted that "The faddists have produced some extraordinary things in the way of literature, but nothing more freakish has made its appearance in the last half century than *The Lark*." The Washington, D.C. *Capital* noted, "In both type and illustration there is much that people have dreamed before, but surely never attempted to express."

What strikes the modern browser in *The Lark* (as it did some contemporary reviewers) is the quality of feckless preciousness that pervaded the magazine. Even though they were in their fifties and a mite too old to call themselves, as they did, "Les Jeunes," Burgess and some of his collaborators were at least aesthetically young. Something of their precociousness, if that was what they were trying for, showed in their love for ornate rhyme schemes, esoteric references, and paradings of erudition (both true and mock). Some of the unique flavor of "Purple Cow" humor also came from their attitudes and their unblushing self-consciousness. The far-out frivolity was much like that in George Horatio Derby's writings or S. J. Perelman and George S. Kaufman's Marx Brothers scripts. The authors left an exterior, realistic world and entered something very much like the dreams that no one before had "attempted to express," at least humorously, with quite as much determination and energy.

Two of Burgess's "Goop" poems illustrate the childlike simplicity (if not simple-mindedness) of his humor. Their whimsicality approaches meaninglessness, and their frothy quality disguises no higher truths. One celebrates feet:

> My feet they haul me 'round the House;
> They hoist me up the Stairs;
> I only have to steer them and
> They ride me everywheres.

The other, a limerick, is akin to some of Lear's wilder cogitations:

> I wish that my Room had a floor;
> I don't so much care for a Door,
>   But this walking around
>   Without touching the ground
> Is getting to be quite a bore!

While this underlying whimsicality in "Purple Cow" humor was not, to be sure, as irrational as what we now label "absurd," it was marked by something close to modern exploitations of unpredictability. The "Goops" were physically as unreal as the characters in the drawings which Clarence Day used later in *Thoughts Without Words* and *Scenes from the Mesozoic* and as Al Capp's schmoos. Other drawings tended to be as serpentine and arabesque as was necessary to divorce them completely from reality. In the verses, too, a childlike simplicity, more reminiscent of Edward Lear and Lewis Carroll than of traditional American humor, predominated. (A like simplicity marked Oliver Herford's poems and Robert Williams Wood's *How to Tell the Birds from the Flowers*.) Since there was no objective "reality" against which to measure the comic world of *The Lark*, as a predictable result it tried for no satire, no attempts at social reform, and no exploitation of comic antagonisms such as those in fashion earlier. Burgess admitted that there had been an "absolute lack of Realism," along with a deliberate avoidance of satire and parody, in the pages of the magazine.

Significantly, in his remarks in the concluding issue, Burgess also gave some important clues to its elitist standards. Admitting that the periodical was a part of a "revolt against the commonplace," he confessed:

It was at first an escapade—but the echo of its shout of mirth committed it to gayety. It has never been "popular," but something in the quality of its friends gave it repute. *The Lark* was received by the few who had "discovered" it with indulgence.

Several newspaper and periodical reviews of *The Lark* agreed about its peculiarly narrow appeal. A writer for the Richmond *Times* was frankly boggled: "We do not understand upon what the editor of *The Lark* bases anticipation of interest and consequent demand." *The Chap-Book* predicted from Chicago, "Its friends will be appreciative, but there will not be many of them. We must thank the editors for a magazine which can never be 'popular.' " The San Francisco *Examiner* guessed that "this bit of a journal will toss about the studios and clubs for a little time—the fleeting fancy of the few."

The love of fantasy (fantasy, that is, without the appearance of reality that the tall tale had contained) and the sniffs at an appeal to the masses were thought to be impressively "new" attitudes. (They were to have echoes in boasts about hyperexclusiveness in *The New Yorker*'s initial manifesto.) *The Lark* was the most extreme version of the highbrows' demand for humor that would have nothing in common with mere "space writing" levity.

But Burgess's claim that *The Lark* "was not popular enough even to gain the flattery of imitation" is not quite correct. At the time he published it, newspapers were about to experiment with wilder comic strips; only slightly higher-toned periodicals already had pictures of elegant and skillfully drawn Gibson girls and boys engaging in such totally upper-crust pastimes as tennis and high-tea. The cover of the first volume of *The Chap-Book* was adorned with an elegant Regency period Corinthian peering through a monocle—an ancestor (unacknowledged but with a suspicious resemblance) of Eustace Tilley, of the traditional anniversary cover of *The New Yorker*. The old *Life* magazine (itself a comic periodical in its pre-Luce version) launched a sustained attack against realistic writers, as did other comic periodicals. Robert Bridges, an editor of *Life*, sounded almost as uppity as John Kendrick Bangs when he said in 1895, "It isn't a literary crime to write about people who live north of Ninth Street and dress for dinner. . . . Good clothes and a decent life ought not to condemn a man for literary purposes." *M'lle New York* announced it would champion "the aristocracies of birth, wit, learning and art." So, while these periodicals of the late 1890's were not exclusively humorous, they printed a cliqueish, sophisticated brand of humor.

Although a few small coteries of avant-garde editors exploited a militant and mildly deranged urbane humor, a larger group of early-twentieth-century humorists went even further. They

THE

Chap-Book

BEING

A MISCELLANY of Curious and Interesting Songs, Ballads, Tales, Histories, &c. ; adorned with a variety of pictures and very delightful to read ; *newly composed* by MANY CELEBRATED WRITERS ; To which are annex'd a LARGE COLLECTION of Notices of BOOKS.

VOLUME I.

From May 15th to November 1st

A.D. MDCCC XC IV

CHICAGO

Printed for *Stone & Kimball* of the *Caxton Building* *where Shopkeepers, Hawkers, and others are supplied*

Cover of the first volume of *The Chap-Book* (1894).

moved away from the rural presses, got newspaper jobs in population centers such as Chicago and New York, and proceeded to look back with a jaundiced eye at the rural and small-town settings and characters which in the past had been standbys. Long before Sinclair Lewis and H. L. Mencken, other satirists of at least a partially cosmopolitan stripe battered the village, the "average American," and common sense virtues.

In that Western outpost of American bohemia, San Francisco, at the same time that Les Jeunes were printing the first exotic issues of *The Lark*, a man was working who could persuade prac-

Feb.21,1977   **THE** Price 75 cents

NEW YORKER

Eustace Tilley of *The New Yorker* (1925-   ). (©*1925, 1953, The New Yorker Magazine, Inc.*)

tically anyone to cross the street to avoid him. Ambrose Bierce, ironically enough, was William Randolph Hearst's star reporter on the *Examiner*. He eventually made his mark as the author of superb Civil War short stories and Gothic fiction in the tradition of Edgar Allan Poe. But he was also a wit ("Nearly all Americans are humorous," he once said. "If any are born witty, heaven help them to emigrate!"), who previewed many of the tantrums that Mencken would stage. An anglophile of Toryish dimensions, an author of elegant and polished prose who delighted in highfalutin phrases and long latinate words (including such coinages as "microcephalous bibliopomps"), Bierce alternately wielded his pen as if it were a scalpel or a meat-ax. In addition to all his other activities, Bierce—in at least one of his roles—poked with a poison-tipped pen into many virtues of the "common man." He ridiculed boondock mentality and fundamentalist religion; he called the common man a "lout of the stables"; and he disparaged the colloquial speech—the "language of the unlettered hind"—which realistic writers had been using. He called employers of dialect

the pignoramous crew of malinguists, cacophonologists and astrophotographers who think they get close to nature by depicting the sterile lives and limited emotions of the gowks and sodhoppers that speak only to tangle their own tongues, and move only to fall over their own feet.

Bierce's brother claimed that Ambrose was never the same after he suffered a head wound in the Civil War. Whatever the cause, Bierce came out of the war less patriotic. He defined the United States as "a great, broad blackness with two or three small points of light struggling and flickering in the universal blank of ignorance, crudity, conceit, tobacco-chewing, ill-dressing, unmannerly manners and general barbarity."

In his *Devil's Dictionary* (first published in 1906, although he had been compiling its entries since 1881), under *Dullard* he wrote:

Since a detachment of Dullards came over with the Pilgrims in the *Mayflower* and made a favorable report of the country, their increase by birth, immigration, and conversion has been rapid and steady. . . . The intellectual center of the race is somewhere about Peoria, Illinois, but the New England Dullard is the most shockingly moral.

Under *Fool:* "He it was who invented letters, printing, the railroad, the steamboat, the telegraph, the platitude and the circle of the sciences. He created patriotism and taught the nations war—founded theology, philosophy, law, medicine and Chicago."

Under *Slang:* "The grunt of the human hog. . . . A means (under Providence) of setting up as a wit without a capital of sense."

It is not true that Bierce saved all his venom for the average man. He slashed at personal enemies, the Southern Pacific Railroad, Socialists, and women. "Looking at the human circus," Paul Fatout has observed, "he laughed at its clowns and trained seals." But to the extent that his cosmopolitan and mordant "Prattler" columns in the *Examiner* ridiculed native qualities— and gained notoriety for their author—they struck the tone that was being called the "new note" in humor. Bierce remains especially significant because his bitterness, his hatred of mediocrity, his autocratic personality, and his penchant for the grotesque and the abnormal pushed the limits of humor as far as they could go, and sometimes perhaps farther.

At the time Bierce was a California phenomenon, Chicago and New York journalists attracted national attention to their humorous columns. A cluster of much more healthy Chicagoans had the nerve to expect that their city would soon be brimming over with elegance, gentility, and urbanity. And some of the same corrosive attitudes that Bierce expressed in San Francisco turned up in some of the Windy City's humor.

Eugene Field, the spiritual father of Chicago's humorists, embodied contradictions that one might predict in a humorist trying to convert from rusticity to urbanity. A Midwesterner who became famous as a writer for a Colorado newspaper, Field was the author of dialect poems reminiscent of Bret Harte and James Whitcomb Riley. He also translated Horace and Virgil and composed mock Old English ballads. In time, he would be famous for his sentimental poems—"Little Boy Blue" and children's poems—"The Duel" (better known as "The Gingham Dog and the Calico Cat"). But early in his career, he contributed to the Denver *Tribune* outrageous burlesques of the *New England Primer* that gleefully mocked children's do-good readers:

The Cat is Asleep on the Rug. Step on her Tail and See if She will Wake up. Oh, no; She will not wake. She is a heavy Sleeper. Perhaps if you Were to saw her Tail off with the Carving knife you might Attract her attention. Suppose you try.

This is a gun. Is the Gun Loaded? I do not know. Let us Find out. Put the Gun on the table, and you, Susie, blow down one barrel, while you, Charlie, blow down the other. Bang! Yes, it was loaded. Run quick Jennie, and pick up Susie's head and Charlie's lower Jaw before the Nasty Blood gets over the New carpet.

This is a Cock Roach. He is Big, Black, and Ugly. He is Crawling over the Pillow. Do not Say a Word, but lie still and Keep your Mouth open. He will Crawl into Your Mouth and You can Bite him in Two. This will Teach him to be Discreet in the Future.

In Chicago, Field's garnerings from his column in *Culture's Garland* did for Midwestern philistinism and pretensions what

Bierce did for provincialism, though in a different way. Its sub-title was "The Gradual Rise of Literature, Art, Music and Soci-ety in Chicago, and Other Western Ganglia." A frontispiece was labeled, "A Chicago Literary Circle in the Similitude of a Laurel Wreath": it was a ring of sausages. The text itself contained such vitriolic assaults on the Chicago new-rich as this:

> Squire Enos Hapgood, who expired by a vicious mule's kick on the West Side last Monday, was one of the most prominent patrons of lit-erature in the West. Before her death, his wife had been a subscriber to "Godey's Lady's Book" for twenty odd years.

> The line D [in a palmistry chart] is common to the Chicago hand; it argues a fondness for the fine arts, for music, and for all the articles of vertoo—such as piano-fortes, folding-beds, wax flowers, race-horses, perfumery, $4 opera, pug dogs, statuary, Browning's poems, dyspepsia, and lawn tennis. Of late this art-line has got so deep in a great many Chicago hands, that it had to be sewed up by a doctor.

Throughout his column "Sharps and Flats," he parodied his own corny poetry. And for the pleasure or embarrassment of his close friends, he penned privately circulated bawdy poems.

A slightly younger generation of journalists—including George Ade, cartoonist John T. McCutcheon, Opie Read, and Finley Peter Dunne—collected in the 1890's at the Whitechapel Club in Chicago, a rendezvous for boozing, taunting one anoth-er's work, and playing practical jokes. Elmer Ellis writes of this gathering place: "the atmosphere of the club was Bohemian, Rabelaisian, and macabre." Trophies of famous crimes, murder weapons, a coffin-shaped table, and a stuffed owl hanging by a string from the ceiling were parts of the furnishings, and the club itself was named for the area of London where Jack the Ripper currently inspected the innards of his victims. When one of the members, a man named Collins, committed suicide, it is reported that the Whitechaplers smuggled his body to Indi-ana, cremated it on the shores of Lake Michigan, and brought the skull back to Chicago to decorate the clubroom. However much of a tall tale that one might be, the Whitechapel Club was a convivial group of malcontents. George Ade later remembered that "the club was in session almost every evening. . . . It fi-nally went into bankruptcy because it entertained royally and failed to pay the bill."

More important, Charles H. Dennis, recalling the White-chapel Club in the Chicago *Daily News* (July 29, 1936), suggested that "underlying nearly all their talk was a wholesome cynicism, a ferment of disillusionment." That cynicism and disillusionment seeped into the finest humorous productions of any member of the crew except for Dunne's Mr. Dooley—George Ade's *Fables*.

Ade, a Hoosier whose career in Chicago journalism abated when the success of his play *The Sultan of Sulu* lured him to Broadway in 1902, wrote his first fable in 1897 and by 1900 had produced enough to fill a book. During the next two decades he published nine more volumes of fables, plus a number that have never been collected. They were an immediate success.

They were also paradoxical. In most, Ade seemed to be making fun of the pretensions and pomposities of intellectual frauds —devotees of culture, professors and other con men, and people who deviated from the Midwestern norm. At best, he satirized human foibles "warmheartedly."

A bitterness underlying Ade's view of the common man was noticed by Mencken in 1919 when he spoke about "a humor so grotesque that it almost tortures the midriff," and that "up to a certain point it is all laughter, but after that there is a flash of the knife, a show of teeth." The comment foreshadowed emphases of recent critics. Terence Tobin has argued that the fables "captured a nation embarking on a new century, seeking different modes of expression, and willing to trade new morals for old. . . . The fables were often criticisms of tenets held by an America of small towns." And Lee Coyle said in 1964 that the fables revealed "the loneliness of the farm, the destruction of the village, the emptiness of the city, the inadequacy of traditional values, the tedium of life without laughter, the lust for status and culture, the national distrust of ideas and acceptance of prosperity as an ultimate value."

The first two collections, *Fables in Slang* in 1899 and *More Fables in Slang* in 1900, are pretty catholic in the choice of objects for their satire. They deflate pretension, greediness, vanity, self-importance wherever Ade had noticed them. Some attacks are on jerkwater values, common sense, and the inhabitants of small towns, pictured as specific rather than as typical of universal human failure. This is an undercurrent, but it is there. Coyle has pointed out that rural settlements have names like Fodderville, Miasma, Nubbinville, and Dinkusville, and he quotes a fable (in a 1912 collection) which begins, "Out in the Celery Belt of the Hinterland there is a stunted Flag-Station. . . . In this Settlement the Leading Citizens still wore gum Arctics with large Buckles, and Parched Corn is served at Social Functions." "The Fable of How Uncle Brewster was Too Shifty for the Tempter" and "The Fable of the Honest Money-Maker and the Partner of His Joys, Such as They Were" both ridicule the stinginess of rural types. "The Fable of the Regular Customer and the Copper-lined Entertainer" mocks the country customer whose liquid diet had been "Rain Water and Buttermilk all his life." "The Fable of Handsome Jethro, Who was Simply Cut Out to be a Merchant" describes an Illinois farmer in unflattering terms:

The elderly Man was a Yap. He wore a Hickory Shirt, a discouraged Straw Hat, a pair of Barn-Door Pants clinging down over his Plow Shoes. He was shy several Teeth and on his Chin was a Tassel shaped like a Whisk-Broom. If you had thrown a Pebble into this Clump of Whiskers probably you would have scared up a Field Mouse and a couple of Meadow Larks.

Such commentary, in comparison with that of Bierce, is more muted and therefore typical of Chicago humor at the turn of the century. Ade is more robust and earthy than Bierce. He lacks the snobbishness of Burgess and Company, and doesn't traffic in erudition and glitter, as Bangs does. Ade once insisted, "Always I wrote for the 'family trade' and I used no word or phrase which might give offense to a mother and the girls or a professor of English." But thanks to his keen ear for colloquial language, street talk, and vivid phrases, he produced such similes as, "she looked like a Street just before they put on the Asphalt" and "He breathed like a Rusty Valve every time he had to go up a Stairway." He was an expert in dead-pan irony:

Lutie was an Only Child. When Lutie was eighteen her Mother said they ought to do something with Lutie's Voice. The Neighbors thought so too. Some recommended killing the Nerve, while others allowed that it ought to be Pulled.

His erratic capitalization is as often satiric as Germanic; and his straightforward and simple declarative sentences contrast tellingly with Bierce's ornate and elaborate rhetoric.

Probably Ade was less alienated from his culture than his contemporaries treated in this chapter. All the same, he foreshadows Sinclair Lewis, who would use vernacular language, rural speech, and provincial phrases (often with a similar comic use of capital letters) in order to ridicule a speaker and his shopworn point of view. Not surprisingly, S. J. Perelman, whose own keen ear for clichés has been a precious asset, was convinced that "Ade was undoubtedly one of the greatest humorists, if not the most outstanding, America has yet come up with"—one who "influenced all of the 20th Century American humorists in one way or another."

What was an ambivalence in Field, a minor note in Ade, and a major chord in Bangs, Bierce, and Burgess would shortly become a symphony of humorous attitudes. The impulse for urbanity and wit, the fascination with neurotic (if not psychotic) behavior, the alienation from native soil and preference for urban asphalt, and the increased interest in fantasy all simmered at the turn of the century. Only a few years later, when humorists discovered there was no particular reason for rejoicing at their position of superiority, New Yorkers would boil them over.

Between World Wars

> *The trouble now [Paul Bunyan decided] was with the loggers. True men of muscle, the best virtues for them to possess were unquestioning loyalty and faithfulness to their leaders and simple confidence in them. Oratory was good for them when it stimulated these virtues, but ideas were poisonous; for they caused the loggers to become critics and independent thinkers, and their minds were not fitted for such occupations.*
>
> *"Work and discipline will repair the damage," decided Paul Bunyan. "Work is the great consoler, for in it men forget the torments and oppressions of life. And nothing is more tormenting and oppressive to men of muscle than ideas. My loggers shall forget them."*
>
> —James Stevens, *Paul Bunyan* (1925).

37.
Mass Production Comic Demigod

WORLD WAR I, A WATERSHED IN American history comparable with the Revolution, the election of Andy Jackson or the Civil War, buffeted and twisted American literature of several kinds, including humor. Like a character in one comic story who leaped aboard a horse and galloped in every direction, our postwar humor took divergent pathways. The period that gave birth to *The New Yorker* and its confused "Little Men" was also a great one for superefficient "Comic Giants."

A few authors who retold stories about those pre-Civil War comic demigods, Davy, Mike and Mose, had moderate success. And a slew of books about newly appreciated—if not invented— comic demigods won remarkable popularity. Their tall tales featured a Northwoods lumberman, a West Virginia steel driver, a Yankee sea captain, an Oklahoma oil driller, a Texas cowboy, a Nebraska farmer and inventor, a Pittsburgh puddler, and many others.

Journalists and creative writers published stories about these supermen that they had heard or (more often) read, told in earlier versions about the same characters, workers in the same field, or complete strangers to both. More often than writers about Fink and Crockett (though not about Mose), these popularizers invented details and episodes; and diffusion was largely by print. Therefore, though the process resembled oral transmission, livid folklorists have cussed and excommunicated anyone who claimed or believed the productions were folklore. (The leading crusader, in books on which he collects royalties, calls the authors "money-writers," implying that there is some other, more saintly, kind.) Regardless of their origin, the tales appealed to a great many readers. And though, of course, earlier prototypes of happenings and characters often were world-wide, the huge popularity of this sort of fun was an interesting American phenomenon in the 1920's, 1930's, and 1940's.

Typical of the new breed, the most popular and most often imitated, was Paul Bunyan, usually a Northwoods lumberman but in some anecdotes a farmer or oil field worker. Like most newly popular demigods, Paul had no historic prototype and owed most of his fame to writers. In the early 1900's a handful of oral yarns about him circulated in lumbercamps scattered from Maine to the Pacific Northwest. A journalist and rhymster published a few in obscure periodicals before W. B. Laughead, a former lumberjack turned advertising writer, hoisted him to fame. Between 1922 and 1944, Laughead's pamphlets, sandwiching Bunyan yarns between slices of advertisements for a lumber company, hit a total of a hundred thousand copies. Helped by these, by columnists and by feature writers, other money-writers between 1924 and 1936 published seven books about Paul that had national sales. A great many other books, all or in part about the lumberman, followed. On into the 1940's and beyond, advertisements, Paul Bunyan columns, articles, children's books, ballets, operettas, plays, radio dramatizations, animated cartoons, murals, sculptures, and community festivals proved that the lumberman-demigod was popular.

One reason for his appeal becomes clear the minute we read one inventive account of his babyhood. When he was three weeks old, Paul tossed in his sleep and knocked down four square miles of timber. When his floating cradle was anchored offshore near Eastport, Maine, he rocked the thing and set up waves that destroyed towns and threatened to make Nova Scotia an island. When he stepped out, he started the tides in the Bay of Fundy that to this day are world renowned.

Since this was long before Paul got his growth, it is safe to deduce that Paul (like most of the new demigods) was a giant. As such, he belonged to a tribe whose members have repelled, fascinated, and entertained folk everywhere for centuries. Going back to the beginning, mythical histories of a number of countries assure us that the original inhabitants were monstrous men and women who ran things until gods or native heroes overcame them. Surviving giants were famous. At the start of *Pantagruel* (1532), Rabelais listed as his mountainous hero's ancestors fifty-eight renowned giants whose names he had collected from mythology, the Bible, and the literature of the Middle Ages or the early Renaissance. (He tells how one survived Noah's flood even though he was not taken aboard the ark.) If for nothing else, giants had to survive so that little fellows could defeat or befool them—Ulysses versus Polyphemus, David versus Goliath, Brabon versus Antigonus, Corineus versus Gogmagog, and Jack versus the big brute at the top of the beanstalk. The triumphs, one might say, were thingifications of the defeat of an *alazon* by an *eiron*.

Ambivalent as usual, legend makers also admired giants and bestowed giantude on national heroes. Herodotus says Hercules's footprint was about a yard long; Higden claims that King Arthur's eyes were nine inches apart; Sir Gawain, legend has it, completely filled a fourteen-foot grave; Charlemagne and Roland both were said to be enormous; Andrew Jackson (in a poem) was eight feet tall, and his sword was "so long he dragged it on the ground." In boasts, at least, American heroes had pictured themselves as giants—Mike Fink, Davy Crockett, the Child of Calamity. For centuries, many European cities have marched around their local basketwork-and-canvas giants on festive days, and disremembering that the monsters in far-off times menaced their forebears' lives and property, have become quite fond of their effigies. In the 1970's, to celebrate Christmas, Mardi Gras, and other Christian fetes, American civic groups parade papier-mâché giants on floats or haul balloon giants through city streets. Green Giant advertisements in newspapers and on television screens peddle canned and quick-frozen vegetables, "Ho-ho-ho— In the Valley of the Jolly Green Giant!"

Anecdotes—endlessly, some readers feel—demonstrate Paul's gianthood. Like Rabelais, who had Gargantua create rivers with his urinary flow, writers told how Paul, in more sanitary ways, created the Great Lakes, Grand Canyon, Puget Sound, Mount Baker, and other geographical curiosities. Somewhat more amusingly, they developed the motif by incidentally suggesting Paul's size: Hot Biscuit Slim "leans against the toe of the hero's boot and weeps"; Paul "plucks up a young pine tree and brushes his beard" and then "thrusts the tree into his pocket"; two deer and three bears that he slays "only fill one pocket of his mackinaw." Or they bestow giantude by association: Babe, Paul's blue ox, measures forty-two ax handles and a tobacco box between the eyes; Paul's wife helps him dam a stream by pitching in boulders, logs, and a few hills.

A man the size of Paul easily licked legions, and the fact is duly recorded. In 1914, for instance, Douglas Malloch gives a rhymed summary in *The American Lumberman:*

> Paul Bunyan, (you have heard of Paul?
> He was the king pin of 'em all,
> The greatest logger in the land;
> He had a punch in either hand
> And licked more men and drove more miles
> And got more drunk in more new styles
> Than any other peavey prince
> Before, or then, or even since.)

Another popularizer or two gave accounts of Paul's battles. One wrote several pages about Paul's fight with huge Hels Helsen, then rhapsodized about

. . . this conqueror, this victor in that tourney of the Titans, that battle of the behemoths, that riot of the races, that Herculean jaw-hammering, chin-mauling, nose-pounding, side-stamping, cheek-tearing, rib-breaking, lip-pinching, back-beating, neck-choking, eye-gouging, tooth-jerking, arm-twisting, head-butting, beard-pulling, ear-biting, bottom-thumping, toe-holding, knee-tickling, shin-cracking, heel-bruising, belly-whacking, hair-yanking, hell-roaring supreme and incomparable knock-down-and-drag-out fight of all history . . . the mighty leader of the new race of loggers, Paul Bunyan.

The thunderous tussle was on such a whopping scale that it completely disintegrated a mountain and replaced it with the Black Hills of Dakota. All the same, as the tribute to it makes obvious, it follows the pre-Civil War boast-brave-battle-victory patterns.

This hoary plot, as has been said, was no longer *le dernier cri*. And repetitions of it—especially in tales about an unbeatable giant—could not be counted on to enchant readers. By design or good luck, therefore, old-style conflicts play only a small part in comic Bunyaniana.

What we get instead are miles of yarns about Paul's brilliant handling of fantastic logging problems. One spring, for instance, Paul and his crew learned that the river down which they had been driving logs for four weeks was Round River, had no end, and therefore made getting to any sawmill impossible and the logs "a total loss." Paul pondered a while, then called Sourdough Sam, the cook:

"Sam," he says, "make up a good stiff batch of sourdough biscuit dough, and when I get ready, you put it where I tell you to."
And then he goes out right away and spades out a channel through a ridge that's between the river and a lake . . . that's got an outlet. And next mornin' Sam dumps his sourdough in the big tank and hitches Babe to it and hauls it out and dumps it in the river, and it riz right up and filled the channel and floated the logs right out into the lake.

In another episode, one of the fool men in Paul's outfit not only drives someone else's logs downstream; he lets the damned things float down the Mississippi all the way to New Orleans. Paul feeds Babe quantities of salt; Babe gets powerful thirsty; Babe drinks gallons of upper Mississippi water; the logs come rushing upstream, and the day is saved.

The difference between money writers' stories about the gigantic lumberman and most European folktales about giants is gargantuan. In most Old World tales, the benevolent giant (e.g., one of the Greek Titans and the Bohemians' Rübezahl) is the exception. Representative giants are monsters—sadistic people-eaters. Polyphemus ate two of Ulysses's men at every meal until the wanderers escaped from his cave. Another famous giant chanted a rhyme about his cannibalism:

> Fee fi fo fum,
> I smell the blood of an Englishman.
> Be he alive or be he dead,
> I'll grind his bones to make my bread.

Usually European folk giants combined with their viciousness abysmal stupidity. For their weak little opponents, this was a lucky circumstance, since it made it possible for smart little men, Jack the Giant Killer or the Valiant Tailor, say, to think up clever ruses that enabled them to knock off the huge, dim-witted oafs.

Paul Bunyan, as a popularizer says, was "one hero of myth who kept kindness in his heart." He was genial, public-spirited, and funny rather than cruel and frightening. And giant though he was, instead of being a dope and a dupe, he had brains, guile, know-how—equipment that Old World folklore usually reserved for giant killers.

Two American traditions in the field of humor had prepared for Paul's artful dodges—lore about clever heroes and lore about horse-sensible characters.

Not only Yankee peddlers and confidence men but also legendary frontiersmen had proved they were shrewd fellows. Mike Fink, it will be remembered, used hanky-panky to relieve a riverside farmer of his sheep. Another frontier hero, the more reputable and public-spirited Daniel Boone was also smart: habitually he used his head—in legendry, at least—to bamboozle Indians. Caught unarmed in his tobacco shed by red men, he threw dry tobacco in their eyes, and then ran to his cabin and safety. Another time, "determined to kill two Indians with one shot," just because they were there, apparently, Daniel used a strategy that Baron Münchausen and others had hit upon—he waited until they were lined up just right, fired, killed one, and disabled the other. Still another time, when he had been captured, using his "considerable expertness at slight of hand," he "deliberately opened his mouth and affected to swallow a long knife, which at the same instant he threw adroitly into his sleeve." When he "drew forth the knife, as [his captors] supposed, from his body," the frightened savages "marched off, desiring no farther intercourse with a man who could swallow a scalping knife."

The legendary Davy often served his fellows in ways that took athletic skill rather than mental might, such as when he rescued neighbors from varmints and wild men or as a soldier killed eighty-five Mexicans and wounded a hundred and twenty in the battle of the Alamo. But in times of need, he saved the nation or even the universe by combining know-how with his great strength. Take the time Halley's comet headed straight for the United States and scared the natives half to death. Davy's account in the 1837 *Almanack* of how he coped is all the more impressive because it is laconic: "I was appointed by the President to stand on the Alleghany Mountains and wring the Comet's tail off. I did so. . . ." Again, on an "antedeluvian and premature cold" morning when the sun failed to rise and the universe started to freeze, Davy climbed to the peak of Daybreak Hill and saw at once what the trouble was: "The airth had actually friz fast on her axis, and couldn't turn round; the sun had got jammed between two cakes o' ice under the wheels, an' . . . friz fast in his cold sweat." He quickly decided what was needed and acted—poured oil on the earth's axis and the sun's face, "give the airth's cog-wheel one kick backwards, till I got the sun loose," re-established order and saved the whole creation.

How did Davy manage to handle such emergencies—emergencies that, frankly, would baffle most of us? By good luck, despite differences, he had one of the endowments of the real David Crockett—good sound gumption. The historical Crockett, the man who got to Washington because he championed and worked out horse-sensible solutions to problems, was not a stranger to the rootin'-tootin' Davy. After the Alamo, to support a doubtful claim that *Davy Crockett's Almanack 1838* was "published by the heirs of Col. Crockett," the Nashville compilers brazenly launched it with an introduction that they implied Crockett had written before he lit out for Texas:

I was born in a cane brake, cradled in a sap trough, and clouted with coon skins; without being choked by the weeds of education, which do not grow *spontinaciously*—for all the time I was troubled by *young-ness*, my cornstealers were *na'*trally used for other purposes than holding a pen; and *rayly* when I try to write my elbow keeps coming round like a swingle-tree, and it is easier for me to tree a varmint . . . than to write. . . . Of books the divil a one have I read, except Tom Toe and The Axes of the Apostles. And although my I *dears* run through me like an hour glass that never wants turning, if I only know'd how to scrawl the alphabet, I'd soon row some of the larned ones up *Salt River*—for

> Honor and fame from no condition rise;
> Axe well your part and down the tree soon lies.

For it's the grip of a fellow that makes the man; and I'm half chicken-hawk and steel trap. So I will just let you know, reader, what I think about gineral matters and things in particular.

Fakelore though it is, the paragraph says things that the real Crockett might have said or would have been glad to have a ghost writer say for him. And every year, Nashville almanacks and almanacks published elsewhere, in columns for all the months headed "Aspects, &c." laced witty aphorisms—presumably I *dears* of Davy—with data about moon phases, eclipses, holidays, and the like. A couple in the 1840 issue are illustrative. "If you would be rich," one went, "think of saving as well as getting." Another read: "Riches, like manure, do no good till they are spread." The first of these was a recycled proverb: Poor Richard (probably after swiping it somewhere) had put it into one of his almanacks. The second would get laughs from theater and movie audiences of the 1960's and 1970's, when it was intoned by the shrewd matchmaker-heroine of the popular musical comedy, *Hello Dolly!*

Early on, like Davy and David, Paul the superman and Paul the pawky businessman climbed into one skin and collaborated. Laughead, applying his lively imagination, promoted his hero from his job as a lumberman to a position as a super industrialist, and satire against efficiency experts intruded:

When Paul took up efficiency engineering . . . he did not fool around clocking the crew with a stop watch, counting motions and deducting the ones used for borrowing chews, going for drinks, dodging the boss and preparing for quitting time. He decided to cut out the labor altogether.

Other popularizers and adapters enlarged the satire and in their stories had Paul, like real-life tycoons in America and elsewhere, "perfect" one industry and then branch out and succeed in others. He got into farming, cattle raising, mining, oil drilling, government contracting—always thinking big and prospering. When, for instance, Paul built a hotel, he made it a skyscraper "and had the last seven stories put on hinges so's they c'd be swung fer to let the moon go by." He spread it over more than ten acres and had his bell-hops cover the vast spaces on roller skates.

In other words, literary men and women, reworking old stories and lavishly inventing new ones, left the lore of timbercamps far behind. After taking a fierce pounding on their typewriters, the tall tales about Paul Bunyan that emerged had become mock folktales which at times lauded, at other times kidded and satirized, the America of the period as the authors saw it.

The most successful of the popularizers was James Stevens, who wrote articles and books about the comic demigod during two decades. His *Paul Bunyan* (1925) sold well enough to trigger his writing of two more books about the hero. Its sales totaled seventy-five thousand copies, and long excerpts from it and its sequels got into many anthologies.

The discoverer, patron, and guide of James Stevens was a post-World War I phenomenon, the cynical, iconoclastic Henry L. Mencken (1880–1956). When he was writing the stories in the first book, Stevens acknowledged in a letter to this author: "I feel that I am writing them for you"; and the Introduction ended, "Without his help and encouragement the stories would not have been written." Mencken published the first of the tales in his fashionable magazine, *The American Mercury*, sold the idea of commissioning a collection to a prestigious publisher and reviewed the books with enthusiasm.

A few facts about what some historians call "the Age of Mencken" and about this sponsor and admirer of Stevens' Paul Bunyan stories, therefore, will help define them. It was an era when iconoclasm was all the rage. And Mencken, "the bad boy of Baltimore," was a ripsnorting bull in the post-World War I china shop—a blue-ribbon champion in a period of tough competition.

Disillusioned by the cynical peace after a conflict that allegedly would "make the world safe for democracy," leading writers of the 1920's and 1930's blasted every segment of American life. Striking a keynote, thirty intellectuals in 1921 put out a symposium, *Civilization in the United States*, in which they peered into every corner and glumly announced that they had found nary a trace; conformity, mediocrity, and chicanery were blighting the whole countryside. Sinclair Lewis, Sherwood Anderson, James Branch Cabell, and other fiction writers assaulted life on farms, in small towns, in cities; businessmen, industrialists, doctors, politicians, journalists, labor unionists, poets, religionists, and American womanhood. Two devastating panoramas of American life appeared in the same year as Stevens' *Paul Bunyan*—F. Scott Fitzgerald's *The Great Gatsby* and Theodore Dreiser's *An American Tragedy*.

Mencken inspired these fictionists and whooped it up for their writings in unrestrained reviews. In syndicated newspaper columns, magazine pieces and books, he repeated his praises and on his own forcefully shouted similar messages. Wielding tree trunks, truncheons, and slapsticks, he too mowed down—or tried to mow down—group after group. A ravished connoisseur of American and imported words, he hurled memorable invectives at common men (*"booboisie"* and "anthropoids"), elected officials ("crooks," "charlatans"), preachers ("mountebanks," "gaudy zanies"), reformers ("wowsers"), fundamentalists ("the Bible Belt"), pedantic professors ("the Gelehrten"), the whole nation ("the most timorous, sniveling, poltroonish, ignominious mob of serfs and goose-steppers ever gathered under one flag in Christendom since the Middle Ages"). Mencken's trumpetings won warm huzzas and blistering denunciations. Savoring the attacks, he lovingly collected the fiercest and issued a book stuffed with favorite samples, e.g., "a treacherous alien sapping at the vitals of America's proudest and most essential institutions, an indecent buffoon wallowing in obscenity as he howls with glee."

Before Mencken incited him to write at length about Paul Bunyan, Stevens had wonderful chances to hear the tales told by experts. Born in Iowa, brought up there and in Idaho, at age fifteen he started a wandering life as a hobo, day laborer, mule skinner, lumbercamp and mill worker, and World War I infantryman. What some scholars learned by research in books he learned, so he said, by personal visits to "timber-town saloons," which he called "peaceful places": "The fist-and-boot battles and the Big Drunks of loggers were few and tame—compared to the brags of ring-tailed roarers and the pages of popular fiction." When he started Paul's biography, he was a lumber-sorter, "slugging green pine off conveyor chains and piling it on trunks by day; then, shucking mulehide mittens, taking pen in hand each night to write."

In his introduction to the book, Stevens pictured himself as a proletarian folklore buff who had collected many stories in widely scattered bunkhouses and then painstakingly traced them to their origins during "the revolt of the French-Canadians against their young English Queen" in 1837, when a rebel named Paul Bunyon became famous. This hero later ran a Canadian lumbercamp, and stories about him grew. (Stevens learned this, he said, from old-time Canuck informants.) In time, he claimed, the stories seeped southward across the border. American loggers appropriated, told, and naturalized about a hundred traditional ones, rechristened their chief character Bunyan, renamed Bébé the Blue Ox Babe, and brought forth a "true American legend" about a folk hero "absolutely American from head to foot" celebrated by generations of yarnspinners. In every lumbercamp, Stevens said, a chief storyteller "could elaborate on it for hours, building a complete narrative, picturing awe-inspiring characters, inventing dialogue." From several such bards, he announced, he had learned the method he used in the book.

A good deal of this, simon-pure folklorists have proved, was as phony as a three-dollar bill—demonstrable Canadian origin, key stories numbering a hundred, wide diffusion, lumbercamp laureates, Stevens's passion for old bardic traditions. Much more accurate were later—quite different—accounts he gave. In these, he contrasted his ways with those of folklorists and defiantly claimed that he wrote as an artist who "*adopted* folklore for the work of his imagination." This way, he believed (with reason), "comic writers from 1830 to 1860 . . . popularized the simple original lore of Boone, Crockett and Fink," and Mark Twain in *A Connecticut Yankee* monkeyed with the old Camelot idylls to make fun of his world. (With less justification, Stevens claimed

that he followed "especially Joel Chandler Harris, who made up
stories from one folk fable, 'The Tar Baby.' " Actually, the Uncle
Remus narratives were based upon a great many folktales.)

In an autobiographical novel, Stevens showed a lumbercamp
storyteller whom he greatly admired shaping Paul Bunyan
stories, as he himself did, to satirize current stupidities. During
World War I, seeing "how idiotic all the different brands of
making-the-world-better talk are" and deciding that "all the
people on the other side of the Atlantic were making . . . mule-
headed fools out of themselves," this bunkhouse bard "got to telling Paul Bunyan stories around the smudge fire, in ridicule of
all the fighters over in Europe."

Years before Stevens confessed that he went and did likewise,
astute reviewers of his book who knew American literature and
history had caught him with his stance down and described
pretty accurately what he had done. And instead of yelling,
"Fake!" they had approved in principle and had given him two
or three cheers. Constance Rourke, for instance, held that Stevens
did the sort of thing poets always did—"used legends according
to the play of his own fancy." Even the sizable number of stories
he dreamed up entirely on his own, she thought, were "invention kept within the happy bound of substantial tradition," so
that "old and new, [his narratives] have the windy breadth, the
loose and casual structure, the sly pitfalls which everywhere
characterize the Paul Bunyan stories." Carl Van Doren spoke up
for Stevens's electing "deliberately to desert document for art"
and "choose among his materials with a high hand" to make, if
he could, "a burlesque epic out of what was only a collection of
folktales."

Mencken, beaming like a fatuous father ogling a newborn son,
actually praised his protégé for doing something to his stories
that time and again he eloquently denounced other authors for
doing—bowdlerizing them:

as heard in the camps they were overladen with pornographic and
even skatological embellishments [that] Mr. Stevens had to . . .
transmute into something immeasurably softer. It seems to me that he
has done the job with infinite cunning and vast success. The Paul
Bunyan that he presents . . . is still the authentic Polyphemus of the
woods: horrible, hairy, human . . . immensely strong, unflinchingly
honorable, romantically generous.

The scourger of puritanical censorship and Comstockery was concerned that the purification of this book had not robbed it of other great charms—"a simple, ingratiating style . . . rich, wholly masculine humor . . . rapport with the extravagant, Rabelaisian humor of Bunyan himself." Besides, though Stuart Chase darkly suspected him of being a 1920 model radical—an I.W.W., a Wobbly—this protégé of Baltimore's hatchet man satirized exactly those groups, institutions, attitudes, and personalities that Mencken particularly loved to have bludgeoned.

In the first chapter of *Paul Bunyan*, for example, Stevens took a swing at one of Mencken's favorite foes, "the cornfed *intelligentsia*." During his youthful Canadian days, Paul, says this biography, was a scholar who "was not long in learning all the history worth learning" and becoming "as good a figurer as any man could be." When, as he modestly decided, "there was nothing more for him to learn," he spent a long time thinking. His thoughts were jim-dandies. The best of them: "Somewhere in the future a great Work was waiting to be done by him."

The locale that Paul hit upon for this Work was one Mencken extolled in an essay he wrote in 1922, "On Being an American." Ours was the finest homeland in the world for him personally, Mencken said, because—thanks to the lack of competition—making a living was so easy, and because the rascals, hypocrites, and clowns with whom the country teemed were so endlessly amusing. Paul decided he would go to "Real America," his "Land of Opportunity" (Stevens's capitals). So he crossed the border, renamed himself and his ox, and "using the rightful language of Real America," declaimed:

"We are now Real Americans both, hearts, souls and hides. . . . And I'm glad of it! By the holy old mackinaw, and by the hell-jumping, high-tailed, fuzzy-eared, whistling old jeem cris and seventeen slippery saints, I'm *proud* of it, too! . . ."

Then he felt amazed beyond words that the simple fact of entering Real America and becoming a Real American had made him feel so exalted, so pure, so noble, so good. . . . Freedom and Inspiration and Uplift were in the very air . . . , and Babe and Paul Bunyan got more noble feelings in every breath.

"The *boobus Americanus*," Mencken had written, "is a bird that knows no closed season . . . he will always come down to In-

spiration and Optimism [his capitals], whether political, theological, pedagogical, literary, or economic." Paul had joined the
booboisie.

Next, using the prodigious brain that had helped him become
a superlative scholar, Paul pondered "for many days and nights"
how he would obey a command the Real America helpfully
"whispered in his heart" and then "shouted": "To work! Take
advantage of your opportunity!" With a brilliance that Sherlock
Holmes well might envy, Paul ratiocinated his thorny way to a
"Great Idea":

Real America was covered with forests. A forest was composed of trees.
A felled and trimmed tree was a log. Paul Bunyan . . . jumped to his
feet with a great shout.

"What greater work could be done in Real America than to make
logs from trees?" he cried. "Logging! I shall invent this industry and
make it the greatest one of all time!"

The superlative mind that gave him this insight did enable him
to invent the logging industry and introduce one innovation after
another—"the multiplication table, cube root and algebra, . . .
bossmen," competition, "the perfect organization he had always
dreamed about."

Again and again, confronted with apparently unsolvable
problems, he coped. An example: In Utah, when he and his men
tried to log off forests of stonewood trees—

The gritty texture of the stonewood timber dulled the edge of an ax
bit in two strokes. At the end of a twelve-hour day in the woods the
loggers had to sharpen axes for several hours. They were always
fagged out. . . . Paul Bunyan . . . brought all his inventive powers
to the problem. . . . In eleven days and nights he devised eight hundred and five systems, machines and implements, and from this galaxy
he selected a noble tool.

Paul Bunyan's new invention was the double-bitted ax, which is
used everywhere in the woods to-day. Paul Bunyan devised it so that a
faller could chop with one blade, then twist the handle and whet the
other blade on the gritty stonewood with the backward swing.

Other tokens of the great leader's practical sense were a mess
of aphorisms which summed up his keenest insights concerning
men and methods. Sometimes he crowded three into one brief
speech, e.g., "The test of great leadership is originality. . . .

The hero inspires, but the thinker leads. . . . One great idea put into action can set the world afire." Other beauties: "Be true to your pretensions"; "Meals make the man"; "Work is the great consoler, for in it men forget the torments and oppressions of life"; "The best virtues for loggers to possess are unquestioning loyalty and faithfulness to their leaders and simple confidence in them"; "Ideas are poisonous; for they cause the loggers to become critics and independent thinkers."

In contrast to the witty maxims of horse-sense humorists which charmed Americans from the days of Benjamin Franklin to the days of Will Rogers, these puny utterances were remarkably stale, flat, and unprofitable. They were unprofitable, that is, to the loggers, but not to the giant industrialist who was their leader. Stevens—and Paul—constantly talked about the loving kindness of the lumbering tycoon, and the adoration and respect that he got in return, but more than one passage gives the whole show away:

Paul Bunyan's loggers . . . never realized what inventiveness, thought and effort were needed. . . . Nor did Paul Bunyan expect shouted praises and thanks from his loggers. He gave so much to them because he expected much from them. He worked his men twelve hours a day, and, had they thought about it, they would have been astounded by any idea of working less. And they would have been perplexed by any other scheme to ease their lot. . . . A noble breed. . . . He himself told them in a speech . . . that they were "a good band of bullies, a fine bunch of savages."

As a speaker, Paul was not only more condescending; he was even longer-winded, it seems, than most executives. The inspiring oration lasted nine days and eight nights. It ended on Tuesday, and the inspired men slept until the following Sunday.

What Stevens did, it is clear, was so manhandle and expand the Bunyan legendry as to transform it into a romping assault on American hundred percentism, optimism, industrialism, know-how, inventiveness, common sense, altruism and paternalism—all of them subjects for dozens of Mencken's elephantine japes. Other passages in Stevens's books about Bunyan had at other Menckenian targets—puritanism, prohibition, sentimentality, poetry, oratory, pedantry, California boosterism, He-Manhood, and Womanhood. Individuals were satirized, too: Henry

Ford and his so-called ideas, for instance, in passages about a Swedish logger named Ford Fordson.

Stuart Pratt Sherman, who had recently resigned from a University of Illinois professorship to become a full-time book review editor in New York, found fault with *Paul Bunyan* for an interesting reason: "Briefly speaking, Mr. Stevens has converted Paul Bunyan from folklore to farce, prepared it for the motion pictures, the burlesque show, or the comic strips—probably with some dim satirical intention." This "dim" may seem puzzling until one notices that Mencken had made many attacks upon Sherman and his critical attitudes, and one of Stevens's characters, named Professor Sherm Shermson, expresses ideas which weirdly exaggerate beliefs like those of Sherman.

What had happened to the comic American hero since the riproarious days of Mike Fink, Mose, and Davy Crockett shouldn't happen to a god.

[A Colyumnist] *has to deal with*
the most elusive and grotesque material he knows—his own mind.
. . . You may know him by a sunken, brooding eye; clothing marred
by much tobacco, and a chafed and techy humour toward the hour of
5 P.M. . . . Poor soul, he is like one condemned to harangue the vast,
idiotic world through a keyhole.

　　　—Christopher Morley, "Confessions of a 'Colyumist' " (1920).

　　　　　　　　　　For the people who were "ad-
dressed" to success, the Round Table was honeysuckle and roses during
the 'Twenties.

"It must be a boom," Georges, the headwaiter, said to my father one
day, "they order ice cream on top of everything!"

"Uh-huh," said Bob Benchley, when Father told him this glad news,
"and then they grab their lollipops and pitter-patter over to their psy-
chiatrists." 　—Margaret Case Harriman, *The Vicious Circle* (1951).

38.
The Lunatic Fringe:
Colyumnists and
Algonquin Wits

THE PATTERN FOR COMIC DEMI-
god confrontations wasn't the only one that disillusioned post-
World War I intellectuals revised.

New York—as New Yorkers weren't too shy to admit—was by
now the headquarters for the illuminati. The reason, less often
noticed, was that a large share of them had invaded the place.
Like the riffraff from the Midwest, the South, and the Far West
who had captured popular fiction and humor after the Civil
War, a bunch of out-of-town Goths had intruded.

An earlier generation had been more restrained. Back in the
1880's, Eugene Field, out in Denver, had worried about getting too
far Eastward (and cultureward) from earthy rowdiness. He decided (so his biographer, Slason Thomson, says) that he could
safely move a little over half way—to Chicago. That city

was as far East as he could make his home without coming within the
influence of those social and literary conventions that have squeezed so
much of genuine literary flavor out of our literature.

A few years later, though, others seeking their fortunes as professional giggle-merchants had different notions. Franklin P. Adams migrated from Chicago to New York in 1904. A few years later, after an apprenticeship under Joel Chandler Harris in Atlanta, Don Marquis headed in the same direction. Following the First World War, Robert Benchley bumbled in from New England (as did E. E. Cummings, to contribute comic prose to *Vanity Fair*). James Thurber arrived later, from Ohio (via France) in 1926; and other wits converged, like so many worms, on the Big Apple.

Most of the jokesters of the so-called lost generation got jobs on the big newspapers: Adams's "The Conning Tower" ran in the *Tribune* for nine years, then in the *World* for a decade; Marquis's column "The Sun Dial" became a fixture of the *Evening Sun*. Benchley, after helping Adams fill his "Tower" with insane contributions, such as "Do Jellyfish Suffer Embarrassment?," joined Robert E. Sherwood and Dorothy Parker in 1919 at *Vanity Fair*. Christopher Morley's "The Bowling Green" started in the *Evening Post* in 1920, and Alexander Woollcott (once called Louisa M. Woollcott because of his intermittent sentimentality) and George S. Kaufman wrote for the *Times*.

One of the first critics to notice, Carl Van Doren, spotted some hallmarks of the group's humor that distinguished it from "rural" humor, and he suggested antecedents. "They are town wits," he said, "as Addison and Steele were in their merry London, as Irving and Paulding were in the New York of a hundred years ago." They marked, he continued, "the moment when cities began to demand of their wits a more edged, more sophisticated, more varied, and more continuous entertainment than had been demanded among the farms and villages." Being a "town wit," with its sharp edge, sophistication, variety, and constant outpouring, didn't mean, though, that they escaped their own kind of parochialism: "To read them in any distant city is to miss half the points they make, or at least half the freshness of their points."

Of course, there was as much individual variation among these Manhattan wits as there was cohesiveness. We think, though, that it is possible and useful to divide them into two groups: those who called themselves "Colyumnists," retaining vestiges of "native" humor in daily columns; and the members of the Algonquin Round Table (also known as "the Vicious Circle"), whose wit tended to be more caustic, urbane, and neurotic.

When Don Marquis reminisced about his childhood in rural Illinois, he confessed, "I read, every day, Eugene Field's column in a Chicago newspaper; and later George Ade's sketches, and I decided I wanted to do something like that." After he arrived in New York in 1909, he got his chance, and discovered (like many of the literary comedians before him) that it wasn't easy to meet a daily deadline with humorous material:

It sapped my vitality, made corns and bunions on my brain, wrecked my life, and I adored it. . . . I loathe, hate, abhor and dread the column-writing game; I think of it as the most poisonously destructive vice to which any writer may become addicted, and the hardest work to which any human being might contract himself; and at the same time I love it.

Sometimes, he said, "one gets up a column in thirty minutes, depending largely on contributions; at other times I have worked twelve and fifteen hours on one of them."

Marquis solved his dilemma by creating a couple of fictional worlds and a menagerie of comic characters who surfaced in his column, and then filled a series of humorous volumes. These were closer to the native tradition in American humor than anything the other colyumnists produced. Because Marquis, for one thing, was the most socially oriented of the group, his columns touched almost daily on the stupidities and asininities of his times. Archy, the lower-case free-verse poet who transmigrated into the body of a cockroach, was a parody of E. E. Cummings and other modish poets and, in addition, a social commentator whose aberrant punctuation and capitalization (he was forced to jump from the carriage onto the keys of the typewriter in order to satisfy his need for expression) didn't disguise his homespun morality. Among his observations:

> i have noticed
> that when
> chickens quit
> quarreling over their
> food they often
> find that there is
> enough for all of them.

did you ever
notice that when
a politician
does get an idea
he usually
gets it all wrong

everybody has two kinds of friends
one kind tries to run
his affairs for him
and the other kind
well i will be darned if i can remember
the other kind

Archy's labors at the typewriter served another important purpose. By taking up only a few of the spaces down the center of the column and leaving lots of wide, white margin, they satisfied one of Marquis's criteria for column-writing:

A column must have plenty of white space, a challenging make-up, constant variation in typographical style; not only must it catch the eye but it must have points and corners and barbs that prick and stimulate the vision, a surface and a texture that intrigue and cling to and pull at the sight. Franklin P. Adams, of the New York World, is the master hand at this sort of thing.

Marquis, too, managed through Archy's erratic line-division to get about as much variety into the "vision" of his column as is imaginable.

Archy's topicality allowed him to lambast prohibition, companionate marriages (practiced by Mehitabel the cat, whose morals were sub-feline), the League of Nations, contract bridge, and countless other current issues. Even though on many occasions he talked like a crackerbarrel philosopher, Archy was a tormented bug. He had to dodge larger, hungry animals in a hostile universe; he saw things, as he said, from the underside. Also, as Enid Veron observed, he kept "hammering out philosophic verses that belie his puny existence." However wry and sardonic Archy might be about the world around him, that world posed a constant threat to him.

Marquis's fictional worlds also included the rummy Old Soak who, with bartender Al as sidekick, made his way through the column, books, a movie, and a successful play. They included, finally, Hermione and her Little Group of Serious Thinkers— probably the most undeservingly neglected character in Ameri-

there s a dance in the old dame yet

archy and mehitabel. Illustration by George Herriman in Don Marquis, *lives and times of archy and mehitabel*, p. 85, copyright 1930 by Doubleday and Company, Inc. (*Reproduced by permission of Doubleday and Company, Inc.*)

ca's comic pantheon. Hermione, a faddist poseur up to her empty head in all the intellectual vogues of the day, is surrounded by an esoteric group of frauds. These include Fothergil Finch, a poet whose nose provides him with inspiration, and Voke Easeley, who, with nothing more than his Adam's apple, does an imitation of the sunrise on Mont Blanc. Hermione's monologues begin with her newest preoccupation:

We've been going in for Astrological Research lately—our Little Group of Modern Thinkers, you know—and we've picked our own personal stars.

We've been taking up Metabolism lately—our Little Group of Serious Thinkers, you know—and it's wonderful; just simply *wonderful!*

I'm taking up Bergson this week.

Next week I'm going to take up Etruscan vases and the Montessori system.

Oh, no, I haven't lost my interest in sociology.

Only the other night we went down in the auto and watched the bread line.

But Hermione is obviously going to bounce through life unendangered by a single thought.

One thing that keeps Marquis's writings alive and fresh is their fictional context. Alone among the Colyumnists, Marquis embodied his humorous antagonisms, resentments, and points of view without losing an appearance of objectivity.

Two others in the column-editing group—Christopher Morley and Heywood Broun—were more self-centered. In their columns, which were less consistently humorous than those of Marquis, they talked about themselves. Morley, nicknamed "The Old Mandarin" because he was indeed an epicurean, championed good living, strong tobacco, fine food, and old brandy. He wrote highly ornate and precise parodies of esoteric verse forms and was (with the possible exception of S. J. Perelman) the last of the cognoscenti. Gentility, affluence, erudition, and refinement oozed from him. As Van Doren observed, Morley's "comments on the passing show rarely bite and never pulverize. He is bland and lacks the concentration of sardonic wits."

Broun was the author of a column, titled "It Seems to Me," more serious than the others. At least as "socially aware" as Hermione's Little Group, he supported the Scottsboro Boys, Sacco and Vanzetti, and a newsman's union. When he was humorous, he was so for a purpose: "humor is the grit in the evolutionary process," he once said. " 'Does it matter?' is the underlying mood in almost every expression of humor. And of course it does matter."

Examples of Broun's mordant humor: Once an actor was so bad in a play that Broun labeled him the worst in America. When the young man next appeared, Broun said only that his "performance was not up to its usual standard." When Tallulah Bankhead appeared in a flop, Broun told her, "Don't look now, Tallulah, but your show's slipping." And among his comic definitions: "A liberal is a man who leaves the room when the fight starts"; and "Repartee is what you wish you'd said."

At the opposite end of the spectrum from Marquis (though they were good friends) was Franklin P. Adams, both a Colyumnist and (like Heywood Broun) a member of the Algonquin Round Table. Carl Van Doren's appraisal again hit the target:

Mr. Adams is in a strict sense the wit of the group. He is the neatest of them all with his gay verses, the crispest of all with his puns. . . .

Very many of his witticisms are merely verbal; many of them are very trivial and some of them are cheap. . . . He seldom touches public affairs more closely than to point out some misquotation or solecism in a speech by some public man.

And as Robert E. Drennan noted more recently, Adams "wrote in the 'genteel' tradition, excelling in urbanity, high wit, and erudition."

Adams's "The Conning Tower" depended more on contributors than other columns, but a consolation was that the contributions came from, among others, George S. Kaufman, Dorothy Parker, and Alexander Woollcott. One day a week, he himself filled his column with a first-class parody of Samuel Pepys's diary, filled with trivia, name-dropping, and comic contretemps.

Adams's best hold was high wit. He doted on complicated puns. In a word-game which his group played called "I'll give you a sentence," for a sentence containing the word *punctilious*, Adams offered: "A man had two daughters, Lizzie and Tillie, and Lizzie is all right, but you have no idea how punctilious." When the family of one Jonny Madden was discussed in an Algonquin gathering, Adams said that he knew a family who lived nowhere near the Madden family—"Far from the Madden Crowd."

He could deflate his friends. A lady he took to a cocktail party sat on a cane-bottom chair. More accurately, she sat through the cane-bottom until her bottom almost bumped the floor. "I've told you a hundred times," he said sternly, "that's not funny!" When Alexander Woollcott once mused, "Ah, what is so rare as a Woollcott first edition?," Adams answered, "A Woollcott second edition."

Adams saved his vitriolic bons mots for the Vicious Circle, though, and made "The Conning Tower" an outlet for blander, more academic stuff. He excelled in parodies of famous poetry (including the odes of Horace), rewriting Leigh Hunt's "Jennie Kissed Me" in Italian dialect:

> Signor, I gattin' old an' gray,
> But—Rosa keess me yestiday.
>
> Joos' yestiday, w'en I am stan'
> Right here by my peanutta stan',
> A granda lady, beeg an' fine,

Weeth leeps joos' like Eetalia's wine,
Ees com' in soocha fina car
An' ask how mooch peanuttas are.
Her hair so black, her han' so small
I say, "You notta pay at all."
An' she ees joomp from off da seat,
An' keessa me—ow, my, so sweet!
Not like da kees from child or wife,
But deeferent, you bat my life!

Signor, I gattin' old an' gray,
But—Rosa keess me yestiday!

His disjointed paraphrase of Wordsworth's poem was another
marvel:

She dwelt among the untrodden ways
Near Dove Springs Junction;
A girl whom nobody ever praised,
A maiden whose lovers were few.
A dandelion by a mossy boulder,
Fair as a solitary shining star,
She lived unknown.
Few were informed of her death.
But it made a difference to some.
Eh, William Wordsworth?

Such humor depended for appreciation upon a fairly literate
readership.

Since the range from Marquis to Adams is a vast one, it is fair
to ask what yoked the Colyumnists together. One thing was their
self-consciousness. An early issue of the *Saturday Review* (in
1925) commented:

Under all styles its conductor's fundamental attitude is this, "it is my
daily (or weekly) endeavor to conceal from you the fact that I take
myself at all seriously." The true "Colyum" is a perpetual, whimsical
turning-inside-out of the "Colyum" conductor's personality.

Though the conductor swirled through a busy world, what
counted for humor was his own response to that world: "It is the
intimacy of detail, the naked bits of autobiography," Mary Ellis
Opdycke said in the *New Republic*, "that establishes the colyum
of America":

These privacies take on a national importance as soon as they leave
the composing room. The Pacific coast knows what the colyumist likes

for breakfast, almost before he has ordered his supper; his secret sins are syndicated from Texas to Maine. Everything the New York colyumist does become his copy. He eats at one restaurant and notes down the menu in a rondeau; he plays poker or pool and adds up his winnings in his colyum. . . . He meets a girl on the street and quotes what he says to her, and if she is very bright what she says to him. The capital for his colyum is the order of every waking minute of his day, as well as what he has dreamed the night before—if it was fit for print.

The first-person posturings were obvious heritages from the literary comedians and other nineteenth-century newspaper comics.

But, more important, and distinct from the traditional legacy, was the group's cosmopolitanism. Like Bangs and the "Purple Cow" writers, the Colyumnist went in for being intellectual, witty, and urbane. His humor was ephemeral and frothy. Some of the qualities of genteel humor had sneaked from periodicals into the daily newspaper, the bastion of "native" humor.

The large round table that Frank Case installed in the center of the Rose Room at the Algonquin Hotel was a personified, mass-aggression syndrome. Regulars, in addition to Adams and Broun, included Woollcott, Kaufman, Benchley, Dorothy Parker, Robert E. Sherwood, and Edna Ferber. Ring Lardner, Harpo Marx, Jascha Heifetz, Tallulah Bankhead, Ethel Barrymore, Douglas Fairbanks, and out-classed Harold Ross were also predictable squatters there.

They gained their notoriety by keeping their tongues sharper-honed than the knives at the table. Their mastery at the put-down became legendary. When Noel Coward made the mistake of commenting on Edna Ferber's mannish hair-do and suit one noontime, telling her, "You look almost like a man," she replied to the mannered Englishman, "So do you." To a boorish young man who made the mistake of getting too close to Dorothy Parker and bragging, "I can't bear fools," Parker replied, "That's queer. Your mother could." When she was told that her enemy, Clare Booth Luce, was always kind to her inferiors, Mrs. Parker was puzzled. "Where does she find them?" she wondered.

Alexander Woollcott once told a female guest, "You are married to a cuckold." Woollcott was probably the most hysterical member of the group. He threw tantrums, nursed grudges, and insulted friends both at the Table and at the apartment which Dorothy Parker christened "Wit's End." He egomaniacally bossed every social function he attended. His essays, the best of which he collected in *While Rome Burns*, were a peculiar mixture of pathetic sentiment, the bizarre, and the grotesque. He wallowed in details about grisly murders, especially unsolved ones, explaining that such gory doings provided readers with an escape from the humdrum routine of every day. He told ghost stories and recounted anecdotes of strange coincidences and unlikely turns of events. Though usually a genial and genteel essayist, he often used a superior tone and patronized his audience, calling them "my dears," as if they were children. The image which crystallizes is of a witty, urbane storyteller, whistling in the dark and retreating into bathos because of his insecurities.

Even more self-destructive than Woollcott was Ring Lardner, the taciturn, near-mute member of the wits. Lardner had won fame with his slangy baseball stories and letters, but by the mid-1920's, he was foreshadowing most of the qualities of *New Yorker* humor (and for years, in fact, he wrote a column called "Over the Waves" for that magazine). His alcoholism, insomnia, and acute depression led William Bolitho to call him "the greatest and sincerest pessimist America has produced." Clifton Fadiman suggested, "He just doesn't like people. I believe he hates himself; most certainly he hates his characters; and most clearly of all, his characters hate each other. . . . His hatred is not the result of mere crabbedness but of an eye that sees too deep for comfort."

In spite of personal moroseness and fatalism, Lardner produced humor that was increasingly flippant and surreal. His use of the vernacular had been sardonic in his earlier stories, a weapon for depicting the stupidity and insensitivity of rural folk. But Lardner's later humor was in the dead center of the lunatic fringe.

"On Conversation," from his collection *First and Last*, is a dialogue between two men, each of whom repeats his answers to the other's questions without hearing a word of the conversation. Over and over, they jaw the same phrases and sentences:

> "How long since you been back in Lansing?"
> "Me?" replied Butler. "I ain't been back there for twelve years."

"I ain't been back there either myself for ten years. How long since you been back there?"

"I ain't been back there for twelve years."

"I ain't been back there myself for ten years. Where are you headed for?"

"New York," replied Butler. "I have got to get there about once a year. Where are you going?"

"Me?" asked Hawkes. "I am going to New York too. I have got to go down there every little wile for the firm."

"Do you have to go there very often?"

"Me? Every little wile. How often do you have to go there?"

"About once a year. How often do you get back to Lansing?"

"Last time I was there was ten years ago. How long since you was back?"

"About twelve years ago. . . ."

The impression is not just that both men are hard of hearing; rather, it's that both are stark mad.

"Large Coffee," another story in the same collection, combined facetiousness with derangement. A "Mr. Lardner" checked into a hotel to get away from having his "mind . . . constantly distracted by the knowledge that other people were having fun." After knocking on his door for two weeks without getting an answer, the chambermaids decided that he "would need a clean towel if living, and perhaps two of them, if dead." Indeed, the tenant was found on the floor, "his head crushed in by a blow from some blunt instrument, probably another hotel." His demise evidently came about because room service couldn't cope with an order of four cups of coffee for one person. His double order produced two place settings, two cereal bowls, and two plates for bacon and eggs. "Two orders of coffee, but for one person" produced one pot with two cups of coffee. "Double coffee, large coffee, enough coffee for four cups, sixty cents worth of coffee, enough coffee for two people served for one person"; nothing worked. Meanwhile, Mr. Lardner was having other problems. "I spent so much thought yesterday and this morning on what I would have sent up for breakfast that when I sat down at the typewriter, my mind was too tired to work." He decided to order toast instead of plain or sweet rolls "because the sweet ones are too filling and messy, and the plain ones are made in Bethlehem, Pa."

Other occupants of the hotel at whom he peeped were as

strange as Mr. Lardner. "A business woman who looks like Tom Heeney and has a red splotch under her left shoulder blade is occupying the room opposite. She is out all day and goes to bed at eight and reads the Brooklyn telephone directory." And "a mystifying combination of tenants has taken the room across the court. There are two young women and a man. They can't be going to stay in town very long because the women apparently haven't brought anything but nightgowns and when the man isn't in B.V.D.'s. he's out of them." We never do learn what killed him, but the last entry in his diary reads, "I'm pretty sure that late tonight I will lean out the window and holler, 'Hey! Don't you want a fourth for strip bridge?' "

Lardner's 1925 collection, *What of It?*, contains three plays in which nonsense, non-sequiturs, and fractured logic abound. "Clemo Uti—'The Water Lilies' " designates its setting as "The Outskirts of a Parchesi Board." "Taxidea Americana" is "Translated from the Mastoid." "I. Gaspiri (*The Upholsterers*)" contains the famous dialogue

> First Stranger
> Where was you born?
>
> Second Stranger
> Out of wedlock.
>
> First Stranger
> That's mighty pretty country around there.

(And a stage note stipulates, *The curtain is lowered for seven days to denote the lapse of a week.*) At a later date in the history of the American stage, such nonsense would be taken quite seriously; but in 1925, Lardner's zany, capricious humor was a portent.

Mixed with the mordant bitterness were such madcap touches as these we have described. Both Woollcott and Lardner, in different ways, sought a safety-valve from the conventional. Both lashed out at what Henry Steele Commager, referring only to Lardner, called "the irremediable depravity of the ordinary man." Each saw the gauche hypocrisy that underlay the middle-class ethic, the bloodletting that constituted human relationships. Woollcott managed to insulate himself by delving into the bizarre, by using his razor wit to slash the throats of friends and enemies alike, and by taking a superior attitude toward his audience. Lardner, perhaps more honest in confronting the world, found no way to escape, except into a neurosis that, in spite of what seemed to be frivolity, a later generation would call "sick." As Henry Seidel Canby noted, "the most influential magazine of the period among sophisticated intellectuals, the *New Yorker* (founded in 1925) had for its spiritual ancestor the . . . humor of Ring Lardner."

The most obvious element that Lardner passed along to the writers for *The New Yorker* was his reliance on and popularization of abnormal states of behavior. Freud and his followers were beginning to make the same impact on humorous writers that they had made a little earlier on serious novelists. As Frederick J. Hoffman has pointed out in *The Modern Novel in America*:

Psychoanalysis came into the American consciousness because American writers were more than ready for it. It seems a ready-made scientific explanation and extenuation of the American life, as these writers had seen it. From 1910 to 1930, there was a steady growth in curiosity regarding all of the secret recesses. . . .
. . . In its particular literary applications, it took the form of further and further elaborations of the "dream consciousness." The dream state or the condition of revery became more and more important as the crucial means of developing a narrative.

By the late 1920's, Freudianism was a resource for comics as well as novelists. Adams's poem "Song: 'Don't Tell Me What You Dreamt Last Night,' " made fun of the new psychology as early as 1917:

> "Don't tell me what you dreamt last night, I must not
>   hear you speak!
> For it might bring a crimson blush unto my maiden
>   cheek.
> If I were you, that subject is a thing that I'd
>   avoid—
> Don't tell me what you dreamt last night, for I've
>   been reading Freud."

But unlike Adams's spoofing of Freudianism, Lardner accepted its premises. And delusions, repressions, neuroses, dementia, defense mechanisms, paranoia, schizophrenia, and fantasies became the stuff of humor, embodying characters who cannot control their world or their reactions to it.

> *When the revolution comes, it will be everybody against Ross.*
> —Dorothy Parker, as reported by Dale Kramer, 1951.
>
> *What I'm running here is a goddam bughouse. Not a man in the place without a screw loose.*
> —Harold Ross, as quoted by Brendan Gill, 1975.

39.
The New Yorker

HAROLD W. ROSS APPEARED TO be about as unlikely a candidate as anyone could imagine to found the recherché magazine that was to influence chic American humor for a half-century. He was self-taught, unpolished, explosive, and profane. Starting from Aspen, Colorado, and wandering through the West into the First World War, he acquired his training in journalism by editing *Stars and Stripes* (with Adams and Woollcott also on the staff) and its postwar sequels, *The Home Sector* and the *American Legion Weekly*. More often than not, he was a victim of Algonquin wits rather than an assailant; and his "friendship" with the precious Woollcott verged on open warfare. In the midst of a sophisticated crew, even his literacy was subject to doubt: he once asked, it was claimed with a straight face, "Is Moby Dick the whale or the man?"

In spite of malicious testimony of the people who worked under him, though, Ross was really well qualified. First, he was a stickler for correct, precise, and polished language. Fowler's *Dictionary of Modern English Usage* was his Bible. Legend has it that even the shortest pieces written for his magazine underwent the kind of finicky scrutiny that persnickity grammar teachers admire. Second, he had firm and acute notions about where humor was drifting. He had studied the comic periodicals of the early twenties—*Vanity Fair*, *The Smart Set*, *Judge*, *Life*—to learn what was old hat and what was on the rise. His notion that there could be a magazine devoted exclusively to New York audiences was the backbone of his editorial policy. Most important, as his epigraph to this section shows, he knew that he was running an asylum. All in the interests of *The New Yorker*, he petted, cajoled, hired and fired its inmates. This roughneck's dedication produced some giant-size hatreds and feuds, but it also produced "Ross's *New Yorker*."

Beginnings were not promising. Ross borrowed money, and more money, through the first year, when some issues of the magazine were only twenty-four pages long—roughly the equivalent of an airport-terminal guidebook to the city. Advertising was so skimpy that Corey Ford had to write a comic history of the founding of the magazine to fill the inside covers (incidentally, also christening the Regency dandy who adorned the first cover, "Eustace Tilley"). And before *The New Yorker* at long last went into the black in 1928, Ross had borrowed more than seven hundred thousand dollars to keep it from sinking.

A major problem was that Ross could not get his Algonquin pals to become regular contributors. Woollcott, catching the smell of death, declined. F. P. Adams contributed only now and then, and Lardner sent in his third-best stuff—lambastings of suggestive lyrics in songs and of provocative Broadway plays. (Dorothy Parker was later to chaff under the book-review assignment, and Robert Benchley to find Hollywood so diverting that he had to be replaced as drama critic.) Though a number of the Wits appeared as advisory editors on the first masthead (on February 21, 1925), Ross had to recruit unknowns and hope for luck during the magazine's early stages. Early recruits were Helen Hokinson, whose dumbbell club-women cartoons would continue for more than twenty years, and Peter Arno, Rudy Vallee's piano player, who dabbled in art; both literally walked in off the streets. Lois Long, theater editor of *Vanity Fair*, was persuaded to moonlight the nightlife column under the pseudonym "Lipstick." Ellin Mackay (shortly to become Mrs. Irving Berlin) wrote a couple of horsey-set exposés that attracted attention on Park Avenue and pulled in large advertising commitments from B. Altman and Saks Fifth Avenue.

After some experimental fumbling, the segments "Talk of the Town," "Notes and Comments," "Reporter at Large," and "Profiles" became standard. Hemingway, John O'Hara, and Sally

Benson made a few contributions. After three suspicious years, Woollcott imperially consented to write a regular column, "Shouts and Murmurs." Otto Soglow and Mary Petty joined the cartoonists; Ogden Nash began contributing poetry; and in 1931, Frank Sullivan joined the staff, creating his cliché expert Mr. Arbuthnot and, a few years later, his initial Christmas poem.

About the same time, Clarence Day began to supply stories which would later be collected as *Life with Father*. Their success spurred dinner-table talk, swelled the magazine's subscription list, and in time extended far beyond the exclusive *New Yorker* audience. Day, son of a Wall Street broker and graduate of Yale, worked in the New York Stock Exchange, served in the Navy during the Spanish-American War, and became a journalist and writer of sketches, essays, and books. It was not until he wrote this series of family reminiscences, though, that he struck his best and most popular vein. The earlier *God and My Father* and the two *New Yorker* collections, *Life with Father* and *Life with Mother*, were best-sellers. A dramatization based on them had a record run as a play and a reincarnation as a successful movie and, later, as a television series.

Father, as Day pictured him, could have been an old-fashioned horse-sense philosopher if he had had a country upbringing and had learned to say wise things in a witty way. Like Poor Richard, he has formed firm ideas about what is right on the basis of keen thinking and experience. He courageously takes stands and tells what they are. He is irked by those who carry on "all the chuckle-headed talk and rascality in business and politics":

He was always getting indignant about them, and demanding that they be stamped out. . . . And twice a day, regularly, he would have a collision, or bout, with the newspaper; it was hard to see why God had made so many damned fools. . . . I would try to persuade him . . . to accept the world as it was and adapt himself to it, since he could scarcely expect to . . . change the whole earth single-handed. Father listened to this talk with suspicion.

This rugged individual does not find God awe-inspiring; "he seemed to envisage a God in his own image. A God who had small use for emotionalism and who prized strength and dignity. . . . Father and God . . . usually saw eye to eye."

Father's resemblance to old-time rustic oracles is clear. But his depicter's tone contrasts with that of nineteenth-century authors who pictured similar characters. Seba Smith picturing a Jack Downing or William Tappan Thompson picturing a Major Jones, as has been indicated, admired such characters and shared their attitudes. Day, though fond of Father, thinks he's a quaint figure of a bygone day. He questions his standards, laughs at his judgments, and satirizes his outmoded ways.

In most stories, Father's "antagonists" are an irresponsible, flutter-brained family. They don't know what they're doing; they bumble and blunder. But Father fails to get what he wants, while the family flounders to triumph. Mother in particular, conniving, not overly careful with the truth, unsystematic and amoral, outwits him all the time. The contrast is quite striking in one story, in which an old Yankee trick is assigned to Mother as she fights a battle in the continuous war with Father about household accounts. The old-time Yankee cheated his victim because he was shrewd enough to think up the trick. Mother, on the other hand, manages to get away with her con because she is illogical enough to stumble on this way of outwitting her spouse. And Day leaves no doubt that he prefers Mother's way:

"But I gave you six dollars to buy a new pot," Father firmly repeated, "and now I find that you apparently got one at Lewis & Conger's and charged it. . . ."

"So I saved you a dollar," Mother triumphantly said, "and you can hand it right over to me."

"Bah! What nonsense you talk!" Father cried. . . . "What did you do with the six dollars?" . . .

"I spent four dollars and a half for that new umbrella I told you I wanted, and you said I didn't need one, but I did. . . . And that must have been the week," Mother went on, "that I paid Mrs. Tobin for two days' extra washing, so that was two dollars more out of it, which makes six-fifty. There's another fifty cents that you owe me. . . . Well, you can put your hand in your pocket and give me that dollar-fifty this minute," she said. "You owe me that, anyhow."

Father said he didn't have a dollar-fifty to spare and tried to get back to his desk, but Mother wouldn't let him go till he paid her. She said she wouldn't put up with injustice.

Characters who rebel against ancient standards and fail, who are demolished by illogic, by the outside world, and especially by women became the hallmark of other *New Yorker* writers—Benchley, Perelman, and Thurber (whom we will discuss in successive chapters). Unlike earlier horse-sensible characters, these were invariably unable to cope. Psychology had given humorists a fancy name for the illusions that Day pestered Father with: "The literary comedians," Bernard DeVoto said, "presented themselves as Perfect Fools, whereas our [modern] comedians present themselves as Perfect Neurotics. There is no other difference." Even if this is true, the difference is revolutionary.

Ross, helped by Father, Mother, and these comic neurotics, rode a wave of insight and good luck that seemed unlikely ever to crest. During the Depression, Arthur Kober began his Ma and Pa Gross stories, in Jewish dialect and with a Bronx setting. Phyllis McGinley began offering her humorous poetry. When Clifton Fadiman took over the book-review department and stayed at the post for a decade, even it attracted new readers.

At least as much as the comic writers, cartoonists were responsible for charting the outlines of the "New Yorker school of humor." Early on, and consistently, they made fun of the little man collapsing before the outside world and taking refuge in fantasy and daydreams. Peter Arno "sketched," as Brendan Gill has pointed out, "with particular relish the breakdown of mechanical things—trains, planes, ships, and taxicabs." He also portrayed affluent upper-class people (Father's fellow club members, probably) who were outraged at the coming of the Roosevelt administration. His wealthy nightclubbers were almost always skunked. His "Whoops Sisters" were liberated versions of ladies from Dubuque raising the devil. In many ways, Arno was the Cole Porter of the cartoon.

William Steig's long career produced cartoons almost Mittyesque in their fantasy. One long series called "Dreams of Glory" pictured an urchin engaging in much the same sort of wish-fulfillments: the boy, in a cowboy outfit, captures Hitler; he saves a beautiful girl from a giant shark; he provides the testimony that saves the hopeless law case. An entire book of Steig's cartoons focuses on "Mother"—usually a huge Oedipal figure before whom frail, full-grown men weep and plead. His most famous cartoon, which adorned cocktail napkins and highball glasses several decades ago, showed a scowling man backed into a large box, with the trenchant caption, "People are no damn good."

Helen Hokinson's plump club ladies fretted over their billowy hats and their socials—lectures and pageants, mostly—oblivious to and unable to cope with the real world. One of her dowagers, for instance, explains to another, "His father wants him to be a lawyer, but I want him to go into a bank. It's always so nice and cool in a bank."

Mary Petty's intricate draftsmanship of the Victorian upstairs-downstairs, Whitney Darrow's psychiatrist-couch cartoons, and Sam Cobean's men stripping female characters in their dirty imaginations all had the *New Yorker* quality.

Three *New Yorker* cartoonists—Charles Addams, George Price, and Saul Steinberg—are especially helpful in the attempt to define that quality. Addams, with his graveyard humor, emphasized weird and abnormal characters in identifiable situations. His spooky "Addams family" included a father whom readers in the 1940's thought looked amazingly like Thomas E. Dewey, a mother—later named "Morticia"— with a cadaverous, succubus-like quality, and an uncle who was more a shapeless dumpling than a human being. A normal-looking pair of children and a "grandmother" who mostly peered over balconies completed the family. The butler was the spitting image of the Franken-stein monster. Into a wide range of macabre and grotesque situations Addams put his family and its servant. But the cartoons selected for *The New Yorker Album of Drawings, 1925–1975* all have a consistent motif: these repulsively demonic characters were constantly coping in appropriate ways with everyday situations. The mother—alone in the cobwebby haunted house at night—looks over her shoulder and discovers the Frankenstein-monster-butler behind her with a tea tray. "Oh, it's *you!*" she says. "For a moment you gave me quite a start." The family gathers in front of a bay window in the house while a howling storm rages outside. Comments the father, "Just the kind of day that makes you feel good to be alive!"

A crypt in a spooky graveyard had a front door and a sign pointing to the side: "Service Entrance." Two Macbethian witches stir a boiling cauldron, with octopus legs and squirmy animals in it. One witch, pouring the contents of a box into the pot, tells the other, "It's wonderful! All you do is add water." Often, though not exclusively, of course, Addams created humor by placing the bizarre and the grotesque in a maudlin context. As

Wolcott Gibbs said in an introduction to the collection *Addams and Evil*, Addams's world is peopled

with men, beasts, and even machines whose appearance and behavior are terribly at variance with the observable universe. He is, generally speaking, successful to the precise extent to which his creations seem peculiar, disturbing, and even outrageous to the normal, balanced mind.

But in a later scrapbook, *Dear Dead Days*, Addams collected together the monstrosities that exist in the real world. Photographs of freaks, torture instruments, mortuary equipment, and medical dissections were included. Pictures of the electrocution of Tops the renegade elephant, a man who survived a scalping, and the mummies of Guanajuato were high points in the anthology which proved that possibly the morbid, aberrant world was the real one.

George Price reversed the Addams formula, playing with similar contrasts. Taking ordinary, middle- and lower-class characters, he placed them in outlandish situations. He became noted for his bedraggled department-store Santa Clauses and a long series of cartoons involving a floating man, who has levitated halfway between his bed and the ceiling. The last of that series showed the man crumpled on the bed with his wife telling the police, smoking shotgun in her hand, "He never knew what hit him." A whole world of tenement dwellers living in squalid, one-room flats with bare lightbulbs and exposed plumbing provided Price with the kind of incongruity he loved. In one, the mother, dipping stew out of a battered kettle at the stove, tells her unshaven, half-dressed bum of a husband, "Sure, there's something you can do. You can lay out the place cards." In another, the husband and wife are eating at the sleazy dinette set, while another grimy man sniffs at the pot on the stove. "Is it anyone we know?" the couple wonders.

Saul Steinberg was a different breed of artist, but he too had fun with frightening fantasies. A first-rate draftsman, he was hypnotized by lines. Huge, cavernous railway stations and the architectural nightmares of Southern California obsessed him. Passports, diplomas, and other documents which provided the illustrations for almost an entire collection contained nearly, but not quite, legible handwriting. Human bodies have thumb prints or Exit signs for heads. Gigantic allegorical pyramids defy the laws of gravity. Brendan Gill says of Steinberg, "he has much that he wishes to tell us about the unreliability of signs, signals, and symbols. . . . The nature of Steinberg's interior world one can only guess at; it is a vaudeville of tumbling alphabets and numerals, and it is something more. A stranger might fear that the air there was too cold for comfort and perhaps too thin for ordinary folk to breathe."

Whatever else Steinberg's world may be, it has a consistently surreal quality. Nothing is quite what it appears to be. Without being quite ominous, it is at least untrustworthy. Shapes change, objects dissolve, and order seems tantalizingly just out of reach. The artist's eye for perspective distorts the rational and the mundane and produces a suspicious distrust of the tangible.

A newer, post-Ross generation of *New Yorker* cartoonists has carried on some of the traditions these older hands founded. George Booth works the Price vein; Edward Koren is Addamsesque; William Hamilton exploits the vapid, affluent young moderns who are the children of Helen Hokinson's ladies.

As a visual artist, James T. Thurber seemed to be quite a different breed of bird, but in his own way he belonged.

Thurber started as an inept doodler. The legend of his "discovery" by E. B. White as a cartoonist (rather than as a comic writer) goes like this: Thurber drew one of his familiar seals and threw the illustration into a wastebasket. White, his office mate, rescued it, added a caption, and submitted it to the *New Yorker* editors—who immediately rejected it because its whiskers were backward. Later, after Thurber's childlike pictures had been accepted (incredulously, but accepted) by Harper & Brothers to accompany the text of the White-Thurber collaboration *Is Sex Necessary?*, Ross and the staff of the magazine changed their minds about Thurber's art. Almost instantaneously, Thurber's reputation as cartoonist zoomed. His animals became the center of "Our Pet Department," a parody of a question-and-answer column. His unique dogs, who seem to change breed several times in a single picture, became famous.

But mostly, the domestic situations that pitted frail and defenseless little men against menacing big women became Thurber's visual trademark. E. B. White analyzed the type:

Harold Ross, pictured trying to be Eustace Tilley, by Rea Irvin. The bug which here replaced the butterfly is Alexander Woollcott.

When one studies the drawings, it soon becomes apparent that a strong undercurrent of grief runs through them. In almost every instance the man in the picture is badly frightened, or even hurt. These "Thurber men" have come to be recognized as a distinct type in the world of art; they are frustrated, fugitive beings. . . . The *women*, you will notice, are quite different: temperamentally they are much better adjusted to their surroundings than are the men, and mentally they are much less capable of making themselves uncomfortable.

Dorothy Parker said of Thurber's cartoon characters, "All of them have the outer semblance of unbaked cookies." And one man, Harold Ross, never did figure them out.

For that matter, Ross must have wondered about a lot of things that made *The New Yorker* the major comic periodical in America. His famous prospectus, which turned up its nose at the tastes of "the old lady in Dubuque," envisioned a magazine whose "readers will be kept apprised of what is going on in the public and semi-public smart gathering places—the clubs, hotels, cafés, supper clubs, cabarets and other resorts." Added to that *bon vivant* quality would be "the truth and the whole truth without fear and without favor." Ross vowed that his magazine "will print facts that it will have to go behind the scenes to get, but it will not deal in scandal for the sake of scandal nor sensation for the sake of sensation. Its integrity will be above suspicion."

Obviously, something happened to Ross's plan. His cartoonists had given the pages of *The New Yorker* a quality approaching the neurotic. His writers turned the offices into a perpetual April Fool's Day of pranks, practical jokes, and strange shenanigans. The pages of the magazine, too, began—no doubt in spite of all Ross could do—to partake of the same quality as the cartoons. Dorothy Parker, who signed book reviews as "Constant Reader," said of A. A. Milne's Pooh books, "Tonstant Weader Fwowed Up." A special issue of the magazine was contrived to make fun of Ross—with him in the pose of Eustace Tilley, peering through his monocle at a spider who was unmistakably Alexander Woollcott. "I live the life of a hunted animal," Ross once said; and the strain of trying to keep an office full of mischief makers at work caused real and imaginary strains. "I don't want you to think I'm not incoherent," he once told Benchley.

The truth was that by the mid-thirties *The New Yorker*, like the Frankenstein monster, was on its own. Brendan Gill may give too much credit to two cohorts when he says that White and Thurber, "the persona of the magazine," "is what led to its success." The stable was full of thoroughbreds, and Robert Benchley and S. J. Perelman gave as much to the tone of dementia praecox as anyonè else.

> *Sheer madness is, of course, the highest possible brow in humor.*   —Robert Benchley, 1926.

> *Benchley got off to a fast start ahead of all of us on* The New Yorker, *and our problem was the avoidance of imitation. . . . Benchley beat me to a lot of things. . . . His day dreamer, cool and witty on the witness stand (1935) and in heroic peril (1932) antedated a little old day dreamer of my own named Mitty.*   —James Thurber, 1949.

40.
Benchley and
Perelman

WHEN ROBERT BENCHLEY moved from the staff of *Life* to *The New Yorker* in the late 1920's, he brought with him a completely formed and fully characterized fictional mask—the Little Man. Over and over in his earliest books—*The Early Worm* and *20,000 Leagues Under the Sea, or David Copperfield*—Benchley had shown his non-hero confronting the outside world.

He had a child, who returned home from summer camp to assault him: "This means that when you go swimming with him he pushes you off the raft and jumps on your shoulders, holding you under water until you are as good as drowned—better, in fact."

This schlemiel was baffled by trivial question-and-answer games and plagued by nightmares in which he was walloped: "I haven't been at a fight for more than three minutes before I begin indulging in one of my favorite nightmares. This consists of imagining that I myself am up in the ring facing the better of the two men."

The Little Man had even been defeated by a necktie:

I pull and yank, take the collar off and rearrange the tie, try gentle tactics, followed suddenly by a deceptive upward jerk, but this gets me nothing. The knot stays loosely off-center. . . . After two minutes of this mad wrenching one of three things happens—the tie rips, the col-

427

lar tears, or I strangle to death in a horrid manner with eyes bulging and temples distended, a ghastly caricature of my real self.

Physically, at least, the Little Man was full grown by 1929.

Ever since his college days, in fact, Benchley had been refining a means of expressing frustration, uncertainty, passivity, and failure. He worked on the *Lampoon* with Gluyas Williams, whose illustrations of the timid Little Man were to accompany the essays in all of Benchley's books. And, adopting the pose of a badly informed and mixed-up pedant, he had delivered a series of bizarre lectures—"Through the Alimentary Canal with Gun and Camera" and the Class Day Ivy Oration—abounding in factual distortions, unintentional plays on words, non sequiturs, and wrenchings of logic.

After college, as Benchley wandered through a number of writing jobs, he perfected the pose of a bumbling idiot disguised as an expert. Book reviews wandered off to discuss subjects in no way related to the books under review. Self-help essays encumbered the reader with monumental and impractical solutions to trivial dilemmas. Drama reviews for *Life*, during the twenties, used the Little Man, as Norris Yates notes, "to depict himself as a bumbling but basically sensible fellow who happened to be sizing up plays instead of selling suits or running an office."

Whatever form of writing Benchley happened to choose, there were some hallmarks of the mask. Essays that were "autobiographical" recorded confrontations with frustrating trivia. Timid, shy, unconfident of both himself and his adjustment to his world, the "I" in them knows beforehand that he is doomed to defeat by mechanical forces and puny but overbearing antagonists—pigeons and parking meters, waitresses, french pastry. In book reviews, inept opera and plays, he debouches on Lardneresque detours of fancy that stumble ahead to total incomprehensibility. The synopsis for "home study" of Act I of the opera *Die Meister-Genossenschaft* goes:

> *The Rhine at Low Tide Just Below Weldschnoffen.*— Immerglück has grown weary of always sitting on the same rock with the same fishes swimming by every day, and sends for Schwül to suggest something to do. Schwül asks her how she would like to have pass before her all the wonders of the world fashioned by the hand of man. She says, rotten. He then suggests that Ringblattz, son of Pflucht, be

made to appear before her and fight a mortal combat with the Iron
Duck. This pleases Immerglück and she summons to her the four
dwarfs: Hot Water, Cold Water, Cool, and Cloudy. She bids them
bring Ringblattz to her. They refuse, because Pflucht has at one time
rescued them from being buried alive by acorns, and, in a rage,
Immerglück strikes them all dead with a thunderbolt.

When the "I" becomes a lecturer whose confident superiority
melts before dates, names and theories, he offers such less than
lucid explanations as this one of "Political Parties and Their
Growth":

> During the early years of our political history the Republican Party
> was the Democratic Party, or, if you chose, the Democratic Party was
> the Republican Party. This led naturally to a lot of confusion, espe-
> cially in the Democratic Party's getting the Republican Party's mail;
> so it was decided to call the Republicans "Democrats" and be done
> with it. The Federalist Party (then located at what is now the corner
> of Broad and Walnut streets and known as "The Swedish Nightin-
> gale") became, through the process of Natural Selection and a gradual
> dropping-off of its rudimentary tail, the Republican Party as we know
> it today.

Little wonder that Thurber once confessed that one of a comic
writer's worst fears was "the suspicion that a piece he has been
working on for two long days was done much better and probably more quickly by Robert Benchley in 1924."

The collection which we think displays Benchley as his most
brilliant is the 1942 volume of reprints, *Inside Benchley*. The
title page shows the Gluyas Williams caricature of Benchley
peering into his bedroom mirror and seeing the image of Wimpy
from *Popeye* reflected there. In the back of the book, we come
upon an utterly worthless Glossary of Kin, Native and Technical
Terms, a list of Abbreviations from the Old and New Testaments
and the Apocrypha, a Bibliography of books in sexual psychology, and an Index which is a page of the New York City telephone directory. Preceding this bufoonery are some of the best
examples of vintage Benchley.

The mock-lecture, "The Social Life of the Newt," points out
that newt courtship occurs "with a minimum distance of fifty
paces (newt measure) between the male and the female. Some
of the bolder males may now and then attempt to overstep the
bounds of good sportsmanship and crowd in up to forty-five

paces, but such tactics are frowned upon by the Rules Committee." In "Cell-formations and Their Work," we are told that

in about 1/150000 of a cubic inch of blood there are some five million
cells afloat. This is, as you will see, about the population of the City of
London, except that the cells don't wear any hats. Thus, in our whole
body, there are perhaps (six times seven is forty-two, five times eight
is forty, put down naught and carry your four, eight times nine is
seventy-two and four is seventy-six, put down six and carry your seven
and then, adding, six, four, three, one, six, naught, naught, naught),
oh, about a billion or so of these red corpuscles alone, not counting over-
head and breakage.

Perhaps even less information comes across in "The Romance of
Digestion." This essay reveals a lecturer trying to get cute: The
teeth and the tongue ("which we may call the escalator of the
mouth or Nature's nobleman for short") "toss the food back and
forth between them until there is nothing left of it, except the
little bones which you have to take out between your thumb and
forefinger and lay on your butter-plate":

And now comes the really wonderful part of the romance which is
being enacted right there under your very eyes. A chemical reaction
on the tongue presses a little button which telegraphs down, down,
down, 'way down to the cross old stomach and says: "Please, sir, do
you want this food or don't you?" And the Stomach, whom we shall
call "Prince Charming" from now on, telegraphs (or more likely
writes) back: "Yes, dear!" or "You can do what you like with it for all
of me. . . ."
   The food is then placed on a conveyor, by means of which it is taken
to the Drying Room, situated on the third floor, where it is taken apart
and washed and dried, preparatory to going through the pressing machines. These pressing machines are operated by one man, who stands
by the conveyor as it brings the food along and tosses it into the vats.
Here all rocks and moss are drawn off by mechanical pickers. . . .
From here the food is taken to the Playroom where it plays around
awhile with the other children until it is time for it to be folded by the
girls in the bindery, packed into neat stacks, and wrapped for shipment
in bundles of fifty. . . . The by-products are made into milk-bottle
caps, emery wheels, and insurance calendars, and are sold at cost.

The utterly inappropriate names ("Nature's nobleman" and
"Prince Charming"), the unexpected and irrational non sequiturs, the anti-climaxes, incongruous catalogues, associational
leaps, and childlike but confusing "explanations" of the lecturer
produce an effect close to hallucination.

Inside Benchley also includes one of the author's finest parodies, "Family Life in America," a take-off on the Naturalistic novel and others in the modes of Dickens and H. G. Wells. "More Songs for Meller" recalls George H. Derby in summaries of Spanish songs that Senorita Meller sings; for instance:

> (3) La Guia
> (The Time-Table)
> It is the day of the bull fight in Madrid. Everyone is cock-eyed. The bull has slipped out by the back entrance to the arena and has gone home, disgusted. Nobody notices that the bull has gone except Nina, a peasant girl who has come to town to sell her father. She looks with horror at the place in the Royal Box where the bull ought to be sitting and sees there instead her algebra teacher whom she had told that she was staying at home on account of a sick headache. . . .

All of Senorita Meller's songs are equally surreal.

Most important, there is a whole series of minor dilemmas before which the Little Man quails. Pushed by uneasiness into a spoonerism in "Coffee, Megg and Ilk, Please," the "I" tells about his abject terror before any workingman. "I become servile, almost cringing. . . . When, for instance, I give an order at a soda fountain, if the clerk overawes me at all, my voice breaks into a yodel." "The Tooth, the Whole Tooth, and Nothing but the Tooth" records the terror of a dentist appointment: "Of course, there is always the chance that the elevator will fall and that you will all be terribly hurt. . . . Things don't work as happily as that in real life." "Kiddie-Kar Travel," "The Last Day," "Traveling in Peace" ("I myself solved the problem of shipboard conversation by traveling alone and pretending to be a deaf-mute"), and "Howdy, Neighbor!" record the anguish of train travel, packing up at the end of vacation, ship travel, and visiting with friends. " 'Ask that Man' " confronts the awesome trauma of getting directions from strangers. Ordered by his wife to ask which train went to Boston, the Little Man approaches the stationmaster and "simulating conversation with him, I really asked him nothing":

> Eight months later we returned home. . . .
> From Arkansas, we went into Mexico, and once, guided by what I told her had been the directions given me by the man at the news-stand in Vera Cruz, we made a sally into the swamps of Central America in whatever that first republic is on the way south.

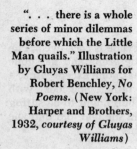

"... there is a whole series of minor dilemmas before which the Little Man quails." Illustration by Gluyas Williams for Robert Benchley, *No Poems*. (New York: Harper and Brothers, 1932, *courtesy of Gluyas Williams*)

"The only trouble was that the cab didn't see me hail it, and drove right by."

Whether he blusters, bumbles, or lies deliberately, the Little Man is trapped. Neither the common sense of his crossroads antecedents nor the logic and erudition of the urban wits gets him out of his predicaments.

It's noteworthy, too, that Benchley managed to transfer many of the qualities of the Little Man from the rarefied atmosphere of *The New Yorker* and other highbrow periodicals to the mass media. Robert Redding, looking at Benchley's movie career in *Starring Robert Benchley*, argues convincingly that when Benchley played the role of lecturer, "his monologue . . . invariably took some unexpected and inexplicable turns; then the speaker's words or manner might betray an awareness that all was not going well, but as often he would briskly proceed, apparently satisfied that his outlandish discourse was altogether lucid and instructive." Redding sees Benchley in other movies becoming "Joe Doakes," "a fumbling, ineffectual, supposedly average citizen, reenacting trivial, everyday humiliations of the sort that, again, most of his viewers could recognize. They watched him being intimidated, or defeated outright, by supercilious clothing salesmen, uniformed attendants, precocious children, malevolent ironing boards and furnaces and window shades." In the film of his most famous lecture, "The Treasurer's Report," a substitute completely messes up the annual financial statement before the members of his organization.

That Benchley was able, almost singlehandedly, to define the character of the Little Man is possibly less important than that he managed to find a sympathetic audience among the middle-class moviegoers of the late thirties and forties. His popular success suggests that his "sheer madness" was in fact recognizable to brows of all levels in America. Something of the futility, the hopeless bravado, the glorious confusion, and the lurking terror that Benchley embodied in his invention struck universal chords.

Part of the explanation may be that his subjects were everyday annoyances. His language, while it was formal rather than colloquial, imitated the hesitancy and informality of spoken English. His allusions—though they frequently required special knowledge on his reader's part—never soared over the common man's head into the stratosphere. Though Benchley did a beautifully faithful rendition of "The Secret Life of Walter Mitty" for radio in 1940, his own zaniness never quite reached the clinical level that Thurber's Mitty did. Benchley managed to walk a razor edge between in-group faddishness and universal appeal. He came closest to clinical schizophrenia in one story, "My Subconscious," when he wrote, "One of the many reasons for my suspecting that I am headed for the last break-up . . . is my Subconscious is getting to be a better man than I am." But, he had to confess, "on the whole, my Subconscious makes a much better job of things than I do."

S. J. Perelman was heir to several elements of the style of what Benchley himself called the "dementia praecox" school of humor. Benchley praised Perelman for doing "to our weak little efforts at 'crazy stuff' what Benny Goodman has done to middle-period jazz. He swung it. To use a swing phrase, he took it 'out of the world.' And there he remains, all by himself."

By the early thirties, after a youth in Rhode Island, college years at Brown (where he edited the comic magazine), and apprentice work at *Judge* when Ross was a co-editor of that magazine, Perelman was ready for a varied career. He wrote and collaborated on scripts for the Marx Brothers, including *Duck Soup*;

he did sketches for reviews and scripts for the movies, and from 1931 on, contributed to *The New Yorker*.

Like Benchley, Perelman—especially in his earlier writings— exploited the antics of a persona gone mad in a world that also had gone mad. But the Perelman character had some significant differences from Benchley's Little Man. Benchley's Little Man looked in the mirror and saw Wimpy; Perelman's creation saw "a man who looks like Ronald Colman and dances like Fred Astaire." On another occasion, he describes himself: "I am a fairly typical Yankee who looks like Gary Cooper, sings like Frank Sinatra and dances like Fred Astaire." His delusions tended as often to be those of grandeur as of persecution.

"Benchley" pretended to have wisdom he didn't have in lectures; "Perelman" sprinkles his daily conversation with exotic foreign words and obscure allusions, as when he tells his maid, who has observed that "You mus' be crazy":

"But aren't we all?" I reminded her with a charming smile. *"C'est la maladie du temps*—the sickness of the times—don't you think? *Fin-de-siècle* and lost generation, in a way. 'I should have been a pair of ragged claws scuttling across the floors of silent seas.' How well Eliot puts it! D'ye ever see any of the old *transition* crowd?"

All this to impress a maid!

Or perhaps the comic "Perelman" has been brainwashed. Many of his fantasies, it seems clear, come from taking literally the make-believe world of commercial advertising or Hollywood. He reads, for instance, in *Harper's Bazaar* the suggestion, "Why don't you try the effect of diamond roses and ribbons flat on your head, as Garbo wears them when she says good-bye to Armand in their country retreat?" Obeying the advice when he goes to collect the day's mail at the post office,

Piling my head high with diamond roses and ribbons, I pulled on a pair of my stoutest *espadrilles* and set off, my cat frisking ahead of me with many a warning cry of "Here comes my master, the Marquis of Carabas!" We reached the post office without incident, except for the elderly Amish woman hoeing cabbages in her garden. As I threw her a cheery greeting, Goody Two-shoe looked up, gave a rapid exhibition of Cheyne-Stokes breathing, and immediately turned to stone. In case you ever get down that way, she is still standing there, slightly chipped but otherwise in very good condition, which is more than I can say for the postmaster. When I walked in, he was in process of spitting into the top drawer, where he keeps the money-order blanks. One look at

Boxholder 14 and he went out the window without bothering to raise the sash. A second later I heard a frightened voice directing a small boy to run for the hex doctor next door to the Riegels'. I spent the night behind some willows, . . . but it was a matter of months before I was able to convince the countryside that I had a twin brother, enormously wealthy but quite mad, who had eluded his guards and paid me a visit.

Even more often, reading advertising, unusual books, and newspaper stories sends the Perelman character into a daydream during which, using a cast of frenzied and surreal characters, he dramatizes the exaggerations. Again like Benchley, he makes associations that lead him to wrench words into puns and feckless combinations:

The color drained slowly from my face, entered the auricle, shot up the escalator, and issued from the ladies' and misses' section into the housewares department.

"Have a bit of the wine, darling?" queried Diana solicitously, indicating the roast Long Island aeroplane with apple-sauce. . . . Soon we were exchanging gay bantam over the mellow Vouvray, laughing as we dipped fastidious fingers into the Crisco parfait for which Diana was famous. Our meal finished, we sauntered into the rumpus room and Diana turned on the radio. With a savage snarl the radio turned on her. . . .

The conductor . . . told me he had been riding on trains for so long that he had begun to smell like one, and sure enough, two brakemen waved their lanterns at him that night and tried to tempt him down a siding in Kansas City.

Living almost entirely on cameo brooches and the few ptarmigan which fell to the ptrigger of his pfowling piece. . . .

Among lesser triumphs: "every nook and granny," "as far as the ground could see the eye was white," and "with a blow I sent him grovelling. In ten minutes he was back with a basket of appetising fresh-picked grovels."

Where the Benchley Little Man doggedly fights the real world in spite of unrelieved failure, the Perelman character is actually propelled into his world of fantasy. Though "Perelman" attempts a bravado much like that of Benchley's lecturer, neither Joe Doakes nor Perelman's cultivated *bon vivant* controls his future or his fate.

In their use of a central character—mostly in first-person narratives—who resembles his creator, who finds the hysteria of his world reflected in the hysteria of his language, and who bumbles his way through a universe conspiring against him, Benchley and Perelman to some extent resemble earlier comics, such as Artemus Ward, Charles Heber Clark, George Horatio Derby and others. (The performance of the typical American humorist, Harry Levin claimed in 1972, "is that of an *eiron*, a self-ironist who dissembles his wit—like Socrates himself, or like Will Rogers . . . or like the accident-prone anecdotists of the *New Yorker.*")

But in the later humor there are some important innovations.

For one thing, clinical psychiatry gave effective names and descriptions for the mad behaviors they describe—neurosis, dementia praecox, manic depressive. For another, neither common sense nor erudition helped them to get along in the world; there was no choice but to suffer humiliation, defeat, and failure. Most significantly of all, the world itself had become so chaotic and unreasonable that instead of feeling comfortably superior, a large segment of readers could identify with these comic types. Their problems, their futile attempts to solve them, and their defense mechanisms for surviving among them seemed all too universal. ("Serious literature," with its anti-heroes and schlemiels, was beginning at the same time to find such characters equally worth exploring.)

Except for the most disguised sort, both Benchley and Perelman stop short of satire. True, they make implicit fun of mass-media hypnosis, of pompous windbags, of the humdrum existence in which the average man measures out his life in coffee spoons or (more likely) jiggers of bourbon. Both parody sentimentalism in literature. Both point out the frailty of contemporary human beings confronting the technological world. Both see something ridiculous in man's fate. But the tidal waves of banter, frivolity, and whimsy prevent most readers from coming away from their *New Yorker*-style material clutching any message.

For the same reasons, both men avoid serious nightmares. Their humor has the possibilities for something like, say, *The Dream Life of Balso Snell*, by Nathanael West (college friend and brother-in-law of Perelman). But the defeats their characters suffer fall short of annihilation—sometimes by microscopic distances, but short, all the same.

[*Humorists*] *have, nobody knows why, a genius for getting into minor difficulties: they walk into the wrong apartments, they drink furniture polish for stomach bitters, they drive their cars into the prize tulip beds of haughty neighbors, they playfully slap gangsters, mistaking them for old school friends. To call such persons "humorists," a loose-fitting and ugly word, is to miss the nature of thir dilemma and the dilemma of their nature. . . .*

Such a writer moves about restlessly wherever he goes, ready to get the hell out at the drop of a pie-pan or the lift of a skirt. His gestures are the ludicrous reflexes of the maladjusted. . . . He talks largely about small matters and smally about great affairs. His ears are shut to the ominous rumblings of the dynasties of the world moving toward a cloudier chaos than ever before, but he hears with an acute perception the startling sounds that rabbits make twisting in the bushes along a country road at night and a cold chill comes upon him when the comic supplement of a Sunday newspaper blows unexpectedly out of an area-way and envelopes his knees.   —James Thurber, 1934.

41.
White and Thurber

BRENDAN GILL HAS TALKED about the "White-Thurber sensibility" which gave *The New Yorker* its basic character. We hope that we have shown that, in fact, an entire chorus-line of comedians provided Ross with the unique flavor he wanted for seasoning. But it is still true that White and Thurber, the most durable of Ross's staff, gave *The New Yorker* its security.

White had a large share in charting *The New Yorker*'s course and, as was no more than fair, the magazine had a large share in charting his. White contributed to early issues, became a part-time editor in 1926 and a full-time handyman or contributor-with-desk-space not long after. Contrary to general belief, he was never an editor and did not have a hand in the selection and editing of manuscripts, but he was, as one colleague put it, "a wheel horse." He did routine reporting and rewrote captions for comic drawings, including Thurber's. At some time, he contributed to nearly every department. He even painted a cover; it showed a sea horse wearing a feedbag. His first job was to edit the items used to fill out columns for magazines and newspapers, writing tag lines which topped the hilarity of their inept or garbled contents. More important, he wrote "Notes and Comment," the opening item of the magazine, which sounded a keynote and became one of its most admired features. As Marc Connally put it, he "brought the steel and music to the magazine."

The matter and manner of some of White's pieces, early and late, show a kinship with other *New Yorker* contributors—Benchley, Frank Sullivan, Thurber, Adams, and others. At the start, contributors had fun shooting barbs at almost any fixed or moving target. They were particularly eager in the 1920's to topple the over-solemn pundits who were cocksure about their solutions for cosmic problems. White and Thurber mocked these deep thinkers with their burlesque, *Is Sex Necessary?* Like Benchley and Thurber caricaturing themselves as ridiculous figures ill at ease in the complex modern world, White is also capable of self deprecation: "In the minds of my friends and neighbors who really know what they are about and whose clothes really fit them, much of my activity has the quality of a little girl playing house." He tells of a struggle he carries on "setting pictures straight; squaring rugs up with the room," and foresees that in his lifelong battle against these inanimate objects he "shall fall at last." In "Dog Training," he recalls how one dog after another has overmastered him. In "Clear Days," he shows a fear that his farm clothes would give him the appearance of a scarecrow, so "I should think twice before I dared stand still in a field of new corn." It is not surprising to find him confessing that he knows what it is to have "one of those days when inanimate objects deliberately plot to destroy a man, lying in wait for him cleverly ambushed, and when dumb animals form a clique to disturb the existing order."

White, then, joins Benchley and others in playfully putting before the reader a character, purportedly the writer, who is poorly equipped to cope with inanimate objects and animals, let alone his fellow men and the complex problems of the modern world.

White's manner, too, has qualities which his cohorts on *The New Yorker* relished. When Thurber defined humor as "a kind of emotional chaos told about calmly and quietly in retrospect," he was talking about the kind of comedy created by a writer who was composed and undemonstrative, because he was removed by time from the events he was describing. Paradoxically, White and some other writers for the aggressively modern *New Yorker* often, by being calm, quiet and retrospective, tended to achieve aloofness somewhat like that of old-time essayists—the detached "Spectators" and "Observers" of the eighteenth century or, more accurately, the less aloof De Quinceys and Hazlitts of the nineteenth century.

Lightness of tone and polish have always been standard equipment for *vers de societé* such as White wrote when he broke into *The New Yorker* and later included in *The Lady is Cold* and *The Fox of Peapack, and Other Poems.* The same qualities have generally distinguished his prose. Even when writing about farming, he was a quiet-voiced man about town. His usage is faultless, and though he seems to be writing with careless ease, he weighs his every word and finds it wanted. In many ways, then, White belongs right in there with other writers for Ross's magazine.

In other ways, his writings have interesting likenesses with those of comic writers who, for the most part, lived and wrote in the earlier America of farms, woodlands, and pawky, horse-sense philosophy. So instead of tabbing him with a *New Yorker* label, Henry Seidel Canby, that veteran biographer and classifier of American authors, "placed him . . . unhesitatingly . . . in the main stream of the homely American humorists, which begins in the eighteenth century and, regarded as literature, includes Franklin, as well as wisecrackers like Artemus Ward; and Thoreau and Mark Twain and Don Marquis and Robert Frost."

Nowhere in White, for instance, can you catch him showing a book-learned city man's contempt for farm and frontier ways of learning and reaching decisions; and from the record, it appears that he felt no such contempt. More often than not, his thinking has a homespun quality reminiscent of the old-timers.

Further, his comic pictures of himself as a poor innocent put upon by inanimate things and arrogant animals, and confused by life's complexities, are not, he has learned, permanent likenesses. On the day when everything is going wrong—separator, lantern, grain sack, weather, lamb, cow, cook, and child—as a result of his experience, he realizes that the condition is temporary: "I'm not fooled any more by an ill wind and a light that fails. My memory is too good."

Having won such assurance, White can, and does, believably resemble the humorists of gumption in another way. Aided by native wit and experience, he confidently forms opinions and comes right out with them. Humorous writing, he finds, "plays, like an active child, close to the big hot fire which is Truth. And sometimes the reader feels the heat." Self-mocking and equable though he usually is, White often conducts heat. He warmly resents sentimentality, unction, pretense, regimentation, parochialism, exploitation (of movie queens and laborers alike), prejudice, and other sins of the body politic. Usually, like earlier native satirists, he makes his attack tell by using a jocular approach; he has equated gaiety with "truth in sheep's clothing." But on occasion, as in the essays "Freedom" and "The Wave of the Future," he is steered as unrelentingly into a form of seriousness like that of Thoreau denouncing slavery or Mark Twain clobbering imperialism.

Many times, White relies on traditional comic devices. Dry Yankee wit, like that of Thoreau and other New England humorists; paradox; homely figures of speech; understatement; anticlimax; humanized animals; the occasional use of the vernacular for color and comic emphasis—all are evident:

> In a free country it is the duty of writers to pay no attention to duty.

> A true poem contains the seed of wonder; but a bad poem, egg-fashion, stinks.

> The poet's dream of cattle winding slowly o'er the lea is a pleasant idyll, but the bald fact is that you suddenly find yourself with a heifer who shuns the bull, lavishes kisses on a horse, and eats cardboard.

> When I answer his [dachshund's] peremptory scratch at the door and hold the door open for him to walk through, he stops in the middle and lights a cigarette, just to hold me up.

White thus appears to belong with both the citified New Yorkers and countrified humorists. He combines the self-deprecation, the uneasiness in a chaotic world, the book-learning, the worldliness, and the polish of the former with the self-assurance, the gumption, the earthiness, and the patois of the latter.

James Thurber shows some of the same minglings. The self-portrait at the start of this chapter strikes the major note: a humorist is bedeviled by neuroses, cowed before the insignificant things in his world, and indifferent to the cosmic ones. He loses and loses and loses his combats with machines, women, and animals until defeat becomes permanent. That picture was reinforced by *My Life and Hard Times*, a comic autobiography which collected some of the insanest family members ever to taint a bloodline. It was also reinforced by Thurber's actual life story (poignantly and voluminously recorded in 1975 by Burton Bernstein: blindness, a disastrous marriage, alcoholism, impotence). Wilfrid Sheed has suggested that

where Thurber had used edginess as a purely comic device . . . with White it was a simple statement of fact. He is, it seems, so finely strung that keeping his sanity has been a struggle at times and writing brightly for The New Yorker a potential torture. No wonder his stuff seemed almost preternaturally sane and well-balanced. It had to.

Nevertheless, of all the *New Yorker*'s collection of Little Men, Thurber probably came closest to a truthful description of himself.

But before we examine that aspect of Thurber's career, it is important to notice another, minor one that links him, much like White, to the earlier tradition of American humor.

First, Thurber denied the legend of the madhouse that Ross ran; he insisted that

The New Yorker was not, in fact, the violent loony bin it had been cracked up to be. . . . A group photograph of its editors and resident contributors . . . would have moved the softhearted to send in contributions of food, clothing, money, and inspirational literature.

And when he got some bad reviews and comments on *The Years with Ross*, he wrote White an amazingly heroic sentiment: "My heart is not made of the stuff that breaks, my mind of the stuff that cheapens, my soul of the stuff that is on sale to the devil."

His writings, too, had some heroic moments. His play *The Male Animal* (co-authored with Elliot Nugent) shows a henpecked English professor, a fumbler bogged down in futility, who reaches a noble and heroic stature by reading Vanzetti's last letter to his English class in spite of threats from the board of regents. *The Wonderful O*, one of Thurber's late fairytales, has as its moral, in Bernstein's words, "the importance of never losing hope, love, valor, and freedom." Another fable, *The White Deer*, has its main character, Jorn (recognizably Thurber himself), win the hand of the deer-princess over his rivals. And White has said of a third fairytale, "The book of his I like best is 'The Last Flower.' In it you will find his faith in the renewal of life, his feeling for the beauty and fragility of life on earth."

Even earlier than these, in more traditional *New Yorker* pieces, Thurber's version of the Little Man manages to win an occasional victory. In "The Unicorn in the Garden," the husband plots a hoax—that there is a unicorn grazing among the roses. By his craft and deadpan persistence, he convinces his wife that he is crazy. But when the psychiatrist arrives, the man denies he ever saw such goings-on:

"Of course not," said the husband. "The unicorn is a mythical beast." "That's all I wanted to know," said the psychiatrist. "Take her away. I'm sorry, sir, but your wife is as crazy as a jay bird."

The same formula works in "The Catbird Seat," when Mr. Martin's job is endangered by the efficiency expert, Mrs. Ulgine Barrows. Martin appears after work at Mrs. Barrows's apartment, plotting to kill her, but "somewhere in the back of his mind a vague idea stirred, sprouted. . . . The idea began to bloom, strange and wonderful." So Mr. Martin, a milquetoast, begins *his* hoax. He plots the death of his employer, admits to taking heroin, and sticks out his tongue at Mrs. Barrows. The next day, when she reports his behavior to the boss, Mrs. Barrows is fired on the spot. Such cunning harkens back to the *eiron* defeating the *alazon* and to the sensible character tall-tale-telling his way out of a predicament in earlier humor.

We don't propose to exaggerate Thurber's positive side. Optimism, workable common sense, and reliable mother wit are much rarer in his humor than in White's. Still, they do crop up occasionally.

The main thrust of Thurber's writings was, of course, in the opposite direction. His reminiscences build up the image of a man doomed to perpetual defeat. It began at an inauspicious birth:

The house, which is still standing, bears no tablet or plaque of any description, and is never pointed out to visitors. Once Thurber's mother, walking past the place with an old lady from Fostoria, Ohio, said to her, "My son James was born in that house," to which the old lady, who was extremely deaf, replied, "Why, on the Tuesday morning train, unless my sister is worse." Mrs. Thurber let it go at that.

His fictional family contained a cousin who believed he was going to stop breathing when he fell asleep and wanted to be awakened during the night to be sure he was alive. Another member was an aunt who was convinced that a burglar was going to

blow chloroform under her door through a tube. To avert this calamity—for she was in greater dread of anesthetics than of losing her household goods—she always piled her money, silverware, and other valuables in a neat stack just outside her bedroom, with a note reading: "This is all I have. Please take it and do not use your chloroform, as this is all I have."

Grandfather had spells of believing he was still fighting the Civil War; and Grandmother "lived the latter years of her life in the horrible suspicion that electricity was dripping invisibly all over the house. It leaked, she contended, out of empty sockets." Mother was convinced that the Victrola was going to explode and always took the telephone off the hook when it stormed. And according to Grandfather, one of young Thurber's uncles died of the chestnut blight in 1866.

Under the circumstances, it isn't surprising that the fictional Thurber reached maturity in fragile shape. His misadventures included dashing into a garage because one of the dials on his mysterious automobile was registering 1560, only to have the mechanic tell him, "That's your radio dial, Mac. . . . You got her set at WQXR." His maid Della concludes that "His mind works so fast his body can't keep up with it." The "real" Thurber might note "the little fusses at the breakfast table, the routine troubles at the office, the familiar anxieties over money and health—the welter of workaday annoyances which all of us meet with and usually conquer without extravagant wear and tear," but the "fictional" Thurber confesses, "you could send an owl into my room, dressed only in the feathers it was born with, and no monkey business, and I would pull the covers over my head and scream." He catalogues things "of which I stand in constant dread: boats coming down rocks, people being teleported, statues dripping blood, old regrets and dreams in the form of Luna moths fluttering against the windows at midnight." "No man," the creation believes, "who has wrestled with a self-adjusting card table can ever be quite the man he once was."

As for adjusting, forget it. The self-help books spoofed in *Let Your Mind Alone!* don't work. He contemplates the suggestion that he spend one hour daily not talking except to answer questions:

No hour of the day goes by that I am not in some minor difficulty which could easily become major if I did not shout for help. Just a few hours ago, for example, I found myself in a dilemma that has become rather familiar about my house: I had got tied up in a typewriter ribbon. The whole thing had come unwound from the spool and was wound around me. . . . To have gone a whole hour waiting for someone to show up and ask me a question could not conceivably have improved my mind.

But he is convinced that the battle between humans and machines isn't his alone:

There goes a man who picked up one of those trick matchboxes that whir in your hands; there goes a woman who tried to change a fuse without turning off the current; and yonder toddles an ancient who cranked an old Reo with the spark advanced. Every person carries in his consciousness the old scar, or the fresh wound, of some sort. . . . In none of these people have I discerned what I would call a neurosis, an "exaggerated" fear; I have discerned only a natural caution in a world made up of gadgets that whir and whine and whiz and shriek and sometimes explode.

He decided, in *Let Your Mind Alone!*, that "I would be the last person to say that madness is not a solution."

Thurber's unique contribution to the profile of the Little Man was his famous series of cartoons called "The War Between Men and Women." (The seventeen cartoons in the sequence showed pitched battles ending with the startling surrender of the women.) As early as his collaboration with White, *Is Sex Necessary?*, those battle lines had been drawn. Of the myth of the ineffability of woman, Thurber says in the Preface:

To destroy it would be to put the female properly in her place, as a plain, unadorned unit in the senseless but unending pattern of biologi-

cal continuity. Romantic love would disappear. Life would be simplified. Neuroses would vanish. But Man clings to his ancient and silly
value. . . . It has subordinated him to Woman, for one thing. . . .

He explained further on that "The female, equipped with a Defense far superior in polymorphous ingenuities to the rather simple Attack of the male, was prepared. She developed and perfected the Diversion Subterfuge. Its purpose was to put Man in
his place. Its first manifestation was fudge-making." From there
it just gets worse.

In his essay "The Case Against Women," Thurber itemized
the reasons for his problem: "In the first place, I hate women because they always know where things are. . . . Another reason
I hate women (and I am speaking, I believe, for the American
male generally) is that in almost every case where there is a sign
reading 'Please have exact change ready,' a woman never has
anything smaller than a ten-dollar bill." Other aversions: "Another spectacle that depresses the male and makes him fear
women, and therefore hate them, is that of a woman looking another woman up and down, to see what she is wearing"; "I . . .
hate women because they almost never get anything exactly
right"; "I hate women because, while they never lose old snap-
shots or anything of that sort, they invariably lose one glove." As
an indictment, it is spectacular in its triviality.

In his third-person short stories, Thurber carried his bill of
particulars further. There, the antagonism becomes downright
hostility, with a series of Little Men bested and benumbed by
their female opposites. A few samples: in "A Couple of Hamburgers," an antagonistic couple drives in the rain, looking for
a place to eat. They can't agree on a diner (they can't agree on
anything); she doesn't like one because it sits at an angle from
the road and "They're cheaper, because they fitted them into
funny little pieces of ground." Angered at her illogic, the man
eats hamburgers, with lots of onions, at a greasy spoon while she
waits in the car. He has apparently triumphed; but she heard the
sound of "safety pins in a tumbler" which means a bearing in
the engine is burning out. And with a smile on her lips, "she relaxed against the back of the seat content to wait."

"The Breaking Up of the Winships" took place because the
wife thought Greta Garbo was the greatest actress in the world

Home à la Thurber. Drawing originally printed in *The New Yorker.* (*Copyright © 1943 James Thurber; copyright © 1971 Helen W. Thurber and Rosemary Thurber Sauers. From* Men, Women and Dogs, *New York: Harcourt Brace Jovanovich*)

but her husband—who takes to drink and gets "a wild light in his eye"—nominated Donald Duck. In "The Curb in The Sky," Charlie Deshler makes the mistake of marrying Dorothy, whose only problem is that she likes "to finish sentences for people. Sometimes she finished them wrongly, which annoyed the person who was speaking, and sometimes she finished them correctly, which annoyed the speaker even more." The only way that Charlie can get to finish a story is to relate what happened in his dreams. But

any psychiatrist will tell you that at the end of the way Charlie was going lies madness in the form of monomania. You can't live in a fantastic dream world, night in and night out and then day in and day out, and remain sane. The substance began to die slowly out of Charlie's life, and he began to live entirely in shadow. . . .

After a month or two, Charlie finally had to be sent to an asylum. . . .

But, even there, Dorothy comes to visit and correct him, while "he looked quite mad."

Even in Thurber's fables and cartoons, the battle wages. In "The Shrike and the Chipmunks," the efficient female chipmunk gets her husband and herself killed by the shrike, because of her demands that he go outside and get some exercise. *"Moral: Early to rise and early to bed makes a male healthy and wealthy and dead."* And the most trenchant cartoons in *Men, Women and*

Dogs are the ones in which meek, docile males are browbeaten by large, scowling, aggressive females. "Well, I'm Disenchanted, Too. We're *All* Disenchanted"; "Yoo-hoo, It's Me and the Ape Man"; "It's Our *Own* Story *Exactly!* He Bold as a Hawk, She Soft as the Dawn," these amazons proclaim about their mousy, browbeaten, and incredulous husbands. Most poignant of all, "House and Woman" shows a tiny man recoiling in horror before a large house that transforms itself into the face of a threatening woman.

White and Thurber both explore the same world, then, as Benchley and Perelman, but there is a significantly different quality to their depictions of the Little Man. Each depends less upon verbal gymnastics, the "dementia praecox" manner of telling the story. Those unexpected puns, wordplays, and free-associational leaps so frequent in Benchley and Perelman are rarer in White and Thurber. Common sense and a search for logic and order makes their humor less irrational. Somehow, White and Thurber don't give the impression of having quite gone over the brink.

Of course, in addition to "The Curb in the Sky," there is an exception. Of all Thurber's works and of all the *New Yorker* humor telling the miseries of the Little Man, the most famous, popular, and durable is "The Secret Life of Walter Mitty"—worth, we think, a chapter all its own.

> *The original of Walter Mitty is every other man I have ever known. When the story was printed . . . twenty-two years ago six men from around the country . . . wrote and asked me how I got to know them so well.*
> —James T. Thurber, Letter to Mrs. Robert Blake, April 7, 1961.

42.
"The Secret Life of Walter Mitty"

SOON AFTER JAMES THURBER'S "The Secret Life of Walter Mitty" was published in *The New Yorker* in 1939, fans spread the news that it was one of the author's best stories. *The Reader's Digest* reprinted it for millions of readers, few of whom subscribed to *The New Yorker* or even liked it. By the time the piece came out as an item in *My World— And Welcome to It* in 1942, it was Thurber's most popular opus. Reviewers of the collection said so in newspapers, magazines, and a nationally broadcast radio interview, "Of Men and Books." In articles about the humorist, both *Time* and *Newsweek* gave "Mitty" special mention.

A paperback World War II Armed Services Edition of *My World—And Welcome to It* was passed around to hundreds of thousands of GIs, gobs, and airmen. There is proof that they went for the story. They formed Mitty clubs in both the Atlantic and the Pacific theaters; names of characters in the story were given to bombers; catch phrases in it were used as passwords.

Collections of American humor, and high school and college textbook anthologies, used "Mitty" to represent its author. A recent biographer of Thurber with access to royalty statements believes that reprint permissions brought the author more money per word than those for any other story, serious or humorous, ever netted by any other writer. In due time, the piece was dramatized in six forms, some quite popular—as a radio playlet, a movie, a revue sketch, an opera, an off-Broadway musical, and a segment of a one-man evening-long impersonation of Thurber.

The name Mitty joined those of Hercules, Judas, Romeo, Don Quixote, Don Juan, Mrs. Malaprop, Frankenstein, Scrooge, Sherlock, Pollyanna, and Babbitt as a part of common English and American speech. *Lancet*, a British medical journal, spoke of "the Walter Mitty syndrome," a Pakistani newspaper editorial of "Walter Mitty types." In the 1970's a television sportscaster reporting a Rams-Raiders football game casually talked about his viewers' "playing Walter Mitty"; a Washington, D.C., politician barked at a columnist for suffering from "a Walter Mitty complex"; and a writer in the *New York Times* (February 8, 1976) began an analysis of the supersonic transport with a reference to "Walter Mitty, man repressed, searching for fulfilment." None of these stopped to explain the reference.

Why the popularity?

For a start, the story skillfully treats an overbearing wife and her victimized mate, an eternally amusing contretemps. Thanks to the unseemly actions of a few formidable matrons and libels by male chauvinist pigs, jests about bossy dames and their henpecked consorts must have started soon after marriage did. They never ended. Legendary japes told how Noah's nagging wife drove her husband to drink both before and after their famous cruise. Xanthippe yapped at Socrates. The Wife of Bath put all her husbands in their places. Farces and jokebooks through the centuries teemed with variations on the motif. (Translation from a 1574 Spanish jokebook in a British jestbook of 1595: "A shrewish wife chid her husband out-of-doors, and he stepping forth into the street stumbled with his nose into the gutter; and rising up again, he said, 'Better here yet, than within-doors.' ")

In eighteenth-century America, Rip Van Winkle had a termagant Dame. Later, though Mark Twain and William Dean Howells were blessed with invalid wives who were neither hot-tempered nor energetic enough to become successful as shrews, both writers pictured them as fire-snorting dragons who made their spouses' lives hell on earth. (Van Wyck Brooks failed to see that Twain was joking, and wrote that a raging Mrs. Clemens ruined her poor husband's career.) In the twentieth century, inexorable wives and quaking husbands have peopled radio and television situation comedies; in comic strips Mrs. Mutt squelched Mutt, Maggie endlessly bossed Jiggs, and Dogpatch's Mammy tyranized over Pappy. In Joyce's *Ulysses* (1922), Molly Bloom harrassed Leopold Bloom; in his best-seller *Dodsworth* (1929), Sinclair Lewis celebrated the bitcheries of Fran, a domineering American wife.

A second appeal: the meek Little Man, married or not, had recently become a favorite figure in American humor. Charlie Chaplin had made his version of this type famous in America and throughout the world. A comic strip called "The Timid Soul" had made one Casper Milquetoast widely known. By 1925, at least seven popular American writers had pictured the character again and again: Norris W. Yates, in *The American Humorist* (Ames, 1964) cites Stephen Leacock, Clarence Day, Robert Benchley, Donald Ogden Stewart, Simon Strunsky, Alexander Woollcott, and Heywood Broun. Several of them, as has been indicated, were writers for *The New Yorker*.

A third appeal: little Walter Mitty is fashionably neurotic. Beginning in 1919, when Sherwood Anderson stocked *Winesburg, Ohio* with abnormal, put-upon folk who were bedeviled by complexes and phobias, psychology—almost all of it Freudian— had become the "in" thing among the literati and even some of the hoi polloi. Novels, dramas (O'Neill's, for instance), debunking biographies, and histories of literature (Lewisohn's, for instance) teemed with the insights of amateur but cocky psychoanalysts. So did humor. About the same time, Charlie Chaplin was saying:

> Modern humor frightens me a little. The Marx Brothers are frightening. Thurber, [Donald Ogden] Stewart, Joe Cook, Benchley—yes, all of them. They say, "All right, this is how we live and we'll write that way." They go in for being crazy. . . . They say, "All right, you're insane, we'll appeal to your insanity." They make insanity the convention. They make humor a premise.

Again, *New Yorker* authors were right in there pitching; a typical book was titled *A Bed of Neuroses*.

At intervals, Mitty escapes from the unhappy world by daydreaming, conjuring up visions in which he triumphs by performing sensational deeds of derring-do, know-how, reasoning, and courage.

Fantasizing was not a new invention. It had been used over the years in American humor, and contrasts between the ways older and more recent humorists played with it help define the humor that was fashionable when poor Mitty's story was given to the world.

Pre-Civil War ring-tailed roarers, it will be remembered, in their vauntings magnified the strength and skill they could use to whomp any men or beasts dumb enough to defy them. Although these roughs exaggerated, they truly *were* superb scufflers. Postwar alazons knew in *their* hearts that their boasts were bluffs, and had enough sense to avoid any testing of them. Taking a further step, Mitty and his repressed ilk were too meek even to *try* to bluff. They therefore kept their little mouths shut. But in brooding silence, they caressed and enlarged the splendors of their impossible imaginings.

The comic quality of their flights of fancy was underlined because, simultaneously, a noisy American cult was preaching aggression. Its leading spirit, Dale Carnegie, wrote its Bible, *How to Win Friends and Influence People*, in 1936, and during the two years before "Mitty" appeared, he broadcast a series of radio programs called "Getting Ahead." (The same incongruity would still be good for laughs in the 1970's. Robert Ringer's *Winning through Intimidation* became a best-seller; movie and television tough guys massacred multitudes; and in the "Peanuts" comic strip, tiny beagle Snoopy lay atop his little dog-house and dreamed an impossible dream that he was a heroic aviator knocking down scores of enemy planes.)

Daydreaming with a function—to escape unhappiness—had also turned up in earlier comic writings. Again, when the old instances are put alongside the extravaganzas Mitty concocted, the contrast helps discriminate the comedy of the later era.

A century before Thurber's piece, a famous antebellum sketch by Longstreet had shown a frontier youngster in Georgia blissfully dreaming that he was decimating a gigantic and fierce opponent in a no-holds-barred scrimmage. And sixty years before "Mitty," Tom Sawyer, made unhappy by Becky Thatcher, assuaged his sorrow by taking off in flights of fancy:

. . . he would be a soldier, and return after long years, all warworn and illustrious. No—better-still, he would join the Indians, and hunt buffaloes and go on the warpath in . . . the Far West, and away in the future come back a great chief, bristling with feathers, hideous with paint, and prance into Sunday-school, . . . and sear the eyeballs of all his companions with unappeasable envy. But no, there was something even gaudier than this. He would be a pirate! . . . How gloriously he would go plowing the dancing seas, . . . with his grisly flag flying at the fore!

But the pre-Civil War humorist and Mark Twain had both found the dreaming comic because it was a child's way, inappropriate for an adult.

Professional psychiatrists in post-World War I days spread the word that many a boy who became a man failed to put aside childish things. Even lay persons were informed that dreams and fantasies often compensated for repressions. Highbrow plays and lowbrow comic strips had fun with dream sequences. When George F. Babbitt, the frustrated protagonist of Sinclair Lewis's novel, escaped into slumberland,

Instantly he was in the magic dream. He was somewhere among unknown people who laughed at him. He slipped away, ran down the paths of a midnight garden, and at the gate the fairy child was waiting. Her dear and tranquil hand caressed his cheek. He was gallant and wise and well-beloved: warm ivory were her arms; and beyond perilous moors the brave sea glittered.

So "Mitty" plays with many popular motifs of the 1920's and 1930's.

It is also as representative of its author as any piece one can find—"a supreme distillation," as his latest biographer puts it, "of Thurber people and Thurber themes." The humorist, a few months before his death, told a friend on *The New Yorker* what he thought would make an appropriate obituary: "the best, and most honest tribute, when the day comes, would simply be the reprinting of 'The Secret Life of Walter Mitty,' with a brief note saying that I requested it in my will." The magazine followed the request. In an additional notice, E. B. White called an expression that his old friend had used "pure Mitty," and mentioned that the story about Mitty was the one for which, quite properly, Thurber was best known.

A few years before he wrote his most famous piece, the author told Max Eastman that his humor was "about" one thing: "beaten-down married people." "The American woman is my theme, and how she dominates the male, how he tries to go away but always comes back for more. . . ." Thurber once said that "the little man" was "a genus sometimes called, around [*The New Yorker*] office, the Thurber husband." White described his colleague's men as "frustrated, fugitive beings, at times . . . too humble or meek to move."

In addition to his wife, other associates and nonhuman forces make Mitty meek. Like every male in Thurber stories who has a confrontation with an automobile, this poor devil is baffled by his car, handles it ineptly, irks a cop, and is blasted by the contemptuous snorts of garagemen and parking attendants.

Obviously he is equipped with an affliction known to all amateur psychoanalysts of his era—an inferiority complex. Thurber was as hooked on psychology as most of his contemporaries. His first book, as noted, was a collaboration with White that parodied popularizations of Freud—*Is Sex Necessary?* (1929); his 1937 *Let Your Mind Alone* kidded both psychology and inspirational books. Introducing a collection of his drawings, he made a comment on them that also fit his writings: "I am concerned with the beast inside"—one of the disturbing fauna that have "emerged from the shameless breeding ground of the idle mind." As an admirer of Henry James, he almost had to think as he wrote of his idol's famous story, "The Beast in the Jungle," in which the said beast is a "huge and hideous" hallucination rampant in John Marcher's mind.

He was as aware as his contemporaries were of the way such worms as Mitty escaped by daydreaming. Quite possibly he had noticed this kind of reaction before he encountered psychological treatises. As a one-eyed nervous and shy junior high school student, he wrote a class prophecy about a trip that the class would take far in the future on a Seairoplane. In its course, he fantasized, he would save everybody's life in mid-air by walking out on a beam and tugging free a rope caught in the machinery.

Was "Mitty," then, autobiographical? A biographer ticks off many differences between the Little Man of the illustrations that Thurber drew (and the story) and his creator:

. . . the typical man in his pictures—diminutive, bald, and pince-nezed, bears no resemblance at all to Thurber. . . . Thurber was six foot, one and a half inches tall, with a short, cropped mustache and a thick head of often unruly hair. James E. Pollard noted his youthful look and erect carriage at sixty-six.

Several others who knew the real-life Thurber spoke of his different qualities—"firm handgrasp and confident voice . . . a man who knew what he wanted. . . . I have never seen him defeated, or even perceptibly disconcerted by [life]. The essence of Mitty and Monroe [another Thurber character] is that they are, so to speak, driven underground by more confident personalities; the essence of Thurber is such that in any real contest of personalities everybody else would be well advised to take to the hills." Contemporaries nominated as the real-life originals of Mitty both of the author's brothers—or maybe he had in mind just one of them, or the chief editor of *The New Yorker*. Thurber said that the prototype was "every *other* man that I have ever known." He was very proud of the character's universality. In an interview in the New York *Herald Tribune* on November 3, 1957, he told about revising the first draft so that a scene involving the Stork Club and Mitty's defeat of Hemingway in a brawl was removed because he was persuaded that nothing so topical should be included. Beyond any doubt, Thurber had shared a good many of the meek Little Man's traits. At any rate, Mitty was one of a long roll call of Thurber anti-heroes who were neurotic and escaped into fantasies—Monroe, Bidwell, Trinway, Kinstry, Pendly, and Bruhl. Throughout the humorist's career, moreover, as Gerald Weales claims, just as he does in this story, Thurber "insists on being rational in the cause of irrationality—at least insofar as that word can stand for fantasy, variety, openness, surprise, and a healthy distrust of all rules."

As in the great narratives of Henry James, the most important happenings in "Mitty" are not physical but mental. The physical action makes for as dull a story as anyone can imagine: Walter Mitty drives his wife from their country home in Connecticut to nearby Westbury, leaves her at a hairdresser's, takes the car to a parking lot, does some shopping, waits for her in a hotel lobby, walks with her toward the parking lot, stands beside a drugstore wall while she goes in to make some purchases, lights a cigarette, and steps into the rain. Mrs. Mitty nags him all the time she is with him, a policeman snaps at him, a car parker is contemptuous of his driving, and a passing woman laughs at him. Dullsville.

More significant episodes in the story, the ones that provide the chief incongruities, are Mitty's responses to frustrations, slights, and affronts. He responds by dreaming of himself in important roles handling dramatic situations far better than he handles those of his workaday world. And the contrasts between humiliations by cops, car parkers, salespeople, his bitchy spouse, and trivia such as overshoes and puppy biscuits, on the one hand, and his deeds in heroic imaginings, on the other hand, are ludicrous.

In his visions, Mitty is in full control.

He is a Commander readying his crew for a run through a hurricane aboard "an eight-engined Navy hydroplane," an "SN202."

He is a great physician preparing to perform difficult surgery.

He is a man on trial for murder who gives sensational testimony—testimony that makes monkeys out of the attorneys and wins the caresses of "a lovely, dark-haired girl."

He is Captain Mitty of the United States Air Force, deciding to fly a two-man bomber all alone, "forty kilometers through hell," to "get that ammunition dump."

Finally, he is a captive of the enemy calmly standing against a wall before a firing squad.

Ironically, the poor little fellow is completely unable to escape from the tyranny of actuality even when he is fantasizing.

His driving of his car—too fast, his wife claims—triggers his vision of a dash, by hydroplane, over storm-tossed seas. His wife speaks of a Dr. Renshaw and scolds Walter for not wearing his gloves, and he drives past a hospital. Soon he imagines himself a surgeon who enters the hospital, doffs his gloves, reassures a "distraught and haggard" Dr. Renshaw, and dons thin surgeon's gloves so that he may operate (while awed experts watch) on an important patient. Promptly after he thinks of wearing his right arm in a sling, worries about his forgetfulness, and hears a newsboy "shout something about a Waterbury trial," he envisions himself in a courtroom facing a district attorney who says, "Perhaps this will refresh your memory," and boasting that even with his right arm in a sling he can shoot and kill. He scans a magazine article about the German air force and its bombers, and at once thinks of himself as a daring flyer deciding to blast a German ammunition dump. Finally, as he stands by a wall, sees rain start to fall, and lights a cigarette—

He put his shoulders back and his heels together. "To hell with the handkerchief," said Walter Mitty scornfully. He took one last drag on his cigarette and snapped it away. Then, with that faint, fleeting smile playing about his lips, he faced the firing squad; erect and motionless, proud and disdainful, Walter Mitty the Undefeated, inscrutable to the last.

Thurber indicated a second way even Mitty's imaginings are enslaved by outside forces when he said he himself had once thought of wandering around the South Seas "like a character out of Conrad, silent and inscrutable," using adjectives close to those in the final paragraphs of both *Lord Jim* and "Mitty." Conrad's great novel is far and away the best literary work from which Mitty swipes details; but the man makes up for his pitiful ignorance by plagiarizing every one of his dreams. Other sources of his extravaganzas are second or third-hand trash—clichés purloined from melodramatic fiction, movies, and radio plays. Trashy doctor stories, long popular, had overworked many details of the hospital scene. The courtroom stuff came from opera such as Erle Stanley Gardner's Perry Mason whodunits and a play, *The Trial of Mary Dugan*. From a recent movie, *The Dawn Patrol*, Mitty lifted data about bombers and dialogue for the Air Force dream: "Van Richtman's circus is between here and Saulier," and "Somebody's got to get that ammunition dump." In many a war dramatization, unruffled heroes flipped away cigarettes, stood before walls, and defied firing squads.

The exhausted but inflated language of Mitty's flummeries often comes straight from the parodied works: ". . . heavily braided white cap pulled down rakishly over one cold gray eye . . . the grave, uncertain faces of the two great specialists. . . . Pandemonium broke loose in the courtroom. A woman's scream rose above the bedlam and suddenly a lovely, dark-haired girl was in Walter Mitty's arms . . . 'You miserable cur!' " These larger-than-life free-wheeling whim-whammies are cheek-by-jowl with Mrs. Mitty's deflating, reasonable, matronly instructions, flatly commonplace in their phrasing: "You're driving too fast! . . . Remember to get those overshoes. . . . Why don't you wear your gloves? . . . I'm going to take your temperature when I get you home." The juxtaposition underlines the florid quality of Mitty's maunderings.

There is a third way that—try though he does to leave Mrs. Mitty's ordered world—Mitty is imprisoned by his limited knowledge of the worlds into which he tries to project himself. What he says about a "Webley-Vickers 50.80 automatic" in his cross-examination pipe dream and his World War II dugout fantasy shows that he is completely uninformed about the weapon.

An expert on firearms points out that, especially in the context, it is an impossible conglomeration. For instance: "The '50.80' is the description of a very powerful black powder *rifle* suitable for African big game and weighing about twelve pounds. The '50' means the bore is a half an inch in diameter and the '80' means that the cartridge case holds eighty grains of powder." The same authority finds "just plain silly" Mitty's boast that, holding this peculiar weapon in his left hand, he "could have killed Gregory Fitzhurst at three hundred feet" since "Any modern arm, rifle or pistol, could kill a man at a hundred yards if the shooter can hold it."

When Mitty tries to climb into a surgeon's gown, he can do nothing but fling around inappropriate or even non-existent medical terms. His alter ego's brilliant book, which established his reputation, deals with streptothricosis. He is to operate on Wellington McMillan's ductal tract, afflicted with tertiary obstreosis, made even worse because it is complicated by coreopsis. Writes Dr. Alvin R. Tarlov, Chairman and Professor of the Department of Medicine, Pritzker School of Medicine, the University of Chicago: "I have checked the medical reference sources completely, and find no entries for streptothricosis, obstreosis or coreopsis. In our department, we have many specialists in the obscure, . . . but none ever heard of these. . . . I doubt that Wellington McMillan made it." Coreopsis, however, is a scientific term in a nonmedical area: probably Mitty came upon it in a seed catalogue, since it is the Latin name of a composite flower.

Vague about the nature of a Navy hydroplane and an anesthetizer, Mitty equips each with "a row of [complicated or glistening] dials." And unable even to guess how a hydroplane engine, an anesthetizer, or "new flame-throwers" sound, he has them all—with minor variations—go "pocketa-pocketa-pocketa"—a noise he has apparently decided any fool machine is likely to make.

A fact that is as comic as it is pathetic: Mitty himself has to be aware that his imaginings are completely ersatz. He cannot avoid the knowledge that he is bluffing—that he glosses over his abysmal ignorance either by being vague or by flinging in fake technical terms gathered in impossible places. Even so, he usually lacks the nerve to go whole hog. Except in the courtroom fantasy and the final vision, he is not performing a heroic deed but merely *preparing* to perform it.

Although the dreams are alike, there are rather grim progressions embodied in them. The hero of the first fantasy bears no name: he is simply "The Commander." In later soarings, the star is, successively, Dr. Mitty, Walter Mitty, Captain Mitty, and then the palpable Walter Mitty in person as he stands besides a drugstore wall in the actual city of Waterbury, Connecticut. Stephen A. Black sees a development that is significant:

The clichés lead him farther and farther away from life. The more he depends on the escape they afford, the less possibility there is of his confronting his real problems. . . . The increasing peril of each dream seems to imply a weakening in Mitty's hold on life.

The weakening is accompanied by an increasing immersion in dreams, and the dreams move toward Mitty's annihilation. The first time Mrs. Mitty recalls her spouse from his never-never land, he has trouble getting back to reality, but he makes it:

"Not so fast! You're driving too fast!" said Mrs. Mitty. . . . "Hmm?" said Walter Mitty. He looked at his wife, in the seat beside him, with shocked astonishment. She seemed grossly unfamiliar, like a strange woman who had yelled at him in a crowd. . . . Walter Mitty drove on toward Waterbury in silence, the roaring of the SN202 . . . fading in the remote, intimate airways of his mind.

As one new fantasy follows another, differences between reality and vision decrease. Details from the real world mingle with wild evocations, and vice versa. Gloves, doctors, daisies, arm slings, law suits, and magazine articles, all of them realities, keep invading Mitty's trances. After the Mitty of the courtroom fantasy has called his imagined lawyer a cur, his flesh-and-blood *Doppelgänger*, newly returned to reality, remembers that he has to buy dog biscuits, and a passing woman says: "That man said 'Puppy biscuit' to himself." Mrs. Mitty awakens her mate from his aviation dream and starts her usual bickering. Mitty, for a fleeting instant brave—even though he is back in the actual world—says something that applies to both that world and fantasy land: "Things close in . . . I was thinking." And in the final paragraph, as the living, breathing Mitty of actuality snaps away his palpable cigarette and bravely faces the imaginary firing squad, the distinction between dream and reality dissolves for him. At the very moment when pitiful little Walter Mitty has his rendezvous with death, his reality and his fantasy are one.

"You're tensed up again," sensible Mrs. Mitty has told him. "I wish you'd let Dr. Renshaw look you over. . . . I'm going to take your temperature when I get you home."

Whether the thermometer shows the temperature is high or not, she will do well to have Dr. Renshaw come around.

Or better still, a psychiatrist.

Modern
Humor

> *—Yes, sir, doctor, I know as well as anybody that you're a mighty busy man, . . . but this here business about that husband of mine a-losin' his manhood is life or death, that's all there is to it. . . . this can't wait a minute longer, or he's liable to do something desperate to himself. He ain't the kind of a man that can take a thing like that like it was a plain ordinary misery somewhere in him, no, sir. He's always been broody and headstrong, and the way he sets around a-mutterin' to himself and a-glarin' at the gun over against the wall and a-pindlin' away like he's a-doin', I'm scared to be around him. . . . You ain't got any notion how deep a thing like this takes ahold on him. Yes, sir, impotency. Well, the first time we noticed it was along yesterday afternoon, and then a couple a times last night, and again this morning; and it's come to the point now that he's . . .* —H. L. Davis, 1952.

43.
Humor in Fiction

ONE FORCE WHICH SHAPED much of our humor—including that in sketches, short stories, and novels—from the start kept right on doing so—oral storytelling. This influence, instead of ending with the reign of the group of fiction writers called local colorists, survived to the very present. The framework structure and the mock oral tale, both with the long stretches of vernacular narration so popular through the nineteenth century, continued to offer proof that oral storytelling continued to be an influence. As the sketchy survey that follows will show, humor-studded fiction in this tradition kept on winning popularity or awards. As often as not, it won both.

At the turn of the century, Edward Noyes Westcott's *David Harum* (1898, 1900) in twenty months piled up 500,000 sales (rough equivalent today: 1,330,000). It sold briskly for decades—about 1,250,000 copies by 1965—thanks largely to many amusing tales in rustic dialect told by horse-sensible David and his pawky sister. In the movie, Will Rogers was type-cast as horsetrader Harum. Central New York was its setting, but the decade 1900–1910 was a great one for Far Western oral tales— or facsimilies—in frameworks. Owen Wister's *The Virginian* (1902), reprinted fifteen times in nine months, was not only a bestseller (1,736,000 copies by 1965) but also the source of a play performed for decades, three movies, and an interminable television series. The most amusing and best-remembered parts were based upon oral stories, and three crucial chapters told word-for-word about a tall-tale-telling contest between the villain and the hero. In one, cowhand Trampas takes in the Eastern narrator with a whopper about a woman who saved his life after a big snake with eight rattles attacked him:

"And she whipped out one of them Injun medicine stones . . . and she clapped it onto my thumb, and it started right away. . . . And when it had sucked the poison out of the wound, off it falls . . . by itself! . . . I never knowed how excited she had been till afterward. She was awful shocked."

"I suppose she started to talk when the danger was over," said I, with deep silence around me.

"No; she didn't say nothing to me. But when her next child was born, it had eight rattles."

Din now rose wild in the caboose. They rocked together . . . And I joined them. Who could help it? It had been so well conducted from the imperceptible beginning. Fact and falsehood blended with such perfect art. And this last, an effect so new made with such world-old material! I cared nothing that I was the victim, and I joined them. . . .

Between 1897 and 1913, Alfred Henry Lewis, who figured in the chapter on local colorists, published six popular volumes of meandering yarns told in dialect by one "Old Cattleman" about Arizona frontiersmen. And between 1903 and 1905, Andy Adams published three novels that served as a framework for twenty-nine yarns spun by cowboys resting after a hard day. Adams followed these with *Cattle-Brands* (1906), subtitled "a Collection of Western Camp-fire Stories"—boxed narratives in which "the sound of the voice and the turns of everyday speech . . . racy and full of localisms," are heard. Adams is still admired and reprinted as both an artist and the most authentic portrayer of Texas cowmen.

Texas was long the home of O. Henry, who rose to fame during the same decade and was popular and respected as a short story writer until about 1930. While serving a three-year sentence for embezzlement, he began his career by writing down stories he heard fellow prisoners tell, and until he died in 1910, he constantly used oral sources. (Many, like anecdotes, ended with snappers.) A group of stories still relished by faithful fans are framed reminiscences of wandering con man Jeff Peters, most of them included in *The Gentle Grafter* (1908). Sample frame:

> On an east-bound train I went into the smoker and found Jefferson Peters. . . . Jeff is in the line of unillegal graft. He is not to be dreaded by widows and orphans; he is a reducer of surplusage. His favorite disguise is that of the target-bird at which the spendthrift or the reckless investor may shy a few inconsequential dollars. He is readily vocalized by tobacco; so, with the aid of two thick and easy-burning brevas, I got the story of his latest Autolycan adventure.

O. Henry collected similar stories, many of them tall tales, about and by other characters, in books that sold several million copies. As a sign of the high rating critics gave him, the prestigious "O. Henry Memorial Award Prizes" were set up in 1919.

Authors of the 1920's cut down on framework stories. But they wrote mock oral stories which were popular and critical successes—Don Marquis's Old Soak and comic biblical stories; Roark Bradford's Negro dialect legends about "ol' man Adam and his chillun" (which were made over into a Pulitzer Prize-winning play, *The Green Pastures*); and Ring Lardner's warmly applauded short stories in Midwestern-cum-Phunny-Phellow dialect. The form migrated to citified settings in some of Lardner's cynical dramatic monologues and Anita Loos's *Gentlemen Prefer Blondes*. (The Loos women in the latter piece lived on in two musical comedies and a very funny movie.)

The 1920's brought vernacular tall tales about Paul Bunyan by Esther Shephard. This heralded the rediscovery, or the invention, in the 1930's, of several comic demigods, and the publication of stories, mostly in dialect, about them—John Henry, Mike Fink, Davy Crockett, Old Stormalong, and Febold Feboldson. The 1930's also saw Stephen Vincent Benét's imaginative yarns

about Paul Revere, Dan'l Webster, the Fool-Killer, the Cape Cod
Sea Serpent, and others that he called "our own folk-gods and
giants and figures of earth." Hear Benet's familiar lore about
Dan'l Webster:

There were thousands that trusted him right next to God Almighty,
and they told stories about him that were like the stories of patriarchs
and such. They said, when he stood up to speak, stars and stripes
came right out in the sky, and once he spoke against a river and made
it sink into the ground. They said, when he walked the woods with his
fishing rod, Killall, the trout would jump out of the streams right into
his pockets, for they knew it was no use putting up a fight against
him; and when he argued a case, he could turn on the harps of the
blessed and the shaking of the earth underground.

Dorothy Parker wrote dramatic monologues of big blondes and
brunettes with big problems. H. L. Davis's Pulitzer Prize-
winning *Honey in the Horn* spaced tall tales through a meandering narrative about pioneer Oregon. Thornton Wilder's
Heaven's My Destination, a monologue by that legendary figure,
the traveling salesman, showed the author's skill with dialect.
This skill he used best in the 1938 Pulitzer Prize-winning play,
Our Town, in comments by the Stage Manager, an old-fashioned
Yankee sage.

During the 1940's Jesse Stuart's *Taps for Private Tussie*, a
story, humorous for the most part, told by a teen-age Kentucky
farm boy—was cheered by critics and sold a million copies. William Saroyan's *Adventures of Wesley Jackson* had a similar,
though somewhat older, vernacular narrator. Beginning in the
World War II years, Jesse B. Simple spoke for blacks in monologues by Langston Hughes; he kept writing these into the 1960's.
Simple wrote a letter to Dr. Butts, called a black leader, in which
this was a representative passage:

Dr. Butts, I am glad to read that you writ an article in *The New
York Times*, but also sometime I wish you would write one in the
colored papers and let me know how to get out from behind all these
buts that are staring me in the face. I know America is a great country
but—and it is that *but* that has been keeping me where I is all these
years. I can't get over it, I can't get under it, and I can't get around it,
so what am I supposed to do? If you are leading me, lemme see. Because we have too many colored leaders now that nobody knows until
they get from the white papers to the colored papers and from the

colored papers to me who has never seen hide nor hair of you. Dear Dr. Butts, are you hiding from me—and *leading* me, too?

The 1950's brought J. D. Salinger's *The Catcher in the Rye*, for years the book most admired by the younger generation; they helped its sales reach 5 million copies. Here, a prep school prototype of Huck Finn told in his own vulgar and funny style about his misadventures during a weekend in New York. H. L. Davis's *Winds of the Morning*, a book club selection, sprinkled its pages with vernacular anecdotes. (One is quoted at the start of this chapter.) The 1950's also brought several novels by Mark Harris or (their title pages said) by illiterates whose battered grammar and punctuation Harris edited; Saul Bellow's picaresque *Adventures of Augie March*; Eudora Welty's *The Ponder Heart*, honored with the Howells Medal for fiction; and Vance Randolph's five volumes of homespun Ozark anecdotes. Mac Hyman's *No Time for Sergeants* was a book club choice, a bestseller for two years (2,400,000 copies), and the source of a Broadway hit, a movie, and a television series. Robert Lewis Taylor's *The Travels of Jaimie McPheeters* came along at the end of the decade, and a number of reviewers remarked on its resemblance to *Huckleberry Finn*.

The success of this book (bestseller, Pulitzer Prize) encouraged its author to follow it during the 1960's with two more popular novels narrated by amusing, illiterate teen-agers. In *Journey to Matecumbe*, one of them told about the spiel of Dr. Snodgrass in Bosky Dell, plugging trusses he was selling—devices invented by a hundred-and-forty-year-old Choctaw Indian chief:

"I was totally unable to walk till I was twenty-four years old! . . . double hernia . . . with complications of fibrosis, osteojaundice, and yaws. . . . I was running, leaping streams . . . within a week after I put these trusses on."
Dr. Snodgrass then told the crowd a little about hernia, and I was glad to hear it, because I'd never exactly realized what it was, before. He explained how the muscles in the outside stomach, or peritonitis, got inflamed from eating the wrong kind of food, and caused a swelling . . . where the legs joined the body part . . . at the worst, your legs fell off.

In the same decade, William Price Fox's *Southern Fried* stories followed the tradition; Thomas Berger's *Little Big Man*, with an elaborate framework; and Charles Portis's mock oral *True Grit* were bestsellers and the sources of well-attended motion pictures. Bawdier comic successes used vulgar narrators in long comic stretches—Robert Gover, *The $100 Misunderstanding* (Kitten's monologues) and Gore Vidal, *Myra Breckenridge* (Buck Loner's tape recordings).

The 1970's kept the trend going in more seemly novels. David Wagoner's Andrew Jackson Holcomb, Jr., in *Where Is My Wandering Boy Tonight?* told about his growing up in Wyoming; Eudora Welty's *Losing Battles*, nominated for a National Book Award, was made up almost entirely of yarns told by rural Mississippi family members at a reunion. In the summer of 1971, David Freeman's *U.S. Grant in the City* mounted to comic heights in a Bowery bum's sagebrush tall tales. In Joe D. Brown's *Addie Pray*, an adolescent orphan girl told a picaresque story which became a book club selection and the source of an award-winning movie, *Paper Moon*. Philip Roth's *The Great American Novel*, which followed shortly, put together some superb tall tales. And Saul Bellow's *Humboldt's Gift*, written largely in the vernacular by the earthy and funny Charles Citrine, won fine reviews and a Pulitzer Prize, and helped Bellow toward the Nobel Prize for literature, which he received in 1976.

This catalogue must not end without at least a glance at a group of books that belong high on it—books by the most admired of all the modern American writers who used framework narratives and mock oral tales—William Faulkner. Works in which he made lavish use of these forms spanned the period between the 1920's and the 1960's. They included both short stories and novels, notably, *The Sound and the Fury* (Jason's segment), *As I Lay Dying* (entirely told in mock oral narratives), the Snopes trilogy—*The Hamlet*, *The Town*, and *The Mansion*— and the bestselling *The Reivers*.

The last of these the author himself proudly called "one of the funniest books I ever read," and he was fond of the humor in his other writings. Very early in his career—in 1926—he said it was "a pity" that American artists were taking their work and themselves too seriously to make "prevalent in their art . . . one priceless universal trait . . . national and indigenous"—our humor.

Evidence bolsters the guess that the Nobel laureate followed the implied advice. He studied and often praised his country's writers of comedy. We have quoted his extravagant praise of Thorpe's "The Big Bear of Arkansas" and George W. Harris's Sut Lovingood. He ranked not only Sut but also Huck and Jim with such great comic characters as Sarah Gamp, Mercutio, Don Quixote, Sancho Panza, and Falstaff—all his favorites, he said. His library shelves held books that have a variety of places in histories of our humor—by Washington Irving, George Washington Harris, Mark Twain, Joel Chandler Harris, Bret Harte, James Branch Cabell, S. J. Perelman, Eudora Welty, and Nathanael West—plus compilations of current jokes. He told "The Legend of Sleepy Hollow" to his children in his own words. In informal talk, he quoted Johnson J. Hooper, praised other Southwestern humorists, and expressed great admiration for J. D. Salinger. He had as acquaintances Benchley, Thurber, Parker, and other *New Yorker* writers.

Faulkner made some of his most obvious uses of traditional humor in the Snopes trilogy. Look at the Mississippi-style payoff of a yarn with analogues scattered across nearly two centuries. Following a rainstorm, a horse-trader finds that he has been gypped:

"The horse!" I hollered. "He's changing color!"
"He was sober then. We was both outen the wagon then and Ab's eyes popping and a bay horse standing in the traces where he had went to sleep . . . a black one. He put his hand out like he couldn't believe it was even a horse and touched it at a spot where the reins must every now and then just barely touched it . . . and next I knowed that horse was plunging and swurging. . . . Then there was the sound like a nail jabbed into a big bicycle tire. It went *whishhhhhhhhhh* and then the rest of that shiny fat black horse we had got from Pat Stamper vanished. I dont mean me and Ab was standing there with just the mule left. We had a horse too. Only it was the same horse we had . . . swapped Beasley Kemp the sorghum mill and the straight stock for two weeks ago.

The speaker is an early-twentieth-century peddler—a sewing-machine agent whose leisurely yarns fill many pages in the three Snopes novels—V. K. Ratliff. Introducing him early in *The Hamlet*, Faulkner says that he wanders around the countryside, stopping now and then to sell machines, join natives in sundry activities, watch them in others, and collect and swap livestock, tools, musical instruments, messages, gossip, news, and stories:

> He spoke in a pleasant, lazy, equitable voice which you did not discern at once to be even more shrewd than humorous. . . . On successive days and two counties apart the splashed and battered buckboard and the strong mismatched team might be seen tethered in the nearest shade and Ratliff's bland affable ready face and his neat tieless blue shirt one of the squatting group at a crossroads store, or—and still squatting and still doing the talking apparently though actually doing a good deal more listening than anybody believed until afterward— among the women surrounded by laden clotheslines and tubs and blackened wash pots beside springs and wells, or decorous in a splint chair on cabin galleries, pleasant, affable, courteous, anecdotal and impenetrable.

Ratliff is of the race of Poor Richard, Jack Downing, Hosea Biglow, Jim Doggett, and Major Jones. His favorite saying is, "Man aint really evil, he jest aint got any sense." He is a fine storyteller because he knows human nature in general and the men and women of the county in particular, and can talk knowingly and humorously about both.

Another *eiron*-storyteller, twelve-year-old Charles Mallison of *The Town*, is more like Huck Finn or Holden Caulfield. Faulkner explained why he gave him the job of telling some of the story:

> I thought it would be more amusing as told through the innocence of a child that knew what he was seeing but had no particular judgment about it. That something told by someone that don't know he is telling something funny is sometimes more amusing than when it's told by a professional wit who is hunting around for laughs.

The boy's completely solemn description of Eck Snopes's funeral illustrates. All of Eck except a neckpiece got redistributed and disappeared in an oil tank explosion that his stupid bungling brought about. But his brother Masons, Charles says, had a funeral complete with a Baptist preacher and flowers—"buried the neck-brace anyway, in a coffin all regular . . . and the Masons in their aprons dropping a pinch of dirt into the grave and saying 'Alas my brother' . . . and the tank was insured so when the oil company got through cussing Mr Snopes for being a grown man with no more sense than that, they gave Mrs Snopes a thousand dollars to show that they were sorry for her even if she married a fool."

The Reivers, published in 1962, the year of Faulkner's death, is told throughout in the words of an innocent and amoral boyish narrator who, like Huck Finn, Charles Mallison, and other such adolescent favorites, is ludicrous because he "don't know he is telling something funny."

So many critics have written about Faulkner's close kinship with antebellum Southwestern humorists that it is now taken for granted. Recently, several critics have gone further. They have said that this man, for whom humor and humorists were so important, also had ties with other comic schools. Matthew Wood Little, in his doctoral dissertation, "Faulkner and American Humor: Traditions and Innovations" (1975), thoroughly documents their claims and even expands them. Like other scholars who survey a single aspect of an author, Little may have stretched things somewhat. But his findings and the evidence he offers for them are impressive. He summarizes the wide-ranging relationships:

The humor in Faulkner's major novels ranges from black humor to crackerbox philosophy to description of regional peculiarities of northern Mississippi to broad satire of American society to tall tales to sophisticated intellectual humor to the humor of the comic strip; and Faulkner often not only includes, but also modifies and synthesises, several such disparate modes of humor within single works.

In one of Little's most innovative chapters, he looks carefully at the author's *As I Lay Dying* and finds frequent telling resemblances to the comedy of the Algonquinites and *New Yorker* contributors—the "dementia praecox" school, as he (and some of its members) call it. To show that the Bundrens, whose story it tells, like so many "Benchleys," are big-scale bumblers, he ticks off casualties of the funeral which is their joint endeavor: "one horse, two mules, a broken leg, a barn full of hay, a lot of hunger, a lot of money, the outrage of most of the neighbors, a lot of general suffering and anguish, and the loss of one able-bodied farmhand to the local madhouse." The madhouse bit relates to the fact, like so many Lardner characters, the Bundrens have all sorts of foibles and mental hangups. Like so many Walter Mittys, the men, women and children in the book juggle, without distinguishing, fantasy and reality. And since this is a novel stressing comic aspects of dying, death, decay, and burial, its relationship with sick or black humor is clear. Intermingled with highbrow elements, Little notices, are many that are usually found in lowbrow humor. So "an interesting combination of two generally divergent modes" gives the novel "broader implications than anything in either Southwestern or *New Yorker* humor."

Faulkner's habit is to develop serious themes by integrating comedy with his somber and even tragic fictions. In *Light in August*, for instance, he hands over to vernacular comic storytellers a pair of crucial chapters. The first of them, Chapter 15, quotes the earthy talk of clerks, loafers, and farmers around their supper tables and in the shadowed yards of the rural Mississippi community. The country folk have fun putting together a sidesplitting tale about what must have been a pathetic meeting between a frustrated old pair, Uncle Doc Hines and his wife, and Joe Christmas. Satirical and contemptuous, the storytellers get laughs by saying that the doddering old man "hollered," "screeched," "slobbered," "shook," and "flopped," and by comparing him with a hypnotist's stooge and a runaway from a crazy house. They caricature Mrs. Hines by calling her fat and dowdy and likening her face to a balloon on which Katzenjammer Kids have painted a funny phiz. They gloat as they show her shutting up her bombastic little spouse, planting him in a chair, and making him stay put. By showing the community's bitter intolerance, the jocose telling repeats a motif that runs through the whole book.

The placing of the other chapter gives it a particular emphasis: it ends the novel. And the circumstances of the telling, indicated in the frame, make for meaningful contrasts. A furniture dealer who has helped hitchhikers Lena Grove and Byron Bunch on their journey talks about the encounter to his passionate young wife between couplings. The pair's earthy quips about their relish of sex contrast starkly with the husband's story about Byron's timid try at seducing Lena, her disdainful but calm refusal, and—even after the turndown—his hangdog return to her side. Set in such an incongruous frame and stressing ludicrous details, the anecdote summarizes a comparison that runs through the whole book and illuminates for the last time a central theme.

In his combination of slapstick and subtle humor in fiction that develops tragic or disillusioned themes, Faulkner foreshadowed practices that would become widespread after 1945. James E. Miller, Jr., has suggested "the nature of the world in . . . the American novel as it gradually evolved after World War II and as it now appears":

America's machine-made, jet-propelled, plastic-comfortable world transfigured into nightmare, evoking feelings of horror mingled with a strong sense of the ridiculous—such is the nature in broad outline of novels written by . . . post-World War II novelists. . . . Now I would not claim that . . . contemporary novelists are all alike, or that they equally emphasize the . . . nightmarish world or disoriented sensibility. . . . Nor would I claim that these elements are radically new in literature. What I do want to suggest is that for the first time in our literature, after World War II, the world that dominated our fiction was sick, hostile, or treacherous, and that the recurring stance of the modern fictional hero reflected some mixture of horror, bewilderment, and sardonic humor—or, to use the popular term, alienation. The common pattern of action which recurred was the pattern of the quest, the quest absurd in a world gone insane or turned opaque and inexplicable, or become meaningless. . . . The nightmare world, alienation and nausea, the quest for identity, and the comic doomsday vision—these are the four elements that characterize recent American fiction.

Although the ingredients that they use differ greatly, at least twenty-five "semi-randomly selected . . . contemporary American novelists," Miller finds, follow this prescription. He lists them. We place their names in a footnote, and add seven names of novelists who joined the group, for the most part, during the decade after he made his list.*

Miller mentions as causes for the large role played by outraged, absurd, and almost hysterical humor in recent fiction the destruction of World War II, the awareness of a nuclear bomb

* Miller's list: James Baldwin, John Barth, Saul Bellow, William Burroughs, Truman Capote, J. P. Donleavy, Ralph Ellison, Joseph Heller, John Hawkes, James Jones, Jack Kerouac, Ken Kesey, Norman Mailer, Bernard Malamud, Carson McCullers, Wright Morris, Flannery O'Connor, Reynolds Price, James Purdy, Thomas Pynchon, Philip Roth, J. D. Salinger, Terry Southern, William Styron, John Updike. Additions: Donald Barthelme, Richard Brautigan, John Gardner, Jerzy Kosinski, Ishmael Read, Gore Vidal, Kurt Vonnegut.

capable of destroying civilization, and general disillusionment. He finds that literary causes were also important, notably proletarian novels and the theater of the absurd. We would add, as a different kind of literary source, the work of such figures as T. S. Eliot, Robert Frost, e.e. cummings, and others who wrote poems using "serious humor" long before World War II.

Richard Boyd Hauck, in *A Cheerful Nihilism* (1971), repeats Miller's list with approval, since it helps him tell the story of the "absurd" in American humorous fiction from early times to the present. Hauck's definition of the "absurd" varies somewhat as he examines different periods. But near the end of his study he cites "an emblematic joke, one of the keenest to be found anywhere in American literature," which illustrates well the "absurdist humor" widely used by novelists today. Philip Castle, in Kurt Vonnegut's *Cat's Cradle* (1963), is remembering how, during a terrible plague, he and his father walked among bodies piled high inside and outside of a jungle hospital:

"It was all we could do to find a live patient to treat. In bed after bed we found dead people.

"And Father started giggling," Castle continued.

"He couldn't stop. He walked out into the night with his flashlight. He was still giggling. He was making the flashlight beam dance over all the dead people stacked outside. He put his hand on my head, and do you know what that marvelous man said to me?" asked Castle.

"Nope."

" 'Son,' my father said to me, 'someday this will all be yours.' "

Hauck also finds useful for his summary one of Portnoy's complaints to his psychoanalyst. He is sore at standup comedians who erase the painful elements from their jokes because they neglect the absurdist aspects of life:

Spring me from this role I play of the smothered son in the Jewish joke! . . . it *hoits,* you know, there is pain involved. . . . Doctor, *please,* I can't live any more in a world given its meaning and dimension by some vulgar nightclub clown. By some—some *black humorist!* . . . Stories of murder and mutilation! . . . The macabre is very funny on the stage—but not to live it, thank you! So just tell me how, and I'll do it!

Portnoy's chronicler, Philip Roth, hasn't been guilty of omitting this element from a fiction of his, *The Great American Novel*, which we discuss next.

The comedy in The Great Ameri-
can Novel *exists for the sake of no "higher" value than comedy itself;
the "redeeming" value is not social or cultural reform, or moral instruction, but for* comic inventiveness. *Destructive, or lawless, playfulness
—and for the fun of it. . . . It was . . . a matter . . . of discovering in baseball the means to dramatize* the struggle *between the benign national myth of itself that a great power prefers to perpetuate,
and the relentlessly insidious, very nearly demonic reality. . . .*

*Now the discovery of thematic reverberations, of depth, of overtone,
finally of meaning, . . . would seem to contradict what I have said
about wanting fundamentally to be unserious; and it does.*

—Philip Roth, 1973.

44.
The Great
American Novel

Comic skirmishes between
the genteel and the learned, on the one hand, and the unpolished
and untutored, on the other, in this country have lasted for at
least two and a half centuries. We have seen them turning up
again and again. Teen-age Ben Franklin had his earliest alter
ego, Silence Dogood, speak sharply against collegians and professors. Pedants collided with Dutch burghers, Yankees and settlement roughs in Irving's pages. Parson Wilbur's erudite epistles
set off Hosea Biglow's Yankee lingo poems. Educated reporters
wrote polished frameworks that were incongruous because they
were cheek by jowl with Southwestern vernacular tall tales.
Scientists, pontificating lecturers, and local colorists contrasted
amusingly with Far Western humorists, Phunny Phellows, and
rustics of various regions. Urban wits showed up quirks of clodhoppers and square ladies in Dubuque.

Beginning in 1939, thanks to an arresting article by Philip
Rahv, a new statement about the old opposition received widespread discussion. Writing not about American humor but about
American literature, Rahv in "Paleface and Redskin" noticed that
a great many of our writers might usefully be classified as one or

the other: "The paleface [such as T. S. Eliot and Henry James] continually hankers after religious norms, tending toward a refined estrangement from reality. . . . at his highest level the paleface moves in an exquisite moral atmosphere, at his lowest he is genteel, snobbish, and pedantic." As for redskins, such as Whitman, Twain, Anderson and Wolfe: "Their reactions are primarily emotional, spontaneous, and lacking personal culture. . . . In giving expression to the vitality and to the aspirations of the people, the redskin is at his best; but at his worst he is a vulgar anti-intellectual, combining aggression with conformity, reverting to the crudest forms of frontier psychology."

Philip Roth found it useful, some years later, to quote Rahv's classification when explaining the nature of some very funny books that he had written. Roth made a stir as a fiction writer and critic when he was twenty-three, and by the time he was twenty-six, in 1959, his articles and fictions about what he called "a cockeyed world" had won him recognition as one of the country's leading writers. In 1973, in "Reading Myself," a self-conducted interview which enabled him, conveniently, to both ask and answer questions, Roth, now forty, surveyed his career. He started, he believed, pretty much in the paleface camp. He wrote his stories and novels in the tradition of James, Tolstoy, Flaubert and Mann, "whose appeal was as much in their heroic literary integrity as in their works."

Roth was somewhat uneasy, though, about what he had written, because (as some delightful low humor that had intruded into his fiction showed) he had affinities with the redskins—"the aggressive, the crude, and the obscene." As a kid, he had loved the schlemieldom of a vaudeville and nightclub standup comic, Henny Youngman. Later he had gone for "Jake the Snake H., a middle-aged master of invective and insult, and repository of lascivious neighborhood gossip," and "Arnold G., an unconstrained Jewish living-room clown whose indecent stories of failure and confusion in sex did a little to demythologize the world of the sensual for me in early adolescence." He decided that "it was to the low-minded and their vulgarity that I owed no less allegiance than I did to the high-minded with whom I truly did associate my intentions." But though he owed them no *less* allegiance, he also owed them no *more*. He was "fundamentally ill at ease in, and at odds with, both worlds." He found himself in the position of a "redface"—"sympathizing equally with both parties in their disdain for the other, and as it were recapitulating the argument within the body of his own work." In *Portnoy's Complaint* (1969), *Our Gang* (1971), and *The Great American Novel* (1972), though both parties were active, there was much more of the Roth who had alliances with redskins than there had been in his earlier works. (We omit consideration of two largely humorous books written after *The Great American Novel*—*The Breast* and *My Life as a Man*.)

Like his part-time idol, Henry James, Roth has always been more articulate than most fiction writers about his aims and methods. So he watched and described himself moving toward "the comic 'recklessness' that I've identified with my old mentor, Jake the Snake." *The Great American Novel* in some ways was a climax. Jake's subversive influence, Roth guessed, "could not develop to its utmost, until the *subject* of restraints and taboos had been dramatized in *a series of increasingly pointed fictions* that revealed the possible consequence of banging your head against your own wall" [our italics].

The move from paleface territory to *Portnoy's Complaint* took several steps. "On the Air" told about "a series of grotesque adventures . . . as extreme in their comedy" as anything that would go into the novel; but it stopped when it was "only a story." A two-hundred-page manuscript used "jokey dialogue and comedy that had the air of vaudeville turns"—something Roth "liked and hated to lose"; but since he wasn't satisfied with it, he didn't publish it. A play with funny moments and laughable dialogue that he relished "lacked precisely the kind of inventive flair" that he wanted. More steps eventually carried the author to the actual start of the writing. He defined his final step as that of "discovering Portnoy's voice—or more accurately his mouth—and discovering along with it, the listening ear: the silent Dr. Spielvogel." In other words, what at last made composition possible was Roth's invention of a framework which, barring the final sentence, was implied but not dramatically represented. Except for that sentence, the book was a mock oral tale.

Reading this dramatic monologue, antiquarians who garner old jokes will recognize a slew of familiar friends. *Portnoy* is stuffed with Jewish-mother-and-son jokes, such as the tall talk of one momma about Her Son the Doctor: "he's so important . . . that in every single city in Europe that [he and his family] visited he was asked by the mayor himself to stop and do an impossible operation on a brain in hospitals that they had built for him right on the spot." Portnoy, for the most part, is a traditional schlemiel; but even when he isn't one, he comically pretends to be. Naomi's description of his "ghetto humor," as she calls it, summarizes not simply a Jewish but also an American comic dynasty: "Everything you say is somehow always twisted, some way, or another, to come out 'funny'. . . . In some little way or other, everything is ironical, or self-depreciating." Naomi, "the Heroine, that hardy, red-headed, freckled, ideological hunk of girl," gives Alex a chance to be an updated *alazon* when he tries to rape her. Having with great difficulty forced her body down beneath him, the bluffing braggart loftily tells her she must submit: "Down, down with those patriotic khaki shorts . . . unlock your fortressy thighs! Make ready, Naomi!" Then, since he is impotent—"But of course I couldn't." Though the 1969 version plays up not fighting strength but virility, the boast is about physical prowess, just as it had been a hundred and fifty years earlier.

As with *Portnoy*, both written and oral humor helped Roth write his ferocious *Our Gang*. This time, he converted his "indignation and disgust," as he put it, "from raw, useless emotion to comic art." This savaging pre-Watergate satire against Richard Nixon, his attitudes and his associates, credited literary antecedents in two epigraphs, one from Jonathan Swift's masterpiece, *Gulliver's Travels*, and the other from George Orwell's "Politics and the English Language." In interviews, Roth spoke of James Russell Lowell's *Biglow Papers* and the Nasby letters as native forerunners. He also mentioned as models for his "broadly comic" book the antics of Charlie Chaplin, Laurel and Hardy, Olson and Johnson, Abbott and Costello, and the Three Stooges. Finally, a book containing speeches and monologues by "Trick E. Dixon," using as it does many of its model's favorite locutions, almost had to be shaped by impressionists, notably the vicious David Frye, who had been using them lavishly in television shows and night club acts.

A number of readers found this book hilarious, and as *The White House Transcripts* show, it was prophetic. But its ferocity, like that of Northern and Southern Civil War satirists, made it amusing only to those who shared the author's hatreds; and five years after it came out, its topicality makes reading it tough going. It was useful, though, as a cathartic, and its surrealistic fantasies—particularly those of its last two chapters—exercised inventive powers that would be used to the utmost in *The Great American Novel*.

Literary and oral influences, this highly self-conscious artist makes clear, affected this novel. Roth mentions three "gifted writers" who had "gotten quite a yield" from baseball as material for fiction—Ring Lardner, Mark Harris, and Bernard Malamud. He may not have encountered—or he possibly forgot—a fantastic short story that Thurber first published in 1942, "You Could Look It Up," worth mentioning because, like Roth, Thurber had a midget play on a struggling baseball team. Possibly he didn't see the hit musical *Dam Yankees* (1955), or the novel it dramatized, which melded the Faust legend with a pennant race. He shows no awareness of Robert Coover's *The Universal Baseball Association, Inc.* (1969), about a lunatic farther gone than Roth's, who dreamed up a wonderful baseball team and details concerning its fantastic games. Again, he could have missed Claude Brion Davis's prior use—almost—of Roth's title when he wrote *"The Great American Novel"* (in quotes), in which, like Roth, Davis had a journalist try to create the elusive masterpiece. (Even if Roth knew none of these, it is worth noticing that other writers used quite similar gambits.) But Roth did mention in his "Acknowledgements" *The Fireside Book of Baseball* and *Percentage Baseball* as books from which he borrowed incidents. And since burlesques and parodies dot the pages, one can easily spot writings running back to the Middle Ages and down to the present as acknowledged and unacknowledged forebears.

In his "Acknowledgements," Roth also credits an oral "source": "The tape-recorded recollections of professional baseball players that are deposited at the Library of the Hall of Fame in Cooperstown . . . have been a source of inspiration to me while writing this book, and some of the most appealing locutions of these old-time players have been absorbed into the dialogue." Although Portnoy poor-mouths them, he proves by commenting on them that his creator was familiar with standup comedians Sam Levenson, Myron Cohen, Henny Youngman, and Milton Berle. George Plimpton in a 1969 interview asked Roth whether he might have echoed Lenny Bruce's comic routines. The novelist said that he thought well of Bruce as a mimic and social commentator, but guessed that a literary work—Kafka's *Metamorphosis*—had influenced *Portnoy* more. Bruce's biographer, Albert Goldman, however, described Roth's performances in private gatherings that were quite Bruce-like:

Philip Roth . . . was a fantastically funny man years before *Portnoy's Complaint* was published. He broke up his friends at parties, flew off in conversation into marvelous fantasies, did all sorts of voices and dialects, rehearsed old radio shows, exhibited exactly the same sense of timing, meter and delivery as any professional comedian.

This sounds like Alex Portnoy on the couch or the author quoted at length in *The Great American Novel*, Word Smith.

A forty-five page "Prologue"—proportionately one of the lengthiest "frames" for a boxed narrative in the history of our humor—introduces Smitty, an eighty-seven-year-old ex-sportswriter. His three-hundred-and-thirty-five page novel and six-page "Epilogue" follow.

Smith describes himself in the "Prologue": "Short-winded, short-tempered, short-sighted as he may be, soft-bellied, weak-bladdered, . . . anemic, arthritic, diabetic, dyspeptic, sclerotic, in dire need of a laxative, . . . *and in perpetual pain*." As this brief sample of his prose suggests, Word Smith is fond of alliterations—as fond, in fact, as Rabelais, who on occasion alliterated pages at a time. The old fellow's psychiatrist calls Smith's use of the device "an orgy [that] strikes me as wildly excessive and just a little desperate." This verbal tic and a great many others are signs that this inmate of the Valhalla Home for the Aged is as loopy as a scenic railway. He is a mess of aberrations—a sick, talky, vicious, dirty-minded, sadistic, racist, chauvinistic pig with a persecution complex and an aggravated case of paranoia.

It may be instructive to look at a short parade of American comic narrators: (1) the pedantic but witty Diedrich Knickerbocker (1809); (2) the imaginative, self-deceiving Jim Doggett

(1841); (3) the drunken Copperhead and political freewheeler Nasby (1861); (4) gently teched but sweet and harmless Jim Baker (1880); (5) bumbling, phobia-ridden "Benchley" of *The New Yorker* (1925); (6) crafty and ornery Jason Compton of *The Sound and the Fury* (1929); (7) Smitty. This sketchy little survey is too incomplete to allow more than a very broad—but we think informative—generalization: The tendency is not to make our humorous storytellers more and more lovable; it is to make them more and more complex.

The obsession that forces Smitty to write his novel is the belief that he has a mission: to give the world a history that evil forces have suppressed—that of a forgotten major baseball organization, the Patriotic League, and more particularly, its fabulous team, the Rupert Mundys of Port Ruppert, New Jersey. The Dies Committee's vile persecutions and fiendish machinations, he is sure, brought about not only the dissolution of the league and the imprisonment of ten of its players but also the purge of every single trace of its glorious history. To make sure of this, no effort has been spared: even the names of the league's cities were changed. Who, except Smitty, ever heard of Asylum, Ohio; Terra Incognita, Wyoming; Kakoola, Wisconsin; and Port Ruppert, New Jersey? See?

To restore the suppressed truth, moving at the pace that suits him, pausing to elaborate whenever he pleases, detouring any time he likes, Smitty gives us his fantastic chronicle.

It seems that there was this third big league, dominated for years by the Mundys. Came World War II. The Port Ruppert stadium was taken over by the government to help with the war. So the homeless Mundy team had to go on an unending road trip. The team wasn't in the best shape for such a heroic odyssey. Decimated by the war and no longer prosperous, this permanent visiting team was a ramshackle crowd that got ramshackler. It included fifty-year-old veterans reactivated after retirement, a refugee from a Japanese league, a one-armed outfielder, a peg-legged catcher, a teen-age genius, an alcoholic ex-con man, a midget pitcher, and so on. Smitty told the wonderful but tragic tale of its past and its final struggles. That was his "great American novel."

It would be pleasant to report that Smitty's opus is to be pub-

lished, that truth as he tells it is to prevail, and that the author's
genius is to be recognized. His pitiful "Epilogue" shows all too
clearly that, thanks to the conspiracy of a new persecuting group,
the masterpiece will never see print. Twenty-seven publishers
have fobbed him off with weak excuses. One letter turned it
down because its "treatment of blacks, Jews, and women, not to
mention the physically and mentally handicapped, is offensive
in the extreme; in a word, sick." Another tells the author:

I am returning your manuscript. Several people here found portions
of it entertaining, but by and large the book seemed to most of us to
strain for its effects and to simplify for the sake of facile satiric comment the complexities of American political and cultural life.

As the alliterative sad saga stops, Smitty is sending off a screed
to the chairman of the People's Republic of China in a desperate
(and surely futile) attempt to get his history published in Pe-
king.

Our knowledge of Roth, like that of Faulkner, has been enriched by a recent study. This is Bernard F. Rodgers's University
of Chicago doctoral dissertation, "Stalking Reality: The Fiction
of Philip Roth" (1974), for the most part unpublished. One article based upon it, *"The Great American Novel* and 'The Great
American Joke,' " published in *Critique*, 16 (December 1974),
12–29, includes and supplements what follows. Rodgers makes a
good case for his claim that when Roth decided to join the red-
faces and wrote this book, he "employed comic techniques which
echo the raucous and ribald quality of nineteenth-century native
American humor and twentieth-century popular comedy."

It is impossible for us (or Rodgers) to know how consciously
he did this. Writers, since each is unique, create in many ways.
Our guess is that even so self-conscious an artist as Roth, though
he knows American humor well, when he became playful and
outrageous gave little or no thought to "models" or "influences"
or "echoes." But we do not know. We can only say, with Rodgers, that in a very individual way he wrote in the styles of old
and new schools, and adapted them to serve his purposes.

One kinship is with antebellum Southwestern humor. Its creators had as a chief outlet a magazine for men dealing with
sports, the stage and literature. Two instalments of Roth's novel

came out in *Sports Illustrated* and *Esquire*. Like Roth's, the older
humor of *The Spirit of the Times* is masculine, exuberant, vulgar, and full of sheer animal spirits. Both the older comedy and
Roth's are characterized by irreverence, profanity, physical dis-
comfort, scatology, and even obscenity. Both here and in the
older humor, boasts and tall tales abound. One of many instances: Gil Gamish, legendary pitcher for the Mundys, takes his
place alongside Mike, Davy, Mose, and Corpse Maker. "I'M GIL
GAMESH!" he would yell, in capital letters. "I'M AN IMMORTAL,
WHETHER YOU LIKE IT OR NOT!" Let a strong batter step to the
plate, and Gil would become obnoxious:

"You couldn't lick a stamp. You couldn't beat a drum." . . . Then,
sneering away, he would lean way back, kick that right leg up sky-
high like a chorus girl, and that long left arm would start coming
around by way of Biloxi—and next thing you knew it was strike one.
He would burn them in just as beautiful and nonchalant as that, three
in a row, and then exactly like a barber, call out, "Next!" He did not
waste a pitch, unless it was to throw a ball at a batter's head, and he
did not consider that a waste.

The legendary Davy Crockett, storytellers claimed, topped his
earlier fantastic feats after the world thought he had died at the
Alamo. Gil, too, after his death was reported was immortalized
in stories that placed him everywhere—riding the rails in Indi-
ana, tending bar in Florida, singing grand opera (for God's sake)
in cities with big auditoriums. Roth has him actually turn up toward the end of the book, now a double agent from Russia, as
mean and ornery as ever.

Roth, guiding Smitty's pen, proves that he has perfected an
art which American storytellers tenderly nourished from the
start—that of developing scenes with multitudinous, apt details
that almost convince because they seem inevitable. A wide detour—one of many that Smitty takes—brings a leisurely history
of the Mosquito Coast League of Nicaragua. Its teams, we learn,
are far worse off than the Mundys. They are made up of "native
boys," sailors who have jumped ship, unemployed spitballers and
"assorted nuts and desperadoes"—fugitives from decent society.
The picture of their sordid lifestyle has the ring of absolute
truth:

Carried from village to village on mules, sleeping in filth with the
hogs and the chickens, or in hovels with toothless Indians, these men

quickly lost whatever dignity they may once have had as ballplayers and human beings; and then, to further compromise themselves and the great game of baseball, they took to drinking a wretched sort of raisin wine between innings, which altered the pace of the game immeasurably. But the water tasted of rats and algae, and center field in the dry season in Guatemala is as hot as center field must be in Hell— catch nine innings in Nicaragua in the summer, and you'll drink anything that isn't an out-and-out poison. Which is just what the water was. They used it only to bathe their burning feet. Indian women hung around the foul lines, and for a penny in the local currency could be hired for an afternoon to wash a player's toes and pour a bucketful of the fetid stuff over his head when he stepped up to bat. Eventually these waterwomen came to share the benches of the players, who fondled and squeezed them practically at will. . . .

Anyone who suspects Smitty is a loon who has dreamed up his "history" surely must waver when he reads this vivid and authoritative passage.

The overall construction of *The Great American Novel* is picaresque—loosely linked episodes, brief tall tales, anecdotes, vignettes, sketches such as Southwestern writers of humor ordinarily (though not exclusively) wrote. As the older group did, Roth —or Smitty—likes a climactic ordering for a tall tale: one of his best uses of it is in his history of Gil's more and more incredible pitching feats. And much of the language reminds a reader who knows Southwestern humor of its phrasings. (This may well be, of course, because of the common influence of oral speech. Transcripts of the tapes that Roth credits, when compared with the book, show that the author joyously glaumed onto many of the salty phrasings of reminiscing ballplayers.)

Smitty, himself an ex-newspaper columnist, is also a great one to write in the fashion of the Phunny Phellows and the Algonquinites. Verbal acrobatics—puns, malapropisms, alliterations, incongruous catalogues, afflicted logic, contorted sentences—dot the pages. In just one of many innumerable plays on words, Smitty says he would "rather be a writer than President." A host of names in addition to that of Word Smith are puns—Base Baal, Spit Baal, Angela Trust and others. Smitty's belief in the world-shaking importance of his scrimy team inevitably brings anticlimactic sequences. Listing scenes of great achievements, he swoops from the Runnymede of the Magna Carta and the Philadelphia of the Declaration of Independence to the Mundy Park of his heroes' triumphs, and on the same page he talks of "notables ranging from Secretary of War Stimson and Governor Edison to the Mayor of Port Ruppert, Boss Stuvwxyz."

Like the writings of the literary comedians and the *New Yorker* crowd, too, this book is stuffed with burlesques and parodies. Victims cover a prodigious range—the Bible, ancient epics, Chaucer, Henry Fielding, classic American fictionists such as Poe, Hawthorne and Twain, Joseph Conrad's "Heart of Darkness," Henry James, and Roth's contemporaries (Bellow, Malamud, stuffy book reviewers, Richard Nixon, and Edward Kennedy). The very first sentence in the "Prologue," "Call me Smitty," shows that Herman Melville will be among the victims; and a high point is a parody of Ernest Hemingway doing a parody of *Moby-Dick*.

So what was new in *The Great American Novel?*

Obviously, there were no spanking new ingredients. Now that Americans have been creating humor for more than two hundred years, precedents can easily be found for all the comic elements in today's writings. But even so, there have been qualitative and quantitative changes.

Southwestern humor in the antebellum period, to be sure, was irreverent, scatological, and obscene; but one must add, *for the times*. The times have changed, especially since World War II, and these elements are now used in a far less restrained fashion. Even readers who aren't shocked by the earlier vulgarity and frankness may well be distressed by much of the humor of the 1972 novel. Rodgers's summary suggests some deviations:

Midgets, dwarfs, dimwits, cripples, one-armed and one-legged characters swarm through the pages of *The Great American Novel* and typically tasteless—and hilarious—fun is made of their physical maladies. At the same time, prostitution, vaginal odors, sexual perversity, urination, flatulence, and various forms of physical pain and punishment are freely and comically treated in ways designed to offend the squeamish.

Something like what happened to Norman Mailer perhaps happened to Roth:

Mailer [said Mailer, writing about himself in the third person] never felt more like an American than when he was naturally obscene—all the gifts of the American language came out in the happy play of obscenity. . . . So after years of keeping obscene language off to one corner of his work . . . he had kicked goodbye . . . to the old literary corset of good taste, letting the sense of language play on obscenity as freely as it wished . . . with the happiest beating of wings—it was the first time his style seemed at once very American to him and very literary in the best way. . . .

Both Roth/Smitty's frank language, and the dialogue of his unrestrained jocks, quite possibly seem not only more "American" but also more lifelike to readers in the present uncensored era.

Inventive old-time yarnspinners, like all the best liars, made their most outrageous extravaganzas seem believable by peppering them with concrete details. So did Roth, but in step with today's "tell-all" fictionists, he piled up more naturalistic details. The passage about the Mosquito League quoted above illustrates this tendency; so do numerous others.

Some touches give an aspect of reality to Smitty's wild story in a way that is fashionable and that some critics have called novel. Walter Kerr in 1976 wrote:

With increasing freedom, and a malicious playfulness, writers of fiction—writers who are supposed to imagine their characters—have been reaching out into real life, picking up people who actually lived, shaking them free of their strictly factual accoutrements, and scrambling them together with the unreal, imagined figures they *have* invented. They're cross-breeding fact and any degree of fantasy they care to apply, meshing history and improvisation with a deadpan impertinence.

He cites as an early example the drama *Travesties* by Tom Stoppard, which has Lenin, James Joyce, and Tristan Tzara meet up with an imagined character. He also notices that following the staging of the Briton's play, the American Nicholas Meyer wrote *The Seven Percent Solution* and *The West End Horrors*, in which the fictitious Sherlock Holmes and Dr. Watson have meetings and adventures with the historical Sigmund Freud, Bernard Shaw, and Sir Arthur Sullivan. And he discusses the bestselling E. L. Doctorow's *Ragtime*, which intermingles Harry Houdini, Evelyn Nesbit, and Stanford White with completely imagined characters. His suggestion is that when the real is shoved up against the imagined, it is shown to be "just as subject to manipulation and hence not really any truer." Fictitious writing, Kerr guesses, is "trotting out its own created legends to show that they have just as much continuing life in them as the vague folk in the history books."

The comment evokes this response: the gambit isn't all that new. Historical-play writers and historical novelists always did something similar. The historical Prince Hal romped with the fictitious Falstaff; the Four Musketeers mingled with Richelieu, Louis XIII, and the Queen of France; the fictitious Pauper changed places with the historic Prince. Even fictitious characters who mingled with more recent historical figures weren't novel. Upton Sinclair's Lanny Budd novels (1940–1949) had their hero meet historical characters active and famous between 1913 and 1945 all over the world. Even our old-time comic figures met real contemporaries: Jack Downing was the pal of several Presidents; Artemus Ward met Abe Lincoln and gave him some good advice.

Smitty starts nothing entirely new, therefore, when he says that he has been a crony and speech polisher for four Presidents and ties his unbelievable "history" to actual history. In his account, Black Jack Pershing and William Howard Taft help General Oakhurst become president of the Patriotic League; Bob Hope cracks jokes before GI's in army bases through the world about the wandering Mundys, and so on. The device isn't new. But the way it is used, and the gilt that it acquires by association, enable it to deliver a modern-day message.

Roth, helpful as usual, has talked about his use—or Smitty's— of factual matter in his all-but-incredible yarn. "The paranoid fantasist Word Smith," Roth says, was created because his amanuensis·wanted him to describe "what America is really like to one like *him*." He wanted a narrator "like him," he specified, because Smitty's distorted vision is representative: "His is not so unlike the sort of fantasies with which the national imagination began to be plagued during the last demythologizing decade of disorder, upheaval, assassination and war." What does he mean by "demythologizing?" It is the process by which "venerable institutions and beliefs" in war aims, foreign policies, Camelot and men in high offices—in "what was assumed to be beyond reproach—became the target for blasphemous assault." Baseball, itself a "venerable institution," could, he decided, furnish "a counterhistory, or *countermythology*":

It was not a matter of demythologizing baseball—there was nothing in that to get fired up about—but of discovering in baseball the means to dramatize *the struggle* between the benign national myth of itself that a great power prefers to perpetuate, and the relentlessly insidious, very nearly demonic reality (like the kind we had known in the sixties) that simply will not give an inch in behalf of that idealized mythology.

In the last pages of his narrative, Smitty has the Dies Committee haul up and try the Mundys for Communist activities, find them guilty, and destroy them. Roth "anchored the book" in these investigations, he explains, "to establish a kind of passageway from the imaginary that seems real to the real that seems imaginary, a continuum between the credible incredible and the incredible credible." The intermingling of the wildly imagined and the factual so characteristic of the old tall tales here achieves "thematic reverberations, . . . depth, . . . overtone, finally . . . meaning."

"Ultimately, all jokes, parables, lies, and in fact all fictions and fables of whatever sort," says G. Legman, "are simply the decorative showcases of their tellers' anxieties, their repressions, and generally of their neuroses . . . being juggled with onstage to beg the audience's applause." Smitty's history is a showcase for a cartoon of America. That editor who turned it down because of its "satiric comment [on] the complexities of American political and cultural life" knew what he was talking about.

With this in mind, a reader can notice how Roth made its ingredients contribute to the book's "reverberations." Smitty is nostalgic—as nostalgic as the postbellum local colorists were; but bygone scenes that he recalls are anything but idyllic. What he believes was baseball's golden age is funny, to be sure; but it is also brutal, ugly, and obscene. Its heroes are dwarfs, cripples, perverts, and freaks. These are Smitty's comic demigods. Their astonishing feats, like those of a mental asylum team in one episode, are "as low as low can be." They enact for our laughter what Saul Bellow in *Herzog* calls "the degraded clowning of this life through which we are speeding."

Laughable gyrations of language also help "demythologize."

Players' names recall gods—Astarte, Baal, Demeter, Roland Agni (cf. Agonistes) and lesser deities; but given names—Frenchy, John, Deacon, and the like—ground them and encourage readers to make uncomplimentary contrasts. The profanity, obscenity, and scatology pollute the atmosphere of Smitty's never-never land.

Parodies of great fictional works help the impeachment. Roth ended his self-interview by saying why Smitty, loopy though he was, was on target when he put himself in a class with Hawthorne and Melville. These two also tried to write "the great American novel," and "Smitty's book, like those of his illustrious forebears, attempts to imagine a myth of an ailing America; my own is to some extent an attempt to imagine a book about imagining that American myth."

I hear America swinging,
The carpenter with his wife or the mason's wife, or even the
mason,
The mason's daughter in love with the boy next door, who is in
love with the boy next door to him,
Everyone free, comrades in arms together, freely swinging. . . .
　　　　　　—Peter De Vries, *I Hear America Swinging* (1976).

"I'm now interested in taking a story, fantastic and improbable, and trying to get to the bottom of it, to make it seem not only real, but inevitable."　　　—Stanley Kubrick, discussing *Dr. Strangelove*, 1964.

45.
Up from the
Underground

THROUGHOUT THE NINETEENTH century in the United States (as elsewhere), a current of humor aimed at the popular audience ran deep and swift to what would later be called "middlebrow" and "lowbrow" consumers. Charles Farrar Browne made the Cleveland *Plain Dealer* famous throughout the country; David Ross Locke performed a similar service for the Toledo *Blade;* Charles Henry Smith's writings for the Atlanta *Constitution* were quoted nationwide. Phunny Phellows lifted to prominence the Burlington, Iowa, *Hawkeye;* the Laramie, Wyoming, *Boomerang;* the Danbury, Connecticut, *News;* the Denver, Colorado, *Tribune;* and other previously unknown newspapers. Practically all the big newspapers had columnists who were famous from coast to coast. Following Browne's example, many became platform comedians who earned at least as much money on the lecture circuit as they did from their columns and books. There were also minstrel shows which carried burlesque "Abyssinian dramas" through the countryside, poking fun at the classics by reducing them to black dialect. And many of the thriving comic periodicals—*Life*, *Puck*, and *Judge*—exploited the potential of visual humor, the cartoon, during the latter half of the century.

But it was not until the media explosion of the late nineteenth and early twentieth centuries that outlets for popular humor could be nationalized. Syndication of newspaper columns combined with telegraphy to spread comic relief almost instantaneously throughout the country. William Randolph Hearst experimented with the comic strip, a sequential arrangement of cartoons that had the rudimentary trappings of plot, action, characterization, and consistency, beginning with "Hogan's Alley" featuring The Yellow Kid, in 1894. Early movies, early phonograph cylinders and records, and—slightly later—network radio added options to the humorist who wanted to reach a popular audience. Now, television, long-playing recordings, road-show engagements, and closed-circuit movies bring popular humor to every American old enough to turn a dial or focus his eyes.

From the days of the silent movie and vaudeville, the chief attribute of many popular humorists has been some kind of visual trademark: Chaplin's penguinesque waddle; Buster Keaton's moony stare; Harry Langdon's white, girlish face; Oliver Hardy's "slow burn" of anger and Stan Laurel's placid smile; Durante's nose; Groucho's eyebrows and painted mustache; and Will Rogers's meandering, sly grin. There was a comfortable and reliable repetitiousness about these devices for comedy. The critical "pause," the deadpan seriousness, and the inane repetition that Mark Twain had championed in "How to Tell a Story" as one of the chief resources for the storyteller's art could be enjoyed by wide audiences. Krazy Kat could be counted on to get brained by Ignatz Mouse in the final comic-strip square with the same eternal brick.

Sound effects could get repeated laughs, too. Jack Benny clicked lock after lock to open his money vault; Fibber McGee's hall closet could always be depended on to disgorge a noisy avalanche of odds and ends that allowed for an extended comic catalogue. Bud Abbott would never manage to explain anything to Lou Costello by simple logic, and Sylvester and the coyote would never catch Tweety Pie or the roadrunner. This dependence on familiarity may have lulled, rather than shocked, the audience but it also produced some comic characters who became a part of middle-class American folklore, whose deaths (those of Will Rogers and Jack Benny, for instance) were universally mourned.

Familiar, too, were a number of comic types that popular-culture humor exploited. It was not surprising that the traditional homespun bumpkin (Li'l Abner, Ma and Pa Kettle, the Beverly Hillbillies) remained stereotypes championing homely sagacity in the face of egghead logic; and a popular radio show (disastrously revived for television) emphasized that "It Pays to be Ignorant." The domestic sketch, honed and refined by Phunny Phellows in the 1870's, continued to appeal in "Jiggs and Maggie," "Gasoline Alley," the various Lucille Ball shows, and "The Easy Aces" on radio. Stuffed shirts and other types of pedants—Major Hoople, Groucho's adversary Margaret Dumont, or Gale Gordon in almost all of his television roles—continued to be frustrated and comically demolished. And the Little Man of *New Yorker* humor retained his comic charm in his many popular incarnations: Fibber McGee, Casper Milquetoast, Sad Sack, Ziggy, Dagwood, Wally Cox, and Don Knotts. Comic dialects (Amos 'n' Andy, Fred Allen's "Allen's Alley" radio segment, the Baron, the Mad Greek, Jerry Colona, and Sid Caesar's German professor) brought laughs, as did the dependable comic types—henpecked husbands, overeager spinsters, mischievous children, and humanized animals.

Popular humor, as a rule, resolutely refused to indulge in biting political satire, social criticism, or other indictments of the Establishment. There were occasional exceptions: Chaplin's *The Great Dictator;* Spike Jones's record "Der Führer's Face"; many of the early "Orphan Annie" comic strips—though not the radio serial; and some Depression-oriented comics like "Apple Mary" —later sweetened into "Mary Worth." Generally, though, whatever the medium, popular humor enforced and championed the values of the middle class which constituted its audience. It is curiously true, for instance, that comic-strip readers detected something different and disturbing about Pogo or Li'l Abner when Walt Kelly and Al Capp began to infuse social or political satire into those strips.

In contrast to this bland, essentially non-threatening mode of humor, Henry Miller, the audacious literary terror of the 1930's and 1940's, was prophetic. His depiction of sexual battles between men and women was a franker version of much *New Yorker* humor. In *The Literature of Silence* (1968), Ihab Hassan has called Miller's *Sexus* (1949) a "diary of a weak man who transforms his weakness into a fumbling, maudlin, awed reverence for life."

Miller's sexual fantasies were cock-and-bull versions of a favorite Old Southwestern theme. They celebrated bodily functions —aromas, tastes, and sensations—with an earthy and obsessive realism, while they soared to the level of tall tales with their sexual gymnastics and insatiability.

Miller focused on the shock value of four-letter words "calculated to be as disturbing as possible to the sensitive reader," according to William A. Gordon (in *The Mind and Art of Henry Miller*, 1967), who also noted that Miller deliberately spent much of his writing energy describing "almost unerringly what in the American culture has been least acceptable." As a crusader for shucking inhibitions and moral hypocrisy, Miller foreshadowed many later underground comics. Even his own definition of comedians (in *Sexus*)—they try "to create the illusion of a world in which the Unconscious rules supreme. . . . At every performance [they slay] the censor who stands like a ghost on the threshold of the subliminal self"—has the ring of Lenny Bruce and George Carlin.

It would be an oversimplification to say that counterculture humor burst into existence spontaneously in the 1950's. Allen Sherman's tedious *The Rape of the A*P*E* (American Protestant Ethic) lists manifestations. But, since the late 1950's and early 1960's, intense sociologists, concerned educators, and harassed parents have become fascinated with what they describe (usually to deplore) as the underground culture in America. The underground is generally youthful (or, some would say, infantile), intellectually elitist, and hostile to the values of dominant American culture. Several unpopular wars splintered the patriotic unity the country had felt during World War II; the various Kinsey reports appeared to chart convincingly the sexual hypocrisy of the American public; and a number of courts began redefining interpretations of freedom of speech, obscenity, and pornography. Pot, the pill, and Chairman Mao all belonged in there somewhere, along with Timothy Leary, William Kunstler, and other not-too-youthful "revolutionaries." The Yippies, the Free Speech Movement, organic vegetables grown in transcendental communes, and the ultimate distortion, Charles Manson, were all part of the underground. But what is important here is that when members of the counterculture were not overwhelmed with their own high seriousness, they managed to produce a vitally important humor to shock and satirize the System.

Just before his death, James Thurber wrote,

I am worried about the current meanings of the word "funny." It now means ominous, as when one speaks of a funny sound in the motor; disturbing, as when one says that a friend is acting funny; and frightening, as when a wife tells the police that it is funny, but her husband hasn't been home for two days and nights.

Agreeing with this, Robert Ruark suggested in the late 1950's that something was happening to humor that reflected "a psychoneurotic-cesspool state of mind." What Thurber and Ruark apparently noticed was the beginning of the comic underground. Originally it had centered in New York and San Francisco. Paul Krassner's *The Realist* was its magazine; Terry Southern was the high-priest, mocking incest in *Candy*, material wealth in *The Magic Christian*, death in his film script of *The Loved One*, and even pornography in *Blue Movie*. Lenny Bruce, with his string of arrests for offending the decency of his audience and his death from an overdose of heroin, was its martyr. He was also the prototype for a legion of imitators—Richard Pryor and Freddie Prinze, among the best of them—who followed in his steps from the Gate of Horn to the hungry i, imitating his manners, gestures, timing, and material.

Little that was new in technique distinguished underground humor. The X-rated animated cartoon "Fritz the Cat" used humanized animals in the ancient tradition. Comic strip artists like R. Crumb (whose *Mr. Natural* provided the motto "Keep on Truckin'" for a college generation); Dan O'Neill and his Odd Bodkins (which reproduced a psychedelic fantasy world induced by a magic cookie); or Gary Trudeau (whose "Doonesbury" rose from the Yale underground to national prominence and syndication) employed basically realistic techniques mixed with elements of fantasy—and, indeed, Disney's 1941 movie *Fantasia* seemed to many the foreshadowing of one element of underground culture. Stand-up comics indulged in the dramatic monologues and dialogues of earlier generations; but the Firesign Theater, with several levels of dramatization occurring at once and integrated with one another by elaborate and zany puns and wordplays, produced records which some of its fanatical admirers insisted could be understood fully only if the listener were turned on. The effects in their most popular records—"Waiting for the Electrician or Someone Like Him," "Don't Crush that Dwarf, Hand Me the Pliers," and "I Think We're All Bozos on This Bus"—were essentially Joycean in their fluid verbal agility, or at least reminiscent of the Marx Brothers scripts by Kaufman or Perelman.

What is most significant about counterculture humor is that, in spite of all its efforts to escape dilution and preserve exclusiveness, it managed to invade the media which, it thought, were closed to it and to gain at least some acceptance by the very level of culture which it thought was its target. It was impossible to sustain the elite aloofness. *The Realist* moved to San Francisco and became a popular magazine with a reported readership of sixty thousand—and very little humor. Helen Gurley Brown turned the soporific *Cosmopolitan* into a swinging magazine which published *Myra Breckenridge* and in one issue included a demure nude centerfold of Burt Reynolds as a bonus. Bizarre Records, which released Lenny Bruce's "Berkeley Concert" album, announced on its blurb that "we make records that are a little different. We present musical and sociological material which the important record companies would probably not allow you to hear." This longing for rejection was satisfied as long as Lenny Bruce got arrested, or *The Realist* was forbidden the use of the United States mail, or *Candy* had to be smuggled into the United States in its Olympia Press edition.

But Broadway produced the all-nude *O, Calcutta* and off-Broadway staged the fantasy, *The Beard*. Moviegoers reveled in *Dr. Strangelove*; they formed lines to see *Where's Poppa?* and *Harold and Maude* (and made Ruth Gordon the unanimous choice for the top comedienne of the 1970's); they paid roadshow prices to see Mel Brooks's *Blazing Saddles* and *Young Frankenstein*. And in X-rated movies like *Deep Throat* and *It Happened in Hollywood*, even kinky sex became funny.

Because television remained the last stronghold of conservative humor, it was totally absurd for Thomas Swafford of CBS to claim in 1973 that "TV comedy has covered every subject except sodomy, bestiality, and necrophilia." But even television loosened up. Carroll O'Connor's Archie Bunker in "All in the Family" first managed to tackle previously tabooed subjects on prime time and thereby win great acclaim. The series was followed by "Maude," "Chico and the Man," and the raunchy (though short-lived) "Hot L Baltimore." And although the Smothers Brothers' show might be cancelled for its political satire, "M*A*S*H" enjoyed a long popularity with its assault on the military. Carol Burnett and Harvey Korman indulged in occasional off-color skits on her show; and the late-night talk-show host Johnny Carson included among his guests practically all of the controversial comedians. By 1976, even old-timers were staying up late to watch the "shocking" humor of "Mary Hartman, Mary Hartman" and "Saturday Night Live," and, in 1977, "Soap."

Even a cartoonist like Gahan Wilson, the inheritor of Charles Addams's graveyard, could syndicate his material in the Sunday comics section of newspapers. And the bizarre extravaganza called the *Lampoon* could convert from *Harvard* to *National* and appear on newsstands everywhere. By the end of 1969, Paul Krassner could complain in *The Realist*, "Over the past decade, the climate has changed so much that articles and cartoons which once might have ended up in these pages now appear instead . . . in . . . *Playboy*, *Esquire* and, yup, the *Wall Street Journal*."

In spite of its similarities to popular-culture humor and its invasion of popular media, underground humor, predictably enough, made some distinct assumptions and had certain biases which were quite different from those of popular-culture humor. It was, to begin with, intensely satiric in its own unusual way. It made fun of the traditional minority stereotypes by exaggerating and dramatizing them with the use of dialect—by Dick Gregory and Richard Pryor, for example, with blacks and Bill Dana and Freddie Prinze with Latinos. It shot at topical targets, beginning with Mort Sahl's nightclub routines, newspaper in hand for source material, and Lily Tomlin, in her role as the "tasteful" guardian of WASP decorum on "Laugh-In." After Kennedy, American Presidents became objects, once more, of both official and personal attacks. Johnson, Nixon, and Ford admittedly offered irresistible invitations to assault; but underground humorists also opposed the draft, the war in Vietnam, the marijuana laws, Victorian (and post-Victorian) morality, racism, sexism, and almost any standard which the Establishment (or their interpretation of the Establishment) cherished. Among the fascinating discoveries of the Underground was a "new" brand of humor involving racial minorities and women.

From the nineteenth century on, ethnic and racial minorities had been the butts of American humor that ranged from gentle to vicious. Poems and sketches using foreign dialects flourished as part of the local color and Phunny Phellow movements (e.g., Charles Godfrey Leland's "Hans Breitman" verses, Charles Follen Adams's "Yawcob Strauss's" monologues, and Dunne's "Mr. Dooley" pieces). Blacks from early times were stereotyped as lazy, superstitious, and simple-minded. In books, stories, and especially stage performances, the black was a sure-fire comic character. (Gary Engle's edition of "Ethiopian Dramas," tail-pieces to minstrel shows, shows blackface actors burlesquing Shakespeare in plays with titles such as "Desdemonum" and "Julius the Snoozer" and Longfellow in "De Maid ob de Huncpuncas.")

By the middle of the twentieth century this kind of ethnic deprecation had been shelved because it was considered tasteless and bigoted. But in the 1960's and 1970's, startlingly, the minorities themselves began to engage in self-ridicule—and that was acceptable. *Huckleberry Finn* could get banned as required reading in a Chicago suburb in 1976 for using the word "nigger," but Dick Gregory could title a book with the word—and without a groan from his integrated audience. A Secretary of Agriculture could be forced to resign for making an off-color comment that Red Foxx's audiences would have cheered. Domestic situation-comedy routines that were criticized when "Amos 'n' Andy" used them in blackface radio shows and movies flooded television in "The Jeffersons" and "Sanford and Son." Bill Cosby and Flip Wilson delivered monologues over national hookups using the very stereotypes (Fat Albert and Geraldine) that would have led to mayhem on the spot if a white comedian uttered them.

In a way, such comedy ridiculed white bigotry by exaggerat-

Mr. Dooley, a Chicago
saloonkeeper, commented
in an Irish brogue on na-
tional affairs. Drawing by
E. W. Kemble for *Mr.
Dooley's Philosophy*
(1900).

ing the very prejudices on which that bigotry had been based
(much as Americans had exaggerated their foibles to kid jaundiced foreign travelers during the eighteenth and nineteenth
centuries). It also provided a healthy kind of humor which revealed unfamiliar cultural, economic, and racial quirks to a
broader and broader audience.

When a Massachusetts lady, Anne Bradstreet, wrote humorously in the seventeenth century, she didn't make fun of women
or, in fact, of other creatures that female writers kid today. Her
poems about her spouse, which were worshipful even though he
was a politician, and about her children, which were affectionate
even though there were eight (!) of them, in retrospect justify

the advertising slogan, "You've come a long way, baby." Eighteenth-century Sarah Kemble Knight managed to be irreverent and to crack jokes about people, including women, who amused her because they differed from the folk of her hometown, Boston. And Caroline Kirkland in 1839 satirized Michigan pioneers, including women, because they were less couth than the folk of her native New York.

In the era of the Phunny Phellows, Marietta Holley edged closer to today's women comic writers when she created and quoted a Phunny Phemale, "Josiah Allen's Wife," Samantha. Ms. Holley, a feminist, satirized religious hypocrisy, political skulduggery, and male chauvinism. But she was an unschooled rustic with sound mare sense, a Christian, a loving wife and a model housekeeper, and therefore could never have become as popular today as she did during her lifetime.

Harbingers of the modern women humorous writers were poets Edna St. Vincent Millay and Dorothy Parker, who sloughed off rusticity, cultivated wit, and wryly bemoaned not only women's but their own personal frailties. Parker—in her talk, if not in print—was broadly humorous and gamy. As barriers tumbled, women authors became much franker. The most popular author of housewifely humor, Erma Bombeck, wrote in her syndicated columns and books about toilet training, smelly kids, chauvinistic husbands, and sexual fantasies which her predecessors only a few years earlier wouldn't dream of telling the world they enjoyed. In the mid-seventies, her syndicated column appeared in scores of newspapers, and her book, *The Grass is Always Greener over the Septic Tank* (1977), for many weeks was on bestseller lists. Erica Jong's *Fear of Flying* (1973), which lived up to blurbs saying it was "dazzlingly uninhibited" and to reviewers' praises for "extending the tradition of *Portnoy's Complaint*," was horny, funny, and popular. In hardcover and paperback editions, it sold more than five million copies. Deanne Stillman and Anne Beatts in 1976 published what they called (incorrectly) the first collection of humor by women only. Delicately, they called it *Titters*, and made sure that everybody who opened it noticed its pun by labeling sections illustrated with whole pages of full-color photographs labeled "Knockers, Melons, Jugs, Boobs" and the like. "You see," said the editors, "we think

Illustration by Loretta Krupinski for Erma Bombeck, *I Lost My Everything in the Post-Natal Depression* (Garden City: Doubleday, 1973.)

that women should be allowed to be outrageous. . . . Then is nothing sacred? Maybe something is, but personally we doubt it."

Thus, outrageous comedy about minorities and women that had once been in the worst possible taste floated up from the underground. Racist comic series were shown on television screens, and families watched them and chuckled. Prestigious publishing houses happily printed Bombeck, Jung, Stillman, and Beatts, and boasted in advertisements that they were selling well.

Such shifts in values presented a major problem for counter-culture humorists: the Establishment refused all too often to become outraged. The permissive 1970's tolerated comic assaults on its standards, often in words previously felt to be improper for mass consumption. The pill, Watergate, political assassinations—whatever the cause, the humorist-in-revolt was hard put to stay antagonistic. Eventually, when Mort Sahl hopefully asked his audience, "Let's see, is there anybody I haven't offended?" the sad answer was, "Practically everybody."

Constant shifts such as these account for the ephemeral nature of underground humor. Satirical and topical, it moved from one objective to another almost too fast for the naked eye. Its practitioners disappeared. Like Lenny Bruce or Richard Fariña (*Been Down So Long It Looks Like Up to Me*), they died. Or they were spoiled by success, like Don Addams ("Get Smart") and Red Foxx. Or they turned deadly serious, like Dick Gregory and Ken Kesey. Somehow, those trademarks of familiarity

which distinguished popular comics never had a chance to jell
for the counterculture satirists.

As a result, their comic routines often were primarily oral
rather than visual, depending on sound effects and dialect or
dialogue (the latter most successfully in the acts of Mike Nichols
and Elaine May). Their media were unpredictable. *The Realist*
became serious, while *Cosmopolitan* "turned on and tuned out";
and "All in the Family" and "Maude" struggled desperately to
find "controversial" topics to convert to humor.

Possibly what occurred was the acceptance of the underground's own special morality by mainstream American culture.
"Do your own thing," "Make love, not war," "Black is beautiful," "Peace" and similar beatitudes of the underground simply
gained acceptance when the variant lifestyle, with an intensely
ethical perspective all its own, became familiar, comfortable, and
a lot less revolutionary than it first appeared to be. For humor, it
was a healthy transfusion.

A third strand of contemporary humor braided itself with
popular and underground humor in the post-World War II
period—one which many commentators would not consider
"healthy" by any standard. Conrad Knickerbocker coined the
term "black humor" to describe a phenomenon he noticed in a
number of novelists who began writing after the war; but
neither he nor anyone else has managed to define the exact qualities of black humor to the satisfaction of anyone else. The adjectives *sick*, *absurd*, *apocalyptic*, and *nihilistic* are flung indiscrim-
inately into discussions of it, and critics nominate fantasies by
Donald Barthelme (like *Snow White*) and realistic novels like
Philip Roth's *Portnoy's Complaint* for inclusion in the category.
We need not be afraid, therefore, that we will make the definition
any murkier.

To begin, we might consider what constitutes the blackness of
black humor. What prompted *Time* magazine to conclude that
a form of humor, as early as 1959, came "so close to real horror
and brutality that audiences wince even as they laugh"? The
brand of gothic humor, which we have noticed earlier, flourished
simultaneously with early American humor; Poe's "Hop-Frog"
is a sample. Postbellum descendants were Ambrose Bierce's satanic sketches like "Oil of Dog," and Eugene Field's *Tribune
Primer*. In the twentieth century there has been a long tradition

of queasy jokes about Helen Keller, Little Willie, the little moron, and Polacks. Cartoons in the 1930's made fun of black and Jewish minorities, and harelip jokes charmed and challenged as masterful a humorist as H. Allen Smith.

This tradition has a norm: the exploiting of a variation from an acceptable median. Before the twentieth century began, Mark Twain said enigmatically, "There is no humor in heaven." Over fifty years later, Lenny Bruce said in his autobiography that "the healthy comic would never offend . . . unless you happen to be fat, bald, skinny, deaf or blind." Both comments appear to suggest that a typical audience does not mind humor based on deformity, physical imperfection, or other variations from that acceptable median. It is possible to shout at human frailty as long as the imperfect variant is the target. Where everyone is perfect, Mark Twain perhaps meant to say, there is no basis for comic incongruity. And only where there were deviations from the norm, Lenny Bruce possibly meant, is there a potential for "healthy" humor.

But Bruce then offered the opinion that "Everything is rotten—mother is rotten, God is rotten, the flag is rotten." He even suggested that Lenny Bruce was rotten when he confessed, "I am heinously guilty of the paradoxes I assail in our society." This seems to suggest a new perspective—humor can attack not only the misfits and peculiar variants from the norm, but also the norm itself, somehow universalizing its assault until it slugs everyone—even the audience paying the standup comedian for the privilege of being insulted.

This quality of universal condemnation is something that many felt was unusual in American humor. It bothered Walter Kerr when he reviewed the play *Lenny* in 1971. The traditional comic, Kerr said, was

the sane man, the norm, the champion of common sense, the fellow who sees the clown's disproportion *as* a disproportion and puts it into a proper, and hence, hilarious, perspective for us. Making his own sanity the measure of the insanity all about him, he serves as cool distancer, standing securely on the brink of disaster and pointing his finger at the clown who teeters over, and finally into it.

Had Lenny Bruce been alive in 1971, we know whom he would have pointed his finger at—and which finger he would have pointed. Because, in spite of an enormous body of earnest and pretentious commentary about Bruce's function as a "satirist," the essential fact about his humor is its lack of a satiric target and its complete indifference to reform. "The truth is what is, not what should be," Bruce said; "what should be is a dirty lie." Universal human frailty was his subject matter: all religions, any minority and the majority as well, sexual hypocrisy, and sacred cows of any color. Most obviously, Bruce used his audience as his comic foil, antagonistically and belligerently taunting it with topics that would offend it.

Kenneth Tynan, in his foreword to Bruce's *How to Talk Dirty and Influence People*, describes a typical occasion. A group of affluent Londoners listened to the American comic's jokes about miscegenation, fallout, and masturbation. "Suddenly Bruce ventured on the subject of cigarettes and lung cancer. At once, as if in obedience to some tribal summons, the brisk, pink, stockbroker host sprang to his feet. 'All right,' he said tersely, 'Susan, Charles, Sonia! Cancer! Come on! *Cancer!* All out!' And meekly, in single file, they marched out through the door." Like a surgeon performing an exploratory operation, Bruce used the scalpel of his wit to uncover the one tabooed subject at which his listeners refused to chuckle good-naturedly.

At least one source of this pessimism, whether Bruce realized it or not, was probably a handful of serious novelists, including Melville, some post-World War I French existentialists (who could never be mistaken for humorists), and the later Mark Twain. Like Bruce, they despaired of human perfectability, wrote works which were greeted with puzzled antagonism by their audiences, and specialized in subjects that were significant for their refusal to abide by the acceptable norms and formulas for their modes of writing. And even now, most discussions of black humor focus upon a number of "serious" novelists—Heller, Barth, Vonnegut, Pynchon, Hawkes—whose blackness is not in doubt, but whose humor might well be debatable.

Bruce managed to do two significant things with the black despair of his predecessors. First, he actually made it often funny, adding the "humor" half to the term by a number of comic strategies: He insisted that the language he used was universally understood. He proclaimed the universality, too, of the ludicrous behavior he described. He confronted tabooed subjects with an honesty that made something intimate and confessional about his routine. Although his audiences might squirm, they could also laugh at the sincerity and accuracy of Bruce's material. He also managed to broaden its appeal to the mass media of stand-up nightclub comedy and long-playing recordings. Admittedly, Bruce appealed to an elitist audience, the thin sliver of society willing to be shocked to laughter by its own absurdity and duplicity. And admittedly, Bruce, at his worst, was too overwhelmed by his crusade for linguistic honesty (his own euphemism for four-letter words), his harassment by the police, and his legal battles over his drug habit to maintain a vital comic detachment. But his mimicry, his studied air of improvisation, and his comic imagination could work beautifully to expose and startle his audience.

Before we look at some purer versions of popular, underground, and black humor, the comic ricochet of black humor from serious fiction to the popular humor and then back to the contemporary novel is notable enough to deserve some consideration.

What appears to be clear is that the earliest versions of "black humor" were some post-World War II novels, like *Catch-22*, *V.*, and *Mother Night*, in which it is impossible to miss the indignation, the bitterness, and the sense of quiet desperation that Heller, Pynchon, and Vonnegut, respectively, convey. Heller's novel pits one sane man against the insane bureaucratic war machine; Pynchon asks complicated philosophical questions about cause-and-effect relationships and the fabric of intelligible history; in his bitterest novel Vonnegut explores the question of crime, guilt, and atonement. Each book asks serious questions about fundamental issues, even if the solution is only futile laughter. Each lingers in the memory, each requires close reading and re-reading. Whatever the protagonists Yossarian, Stencil, and Howard Campbell and their frustrations mean, we as readers are aware that they mean something and that their histories are woven from the rich material of the serious and the universal.

By contrast, Richard Fariña's *Been Down So Long It Looks Like Up to Me*, Gore Vidal's *Myra Breckenridge*, and Philip Roth's *Portnoy's Complaint* are examples of what Leslie Fielder has recently called "the pop novel." They are self-destructing,

instant-throwaway books, lacking elaborate textures, ambigui-
ties, or viable moral choices which could result in the reader's
identification with the protagonist or condemnation of the antagonist. They are, in effect, slick. Gnossos Pappadopolis loses his
fight for immunity, but in a world so sophomoric that it is difficult to care one way or the other. Myra's search for identity is,
purely and simply, a search for genitalia, a comic metaphor but
hardly a universal one. *Portnoy* does not persuade us to stamp
out Jewish mothers, and does not intend to.

But the point is not that this recent trio of novels lacks literary
merit; it is, instead, that none of them is based upon what, until
recently, had been at least an attempt at universality on the part
of black humorists. Very little lurks behind the masturbation,
sodomy, and venereal disease of these three novels which could
be called, even in disguise, serious. Middle-class values are not
ridiculed; the "silent majority" is not depicted antagonistically;
there is nothing elitist about the tensions. Fariña, Vidal, and
Roth have written burlesque shows rather than sermons. In
short, these books aim at a middle-class audience by avoiding
historical or philosophical allusions, complex psychological insights, or murky literary embellishments.

Nor, for that matter, are the values of mass-audiences held
up to ridicule. What are we to make of Myra's transformation,
for example? He/she tells us in the last chapter of *Myra Breckenridge* that

> For over three years now we have been living in the San Fernando
> Valley on what they call a ranch but is actually just a few acres of
> date palms and lemon trees. The house is modern with every con-
> venience and I have just built an outdoor barbecue pit which is much
> admired by the neighbors, many of whom are personalities in show
> business or otherwise work in some capacity or other in the Industry.
> Ours is a friendly community, with many fine people to share interests
> with.

The description continues for several pages, in none of which is
there a hint of the condemnation, satire, or comic attack on the
values which writers have been ridiculing at least since *The Day
of the Locust*. The style is flat, objective, even depersonalized.
The sting which was immediately discernible in the earlier three
books is gone.

In addition, the three recent novels are closer approximations of reality and depend less upon fantastic elements than the earlier three. In *Catch-22*, time and chronology become puzzles which the reader must piece together; Heller challenges and dares us to make sense of the materials. In *V.*, the history of the twentieth century is the canvas, the Western world is the setting, and Stencil's search for order and meaning is played against the senseless counterpoint of the Whole Sick Crew. Howard Campbell is what he pretends to be—but he has pretended to be the man solely responsible for the Second World War. When he and several minor characters stop pretending, stop existing at their own levels of fantasy, they are destroyed. Hope exists in the person of a Blue Fairy Godmother. Neither time nor space is predictable in worlds populated by ubiquitous whores with knives who will not listen to reason, by a giant rat named Veronica and a mysterious woman with a glass eyeball containing a clock, or by the members of The Iron Guard of the White Sons of the American Constitution. All syllogisms are nonsequiturs. Causes create no effects or the opposite effects of the predictable ones. Yossarian, Stencil, and Howard Campbell ask important questions in a world that is one half a painting by Bosch and the other half Alice in Wonderland. It refuses to answer the questions and frequently refuses even to hear them. Pynchon in *V.* mentions that each person "built his own rathouse of history's rags and straws," and Howard Campbell's definition of the mind of his world is

the cuckoo clock in Hell—keeping perfect time for eight minutes and thirty-three seconds, jumping ahead fourteen minutes, keeping perfect time for six seconds, jumping ahead two seconds, keeping perfect time for two hours and one second, then jumping ahead a year.

Such surreal fantasy—especially when the protagonist attempts unsuccessfully to confront and conquer it—hearkens back to the Walter Mittys, the Balso Snells, and the Benchley persona of the genteel, high-culture humorists of the *New Yorker* mode of comedy; but the external world has become as paranoid as the protagonist. The effect is chilling because these writers distort both their characters and their nightmare environments.

Gnossos, Myra, and Portnoy are attempting to frame basic

questions, too, of course, about identity and self-preservation in a hostile world. But that world is visible and real; it fights by recognizable and acceptable rules. Gnossos, Myra, and Portnoy may make bad choices, but we realize that they do have choices to make and that they are somehow rewarded or punished sensibly and equitably. In a way, the superficiality of the three recent novels facilitates our recognition of, and our sense of superiority to, the essentially comfortable patterns of action and response in *Been Down So Long* . . . , *Myra Breckenridge*, and *Portnoy's Complaint*.

One reason for accepting the characters and actions in the recent novels as more real is that they are more purely physical—indeed, more sensual—than the intellectualized patterns of the earlier novels. In *The Floating Opera*, Todd Andrews announces his definition of quint-essential humor:

Nothing is *intrinsically* funny, to be sure, but to me nothing is so consistently, profoundly, earth-shakingly funny as we animals in the act of mating. Reader, if you are young and would live on love; if in the flights of intercourse you feel that you and your beloved are fit models for a Phidias, for a Michelangelo—then don't, I implore you, be so foolish as to include among the trappings of your love-nest a good plate mirror. For a mirror can reflect only what it sees, and what it sees is screamingly funny.

Fariña, Vidal, and Roth have made that injunction their *modus operandi* in these three novels; most of the time Gnossos, Myra, and Portnoy define their worlds in sexual terms. By their orgasms ye shall know them. Gnossos loses his Immunity when he cuts a hole in a condom to get Kristen pregnant and gets gonorrhea instead (surely it is the only condom in all literary history that was really "sold for the prevention of disease only"). Myra's "rape" of Rusty eventually earns Myron his ranch house, Mary Ann, and all the trappings of normal mediocrity. Portnoy, though he may require the psychiatrist's couch (possibly as a status symbol rather than for therapeutic help), also gets, as he himself acknowledges, the complete realization of all his sexual fantasies in the willing person of the Monkey.

Just as actions produce intelligible reactions and responses in the recent novels, settings and allusions and frames of reference are familiar, even lowbrowed. (The mention of Phidias and

Michelangelo in the quotation from Barth above would be most inappropriate in the context of Gnossos, Myra, or Portnoy.) Portnoy lives in the urban Jewish setting, complete with dominating mother, which is fast becoming the traditional setting for all American literature. Myra analogizes and symbolizes her actions with B-grade movies of the 1930's and 1940's. The basic images of *Been Down So Long* . . . derive from *Winnie the Pooh*; and among Gnossos's talismans is a Captain Midnight Code-O-Graph. We are in a popular-culture framework, in short, which is comfortably undemanding, and we as readers move in it with assurance. They do not require the defensiveness the reader feels in the unpredictable fantasy worlds of *Catch-22*, *V.*, or *Mother Night*. And they do not demand intellectual effort by the reader to penetrate and unravel their mysteries. They exploit the reality of the commonplace.

Finally, there is the question of optimism in the recent novels versus pessimism in the earlier ones. At the very least, the major characters of the three recent books are presented at a level that makes serious concern about them difficult. Campbell's suicide, Stencil's futile and irrational search for meaning and identity in a letter of the alphabet, and Yossarian's paddling in a rubber lifeboat from the middle of the Mediterranean toward Sweden (one of the most hopeless conclusions in modern literature) affect us with their despair and meaninglessness because they are the acts of intelligent men. The defeats (if that is what they are) of Gnossos, Myra, and Portnoy are mitigated, though. These novels, like some others which Richard Hauck mentions in *A Cheerful Nihilism*, "always imply a nonabsurd solution to difficulties that are absurd only in context." Perhaps this is not optimism in any traditional sense; certainly these are not novels with "happy endings." But hovering, somehow echoing, throughout them are the implications of order, control, and choice. Solutions exist, even if Myra, Gnossos, and Portnoy do not quite find them.

The reason for our sense of optimism is quite simple. We, as readers, are allowed to feel that traditional and comfortable superiority to the characters which produces one well-recognized mode of humor. We see the nonabsurd solutions to the dilemmas of *Portnoy*, *Myra Breckenridge*, and *Been Down So Long* . . .

because the dilemmas are distinctly not universal and the characters are not emblematic of a universal condition of hopelessness and despair. Perhaps we are shocked by the explicitness of the language, the physical description, or the hedonism of the worlds of this fiction, but we are not threatened because we know somehow that the fictional world is not *our* world. When Gnossos says that he wants to be a "maker of mirrors," implying presumably that he wishes to hold up an accurate image or a true reflection to everyone who looks at him, not even Heffalump listens to him. Nor, for that matter, do we. Unlike the archetypical and universalized worlds of *Catch-22*, *V.*, and *Mother Night*, we are certain that we would never see ourselves reflected in Gnossos's mirror. (In much the same way, Terry Southern's latest novel, *Blue Movie*, does not endanger any of our stereotypes as *Candy* did; we expect Hollywooders to be depraved, but not the girl next door!)

However elusive the term "black humor" is (and perhaps Roth, Fariña, and Vidal are experimenting with dark gray humor instead), in its purest forms it is a distinct strain from traditional popular humor and underground humor. And it allows for an even wider range of potential comic mixtures that the contemporary humorist can exploit.

"You young men have too many jokes. When there are no jokes, you have nothing left."

"Fortunately there are always more jokes," the ugly young man remarked.

"I don't believe it—I believe things are getting more serious. You young men will find that out."

"The increasing seriousness of things—that is the great opportunity of jokes."

"They will have to be grim jokes," said the old man.

—Henry James, *Portrait of a Lady* (1881).

46.
Cinema, Cartoon, and Stand-up Comic

W. C. FIELDS IS ONE OF THE FEW popular comics whose legend has survived and grown since his death in 1946. His early movies draw crowds around the country; posters showing his characteristic bulbous nose and shifty glance adorn dormitory walls; and in the mid-1970's, biographies and reminiscences of him were still pouring off presses and a feature-length movie purported to unfold his biography. Among the many forerunners for his blustering buffoonery were Nutmeg, the Yankee peddler in Alphonso Wetmore's play *The Pedlar* (1821), and Mark Twain's Colonel Sellers in *The Gilded Age* (1873), both of whom used elaborate speeches and inflated rhetoric for comic purposes. But Fields, with the help of the movie screen, pulled out all the stops. Not only was his speech convoluted, euphemistic, and highflown; but his pauses, his double-takes, his throwing away of comic snappers in an almost inaudible mutter, his repetition of comic situations (like "It ain't a fit night out for man nor beast" in *The Fatal Glass of Beer*), and a catalogue of unique mannerisms all stamped him as spectacular.

A long line of vaudeville performances preceded an equally long succession of comic movies, including a totally felicitous

Mr. Micawber. But Fields's screenplay of *The Bank Dick* (written under the pseudonym "Mahatma Kane Jeeves") shows as well as any other movie the typical Fieldsian comedy. The plot, predictably enough, involves a frustrated con man, whose every attempt at getting suckers to bite fails. Fields, as Egbert Souse ("Soozay—accent grave over the 'e,' " he has to keep reminding other characters), unwittingly captures a bank robber, is rewarded with the job of security guard, has his prospective son-in-law embezzle $700, foils a prissy auditor (played by one of the unsung heroes of comic movies, Franklin Pangborn) in his attempt to balance the bank books, and finally captures a second bank robber after a mad chase reminiscent of the Keystone Kops. He receives ten thousand dollars for a bizarre movie script he has invented along the way and another five thousand dollars for capturing the two thieves. But, unregenerate to the last, he refuses to go to work, and the final scene shows him ogling a pretty chickadee who has managed to divert his attention throughout the entire movie. The wild chase, the madcap adventures, the domestic problems (when his wife asks Egbert if married people live longer, he snarls back at her, "No, it just seems longer"), and the predictable assault on a small child—a boy with a cowboy pistol—which became a Fields trademark are all present in *The Bank Dick*. So are jokes about Egbert's nose, his laziness, and similar dependable standbys.

A central running joke pervades the script, like the repeated line in *The Fatal Glass of Beer:* on six occasions, Egbert walks past a broken-down automobile. The first time, as a predictable authority on car repairs, all the while maintaining his composure and behaving with absolute politeness, he advises the chauffeur, turns a bolt, and watches the engine fall out. On the second occasion, the chauffeur is valiantly trying to replace the engine; the third time, the chauffeur is sitting on the back seat, and the little lady is under the hood. The fourth pass-by finds the lady greasy and so infuriated that she hits Egbert with a wrench. On the fifth occasion, the car is empty with a "For Sale" sign on it, and Egbert and the crook steal it for the getaway car; later, Egbert captures the thief by sending him under the hood and dropping the engine on him. Finally, in the last scene of the script, Egbert finds another disabled car with a man working on it, hesitates, and decides not to offer his assistance. This repetition-with-variation exploiting of humor gives some consistency to a film that otherwise depends on one-liners and almost non-sequential skits.

Most important of all for the humor of *The Bank Dick*, however, are those bursts of imaginative fustian that, like all of Field's characters, Egbert cannot resist. His rhetoric soars in beautiful imitations of the tall tale to outrageous heights. When a friend is about to swat a fly on a bar counter, Egbert declaims,

Don't hurt that fly—that's Old Tom—they named a gin after him. That fly followed me out here from the show. . . . He used to drive the chariot races in the flea circus. . . . One afternoon in a small town outside of Hoosic Falls, when I was ignominiously dragged off to the local bastille and placed in durance vile at the behest of a blackguard regarding the loss of his silver timepiece, . . . Old Tom, feeling he was implicated—remembering the adage—"Time Flies" . . . stuck his left hind leg into the Governor's inkwell, dragged it above the dotted line, forging the Governor's signature. The Governor's secretary, unware of the hoax, inadvertently picked up the document, gave it to a messenger and sent it to the warden who released me with profuse apologies. I love that fly.

When a reporter interviews Egbert about his capture of the first robber—an event to which Egbert only accidentally contributed—Egbert provides the following summary:

Exclusive to the Lompoc *Beagle:* In a sensational display of courage, Egbert Souse, prominent citizen and father of Myrtle Souse of this city, today routed a pair of ferocious criminals with larcenous intentions toward the lettuce of the National bank. . . . Drawing his own revolver, which he carried for such emergencies, he struck the felon—said to be the notorious Repulsive Rogan—over the head with the butt of his trusty weapon, felling him to the earth. . . . The other ruffian, alleged to be Filthy McNasty—known as The Wild Cat, and wanted in every state in and out of the Union—swung an assagai of razor-edge sharpness at Mr. Souse's neck. . . . Mr. Souse, who claims the distinction of fighting a draw with John L. Sullivan in a back bar room in 1896, dodged the blow and kicked Filthy McNasty in the kidney. McNasty ran down Lompoc Boulevard screaming with pain. He is still at large—minus a kidney.

And when he is attempting to impress the stenographer at the bank, he explains, "In my school days, my chums used to call me 'Gritty'—'Gritty Souse.' Catching those crooks was due to my athletic training in my not-so-long-ago younger days. . . . I used to have the figure of the Apollo Belvedere . . . golden hair that hung to my knees. I was known as Young Curlilocks, or Killer Claude. . . . It wouldn't take me two days to get right back in that same condition again, if I took a little exercise and laid off sen-sen. . . . Fought Sullivan 108 rounds to a draw in Oswego, New York, on the 4th of July. Everyone said I was robbed of the decision."

The "facts" in these monologues are particularly outrageous when a viewer has the opportunity to see and hear the speaker. Neither courage nor beauty is a part of Egbert's charm. He's too smart to risk his neck, too tricky, too full of knowledge learned from defeat. His face is pig-like except for the big nose; his belly is rotund; he even has trouble walking. The ridiculousness is heightened by command of multi-syllabled words, esoteric terms, and total resistance to the truth. And Fields managed to create a hilarious incongruity by delivering his tales of high adventure or deering-do in a hard drinker's nasal voice that was almost a monotone, never heightened and frequently muttered, never sped up with excitement and almost always drawled in languid, incomplete sentences. It was bombast muted and almost thrown away.

This is the modern descendant of Mike Fink, Davy Crockett, Mose the Fireman, the Corpse Maker, Yankee peddlers, medicine show spielers, Simon Suggs, and Colonel Sellers and the Gentle Grafter. His physical presence marks him as a bluffer, as Penelope Gilliat says:

He is one of life's losers, and the hell with it. He is not in the race. Fields is truly stylish and his own man, . . . hiding affliction under a far-off and sulphurous view all his own. . . . Fields is a smoldering independent who asks no pity and who saves himself with eccentrically conceived and harmless vengeances. . . . He plays the muttering straight man to life, the counterblow to a punch in the stomach. His retorts are conceived for himself alone, like his endearments and his curses.

He enriches and individualizes one of the great traditions of American humor.

It is worthwhile to notice that *The Bank Dick* ends neatly and without controversy: the crooks are caught, the money is returned to the bank, Egbert's daughter is married, and his family gives him more respect than when the movie began. If a ne'er-do-well manages to accumulate fifteen thousand dollars, it is not, at any rate, through the success of one of his con-man schemes. If Egbert is incorrigible, he is not a danger to the system. Fields once proposed that

I never saw anything funny that wasn't terrible. If it causes pain, it's funny; if it doesn't, it isn't. I try to hide the pain with embarrassment, and the more I do that, the better they like it. But that doesn't mean they are unsympathetic. Oh no, they laugh often with tears in their eyes.

If it is difficult to swallow that definition in terms of Fields's own brand of humor, it is clear that it does have importance for the other strands of contemporary mass-media humor.

In 1972, when Art Buchwald wrote a short introduction to a collection of Garry Trudeau's cartoons called *Still a Few Bugs in the System*, Buchwald predicted, "As with all anti-Establishment figures, Mr. Trudeau will soon be an honored member of the Establishment, if he is not already." By 1975, President Gerald Ford could tell the Radio and Television Correspondent Association annual dinner, "There are only three major vehicles to keep us informed as to what is going on in Washington: the electronic media, the print media, and *Doonesbury* . . . not necessarily in that order." And in May of the same year, when *Doonesbury* became the first comic strip ever to receive the Pulitzer Prize, its publisher took a large ad in the *New York Times Book Review* to extend condolences to Trudeau's cast of characters. It was nice, said Holt, Rinehart & Winston, for Trudeau to be honored, "but it's quite another thing when the Establishment clutches all of Walden Commune to its bosom."

The cast of *Doonesbury* characters, though they lived on the Yale campus when they first appeared in 1968, would have been recognizable in the Haight-Ashbury of San Francisco, Berkeley's Telegraph Avenue, Greenwich Village, or the plaza in Taos. Megaphone Mark Slackmeyer, the campus radical; Calvin, the black activist; Joanie Caucus, the women's libber; Zonker Harris; Rufus, the tricky ghetto public-schooler—these or their troubles

DOONESBURY
Politics in the Funny Papers

Doonesbury's cast of characters surrounding Uncle Duke, clockwise from bottom left: Mark Slackmeyer, B. D., Joanie Caucus, Michael J. Doonesbury, Virginia, and Zonker.

became all too familiar to the Establishment during the Democratic National Convention of 1968, the student riots and sit-ins of the late 1960's, and the anti-war protests during the Vietnam War. Although by the mid-1970's the entire gallery seemed slightly anachronistic, in that seething earlier period Trudeau's comic use of them and, more impressively, his getting the Establishment to clutch them to its collective bosom, was no small achievement.

One thing that underlies all of Trudeau's characters is their constant frustration. No one achieves his goals, and very few even manage a victorious skirmish. Mark Slackmeyer constantly has his radical demands met in ways that produce frustration. When Mark's mother asks his position on material wealth and private ownership, Mark replies, "Surely, you must know, Mother! To me, earthly belongings are the curse of mankind! On this point Marx, Gandhi, Christ and I all agree!" "I'm glad you feel that way, Mark," his mother replies, "I just backed over your motorcycle." When Calvin, the militant black, tells a campus rally, "If justice is to be attained, the status quo must be annihilated! Every building in town must be eradicated in due haste!," his white undergraduate listeners respond, "Right on!," "Yeah!," Right one!" Then Calvin says, "Yea, we must burn down every last building on our own campus!" A subdued and shocked audience asks meekly, "Even the fraternities?" And when the Yalies march on to Washington to demonstrate for peace, Mark discovers that only a fashion reporter for the *Washington Post* covers his activities: "The moratorium committee had one of their gloriously kinky rallies yesterday. It was a smasho day of sunshine as masses of those delicious doves did their thing. . . . There on hand was Mark Slackmeyer, of the Forest Hill Slackmeyers. Every little thing about him was so, so right on that his crowd is sure to be the right one. . . . A word about his darling, kinky hairstyle. . . ."

Such humor raises a vital question: which is it, the Establishment or the undergraduate radical, that is in fact the target of Trudeau's satire? In these early anti-Establishment strips, are upper-class radical chic, communal impulses, and self-aggrandizement by ghetto blacks actually the sources of the humor? (A similar question might be posed for "All in the Family," which received the approval of both the blue- and open-collar segments of the television audience, or of Tom Lehrer's early songs, or Elaine May's one-act satire "Adaptation.")

What appears to us to be true is that, in ways reminiscent of the Little Man of *New Yorker* humor, Trudeau's characters face a system so formidable and so indifferent to their social impulses that it can afford to ignore their calls for reform. Constantly misunderstood, usually ignored or ostracized, almost always defeated, these underground characters exploit the huge gulf between their idealistic goals and their actual frailties. And even if their creator's technique deflects some of the sting of the humor, there is a sense in which showing idealistic intentions greeted with a bored yawn and a shrug provides a significant indictment.

And, of course, there are Michael J. Doonesbury, Mark Slackmeyer's parents, B. D. the star quarterback, and *his* parents who, even as early as *Still a Few Bugs in the System*, provide the satiric target for much of Trudeau's humor. When Doonesbury, the born loser, watches Gloria Steinem, to the accompaniment of Slackmeyer's women's-lib commentary, his only response to the picture on television is, "Nice legs." When B. D.'s father is laid off from his job at the fighter-plane factory, B. D. encourages him with a promise that "There'll be other wars, there'll be other F100s to build. . . . Sure, Dad, we'll have another war, you'll see! Our country will prosper once again!" And Doonesbury himself carries the comic-strips outside the realm of satire by being the eternal turkey. He always fails with co-eds; he talks to his mirror—which talks back to him; and he is laughed out of his sensitivity group when he confesses that he tells his secrets to his teddy bear. When, after an especially bad week at school, he prepares to dissect a frog in his biology class, Doonesbury wonders what else can go wrong; and from the lab table comes the voice, "Hi. I'm Leonard, the talking frog."

In the cartoons after his Yale days, Trudeau focused on the Vietnam War, Watergate, and national politics more narrowly than in his earliest books. But the underlying principle remained relatively stable. By tempering his satiric attack (unlike, say, Jules Feiffer) and reflecting some of his humor back upon the spokesmen for the counterculture, Trudeau from the start hit upon a formula that drew some of its venom. By universalizing many of his underground types, he helped the Establishment discover funny aspects of itself. The alternative lifestyle turned out to be, in many ways, infected with the same limitations, despairs, and quirks as those bedeviling the middle-class. And the impulse for reform was both muted and diluted by non-satiric strips that forced *Doonesbury* to rise up from the underground to national prominence. Buchwald predicted, "in the very near future we will be seeing Doonesbury Sweatshirts, B. D. Star Quarterback Football Games, Megaphone Mark Campus Radical Ashtrays, and God knows how many boxes of Hallmark 'Calvin' greeting cards." And though Trudeau has honed the edge of his satire with more recent collections (*The President Is a Lot Smarter Than You Think*, *But This War Had Such Promise*, and *Dare to be Great, Ms. Caucus* notable among them), he has kept those qualities which endeared him to the Establishment.

In its broad outlines, then, what we have been discussing as popular humor makes gentle fun of the mass audience or ridicules the "minority" variant from that group. Underground humor, more satiric in its general direction and more willing to make protagonists of unusual (and in some sense, unacceptable) character types, suggests in varying decibels of hostility the possibility of improving and reforming the mass audience. What Bruce and other popular humorists who have popularized black humor have undertaken is an assault on audiences through various shock tactics without suggesting corrective reform. One publisher of pornography defined his function as "working toward the last gasp." "We will," he promised, "publish a book that will make the public gasp for the last time. When we do, we will have reached a more adult civilization." Bruce, similarly though more stridently, cried for honesty.

To achieve his comic goals, Bruce used many of the techniques which a century earlier distinguished Sut Lovingood. During his heyday in the late 1950's, Bruce made hostile fun of popular idols, even at the moment of the assassination daring to question Jackie Kennedy's behavior. He ridiculed white Southerners, blacks, and earnest Northern liberals. One of his more famous early lines defended Leopold and Loeb's murder of Bobby Frank—he was a snotty kid, anyway. To the colloquial level of much American humor, he added the four-letter language of basically masculine society. Like Sut, he was fascinated by sex and scatology; and like Sut, he took a dim view of sheriffs, law courts, and theologians who tried to repress him. And, finally, like Sut's remarks, what he said was "horrible" only if a listener or reader disagreed with the underlying beliefs of both about human nature.

Bruce's typical routine was a running commentary, sometimes essentially satiric in its thrust, in his own voice. But in a feigned improvisation (which he had in fact refined, like Mark Twain, through a string of performances), he would remember a situation that he would "dramatize" in a number of voices and dialects. These "bits," as he called them, began like a tall tale, were grounded in fact and based on believable premises. In technique, it was as if Mort Sahl (who always addresses his audiences in his own "voice") suddenly became Jonathan Winters (who almost never uses his own voice), moving from current and realistic commentary into the bizarre and surreal world of fantasy. What if the Lone Ranger was sexually attracted to Silver? What if Hitler had been chosen as Chancellor of Germany by a promotion agency? And what if the big business of religion in America formed a corporation to sell itself by Madison Avenue tactics? That premise developed into one of Bruce's most famous routines, "Religions, Inc."

Bruce's theories of his comedy, as he discussed them in *How To Talk Dirty and Influence People* (1965, a year before his death), contrasted his own brand of humor with that of what he called "the healthy comedian": "the comedians who used to do the harelip jokes, or the moron jokes . . . the healthy comedians who told good-natured religious jokes that found Pat and Abie and Rastus outside of Saint Peter's all listening to those angels harping in stereotype." By contrast, Bruce said, "all my humor is based upon destruction and despair. . . . The kind of comedy I do isn't, like, going to change the world." Thus, instead of picking upon a minority as "healthy" comedians did, Bruce used universal human frailty as his target and the "intellectual dishonesty" that made hypocrites out of the members of his audience. ("There is only what *is*," he said. "The what-*should*-be never did exist, but people keep trying to live *up* to it. There is only what *is*.")

"Religions, Inc." assaulted practically every organized religious faith in the United States with one-liners and longer monologues attacking commercialism and mercenary tactics. Acting out the first great meeting of the salesmen of religion, Bruce used a number of different voices to imitate the fundamentalist holy roller ("Ah'm dumb, ah tol them, ah'm very dumb, AH'VE GOT TWO LINCOLN CONTINENTALS! THAT'S HOW GODDAMN DUMB AH AM!"), the rabbi ("I think we should subdivide"), and the religious novelty salesman, who has

a beautiful selluh—the gen-yew-ine Jewish-star-lucky-cross-cigareet-lighter combined; and we got the kiss-me-in-the-dahk mezuzah; and the wawk-me-tawk-me camel; and these wunnerful lil cocktail nap-kins with some helluva sayings theah—"Anuthuh mahtini faw Muthuh Cabrini."

To end the "bit," Oral Roberts receives a phone call (collect) from Pope John. Roberts congratulates the Pope on his election to the papacy: "That puff of white smoke was a genius stroke. . . . We got an eight-page layout with Viceroy—'The New Pope Is A Thinking Man.' " And he conveys to the Pope a request from Billy Graham: "Billi wants to know if yew can get him a deal on one o those Dago spawts cahs." Then, in true vaudeville spirit, he whispers,

Oh, lissen heah: ah'm sendin ovuh a real winnuh—kid bout twenny-three from Rodondo Beach. Greatest showman you've evuh seen. We grossed seventi-three thousand dollahs in four days in Oakland. Great boy. . . . Well, he does Throwin Away the Crutches and See Again. Good timing, knows when to quit. He can really knot up they dayyim legs. . . .

Roberts then offers to book the Pope onto a West Coast television show—"Jus wave, thass awl. Wear the big ring." And in the final line of the "bit," he reassures Pope John, "NO, NOBODY KNOWS YOU'RE JEWISH!"

By now, Bruce's routine must seem fairly innocuous to most readers. But he was arrested for performing it in Chicago in 1962. (It is equally a sign of the liberal times that Dustin Hoff-man's movie Lenny could draw great crowds in towns where Bruce himself would have been banned or arrested.) But in the 1960's, both the form and the content of Bruce's routine were ap-parently scandalous. For one thing, he burlesqued the conven-tions of all major religious sects—Catholic, Protestant, and Jew-ish. He ridiculed the commercialism, the "showmanship," and the self-aggrandisement of the major theological figures of his

day. Not only did he attack each sect individually through caricature of their leaders, but he also fantasized a conspiracy, for
profit, between groups whose spirit is much less than ecumenical
in fact. The irreverence extends to the dialects of Bruce's speakers, too. The Pope's only lines are *"Dominus vobiscum populus
succubus"*; the rabbi speaks with a British accent; and the fundamentalists are loudly profane and ungrammatical. As a comprehensive assault on the beliefs of his listeners, "Religions, Inc."
leaves no hiding places.

In both this routine, and more explicitly in others employing
four-letter words, Bruce brought to culmination the mode of humor that assaulted its audience's own sensitivities and sensibili-
ties, particularly in the areas of sex and theology. (Throughout
his entire career, Bruce as a humorist was consistently apoliti-
cal.) His boldness was especially dramatic, because he dared to
take his brand of humor out of the locker room into the popular
market, with nightclub appearances, records, and concerts—not
to mention highly publicized court trials.

Quite possibly the medium that Bruce assaulted was first
breached with Elliot White Springs' shocking advertisements for
Springmaid sheets in the early 1950's. Voices rose in complaint
when an advertisement showed an exhausted Indian brave col-
lapsed on a sheet, while a voluptuous maiden walked away, with
a seductive look on her face. The caption: "A Buck Well Spent on
a Springmaid Sheet." (Springs discussed his campaign and the
outraged response in his 1954 book, *Clothes Make the Man*.)
Similar innuendoes dotted other advertising in radio, and television. Dick and Tom Smothers had a famous television routine, in
which Tommy tells about falling into a chocolate vat at a candy
factory and yelling "Fire, Fire" because nobody would come rescue him if he hollered "Chocolate, Chocolate!" It was in fact a
cleaned-up version of a yarn in George Milburn's 1936 novel
Catalogue, in which a character who plummets into a septic tank
at night yells "Fire, Fire" because no one would pay any attention if he yelled, "Shit, Shit."

Bruce, however, did not stop with smutty insinuations. His
"bits" on "Tits and Ass," his poem "To Come," and his casual
speech were peppered with four-letter words of erotic and scatological nature. He rejoiced in one of his routines because

Lenny Bruce, drawing by Jay Lynch. (© *Douglas Communications Corp.*)

Webster's Third Unabridged—not *the Dictionary of American Slang*, but I mean the public school dictionary—has the word "bullshit" in it, in your public school. And it says, "bullshit: nonsense." It has p-r-i-c-k in it. It says, "a disagreeable person." It has "shit" in it—"inferior." It has "pissed off"—"angry."

He could have taken some of the credit for those entries as a result of his sustained assault on double standards and hypocrisy.

In the last stages of his career, Bruce became increasingly shrill, uncomic, and obsessed with the legal ramifications of his many arrests (especially in such late appearances as "The Berkeley Concert"). But at his best, he evoked laughter that was novel if not unprecedented because of its mixture of shock and embarrassment. Familiar as we are today with the kinds of comedy Bruce pioneered, we may tend to forget both the primal source for it and also the pain and harassment needed to make it a part of our humorous legacy.

Afterword

> *We turn . . . to statistical proba-*
> *bilities for hope. With as many human beings alive now as have ever*
> *lived on earth before, we trust in resurgence. Genius may be exercising*
> *itself in nuclear physics and biochemistry, but there will be enough*
> *left over for the arts, including comedy. Men of comic intelligence and*
> *imagination will find their way back to the motives and resources.*
> *. . . The talented and inspired are all about us, and will arrive at first*
> *principles either on the basis of present-day critical imperatives or,*
> *which is more likely, on their own. They will make decline or fall*
> *temporary.*
> *They always have.*
>
> —Jesse Bier, 1968.

EARLY IN THIS STUDY, WE glanced at Mrs. Trollope's dismal survey of humor—or rather, non-humor—in the doleful America of 1831. People, she said, stayed away from comedies in droves; humorous magazines quickly flopped; everybody was a sourpuss; the reader who tried to find "keenly cutting satire" anywhere just couldn't: "Jonathan is a very dull boy . . . compared with Americans, we [English] are whirligigs and tetotums. . . ."

In 1839, updating a new edition of her book, the English lady wrote a footnote that took back her gripe. This rebuke, she said, "must never be repeated" because at last she had seen some pieces that "prove, much beyond . . . contradiction, that humour, rich and original, does exist in the United States, and . . . when such a treat is given them, the people know how to enjoy it." What fetched her were some writers of Yankee humor. One amusing fellow was facetious about the Bank of the United States, "and if American citizens are gay spirited enough to enjoy wit that expends itself on such a grave subject, . . . it is easy to predict, that, in the progress of time . . . they will chuckle at, and enjoy wit, otherwise employed."

The sequence that came this early has been repeated many

times. American humor has been autopsied, only to hop spryly from its deathbed blowing a raspberry salute. E. C. Stedman in 1873 forecast an immediate funeral; Thurber did the same in 1962, Melvin Maddocks in 1970. In 1972, Clifton Fadiman chanted his little dirge: "It's getting harder and harder to be funny in the America of the seventies. Art Buchwald and a few others still command the secret, but the whole drift of things is clearly not on their side."

A look back often shows that viewers-with-alarm failed to glimpse one of three developments: Some old-style humorists making tardy entrances; our phoenix-like comedy rising from the ashes in a brand-new—more often, a semi-new—guise; or as a third possibility, that both these reincarnations were taking place at the same time.

Mrs. Trollope, we now can see, in 1831 missed a host of historic loomings. She was quite unaware that astonishing tales which funereal-phizzed natives told her were playful lies of a sort soon to be called "typical American humor." Mike Fink's fame was spreading. Congressman David Crockett had made a big stir in Washington, and yarns about Davy splattered newspapers everywhere. James K. Paulding's comedy, *The Lion of the West*, which (with an assist by John Wesley Jarvis) caricatured the man from the canebrakes, had been revised and was ready for popularity that would last for decades. Seba Smith was publishing letters from his Yankee bumpkin Jack Downing in his little Portland, Maine, newspaper, and newspapers elsewhere were picking them up. The first of a long line—*The American Comic Almanac for 1831*—containing humor from several sections, was being pored over daily by families in thousands of homes. What the world would call distinctively American humor was being born, and sharp-eyed Mrs. Trollope saw no sign of the lying in.

In 1873, the year of Stedman's elegy, both Phunny Phellows and local colorists were taking charge of the humor production line. (Stedman was too much of a Paleface to appreciate either group.) In the 1960's and 1970's, our comic creations were turning black; and black humor wasn't everybody's bottle of ink.

Though we have not happened to run across one, we are willing to bet that shortly before 1915, some pundit was saying confidently that horse-sensible humor of the sort supplied by Poor Richard, Hosea Biglow, Major Jones, Josh Billings, Mark Twain, and hosts of others had been finally played out. But 1915 was the year when the most popular of all such comic dispensers of gumption rose to fame. He would be America's best known humorist for the next two decades.

This was an Oklahoma-born ex-cowboy, ex-Wild-West-show-lariat-twirler and ex-vaudeville-performer: Will Rogers. In 1915, Will became a star in Florenz Ziegfield's *Midnight Frolic* by chewing gum, performing rope-tricks, and pausing now and then to drawl amusing comments on current events.

Anyone who had met up with the breed would soon see that, though he had unique charms, Rogers had all the brand marks. His outfit—battered broadbrim hat, bandana scarf, shirtsleeves and chaps—was that of a proletarian. "Grammar and I get along like a Russian and a bathtub," he boasted; and his store of words and frequently flawed spelling helped prove that he hadn't been besmirched by too much education. "Maybe ain't ain't so correct," he allowed, then he went on to state the time-hallowed American belief that book learning got you nowhere: "But I notice that lots of folks who ain't usin' ain't ain't eatin'." Will knew why he himself was doing better: "I've been eating pretty regular, and the reason I have been is because I stayed an old country boy." Will had chummy chats with Presidents reminiscent of those that old country boys Jack Downing and Artemus Ward said they had.

But because there was enough that was new about Will to keep him from seeming too old-hat, in time he was getting laughs from more of his countrymen than any humorist before him, including Mark Twain, had reached. He came from a recent frontier that Western novels, plays, and movies had made glamorous: Will was the first great *cowboy* comedian to come along. That wasn't all he had going for him. More Americans than ever were there to be reached—and more media could reach them—than ever. Rogers got into all the acts that were available. He did his stuff on Broadway, not only in the *Frolics* but also in the *Follies*. He was booked into vaudeville circuits, movie-palace stage shows, and lecture halls. He was in movies—first silents, when his cracks were captions between segments, then talkies. The airwaves carried his shrewd comments. He wrote books, magazine articles and columns, the last for newspapers with forty million readers. News stories and newsreels told how in the Era of Beautiful Nonsense he turned Downing's and Ward's fancied encounters into actualities; he had real-life kidding sessions with Calvin Coolidge and his wife. He appeared by invitation before national conventions. So Rogers initiated impudent familiarities with White House denizens and leading politicians that professional wits would continue into the 1970's.

When Rogers died in a plane crash in August, 1935, public mourning outdid any in the past for an American humorist. Newspapers filled pages with Rogers's life story; a national radio hookup broadcast a memorial service; and in the Senate, Majority Leader Robinson rose to say: "Probably the most widely known citizen in the United States and certainly the best beloved met his death some hours ago in a lonely and faraway place."

In their elegies for Rogers, editorial writers mentioned their regret that with his passing, something important for two centuries had ended—a procession of immensely popular laugh-provoking philosophers who wore leather aprons, homespun, buckskin, or shirtsleeves. As usual, the funeral notices were premature. For in 1958, another unofficial commentator-at-large brought out an amusing book, *Only in America*, and alert journalists at once welcomed its author, Harry Golden, to the long parade.

Editorialists cited the humorist's scheme to end segregation just by taking the seats out of all Southern classrooms. ("One of the best solutions to the problem we have heard yet."—Greenville, N.C., *Daily Register* and twelve other newspapers.) Scores of reviewers liked this or his explanation that Rome fell because wives were left at home with "Senators and 4-Fs." They saw Golden as a man who mingled ghetto wisdom and Yankee or Southern horse sense.

We don't use the phrase "scores of reviewers" irresponsibly here. In 1961, Theodore Solotaroff read hundreds of pieces about Golden, his first book and other Golden books, and then wrote a valuable survey, "Harry Golden and the American Audience." We are in Solotaroff's debt for much that follows.

Golden, born in the ghetto and reared and educated in New

York City, did well enough in business there to be able to move to Charlotte, N.C., and at age forty launch his own newspaper. *The Carolina Israelite*, which he published and mostly wrote, because of its ethnic quality, its place of origin, and its shrewd and witty attacks on prejudice, parochialism, and conservatism, attracted readers far away from North Carolina. *Only in America*, a collection of *Israelite* skits, sketches, and editorials, sold 250,000 hardback copies and 1,750,000 paperback copies. Golden capitalized on its success by publishing ten other books in the next seven years. He was featured on all the television talk shows. Solotaroff's scrutiny of reviews convinced him that this "Jewish Will Rogers," as Golden was called again and again, succeeded, for one thing, because he followed two traditions that had long been popular—that of the group exploiting "the idiom and folkways of the Yankee farmer, the Southwest hunter or adventurer, the Far Western prospector and gambler," and that of the group speaking in dialect for urban European immigrants—humorists who relied "upon the ethnic rather than regional coloring, . . . using the immunity of the clown to make some telling hits on [America's] political, social, or moral follies."

Golden had additional appeals, though, that reviewers kept mentioning. "I use Jews as examples," Golden explained, "and rely upon Gentiles to get the point." "The Jewish slant," Solotaroff noticed, "is decidedly in vogue." Solotaroff doesn't say why, but we suggest that the nation's raft of superb Jewish writers and the heroic history of spunky little Israel had created much good will. Reviewers also went for Golden's fond pictures of life during his boyhood, distinguishable, says Solotaroff, "from the suburban 'picture-window ghettos' of today . . . not so much [by] the noise, the grinding penury, the wear and tear on the nerves, but rather [by] the vividness, energy, aspiration, discipline, and finally the warmth of its life—that is, precisely those qualities which are said to be declining in the modern middle-class family and suburb." A final appeal often mentioned: "Golden's anecdotes are crammed with little details of what the Lower-East-Side Jews ate and slept on and took for medicine, of how they courted, voted, and shopped," satisfying "both Jewish nostalgia and Gentile curiosity." Ethnic individuality such as this, as both the humorist and his admirers kept saying, was all too clearly on the wane. The comment, of course, suggests that with the appeal of his good old gumption, Golden combined an attractiveness much like that of those specialists in nostalgia, the post-Civil War local colorists.

Despite the fact that in 1961 Golden's third book, *Enjoy! Enjoy!* was greeted with one review that read, "Enough! Enough!," he continued to be popular well into the 1960's. During the 1970's another pair of horse-sensible wits—one of them posthumously—became popular. Again, current developments helped. Activists' demonstrations against politicians and policies, plus reporters' exposés of scandals, led to widespread disillusionment with politicians unmatched since the badly tarnished Gilded Age. There was a longing for the rediscovery of at least some public figures who weren't splattered. Televised senatorial hearings on Watergate were avidly watched for hours by millions. A white-haired, wrinkled North Carolina Senator, Sam Ervin, full of years, chaired the hearings. Watchers decided that he had probity such as they yearned for and—as an extra dividend—charm and wit. Every so often he drawled a homely aphorism, a thoroughly countrified phrase, or a well-put wry comment of an old-fashioned sort that made viewers chuckle. Ervin became the hero of the hour, and a book of his hastily collected Deep Southern anecdotes and quidities piled up sales.

Also in the 1970's, a pair of books about the late Harry Truman were warmly appreciated—Margaret Truman's biography, quoting pages of frank letters and salty talk, and Merle Miller's *Plain Speaking*—transcriptions of taped commentaries, often picturesque, profane, and even feistier. The books, reviewed with cheers, hit lists of bestsellers. While many passages were not witty, those that were had the ring and the appeal of Missouri cornfield badinage: "Haven't had a crisis for two weeks. Looks like the country is going to hell or Republican." Though Will Rogers would have used a euphuism instead of "hell," the cowboy might have said very much the same thing to his idolators half a century earlier.

These resurrections and others make it safe to guess that some types of American humor that have been elegized are merely estivating. When for some reason audiences have come to want them again, if they are adapted in timely ways, they will be produced and applauded.

Now put a few dates side by side. Will Rogers's great years

were the 1920's. But that was the decade when *The New Yorker* came into the world, spoiling to displace the hick humor of the farm and the frontier. Instead of vamoosing, until the middle of the next decade Will kept winning more and more success.

It was between 1958 and the mid-1960's that Harry Golden made a hit by giving two-and-a-half cheers for what could happen *Only in America*. But looking back in 1968 at what was Golden's triumphant period, Jesse Bier saw black and sick humor reaching a climax: "In the scatological and obscene blasphemy of the most notorious night-club comedian of the moment, Lenny Bruce, . . . fierce contempt for the sacred and simple extreme hypocrisies of American life turned inevitably shrill and extreme [in] radical hysteric humor that screams instead of laughs. . . ." Golden's great decade was also that of *Catch-22* and *One Flew Over the Cuckoo's Nest*. And the same decade cast abroad the corn of pro-Establishment Senator Ervin and Harry Truman.

These concatenations illustrate something that a student of our humor sees happening time after time. Irreverent and irresponsible humorists, even less accommodating than other creative men and women, do not decamp when any fool can plainly see that in the interest of historical neatness they should absquatulate at once. As long as they get laughs, they don't at all mind being anachronisms.

As recently as 1976, two television comics demonstrated this fact when they appeared in nationally broadcast spectaculars that gave reprises of their careers—Lucille Ball and Bob Hope. Hope wrote (or at least signed) an article, "A Funny Thing about Comedy," and Ball gave Karl Fleming a long interview. Both confidently came up with formulas for comedy.

Hope's ingredients were "material, mellowed and ripened over the years," plus tried-and-true devices—facial expressions, pauses timed "to the tenth of a second," "speed of delivery," "topicality," and an endless puncturing of "the big guy's dignity." "The basics," he summarized, "are still here." Ball's recipe included carefully elaborated scripts, "close attention to detail," and "stories and characters that merely exaggerate the fantasies, foibles and troubles of the ordinary middle-class harried American housewife . . . great identification with millions of people who . . . can tell that the boss's hat is being knocked off. . . . We just took ordinary situations and exaggerated them." Each of these formulas is as antiquated as our newly naturalized humor was—or, in fact, as the non-naturalized Old World humor was—in the far-off past. Both of these "old-fashioned" comics were quite firm about two kinds of funmaking that they would shun—the kind downgrading races and the kind degrading sex.

Ball said she saw nothing funny about the series "All in the Family," in which the chief clown constantly talked about his violent racial antipathies: "I object to the show's bringing certain words—the racial epithets—back into our vocabulary. . . . I think any kind of racial put-down is wrong." Hope refused to raise from the dead ethnic comedy which he thought had passed away with vaudeville—"Polish jokes, Irish jokes, jokes about blacks, Indians, Jews."

Ball had no kind words for comic series that played up "violence and rolling-around-in-the-bed sex": "I don't understand what 'Mary Hartman' is about, or why. A kid being electrocuted in the bathtub is supposed to be comedy? . . . Their subject matter is very questionable, not funny. Monotonous, perhaps." The sex jokes that Hope noticed were "in" didn't appeal to him. "To my mind, it's very difficult to find a really good sex joke because the closer you get to the subject, the tougher it is not to be raunchy. I like to keep my distance. . . . the deliberate use of four-letter words to get laughs is a cop-out."

If long, triumphant careers gave anyone the right to say what was funny and what wasn't, this pair were set. Both had starred in stage shows and movies, and both had done well on radio and on television (twenty-five years for Ball, twenty-seven for Hope). Although the Ball anniversary show was two hours long and the Hope show four, each in its prime-time slot drew more watchers than any competing show. On and on into the 1970's, Ball situation comedy segments taped over the years were rerun, watched by three generations, and given top ratings. Hope began each of his performances with a barrage of horse-sensible witticisms about the day's events, then enacted a series of sketches which showed his boasts that he was a sex pot, an athlete or a hero were bluffs. Thanks to these old formulas, Hope regularly filled college auditoriums, convention halls, army camp bleachers, and county and state fair grandstands. And each time he did a televised special—four or more a year—he hogged the watching audience. So well into the 1970's, "old-fashioned" comedy, as exemplified by this aging pair, was sensationally successful.

But "All in the Family" and "Mary Hartman, Mary Hartman," the television series that Ball wouldn't have any truck with, one playing up extreme racism and the other multifarious sex, were also getting top ratings. Ethnic materials were coining fortunes for standup comedians—to name a few of many, Polish Bobby Vinton, Latino Freddy Prinze, Jewish Woody Allen, Myron Cohen, Sam Levinson and Don Rickles, black Bill Cosby, Red Foxx, Dick Gregory, Richard Pryor, and Jimmy Walker. And as Hope acknowledged, though he couldn't get laughs with explicit sexual jokes, japes about scatology, voyeurism, impotence, rape, fornication, seduction, exhibitionism, and adultery by others or even dramatized were very big. Novels, short stories, jokebooks, stage plays, musicals, records, and television series were battening on both kinds of comedy.

In other words, at one and the same time, quite antithetical types of fun were flourishing in the United States. Some omnivorous consumers, perhaps, relished any kind of funmaking put before them. But others—including some who hated Ball and Hope and some who doted on them—were more choosy. While we have conducted no poll, we are willing to wager that there are several audiences, each big enough to furnish great bodies of customers for a favorite type of fun. And any country which can simultaneously cherish such clashing ways of getting laughs isn't likely to exhaust all its comic veins.

Another thing: There is no blinking the fact that two American national resources are pretty sure to keep on nourishing our humor.

One is our vibrant, innovative, and expressive language. In his posthumously published *Arts of Arthur and His Knights*, the late John Steinbeck eloquently characterized this rich possession:

This is a highly complicated and hugely communicative language . . . a new thing under the sun. . . . The frames have grown out of ourselves but have used everything that was there before. But most of all it has an ease and flow and a tone and a rhythm which is unique in the world. There is no question where it comes from, its references, its inventions, its overtones grew out of this continent and out of our twenty generations here. It is English basically but manured and seeded with Negro, Indian, Italian, Spanish, Yiddish, German, but so mixed and fermented that something whole has emerged.

Constantly enlivened by oral stories and exchanges, and endlessly enriched by talk-like inventions of imaginative folk journalists, our humor has a good chance to be sustained in the future by our wonderful native language.

A second favorable circumstance was noticed by H. L. Mencken in 1922, when that fervent patriot was gloating about this country's unending charm for anyone with "my congenital weakness for comedy of the grosser varieties":

The United States . . . avoids diligently all the kinds of clowning which tire me most quickly . . . and lays chief stress upon the kinds which delight me unceasingly—for example, the ribald combats of demagogues, the exquisitely ingenious operations of master rogues, the pursuit of witches and heretics, the desperate struggles of inferior men to claw their way into Heaven. We have clowns in constant practice among us who are as far above the clowns of any other great state as [the heavyweight champion of the world] is above a paralytic—and not a few dozen or score of them, but whole droves and herds. Human enterprises . . . are here lifted to such vast heights of buffoonery that contemplating them strains the midriff almost to breaking. . . . Here the buffoonery never stops.

With such an inexhaustible cornucopia of funny men (and nearly as many funny women) just waiting to be celebrated and laughed at, how can American humor ever fade away?

References

As a rule, when primary and secondary sources are clearly indicated in the text, they aren't listed again here. Numerals refer to chapters, e.g., "1" to "1. The Lies of the Land."

PAGES 3-16

1. The chief collection of early accounts of visits to America is Richard Hakluyt, *The Principall Navigations, Voiages, Traffiques and Discoveries of the English Nation,* 12 vols. (Glasgow, 1903–1905). Jane Louise Mesick, *The English Traveler in America, 1785–1835* (New York, 1922) has a good bibliography and a useful discussion of later works. Also useful: Howard Mumford Jones, *O Strange New World* (New York, 1965); James R. Masters on *Tall Tales of Arkansas* (Boston, 1943); Percy G. Adams, *Travellers and Travel Liars* (Berkeley, 1962); *The Traveller's Eye,* ed. Dorothy Carrington (New York, 1947). An illuminating two-part article is James R. Masterson, "Travelers' Tales of Colonial Natural History," *Journal of American Folklore,* 59 (1946), 51–67, 174–188.

Supplementing the discussion in Masterson's book of ferocious Westerners are a number of passages in Mody Boatright, *Folk Laughter on the American Frontier* (New York, 1949). The early libels mentioned are in *Diedrich Knickerbocker's A History of New York* (1809), Book IV, ch. iv, and James K. Paulding, *John Bull and Brother Jonathan* (1812, 1833), ch. xviii.

Martin Roth, *Comedy in America: The Lost World of Washington Irving* (Port Washington, 1976), which appeared after this section was written, has fine material on American versions of Cockaigne.

2-4. William Carew Hazlitt, "Introduction" to *The New London Jest Book,* an anthology of ancient jokes (London, 1871), briefly and informally gives the history of the genre. F. P. Wilson, "The English Jestbooks of the Sixteenth and Early Seventeenth Centuries," *Huntington Library Quarterly,* 2 (1939), 119–158, is more detailed and is well documented. John Wardroper, "Introduction," "Notes," and "Appendix" in *Jest Upon Jest* (London, 1970), subtitled "A Selection from the Jestbooks and Collections of Merry Tales published from the Reign of Richard III to George III," are invaluable. A number of facsimiles and reprints of *Joe Miller's Jests* (1739) and *Baron Münchausen's Narrative* (1786) have been published.

Harry B. Weiss, *A Brief History of American Jest Books* (New York, 1943), furnishes much information about such compilations. James R. Masterson, *Tall Tales of Arkansas* (Boston, 1943), details the history of *On a Slow Train through Arkansaw* and contains useful lore about perennial jokes. Richard M. Dorson, *Jonathan Draws the*

Long Bow (Cambridge, 1946), contains many Yankee anecdotes. Daniel Hoffman, *Form and Fable in American Fiction* (New York, 1961), and Tristram Potter Coffin, *Uncertain Glory* (Detroit, 1971), add lore about Yankee peddlers, and the former book discusses confidence men. P. T. Barnum, *The Humbugs of the World: An Account of Humbugs, Delusions, Impositions, Quackeries, Deceit and Deceivers Generally, in All Ages* (New York, 1966), is a treatise, if not by a scholar, by an expert. Susan Kuhlman, *Knave, Fool, and Genius* (Chapel Hill, 1973), concerns the confidence man in nineteenth-century American fiction.

The travel books by Frances Trollope and Charles Dickens were, respectively, *Domestic Manners of the Americans* (1832, 1839) and *American Notes for General Circulation* (1842). Vance Randolph's version of the story about the discriminating drinkers is in *Sticks in the Knapsack* (New York, 1858); notes supply details about other versions. Jan Harold Brunvand's statements about what happened to anecdotes in America are in his *The Study of American Folklore* (New York, 1968).

The Yankee author who praised "*over*-heard" stories was John Neal, in "Story-Telling," *New-England Magazine*, 8 (1835), 9. Andrew Lang's remarks about our story-swapping and its influence occur in "Western Drolls," *Lost Leaders* (New York, 1889), pp. 186-87. The traveler who was surprised by the coachman's easy ways was John Lambert; his book was *Travels Through Canada and the United States . . . 1806, 1807 and 1808* (3d. ed., London, 1816). Bret Harte's "The Rise of the 'Short Story' " appeared in *Cornhill*, n.s. 7 (1899), 3; Joel Chandler Harris praised oral humor in "Humor in America," *American Wit and Humor* (New York, 1909), I, xxii-xxiii. Statements about three common plot patterns in oral narratives are documented in Walter Blair, " 'A Man's Voice Speaking'," *Veins of Humor*, Harvard English Series 3 (Cambridge, 1972), pp. 197-99.

Daniel J. Boorstin, *The Americans: The Colonial Experience* (New York, 1958), and *The National Experience* (New York, 1965), discusses the diffusion of literacy, journalism, and subliterature: his bibliography is extensive. Theodore Hornberger, *American Literature: a Brief History* (Glenview, 1974), pp. 23-4, 36-7, 62 provides facts about colonial publications. Ben C. Clough's praise for the imagination of journalists is in the "Introduction," *The American Imagination at Work* (New York, 1947). H. L. Mencken credits professional writers for creative tall talk in *The American Language*, abridged by R. McDavid (New York, 1963), p. 149. The paragraph by Uncle Josh, the first version of which appeared in 1839, is quoted from Seba Smith, *My Thirty Years Out of the Senate* (New York, 1859).

John Bristed deplores the extent of Americans' national vanity in *The Resources of the United States of America* (New York, 1818), pp. 460-61. Clarence Gohdes cites statements that American humor and exaggeration are synonymous in *American Literature in Nineteenth-*

Century England (Carbondale, 1963); Max Eastman cites the same belief in *The Enjoyment of Laughter* (New York, 1936). Constance Rourke generalizes about American humor in the course of an exchange with DeLancey Ferguson, *American Scholar*, 4 (1935), 41-9, 249-54, 380-82. Mary Silverstein called our attention to the tall tale in the midst of many humorless items in *American Railroad Journal*, 26 (August 6, 1853), 509.

5-7. Though bowdlerized and incomplete, *The Writings of Benjamin Franklin*, ed. Albert H. Smyth, 10 vols. (New York and London, 1905-1907), was long the best available edition. *The Papers of Benjamin Franklin*, ed. Leonard W. Labaree and others (New Haven, 1959-   ), when completed, will supplant it. *Benjamin Franklin's Letters to the Press, 1758-1775*, ed. Verner W. Crane (Chapel Hill, 1950), is invaluable for a vital period. Carl Van Doren, *Benjamin Franklin* (New York, 1938), continues to be an outstanding biography.

Two former students became highly instructive teachers of the former teacher who wrote this chapter—Richard E. Amacher, "Introduction" to *Franklin's Wit and Folly*, which he edited (New Brunswick, 1953), and *Benjamin Franklin* (New York, 1962); Larzer Ziff, "Introduction" to *Selected Writings of Franklin* (New York, 1959) and *Puritanism in America* (New York, 1973). Also very useful were Lewis Leary's chapter on Franklin in *The Comic Imagination in American Literature* (New York, 1973) and an expanded version which he made available before it appeared in book form. Professor Amacher kindly gave the chapter a careful reading and the author helpful suggestions.

Other useful secondary studies, in order of their writing included: John Adams, *Works*, ed. C. F. Adams (Boston, 1850-1856), I, 649-64; IX, 485-86: C. A. Sainte-Beuve, "Benjamin Franklin," in *Portraits of the Eighteenth Century*, tr. Katharine P. Wormeley (New York, 1964), pp. 311-75; Moses Coit Tyler, *A History of American Literature During the Colonial Time* (New York, 1890) and *The Literary History of the American Revolution* (New York, 1941); Frank Luther Mott and Chester I. Jorgenson, "Introduction" and "Notes" to *Benjamin Franklin Representative Selections* (Cincinnati, 1936); John F. Ross, "The Character of Poor Richard: Its Sources and Alteration," *PMLA*, 55 (1940), 785-94; George F. Horner, "Franklin's Dogood Papers Re-examined," *Stud. in Phil.*, 37 (1940), 501-23; Richard D. Miles, "The American Image of Benjamin Franklin," *Amer. Quar.*, 9 (1957), 118-35; Bruce I. Granger, *Benjamin Franklin, An American Man of Letters* (Ithaca, 1964).

Aristotle, *Nichomachean Ethics* 1108a 22; Lane Cooper, *An Aristotelian Theory of Comedy* (New York, 1923); Max Eastman, *The Enjoyment of Laughter* (New York, 1936); and Northrup Frye, *Anatomy of Criticism* (Princeton, 1957) discuss the *eiron* authoritatively.

8. On Defoe, a perceptive study is James Sutherland, *Daniel Defoe*

a Critical Study (Cambridge, 1971). For Defoe and Swift, essays by the two authors of the following were valuable: Maximillian E. Novak and Herbert J. Davis, *The Uses of Irony* (Los Angeles, 1966). These writings on Swift were very helpful: James Sutherland, "Forms and Methods in Swift's Satire," in *Jonathan Swift: A Dublin Tercentenary Tribute* (Oxford, 1967), pp. 61-77; Edward W. Rosenheim, Jr., *Swift and the Satirist's Art* (Chicago, 1963), and Wayne Booth's discussion of "A Modest Proposal" in *The Rhetoric of Irony* (Chicago, 1974).

9. The three monologists mentioned in the second paragraph of Chapter 9 were Mathews, Hackett and Hill; the burlesque travel book was Paulding's *John Bull in America;* the sketches were Longstreet's "Little Ben" stories; the plays were Peake's *Jonathan Doubikins* (revised as *Jonathan in England*), the anonymous *Jonathan in New York,* Colman's *Sylvester Daggerwood* (as revised), Moncrieff's *M. Mallet,* Dunlap's *A Trip to Niagara,* and Paulding's *Lion of the West* (revised as *The Kentuckian* and *A Trip to New York*).

Harold E. Dickson, *John Wesley Jarvis, American Painter* (New York, 1949), is the best biography. Dickson's "A Note on Charles Mathews's Use of American Humor," *American Literature,* 12 (March, 1940), 78-83, adds useful information about Jarvis, as do Albert H. Marckwardt, "The Chronology and Personnel of the Bread and Cheese Club," *American Literature,* 6 (1935), 389-399; John Neal, "Speculations of a Traveller," *Blackwood's Magazine,* 16 (1824), 91-93; "American Writers, Part 2," *Blackwood's,* 16 (1824), 418; "Sketches of American Character . . . Mr. Mathews' Trip to America," *European Magazine,* n.s. 1 (1826), 179-87; and Benjamin Lease, *That Wild Fellow John Neal* (Chicago, 1972). Dunlap's *History of the Rise and Progress of the Arts of Design in the United States* (New York, 1834), II, 72-96, treats Jarvis at length, tries to retell some of his stories, and confesses that he has failed. Audubon's article about Jarvis, "The Original Painter," was published in *Birds of America* (Edinburgh, 1831-1839).

Mrs. Mathews, *Memoirs of Charles Mathews, Comedian* (London, 1839), is a four-volume work about Mathews's life, his performances, and comments on them by contemporaries. There are two rather full summaries of "A Trip to America," including dialogue and song texts—*Mathews in America* and *Sketches of Mr. Mathews's Celebrated Trip to America.* Francis Hodge, *Yankee Theatre* (Austin, 1964), provides fine accounts of the careers of Mathews, Hackett, and Hill. The same author's "Charles Mathews Reports on America," *Quarterly Journal of American Speech,* 36 (1950), 492-99, covers the actor's United States tour. Walter Blair, "Charles Mathews and His 'Trip to America,'" *Prospects,* ed. Jack Salzman (New York, 1976), II, 1-23, deals with the sources of "A Trip" and Mathews's influences on American humor.

Only fragments of James K. Paulding, *The Lion of the West,* and its revised versions were available to scholars until a copy of the third version was discovered in the British Museum and published as *The Lion of the West, Retitled The Kentuckian, or A Trip to New York,* ed. James N. Tidwell (Stanford, 1954). Joseph J. Arpad wrote about it in "John Wesley Jarvis, James Kirke Paulding, and Colonel Nimrod Wildfire," *New York Folklore Quarterly,* 21 (1965), 92-106, and in "The Fight Story: Quotation and Originality in Native American Humor," *Journal of the Folklore Institute,* 10 (1973), 141-72. John Q. Anderson, "Some Migratory Anecdotes in American Folk Humor," *Mississippi Quarterly,* 25 (1972), traces "the hat-in-the-mud anecdote" during a period of a hundred and sixty years, "moving back and forth between oral tradition and print"; he finds tellings in 1797, 1820, 1830, 1833, 1850, 1856, 1879, 1903, 1910, 1943, 1949, and 1951.

10-13. Alphonse Wetmore, *The Pedlar,* first published in St. Louis in 1821, has been reproduced in facsimile, ed. S. C. Osborn (Lexington, 1955.) *Half Horse Half Alligator: The Growth of the Mike Fink Legend,* ed. Walter Blair and F. J. Meine (Chicago, 1956), contains a lengthy bibliography of treatments of Mike Fink, texts of most of the original printed stories about him, and an Introduction that discusses the historical Fink and the narratives about him. Passages about Mike and snatches of dialogue that we have quoted here will be found in this book.

Books published during David Crockett's lifetime that dealt more or less authoritatively with his biography (usually less) include, notably: *The Life and Adventures of Colonel Crockett of West Tennessee* (Cincinnati, 1833), also published as *Sketches and Eccentricities of Colonel David Crockett,* probably written by Mathew St. Clair Clarke; *A Narrative of the Life of David Crockett* (Philadelphia, 1834), an "autobiography" written with assistance, probably that of Thomas Chilton; and a hack job to which the Tennesseean contributed, *An Account of Colonel Crockett's Tour to the North and Down East* (Philadelphia, 1835). Soon after Crockett's death, a book purporting to make available the hero's diary appeared—*Col. Crockett's Exploits and Adventures in Texas* (1836)—actually the work of Richard Penn Smith. The best modern biography is James Atkins Shackford, *David Crockett, the Man and the Legend* (Chapel Hill, 1956). Walter Blair, "Six Davy Crocketts," *Southwest Review,* 25 (1940), 443-62, reprinted as a chapter in *Horse Sense in American Humor* (Chicago, 1942), pp. 24-50, discusses the varied images of the man and the reasons for their variety. Walter Blair, *Davy Crockett—Frontier Hero* (New York, 1955), distinguishes aspects that are indicated in the subtitle: "The Truth as He Told It—The Legend as Friends Built It."

For discussion of the comic Davy, contemporary and posthumous newspaper items of the 1830's and the Crockett almanacs were read. Constance Rourke, *Davy Crockett* (New York, 1934), gives a list of these. Anecdotal matter in *The Crockett Almanacks Nashville Series*

1835-1838 was edited by F. J. Meine (Chicago, 1955), and a selection of stories from these and later issues, by anonymous journalists, was compiled by Richard M. Dorson in *Davy Crockett, American Comic Legend* (New York, 1939).

Dorson's article, "Mose the Far-Famed and World-Renowned," *American Literature,* 15 (1943), 288-300, provides a detailed account of fictional, dramatic, and journalistic writings about Mose and a good bibliography.

Aristotle's definition of the *alazon* is in *Nichomachean Ethics,* 1127^a, 21-25; 1127^b, 9-20; and 1108^a, 23-24. See also *Tractatus Coisilinianus,* F. M. Cornford, *The Origin of Attic Comedy* (London, 1914), pp. 137-38; Max Eastman, *The Enjoyment of Laughter* (New York, 1936), pp. 192-94; Northrup Frye, *Anatomy of Criticism* (Princeton, 1957), pp. 39, 172, 176, 365.

The long footnote cites works in which the braggart soldier was a character. Daniel C. Boughner, *The Braggart in Renaissance Comedy* (Minneapolis, 1954), is a superb study which discusses at length Capitano Spavento. Francesco Andreini, *La Bravura del Capitano Spavento* (Venezia, 1607), contains the captain's boasts. Flamino Scala, *Scenarios of the Commedia dell' Arte,* tr. Henry F. Salerno (New York, 1967), outlines the action of fifty plays, forty-two of which involve the braggart captain. Marvin T. Herrick, *Italian Comedy in the Renaissance* (Urbana, 1960), is a valuable study.

The play by Frank Murdoch and Frank Mayo, *Davy Crockett; Or, Be Sure You're Right, Then Go Ahead,* is in the series *America's Lost Plays* (Princeton, 1942).

Professor George Kernodle of the University of Arkansas read Chapters 12 and 25, and offered detailed criticisms.

14-15. A discussion of the traditional grouping of Down East and Old Southwest humor is in Walter Blair, *Native American Humor* (New York, 1937, and San Francisco, 1960), pp. 38-101. Some contradictions between rigid stereotypes are explored by Daniel Boorstin's *The Americans: The National Experience* (New York, 1965), which labels Jack Downing "omni-partisan" (p. 322); Marquis James's *The Life of Andrew Jackson* (Indianapolis, 1938), which reports Jackson's admiration for the Downing letters (II, 641); and Louis J. Budd, "Gentlemanly Humorists of the Old South," *Southern Folklore Quarterly,* 27 (1953), which notices Longstreet's ridicule of both the Georgia gentry and the cracker (p. 233).

Norris Yates, *William T. Porter and The Spirit of the Times* (Baton Rouge, 1957), and Richard B. Hauck, "The Literary Content of the New York *Spirit of the Times,* 1831-1856" (unpublished Ph.D. dissertation, Urbana: University of Illinois, 1965), examine the non-political content of that periodical.

Lewis Leary's essay on Washington Irving in *The Comic Imagination in American Literature* (New Brunswick, 1973) is an excellent recent survey of Irving's comic material; Marvin E. Mengeling's "The Gross Humor of Irving's Diedrich Knickerbocker," *Studies in American Humor*, 1 (October 1974), 66-72, catalogues Irving's penchant for the bawdy and smutty; Martin Roth's *Comedy and America: The Lost World of Washington Irving* (Port Washington, 1976) relates Irving to European predecessors and major nineteenth-century American successors.

16-17. Brom Weber's collection, *An Anthology of American Humor* (New York, 1962) contains an admirable and easily accessible sample of colonial humor; a valuable study that appeared too late to serve us is M. B. Stowell, *Early American Almanacs* (New York, 1977). George Lyman Kittredge's *The Old Farmer and His Almanack* (Boston, 1904) remains a basic study. Emerson's essay "The Comic" first appeared in book form in *Letters and Social Aims* in 1875. "Book One, The Knickerbocker Set" in Perry Miller's *The Raven and the Whale* (New York, 1956) is a concise history of that journal.

Richard M. Dorson's *Jonathan Draws the Longbow* (Cambridge, 1946) looks at versions of the New Englander as an atypical tall-tale-teller; and Cecil D. Eby's chapter on Yankee humor in *The Comic Imagination in American Literature* is a helpful summary.

Allen Walker Read reprints and analyzes George W. Arnold's Joe Strickland letters in "The World of Joe Strickland," *Journal of American Folklore*, 76 (1963), 277-308. Jack Downing gets an entire chapter in Walter Blair, *Horse Sense in American Humor* (Chicago, 1942), pp. 51-76, as does Major Joseph Jones (pp. 107-22).

18-19. Although we've tried to avoid purely geographical limitations, the subversive character in American humor coincides impressively with the humor of the Old Southwest. Franklin Meine's *Tall Tales of the Southwest*, Walter Blair's *Native American Humor*, and Hennig Cohen and William Dillingham's *Humor of the Old Southwest* are three anthologies of basic materials. An enormous number of writers in addition to the ones mentioned in this section were members or fellow-travelers of the school, and the most recent bibliography of the swelling scholarship about them is the checklist by Charles E. Davis and Martha B. Hudson in *The Frontier Humorists*, ed. M. Thomas Inge (Athens, Georgia, 1975), pp. 303-23.

20. Discussions of the relationship between Thorpe's story and Faulkner's "The Bear" include Carvel Collins, "Faulkner and Certain Southern Fiction," *College English*, 16 (November 1954), 96, and Francis Lee Utley, "Pride and Humility," in *Bear, Man and God* (New York, 1971), pp. 170-171. Early discussions of "The Big Bear" which were drawn upon include Blair, *Native American Humor*, pp. 91-95, and "The Technique of 'The Big Bear of Arkansas,' " *Southwest Review*, 28 (Summer, 1943), pp. 426-435. A fine biography, supplemented with a detailed bibliography, usefully discusses the story—Milton Rickels, *Thomas Bangs Thorpe, Humorist of the Old Southwest*

(Baton Rouge, 1962), pp. 49-62. Yates, *William T. Porter and the Spirit of the Times* subtitled "A Study of the 'Big Bear' School of Humor" and Richard Boyd Hauck's University of Illinois doctoral dissertation, "Literary Content of the New York *Spirit of the Times*" (1965), are good on the tall tale as a genre and on Thorpe's masterpiece. The latter discussion of the story (pp. 226-232) differs somewhat from the one offered here. J. A. Leo Lemay, "The Text, Tradition, and Themes of 'The Big Bear of Arkansas,'" *American Literature*, 47 (November, 1975), 321-42, contains much valuable information about the story and its background. Lemay's reading also differs from ours. Neil Schmitz, "Tall Tale, Tall Talk," *American Literature*, 48 (January, 1977), which appeared after this chapter was completed, discussed Thorpe's story most recently.

21. Sut Lovingood had his own periodical, *The Lovingood Papers*, which printed hitherto unpublished stories and scholarly articles on its subject. Milton Rickels, in *George Washington Harris* (New York, 1964) and "The Imagery of George Washington Harris," *American Literature*, 31 (1959), 173-87 offers sustained critical insights. Edmund Wilson's fainthearted comments first appeared in "Poisoned!" *The New Yorker*, 31 (May 7, 1959), 150-59. M. Thomas Inge's edition of the *Yarns*, together with the material not included in the first edition, is available in paperback.

22. For "The Last Frontier," these were useful studies: Kevin Starr, *Americans and the California Dream 1850-1915* (New York, 1973). C. Grant Loomis, "California Fertility Lore: 1848-1858," *California Folklore Quarterly*, 5 (1946), 329-33, "A Tall Tale Miscellany, 1830-1866," *Western Folklore*, 6 (1947), 28-41, and "'Tough' Californians," *Western Folklore*, 6 (1947), 108-11; J. Ross Browne, *A Peep at Washoe and Washoe Revisited* [originally published 1860-1864] (Balboa Island, 1959).

23. George R. Stewart, *John Phoenix Esquire* (New York, 1937), Derby's best biography, contains matter not included in Derby's two books, *Phoenixiana* (1855) and *The Squibob Papers* (1865). John Kendrick Bangs discussed the writer in "Introduction" to a 1903 edition of *Phoenixiana;* F. L. Pattee in *American Literatures Since 1870* (New York, 1915); Franklin D. Walker in *San Francisco's Literary Frontier* (New York, 1939; revised ed. Seattle, 1969).

24. J. Cecil Alter, *James Bridger* (Salt Lake City, 1925), is the most detailed and informative biography: it reprints Grenville Dodge's valuable *Biographical Sketch of James Bridger* (New York, 1905). Old Gabe and his stories also are treated in W. F. Raynolds, *Report on the Exploration of the Yellowstone River* (1861); Henry Inman, *The Old Sante Fe Trail* (New York, 1897); J. L. Humfreville, *Twenty Years Among Our Hostile Indians* (New York, 1903); H. M. Chittenden, *The Yellowstone Park* (Cincinnati, 1920); and Bernard DeVoto, *Across the Wide Missouri* (Boston, 1957).

Writings of William Wright and sources of information about him: Dan De Quille, *History of the Comstock* (1889); *The Washoe Giant in San Francisco*, ed. Franklin Walker (San Francisco, 1938); Richard G. Lillard, *Desert Challenge* (New York, 1942) and "Dan De Quille, Comstock Reporter and Humorist," *Pacific Historical Review*, 13 (1944), 251-59; C. Grant Loomis, "Tall Tales of Dan De Quille," *California Folklore Quarterly*, 5 (1946), 26-71; Oscar Lewis, "Introduction" to De Quille's *History of the Big Bonanza* [originally published in 1876] (New York, 1947, 1953); *Thompson and West's History of Nevada* [1881], ed. D. F. Myrick (Berkeley, 1958); *Mark Twain of the Enterprise*, ed. H. N. Smith (Berkeley, 1957); Paul Fatout, *Mark Twain in Virginia City* (Bloomington, 1964).

25. Harry Birdoff, *The World's Greatest Hit—"Uncle Tom's Cabin"* (New York, 1947), contains much information about the history of the play. Edmund Wilson, *Patriotic Gore* (New York, 1962), has a chapter on Harriet Beecher Stowe and numerous references to *Uncle Tom's Cabin*.

J. J. Arpad traces variations of "The Fight" in a recent article, *Journal of the Folklore Institute*, 10 (1973), 141-72. Mody Boatright discussed the frontier boast and its dwindling relationship to fisticuffs and mayhem in *Folk Laughter on the American Frontier* (New York, 1949). The stories about Mike Fink's defeat are gathered in *Half Horse Half Alligator*, cited as a source for Chapter 10.

26. An early general study that still is illuminating was that in F. L. Pattee, *A History of American Literature Since 1870* (New York, 1915). Claude M. Simpson, ed. *The Local Colorists* (New York, 1960) is a fine anthology with a superior introduction and a valuable selective bibliography. Harry R. Warfel and G. Harrison Orians, eds. *American Local-Color Stories* (New York, 1941), with two and a half times as many pages covers a longer period (1834-1903 compared with the period 1868-1897), and contains many more stories. R. D. Rhode's *Setting in the American Short Story of Local Color* (The Hague, 1975) is definitive.

John R. Adams, *Harriet Beecher Stowe* (New York 1963), though it undervalues Stowe's writings, provides a useful survey and a good bibliography. A well-documented biography is Forest Wilson, *Crusader in Crinoline* (Philadelphia, 1941). Alice C. Crozier, *The Novels of Harriet Beecher Stowe* (New York, 1969) is a fine critical study, but doesn't treat the author's best local color work since it is made up of short stories—*Oldtown* [or *Sam Lawson's*] *Fireside Stories*.

The definitive biography of Bret Harte is George R. Stewart, *Bret Harte: Argonaut and Exile* (Boston, 1931). Joseph B. Harrison edited *Bret Harte: Representative Selections* (New York, 1941), which has an excellent introduction, well-chosen stories and a good bibliography. A plea for the author's rehabilitation is Richard O'Connor, *Bret Harte: A Biography* (Boston, 1966).

Other useful studies of local colorists include Edmund Wilson, *Patriotic Gore* (New York, 1962); Eugene Current-Garcia, *O. Henry (William Sydney Porter)* (New York, 1965); Paul M. Cousins, *Joel Chandler Harris: A Biography* (Baton Rouge, 1968); Arlin Turner, *George W. Cable: A Biography* (Durham, 1956) and William Randel, *Edward Eggleston* (New York, 1963). Wade Hall's *The Smiling Phoenix, Southern Humor from 1865 to 1914* (Gainesville, Florida, 1965) focuses specifically on those Local Color humorists from Beneath the Line.

27. Useful general discussions of Phunny Phellow humor: Will M. Clemens, *Famous Funny Fellows* (Cleveland, 1882); Melville D. Landon, *Kings of the Platform and Pulpit* (Chicago, 1891); F. L. Pattee, "The Laughter of the West," *American Literature Since 1870* (New York, 1915), pp. 25-44; Jennette Tandy, *Crackerbox Philosophers in American Humor and Satire* (New York, 1925); Walter Blair, "Burlesques in Nineteenth-Century Humor," *American Literature*, 2 (1930), 236-47; "Popularity of Nineteenth-Century Humorists," *Ibid.*, 3 (1931), 175-94.

The most comprehensive studies of Charles Farrar Browne: Don C. Seitz, *Artemus Ward* (New York, 1919); John Q. Reed, "Civil War Humor: Artemus Ward," *Civil War History*, 2 (1956), 87-101; John C. Austin, *Artemus Ward* (New York, 1964); Edward P. Hingston, *The Genial Showman* (1870), ed. with an Introduction by Walter Muir Whitehall (Barre, Mass., 1971); Brom Weber, "The Misspellers," *The Comic Imagination in American Literature* (New Brunswick, 1973), pp. 127-38.

28. Leading studies of Henry Wheeler Shaw: F. S. Smith, *Adventures of Josh Billings* (New York, 1883); Cyril Clemens, *Josh Billings, Yankee Humorist* (Webster Groves, 1932); Donald Day, *Uncle Sam's Uncle Josh* (Boston, 1953).

Charles Henry Smith has been treated best in Annie May Christie, "Charles Henry Smith, 'Bill Arp,' " University of Chicago doctoral dissertation, 1952. The published portion of this is "Civil War Humor: Bill Arp," *Civil War History*, 2 (1956), 103-19.

The best studies of David Ross Locke: Cyril Clemens, *Petroleum Vesuvius Nasby* (Webster Groves, 1936); Joseph Jones, "P. V. Nasby Tries the Novel," *Texas Studies in English*, 30 (1951), 202-18; Joseph Jones, "Introduction" to *The Struggles of Petroleum V. Nasby* (Boston, 1963), pp. xiii-xxvi; James C. Austin, *Petroleum Vesuvius Nasby (David Ross Locke)* (New York, 1965); John M. Harrison, *The Man Who Made Nasby* (Chapel Hill, 1969).

29-31. The book by John Wardroper that is cited twice is *Jest Upon Jest* (London, 1970).

Mark Twain's "The Petrified Man," in *Mark Twain's Sketches New and Old* (Hartford, 1875), pp. 238-44, takes up the writing of the hoax and the author's reasons for expecting it to self-destruct. His summary there of the sketch, and True Williams's illustration showing the hands of the stoned creature, are quite inaccurate. For the author's comments on literary borrowings and the echoes of literary works mentioned here, plus others, in *Huckleberry Finn*, see Walter Blair, *Mark Twain & "Huck Finn"* (Berkeley, 1960). This study traces the writing of the novel from inception to reception.

Most of the quoted horse race stories, except for the 1792 precursor, are cited in Richard M. Dorson's collection, *Jonathan Draws the Long Bow* (Cambridge, 1946), pp. 85-88. The 1792 sketch is in H. H. Brackenridge, *Modern Chivalry* (1792-1815).

Mark Twain's talk about widespread antebellum American boasting is in a passage deleted from *Life on the Mississippi* but included in the Heritage edition of the book (New York, 1944), ed. Willis Wager, p. 405.

Howard Baetzhold discusses likenesses between the Paladin and Falstaff in *Mark Twain & John Bull* (Bloomington, 1970), pp. 258-60. The book cites many instances of Twain's literary borrowing.

For the account of the one-legged goose story told by Boccaccio, Smith, and Twain, see Ernest J. Moyne, "Mark Twain and the Baroness Alexandra Gripenberg," *AL*, 45 (1973), 370-78. The humorist adds a few details in "Private History of the 'Jumping Frog' Story," originally published in the *North American Review* in April 1894. Smith's "Ginger and the Goose" appeared in *Harper's Monthly*, 60 (1882), 638-40. The comments on Riley's soldier story are in Twain's "How to Tell a Story," in *Youth's Companion*, October 3, 1895. John C. Gerber's valuable article on varied "Mark Twain's" is "Mark Twain's Use of the Comic Pose," *PMLA*, 77 (1962), 297-304.

32. Specific sources of all quoted matter are cited in Walter Blair, "Mark Twain's Other Masterpiece, 'Jim Baker's Blue-Jay Yarn,'" *Studies in American Humor*, 1 (1975), 132-46. Relevant materials are in *Mark Twain's Frontier*, ed. J. E. Camp and X. J. Kennedy (New York, 1962), pp. 89-136.

Major critical statements by Mark Twain which are quoted will be found in *Letters*, ed. A. B. Paine (New York, 1917); *Speeches*, ed. A. B. Paine (New York, 1923); *Notebooks* (New York, 1935); *Mark Twain in Eruption*, ed. Bernard DeVoto (New York, 1940); *My Dear Bro*, ed. Frederick Anderson (Berkeley, 1961); and E. J. Moyne, "Mark Twain and the Baroness Alexandra Gripenberg," *AL*, 45 (1973).

Major secondary sources included these critical studies: Bernard DeVoto, *Mark Twain's America* (Boston, 1932), p. 251; Max Eastman, *The Enjoyment of Laughter* (New York, 1948), pp. 76-80; Henry Nash Smith, *Mark Twain: The Development of a Writer* (Cambridge, 1962); William M. Gibson, *The Art of Mark Twain* (New York, 1976), pp. 66-67.

33-34. The fragmentary writings of Mark Twain's later years include several recently published volumes in the *Mark Twain Papers* series published by the University of California Press: *Mark Twain's Which Was the Dream . . .* (1967), ed. John S. Tuckey; *Mark Twain's Mysterious Stranger Manuscripts* (1969), ed. William M. Gibson; and *Mark Twain's Fables of Man* (1972), ed. John S. Tuckey. The complete autobiographical dictations are scheduled for future publication in the same series.

Twain's pessimistic and apocalyptic world view is charted in Roger B. Salomon's *Twain and the Image of History* (New Haven, 1961) and in Richard Boyd Hauck's *A Cheerful Nihilism: Confidence and "The Absurd" in American Humorous Fiction* (Bloomington, 1971), especially pp. 157-66. Hauck's later chapters (especially pp. 201-45) trace the lines of development in modern humor that we have suggested Twain foreshadowed in his later writings. Two briefer studies which examine Mark Twain in modern comic contexts are David F. Burg's "Another View of *Huckleberry Finn*," *Nineteenth-Century Fiction*, 29 (1974), 299-319, and John C. Gerber's *"Pudd'nhead Wilson* as Fabulation," *Studies in American Humor*, 2 (1975), 21-31, which relies upon Robert Scholes' *The Fabulators* (New York, 1967) for its definitions.

35-36. The best recent study of John Kendrick Bangs is in Norris Yates's *The American Humorist: Conscience of the Twentieth Century* (Ames, Iowa, 1964), which classifies him as a "University wit." Bangs's son, Francis Hyde Bangs, has written a predictably adulatory biography, *John Kendrick Bangs, Humorist of the Nineties* (New York, 1941).

Claude Bragdon's reminiscences are in "The Purple Cow Period," *Bookman*, 49 (1929), 475-78. Joseph M. Backus studies Burgess thoroughly in "Gelett Burgess: A Biography of the Man Who Wrote 'The Purple Cow,' " (unpublished Ph.D. dissertation, Berkeley, 1961).

Critical studies of Bierce include Paul Fatout, *Ambrose Bierce, The Devil's Lexicographer* (Norman, Okla., 1951), and M. E. Grenander, *Ambrose Bierce* (New York, 1971). The best edition of the dictionary is *The Enlarged Devil's Dictionary*, ed. Ernest Jerome Hopkins (New York, 1967).

Elmer Ellis's *Mr. Dooley's America* (New York, 1941) surveys the history of the Whitechapel Club; and recent studies of George Ade include Lee Coyle, *George Ade* (New York, 1964), and Terence Tobin's edition of *The Letters of George Ade* (West Lafayette, Ind. 1973).

37. Daniel G. Hoffman, *Paul Bunyan: Last of the Frontier Demigods* (Philadelphia, 1952), gives a bibliography, a detailed history, and a criticism of oral and written narratives about the legendary lumberman. Richard M. Dorson, "Folklore and Fake Lore," attacks the celebrators of Bunyan, and James Stevens, "Folklore and the Artist," defends his own writings about him in juxtaposed articles in *American Mercury*, 70 (March, 1950), 335-349. In "A Gallery of Folk Heroes,"

in *American Folklore* (Chicago, 1959), pp. 199-226, Dorson distinguishes between lore about the Salt River roarers and twentieth-century comic demigods, and holds that Paul Bunyan "filled the psychic need" of "twentieth-century America, ripe and self-confident after defeating the Kaiser and saving the world for democracy."

Much fascinating lore about giants will be found in F. W. Fairholt, *Gog and Magog* (London, 1859).

Biographies of H. L. Mencken that touch on his sponsorship of James Stevens are William Manchester, *Disturber of the Peace* (New York, 1951), and Carl Bode, *Mencken* (New York, 1969, 1970). Mencken's review of Stevens's *Paul Bunyan* appeared in *American Mercury*, 5 (June, 1925), 254-55. Mencken's "On Being an American," one of the best of the summaries he wrote of his prejudices, appeared in *Prejudices: Third Series* (New York, 1922).

Stevens's three books about his hero are *Paul Bunyan* (1925), *Saginaw Paul Bunyan* (1932), *Paul Bunyan's Bears* (1947). The autobiographical novel cited is *Brawnyman* (1926). Stevens wrote a brief autobiography for *Twentieth-Century Authors*, ed. S. J. Kunitz and H. Haycraft (New York, 1942), pp. 1343-44.

38. Carl Van Doren's survey of the colyumnists is "Day In and Day Out," *Century*, 107 (December, 1923), 308-15. The fullest study of Don Marquis is Edward Anthony's *O Rare Don Marquis* (Garden City, 1962). Margaret Case Harriman's informal *The Vicious Circle, The Story of the Algonquin Round Table* (New York, 1951), is filled with anecdotes. An anthology, *The Algonquin Wits*, was edited by Robert E. Drennan (New York, 1968).

Scott Meredith's *George S. Kaufman and His Friends* (New York, 1974) and Ring Lardner's *The Lardners* (New York, 1976) are recent histories of members of the Round Table.

39. Harold Ross has been the subject of much discussion and dispute. Dale Kramer, *Ross and the New Yorker* (Garden City, 1951), James Thurber, *The Years with Ross* (Boston, 1959), and Brendan Gill, *Here at the New Yorker* (New York, 1975), provide the full spectrum of response. Bernard DeVoto's "The Lineage of Eustace Tilley," noting the traditional background of *New Yorker* humorists, appeared in *Saturday Review of Literature*, 16 (September 25, 1937), 3-4.

40. Benchley's career has been the subject of several appraisals. Nathanael Benchley's biography, *Robert Benchley* (New York, 1955), and Norris Yates's *Robert Benchley* (New York, 1968), are the best. Robert Redding's *Starring Robert Benchley* (Albuquerque, 1973) focuses on Benchley's movie career. S. J. Perelman has been the subject of much less critical attention; but we found Louis Hasley's "The Kangaroo Mind of S. J. Perelman," *South Atlantic Quarterly*, 72 (1973), 115-21, provocative.

41. The publication of E. B. White's *Letters* in 1976 produced some reviews that made cogent evaluations of White as a typical *New Yorker*

humorist, especially Anatole Broyard, "Seriously Unserious," *New York Times*, December 7, 1976, and Wilfred Sheed, "Letters of E. B. White," *New York Times Book Review*, November 21, 1976. Burton Bernstein's *Thurber* (New York, 1975) is a massive and definitive biography. Both shorter and more critically orientated are Robert E. Morsberger, *James Thurber* (New York, 1964), and Richard C. Tobias, *The Art of James Thurber* (Athens, Ohio, 1969).

42. Although the discussion chiefly concerns "The Secret Life of Walter Mitty," it refers to other writings by the author. An exhaustive list is available in Edwin T. Bowden, *James Thurber, A Bibliography* (Columbus, 1969).

Secondary studies: In addition to Bernstein's "authorized biography," and other studies of Thurber that were mentioned above, useful books and articles, listed alphabetically according to author, are: Stephen A. Black, *James Thurber: His Masquerades* (The Hague, 1970); Peter De Vries, "James Thurber: The Comic Prufrock," *Poetry*, 63 (December, 1943), 150-59; Max Eastman, *The Enjoyment of Laughter* (New York, 1936), pp. 105, 108, 341-42; Charles S. Holmes, *The Clocks of Columbus* (New York, 1972); Norris W. Yates, *The American Humorist: Conscience of the Twentieth Century* (Ames, 1964); Gerald Weales, "Not for the Old Lady in Dubuque," in *The Comic Imagination in America* (New Brunswick, 1973).

Morrison Worthington provided information about Mitty's naïveté concerning firearms, and Dr. Alvin Tarlov of the University of Chicago commented on the lack of authenticity in Mitty's operating-room fantasy.

43. Much of the discussion of the shaping of fiction by oral humor between 1898 and the present appeared in Walter Blair, " 'A Man's Voice Speaking': A Continuum in American Humor," *Harvard English Studies 3, Veins of Humor*, ed. Harry Levin (Cambridge, 1972), pp. 185-204. In the article a number of the statements are documented.

Matthew Wood Little, "Faulkner and American Humor: Tradition and Innovations," is a University of Chicago doctoral dissertation, unpublished so far except for an article based upon the chapter which was most useful here, *"As I Lay Dying* and "Dementia Praecox' Humor," *Studies in American Humor*, 2 (April, 1975), 61-70.

James E. Miller, Jr., "The Quest Absurd: The New American Novel," appeared in *Quests Surd and Absurd* (Chicago, 1967), pp. 3-30.

Another useful study, part of which is quoted, is Richard Boyd Hauck, *A Cheerful Nihilism: Confidence and "The Absurd" in American Humorous Fiction* (Bloomington, 1971).

44. Philip Roth's discussion of *The Great American Novel*, in the form of a self-interview, is "Reading Myself," *Partisan Review*, 60 (Fall, 1973), 404-17—one of many interviews and articles by him that say illuminating things about his aims and methods. These are listed

by Bernard F. Rodgers, Jr., in *Philip Roth: A Bibliography* (Metuchen, 1974); so are secondary sources on Roth's writings through 1973. More useful to us was Rodgers's "Stalking Reality: The Fiction of Philip Roth," an unpublished University of Chicago doctoral dissertation, June 1974. A more recent study that we have found of value is Sanford Pinsker, *The Comedy that "Hoits"* (Columbia, Mo., 1975). Walter Kerr, "Why Do Authors Mix Fact and Fantasy?" appeared in the *New York Times*, August 29, 1976. The comment on jokes by G. Legman is in his *No Laughing Matter* (New York, 1975), the second of two volumes classifying and commenting on dirty jokes. The first volume is *Rationale of the Dirty Joke* (New York, 1968).

45-46. Gerald Mast's *The Comic Mind* (Indianapolis, 1973) and Donald McCaffrey's *The Golden Age of Sound Comedy* (South Brunswick, N.J., 1974) are histories of film humor in America. Phil Berger's *The World of the Stand-Up Comics* (New York, 1975) is chock full of comic routines. A forthcoming collection of minstrel-show "Ethiopian drama" has been edited by Gary D. Engle.

Discussions of black humor include Max Schulz, *Black Humor Fiction of the Sixties* (Athens, Ohio, 1973) and critical materials in two anthologies: *Black Humor*, ed. Bruce Jay Friedman (New York, 1963), and *The World of Black Humor*, ed. Douglas M. Davis (New York, 1967). Stanley Trachtenberg's "Counterhumor: Comedy in Contemporary American Fiction," *Georgia Review*, 27 (1973), 33-48, is an excellent overview.

W. C. Fields's *The Bank Dick* has been printed with many stills from the film, as a "Classic Film Strip" (New York, 1973). Doonesbury was honored as the cover story in *Time*, February 9, 1976, pp. 57-66. A substantial bibliography concerning Lenny Bruce as much in his role as martyr as in the one as comic is proliferating. His autobiography, *How to Talk Dirty and Influence People*, was serialized in *Playboy* and published as a book (Chicago, 1965). *The Essential Lenny Bruce*, ed. John Cohen (New York, 1967), contains the sometimes flawed transcriptions of all of the most famous stand-up routines and had gone into nine printings by August, 1974. An over-long biography is Albert Goldman, *Ladies and Gentlemen . . . Lenny Bruce* (New York, 1974).

Afterword. The predictions mentioned in the third paragraph may be found in *Life and Letters of Edmund Clarence Stedman* (New York, 1910), I, 447; James T. Thurber, "The Future, If Any, of Comedy," *Harper's Magazine*, 223 (1961), 40-45; Melvin Maddocks, "We Are Not Amused—and Why," *Time*, July 20, 1970, pp. 30-31; Clifton Fadiman, "Foreword," *The Reader's Digest Treasury of American Humor* (New York, 1972), p. xviii.

Books about Will Rogers include Betty Rogers, *Uncle Clem's Boy* (New York, 1940), and *The Autobiography of Will Rogers*, ed. Donald Day (New York, 1949).

Theodore Solotaroff, "Harry Golden and the American Audience," is included in *The Red Hot Vacuum* (New York, 1970), pp. 50-70.

Bob Hope, "A Funny Thing About Comedy" appeared in the *New York Times*, October 24, 1976; Karl Fleming, "Lucille Ball Looks Back on 25 Years of Laughter," *ibid.*, November 28, 1976.

H. L. Mencken's loving words about low comedy as a great American treasure are from "On Being an American," *Prejudices—Third Series* (New York, 1922, 1949).

Index

Main entries for major humorists and comedians who used pseudonyms are listed under the more familiar name. Comic strips, movies, and Broadway plays appear under their titles. We have not attempted to list all the casual allusions to such major figures as Franklin, Crockett, or Mark Twain. Categories and schools of humor are all listed under "Humor."

Jewett, Sarah Orne, 265
"Jiggs and Maggie," 449, 489
Joe Miller's Jests, 17-18, 104, 127
Johnson, Burges, 370, 371
Johnson, Lyndon B., 494
Johnson, Samuel, 61, 63, 231, 294, 373
Johnston, Charles, 370
Johnston, Richard Malcolm, 265
Jones, Howard Mumford, 5
Jones, James, 470
Jones, Spike, 489
Jong, Erica, 496
Jonson, Ben, 6, 48, 130, 134, 231, 233, 314
Jorgenson, Chester E., 61
Josephus, 294
Josselyn, John, 26, 70
Joyce, James, 450, 482, 492
Judge, 275, 417, 433, 487
Judson, E. Z. C., 240
Juvenal, 327

Kafka, Franz, 477
Kaufman, George S., 377, 405, 410, 412, 492
Keaton, Buster, 488
Keller, Helen, 499
Kelly, Walt, 15, 489
Kendall, George W., 158
Kennedy, Edward, 482
Kennedy, Jacqueline, 515
Kennedy, John F., 493
Kernodle, George, 142
Kerouac, Jack, 470
Kerr, Walter, 483-84, 499
Kesey, Ken, 15, 470, 497, 526
"Kettle, Ma and Pa," 177, 489
King, Grace, 265
Kinsey, Alfred, 490
Kipling, Rudyard, 341
Kirtland, Caroline Matilda, 265, 496
Kliewer, Warren, 21
Knickerbocker, Conrad, 498
Knickerbocker Magazine, 177-78, 181, 203, 225, 241
Knight, Sarah Kemble, 68, 496
Knotts, Don, 489
Kober, Arthur, 421
Koren, Edward, 424
Korman, Harvey, 493
Kosinski, Jerzy, 359, 470
Kramer, Dale, 417
Krassner, Paul, 491, 493
"Krazy Kat," 488

Krylov, Ivan, 341
Kubrick, Stanley, 487
Kunstler, William, 490

Lamb, Charles, 177
Lampton, W. J., 289
Lancet, 449
Landon, Melville, 274, 289
Lang, Andrew, 27, 28-29, 41
Langdon, Harry, 488
Lanigan, George T., 289, 341
Lantern, 275
Laramie *Boomerang*, 487
Lardner, Ring, 412, 413-16, 418, 462, 468, 476
The Lark, 375-79, 380
L'Arkitecture Moderne, 376-77
Laughead, W. B., 389, 395
"Laugh In," 493
Laurel, Stan, 475, 488
Lawrence, D. H., 55
Leacock, Stephen, 29, 450
Lear, Edward, 276, 378
Leary, Lewis, 88, 91, 174
Leary, Timothy, 490
Lecky, W. E. H., 308
Legman, Gershon, 17, 104, 485
Lehrer, Tom, 513
Leland, Charles Godfrey, 494
Lemierre, Antoine-Marin, 119
Lenin, Nikolai, 483
Lenny, 499, 517
Leopold, Nathan, 515
Lesage, Alain René, 48, 308, 327-28
Lessing, Gotthold, 340
L'Estrange, Roger, 340
Lever, Charles, 231
Levin, Harry, 436
Levinson, Sam, 477, 528
Levinson, W. H., 289
Lewis, Alfred Henry, 265, 267, 461
Lewis, C. B., 289
Lewis, Henry Clay, 199
Lewis, Meriwether, 70
Lewis, Sinclair, 50, 267, 372, 380, 387, 397, 450, 452
Lewisohn, Ludwig, 450
Life, 275, 379, 417, 427, 428, 484
Lincoln, Abraham, 43, 88, 114, 157, 230, 287, 293, 487
Little, Matthew W., 468-69
"Little Orphan Annie," 489
Locke, David Ross, *see* "Nasby, Petroleum V."